Excursions in
Modern Mathematics

PEARSON

ALWAYS LEARNING

Peter Tannenbaum

Excursions in Modern Mathematics

Fourth Custom Edition for Eastern Connecticut State University

Taken from:
Excursions in Modern Mathematics, Eighth Edition
by Peter Tannenbaum

*Finite Mathematics for Business, Economics, Life Sciences,
and Social Sciences*, Twelfth Edition
by Raymond A. Barnett, Michael R. Ziegler, and Karl E. Byleen

Cover Art: Courtesy of Photodisc/Getty Images.

Taken from:

Excursions in Modern Mathematics, Eighth Edition
by Peter Tannenbaum
Copyright © 2014, 2010, 2007 by Pearson Education, Inc.
Published by Pearson
Boston, Massachusetts 02116

Finite Mathematics for Business, Economics, Life Sciences, and Social Sciences
by Raymond A. Barnett, Michael R. Ziegler, and Karl E. Byleen
Copyright © 2011, 2008, 2005 by Pearson Education, Inc.
Published by Pearson
Boston, Massachusetts 02116

This special edition published in cooperation with Pearson Learning Solutions.

All trademarks, service marks, registered trademarks, and registered service marks are the property of their respective owners and are used herein for identification purposes only.

Pearson Learning Solutions, 501 Boylston Street, Suite 900, Boston, MA 02116
A Pearson Education Company
www.pearsoned.com

Printed in the United States of America

1 2 3 4 5 6 7 8 9 10 V056 17 16 15 14 13

000200010271784661

SR

PEARSON   ISBN 10: 1-269-34188-X
           ISBN 13: 978-1-269-34188-2

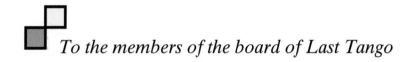 *To the members of the board of Last Tango*

Contents

Taken from: *Excursions in Modern Mathematics*, Eighth Edition, by Robert Tannenbaum.

PART 2 Management Science

5 The Mathematics of Getting Around 138
Euler Paths and Circuits

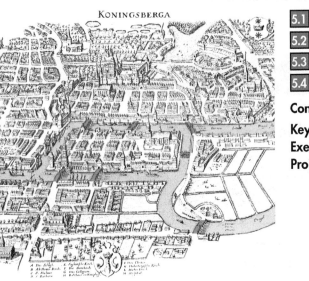

6 The Mathematics of Touring 174
Traveling Salesman Problems

PART 3 Growth

PART 5 Statistics

Taken from: *Finite Mathematics for Business, Economics, Life Sciences, and Social Sciences*, Twelfth Edition, by Raymond A. Barnett, Michael R. Zieger, and Karl E. Byleen.

Taken from:
Excursions in Modern Mathematics, Eighth Edition, by Robert Tannenbaum

Preface

This book started more than 20 years ago as a set of lecture notes for a new, experimental "math appreciation" course (these types of courses are described, sometimes a bit derisively, as "math for poets"). Over time, the lecture notes grew into a book and the "poets" turned out to be social scientists, political scientists, economists, psychologists, environmentalists, and many other "ists." Over time, and with the input of many users, the contents have been expanded and improved, but the underlying philosophy of the book has remained the same since those handwritten lecture notes were handed out to my first group of students.

Excursions in Modern Mathematics is a travelogue into that vast and alien frontier that many people perceive mathematics to be. My goal is to show the open-minded reader that mathematics is a lively, interesting, useful, and surprisingly rich human activity.

The "excursions" in *Excursions* represent a collection of topics chosen to meet the following simple criteria.

> 66 To most outsiders, modern mathematics is unknown territory. Its borders are protected by dense thickets of technical terms; its landscapes are a mass of indecipherable equations and incomprehensible concepts. Few realize that the world of modern mathematics is rich with vivid images and provocative ideas. 99
>
> – Ivars Peterson,
> The Mathematical Tourist

- **Applicability.** There is no need to worry here about that great existential question of college mathematics: What is this stuff good for? The connection between the mathematics presented in these excursions and down-to-earth, concrete real-life problems is transparent and immediate.*

- **Accessibility.** As a general rule, the excursions in this book do not presume a background beyond standard high school mathematics—by and large, intermediate algebra and a little Euclidean geometry are appropriate and sufficient prerequisites. (In the few instances in which more advanced concepts are unavoidable, an effort has been made to provide enough background to make the material self-contained.) A word of caution—this does not mean that the excursions in this book are easy! In mathematics, as in many other walks of life, simple and basic is not synonymous with easy and superficial.

- **Modernity.** Unlike much of traditional mathematics, which is often hundreds of years old, most of the mathematics in this book has been discovered within the last 100 years, and in some cases within the last couple of decades. Modern mathematical discoveries do not have to be the exclusive province of professional mathematicians.

- **Aesthetics.** The notion that there is such a thing as beauty in mathematics is surprising to most casual observers. There is an important aesthetic component in mathematics, and just as in art and music (which mathematics very much resembles), it often surfaces in the simplest ideas. A fundamental objective of this book is to develop an appreciation of the aesthetic elements of mathematics.

Outline

The excursions are organized into five independent parts, each touching on a different area where mathematics and the real world interface.

- **Part 1 Social Choice.** This part deals with mathematical applications to politics, social science, and government. How are *elections* decided? (Chapter 1); How

---

*Just days before this edition went to press, the American mathematician Lloyd S. Shapley—whose method for computing power is discussed in Chapter 2—was awarded the 2012 Nobel Prize in Economics.

can the *power* of individuals, groups, or voting blocs be measured? (Chapter 2); How can assets commonly owned be *divided* in a *fair* and equitable manner? (Chapter 3); How are seats *apportioned* in a legislative body? (Chapter 4).

- **Part 2 Management Science.** This part deals with questions of efficiency—how to manage some valuable resource (time, money, raw materials) so that utility is maximized. Examples of the types of applications discussed in this part are: How do we *cover* a network with the least amount of backtracking? (Chapter 5); How do we find the least expensive route that *visits* a specified set of locations? (Chapter 6); How do we create efficient networks that *connect* people or things? (Chapter 7); How do we schedule a project so that it is completed as early as possible? (Chapter 8).

- **Part 3 Growth.** In this part we discuss, in very broad terms, the mathematics of growth and decay, profit and loss. In Chapter 9 we cover mathematical models of *population growth*, mostly biological and human populations but also populations of inanimate "things" like garbage, pollution, etc. Since money plays such an important role in our lives, it deserves a chapter of its own. In Chapter 10 we discuss the basics of *financial mathematics* with particular emphasis on how to make money grow.

- **Part 4 Shape and Form.** In this part we cover a few connections between mathematics and the shape and form of objects—natural or man-made. What is *symmetry*? What *types* of symmetries exist in nature and art? (Chapter 11); What kind of geometry lies hidden behind the *kinkiness* of the many irregular shapes we find in nature? (Chapter 12); What is the connection between the *Fibonacci numbers* and the *golden ratio* (two abstract mathematical constructs) and the *spiral* forms that we regularly find in nature? (Chapter 13).

- **Part 5 Statistics.** In one way or another, statistics affects all our lives. Government policy, insurance rates, our health, our diet, and our political lives are all governed by statistical information. This part deals with how the statistical information that affects our lives is collected, organized, and interpreted. What are the purposes and strategies of *data collection*? (Chapter 14); How is data *organized, presented,* and *summarized*? (Chapter 15); How do we use mathematics to measure *uncertainty* and *risk*? (Chapter 16); How do we use mathematics to model, analyze, and make predictions about *real-life, bell-shaped* data sets? (Chapter 17).

New in This Edition

- **Hello Chapter 17.** For its first seven editions, this book consisted of 16 chapters organized in four parts, four chapters in each part. Nice symmetry, not much flexibility. This edition is the first break with the four-by-four model: 17 chapters organized into five parts (4, 4, 2, 3, 4 chapters, respectively). What in the seventh edition was a mini-excursion in Population Growth has been upgraded to full chapter status (Chapter 9) in this edition. Combined with the chapter on Financial Mathematics (Chapter 10), these two form a new Part 3.

- **Really Real Examples.** This edition has over 300 examples, many of them new. Among the new examples is a renewed focus on *real-life events and real-life data* (as opposed to examples involving a real-life application but illustrated with an imaginary situation and made-up data—something that is often unavoidable since real-world data can be messy, noisy, and big). Approximately 25% of the examples in this book are now really real (application, story, data—the works). The examples cover a wide swath of life—popular culture, sports, politics, government, society, the environment, health, and finance.

- **Exercises.** This edition has over 1250 exercises, and about 20% are new. There are approximately 1000 Walking exercises, and they are now organized into sections that match the sections in the chapter. This should greatly facilitate the scheduling of assignments. Running exercises will challenge students' ability and are revised in this edition to make them less rigorous, yet still challenging.

- **Glossary of Key Concepts.** The end of each chapter now includes a glossary with a short definition or explanation of the key concepts in the chapter providing ease of study and review.

- **Goodbye Mini-Excursions, etc.** In spite of the addition of a new chapter, this edition is shorter than previous editions. This miracle was accomplished by pruning some chapters and moving discretionary material such as biographical profiles, references, and some of the mini-excursions to MyMathLab®.

- **MyMathLab** for the Eighth Edition offers new features that make the online assessment more closely tied to the text's approach.

  - **Applets,** designed by the author, help students visualize the more difficult concepts. These can be assigned as media assignments in MyMathLab. Applet references appear as margin notes in the text directing students to the MyMathLab course.

  - **New assignable MathXL® exercises** relate to the applets, so students explore the concepts and develop their understanding using these applets and then answer related MathXL questions.

  - **A Ready-To-Go** MyMathLab Course is available, which offers the same robust experience as a standard course but makes course set-up even easier.

In addition to the changes listed above, most chapters have undergone a significant revision for this edition. The following is a chapter-by-chapter list of major changes:

- **Chapter 1.** Arrow's fairness criteria are now discussed together in one section at the end of the chapter. This reorganization allows for more flexibility in teaching this chapter. Instructors who want to cover the fairness criteria and Arrow's Impossibility Theorem in more detail can now do so; instructors who prefer to skip this part of the material can seamlessly do so as well. Many new examples of voting situations from popular culture, sports, and politics have been added.

- **Chapter 2.** There is a new section that covers the enumeration of subsets and permutations. This puts all the mathematics used in the chapter in one place.

- **Chapter 3.** A subsection on Auctions, Reverse Auctions, and Negative Bidding has been added to Section 3.5 The Method of Sealed Bids.

- **Chapter 4.** A new section on the Huntington-Hill method (Section 4.5) has been added. Adams's and Webster's methods have been combined into one section (Section 4.4). The quota rule and the apportionment paradoxes are now organized into a single section at the end of the chapter (Section 4.6).

- **Chapter 5.** Euler's theorems and Fleury's algorithm are now combined into a single section (Section 5.3), and a more detailed discussion of the topic of semi-eulerization of graphs has been added (Section 5.4).

- **Chapter 6.** This chapter has undergone a significant reorganization. There are fewer sections and the algorithms (brute-force, nearest-neighbor/repetitive nearest-neighbor, and cheapest-link) are now covered in separate sections.

- **Chapter 7.** The topic of Maximum Spanning Trees has been added. By popular demand, the material on shortest networks is gone. The chapter has been greatly streamlined.

- **Chapter 8.** Critical paths and the critical-path algorithm are now combined into a single section (Section 8.5). The old section on scheduling with independent tasks has been deleted.
- **Chapter 9.** This is a new chapter. Much of the material is taken from Mini-Excursion 3 in the seventh edition, but with a much greater emphasis on sequences in general and population sequences in particular.
- **Chapter 10.** This chapter has been completely rewritten. The emphasis of this chapter now is on the real-life applications of money management. Savings, investment, and consumer debt are the primary topics discussed.
- **Chapter 13.** This was Chapter 9 in previous editions. There is a bigger focus now on the mathematical properties of Fibonacci numbers and the golden ratio.
- **Chapter 14.** This chapter (old Chapter 13) has been reorganized into three major themes (enumeration, measurement, and cause-effect). Each of these themes corresponds to a section of the chapter. Many real-life examples have been added.
- **Chapter 15.** This chapter is a minor reorganization of the material in the old Chapter 14 with many new really real examples added.
- **Chapter 16.** This chapter now includes two new sections—one introduces expected values (Section 16.4), the other applies the concept of expected value to the measurement of risk (Section 16.5). Some of the material comes from the old Mini-Excursion 4, but several new examples have been added. This chapter is quite a bit longer than the old Chapter 15 it replaces.
- **Chapter 17.** This chapter (previously Chapter 16) has been streamlined into four sections. There is now much more emphasis on modeling real-world approximately normally distributed data with the properties of normal distributions. Several really real examples have been added.

A Final Word to the Reader

66 It's not what you look at that matters, it's what you see. 99

– *Henry David Thoreau*

My goal in writing this book is to shine a small light on all that mathematics can be when looked at in the right way—useful, interesting, subtle, beautiful, and accessible. I hope that you will see something of that in this book.

Peter Tannenbaum

Supplementary Materials

Student Supplement

Student Resource Guide
Dale R. Buske, St. Cloud State University
ISBN 13: 978-0-321-83721-9; ISBN 10: 0-321-83721-5

- In addition to the worked-out solutions to odd-numbered exercises from the text, this guide contains "selected hints" that point the reader in one of many directions leading to a solution and keys to student success, including lists of skills that will help prepare for the chapter exams.

Instructor Supplements

Instructor's Edition
ISBN 13: 978-0-321-83720-2; ISBN 10: 0-321-83720-7

- Includes answers to all Walking and Jogging exercises in a separate section in the back of the book.

The following supplements are ONLINE ONLY and are available for download in the Pearson Higher Education catalogs or inside your MyMathLab course:

Instructor's Guide and Solutions Manual
Dale R. Buske, St. Cloud State University

- Contains solutions to all the exercises in the text as well as a variety of resources for in-classroom use.

Instructor's Testing Manual
Joseph P. Kudrle, University of Vermont

- Contains four alternate tests per chapter. Two have multiple-choice exercises, and two have free-response exercises.

Insider's Guide

- Includes resources designed to help faculty with course preparation and helpful teaching tips.
- Includes learning outcomes, skill objectives, ideas for the classroom, worksheets, and project ideas from current users of the text.

PowerPoint® Lecture Slides

- Fully editable classroom presentations cover important topics and example from the text.

TestGen®

TestGen® (*www.pearsoned.com/testgen*) enables instructors to build, edit, print, and administer tests using a computerized bank of questions developed to cover all the objectives of the text. TestGen is algorithmically based, allowing instructors to create multiple but equivalent versions of the same question or test with the click of a button. Instructors can also modify test bank questions or add new questions. The software and testbank are available for download from Pearson Education's online catalog.

Online Resources

MyMathLab®

Online Course (access code required)

MyMathLab delivers **proven results** in helping individual students succeed.

- MyMathLab has a consistently positive impact on the quality of learning in higher education math instruction. MyMathLab can be successfully implemented in any environment—lab-based, hybrid, fully online, traditional—and demonstrates the quantifiable difference that integrated usage has on student retention, subsequent success, and overall achievement.
- MyMathLab's comprehensive online gradebook automatically tracks your students' results on tests, quizzes, homework, and in the study plan. You can use the gradebook to quickly intervene if your students have trouble, or to provide positive feedback on a job well done. The data within MyMathLab is easily exported to a variety of spreadsheet programs, such as Microsoft Excel. You can determine which points of data you want to export and then analyze the results to determine success.

MyMathLab provides **engaging experiences** that personalize, stimulate, and measure learning for each student.

- **Exercises:** The homework and practice exercises in MyMathLab are correlated to the exercises in the textbook, and they regenerate algorithmically to give students unlimited opportunity for practice and mastery. The software offers immediate, helpful feedback when students enter incorrect answers.

- **Multimedia Learning Aids:** Exercises include guided solutions, sample problems, animations, videos, and eText clips for extra help at the point of use.

- **Expert Tutoring:** Although many students describe the whole of MyMathLab as "like having your own personal tutor," students using MyMathLab do have access to live tutoring from Pearson, from qualified math and statistics instructors who provide tutoring sessions for students via MyMathLab.

And, MyMathLab comes from a **trusted partner** with educational expertise and an eye on the future.

- Knowing that you are using a Pearson product means knowing that you are using quality content. That means that our eTexts are accurate and our assessment tools work. Whether you are just getting started with MyMathLab or have a question along the way, we're here to help you learn about our technologies and how to incorporate them into your course.

New in the MyMathLab course

- A new type of problem making the Applets assignable, helping to assess understanding of the concepts and the applications of the applet.

- Applets integrated into the multimedia textbook.

- An Image Resource Library contains art from the text for instructors to edit provided PowerPoints, create their own presentations, or handouts.

To learn more about how MyMathLab combines proven learning applications with powerful assessment, visit **www.mymathlab.com** or contact your Pearson representative.

MyMathLab®   **Ready-to-Go Course (access code required)**

These new Ready-to-Go courses provide students with all the same great MyMathLab features but make it easier for instructors to get started. Each course includes pre-assigned homeworks and quizzes to make creating your course even simpler. Ask your Pearson representative about the details for this particular course or to see a copy of this course.

MathXL®   **Online Course (access code required)**

MathXL® is the homework and assessment engine that runs MyMathLab. (MyMathLab is MathXL plus a learning management system.)

With MathXL, instructors can:

- Create, edit, and assign online homework and tests using algorithmically generated exercises correlated at the objective level to the textbook.

- Create and assign their own online exercises and import TestGen tests for added flexibility.

- Maintain records of all student work tracked in MathXL's online gradebook.

With MathXL, students can:

- Take chapter tests in MathXL and receive personalized study plans and/or personalized homework assignments based on their test results.

- Use the study plan and/or the homework to link directly to tutorial exercises for the objectives they need to study.

- Access supplemental animations and video clips directly from selected exercises.

MathXL is available to qualified adopters. For more information, visit our website at www.mathxl.com, or contact your Pearson representative.

Acknowledgments

This edition benefited from the contributions and opinions of a large number of people. Special thanks to Dale Buske and Katie Tannenbaum, who read early drafts of the manuscript and provided many useful comments and suggestions, and to Dale Buske Deidre Smith, and Karla Karstens for their valuable contributions to the new and updated exercise sets.

The following is a list of reviewers for the last two editions (asterisks indicate reviewers of this eighth edition).

Lowell Abrams, *George Washington University*
*Diane Allen, *Idaho State University*
Erol Barbut, *Washington State University*
*Gregory Budzban, *Southern Illinois University*
*Lynn Clark, *Westfield State University*
*Irene C. Corriette, *Cameron University*
*Robert V. DeLiberato, *Saint Joseph's University*
Lauren Fern, *University of Montana*
Karla Karstens, *University of Vermont*
*Lynne H. Kendall, *Regis University*
Randa Lee Kress, *Idaho State University*
*Diana Lee, *Highline Community College*
Margaret A. Michener, *University of Nebraska at Kearney*
Mika Munakata, *Montclair State University*
Kenneth Pothoven, *University of South Florida*
Salvatore Sciandra Jr., *Niagara County Community College*
Deirdre Smith, *University of Arizona*
*Paul K. Swets, *Angelo State University*
W. D. Wallis, *Southern Illinois University*
*Cathleen M. Zucco-Teveloff, *Rowan University*

Many people contributed to previous editions of this book. Special thanks to Robert Arnold, Dale Buske (again), and to the following reviewers: Teri Anderson, Guanghwa Andy Chang, Carmen Artino, Donald Beaton, Terry L. Cleveland, Leslie Cobar, Crista Lynn Coles, Kimberly A. Conti, Ronald Czochor, Nancy Eaton, Lily Eidswick, Kathryn E. Fink, Stephen I. Gendler, Marc Goldstein, Josephine Guglielmi, Abdi Hajikandi, William S. Hamilton, Cynthia Harris, Harold Jacobs, Peter D. Johnson, Stephen Kenton, Tom Kiley, Katalin Kolossa, Jean Krichbaum, Thomas Lada, Kim L. Luna, Mike Martin, Thomas O'Bryan, Daniel E. Otero, Philip J. Owens, Matthew Pickard, Lana Rhoads, David E. Rush, Shelley Russell, Kathleen C. Salter, Theresa M. Sandifer, Paul Schembari, Marguerite V. Smith, William W. Smith, Hilary Spriggs, David Stacy, Zoran Sunik, John Watson, and Sarah N. Ziesler.

Last, but not least, the *real movers and shakers* that made this new edition possible and deserve special recognition: mover and shaker in-chief (and Senior Acquisitions Editor) Marnie Greenhut, Executive Marketing Manager Roxanne McCarley, Senior Project Manager Patty Bergin, Senior Content Editor Elizabeth Bernardi, Assistant Editor Elle Driska, Marketing Assistant Caitlin Crain, Media Producer Aimee Thorne, and Project Manager at Cenveo Publisher Services, Sherry Berg.

PART 1

Social
Choice

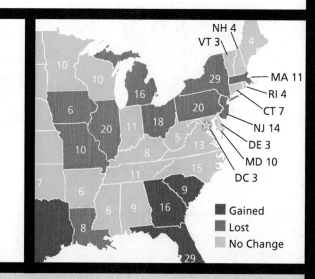

NH 4
VT 3

4

10

10

29

MA 11

16

RI 4

20

CT 7

6

20

11

18

NJ 14

10

5

13

DE 3

8

MD 10

7

11

15

DC 3

6

9

6

9

16

8

29

Gained
Lost
No Change

1 The Mathematics of Elections

The Paradoxes of Democracy

Whether we like it or not, we are all affected by the outcomes of elections. Our president, senators, governors, and mayors make decisions that impact our lives in significant ways, and they all get to be in that position because an election made it possible. But elections touch our lives not just in politics. Academy Awards, *American Idol*, Heisman trophies, football rankings—they are all decided by means of an election. Even something as simple as deciding where to go for dinner might require a mini-election.

We have elections because we don't all think alike. Since we cannot all have things our way, we vote. But *voting* is only the first half of the story, the one we are most familiar with. As playwright Tom Stoppard suggests, it's the second half of the story—the *counting*—that is at the heart of the democratic process. How do we sift through the many choices of individual voters to find the collective choice of the group? More important, how well does the process work? Is the process always fair? Answering these questions and explaining a few of the many intricacies and subtleties of *voting theory* are the purpose of this chapter.

But wait just a second! Voting theory? Why do we need a fancy theory to figure out how to count the votes? It all sounds pretty simple: We have an election; we count the ballots. Based on that count, we decide the outcome of the election in a consistent and fair manner. Surely, there must be a reasonable way to accomplish this! Surprisingly, there isn't.

In the late 1940s the American economist Kenneth Arrow discovered a remarkable fact: For elections involving three or more candidates, there is no consistently fair democratic method for choosing a winner. In fact, Arrow demonstrated that *a method for determining election results that is always fair is a mathematical impossibility*. This fact, the most famous in voting theory, is known as *Arrow's Impossibility Theorem*.

> **❝ It's not the voting that's democracy; it's the counting. ❞**
>
> – *Tom Stoppard*

This chapter is organized as follows. We will start with a general discussion of *elections* and *ballots* in Section 1.1. This discussion provides the backdrop for the remaining sections, which are the heart of the chapter. In Sections 1.2 through 1.5 we will explore four of the most commonly used *voting methods*—how they work and how they are used in real-life applications. In Section 1.6 we will introduce some basic principles of fairness for voting methods and apply these *fairness criteria* to the voting methods discussed in Sections 1.2 through 1.5. The section concludes with a discussion of the meaning and significance of Arrow's Impossibility Theorem.

3

1.1   The Basic Elements of an Election

Big or small, important or trivial, *all* elections share a set of common elements.

- **The candidates.** The purpose of an election is to choose from a set of *candidates* or *alternatives* (at least two—otherwise it is not a real election). Typically, the word *candidate* is used for people and the word *alternative* is used for other things (movies, football teams, pizza toppings, etc.), but it is acceptable to use the two terms interchangeably. In the case of a generic choice (when we don't know if we are referring to a person or a thing), we will use the term *candidate*. While in theory there is no upper limit on the number of candidates, for most elections (in particular the ones we will discuss in this chapter) the number of candidates is small.

- **The voters.** These are the people who get a say in the outcome of the election. In most democratic elections the presumption is that all voters have an equal say, and we will assume this to be the case in this chapter. (This is not always true, as we will see in great detail in Chapter 2.) The number of voters in an election can range from very small (as few as 3 or 4) to very large (hundreds of millions). In this section we will see examples of both.

- **The ballots.** A ballot is the device by means of which a voter gets to express his or her opinion of the candidates. The most common type is a paper ballot, but a voice vote, a text message, or a phone call can also serve as a "ballot" (see Example 1.5 *American Idol*). There are many different forms of ballots that can be used in an election, and Fig. 1-1 shows a few common examples. The simplest form is the **single-choice ballot**, shown in Fig. 1-1(a). Here very little is being asked of the voter ("pick the candidate you like best, and keep the rest of your opinions to yourself!"). At the other end of the spectrum is the **preference ballot**, where the voter is asked to rank *all* the candidates in order of preference. Figure 1-1(b) shows a typical preference ballot in an election with five candidates. In this ballot, the voter has entered the candidates' names in order of preference. An alternative version of the same preference ballot is shown in Fig. 1-1(c). Here the names of the candidates are already printed on the ballot and the voter simply has to mark first, second, third, etc. In elections where there are a large number of candidates, a **truncated preference ballot** is often used. In a truncated preference ballot the voter is asked to rank some, but not all, of the candidates. Figure 1-1(d) shows a truncated preference ballot for an election with dozens of candidates.

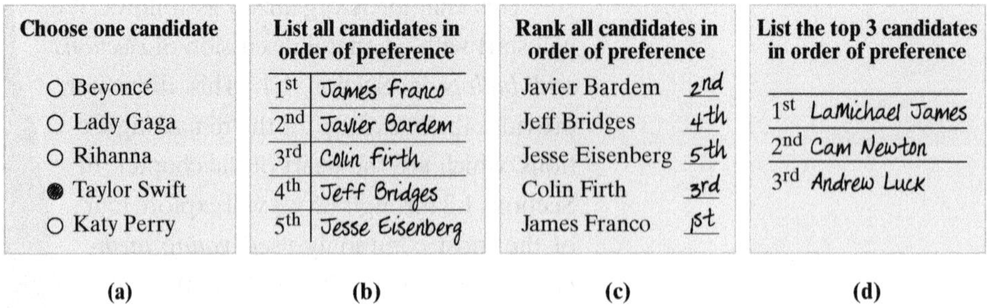

Choose one candidate	List all candidates in order of preference	Rank all candidates in order of preference	List the top 3 candidates in order of preference
○ Beyoncé ○ Lady Gaga ○ Rihanna ● Taylor Swift ○ Katy Perry	1st James Franco 2nd Javier Bardem 3rd Colin Firth 4th Jeff Bridges 5th Jesse Eisenberg	Javier Bardem 2nd Jeff Bridges 4th Jesse Eisenberg 5th Colin Firth 3rd James Franco 1st	1st LaMichael James 2nd Cam Newton 3rd Andrew Luck
(a)	(b)	(c)	(d)

FIGURE 1-1 (a) Single-choice ballot, (b) preference ballot, (c) a different version of the same preference ballot, and (d) truncated preference ballot.

- **The outcome.** The purpose of an election is to use the information provided by the ballots to produce some type of outcome. But what types of outcomes are possible? The most common is **winner-only**. As the name indicates, in a winner-only election all we want is to find a winner. We don't distinguish among the nonwinners. There are, however, situations where we want a broader outcome than just a winner—say we want to determine a first-place, second-place, and third-place candidate from a set of many candidates (but we don't care about fourth place, fifth place, etc.). We call this type of outcome a **partial ranking**. Finally, there are some situations where we want to rank *all* the candidates in order: first, second, third, . . . , last. We call this type of outcome a **full ranking**, or just a **ranking** for short.

■ **The voting method.** The final piece of the puzzle is the method that we use to tabulate the ballots and produce the outcome. This is the most interesting (and complicated) part of the story, but we will not dwell on the topic here, as we will discuss voting methods throughout the rest of the chapter.

It is now time to illustrate and clarify the above concepts with some examples.

We start with a simple example of a fictitious election. This is an important example, and we will revisit it many times throughout the chapter. You may want to think of Example 1.1 as a mathematical parable, its importance being not in the story itself but in what lies hidden behind it. (As you will soon see, there is a lot more to Example 1.1 than first meets the eye.)

EXAMPLE 1.1 THE MATH CLUB ELECTION (WINNER-ONLY)

The Math Appreciation Society (MAS) is a student club dedicated to an unsung but worthy cause: that of fostering the enjoyment and appreciation of mathematics among college students. The MAS chapter at Tasmania State University is holding its annual election for club president, and there are four *candidates* running: Alisha, Boris, Carmen, and Dave (*A*, *B*, *C*, and *D* for short).

Every member of the club is eligible to vote, and the vote takes the form of a *preference ballot*. Each voter is asked to rank each of the four candidates in order of preference. There are 37 *voters* who submit their ballots, and the 37 *preference ballots* submitted are shown in Fig. 1-2.

Ballot	Ballot	Ballot	Ballot	Ballot	Ballot	Ballot	Ballot	Ballot	Ballot	Ballot	Ballot	Ballot	Ballot	Ballot	Ballot	Ballot	Ballot
1st A	1st B	1st A	1st C	1st B	1st C	1st A	1st B	1st C	1st A	1st C	1st D	1st A	1st A	1st C	1st A	1st C	1st D
2nd B	2nd D	2nd B	2nd B	2nd D	2nd B	2nd B	2nd D	2nd B	2nd B	2nd B	2nd C	2nd B	2nd B	2nd B	2nd B	2nd B	2nd C
3rd C	3rd C	3rd C	3rd D	3rd C	3rd D	3rd C	3rd C	3rd D	3rd C	3rd D	3rd B	3rd C	3rd C	3rd D	3rd C	3rd D	3rd B
4th D	4th A	4th D	4th A	4th A	4th A	4th D	4th A	4th A	4th D	4th A	4th A	4th D	4th D	4th A	4th D	4th A	4th A

Ballot	Ballot	Ballot	Ballot	Ballot	Ballot	Ballot	Ballot	Ballot	Ballot	Ballot	Ballot	Ballot	Ballot	Ballot	Ballot	Ballot	Ballot	Ballot
1st C	1st A	1st D	1st D	1st C	1st C	1st D	1st A	1st D	1st C	1st A	1st D	1st B	1st A	1st C	1st A	1st A	1st D	1st A
2nd B	2nd B	2nd C	2nd C	2nd B	2nd B	2nd C	2nd B	2nd C	2nd B	2nd B	2nd C	2nd D	2nd B	2nd D	2nd B	2nd B	2nd C	2nd B
3rd D	3rd C	3rd B	3rd B	3rd D	3rd D	3rd B	3rd C	3rd B	3rd D	3rd C	3rd B	3rd C	3rd C	3rd B	3rd C	3rd C	3rd B	3rd C
4th A	4th D	4th A	4th A	4th A	4th A	4th A	4th D	4th A	4th A	4th D	4th A	4th A	4th D	4th A	4th D	4th D	4th A	4th D

FIGURE 1-2 The 37 preference ballots for the Math Club election.

Last but not least, what about the *outcome* of the election? Since the purpose of the election is to choose a club president, it is pointless to discuss or consider which candidate comes in second place, third place, etc. This is a *winner-only* election.

EXAMPLE 1.2 THE MATH CLUB ELECTION (FULL RANKING)

Suppose now that we have pretty much the same situation as in Example 1.1 (same candidates, same voters, same preference ballots), but that the election is to choose not only the president of the club but also a vice-president, a treasurer, and a secretary. According to the club bylaws, the president is the candidate who comes in first, the vice-president is the candidate who comes in second, the treasurer is the candidate who comes in third, and the secretary is the candidate who comes in fourth.

Given that there are four candidates, each candidate will get to be an officer, but there is a big difference between being elected president and being elected treasurer (the president gets status and perks; the treasurer gets to collect the dues and balance the budget). In this version how you place matters, and the outcome should be a full *ranking* of the candidates.

| **EXAMPLE 1.3** | THE ACADEMY AWARDS

The Academy Awards (also known as the Oscars) are given out each year by the Academy of Motion Picture Arts and Sciences for Best Picture, Best Actress, Best Actor, Best Director, and many other, lesser categories (Sound Mixing, Makeup, etc.). The election process is not the same for all awards, so for the sake of simplicity we will just discuss the selection of Best Picture.

The *voters* in this election are all the eligible members of the Academy (approximately 6000 voters—5755 for the 2011 awards). After a complicated preliminary round (a process that we won't discuss here) ten films are selected as the nominees—these are our *candidates*. (For most other awards there are only five nominees.) Each voter is asked to submit a preference ballot ranking the ten candidates. There is only a winner (the other candidates are not ranked), with the winner determined by a voting method called plurality-with-elimination that we will discuss in detail in Section 1.4. (The winner of the 2011 Best Picture Award was *The Artist*.)

The part with which people are most familiar comes after the ballots are submitted and tabulated—the annual Academy Awards ceremony, held each year in late February. How many viewers realize that behind one of the most extravagant and glamorous events in pop culture lies an election?

| **EXAMPLE 1.4** | THE HEISMAN TROPHY

The Heisman Memorial Trophy Award is given annually to the "most outstanding player in collegiate football." The Heisman, as it is usually known, is not only a very prestigious award but also a very controversial award. With so many players playing so many different positions, how do you determine who is the most "outstanding"?

In theory, any football player in any division of college football is a potential *candidate* for the award. In practice, the real candidates are players from Division I programs and are almost always in the glamour positions—quarterback or running back. (Since its inception in 1935, only once has the award gone to a defensive player—Charles Woodson of Michigan.)

There are approximately 930 *voters* (the exact number of voters varies each year). The *voters* are members of the media plus all past Heisman award winners still living, plus one vote from the public (as determined by a survey conducted by ESPN). Each voter submits a *truncated preference ballot* consisting of a first, second, and third choice (see Fig. 1-1[d]). A first-place vote is worth 3 points, a second-place vote 2 points, and a third-place vote 1 point. The candidate with the most total points from all the ballots is awarded the Heisman trophy in a televised ceremony held each December at the Downtown Athletic Club in New York.

While only one player gets the award, the finalists are ranked by the number of total points received, in effect making the *outcome* of the Heisman trophy a *partial ranking* of the top four (sometimes five) candidates. (For the 2011 season, the Heisman Trophy went to Robert Griffin III, Baylor; second place to Andrew Luck, Stanford; third place to Trent Richardson, Alabama; fourth place to Montee Ball, Wisconsin; and fifth place to Tyrann Mathieu, LSU.)

EXAMPLE 1.5 *AMERICAN IDOL*

The single most watched program in the history of American television is *American Idol*, a singing competition for individuals (as opposed to *The X-Factor*, a similar singing competition that allows for groups as well as individuals). Each year, the winner of *American Idol* gets a big recording contract, and many past winners have gone on to become famous recording artists (Kelly Clarkson, Carrie Underwood, Taylor Hicks). While there is a lot at stake and a big reward for winning, *American Idol* is not a winner-only competition, and there is indeed a ranking of all the finalists. In fact, some nonwinners (Clay Aiken, Jennifer Hudson) have gone on to become great recording artists in their own right.

The 12 (sometimes 13) candidates who reach the final rounds of the competition compete in a weekly televised show. During and immediately after each weekly show the voters cast their votes. The candidate with the fewest number of votes gets eliminated from the competition, and the following week the process starts all over again with one fewer candidate (on rare occasions two candidates are eliminated in the same week—see Table 1-11). And who are the *voters* responsible for deciding the fate of these candidates? Anyone and everyone—you, me, Aunt Betsie—we are all potential voters. All one has to do to vote for a particular candidate is to text or call a toll-free number specific to that candidate ("to vote for Carly, call 1-866-IDOLS07," etc.). *American Idol* voting is an example of democracy run amok—you can vote for a candidate even if you never heard her sing, and you can vote as many times as you want.

By the final week of the competition there are only two finalists left, and after one last frenzied round of voting, the winner is determined. (For the 2011 *American Idol* competition there were nearly 750 million votes cast. Table 1-11 shows a summary of the results.)

Examples 1.1 through 1.5 represent just a small sample of how elections can be structured, both in terms of the ballots (think of these as the *inputs* to the election) and the types of outcomes we look for (the *outputs* of the election). We will revisit some of these examples and many others as we wind our way through the chapter.

Preference Ballots and Preference Schedules

Let's focus now on elections where the balloting is done by means of preference ballots, as in Examples 1.1 and 1.2. The great advantage of preference ballots (compared with, for example, single-choice ballots) is that they provide a great deal of useful information about an individual voter's preferences—in both direct and indirect ways.

Ballot	
1st	*C*
2nd	*B*
3rd	*D*
4th	*A*

FIGURE 1-3

To illustrate what we mean, consider the preference ballot shown in Fig. 1-3. This ballot directly tells us that the voter likes candidate *C* best, *B* second best, *D* third best, and *A* last. But, in fact, this ballot tells us a lot more—it tells us unequivocally which candidate the voter would choose if it came down to a choice between just two candidates. For example, if it came down to a choice between, say, *A* and *B*, which one would this voter choose? Of course she would choose *B*—she has *B* above *A* in her ranking. Thus, a preference ballot allows us to make relative comparisons between any two candidates—*the candidate higher on the ballot is always preferred over the candidate in the lower position*. Please take note of this simple but important idea, as we will use it repeatedly later in the chapter.

The second important idea we will use later is the fact that the relative preferences in a preference ballot do not change if one of the candidates withdraws or is eliminated. Once again, we can illustrate this using Fig. 1-3. What would happen if for some unforeseen reason candidate *B* drops out of the race right before the ballots are tabulated? Do we have to have a new election? Absolutely not—the old ballot simply becomes the ballot shown on the left in Fig. 1-4. The candidates above *B* stay put and each of the candidates below *B* moves up a spot.

Ballot		Ballot
1st *C*		1st *C*
~~2nd *B*~~	→	2nd *D*
3rd *D*		3rd *A*
4th *A*		

FIGURE 1-4

In an election with many voters, some voters will vote exactly the same way—for the same candidates in the same order of preference. If we take a careful look at the 37 ballots submitted for the Math Club election shown in Fig. 1-2, we see that 14 ballots look exactly the same (*A* first, *B* second, *C* third, *D* fourth), another 10 ballots look the same, and so on. So, if you were going to tabulate the 37 ballots, it might make sense to put all the *A-B-C-D* ballots in one pile, all the *C-B-D-A* ballots in another pile, and so on. If you were to do this you would get the five piles shown in Fig. 1-5 (the order in which you list the piles from left to right is irrelevant). Better yet, you can make the whole idea a little more formal by putting all the ballot information in a table such as Table 1-1, called the **preference schedule** for the election.

Ballot	Ballot	Ballot	Ballot	Ballot
1st *A*	1st *C*	1st *D*	1st *B*	1st *C*
2nd *B*	2nd *B*	2nd *C*	2nd *D*	2nd *D*
3rd *C*	3rd *D*	3rd *B*	3rd *C*	3rd *B*
4th *D*	4th *A*	4th *A*	4th *A*	4th *A*
14	10	8	4	1

FIGURE 1-5 The 37 Math Club election ballots organized into piles.

Number of voters	14	10	8	4	1
1st	*A*	*C*	*D*	*B*	*C*
2nd	*B*	*B*	*C*	*D*	*D*
3rd	*C*	*D*	*B*	*C*	*B*
4th	*D*	*A*	*A*	*A*	*A*

■ TABLE 1-1 Preference schedule for the Math Club election

We will be working with preference schedules throughout the chapter, so it is important to emphasize that a preference schedule is nothing more than a convenient bookkeeping tool—it summarizes all the elements that constitute the input to an election: the candidates, the voters, and the balloting. Just to make sure this is clear, we conclude this section with a quick example of how to read a preference schedule.

EXAMPLE 1.6 THE CITY OF KINGSBURG MAYORAL ELECTION

Number of voters	93	44	10	30	42	81
1st	*A*	*B*	*C*	*C*	*D*	*E*
2nd	*B*	*D*	*A*	*E*	*C*	*D*
3rd	*C*	*E*	*E*	*B*	*E*	*C*
4th	*D*	*C*	*B*	*A*	*A*	*B*
5th	*E*	*A*	*D*	*D*	*B*	*A*

■ TABLE 1-2 Preference schedule for the Kingsburg mayoral election

Table 1-2 shows the preference schedule summarizing the results of the most recent election for mayor of the city of Kingsburg (there actually is a city by that name, but the election is fictitious). Just by looking at the preference schedule we can answer all of the relevant input questions:

- *Candidates*: there were five candidates (*A*, *B*, *C*, *D*, and *E*, which are just abbreviations for their real names).

- *Voters*: there were 300 voters that submitted ballots (add the numbers at the head of each column: $93 + 44 + 10 + 30 + 42 + 81 = 300$).

- *Balloting*: the 300 preference ballots were organized into six piles as shown in Table 1-2.

The question that still remains unanswered: Who is the winner of the election? In the next four sections we will discuss different ways in which such output questions can be answered.

Ties

In any election, be it a *winner-only* election or a *ranking* of the candidates, ties can occur. What happens then?

In some elections the rule is that ties are allowed to stand and need not be broken. Here are a few interesting examples:

- In the 1968 Academy Awards, Katharine Hepburn and Barbra Streisand tied for Best Actress. Both received Oscars.

- In the 1992 Grammy Awards, Lisa Fischer and Patti La Belle tied for Best Female R&B Vocal Performance and shared the award.

- In the 1979 National League MVP balloting, Keith Hernandez and Willie Stargell tied for first and shared the award.

- In the 2011 *American Idol* competition, Thia Megia and Naima Adepapo tied for 10th place. They were declared as sharing the 10th–11th position (see Table 1-11).

In other situations, especially in elections for political office (president, senator, mayor, city council, etc.), ties cannot be allowed (can you imagine having co-mayors?), and then a tie-breaking rule must be specified. The Constitution, for example, stipulates how a tie in the Electoral College is broken, and most elections have a set rule for breaking ties. The most common method for breaking a tie for political office is through a runoff election, but runoff elections are expensive and take time, so many other tie-breaking procedures are used. Here are a few interesting examples:

- In the 2009 election for a seat in the Cave Creek, Arizona, city council, Thomas McGuire and Adam Trenk tied with 660 votes each. The winner was decided by drawing from a deck of cards. Mr. McGuire drew first—a six of hearts. Mr. Trenk (the young man with the silver belt buckle) drew next and drew a king of hearts. This is how Mr. Trenk became a city councilman.

- In the 2010 election for mayor of Jefferson City, Tennessee, Rocky Melton and Mark Potts tied with 623 votes each. The decision then went to a vote of the city council. Mr. Potts became the mayor.

- In the 2011 election for trustees of the Island Lake, Illinois, village board, Allen Murvine and Charles Cernak tied for one of the three seats with 576 votes each. The winner was decided by a coin toss. Mr. Cernak called tails and won the seat.

Ties and tie-breaking procedures add another layer of complexity to an already rich subject. To simplify our presentation, in this chapter we will stay away from ties as much as possible. In the rare example where a tie occurs, we will assume that the tie does not have to be broken.

The Plurality Method

The **plurality method** is arguably the most commonly used and simplest method for determining the outcome of an election. With the plurality method, all that matters is how many first-place votes each candidate gets: In a *winner-only* election the candidate with the most first-place votes is the winner; in a *ranked* election the candidate with the most first-place votes is first, the candidate with the second most is second, and so on.

For an election decided under the plurality method, *preference ballots* are not needed, since the voter's second, third, etc. choices are not used. But, since we already have the preference schedule for the Math Club election (Examples 1.1 and 1.2) let's use it to determine the outcome under the plurality method.

EXAMPLE 1.7   THE MATH CLUB ELECTION UNDER THE PLURALITY METHOD

Number of voters	14	10	8	4	1
1st	A	C	D	B	C
2nd	B	B	C	D	D
3rd	C	D	B	C	B
4th	D	A	A	A	A

■ **TABLE 1-3**   Preference schedule for the Math Club election

We discussed the Math Club election in Section 1.1. Table 1-3 shows once again the preference schedule for the election. Counting only first-place votes, we can see that A gets 14, B gets 4, C gets 11, and D gets 8. So there you have it: In the case of a *winner-only* election (see Example 1.1) the winner is A (Headline: "Alisha wins presidency of the Math Club"); in the case of a *ranked election* (see Example 1.2) the results are: A first (14 votes); C second (11 votes); D third (8 votes); B fourth (4 votes). (Headline: "New board of MAS elected! President—Alisha; VP—Carmen; Treasurer—Dave; Secretary—Boris.")

The vast majority of elections for political office in the United States are decided using the plurality method. The main appeal of the plurality method is its simplicity, but as we will see in our next example, the plurality method has many drawbacks.

EXAMPLE 1.8   THE 2010 MAINE GOVERNOR'S ELECTION

Like many states, Maine chooses its governor using the plurality method. In the 2010 election there were five candidates: Eliot Cutler (Independent), Paul LePage (Republican), Libby Mitchell (Democrat), Shawn Moody (Independent), and Kevin Scott (Independent). Table 1-4 shows the results of the election. Before reading on, take a close look at the numbers in Table 1-4 and draw your own conclusions.

Candidate	Votes	Percent
Eliot Cutler (Independent)	208,270	36.5%
Paul LePage (Republican)	218,065	38.2%
Libby Mitchell (Democrat)	109,937	19.3%
Shawn Moody (Independent)	28,756	5.0%
Kevin Scott (Independent)	5,664	1.0%

Source: The New York Times, *www.elections.nytimes.com/2010/results/governor*

■ **TABLE 1-4**   Results of 2010 Maine gubernatorial election

A big problem with the plurality method is that when there are more than two candidates we can end up with a winner that does not have a *majority* (i.e., more than 50%) of the votes. The 2010 Maine gubernatorial election is a case in point. As Table 1-4 shows, Paul LePage became governor with the support of only 38.2% of the voters (which means, of course, that 61.8% of the voters in Maine wanted someone else). A few days after the election, an editorial piece in the *Portland Press Herald* expressed the public concern about the outcome.

> *The election of Paul LePage with 38 percent of the vote means Maine's next governor won't take office with the support of the majority of voters—a situation that has occurred in six of the last seven gubernatorial elections .... Some people ... say it's time to reform the system so Maine's next governor can better represent the consensus of voters.* (*Is Winning an Election Enough?* Portland Press Herald, Nov. 10, 2010)

The second problem with the Maine governor election is the closeness of the election: Out of roughly 571,000 votes cast, less than 10,000 votes separated the winner and the runner-up. This is not the plurality method's fault, but it does raise the possibility that the results of the election could have been *manipulated* by a small number of voters. Imagine for a minute being inside the mind of a voter we call Mr. Insincere: "Of all these candidates, I like Kevin Scott the best. But if I vote for Scott I'm just wasting my vote—he doesn't have a chance. All the polls say that it really is a tight race between LePage and Cutler. I don't much care for either one, but LePage is the better of two evils. I'd better vote for LePage." The same thinking, of course, can be applied in the other direction—voters afraid to "waste" their vote on Scott (or Moody, or Mitchell) and insincerely voting for Cutler over Le Page. The problem is that we don't know how many *insincere votes* went one way or the other, and the possibility that there were enough insincere votes to tip the results of the election cannot be ruled out.

While all voting methods can be manipulated by insincere voters, the plurality method is the one that can be most easily manipulated, and insincere voting is quite common in real-world elections. For Americans, the most significant cases of insincere voting occur in close presidential or gubernatorial races between the two major party candidates and a third candidate ("the spoiler") who has little or no chance of winning. Insincere voting not only hurts small parties and fringe candidates, it has unintended and often negative consequences for the political system itself. The history of American political elections is littered with examples of independent candidates and small parties that never get a fair voice or a fair level of funding (it takes 5% of the vote to qualify for federal funds for the next election) because of the "let's not waste our vote" philosophy of insincere voters. The ultimate consequence of the plurality method is an entrenched two-party system that often gives the voters little real choice.

The last, but not least, of the problems with the plurality method is that a candidate may be preferred by the voters over all other candidates and yet not win the election. We will illustrate how this can happen with the example of the fabulous Tasmania State University marching band.

EXAMPLE 1.9   THE FABULOUS TSU BAND GOES BOWLING

Tasmania State University has a superb marching band. They are so good that this coming bowl season they have invitations to perform at five different bowl games: the Rose Bowl (*R*), the Hula Bowl (*H*), the Fiesta Bowl (*F*), the Orange Bowl (*O*), and the Sugar Bowl (*S*). An election is held among the 100 band members to decide in which of the five bowl games they will perform. Each band member

Number of voters	49	48	3
1st	R	H	F
2nd	H	S	H
3rd	F	O	S
4th	O	F	O
5th	S	R	R

■ **TABLE 1-5**   Preference schedule for the band election

submits a preference ballot ranking the five choices. The results of the election are shown in Table 1-5.

Under the plurality method the winner of the election is the Rose Bowl (R), with 49 first-place votes. It's hard not to notice that this is a rather bad outcome, as there are 51 voters that have the Rose Bowl as their last choice. By contrast, the Hula Bowl (H) has 48 first-place votes and 52 second-place votes. Simple common sense tells us that the Hula Bowl is a far better choice to represent the wishes of the entire band. In fact, we can make the following persuasive argument in favor of the Hula Bowl: If we compare the Hula Bowl with any other bowl on a *head-to-head* basis, the Hula Bowl is always the preferred choice. Take, for example, a comparison between the Hula Bowl and the Rose Bowl. There are 51 votes for the Hula Bowl (48 from the second column plus the 3 votes in the last column) versus 49 votes for the Rose Bowl. Likewise, a comparison between the Hula Bowl and the Fiesta Bowl would result in 97 votes for the Hula Bowl (first and second columns) and 3 votes for the Fiesta Bowl. And when the Hula Bowl is compared with either the Orange Bowl or the Sugar Bowl, it gets all 100 votes. Thus, no matter with which bowl we compare the Hula Bowl, there is always a majority of the band that prefers the Hula Bowl.

Marie Jean Antoine Nicolas Caritat, Marquis de Condorcet (1743–1794)

A candidate preferred by a majority of the voters over every other candidate when the candidates are compared in head-to-head comparisons is called a **Condorcet candidate** (named after the Marquis de Condorcet, an eighteenth-century French mathematician and philosopher). Not every election has a Condorcet candidate, but if there is one, it is a good sign that this candidate represents the voice of the voters better than any other candidate. In Example 1.9 the Hula Bowl is the Condorcet candidate—it is not unreasonable to expect that it should be the winner of the election. We will return to this topic in Section 1.6.

1.3 The Borda Count Method

The second most commonly used method for determining the winner of an election is the **Borda count method**, named after the Frenchman Jean-Charles de Borda. In this method each place on a ballot is assigned points. In an election with N candidates we give 1 point for *last* place, 2 points for *second from last* place, and so on. At the top of the ballot, a *first-place* vote is worth N points. The points are tallied for each candidate separately, and the candidate with the highest total is the winner. If we are ranking the candidates, the candidate with the second-most points comes in second, the candidate with the third-most points comes in third, and so on. We will start our discussion of the Borda count method by revisiting the Math Club election.

EXAMPLE 1.10 THE MATH CLUB ELECTION (BORDA COUNT)

Table 1-6 shows the preference schedule for the Math Club election with the Borda points for the candidates shown in parentheses to the right of their names. For example, the 14 voters in the first column ranked A first (giving A 14 × 4 = 56 points), B second (14 × 3 = 42 points), and so on.

Number of voters	14	10	8	4	1
1st (4 points)	A (56)	C (40)	D (32)	B (16)	C (4)
2nd (3 points)	B (42)	B (30)	C (24)	D (12)	D (3)
3rd (2 points)	C (28)	D (20)	B (16)	C (8)	B (2)
4th (1 point)	D (14)	A (10)	A (8)	A (4)	A (1)

■ **TABLE 1-6** Borda points for the Math Club election

When we tally the points,

> A gets 56 + 10 + 8 + 4 + 1 = 79 points,
>
> B gets 42 + 30 + 16 + 16 + 2 = 106 points,
>
> C gets 28 + 40 + 24 + 8 + 4 = 104 points,
>
> D gets 14 + 20 + 32 + 12 + 3 = 81 points.

The Borda winner of this election is Boris! (Wasn't Alisha the winner of this election under the plurality method?)

If we have to rank the candidates, B is first, C second, D third, and A fourth. To see what a difference the voting method makes, compare this ranking with the ranking obtained under the plurality method (Example 1.7).

EXAMPLE 1.11 THE 2011 HEISMAN AWARD

For general details on the Heisman Award, see Example 1.4. The Heisman is determined using a Borda count, but with *truncated preference ballots*: each voter chooses a first, second, and third choice out of a large list of candidates, with a first-place vote worth 3 points, a second-place vote worth 2 points, and a third-place vote worth 1 point.

Table 1-7 shows a summary of the results of the 2010 Heisman ballot. The table shows the number of first-, second-, and third-place votes for each of the four finalists; the last column shows the total point tally for each. Notice that Table 1-7 is not

Player	1st (3pts.)	2nd (2pts.)	3rd (1 pt.)	Total points
Robert Griffin III	405	168	136	1687
Andrew Luck	247	250	166	1407
Trent Richardson	138	207	150	978
Montee Ball	22	83	116	348
Tyrann Mathieu	34	63	99	327

Source: Heisman Award, *www.heisman.com/winners/r-griffin11.php*

■ **TABLE 1-7** 2010 Heisman Trophy: top four finalists

a preference schedule. Because the Heisman uses truncated preference ballots and many candidates get votes, it is easier and more convenient to summarize the balloting this way.

The last column of Table 1-7 shows the ranking of the finalists: Robert Griffin III (Baylor) won the Heisman easily, Andrew Luck (Stanford) was second, Trent Richardson (Alabama) was third, Montee Ball (Wisconsin) was fourth, and Tyrann Mathieu (LSU) was fifth.

Many variations of the standard Borda count method are possible, the most common being using a different set of values for the positions on the ballot. We will call these **modified Borda count** methods. Example 1.12 illustrates one situation where a modified Borda count is used.

EXAMPLE 1.12 | THE 2010 NATIONAL LEAGUE CY YOUNG AWARD

The Cy Young Award is an annual award given by Major League baseball for "the best pitcher" in each league (one award for the American League and one for the National League). For the National League award there are 32 *voters* (they are baseball writers—two from each of the 16 cities having a National League team), and each voter submits a truncated preference ballot with a first, second, third, fourth, and fifth choice. The modification in the Cy Young calculations (in effect for the first time with the 2010 award) is that first place is worth 7 points (rather than 5). The other places in the ballot count just as in a regular Borda count: 4 points for second, 3 points for third, 2 points for fourth, and 1 point for fifth. The idea here is to give extra value to first-place votes—the gap between a first and a second place should be bigger than the gap between a second and a third place.

Pitcher	1st (7 pts.)	2nd (4 pts.)	3rd (3 pts.)	4th (2 pts.)	5th (1 pt.)	Total points
Roy Halladay (PHI)	32	0	0	0	0	224
Adam Wainwright (STL)	0	28	3	0	1	122
Ubaldo Jimenez (COL)	0	4	19	8	1	90
Tim Hudson (ATL)	0	0	3	13	4	39
Josh Johnson (FLA)	0	0	5	5	9	34

Source: Baseball-Reference.com, *www.baseball-reference.com/awards/awards_2010.shtml*

■ **TABLE 1-8** 2010 National League Cy Young Award: top five finalists

Table 1-8 shows the top five finalists for the 2010 National League Cy Young award. An unusual thing happened in this election—Roy Halladay (Phillies) was the unanimous first choice of all 32 voters, thus garnering the maximum possible points ($32 \times 7 = 224$), a very rare event indeed.

In real life, the Borda count method (or some variation of it) is widely used in a variety of settings, from individual sport awards to music industry awards to the hiring of school principals, university presidents, and corporate executives. It is generally considered to be a much better method for determining the outcome of an election than the plurality method. In contrast to the plurality method, it takes into account the voter's preferences not just for first place but also for second, third, etc., and then chooses as the winner the candidate with the best average ranking—the best compromise candidate, if you will.

1.4 The Plurality-with-Elimination Method

In the United States most municipal and local elections have a majority requirement—a candidate needs a majority of the votes to get elected. With only two candidates this is rarely a problem (unless they tie, one of the two candidates must have a majority of the votes). When there are three or more candidates running, it can easily happen that no candidate has a majority. Typically, the candidate or candidates with the fewest first-place votes are eliminated, and a runoff election is held. But runoff elections are expensive, and in these times of tight budgets more efficient ways to accomplish the "runoff" are highly desirable.

A very efficient way to implement the runoff process without needing runoff elections is to use preference ballots, since a preference ballot tells us not only which candidate the voter wants to win but also which candidate the voter would choose in a runoff (with one important caveat—we assume the voters are consistent in their preferences and would stick with their original ranking of the candidates). The idea is to use the information in the preference schedule to eliminate the candidates with the fewest first-place votes one at a time until one of them gets a majority. This method has become increasingly popular and is nowadays known under several different names, including *plurality-with-elimination, instant runoff voting* (IRV), *ranked choice voting* (RCV), and the *Hare method*. For the sake of clarity, we will call it the plurality-with-elimination method—it is the most descriptive of all the names.

Here is a formal description of the **plurality-with-elimination method**:

- **Round 1.** Count the first-place votes for each candidate, just as you would in the plurality method. If a candidate has a majority of first-place votes, then that candidate is the winner. Otherwise, eliminate the candidate (or candidates if there is a tie) with the *fewest* first-place votes.

- **Round 2.** Cross out the name(s) of the candidates eliminated from the preference schedule and transfer those votes to the next eligible candidates on those ballots. Recount the votes. If a candidate has a majority then declare that candidate the winner. Otherwise, eliminate the candidate with the fewest votes.

- **Rounds 3, 4, . . .** Repeat the process, each time eliminating the candidate with the fewest votes and transferring those votes to the next eligible candidates. Continue until there is a candidate with a majority. That candidate is the winner of the election.

   In a ranked election the candidates should be ranked in reverse order of elimination: the candidate eliminated in the last round gets second place, the candidate eliminated in the second-to-last round gets third place, and so on.

EXAMPLE 1.13 THE MATH CLUB ELECTION (PLURALITY-WITH-ELIMINATION)

Let's see how the plurality-with-elimination method works when applied to the Math Club election. For the reader's convenience Table 1-9 shows the preference schedule again.

Number of voters	14	10	8	4	1
1st	A	C	D	B	C
2nd	B	B	C	D	D
3rd	C	D	B	C	B
4th	D	A	A	A	A

■ **TABLE 1-9**   Preference schedule for the Math Club election

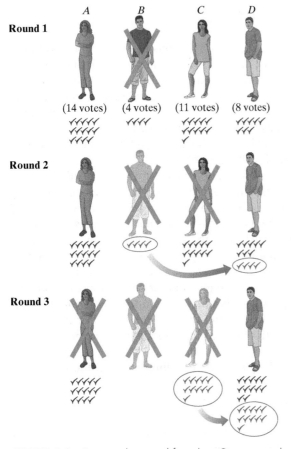

Round 1

Round 2

Round 3

FIGURE 1-6 Boris is eliminated first, then Carmen, and then Alisha. The last one standing is Dave.

Round 1.

Candidate	A	B	C	D
Votes	14	4	11	8

B has the fewest first-place votes and is eliminated first (Fig. 1-6).

Round 2. After B is eliminated, the four votes that originally went to B are transferred to D (per column 4 of Table 1-9). The new tally is

Candidate	A	C	D
Votes	14	11	12

In this round C has the fewest first-place votes and is eliminated.

Round 3. The 11 votes that went to C in round 2 are all transferred to D (per columns 2 and 5 of Table 1-9). The new tally is

Candidate	A	D
Number of first-place votes	14	23

The winner of the election is D! For a ranked election we have D first, A second (eliminated in round 3), C third (eliminated in round 2), and B last (eliminated in round 1).

Our next example illustrates a few subtleties that can come up when applying the plurality-with-elimination method.

EXAMPLE 1.14   THE CITY OF KINGSBURG MAYORAL ELECTION

Table 1-10 shows the preference schedule for the Kingsburg mayoral election first introduced in Example 1.6. To save money Kingsburg has done away with runoff elections and now uses plurality-with-elimination for all local elections. (Notice that since there are 300 voters voting in this election, a candidate needs 151 or more votes to win.)

Number of voters	93	44	10	30	42	81
1st	A	B	C	C	D	E
2nd	B	D	A	E	C	D
3rd	C	E	E	B	E	C
4th	D	C	B	A	A	B
5th	E	A	D	D	B	A

■ **TABLE 1-10** Preference schedule for the Kingsburg mayoral election

Round 1.

Candidate	A	B	C	D	E
Votes	93	44	40	42	81

Here C has the fewest number of first-place votes and is eliminated first. Of the 40 votes originally cast for C, 10 are transferred to A (per column 3 of Table 1-10) and 30 are transferred to E (per column 4 of Table 1-10).

Round 2.

Candidate	A	B	D	E
Number of first-place votes	103	44	42	111

Now D has the fewest first-place votes and is eliminated. The 42 votes originally cast for D would be transferred to C (per column 5 of Table 1-10), but C has already been eliminated, so the next eligible candidate is E (column 5 again). Thus, the 42 votes are transferred to E.

Round 3.

Candidate	A	B	E
Number of first-place votes	103	44	153

Since this is a winner-only election we are done! E has a majority and is declared the winner. (If this were a ranked election, we would continue on to Round 4, only to determine second place between A and B.)

Several variations of the plurality-with-elimination method are used in real-life elections. One of the most popular goes by the name *instant runoff voting* (also called *ranked choice voting* in some places). Instant runoff voting uses a truncated preference ballot (typically asking for just first, second, and third choice). Once the ballots are cast the process works very much like plurality-with-elimination: the candidate with the fewest first-place votes is eliminated and his votes are transferred to the second-place candidates in those ballots; in the next round the candidate with the fewest votes is eliminated and her votes are transferred to the next eligible candidate, and so on. There is one important difference: unlike regular plurality-with-elimination there is a point at which some votes can no longer be transferred (say your vote was for candidates X, Y, and Z —if and when all three of them are eliminated there is no one to transfer your vote to). Such votes are called *exhausted votes* and although perfectly legal, they don't count in the final analysis.

Instant runoff voting is used in several U.S. cities in elections for mayor and city council, including San Francisco, Minneapolis, St. Paul, and Oakland, California, as well as in elections for political office in Australia, Canada, Ireland, and New Zealand. We will illustrate how instant runoff voting works with the 2010 election for mayor of Oakland.

EXAMPLE 1.15 THE 2010 OAKLAND MAYORAL ELECTION

In 2010 the city of Oakland, California introduced instant runoff voting for the first time in all city elections with three or more candidates.

The election for mayor had 10 candidates. The top three candidates were Don Perata, Jean Quan, and Rebecca Kaplan; the remaining seven candidates had relatively few votes and for simplicity they will be lumped together under the name

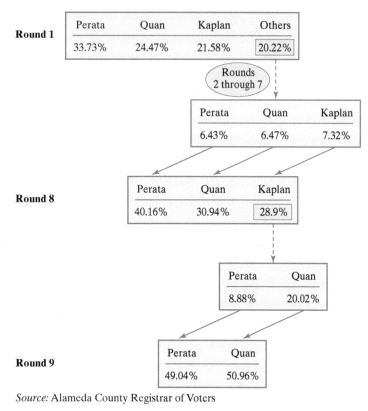

Round 1

Perata	Quan	Kaplan	Others
33.73%	24.47%	21.58%	20.22%

Rounds 2 through 7

Perata	Quan	Kaplan
6.43%	6.47%	7.32%

Round 8

Perata	Quan	Kaplan
40.16%	30.94%	28.9%

Perata	Quan
8.88%	20.02%

Round 9

Perata	Quan
49.04%	50.96%

Source: Alameda County Registrar of Voters

FIGURE 1-7   Results of 2010 Oakland mayoral election

"Others." There were 122,265 ballots cast, with each voter ranking up to three candidates (ballots with just one or two candidates are allowed). Of the original 122,265 ballots, 16,499 were exhausted (more on that later), so the final analysis is based on the 105,766 ballots that really counted. Figure 1-7 shows a summary of how the election went. (To simplify the calculations Fig. 1-7 shows percentages rather than the number of actual votes.) In the first count, Perata had 33.73% of the votes, Quan had 24.47%, Kaplan had 21.58%, and the seven other candidates together had 20.22%. In rounds 1 through 7 all the minor candidates were eliminated one at a time and their votes transferred to the top three candidates or exhausted: 6.43% were transferred to Perata, 6.47% were transferred to Quan, and 7.32% transferred to Kaplan. Round 8 starts with Perata at 40.16%, Quan at 30.94%, and Kaplan at 28.9%. Perata is still the clear leader. Kaplan has the fewest votes (barely) and is eliminated. Kaplan's votes are transferred—8.88% to Perata and 20.02% to Quan. In the final round Quan overtakes Perata 50.96% to 49.04% and is declared mayor of Oakland.

Note that a ballot that did not include either Perata or Quan did not count in the final analysis: at some point before round 9 all of the candidates on that ballot were eliminated, and at that point there was no candidate to transfer that ballot to. This explains the 16,499 exhausted ballots.

As mentioned earlier in this section, the practical advantage of plurality-with-elimination is that it does away with expensive and time-consuming runoff elections. There is one situation, however, where expense is not an issue and delaying the process is part of the game: televised competitions such as *Dancing with the Stars*, *The X-Factor*, and *American Idol*. The longer the competition goes, the higher the ratings—having many runoffs accomplishes this goal. All of these "elections" work under the same variation of the plurality-with-elimination method: have a round of competition, vote, eliminate the candidate (or candidates) with the fewest votes. The following week have another round of competition and repeat the process. This builds up to the last round of competition, when there are two finalists left. Millions of us get caught up in the hoopla. We will illustrate one such election using the 2011 *American Idol* competition.

EXAMPLE 1.16 THE 2011 *AMERICAN IDOL* COMPETITION

We discussed *American Idol* as an election in Example 1.5. Table 1-11 shows the evolution of the 2011 competition. As noted in Example 1.5, the winner is the big deal, but how the candidates place in the competition is also of some relevance, so we consider *American Idol* a ranked election. Working our way up from the bottom of the table, we see that the first candidate eliminated was Ashton Jones. This puts Ashton in 13th place. The second week Karen Rodriguez was eliminated. This puts Karen in 12th place. The third week no one was eliminated (there is a rule that allows the judges to give candidates a free pass to the next round). The fourth week Naima Adepapo and Thia Megia were eliminated in the same round (another mysterious rule). Naima and Thia were declared tied for 10th–11th place.

Winner	→	Scotty McCreery		
Runner-up	→	Lauren Alaina	→	eliminated final week
3rd place	→	Haley Reinhart	→	eliminated week 11
4th place	→	James Durbin	→	eliminated week 10
5th place	→	Jacob Lusk	→	eliminated week 9
6th place	→	Casey Abrams	→	eliminated week 8
7th place	→	Stefano Langone	→	eliminated week 7
8th place	→	Paul McDonald	→	eliminated week 6
9th place	→	Pia Toscano	→	eliminated week 5
10th place ⌉ 11th place ⌋	→	⌈ Naima Adepapo ⌉ ⌊ Thia Megia (tie) ⌋	→	eliminated week 4
12th place	→	Karen Rodriguez	→	eliminated week 2
13th place	→	Ashton Jones	→	eliminated week 1

■ **TABLE 1-11**   2011 *American Idol* results

And so it went for a full three months. In the final week, after a lot of controversy, it came down to Lauren Alaina and Scotty McCreery. Lauren was eliminated last, and Scotty became the 2011 *American Idol*.

1.5 | The Method of Pairwise Comparisons

One of the most useful features of a preference schedule is that it allows us to find the winner of any **pairwise comparison** between candidates. Specifically, given any two candidates—call them X and Y—we can count how many voters rank X above Y and how many rank Y above X. The one with the most votes wins the pairwise comparison. This is the basis for a method called the **method of pairwise comparisons** (sometimes also called *Copeland's method*). For each possible pairwise comparison between candidates, give 1 point to the winner, 0 points to the loser (if the pairwise comparison ends up in a tie give each candidate $\frac{1}{2}$ point). The candidate with the most points is the winner. (If we are ranking the candidates, the candidate with the second-most points is second, and so on.) The method of pairwise comparisons is very much like a round-robin tournament: (1) every player plays every other player once; (2) the winner of each "match" gets a point and the loser gets no points (if there is a tie each gets $\frac{1}{2}$ point); and (3) the player with the most points wins the tournament.

As usual, we will start with the Math Club election as our first example.

EXAMPLE 1.17 THE MATH CLUB ELECTION (PAIRWISE COMPARISONS)

Table 1-12 shows, once again, the preference schedule for the Math Club election. With four candidates, there are six possible pairwise comparisons to consider: (1) A v B, (2) A v C, (3) A v D, (4) B v C, (5) B v D, and (6) C v D. We'll look at (1) A v B and (6) C v D and leave the details of the other four to the reader.

Number of voters	14	10	8	4	1
1st	A	C	D	B	C
2nd	B	B	C	D	D
3rd	C	D	B	C	B
4th	D	A	A	A	A

■ **TABLE 1-12**   Preference schedule for the Math Club election

Pairwise comparison	Votes	Winner
(1) A v B	A (14); B (23)	B
(2) A v C	A (14); C (23)	C
(3) A v D	A (14); D (23)	D
(4) B v C	B (18); C (19)	C
(5) B v D	B (28); D (9)	B
(6) C v D	C (25); D (12)	C
Total points:	$C = 3, B = 2, D = 1, A = 0$	

■ **TABLE 1-13** Pairwise comparisons for the Math Club election

- A v B: The first column of Table 1-12 represents 14 votes for A (A is ranked higher than B); the remaining 23 votes are for B (B is ranked higher than A in the last four columns of the table). The winner of this comparison is B.

- C v D: The first, second, and last columns of Table 1-12 represent votes for C (C is ranked higher than D); the third and fourth columns represent votes for D (D is ranked higher than C). Thus, C has 25 votes to D's 12 votes. The winner of this comparison is C.

We continue this way, checking the results of all six possible comparisons (try it now on your own, before you read on!). Once you are done, you should get something along the lines of Table 1-13 with a summary of the results (a sort of scoreboard, if you will.) From Table 1-13 one can immediately figure out the outcome of the election: In a winner-only election the winner is C (with 3 points); in a ranked election C is first (3 points), B second (2 points), D third (1 point), and A fourth (no points).

		Ranking			
Method	Winner only	1st	2nd	3rd	4th
Plurality	A	A	C	D	B
Borda count	B	B	C	D	A
Plurality with elimination	D	D	A	C	B
Pairwise comparisons	C	C	B	D	A

■ **TABLE 1-14** The outcome of the Math Club election under four different voting methods

If you have been paying close attention, you may have noticed that the results of the Math Club election have been different under each of the voting methods we have discussed—both in terms of the winner and in terms of the ranking of the candidates. This can be seen quite clearly in the summary results shown in Table 1-14. It is amazing how much the outcome of an election can depend on the voting method used!

One more important comment about Example 1.17: Notice that C was the *undefeated* champion, as C won each of the pairwise comparisons against the other candidates. (We already saw that there is a name for a candidate that beats all the other candidates in pairwise comparisons—we call such a candidate a *Condorcet* candidate.) The method of pairwise comparisons always chooses the Condorcet candidate (when there is one) as the winner of the election, but this is not true with all methods. Under the plurality method, for example, you can have a Condorcet candidate that does not win the election (see Example 1.9).

Although the method of pairwise comparisons is a pretty good method, in real-life elections it is not used as much as the other three methods we discussed. In the next example we will illustrate one interesting and meaningful (if you are a football fan) application of the method—the selection of draft choices in the National Football League. Because NFL teams are extremely secretive about how they make their draft decisions, we will illustrate the general idea with a made-up example.

EXAMPLE 1.18 THE NFL DRAFT

The Los Angeles LAXers are the newest expansion team in the NFL and are awarded the first pick in the upcoming draft. The draft committee (made up of coaches, scouts, and team executives) has narrowed down the list to five candidates: Allen, Byers, Castillo, Dixon, and Evans. After many meetings, the draft committee is ready to vote for the team's first pick in the draft. The election is to be decided using the method of pairwise comparisons.

Table 1-15 shows the preference schedule obtained after each of the 22 members of the draft committee submits a preference ballot ranking the five candidates. There is a total of 10 separate pairwise comparisons to be looked at, and the results are shown in Table 1-16 (we leave it to the reader to check the details.)

Number of voters	2	6	4	1	1	4	4
1st	A	B	B	C	C	D	E
2nd	D	A	A	B	D	A	C
3rd	C	C	D	A	A	E	D
4th	B	D	E	D	B	C	B
5th	E	E	C	E	E	B	A

■ **TABLE 1-15**   LAXer's draft choice election

We can see from Table 1-16 that the winner of the election is Allen with 3 points. Notice that things are a little trickier here: Allen is the winner of the election even though the draft committee prefers Byers to Allen in a pairwise comparison between the two. We will return to this example in Section 1.6.

Pairwise comparison	Votes	Winner (points)
A v B	A (7); B (15)	B (1)
A v C	A (16); C (6)	A (1)
A v D	A (13); D (9)	A (1)
A v E	A (18); E (4)	A (1)
B v C	B (10); C (12)	C (1)
B v D	B (11); D (11) ← tie	$B\left(\frac{1}{2}\right); D\left(\frac{1}{2}\right)$
B v E	B (14); E (8)	B (1)
C v D	C (12); D (10)	C (1)
C v E	C (10); E (12)	E (1)
D v E	D (18); E (4)	D (1)
Total points:	$A = 3, B = 2\frac{1}{2}, C = 2, D = 1\frac{1}{2}, E = 1$	

■ **TABLE 1-16**   Pairwise comparisons for Example 1.18

You probably noticed in Examples 1-17 and 1-18 that, compared with the other methods, pairwise comparisons takes a lot more work. Each comparison requires a separate calculation, and there seems to be a lot of comparisons that need to be checked. How many? We saw that with 4 candidates there are 6 separate comparisons and with 5 candidates there are 10. As the number of candidates grows, the number of comparisons grows even more. Table 1-17 illustrates the relation

Number of candidates	4	5	6	7	8	9	10	...	N
Number of pairwise comparisons	6	10	15	21	28	36	45	...	$\frac{N(N-1)}{2}$

■ **TABLE 1-17**   The number of pairwise comparisons

between the number of candidates and the number of pairwise comparisons. The general relation is given by the following useful formula:

$$\text{Number of candidates} = N \Rightarrow \text{Number of pairwise comparisons} = N(N-1)/2$$

1.6   Fairness Criteria and Arrow's Impossibility Theorem

So far, this is what we learned: There are many different types of elections and there are different ways to decide their outcome. We examined four different voting methods in some detail, but there are many others that we don't have time to discuss (a few are mentioned in the exercises). So now comes a different but fundamental question (that may have already crossed your mind):

Kenneth J. Arrow (1921–   )

Of all those voting methods out there, which one is the best? As simple as it sounds, this question has vexed social scientists and mathematicians for centuries, going back to Condorcet and Borda in the mid 1700s. For multi-candidate elections (three or more candidates) there is no good answer. In fact, we now know that there are limitations to *all* voting methods. This is a very important and famous discovery known as **Arrow's Impossibility Theorem**. In this section we will discuss the basic ideas behind this theorem.

In the late 1940s the American economist Kenneth Arrow turned the question of finding an ideal voting method on its head and asked himself the following: *What would it take for a voting method to at least be a fair voting method?* To answer this question Arrow set forth a minimum set of requirements that we will call Arrow's **fairness criteria**. (In all fairness, Arrow's original formulation was quite a bit more complicated than the one we present here. The list below is a simplified version.)

- **The majority criterion.** A majority candidate (i.e., a candidate with a majority of the first place votes) should always be the winner.
- **The Condorcet criterion.** A Condorcet candidate (i.e., a candidate that beats each of the other candidates in a pairwise comparison) should always be the winner.
- **The monotonicity criterion.** If candidate X is the winner, then X would still be the winner had a voter ranked X higher in his preference ballot. (In other words, a voter should not be able to hurt the winner by moving him up in his ballot.)
- **The independence-of-irrelevant-alternatives (IIA) criterion.** If candidate X is the winner, then X would still be the winner had one or more of the *irrelevant alternatives* (i.e., losing candidates) not been in the race. (In other words, the winner should not be hurt by the elimination from the election of irrelevant alternatives.)

The above fairness criteria represent some (not necessarily all) of the basic principles we expect a democratic election to satisfy and can be used as a benchmark by which we can measure any voting method. If a method violates any one of these criteria, then there is the potential for unfair results under that method.

The next set of examples illustrates how *violations* of the different fairness criteria might occur.

EXAMPLE 1.19   THE BORDA COUNT VIOLATES THE MAJORITY CRITERION

Number of voters	6	2	3
1st	A	B	C
2nd	B	C	D
3rd	C	D	B
4th	D	A	A

Table 1-18 shows the preference schedule for a small election. The majority candidate in this election is A with 6 out of 11 first-place votes, but the winner under the Borda count method is B (32 points to A's 29 points).

■ **TABLE 1-18**   Preference schedule for Example 1.19

Essentially what happened in Example 1.19 is that although a majority of the voters had A as their first choice there were also many voters that had A as their last choice (voters either loved A or hated A). Candidate B, on the other hand, was more of a compromise candidate—few first-place votes but enough second- and third-place votes to make a difference and beat A. It is not hard to see how similar violations of the majority criterion might often happen under the Borda count method.

EXAMPLE 1.20   THE PLURALITY METHOD VIOLATES THE CONDORCET CRITERION

Number of voters	49	48	3
1st	R	H	F
2nd	H	S	H
3rd	F	O	S
4th	O	F	O
5th	S	R	R

Let's revisit Example 1.9 (The Fabulous TSU Band Goes Bowling). Table 1-19 shows the preference schedule once again. In this election the Hula Bowl is the Condorcet candidate (see Example 1.9 for the details), but the winner under the plurality method is the Rose Bowl.

■ **TABLE 1-19**   Preference schedule for Example 1.20

Example 1.20 illustrates how, by disregarding the voters' preferences other than first choice, the plurality method can end up choosing a clearly inferior candidate (the Rose Bowl) over a Condorcet candidate (the Hula Bowl).

EXAMPLE 1.21   PLURALITY-WITH-ELIMINATION VIOLATES THE MONOTONICITY CRITERION

This example comes in two parts—a before and an after. The "before" part shows how the voters intend to vote just before they cast their ballots. Table 1-20(a) shows the preference schedule for the "before" election. If all voters vote exactly as shown in Table 1-20(a), C will be the winner under the plurality-with-elimination method (B is eliminated in the first round and the 8 votes for B get transferred to C in the second round).

Number of voters	7	8	10	2
1st	A	B	C	A
2nd	B	C	A	C
3rd	C	A	B	B

(a)

Number of voters	7	8	10	2
1st	A	B	C	C
2nd	B	C	A	A
3rd	C	A	B	B

(b)

■ **TABLE 1-20**   Preference schedules for Example 1.21 (a) before the change and (b) after the change

Now imagine that just before the ballots are cast the two voters represented by the last column of Table 1-20(a) decide to move C from second place to first place on their ballots. This is a change favorable to C, and we would not expect it to change the outcome (as C would have won anyway). But now the preference schedule looks like Table 1-20(b). In this election A is eliminated in the first round, the 7 votes for A are transferred to B, and B wins the election!

Looking at Example 1.21 in retrospect we can say that C lost the election because of *too many* first-place votes! (Had C been able to talk two of his supporters into placing him in second place and A in first place he would have won the election.) This kind of perverse reversal of electoral fortunes is what the monotonicity criterion seeks to prevent. When the monotonicity criterion is not satisfied we can imagine candidates campaigning *not* to get too many first-place votes!

| **EXAMPLE 1.22** | PAIRWISE COMPARISONS VIOLATES THE IIA |

Number of voters	2	6	4	1	1	4	4
1st	A	B	B	C	C	D	E
2nd	D	A	A	B	D	A	C
3rd	C	C	D	A	A	E	D
4th	B	D	E	D	B	C	B
5th	E	E	C	E	E	B	A

■ **TABLE 1-21**   LAXer's draft choice election: Original preference schedule

This example is a continuation of Example 1.18 (The NFL Draft). Table 1-21 is a repeat of Table 1-15. We saw in Example 1.18 that the winner of the election under the method of pairwise comparisons is Allen (you may want to go back and refresh your memory). The LAXers are prepared to make Allen their number-one draft choice and offer him a big contract. Allen is happy. End of story? Not quite.

Just before the announcement is made, it is discovered that one of the irrelevant alternatives (Castillo) should not have been included in the list of candidates. (Nobody had bothered to tell the draft committee that Castillo had failed the team physical!) So, Castillo is removed from the preference schedule and everything is recalculated. The new preference schedule is now shown in Table 1-22 (it is Table 1-21 after C is removed). Table 1-23 shows the result of the six pairwise comparisons between Allen, Byers, Dixon, and Evans. We can see that the winner of the election is now Byers! Other than Byers, nobody is happy!

Number of voters	2	6	4	1	1	4	4
1st choice	A	B	B	B	D	D	E
2nd choice	D	A	A	A	A	A	D
3rd choice	B	D	D	D	B	E	B
4th choice	E	E	E	E	E	B	A

■ **TABLE 1-22**   Preference schedule after C is removed

Pairwise comparison	Votes	Winner
A v B	A (7); B (15)	B
A v D	A (13); D (9)	A
A v E	A (18); E (4)	A
B v D	B (11); D (11)	tie
B v E	B (14); E (8)	B
D v E	D (18); E (4)	D
Total points:	$B = 2\frac{1}{2}$, $A = 2$, $D = 1\frac{1}{2}$, $E = 0$	

■ **TABLE 1-23** *Pairwise comparisons for Example 1.22*

Example 1.22 illustrates a typical violation of the IIA: The elimination of an irrelevant alternative (Castillo) penalized Allen and made him lose an election he would have otherwise won and rewarded Byers, allowing him to win an election he would have otherwise lost. Clearly this is not fair, and the independence of irrelevant alternatives criterion aims to prevent these types of situations.

Criterion	Plurality	Borda count	Plurality-with-elimination	Pairwise comparisons
Majority	✓	Yes	✓	✓
Condorcet	Yes	Yes	Yes	✓
Monotonicity	✓	✓	Yes	✓
IIA	Yes	Yes	Yes	Yes

■ **TABLE 1-24** *Summary of violations of the fairness criteria. ("Yes" indicates that the method violates the criterion.)*

The point of the four preceding examples is to illustrate the fact that each of the voting methods we studied in this chapter violates one of Arrow's fairness criteria. In fact, some of the voting methods violate more than one criterion. The full story of which fairness criteria are violated by each voting method is summarized in Table 1-24. (For examples illustrating some of the other violations shown in Table 1-24 see Exercises 51 through 55.)

If you are looking at Table 1-24 and asking yourself "So what's the point? Why did we spend so much time learning about voting methods that are so flawed?" you have a legitimate gripe. The problem is that we don't have better options—*every voting method is flawed*. This remarkable fact was discovered in 1949 by Kenneth Arrow and is known as *Arrow's Impossibility Theorem*. To be more precise, Arrow demonstrated that for elections involving three or more candidates *it is mathematically impossible for a voting method to satisfy all four of his fairness criteria*.

In one sense, Arrow's Impossibility Theorem is a bit of a downer. It tells us that no matter how hard we try democracy will never have a perfectly fair voting method and that the potential for unfairness is built into every election. This does not mean that every election is unfair or that every voting method is equally bad, nor does it mean that we should stop trying to improve the quality of our voting experience.

 Conclusion

Elections are the mechanism that allows us to make social decisions in a *democracy*. (In contrast to a *dictatorship*, where social decisions are made by one individual and elections are either meaningless or nonexistent.) The purpose of this chapter is to help you see elections in a new light.

In this chapter we discussed many important concepts, including *preference ballots*, *preference schedules*, *winner-only* versus *ranked elections*, *voting methods*, and *fairness criteria*. We saw plenty of examples of elections—some made-up, some real.

We learned same specific skills such as interpreting a preference schedule and computing the outcome of an election under four different voting methods and variations thereof.

Beyond the specific concepts and skills, there were several important general themes that ran through the chapter:

- *Elections are ubiquitous.* The general public tends to think of elections mostly in terms of political decisions (president, governor, mayor, city council, etc.), but elections are behind almost every meaningful social decision made outside the political arena—Academy Awards, *American Idol*, Heisman Trophy, MVP awards, Homecoming Queen, where to go to dinner, etc.

- *There are many different voting methods.* The outcome of an election can be determined in many different ways. In this chapter we discussed in some detail only four methods: *plurality, Borda count, plurality-with-elimination,* and *pairwise comparisons.* By no means do these four exhaust the list—there are many other voting methods, some quite elaborate and exotic (see, for example, Exercise 70).

- *Different voting methods can produce different outcomes.* We saw an extreme illustration of this with the Math Club election: each of the four voting methods produced a different winner. Since there were four candidates, we can say that each of them won the election (just pick the "right" voting method). Of course, this doesn't happen all the time and there are many situations where different voting methods produce the same outcome.

- *Fairness in voting is elusive.* For a voting method to be considered fair there are certain basic criteria that it should consistently satisfy. These are called *fairness criteria.* We introduced four in this chapter (*majority, Condorcet, monotonicity,* and *independence of irrelevant alternatives*), but there are others (see, for example, Exercises 71 and 72). Each fairness criterion represents a basic principle we expect a democratic election to satisfy. When a voting method violates any one of these criteria then there is the potential for unfair results under that method. All of the voting methods we discussed in this chapter violate at least one (sometimes several) of the criteria, and there is a good reason why: for elections with three or more candidates it is mathematically impossible for any voting method to satisfy all four fairness criteria. This is a simplified version of *Arrow's Impossibility Theorem.*

> 66 The search of the great minds of recorded history for the perfect democracy, it turns out, is the search for a chimera, a logical self-contradiction. 99
>
> – *Paul Samuelson*

One concluding thought about this chapter. One should not interpret Arrow's Impossibility Theorem to mean that democracy is bad and that elections are pointless. The lesson to be learned from Arrow's Impossibility Theorem is that no voting system is perfect, because there are some built-in limitations to the process of making decisions in a democracy. This knowledge was made possible through the power of mathematical ideas.

KEY CONCEPTS

1.1 The Basic Elements of an Election

- **single-choice ballot:** a ballot in which a voter only has to choose one candidate, **4**

- **preference ballot:** a ballot in which the voter has to rank all candidates in order of preference, **4**

- **truncated preference ballot:** a ballot in which a voter only has to rank the top k choices rather than all the choices, **4**

- **ranking (full ranking):** in an election, an outcome that lists *all* the candidates in order of preference (first, second, . . . , last), **5**

- **partial ranking:** in an election, an outcome where just the top *k* candidates are ranked, **5**

- **preference schedule:** a table that summarizes the preference ballots of all the voters, **8**

1.2 The Plurality Method

- **plurality method:** a voting method that ranks candidates based on the number of first-place votes they receive, **10**

- **insincere voting:** voting for candidates in a manner other than the voter's real preference with the purpose of manipulating the outcome of the election, **11**

- **Condorcet candidate:** a candidate that beats all the other candidates in pairwise comparisons, **12**

1.3 The Borda Count Method

- **Borda count method:** a voting method that assigns points to positions on the ballot and ranks candidates according to the number of points, **12**

1.4 The Plurality-with-Elimination Method

- **plurality-with-elimination method:** a voting method that chooses the candidate with a majority of the votes; when there isn't one it eliminates the candidate(s) with the least votes and transfers those votes to the next highest candidate on those ballots, continuing this way until there is a majority candidate, **15**

- **instant-runoff voting:** a variation of the plurality-with-elimination method based on truncated preference ballots, **17**

1.5 The Method of Pairwise Comparisons

- **method of pairwise comparisons:** a voting method based on head-to-head comparisons between candidates that assigns one point to the winner of each comparison, none to the loser, and $\frac{1}{2}$ point to each of the two candidates in case of a tie, **19**

1.6 Fairness Criteria and Arrow's Impossibility Theorem

- **fairness criteria:** basic rules that define formal requirements for fairness—a fair voting method should always satisfy these basic rules, **22**

- **majority criterion:** a fairness criterion that says that when a candidate receives a majority of the first-place votes, that candidate should be the winner of the election, **22**

- **Condorcet criterion:** a fairness criterion that says that when there is a Condorcet candidate then that candidate should be the winner of the election, **22**

- **monotonicity criterion:** a fairness criterion that says that a candidate that would otherwise win an election should not lose the election merely because some voters changed their ballots in a manner that favors that candidate, **22**

- **independence-of-irrelevant-alternatives criterion:** a criterion that says that a candidate that would otherwise win an election should not lose the election merely because one of the losing candidates withdraws from the race, **22**

- **Arrow's Impossibility Theorem:** a theorem that demonstrates that a voting method that is guaranteed to always produce fair outcomes is a mathematical impossibility, **22, 25**

EXERCISES

WALKING

1.1 Ballots and Preference Schedules

1. Figure 1-8 shows the preference ballots for an election with 21 voters and 5 candidates. Write out the preference schedule for this election.

Ballot	Ballot	Ballot	Ballot	Ballot	Ballot	Ballot
1st C	1st A	1st B	1st A	1st C	1st D	1st A
2nd E	2nd D	2nd E	2nd B	2nd E	2nd C	2nd B
3rd D	3rd B	3rd A	3rd C	3rd D	3rd B	3rd C
4th A	4th C	4th C	4th D	4th A	4th E	4th D
5th B	5th E	5th D	5th E	5th B	5th A	5th E

Ballot	Ballot	Ballot	Ballot	Ballot	Ballot	Ballot
1st B	1st A	1st D	1st D	1st A	1st C	1st A
2nd E	2nd B	2nd C	2nd C	2nd B	2nd E	2nd D
3rd A	3rd C	3rd B	3rd B	3rd C	3rd D	3rd B
4th C	4th D	4th A	4th E	4th D	4th A	4th C
5th D	5th E	5th E	5th A	5th E	5th B	5th E

Ballot	Ballot	Ballot	Ballot	Ballot	Ballot	Ballot
1st B	1st C	1st A	1st C	1st A	1st D	1st D
2nd E	2nd E	2nd B	2nd E	2nd E	2nd C	2nd C
3rd A	3rd D	3rd C	3rd D	3rd D	3rd B	3rd B
4th C	4th A	4th D	4th A	4th C	4th A	4th E
5th D	5th B	5th E	5th B	5th E	5th E	5th A

FIGURE 1-8

2. Figure 1-9 shows the preference ballots for an election with 17 voters and 4 candidates. Write out the preference schedule for this election.

Ballot	Ballot	Ballot	Ballot	Ballot
1st C	1st B	1st A	1st C	1st B
2nd A	2nd C	2nd D	2nd A	2nd C
3rd D	3rd D	3rd B	3rd D	3rd D
4th B	4th A	4th C	4th B	4th A

Ballot	Ballot	Ballot	Ballot	Ballot	Ballot
1st A	1st A	1st B	1st B	1st C	1st C
2nd D	2nd C	2nd C	2nd C	2nd A	2nd A
3rd B	3rd D	3rd D	3rd D	3rd D	3rd D
4th C	4th B	4th A	4th A	4th B	4th B

Ballot	Ballot	Ballot	Ballot	Ballot	Ballot
1st A	1st A	1st C	1st B	1st A	1st C
2nd C	2nd D	2nd A	2nd C	2nd D	2nd A
3rd D	3rd B	3rd D	3rd D	3rd B	3rd D
4th B	4th C	4th B	4th A	4th C	4th B

FIGURE 1-9

Exercises 3 through 6 refer to an alternative format for preference ballots in which the names of the candidates appear on the ballot and the voter is asked to put a rank (1, 2, 3, etc.) next to each name [see Fig. 1-1(c)]. (This alternative format makes it easier on the voters and is useful when the names are long or when a misspelled name invalidates the ballot. The main disadvantage is that it tends to favor the candidates that are listed first.)

3. Table 1-25 shows the preference schedule for an election based on the alternative format for the preference ballots. Rewrite Table 1-25 in the conventional preference schedule format used in the text. (Use *A*, *B*, *C*, *D*, and *E* as shorthand for the names of the candidates.)

Number of voters	37	36	24	13	5
Alvarez	3	1	2	4	3
Brownstein	1	2	1	2	5
Clarkson	4	4	5	3	1
Dax	5	3	3	5	4
Easton	2	5	4	1	2

■ **TABLE 1-25**

4. Table 1-26 shows the preference schedule for an election based on the alternative format for the preference ballots. Rewrite Table 1-26 in the conventional preference schedule format used in the text. (Use *A*, *B*, *C*, *D*, and *E* as shorthand for the names of the candidates.)

Number of voters	14	10	8	7	4
Andersson	2	3	1	5	3
Broderick	1	1	2	3	2
Clapton	4	5	5	2	4
Dutkiewicz	5	2	4	1	5
Eklundh	3	4	3	4	1

■ **TABLE 1-26**

5. Table 1-27 shows the preference schedule for an election. Rewrite Table 1-27 using the alternative preference schedule format.

Number of voters	14	10	8	7	4
1st	*B*	*B*	*A*	*D*	*E*
2nd	*A*	*D*	*B*	*C*	*B*
3rd	*E*	*A*	*E*	*B*	*A*
4th	*D*	*E*	*D*	*E*	*C*
5th	*C*	*C*	*C*	*A*	*D*

■ **TABLE 1-27**

6. Table 1-28 shows the preference schedule for an election. Rewrite Table 1-28 using the alternative preference schedule format.

Number of voters	37	36	24	13	5
1st	A	B	D	C	B
2nd	C	A	B	A	D
3rd	B	D	C	E	E
4th	E	C	E	B	A
5th	D	E	A	D	C

■ **TABLE 1-28**

7. An election is held to choose the Chair of the Mathematics Department at Tasmania State University. The candidates are Professors Argand, Brandt, Chavez, Dietz, and Epstein (A, B, C, D, and E for short). Table 1-29 shows the preference schedule for the election.

Number of voters	5	5	3	3	3	2
1st	A	C	A	B	D	D
2nd	B	E	D	E	C	C
3rd	C	D	B	A	B	B
4th	D	A	C	C	E	A
5th	E	B	E	D	A	E

■ **TABLE 1-29**

(a) How many people voted in this election?

(b) How many first-place votes are needed for a majority?

(c) Which candidate had the fewest last-place votes?

8. The student body at Eureka High School is having an election for Homecoming Queen. The candidates are Alicia, Brandy, Cleo, and Dionne (A, B, C, and D for short). Table 1-30 shows the preference schedule for the election.

Number of voters	202	160	153	145	125	110	108	102	55
1st	B	C	A	D	D	C	B	A	A
2nd	D	B	C	B	A	A	C	B	D
3rd	A	A	B	A	C	D	A	D	C
4th	C	D	D	C	B	B	D	C	B

■ **TABLE 1-30**

(a) How many students voted in this election?

(b) How many first-place votes are needed for a majority?

(c) Which candidate had the fewest last-place votes?

9. The Demublican Party is holding its annual convention. The 1500 voting delegates are choosing among three possible party platforms: L (a liberal platform), C (a conservative platform), and M (a moderate platform). Seventeen percent of the delegates prefer L to M and M to C. Thirty-two percent of the delegates like C the most and L the least. The rest of the delegates like M the most and C the least. Write out the preference schedule for this election.

10. The Epicurean Society is holding its annual election for president. The three candidates are A, B, and C. Twenty percent of the voters like A the most and B the least. Forty percent of the voters like B the most and A the least. Of the remaining voters 225 prefer C to B and B to A, and 675 prefer C to A and A to B. Write out the preference schedule for this election.

1.2 Plurality Method

11. Table 1-31 shows the preference schedule for an election with four candidates (A, B, C, and D). Use the plurality method to

(a) find the winner of the election.

(b) find the complete ranking of the candidates.

Number of voters	27	15	11	9	8	1
1st	C	A	B	D	B	B
2nd	D	B	D	A	A	A
3rd	B	D	A	B	C	D
4th	A	C	C	C	D	C

■ **TABLE 1-31**

12. Table 1-32 shows the preference schedule for an election with four candidates (A, B, C, and D). Use the plurality method to

(a) find the winner of the election.

(b) find the complete ranking of the candidates.

Number of voters	29	21	18	10	1
1st	D	A	B	C	C
2nd	C	C	A	B	B
3rd	A	B	C	A	D
4th	B	D	D	D	A

■ **TABLE 1-32**

13. Table 1-33 shows the preference schedule for an election with four candidates (A, B, C, and D). Use the plurality method to

(a) find the winner of the election.

(b) find the complete ranking of the candidates.

Number of voters	6	5	4	2	2	2	2
1st	C	A	B	B	C	C	C
2nd	D	D	D	A	B	B	D
3rd	A	C	C	C	A	D	B
4th	B	B	A	D	D	A	A

■ **TABLE 1-33**

14. Table 1-34 shows the preference schedule for an election with four candidates (A, B, C, and D). Use the plurality method to

(a) find the winner of the election.

(b) find the complete ranking of the candidates.

Number of voters	6	6	5	4	3	3
1st	A	B	B	D	A	B
2nd	C	C	C	A	C	A
3rd	D	A	D	C	D	C
4th	B	D	A	B	B	D

■ **TABLE 1-34**

15. Table 1-35 shows the preference schedule for an election with five candidates (A, B, C, D, and E). The number of voters in this election was very large, so the columns of the preference schedule give the percent of voters instead of the number of voters. Use the plurality method to

(a) find the winner of the election.

(b) find the complete ranking of the candidates.

Percent of voters	24	23	19	14	11	9
1st	C	D	D	B	A	D
2nd	A	A	A	C	C	C
3rd	B	C	E	A	B	A
4th	E	B	C	D	E	E
5th	D	E	B	E	D	B

■ **TABLE 1-35**

16. Table 1-36 shows the preference schedule for an election with five candidates (A, B, C, D, and E). The number of voters in this election was very large, so the columns of the preference schedule give the percent of voters instead of the number of voters. Use the plurality method to

(a) find the winner of the election.

(b) find the complete ranking of the candidates.

Percent of voters	25	21	15	12	10	9	8
1st	C	E	B	A	C	C	C
2nd	E	D	D	D	D	B	E
3rd	D	B	E	B	E	A	D
4th	A	A	C	E	A	E	B
5th	B	C	A	C	B	D	A

■ **TABLE 1-36**

17. Table 1-29 (see Exercise 7) shows the preference schedule for an election with five candidates (A, B, C, D, and E). In this election ties are not allowed to stand, and the following tie-breaking rule is used: *Whenever there is a tie between candidates, the tie is broken in favor of the candidate with the fewer last-place votes.* Use the plurality method to

(a) find the winner of the election.

(b) find the complete ranking of the candidates.

18. Table 1-30 (see Exercise 8) shows the preference schedule for an election with four candidates (A, B, C, and D). In this election ties are not allowed to stand, and the following tie-breaking rule is used: *Whenever there is a tie between candidates, the tie is broken in favor of the candidate with the fewer last-place votes.* Use the plurality method to

(a) find the winner of the election.

(b) find the complete ranking of the candidates.

19. Table 1-29 (see Exercise 7) shows the preference schedule for an election with five candidates (A, B, C, D, and E). In this election ties are not allowed to stand, and the following tie-breaking rule is used: *Whenever there is a tie between two candidates, the tie is broken in favor of the winner of a head-to-head comparison between the candidates.* Use the plurality method to

(a) find the winner of the election.

(b) find the complete ranking of the candidates.

20. Table 1-30 (see Exercise 8) shows the preference schedule for an election with four candidates (A, B, C, and D). In this election ties are not allowed to stand, and the following tie-breaking rule is used: *Whenever there is a tie between two candidates, the tie is broken in favor of the winner of a head-to-head comparison between the candidates.* Use the plurality method to

(a) find the winner of the election.

(b) find the complete ranking of the candidates.

1.3 Borda Count

21. Table 1-31 (see Exercise 11) shows the preference schedule for an election with four candidates (*A*, *B*, *C*, and *D*). Use the Borda count method to

(a) find the winner of the election.

(b) find the complete ranking of the candidates.

22. Table 1-32 (see Exercise 12) shows the preference schedule for an election with four candidates (*A*, *B*, *C*, and *D*). Use the Borda count method to

(a) find the winner of the election.

(b) find the complete ranking of the candidates.

23. Table 1-33 (see Exercise 13) shows the preference schedule for an election with four candidates (*A*, *B*, *C*, and *D*). Use the Borda count method to

(a) find the winner of the election.

(b) find the complete ranking of the candidates.

24. Table 1-34 (see Exercise 14) shows the preference schedule for an election with four candidates (*A*, *B*, *C*, and *D*). Use the Borda count method to

(a) find the winner of the election.

(b) find the complete ranking of the candidates.

25. Table 1-35 (see Exercise 15) shows the preference schedule for an election with five candidates (*A*, *B*, *C*, *D*, and *E*). The number of voters in this election was very large, so the columns of the preference schedule give the percent of voters instead of the number of voters. Use the Borda count method to find the complete ranking of the candidates. (*Hint*: The ranking does not depend on the number of voters, so you can pick any convenient number to use for the number of voters.)

26. Table 1-36 (see Exercise 16) shows the preference schedule for an election with five candidates (*A*, *B*, *C*, *D*, and *E*). The number of voters in this election was very large, so the columns of the preference schedule give the percent of voters instead of the number of voters. Use the Borda count method to find the complete ranking of the candidates. (*Hint*: The ranking does not depend on the number of voters, so you can pick any convenient number to use for the number of voters.)

27. The 2009 Heisman Award. Table 1-37 shows the results of the balloting for the 2009 Heisman Award. Find the ranking of the top four finalists and the number of points each one received (see Example 1.11).

Player	School	1st	2nd	3rd
Toby Gerhart	Stanford	222	225	160
Mark Ingram	Alabama	227	236	151
Colt McCoy	Texas	203	188	160
Ndamukong Suh	Nebraska	161	105	122

Source: Heisman Award, *www.heisman.com/winners/ m-ingram09.php*

■ TABLE 1-37

28. The 2011 NL Cy Young Award. Table 1-38 shows the top 5 finalists for the 2011 National League Cy Young Award. Find the ranking of the top 5 finalists and the number of points each one received (see Example 1.12).

Pitcher	1st	2nd	3rd	4th	5th
Roy Halladay (PHI)	4	21	7	0	0
Cole Hamels (PHI)	0	0	0	2	13
Ian Kennedy (AZ)	1	3	6	18	3
Clayton Kershaw (LA)	27	3	2	0	0
Cliff Lee (PHI)	0	5	17	9	1

Source: Baseball-Reference.com, *www.baseball-reference.com /awards/awards_2011.shtml*

■ TABLE 1-38

29. An election was held using the Borda count method. There were four candidates (*A*, *B*, *C*, and *D*) and 110 voters. When the points were tallied (using 4 points for first, 3 points for second, 2 points for third, and 1 point for fourth), *A* had 320 points, *B* had 290 points, and *C* had 180 points. Find how many points *D* had and give the ranking of the candidates. (*Hint*: Figure out how many points are packed in each ballot.)

30. An election was held using the following variation of the Borda count method: 7 points for first-place, 4 points for second, 3 points for third, 2 points for fourth, and 1 point for fifth. There were five candidates (*A*, *B*, *C*, *D*, and *E*) and 30 voters. When the points were tallied *A* had 84 points, *B* had 65 points, *C* had 123 points, and *D* had 107 points. Find how many points *E* had and give the ranking of the candidates. (*Hint*: Figure out how many points are packed in each ballot.)

1.4 Plurality-with-Elimination

31. Table 1-31 (see Exercise 11) shows the preference schedule for an election with four candidates (*A*, *B*, *C*, and *D*). Use the plurality-with-elimination method to

(a) find the winner of the election.

(b) find the complete ranking of the candidates.

32. Table 1-32 (see Exercise 12) shows the preference schedule for an election with four candidates (*A*, *B*, *C*, and *D*). Use the plurality-with-elimination method to

(a) find the winner of the election.

(b) find the complete ranking of the candidates.

33. Table 1-33 (see Exercise 13) shows the preference schedule for an election with four candidates (*A*, *B*, *C*, and *D*). Use the plurality-with-elimination method to

(a) find the winner of the election.

(b) find the complete ranking of the candidates.

34. Table 1-34 (see Exercise 14) shows the preference schedule for an election with four candidates (A, B, C, and D). Use the plurality-with-elimination method to

(a) find the winner of the election.

(b) find the complete ranking of the candidates.

35. Table 1-35 (see Exercise 15) shows the preference schedule for an election with five candidates (A, B, C, D, and E). The number of voters in this election was very large, so the columns of the preference schedule give the percent of voters instead of the number of voters. Use the plurality-with-elimination method to

(a) find the winner of the election.

(b) find the complete ranking of the candidates.

36. Table 1-36 (see Exercise 16) shows the preference schedule for an election with five candidates (A, B, C, D, and E). The number of voters in this election was very large, so the columns of the preference schedule give the percent of voters instead of the number of voters. Use the plurality-with-elimination method to

(a) find the winner of the election.

(b) find the complete ranking of the candidates.

37. Table 1-39 shows the preference schedule for an election with five candidates (A, B, C, D, and E). Find the complete ranking of the candidates using the plurality-with-elimination method.

Number of voters	8	7	5	4	3	2
1st	B	C	A	D	A	D
2nd	E	E	B	C	D	B
3rd	A	D	C	B	E	C
4th	C	A	D	E	C	A
5th	D	B	E	A	B	E

■ **TABLE 1-39**

38. Table 1-40 shows the preference schedule for an election with five candidates (A, B, C, D, and E). Find the com-

Number of voters	7	6	5	5	5	5	4	2	1
1st	D	C	A	C	D	E	B	A	A
2nd	B	A	B	A	C	A	E	B	C
3rd	A	E	E	B	A	D	C	D	E
4th	C	B	C	D	E	B	D	E	B
5th	E	D	D	E	B	C	A	C	D

■ **TABLE 1-40**

plete ranking of the candidates using the plurality-with-elimination method.

Top-Two IRV. Exercises 39 and 40 refer to a simple variation of the plurality-with-elimination method called top-two IRV. This method works for winner-only elections. Instead of eliminating candidates one at a time, we eliminate all the candidates except the top two in the first round and transfer their votes to the two remaining candidates.

39. Find the winner of the election given by Table 1-39 using the *top-two IRV* method.

40. Find the winner of the election given by Table 1-40 using the *top-two IRV* method.

1.5 Pairwise Comparisons

41. Table 1-31 (see Exercise 11) shows the preference schedule for an election with four candidates (A, B, C, and D). Use the method of pairwise comparisons to

(a) find the winner of the election.

(b) find the complete ranking of the candidates.

42. Table 1-32 (see Exercise 12) shows the preference schedule for an election with four candidates (A, B, C, and D). Use the method of pairwise comparisons to

(a) find the winner of the election.

(b) find the complete ranking of the candidates.

43. Table 1-33 (see Exercise 13) shows the preference schedule for an election with four candidates (A, B, C, and D). Use the method of pairwise comparisons to

(a) find the winner of the election.

(b) find the complete ranking of the candidates.

44. Table 1-34 (see Exercise 14) shows the preference schedule for an election with four candidates (A, B, C, and D). Use the method of pairwise comparisons to

(a) find the winner of the election.

(b) find the complete ranking of the candidates.

45. Table 1-35 (see Exercise 15) shows the preference schedule for an election with five candidates (A, B, C, D, and E). The number of voters in this election was very large, so the columns of the preference schedule give the percent of voters instead of the number of voters. Find the winner of the election using the method of pairwise comparisons.

46. Table 1-36 (see Exercise 16) shows the preference schedule for an election with five candidates (A, B, C, D, and E). The number of voters in this election was very large, so the columns of the preference schedule give the percent of voters instead of the number of voters. Find the winner of the election using the method of pairwise comparisons.

47. Table 1-39 (see Exercise 37) shows the preference schedule for an election with 5 candidates. Find the complete ranking of the candidates using the method of pairwise comparisons. (Assume that ties are broken using the results of the pairwise comparisons between the tying candidates.)

48. Table 1-40 (see Exercise 38) shows the preference schedule for an election with 5 candidates. Find the complete ranking of the candidates using the method of pairwise comparisons.

49. An election with five candidates (*A*, *B*, *C*, *D*, and *E*) is decided using the method of pairwise comparisons. If *B* loses two pairwise comparisons, *C* loses one, *D* loses one and ties one, and *E* loses two and ties one,

  (a) find how many pairwise comparisons *A* loses.

  (b) find the winner of the election.

50. An election with six candidates (*A*, *B*, *C*, *D*, *E,* and *F*) is decided using the method of pairwise comparisons. If *A* loses four pairwise comparisons, *B* and *C* both lose three, *D* loses one and ties one, and *E* loses two and ties one,

  (a) find how many pairwise comparisons *F* loses. (*Hint*: First compute the total number of pairwise comparisons for six candidates.)

  (b) find the winner of the election.

1.6 Fairness Criteria

51. Use Table 1-41 to illustrate why the Borda count method violates the Condorcet criterion.

Number of voters	6	2	3
1st	A	B	C
2nd	B	C	D
3rd	C	D	B
4th	D	A	A

■ TABLE 1-41

52. Use Table 1-32 to illustrate why the plurality-with-elimination method violates the Condorcet criterion.

53. Use Table 1-42 to illustrate why the plurality method violates the IIA criterion. (*Hint*: Find the winner, then eliminate *F* and see what happens.)

Number of voters	49	48	3
1st	R	H	F
2nd	H	S	H
3rd	F	O	S
4th	O	F	O
5th	S	R	R

■ TABLE 1-42

54. Use the Math Club election (Example 1.10) to illustrate why the Borda count method violates the IIA criterion. (*Hint*: Find the winner, then eliminate *D* and see what happens.)

55. Use Table 1-43 to illustrate why the plurality-with-elimination method violates the IIA criterion. (*Hint*: Find the winner, then eliminate *C* and see what happens.)

Number of voters	5	5	3	3	3	2
1st	A	C	A	D	B	D
2nd	B	E	D	C	E	C
3rd	C	D	B	B	A	B
4th	D	B	C	E	C	A
5th	E	A	E	A	D	E

■ TABLE 1-43

56. Explain why the method of pairwise comparisons satisfies the majority criterion.

57. Explain why the method of pairwise comparisons satisfies the Condorcet criterion.

58. Explain why the plurality method satisfies the monotonicity criterion.

59. Explain why the Borda count method satisfies the monotonicity criterion.

60. Explain why the method of pairwise comparisons satisfies the monotonicity criterion.

JOGGING

61. **Two-candidate elections.** Explain why when there are only two candidates, the four voting methods we discussed in this chapter give the same winner and the winner is determined by straight majority. (Assume that there are no ties.)

62. **Equivalent Borda count (Variation 1).** The following simple variation of the Borda count method is sometimes used: A first place is worth $N - 1$ points, second place is worth $N - 2$ points, . . ., last place is worth 0 points (where N is the number of candidates). Explain why this variation is equivalent to the original Borda count described in this chapter (i.e., it produces exactly the same election results).

63. **Equivalent Borda count (Variation 2).** Another commonly used variation of the Borda count method is the following: A first place is worth 1 point, second place is worth 2 points, . . ., last place is worth N points (where N is the number of candidates). The candidate with the fewest points is the winner, second fewest points is second, and so on. Explain why this variation is equivalent to the original Borda count described in this chapter (i.e., it produces exactly the same election results).

64. **The average ranking.** The average ranking of a candidate is obtained by taking the place of the candidate on each of the ballots, adding these numbers, and dividing by the number of ballots. Explain why the candidate with the best (lowest) average ranking is the Borda winner.

65. The 2006 Associated Press college football poll. The AP college football poll is a ranking of the top 25 college football teams in the country and is one of the key polls used for the BCS (Bowl Championship Series). The voters in the AP poll are a group of sportswriters and broadcasters chosen from across the country. The top 25 teams are ranked using a Borda count: each first-place vote is worth 25 points, each second-place vote is worth 24 points, each third-place vote is worth 23 points, and so on. Table 1-44 shows the ranking and total points for each of the top three teams at the end of the 2006 regular season. (The remaining 22 teams are not shown here because they are irrelevant to this exercise.)

Team	Points
1. Ohio State	1625
2. Florida	1529
3. Michigan	1526

■ TABLE 1-44

(a) Given that Ohio State was the unanimous first-place choice of all the voters, find the number of voters that participated in the poll.

(b) Given that all the voters had Florida in either second or third place, find the number of second-place and the number of third-place votes for Florida.

(c) Given that all the voters had Michigan in either second or third place, find the number of second-place and the number of third-place votes for Michigan.

66. The 2005 National League MVP vote. Each year the Most Valuable Player of the National League is chosen by a group of 32 sportswriters using a variation of the Borda count method. Table 1-45 shows the results of the 2005 voting for the top three finalists:

Player	1st place	2nd place	3rd place	Total points
Albert Pujols	18	14	0	378
Andruw Jones	13	17	2	351
Derrek Lee	1	1	30	263

Source: Baseball-Reference.com, *www.baseball-reference.com/awards/awards_2005.shtml*

■ TABLE 1-45

Determine how many points are given for each first-, second-, and third-place vote in this election.

67. The 2003–2004 NBA Rookie of the Year vote. Each year, a panel of broadcasters and sportswriters selects an NBA rookie of the year using a variation of the Borda count method. Table 1-46 shows the results of the balloting for the top three finalists of the 2003–2004 season.

Player	1st place	2nd place	3rd place	Total points
LeBron James	78	39	1	508
Carmelo Anthony	40	76	2	430
Dwayne Wade	0	3	108	117

Source: InsideHoops.com, *www.insidehoops.com/lebron-wins-042004.shtml*

■ TABLE 1-46

Determine how many points are given for each first-, second-, and third-place vote in this election.

68. Top-two IRV is a variation of the plurality-with-elimination method in which all the candidates except the top two are eliminated in the first round (see Exercises 39 and 40).

(a) Use the Math Club election to show that top-two IRV can produce a different outcome than plurality-with-elimination.

(b) Give an example that illustrates why top-two IRV violates the monotonicity criterion.

(c) Give an example that illustrates why top-two IRV violates the Condorcet criterion.

69. The Coombs method. This method is just like the plurality-with-elimination method except that in each round we eliminate the candidate with the *largest number of last-place votes* (instead of the one with the fewest first-place votes).

(a) Find the winner of the Math Club election using the Coombs method.

(b) Give an example that illustrates why the Coombs method violates the Condorcet criterion.

(c) Give an example that illustrates why the Coombs method violates the monotonicity criterion.

70. Bucklin voting. (This method was used in the early part of the 20th century to determine winners of many elections for political office in the United States.) The method proceeds in rounds. **Round 1**: Count first-place votes only. If a candidate has a majority of the first-place votes, that candidate wins. Otherwise, go to the next round. **Round 2**: Count *first- and second-place* votes only. If there are any candidates with a majority of votes, the candidate with the most votes wins. Otherwise, go to the next round. **Round 3**: Count *first-, second-, and third-place* votes only. If there are any candidates with a majority of votes, the candidate with the most votes wins. Otherwise, go to the next round. Repeat for as many rounds as necessary.

(a) Find the winner of the Math Club election using the Bucklin method.

(b) Give an example that illustrates why the Bucklin method violates the Condorcet criterion.

(c) Explain why the Bucklin method satisfies the monotonicity criterion.

RUNNING

71. The Pareto criterion. The following fairness criterion was proposed by Italian economist Vilfredo Pareto (1848–1923): *If every voter prefers candidate X to candidate Y, then X should be ranked above Y.*

(a) Explain why the Borda count method satisfies the Pareto criterion.

(b) Explain why the pairwise-comparisons method satisfies the Pareto criterion.

72. The Condorcet loser criterion. *If there is a candidate who loses in a one-to-one comparison to each of the other candidates, then that candidate should not be the winner of the election.* (This fairness criterion is a sort of mirror image of the regular Condorcet criterion.)

(a) Give an example that illustrates why the plurality method violates the Condorcet loser criterion.

(b) Give an example that illustrates why the plurality-with-elimination method violates the Condorcet loser criterion.

(c) Explain why the Borda count method satisfies the Condorcet loser criterion.

73. Consider the following fairness criterion: *If a majority of the voters have candidate X ranked last, then candidate X should not be a winner of the election.*

(a) Give an example to illustrate why the plurality method violates this criterion.

(b) Give an example to illustrate why the plurality-with-elimination method violates this criterion.

(c) Explain why the method of pairwise comparisons satisfies this criterion.

(d) Explain why the Borda count method satisfies this criterion.

74. Suppose that the following was proposed as a fairness criterion: *If a majority of the voters rank X above Y, then the results of the election should have X ranked above Y.* Give an example to illustrate why all four voting methods discussed in the chapter can violate this criterion. (*Hint*: Consider an example with no Condorcet candidate.)

75. Consider a variation of the Borda count method in which a first-place vote in an election with N candidates is worth F points (where $F > N$) and all other places in the ballot are the same as in the ordinary Borda count: $N - 1$ points for second place, $N - 2$ points for third place, . . . , 1 point for last place. By choosing F large enough, we can make this variation of the Borda count method satisfy the majority criterion. Find the smallest value of F (expressed in terms of N) for which this happens.

PROJECTS AND PAPERS

1 Ballots, Ballots, Ballots!

In this chapter we discussed elections in which the voters cast their votes by means of preference ballots. There are many other types of ballots used in real-life elections, ranging from the simple (winner only) to the exotic (each voter has a fixed number of points to divide among the candidates any way he or she sees fit). In this project you are to research other types of ballots; how, where, and when they are used; and what are the arguments for and against their use.

2 Instant Runoff Voting

Imagine that you are a political activist in your community. The city council is having hearings to decide if the *method of instant runoff voting* (plurality-with-elimination) should be adopted in your city. Stake out a position for or against instant runoff voting and prepare a brief to present to the city council that justifies that position. To make an effective case, your argument should include mathematical, economic, political, and social considerations. (Remember that your city council members are not as well versed as you are in the mathematical aspects of elections. Part of your job is to educate them.)

3 The 2000 Presidential Election and the Florida Vote

The unusual circumstances surrounding the 2000 presidential election and the Florida vote are a low point in American electoral history. Write an analysis paper on the 2000 Florida vote, paying particular attention to what went wrong and how a similar situation can be prevented in the future. You should touch on technology issues (outdated and inaccurate vote-tallying methods and equipment, poorly designed ballots, etc.), political issues (the two-party system, the Electoral College, etc.), and, as much as possible, on issues related to concepts from this chapter (can presidential elections be improved by changing to preference ballots, using a different voting method, etc.).

4 Short Story

Write a fictional short story using an election as the backdrop. Weave into the dramatic structure of the story elements and themes from this chapter (fairness, manipulation, monotonicity, and independence of irrelevant alternatives all lend themselves to good drama). Be creative and have fun.

2 The Mathematics of Power

Weighted Voting

In a democracy we take many things for granted, not the least of which is the idea that we are all equal. When it comes to voting, the democratic ideal of equality translates into the principle of *one person–one vote*. (Our entire discussion of elections in Chapter 1 was based on this premise.) But is the principle of *one person–one vote* always fair? Should *one person–one vote* apply when the *voters* are institutions or governments, rather than individuals?

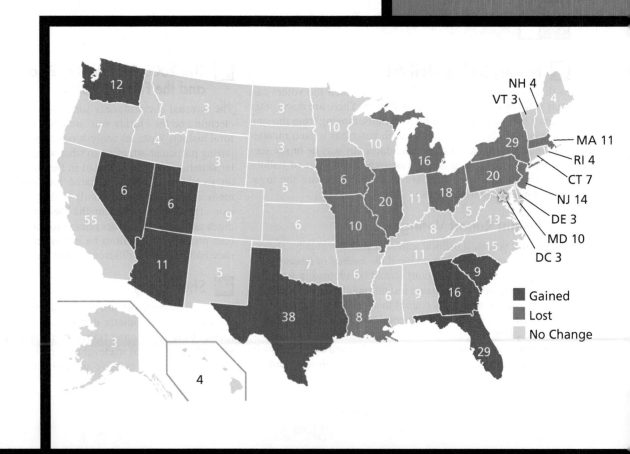

NH 4
VT 3
MA 11
RI 4
CT 7
NJ 14
DE 3
MD 10
DC 3

Gained
Lost
No Change

n a diverse society, voters—be they individuals or institutions—are sometimes not equal, and sometimes it is actually desirable to recognize their differences by giving them different amounts of say over the outcome of the voting. This is the exact opposite of the principle of *one voter–one vote*, a principle best described as *one voter–x votes* and formally called *weighted voting* (the word "weight" here refers to the number of votes controlled by a voter, and not to pounds or kilograms).

Weighted voting is not uncommon—we see examples of weighted voting in shareholder votes in corporations, in business partnerships, in legislatures, in the United Nations Security Council, and in the Electoral College.

The Electoral College, that uniquely American institution used to elect the President of the United States, offers a classic illustration of weighted voting. The Electoral College consists of 51 "voters" (each of the 50 states plus the District of Columbia), each with a weight determined by the size of its Congressional delegation (number of Representatives and Senators). At one end of the spectrum is heavyweight California (55 electoral votes); at the other end of the spectrum are small states (in population) like Wyoming, Montana, North Dakota, and the District of Columbia (3 electoral votes).

Since the point of weighted voting is to give different voters different amounts of influence in the outcome of the voting (i.e., different amounts of power),

> ❝ Each State shall appoint a Number of Electors equal to the whole Number of Senators and Representatives to which the state may be entitled in the Congress. ❞
>
> *– Article II, Section 1, U.S. Constitution*

the key question we will discuss in this chapter is *how does one go about measuring* a voter's power in a weighted voting situation? We will answer this question not once but twice, and in so doing cover some new and interesting mathematics.

Section 2.1 will introduce and illustrate the concept of a *weighted voting system*, a formal way to describe most weighted voting situations. We will learn about *weights*, *quotes*, *dictators*, and *veto power*. Section 2.2 deals with what is known as the *Banzhaf* measure of power. Here we will learn about *coalitions*, *critical players*, and *dummies*. Section 2.3 deals with what is known as the *Shapley-Shubik* measure of power. Here we will learn about *sequential coalitions*, *pivotal players*, and *factorials*. Section 2.4 is essentially a mathematical detour where we will learn about counting *subsets* and *permutations*.

2.1 An Introduction to Weighted Voting

We will use the term **weighted voting system** to describe any formal voting arrangement in which voters are not necessarily equal in terms of the number of votes they control. Unlike Chapter 1, where the discussion focused primarily on elections involving three or more choices, in this chapter we will only consider voting on *yes–no* votes, known as **motions.** Note that any vote between two choices (say *A* or *B*) can be rephrased as a *yes–no* vote (a *Yes* is a vote for *A*, a *No* is a vote for *B*).

Every weighted voting system is characterized by three elements:

■ The players. We will refer to the voters in a weighted voting system as the **players**. The players may be individuals, but they may also be institutions (corporations, governmental agencies, states, municipalities, or countries). We will use *N* to denote the number of players in a weighted voting system, and typically (unless there is a good reason not to) we will call the players $P_1, P_2, \ldots, P_N$. (Think of P_1 as short for "player 1," P_2 as short for "player 2," etc.)

■ The weights. The hallmark of a weighted voting system is that each player controls a certain number of votes, called the **weight** of the player. We will assume that the weights are all positive integers, and we will use $w_1, w_2, \ldots, w_N$ to denote the weights of $P_1, P_2, \ldots, P_N$, respectively. We will use *V* to denote the total number of votes in the system ($V = w_1 + w_2 + \cdots + w_N$). A weighted voting system is only interesting when the weights are not all the same, but in principle we do not preclude the possibility that the weights are all equal.

■ The quota. In addition to the players' weights, every weighted voting system has a *quota*. The **quota** is the *minimum number of votes required to pass a motion*, and is denoted by the letter *q*. While the most common standard for the quota is a *simple majority* of the votes, the quota may very well be something else. In the U.S. Senate, for example, it takes a simple majority to pass an ordinary law, but it takes a minimum of 60 votes to stop a filibuster, and it takes a minimum of two-thirds of the votes to override a presidential veto. In other weighted voting systems the rules may stipulate a quota of three-fourths of the votes, or four-fifths, or even *unanimity* (100% of the votes).

Notation and Examples

The standard notation used to describe a weighted voting system is to use square brackets and inside the square brackets to write the quota *q* first (followed by a colon) and then the respective weights of the individual players separated by commas. It is convenient and customary to list the weights in numerical order, starting with the highest, and we will adhere to this convention throughout the chapter.

Thus, a generic weighted voting system with *N* players can be written as:

$$[q: w_1, w_2, \ldots, w_N] \quad (\text{with } w_1 \geq w_2 \geq \cdots \geq w_N)$$

We will now look at a few examples to illustrate some basic concepts in weighted voting.

EXAMPLE 2.1   VENTURE CAPITALISM

Four partners ($P_1, P_2, P_3,$ and P_4) decide to start a new business venture. In order to raise the $200,000 venture capital needed for startup money, they issue 20 shares worth $10,000 each. Suppose that P_1 buys 8 shares, P_2 buys 7 shares, P_3 buys 3 shares, and P_4 buys 2 shares, with the usual agreement that one share equals one vote in the partnership. Suppose that the quota is set to be two-thirds of the total number of votes.

Since the total number of votes in the partnership is $V = 20$, and two-thirds of 20 is $13\frac{1}{3}$, the actual quota is $q = 14$. Using the weighted voting system notation we just introduced, the partnership can be described mathematically as $[14 : 8, 7, 3, 2]$.

EXAMPLE 2.2 ANARCHY

Imagine the same partnership discussed in Example 2.1, with the only difference being that the quota is changed to 10 votes. We might be tempted to think of this partnership as the weighted voting system $[10 : 8, 7, 3, 2]$, but there is a problem here: the quota is too small, making it possible for both Yes's and No's to have enough votes to carry a particular motion. (Imagine, for example, that an important decision needs to be made and P_1 and P_4 vote yes and P_2 and P_3 vote no. Now we have a stalemate, since both the Yes's and the No's have enough votes to meet the quota.)

In general when the quota requirement is less than simple majority we have the potential for both Yes's and No's to win—a mathematical version of anarchy.

EXAMPLE 2.3 GRIDLOCK

Once again, let's look at the partnership introduced in Example 2.1, but suppose now that the quota is set to $q = 21$, more than the total number of votes in the system. This would not make much sense. Under these conditions no motion would ever pass and nothing could ever get done—a mathematical version of gridlock.

Given that we expect our weighted voting systems to operate without anarchy or gridlock, from here on we will assume that *the quota will always fall somewhere between simple majority and unanimity of votes.* Symbolically, we can express these requirements by two inequalities: $q > V/2$ and $q \le V$. These two restrictions define the range of possible values of the quota:

$$V/2 < q \le V \text{ (where } V = w_1 + w_2 + \cdots + w_N)$$

EXAMPLE 2.4 FEW VOTES, MUCH POWER

Let's consider the partnership introduced in Example 2.1 one final time. This time the quota is set to be $q = 19$. Here we can describe the partnership as the weighted voting system $[19 : 8, 7, 3, 2]$. What's interesting about this weighted voting system is that the *only way a motion can pass is by the unanimous support of all the players.* (Note that P_1, P_2, and P_3 together have 18 votes—they still need P_4's votes to pass a motion.) In this weighted voting system all four players have the same power. Even though P_4 has only 2 votes, his ability to influence the outcome of the vote is exactly the same as that of P_1, with 8 votes. In a practical sense this weighted voting system is no different from a weighted voting system in which each partner has just one vote and it takes the unanimous agreement of the four partners to pass a motion (i.e., $[4 : 1, 1, 1, 1]$).

The surprising conclusion of Example 2.4 is that the weighted voting system $[19 : 8, 7, 3, 2]$ describes a one person–one vote situation in disguise. This seems like a contradiction only if we think of *one person–one vote* as implying that all players have an *equal number of votes rather than an equal say in the outcome of the election.* Apparently, these two things are not the same! As Example 2.4 makes abundantly clear, just looking at the number of votes a player owns can be very deceptive.

EXAMPLE 2.5   MANY VOTES, LITTLE POWER

Four college friends $(P_1, P_2, P_3,$ and $P_4)$ decide to go into business together. Three of the four $(P_1, P_2,$ and $P_3)$ invest \$10,000 each, and each gets 10 shares in the partnership. The fourth partner (P_4) is a little short on cash, so he invests only \$9,000 and gets 9 shares. As usual, one share equals one vote. The quota is set at 75%, which here means $q = 30$ out of a total of $V = 39$ votes. Mathematically (i.e., stripped of all the irrelevant details of the story), this partnership is just the weighted voting system $[30: 10, 10, 10, 9]$.

Everything seems fine with the partnership until one day P_4 wakes up to the realization that with the quota set at $q = 30$ he is completely out of the decision-making loop: For a motion to pass $P_1, P_2,$ and P_3 all must vote Yes, and at that point it makes no difference how P_4 votes. Thus, there is never going to be a time when P_4's votes are going to make a difference in the final outcome of a business decision.

EXAMPLE 2.6   DICTATORS

Consider the weighted voting system $[11: 12, 5, 4]$. Here one of the players (P_1) owns enough votes to carry a motion singlehandedly. In this situation P_1 is in complete control—if P_1 is for the motion, then the motion will pass; if P_1 is against it, then the motion will fail. Clearly, in terms of the power to influence decisions, P_1 has *all* of it. Not surprisingly, we will say that P_1 is a *dictator*.

■ **Dictator.** A player is a **dictator** if and only if *the player's weight is bigger than or equal to the quota.* Since there can only be one dictator, and since the player with the highest weight is P_1, we can conclude that *if there is a dictator, then it must be P_1.* Mathematically speaking, a weighted voting system with a dictator is not very interesting, since all the power is concentrated in the hands of one player. For the rest of this chapter we will restrict our attention to weighted voting systems where there are no dictators.

EXAMPLE 2.7   VETO POWER

Consider the weighted voting system $[12: 9, 5, 4, 2]$. Here P_1 plays the role of a "spoiler"—without the support of P_1 a motion can't pass. This happens because if we remove P_1's 9 votes the sum of the remaining votes $(5 + 4 + 2 = 11)$ is less than the quota $q = 12$. Thus, even if all the other players voted Yes, without P_1 the motion would not pass. In a situation like this we say that P_1 has *veto power*.

In general we will say that a player who is not a dictator has *veto power* if a *motion cannot pass unless the player votes in favor of the motion.* In other words, a player with veto power cannot force a motion to *pass* (the player is not a dictator) but can force a motion to *fail.* If we let w denote the weight of a player with veto power, then the two conditions can be expressed mathematically by the inequalities $w < q$ (the player is not a dictator) and $V - w < q$ (the remaining votes in the system are not enough to pass a motion).

■ **Veto power.** A player with weight w has **veto power** if and only if $w < q$ and $V - w < q$ (where $V = w_1 + w_2 + \cdots + w_N$).

2.2 ▛▜ Banzhaf Power

John F. Banzhaf III (1940–   )

From the preceding set of examples we can already draw an important lesson: In weighted voting the players' weights can be deceiving. Sometimes a player can have a few votes and yet have as much power as a player with many more votes (see Example 2.4); sometimes two players have almost an equal number of votes, and yet one player has a lot of power and the other one has none (see Example 2.5).

To pursue these ideas further we will need a formal definition of what "power" means and how it can be measured. In this section we will introduce a mathematical method for measuring the power of the players in a weighted voting system. This method was first proposed in 1965 by, of all people, a law professor named John Banzhaf III. Banzhaf is a Professor of Public Interest Law at George Washington University, and the founder and executive director of the national antismoking group Action on Smoking and Health. Banzhaf was just 25 years old when he first came up with the ideas we will discuss in this section.

We start our discussion of Banzhaf's method with an application to the U.S. Senate. The circumstances are fictitious, but given party politics these days, not very far-fetched.

EXAMPLE 2.8(a)   THE U.S. SENATE

The U.S. Senate has 100 members, and a simple majority of 51 votes is required to pass a bill. Suppose the Senate is composed of 49 Republicans, 48 Democrats, and 3 Independents, and that Senators vote strictly along party lines— Republicans all vote the same way, so do Democrats, and even the Independents are sticking together.

Under this scenario the Senate behaves as the weighted voting system $[51: 49, 48, 3]$. The three players are the Republican party (49 votes), the Democratic party (48 votes), and the Independents (3 votes).

There are only four ways that a bill can pass:

- All players vote Yes. The bill passes unanimously, 100 to 0.
- Republicans and Democrats vote Yes; Independents vote No. The bill passes 97 to 3.
- Republicans and Independents vote Yes; Democrats vote No. The bill passes 52 to 48.
- Democrats and Independents vote Yes; Republicans vote No. The bill passes 51 to 49.

That's it! There is no other way that a bill can pass this Senate. The key observation now is that the Independents have as much influence on the outcome of the vote as the Republicans or the Democrats (as long as they stick together): To pass, a bill needs the support of *any* two out of the three parties.

Before we continue with Example 2.8, we will introduce some important new concepts.

- **Coalition.** We will use the term **coalition** to describe *any* set of players who might join forces and vote the same way. In principle, we can have a coalition with as few as *one* player and as many as *all* players. The coalition consisting of all the players is called the **grand coalition**. Since coalitions are just sets of players, the most convenient way to describe coalitions mathematically is to use *set* notation. For example, the coalition consisting of players P_1, P_2, and P_3 can be written as the set $\{P_1, P_2, P_3\}$ (but also as $\{P_3, P_1, P_2\}$, $\{P_2, P_1, P_3\}$, etc.—the order in which the members of a coalition are listed is irrelevant).

- **Winning coalition.** Some coalitions have enough votes to win and some don't. Quite naturally, we call the former **winning coalitions** and the latter **losing coalitions**. Since our focus is on weighted voting systems with no dictators, winning coalitions must have at least two players (only a dictator can be in a single-player winning coalition). At the other end of the spectrum, the grand coalition is always a winning coalition, since it controls all the votes. In some weighted voting systems (see Example 2.4) the grand coalition is the only winning coalition.

- **Critical player.** In a winning coalition a player is said to be a *critical player* for the coalition if the coalition must have that player's votes to win. In other words, if we subtract a critical player's weight from the total weight of the coalition, the number of remaining votes drops below the quota. In other words, P is a **critical player** in a winning coalition if and only if $W - w < q$ (where W denotes the weight of the coalition and w denotes the weight of P).

- **Critical count.** For each player we can count the number of times that player is a critical player (i.e., in how many different winning coalitions the player is critical). This number is called the **critical count** for the player.

Coalition	Weight
$\{R, D, I\}$	100
$\{R, \underline{D}\}$	97
$\{\underline{R}, \underline{I}\}$	52
$\{\underline{D}, \underline{I}\}$	51

■ **TABLE 2-1** Winning coalitions for [51: 49, 48, 3] with critical players underlined

EXAMPLE 2.8(b)   THE U.S. SENATE (*CONTINUED*)

We now recast the analysis of the U.S. Senate [Example 2.8(a)] in the language of coalitions, critical players, and critical counts. Table 2–1 shows the four possible winning coalitions, their weights, and the critical players in each winning coalition underlined. (R represents the Republican Party with 49 votes, D represents the Democratic Party with 48 votes, and I represents the Independents with 3 votes.) Note that in the coalition $\{R, D, I\}$ there are no critical players (any two of the three parties can pass a bill by themselves), but in the two-player coalitions both players are critical. The critical count for R is 2 (notice that R is underlined twice in Table 2-1). In a similar manner we can check the critical counts for D and I—they are also 2. In short, all players have a critical count of 2.

We will now introduce the key concept of this section—the *Banzhaf power index*. John Banzhaf introduced this concept in 1965 in a legal dispute involving the Nassau County (New York) Board of Supervisors (more details in Example 2.13). Essentially, Banzhaf argued that it's the *critical count*, and not the *weight*, that truly measures a player's power—if the critical count of X is the same as the critical count of Y then X and Y have the same power; if the critical count of X is double that of Y then X has twice as much power as Y. That's the basic idea. We formalize it with the following two definitions.

- **The Banzhaf power index (BPI).** Let $P_1, P_2, \ldots, P_N$ be the players in a weighted voting system, and $B_1, B_2, \ldots, B_N$ denote their respective *critical counts*. Let $T = B_1 + B_2 + \cdots + B_N$ be the *total critical count*. The **Banzhaf power index (BPI)** of a player is the ratio of the player's critical count over the total critical count T. Using the greek letter β ("beta") to indicate Banzhaf power indexes, we have that the BPI of P_1 is $\beta_1 = \frac{B_1}{T}$, the BPI of P_2 is $\beta_2 = \frac{B_2}{T}$, so on.

- Each Banzhaf power index is a fraction between 0 and 1 and can be expressed either as a fraction, a decimal, or a percent between 0 and 100. You can think of it as a measure of the size of a player's share of the power.

- **The Banzhaf power distribution.** The complete division of the "power pie" among the players based on their Banzhaf power indexes is called the **Banzhaf power distribution** of the weighted voting system. We describe a Banzhaf power distribution by simply listing the power indexes $\beta_1, \beta_2, \ldots, \beta_N$ in order.

Some comments about the numbers in a Banzhaf power distribution. These numbers start out as fractions all having a common denominator T. It is not necessarily a good idea to reduce the fractions to their simplest form—for comparison purposes it is preferable to list all the fractions using a common denominator. As fractions, the numbers in the power distribution must always add up to 1. When T is a large number, decimals or percents provide a more convenient numerical description than fractions, but there is a small price to pay: when converted to decimals or percents, the numbers may not add up to 1 because of round-off errors.

The following is a step-by-step recipe for computing the Banzhaf power distribution of a weighted voting system with N players.

COMPUTING THE BANZHAF POWER DISTRIBUTION

- **Step 1.** Make a list of all possible *winning* coalitions.
- **Step 2.** Within each winning coalition determine which are the *critical* players. (For record-keeping purposes, it is a good idea to underline each critical player.)
- **Step 3.** Find the *critical counts* $B_1, B_2, \ldots, B_N$.
- **Step 4.** Find $T = B_1 + B_2 + \cdots + B_N$.
- **Step 5.** Compute the Banzhaf power indexes: $\beta_1 = \frac{B_1}{T}, \beta_2 = \frac{B_2}{T}, \ldots, \beta_N = \frac{B_N}{T}$.

In the next set of examples we will illustrate how to carry out the above sequence of steps.

EXAMPLE 2.9 BANZHAF POWER IN [4: 3, 2, 1]

Let's find the Banzhaf power distribution of the weighted voting system $[4: 3, 2, 1]$ using the five-step procedure described above. The steps are also summarized in Table 2-2.

Winning coalitions	Weight	Critical players
$\{\underline{P_1}, \underline{P_2}\}$	5	$\underline{P_1}, \underline{P_2}$
$\{\underline{P_1}, \underline{P_3}\}$	4	$\underline{P_1}, \underline{P_3}$
$\{\underline{P_1}, P_2, P_3\}$	6	$\underline{P_1}$
Critical counts: $B_1 = 3$, $B_2 = 1$, $B_3 = 1$		
Banzhaf power: $\beta_1 = \frac{3}{5}, \beta_2 = \frac{1}{5}, \beta_3 = \frac{1}{5}$		

■ **TABLE 2-2** Banzhaf power in [4: 3, 2, 1] winning coalitions with critical players underlined

Step 1. There are three winning coalitions in this weighted voting system. They are $\{P_1, P_2\}$ with 5 votes, $\{P_1, P_3\}$ with 4 votes, and the grand coalition $\{P_1, P_2, P_3\}$ with 6 votes.

Step 2. In $\{P_1, P_2\}$ both P_1 and P_2 are critical; in $\{P_1, P_3\}$ both P_1 and P_3 are critical; in $\{P_1, P_2, P_3\}$ only P_1 is critical.

Step 3. $B_1 = 3$ (P_1 is critical in three coalitions); $B_2 = 1$ and $B_3 = 1$ (P_2 and P_3 are critical once each).

Step 4. $T = 3 + 1 + 1 = 5$.

Step 5. $\beta_1 = \frac{B_1}{T} = \frac{3}{5}$; $\beta_2 = \frac{B_2}{T} = \frac{1}{5}$; $\beta_3 = \frac{B_3}{T} = \frac{1}{5}$. (If we want to express the β's in terms of percentages, then $\beta_1 = 60\%$, $\beta_2 = 20\%$, and $\beta_3 = 20\%$.)

Of all the steps we must carry out in the process of computing Banzhaf power, by far the most demanding is Step 1. When we have only three players, as in Example 2.9, we can list the winning coalitions on the fly—there simply aren't that many—but as the number of players increases, the number of possible winning coalitions grows rapidly, and it becomes necessary to adopt some form of strategy to come up with a list of *all* the winning coalitions. This is important because if we miss a single one, we are in all likelihood going to get the wrong Banzhaf power distribution. One conservative strategy is to make a list of *all* possible coalitions and then cross out the losing ones. The next example illustrates how one would use this approach.

| **EXAMPLE 2.10** | THE NBA DRAFT |

When NBA teams prepare for the annual draft of college players, the decision on which college basketball players to draft may involve many people, including the management, the coaches, and the scouting staff. Typically, not all these people have an equal voice in the process—the head coach's opinion is worth more than that of an assistant coach, and the general manager's opinion is worth more than that of a scout. In some cases this arrangement is formalized in the form of a weighted voting system. Let's use a fictitious team—the Flyers—for the purposes of illustration.

In the Flyers' draft system the head coach (P_1) has 4 votes, the general manager (P_2) has 3 votes, the director of scouting operations (P_3) has 2 votes, and the assistant coach (P_4) has 1 vote. Of the 10 votes cast, a simple majority of 6 votes is required for a Yes vote on a player to be drafted. In essence, the Flyers operate as the weighted voting system $[6: 4, 3, 2, 1]$.

We will now find the Banzhaf power distribution of this weighted voting system using Steps 1 through 5.

Step 1. Table 2-3 shows a list of *all* possible coalitions and their weights with the winning coalitions followed by a check mark. (Note that the list of coalitions is organized systematically—two-player coalitions first, three-player coalitions next, etc. Also note that within each coalition the players are listed in numerical order from left to right. Both of these are good bookkeeping strategies, and you are encouraged to use them when you do your own work.)

Step 2. Now we disregard the losing coalitions and go to work on the winning coalitions only. For each winning coalition we determine which players are critical. Table 2-3 shows the critical players underlined. (Don't take someone else's word for it—please check that these are all the critical players!)

Step 3. We now tally how many times each player is underlined in Table 2-3. These are the critical counts: $B_1 = 5$, $B_2 = 3$, $B_3 = 3$, and $B_4 = 1$.

Step 4. $T = 5 + 3 + 3 + 1 = 12$.

Step 5. $\beta_1 = \frac{5}{12} = 41\frac{2}{3}\%$; $\beta_2 = \frac{3}{12} = 25\%$; $\beta_3 = \frac{3}{12} = 25\%$, and $\beta_4 = \frac{1}{12} = 8\frac{1}{3}\%$.

Coalition	Weight	Coalition	Weight
$\{\underline{P_1}, \underline{P_2}\}$	7 ✓	$\{\underline{P_1}, P_2, P_3\}$	9 ✓
$\{\underline{P_1}, \underline{P_3}\}$	6 ✓	$\{\underline{P_1}, P_2, P_4\}$	8 ✓
$\{P_1, P_4\}$	5	$\{\underline{P_1}, \underline{P_3}, \underline{P_4}\}$	7 ✓
$\{P_2, P_3\}$	5	$\{\underline{P_2}, \underline{P_3}, \underline{P_4}\}$	6 ✓
$\{P_2, P_4\}$	4	$\{P_1, P_2, P_3, P_4\}$	10 ✓
$\{P_3, P_4\}$	3		
Critical counts: $B_1 = 5, B_2 = 3, B_3 = 3, B_4 = 1$			
Banzhaf power: $\beta_1 = \frac{5}{12}, \beta_2 = \frac{3}{12}, \beta_3 = \frac{3}{12}, \beta_4 = \frac{1}{12}$			

■ **TABLE 2-3** Banzhaf power in [6: 4, 3, 2, 1] (✓ indicates a winning coalition)

An interesting and unexpected result of these calculations is that the team's general manager (P_2) and the director of scouting operations (P_3) have the same Banzhaf power index—not exactly the arrangement originally intended.

Shortcuts for Computing Banzhaf Power Distributions

As the number of players grows, listing all the coalitions takes a lot of effort. Sometimes we can save ourselves some of the work by figuring out directly which are the winning coalitions.

EXAMPLE 2.11 [5: 3, 2, 1, 1, 1]

In a weighted voting system with 5 players and no dictators there are 26 possible coalitions (we will discuss this in more detail in Section 2.4). We can save a fair amount of effort by listing only the winning coalitions. A little organization will help: We will go through the winning coalitions systematically according to the number of players in the coalition. There is only one two-player winning coalition, namely $\{P_1, P_2\}$. The only three-player winning coalitions are those that include P_1. All four-player coalitions are winning coalitions, and so is the grand coalition.

Steps 1 and 2. Table 2-4 shows *all* the winning coalitions, with the critical players underlined. (You should double check to make sure that these are the right critical players in each coalition—it's good practice!)

Step 3. The critical counts are $B_1 = 11$, $B_2 = 5$, $B_3 = 3$, $B_4 = 3$, and $B_5 = 3$.

Step 4. $T = 25$.

Step 5. $\beta_1 = \frac{11}{25} = 44\%$; $\beta_2 = \frac{5}{25} = 20\%$; $\beta_3 = \beta_4 = \beta_5 = \frac{3}{25} = 12\%$.

Winning coalition	Weight	Winning coalition	Weight
$\{\underline{P_1}, \underline{P_2}\}$	5	$\{\underline{P_1}, P_2, P_3, P_4\}$	7
$\{\underline{P_1}, \underline{P_2}, P_3\}$	6	$\{\underline{P_1}, P_2, P_3, P_5\}$	7
$\{\underline{P_1}, \underline{P_2}, P_4\}$	6	$\{\underline{P_1}, P_2, P_4, P_5\}$	7
$\{\underline{P_1}, \underline{P_2}, P_5\}$	6	$\{\underline{P_1}, P_3, P_4, P_5\}$	6
$\{\underline{P_1}, \underline{P_3}, \underline{P_4}\}$	5	$\{\underline{P_2}, \underline{P_3}, \underline{P_4}, \underline{P_5}\}$	5
$\{\underline{P_1}, \underline{P_3}, \underline{P_5}\}$	5	$\{P_1, P_2, P_3, P_4, P_5\}$	8
$\{\underline{P_1}, \underline{P_4}, \underline{P_5}\}$	5		
Critical counts: $B_1 = 11$, $B_2 = 5$, $B_3 = 3$, $B_4 = 3$, $B_5 = 3$			
Banzhaf power: $\beta_1 = \frac{11}{25}$, $\beta_2 = \frac{5}{25}$, $\beta_3 = \frac{3}{25}$, $\beta_4 = \frac{3}{25}$, $\beta_5 = \frac{3}{25}$			

■ **TABLE 2-4**   *Banzhaf power in [5: 3, 2, 1, 1, 1]*

EXAMPLE 2.12   THE POWER OF TIEBREAKERS

The Tasmania State University Promotion and Tenure committee consists of five members: the dean (D) and four other faculty members of equal standing (F_1, F_2, F_3, and F$_4$). (For convenience we are using a slightly different notation for the players.) In this committee faculty members vote first, and motions are carried by simple majority. The dean votes *only* to break a 2–2 tie. Is this a weighted voting system? If so, what is the Banzhaf power distribution?

The answer to the first question is Yes, and the answer to the second question is that we can apply the same steps we used before even though we don't have specific weights for the players.

Step 1. The possible winning coalitions fall into two groups: (1) A majority (three or more) faculty members vote Yes. In this case the dean does not vote. These winning coalitions are listed in the first column of Table 2-5. (2) Only two faculty members vote yes, and the dean breaks the tie with a Yes vote. These winning coalitions are listed in the second column of Table 2-5.

Winning coalitions (faculty only)	Winning coalitions (dean breaks tie)
$\{\underline{F_1}, \underline{F_2}, \underline{F_3}\}$	$\{\underline{F_1}, \underline{F_2}, \underline{D}\}$
$\{\underline{F_1}, \underline{F_2}, \underline{F_4}\}$	$\{\underline{F_1}, \underline{F_3}, \underline{D}\}$
$\{\underline{F_1}, \underline{F_3}, \underline{F_4}\}$	$\{\underline{F_1}, \underline{F_4}, \underline{D}\}$
$\{\underline{F_2}, \underline{F_3}, \underline{F_4}\}$	$\{\underline{F_2}, \underline{F_3}, \underline{D}\}$
$\{F_1, F_2, F_3, F_4\}$	$\{\underline{F_2}, \underline{F_4}, \underline{D}\}$
	$\{\underline{F_3}, \underline{F_4}, \underline{D}\}$
Critical counts: 6 for each F; 6 for D	
Banzhaf power: Same for all players $\left(\frac{1}{5} = 20\%\right)$	

■ **TABLE 2-5** Banzhaf power in TSU promotion and tenure committee

Step 2. In the winning coalitions consisting of just three faculty members, all faculty members are critical. In the coalition consisting of all four faculty members, no faculty member is critical. In the coalitions consisting of two faculty members plus the dean, all players, including the dean, are critical. Table 2-5 shows the critical players underlined in each winning coalition.

Step 3. The dean is critical six times (in each of the six coalitions in the second column). Each of the faculty members is critical three times in the first column and three times in the second column. Thus, all players have a critical count of 6.

Steps 4 and 5. Since all five players are critical an equal number of times, they share power equally (i.e., the Banzhaf power index of each player is $\frac{1}{5} = 20\%$).

> ❝ The Vice President of the United States shall be the President of the Senate, but shall have no Vote, unless they be equally divided. ❞
>
> – *Article I, Section 3, U.S. Constitution*

The surprising conclusion of Example 2.12 is that although the rules appear to set up a special role for the dean (the role of tiebreaker), in practice the dean is no different than any of the faculty members. A larger-scale version of Example 2.12 occurs in the U.S. Senate, where the vice president of the United States can only vote to break a tie. An analysis similar to the one used in Example 2.12 shows that as a member of the Senate the vice president has the same Banzhaf power index as an ordinary senator.

Our next example is of interest for both historical and mathematical reasons.

| **EXAMPLE 2.13** | THE NASSAU COUNTY (N.Y.) BOARD OF SUPERVISORS (1960s) |

Throughout the 1900s county boards in the state of New York operated as weighted voting systems. The reasoning behind weighted voting was that counties are often divided into districts of uneven size and it seemed unfair to give an equal vote to both large and small districts. To eliminate this type of unfairness a system of *proportional representation* was used: Each district would have a number of votes roughly proportional to its population. Every 10 years, after the Census, the allocation of votes could change if the population changed, but the principle of proportional representation remained.

In this example we will focus on one specific case: the Nassau County Board of Supervisors in the 1960s. At the time, Nassau County was divided into six districts. Table 2-6 shows the names of the six districts and the number of votes each district had on the Board of Supervisors (based on population data from the 1960 Census). The total number of votes was $V = 115$, and the quota was $q = 58$ (simple majority). Thus, from a mathematical point of view the Nassau County Board of Supervisors could be simply described as $[58: 31, 31, 28, 21, 2, 2]$. We use H1, H2, OB, NH, LB, and GC as shorthand for the six districts.

To simplify the computations that follow we find it convenient to divide the six players into the "Big 3" (H1, H2, and OB) and the "Lesser 3"(NH, LB, and GC). The winning coalitions will be organized into four groups:

	Name (symbol)	Weight
"Big 3"	Hempstead 1 (H1)	31
	Hempstead 2 (H2)	31
	Oyster Bay (OB)	28
"Lesser 3"	North Hempstead (NH)	21
	Long Beach (LB)	2
	Glen Cove (GC)	2
		$V = 115$

■ **TABLE 2-6** Nassau County districts and weights (1960s)

1. Coalitions of the form $\{H1, H2, OB, *\}$. These are coalitions that include each of the "Big 3" and some subset of the "Lesser 3" (i.e., all, just two, just one, or none of the "Lesser 3"). There are eight such coalitions. In these coalitions, none of the players are critical.

2. Coalitions of the form $\{H1, H2, *\}$. These are coalitions that include H1 and H2 and some subset of the "Lesser 3." OB is not included in these coalitions. There are eight such coalitions. In these coalitions H1 and H2 are always critical; the remaining players are never critical.

3. Coalitions of the form $\{H1, OB, *\}$. These are coalitions that include H1 and OB and some subset of the "Lesser 3." H2 is not included in these coalitions. There are eight such coalitions. In these coalitions H1 and OB are always critical; the remaining players are never critical.

4. Coalitions of the form $\{H2, OB, *\}$. These are coalitions that include H2 and OB and some subset of the "Lesser 3." H1 is not included in these coalitions. There are eight such coalitions. In these coalitions H2 and OB are always critical; the remaining players are never critical.

The list above covers all possible winning coalitions. It follows from all of the preceding observations (summarized in Table 2-7) that the critical count for each of the "Big 3" is 16, and the critical count for each of the "Lesser 3" is 0. The Banzhaf power index of each of the "Big 3," therefore, is $\frac{1}{3} = 33\frac{1}{3}\%$, and the Banzhaf power index of each of the "Lesser 3" is 0!

Coalition type	Number of coalitions	Weight
(1) $\{H_1, H_2, OB, *\}$	8	90 or more
(2) $\{\underline{H_1}, \underline{H_2}, *\}$	8	62 or more
(3) $\{\underline{H_1}, \underline{OB}, *\}$	8	59 or more
(4) $\{\underline{H_2}, \underline{OB}, *\}$	8	59 or more
Critical counts: 16 for the "Big 3"; 0 for the "Lesser 3"		
Banzhaf power: $\frac{1}{3} = 33\frac{1}{3}\%$ for the "Big 3"; 0 for the "Lesser 3"		

■ **TABLE 2-7** *Banzhaf power in Nassau County Board of Supervisors (1960s): [58: 31, 31, 28, 21, 2, 2]*

Example 2.13 reinforces the fact that in weighted voting you can have a lot of votes and yet have zero power. A player with votes but zero power is called a **dummy**. In the Nassau County Board of Supervisors Glen Cove, Long Beach, and North Hempstead were all dummies. The supervisors for these three districts attended meetings, participated in discussions, and voted in earnest not realizing that their votes were never relevant. The case of North Hempstead is especially serious—a district with a large population but no representation.

In a series of articles and law filings, John Banzhaf made the case that what was happening in Nassau County to North Hempstead, Long Beach, and Glen Cove (the three dummies) violated the "equal protection" clause guaranteed by the Fourteenth Amendment of the Constitution. Because of Banzhaf's mathematical analysis and legal persistence, in 1993 a federal court made it unconstitutional for county boards to use proportional representation as the basis for weighted voting.

| **EXAMPLE 2.14** | THE UNITED NATIONS SECURITY COUNCIL |

At present, the United Nations Security Council is made up of 15 member nations. Five of the member nations are permanent members: China (CH), France (FR), the Russian Federation (RU), the United Kingdom (UK), and the United States (US). The remaining 10 member nations are nonpermanent members appointed for two-year terms on a rotating basis. We will use a generic symbol NP to describe any nonpermanent member. To pass a motion in the Security Council requires a Yes vote from each of the five permanent members plus at least four additional Yes votes from nonpermanent members. If any one of the permanent members votes No, the motion fails regardless of how many Yes votes it gets. In other words, each of the permanent members has *veto power*. It's clear that the permanent members have more power than the nonpermanent members—but how much more?

Even though we don't have the weights of the players, with the help of a little mathematics we will be able to compute the Banzhaf power distribution. This is a very large weighted voting system, with 15 players and hundreds of winning coalitions, so we don't want to list the winning coalitions.

- **Step 1.** For our purposes, the winning coalitions can be divided into two types: (1) Coalitions with the 5 permanent members plus 4 nonpermanent members (first row of Table 2-8). These are coalitions that just make the cut, and every member of such a coalition is critical. There are 210 coalitions in this group. (2) Coalitions with the 5 permanent members plus 5 or more nonpermanent members (second row of Table 2-8). In these coalitions none of the nonpermanent members is critical (there is slack now for the requirement of a minimum of 4 nonpermanent members). The permanent members continue to be critical. There are 638 coalitions in this group.

Coalition type	Number of coalitions
(1) $\{\underline{CH}, \underline{FR}, \underline{RU}, \underline{UK}, \underline{US}, NP_1, NP_2, NP_3, NP_4\}$	210
(2) $\{\underline{CH}, \underline{FR}, \underline{RU}, \underline{UK}, \underline{US} + 5 \text{ or more NPs}\}$	638

- Total critical count: $T = 210 \times 9 + 638 \times 5 = 5080$
- Critical count for CH, FR, RU, UK, and US: 848 each
- Critical count for all NPs together: $5080 - 848 \times 5 = 840$
- Critical count for each NP $= \frac{840}{10} = 84$
- BPI of each of the 5 permanent members: $\frac{848}{5080} \cong 16.7\%$
- BPI of each of the 10 nonpermanent members: $\frac{84}{5080} \cong 1.65\%$

■ **TABLE 2-8** Banzhaf power in the United Nations Security Council

We now have enough information to find the Banzhaf power distribution in the Security Council, but we will have to do so in a slightly roundabout way (Step 4 before Steps 2 and 3).

- **Step 4.** We will first find the total critical count T. Each of the 210 coalitions of type (1) has 9 critical players. This contributes $210 \times 9 = 1890$ to T. Each of the 638 coalitions of type (2) has 5 critical players. This contributes another $638 \times 5 = 3190$ to T. Adding the two gives $T = 1890 + 3190 = 5080$.

- **Steps 2 and 3.** Each permanent member is critical in each of the 848 winning coalitions. This gives each permanent member a critical count of 848 and accounts for $848 \times 5 = 4240$ of the total. The remaining 840 ($5080 - 4240$) are divided equally among the 10 nonpermanent members, so each nonpermanent member has a critical count of 84.

- **Step 5.** The Banzhaf power index of each permanent member is $\frac{848}{5080} = 16.7\%$; the Banzhaf power index of each nonpermanent member is $\frac{84}{5080} = 1.65\%$.

Example 2.14 has an interesting aftermath. The power of the veto gives the permanent members roughly 10 times as much power as that of the nonpermanent members, and this was not the way that the Security Council was originally intended to work. It took Banzhaf's interpretation of power together with some nice mathematics to figure this out. To make the power distribution more balanced, there are plans in the works to change the current 15-nation arrangement by adding additional permanent members and changing the voting rules.

2.3 Shapley-Shubik Power

In this section we will discuss a different approach to measuring power, first proposed by the American mathematician Lloyd Shapley and the economist Martin Shubik in 1954. The key difference between the Shapley-Shubik measure of power and the Banzhaf measure of power centers on the concept of a *sequential coalition*. In the Shapley-Shubik method the assumption is that coalitions are formed sequentially: Players join the coalition and cast their votes in an orderly sequence (there is a first player, then comes a second player, then a third, etc.).

We will illustrate the main idea with a simple example.

EXAMPLE 2.15 [4: 3, 2, 1] REVISITED

We discussed this weighted voting system in Section 2.2. We will now look at things from a slightly different point of view. Suppose that players join coalitions one at a time and that we want to consider the order in which the players join the coalition. With three players there are six possibilities. (Just for now we will list them in some random order. Later we will try to organize ourselves a little better.)

1. P_2 goes first, P_1 goes second, P_3 goes last. We describe this using the notation $\langle P_2, P_1, P_3 \rangle$. (The $\langle \ \rangle$ is a convenient way to indicate that the players are listed in order from left to right.) This coalition starts with 2 votes, picks up 3 more when P_1 joins (now it has 5 votes), and picks up 1 more vote when P_3 joins. The key observation is that the player who had the pivotal role in making the coalition a winning coalition was P_1. We will call P_1 the *pivotal* player of that coalition.

2. P_3 goes first, P_2 goes second, P_1 goes last. We write this as $\langle P_3, P_2, P_1 \rangle$. This coalition starts with 1 vote, picks up 2 more when P_2 joins (now it has 3 votes), and picks up 3 more when P_1 joins. Once again, it's not until P_1 joins the coalition that there are enough votes to meet the quota. Score another one for P_1!

3. $\langle P_1, P_2, P_3 \rangle$. This coalition starts with 3 votes and gets 2 more votes when P_2 joins. No need to go any further. The pivotal player in this coalition is P_2.

4. $\langle P_1, P_3, P_2 \rangle$. This coalition starts with 3 votes and gets 1 more vote when P_3 joins. That's 4 votes, enough to win. The pivotal player in this coalition is P_3.

5. $\langle P_2, P_3, P_1 \rangle$. This coalition starts with 2 votes and gets 1 more vote when P_3 joins. That's 3 votes, not enough to win. It takes P_1 joining at the end to turn the coalition into a winning coalition. The pivotal player in this coalition is P_1.

6. $\langle P_3, P_1, P_2 \rangle$. This coalition starts with 1 vote and gets 3 more votes when P_1 joins. That's 4 votes, enough to win. The pivotal player in this coalition is P_1.

The six scenarios above cover all possibilities. Going down the list, we can see that in these six scenarios P_1 was the pivotal player four times, whereas P_2 and P_3 were pivotal once each. One could reasonably argue that P_1 has four times as much power as either P_2 or P_3.

We will now formally define some of the ideas introduced in Example 2.15 and end with a definition of Shapley-Shubik power. We will also introduce an important mathematical concept—the factorial of a number. We will discuss factorials in greater detail in Section 2.4, but for now we just need to know what the term *factorial* means.

- Sequential coalition. A **sequential coalition** is an *ordered list* of the players. We write sequential coalitions in the form $\langle P_1, P_2, \ldots, P_N \rangle$. The order of the players is from left to right. A good way to think of a sequential coalition is as a line of people with the head of the line on the left.
- Factorial of N. For any positive integer N, the product of all the integers between 1 and N is called the **factorial** of N and written $N!$. In other words,

$$N! = 1 \times 2 \times 3 \times \cdots \times N.$$

  The exclamation mark after the number indicates a factorial. The reason factorials are relevant to our discussion here is the following: *A weighted voting system with N players has $N!$ sequential coalitions.*
- Pivotal player. When looking at a sequential coalition start counting votes from left to right. At some point (maybe not until the end) there are enough votes to win. The first player that makes this possible is the **pivotal player** in that coalition. Every sequential coalition has *one and only one* pivotal player.
- Pivotal count. For each player we count how many times the player is a pivotal player as we run over all possible sequential coalitions. This gives the **pivotal count** for that player. We use the notation $SS_1, SS_2, \ldots, SS_N$ to denote the pivotal counts of $P_1, P_2, \ldots, P_N$ respectively.
- The Shapley-Shubik power index (SSPI). The **Shapley-Shubik power index** of a player is the ratio of the player's pivotal count over the total pivotal count for all the players. Since with N players there are $N!$ sequential coalitions and since there is exactly one pivotal player in each, the total pivotal count for all players is $N!$. Thus, we can rephrase the definition as: The Shapley-Shubik power index of a player is *the ratio of the player's pivotal count over $N!$.* We will use the Greek letter σ (sigma) to represent the Shapley-Shubik power, so that $\sigma_1, \sigma_2, \ldots, \sigma_N$ denote the Shapley-Shubik power indexes of $P_1, P_2, \ldots, P_N$ respectively.
- The Shapley-Shubik power distribution. The list $\sigma_1, \sigma_2, \ldots, \sigma_N$ of all the Shapley-Shubik power indexes gives the **Shapley-Shubik power distribution** of the weighted voting system. It essentially describes the division of the "power pie" among the players based on their Shapley-Shubik power indexes.

The following is a summary of the steps needed to compute the Shapley-Shubik power distribution of a weighted voting system with N players.

COMPUTING A SHAPLEY-SHUBIK POWER DISTRIBUTION

- **Step 1.** Make a list of the $N!$ sequential coalitions with the N players.
- **Step 2.** In each sequential coalition determine *the* pivotal player. (For bookkeeping purposes underline the pivotal players.)
- **Step 3.** Find the *pivotal counts* $SS_1, SS_2, \ldots, SS_N$.
- **Step 4.** Compute the SSPIs $\sigma_1 = \frac{SS_1}{N!}, \sigma_2 = \frac{SS_2}{N!}, \ldots, \sigma_N = \frac{SS_N}{N!}$.

EXAMPLE 2.16   THE NBA DRAFT REVISITED

In Example 2.10 (The NBA Draft) we computed the Banzhaf power distribution of the weighted voting system $[6\colon 4, 3, 2, 1]$. Now we will find the Shapley-Shubik power distribution.

Steps 1 and 2. Table 2-9 shows the 24 sequential coalitions with P_1, P_2, P_3, and P_4. In each sequential coalition the pivotal player is underlined. (Note that the 24 sequential coalitions in Table 2-9 are not randomly listed—each column corresponds to the sequential coalitions with a given first player. You may want to use the same or a similar pattern when you do the exercises on Shapley-Shubik power distributions.)

$\langle P_1, \underline{P_2}, P_3, P_4 \rangle$	$\langle P_2, \underline{P_1}, P_3, P_4 \rangle$	$\langle P_3, \underline{P_1}, P_2, P_4 \rangle$	$\langle P_4, P_1, \underline{P_2}, P_3 \rangle$
$\langle P_1, \underline{P_2}, P_4, P_3 \rangle$	$\langle P_2, \underline{P_1}, P_4, P_3 \rangle$	$\langle P_3, \underline{P_1}, P_4, P_2 \rangle$	$\langle P_4, P_1, \underline{P_3}, P_2 \rangle$
$\langle P_1, \underline{P_3}, P_2, P_4 \rangle$	$\langle P_2, P_3, \underline{P_1}, P_4 \rangle$	$\langle P_3, P_2, \underline{P_1}, P_4 \rangle$	$\langle P_4, P_2, \underline{P_1}, P_3 \rangle$
$\langle P_1, \underline{P_3}, P_4, P_2 \rangle$	$\langle P_2, P_3, \underline{P_4}, P_1 \rangle$	$\langle P_3, P_2, \underline{P_4}, P_1 \rangle$	$\langle P_4, P_2, \underline{P_3}, P_1 \rangle$
$\langle P_1, P_4, \underline{P_2}, P_3 \rangle$	$\langle P_2, P_4, \underline{P_1}, P_3 \rangle$	$\langle P_3, P_4, \underline{P_1}, P_2 \rangle$	$\langle P_4, P_3, \underline{P_1}, P_2 \rangle$
$\langle P_1, P_4, \underline{P_3}, P_2 \rangle$	$\langle P_2, P_4, \underline{P_3}, P_1 \rangle$	$\langle P_3, P_4, \underline{P_2}, P_1 \rangle$	$\langle P_4, P_3, \underline{P_2}, P_1 \rangle$

■ **TABLE 2-9**   Sequential coalitions for $[6\colon 4, 3, 2, 1]$ (pivotal players underlined)

Step 3. The pivotal counts are $SS_1 = 10$, $SS_2 = 6$, $SS_3 = 6$, and $SS_4 = 2$.

Step 4. The Shapley-Shubik power distribution is given by $\sigma_1 = \frac{10}{24} = 41\frac{2}{3}\%$, $\sigma_2 = \frac{6}{24} = 25\%$, $\sigma_3 = \frac{6}{24} = 25\%$, and $\sigma_4 = \frac{2}{24} = 8\frac{1}{3}\%$.

If you compare this result with the Banzhaf power distribution obtained in Example 2.10, you will notice that here the two power distributions are the same. If nothing else, this shows that it is not impossible for the Banzhaf and Shapley-Shubik power distributions to agree. In general, however, for randomly chosen real-life situations it is very unlikely that the Banzhaf and Shapley-Shubik methods will give the same answer.

EXAMPLE 2.17   A CITY COUNCIL WITH A "STRONG MAYOR"

In some cities the city council operates under what is known as the "strong-mayor" system. Under this system the city council can pass a motion under simple majority, but the mayor has the power to veto the decision. The mayor's veto can then be overruled by a "supermajority" of the council members. As an illustration of the strong-mayor system we will consider the city council of Cleansburg. In Cleansburg the city council has four members plus a strong mayor who has a vote as well as the power to veto motions supported by a simple majority of the council members. On the other hand, the mayor cannot veto motions supported by all four council members. Thus, a motion can pass if the mayor plus two or more council members support it or, alternatively, if the mayor is against it but the four council members support it.

Common sense tells us that under these rules, the four council members have the same amount of power but the mayor has more. We will compute the Shapley-Shubik power distribution of this weighted voting system to figure out exactly how much more. For convenience, we will let P_1 denote the mayor and P_2, P_3, P_4, P_5 denote the four council members.

With five players, this weighted voting system has $5! = 120$ sequential coalitions to consider. Obviously, we would prefer not to have to write them all down. Depending on where the mayor sits on the sequential coalition, we have 5 different scenarios, each consisting of 24 sequential coalitions (Table 2-10).

Type of sequential coalition	Number
1. $\langle P_1, *, \underline{*}, *, * \rangle$	24
2. $\langle *, P_1, \underline{*}, *, * \rangle$	24
3. $\langle *, *, \underline{P_1}, *, * \rangle$	24
4. $\langle *, *, *, \underline{P_1}, * \rangle$	24
5. $\langle *, *, *, *, P_1 \rangle$	24
Pivotal counts: $SS_1 = 48$; $SS_2 = SS_3 = SS_4 = SS_5 = 18$	
Shapley-Shubik power: $\sigma_1 = \frac{48}{120} = 40\%$; $\sigma_2 = \sigma_3 = \sigma_4 = \sigma_5 = \frac{18}{120} = 15\%$	

■ **TABLE 2-10**   Shapley-Shubik power in Cleansburg City Council
(P_1 = mayor, * = city council member)

Notice that the mayor is the pivotal player when he is in the third or fourth position (rows 3 and 4 in Table 2-10). This gives the mayor a pivotal count of 48. The remaining 72 sequential coalitions have city council members as pivotal players (in equal numbers). This gives each city council member a pivotal count of $\frac{72}{4} = 18$.

It follows that the Shapley-Shubik power index of the mayor is $\sigma_1 = \frac{48}{120} = 40\%$ and each of the four council members has a Shapley-Shubik power index of 15%. In conclusion, the Shapley-Shubik power distribution of the Cleansburg City Council is $\sigma_1 = 40\%$, $\sigma_2 = \sigma_3 = \sigma_4 = \sigma_5 = 15\%$.

For the purposes of comparison, the reader is encouraged to calculate the Banzhaf power distribution of the Cleansburg City Council (see Exercise 76).

EXAMPLE 2.18   THE UNITED NATIONS SECURITY COUNCIL REVISITED

In Example 2.14, we computed the Banzhaf power distribution in the United Nations Security Council. In this example we will outline how one might be able to find the Shapley-Shubik power distribution. We will skip a few of the mathematical details as they go beyond the scope of this book.

Recall that the U.N. Security Council has 5 permanent members and 10 nonpermanent members. A motion carries if all 5 permanent members and at least 4 nonpermanent members vote for it. The following is an outline of the computations:

- **Step 1.** There are 15! (about *1.3 trillion*) sequential coalitions of 15 players.

- **Steps 2 and 3.** A nonpermanent member can be pivotal only if it is the 9th player in the coalition, preceded by all five of the permanent members and three nonpermanent members (Fig. 2-1). There are approximately *2.44 billion* sequential coalitions of this type.

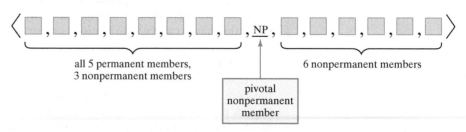

FIGURE 2-1   Sequential coalitions in the U.N. Security Council with pivotal nonpermanent member.

- **Step 4.** The Shapley-Shubik power index of a nonpermanent member is approximately $\frac{2.44 \text{ billion}}{1.3 \text{ trillion}} \approx 0.0019 = 0.19\%$. The 10 nonpermanent members (each with a Shapley-Shubik power index of 0.19%) have together 1.9% of the power pie, leaving the remaining 98.2% to be divided equally among the 5 permanent members. Thus, the Shapley-Shubik power index of each permanent member is approximately 19.64%.

This analysis shows the enormous difference between the Shapley-Shubik power of the permanent and nonpermanent members of the Security Council—permanent members have roughly 100 times the Shapley-Shubik power of nonpermanent members!

| **EXAMPLE 2.19** | THE ELECTORAL COLLEGE (2012, 2016, 2020) |

The president of the United States is allegedly the most powerful person in the world. To get elected president, a candidate must get a majority (270 or more) of the 538 electoral votes in the Electoral College. Electoral votes are assigned to the 50 states and the District of Columbia based on their representation in Congress (i.e., number of electoral votes = number of representatives + 2; the District of Columbia gets 3 votes by law). The first column of Table 2-11 shows the number of electoral votes for each state based on the 2010 Census. These numbers apply to the 2012, 2016, and 2020 presidential elections (they will probably change after the 2020 Census).

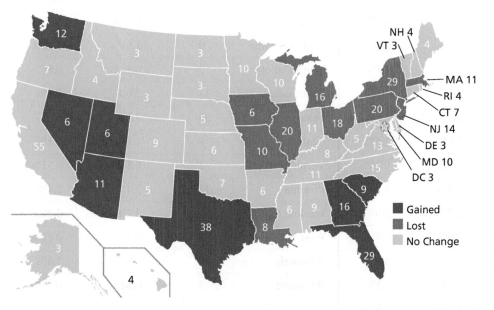

Each state casts all its electoral votes to the winner of the popular vote in that state (there are two small exceptions to this "winner-take-all" rule—Maine and Nebraska allow their electoral votes to be split), and voting typically boils down to two options—the Republican candidate or the Democratic candidate (the last time a third-party candidate received any electoral votes was 1968). If we assume that there are only two choices (Republican or Democrat) and make a slight concession to expediency and assume that Maine and Nebraska do not split their votes, then the Electoral College becomes a very large and complicated weighted voting system (538 total votes, *quota q* = 270, and 51 *players* with *weights* as shown in the first column of Table 2-11).

The power distribution in the Electoral College is one of the many important variables to consider in a presidential campaign (for example in determining the best way to allocate campaign resources and effort among the states). Table 2-11 shows both the Shapley-Shubik and Banzhaf power index of each state in the current Electoral College. It is quite remarkable that the numbers all the way down the list are almost identical. This tells us that the power distribution in the Electoral College is "robust," as both methods tell essentially the same story.

Because the Electoral College is such a large weighted voting system, the calculations of the power indexes in Table 2-11 can only be done using advanced mathematical techniques that go beyond the scope of this book and require some sophisticated software.

■MyMathLab®
The applets *Banzhaf Power* and *Shapley-Shubik Power* are optimized to compute power distributions of very large weighted voting systems like the Electoral College on an ordinary computer.*

*MyMathLab code required.

State	Weight	Shapley-Shubik	Banzhaf		State	Weight	Shapley-Shubik	Banzhaf
Alabama	9	1.64%	1.64%		Montana	3	0.54%	0.55%
Alaska	3	0.54%	0.55%		Nebraska*	5	0.9%	0.91%
Arizona	11	2.0%	2.0%		Nevada	6	1.1%	1.1%
Arkansas	6	1.1%	1.1%		New Hampshire	4	0.72%	0.73%
California	55	11.0%	11.4%		New Jersey	14	2.6%	2.6%
Colorado	9	1.64%	1.64%		New Mexico	5	0.9%	0.91%
Connecticut	7	1.3%	1.3%		New York	29	5.5%	5.4%
Delaware	3	0.54%	0.55%		North Carolina	15	2.8%	2.7%
District of Columbia	3	0.54%	0.55%		North Dakota	3	0.54%	0.55%
Florida	29	5.5%	5.4%		Ohio	18	3.3%	3.3%
Georgia	16	2.9%	2.9%		Oklahoma	7	1.3%	1.3%
Hawaii	4	0.72%	0.73%		Oregon	7	1.3%	1.3%
Idaho	4	0.72%	0.73%		Pennsylvania	20	3.7%	3.7%
Illinois	20	3.7%	3.7%		Rhode Island	4	0.72%	0.73%
Indiana	11	2.0%	2.0%		South Carolina	9	1.64%	1.64%
Iowa	6	1.1%	1.1%		South Dakota	3	0.54%	0.55%
Kansas	6	1.1%	1.1%		Tennessee	11	2.0%	2.0%
Kentucky	8	1.5%	1.5%		Texas	38	7.3%	7.2%
Louisiana	8	1.5%	1.5%		Utah	6	1.1%	1.1%
Maine*	4	0.72%	0.73%		Vermont	3	0.54%	0.55%
Maryland	10	1.8%	1.8%		Virginia	13	2.4%	2.4%
Massachusetts	11	2.0%	2.0%		Washington	12	2.2%	2.2%
Michigan	16	2.9%	2.9%		West Virginia	5	0.9%	0.91%
Minnesota	10	1.8%	1.8%		Wisconsin	10	1.8%	1.8%
Mississippi	6	1.1%	1.1%		Wyoming	3	0.54%	0.55%
Missouri	10	1.8%	1.8%					

*Not bound by "winner-take-all" rule.

■ **TABLE 2-11**   Shapley-Shubik and Banzhaf Power in the Electoral College (2012, 2016, and 2020 Presidential Elections)

2.4 Subsets and Permutations

The goal of this section is to provide a quick primer of basic facts about two very important mathematical concepts: *subsets* and *permutations*. These basic facts turn out to be quite useful when working with coalitions and sequential coalitions. Some of the ideas introduced in this section will be covered again in future chapters.

Subsets and Coalitions

Coalitions are essentially sets of players that join forces to vote on a motion. (This is the reason we used set notation in Section 2.2 to work with coalitions.) By definition, a **subset** of a set is *any* combination of elements from the set. This includes the set with nothing in it (called the *empty set* and denoted by { }) as well as the set with all the elements (the original set itself).

EXAMPLE 2.20 SUBSETS OF $\{P_1, P_2, P_3\}$ AND $\{P_1, P_2, P_3, P_4\}$

Table 2-12 shows the eight subsets of the set $\{P_1, P_2, P_3\}$ and the 16 subsets of the set $\{P_1, P_2, P_3, P_4\}$. The subsets of $\{P_1, P_2, P_3, P_4\}$ are organized into two groups—the "no P_4" group and the "add P_4" group. The subsets in the "no P_4" group are exactly the 8 subsets of $\{P_1, P_2, P_3\}$; the subsets of the "add P_4" group are obtained by adding P_4 to each of the 8 subsets of $\{P_1, P_2, P_3\}$. Thus, adding one more element to the set $\{P_1, P_2, P_3\}$ doubled the number of subsets. Note that the number of subsets of a set is completely independent of the names of its elements, so any set with 3 elements, regardless of what they are called, has 8 subsets, and any set with four elements has 16 subsets.

Subsets of $\{P_1, P_2, P_3\}$	Subsets of $\{P_1, P_2, P_3, P_4\}$	
	"no P_4"	"add P_4"
{ }	{ }	$\{P_4\}$
$\{P_1\}$	$\{P_1\}$	$\{P_1, P_4\}$
$\{P_2\}$	$\{P_2\}$	$\{P_2, P_4\}$
$\{P_1, P_2\}$	$\{P_1, P_2\}$	$\{P_1, P_2, P_4\}$
$\{P_3\}$	$\{P_3\}$	$\{P_3, P_4\}$
$\{P_1, P_3\}$	$\{P_1, P_3\}$	$\{P_1, P_3, P_4\}$
$\{P_2, P_3\}$	$\{P_2, P_3\}$	$\{P_2, P_3, P_4\}$
$\{P_1, P_2, P_3\}$	$\{P_1, P_2, P_3\}$	$\{P_1, P_2, P_3, P_4\}$

■ TABLE 2-12

The key observation in Example 2.20 is that by adding one more element to a set we double the number of subsets, and this principle applies to sets of any size. Since a set with 4 elements has 16 subsets, a set with 5 elements must have 32 subsets and a set with 6 elements must have 64 subsets. This leads to the following key fact:

■ Number of subsets. A set with N elements has 2^N subsets.

Now that we can count subsets, we can also count coalitions. The only difference between coalitions and subsets is that we don't consider the empty set a coalition (the purpose of a coalition is to cast votes, so you need at least one player to have a coalition).

■ Number of coalitions. A weighted voting system with N players has $2^N - 1$ coalitions.

Finally, when computing critical counts and Banzhaf power, we are interested in listing just the winning coalitions. If we assume that there are no dictators, then winning coalitions have to have at least two players and we can, therefore, rule out all the single-player coalitions from our list. There are N different single-player coalitions, which leads to our next fact:

■ Number of coalitions of two or more players. A weighted voting system with N players has $2^N - N - 1$ coalitions of two or more players.

Permutations and Sequential Coalitions

- **Permutation.** A **permutation** of a set of objects is an ordered list of the objects. When you change the order of the objects you get a different *permutation* of those objects.

When the objects are people, a permutation is analogous to having the people form a line: first person, second person, etc. Rearrange the folks in the line and you get a different permutation.

EXAMPLE 2.21 PERMUTATIONS OF P_1, P_2, P_3 AND P_1, P_2, P_3, P_4

The six permutations of P_1, P_2, P_3 are shown at the top of Fig. 2-2. Now imagine that P_4 shows up and we have to add her to the line. We can position P_4 at the back of the line, or in third place, or second place, or at the front of the line (Fig. 2-2). For each of the six permutations of P_1, P_2, P_3 we get four permutations of P_1, P_2, P_3, P_4 depending on where we choose to put P_4. Thus, we have a total of 24 permutations of the 4 objects.

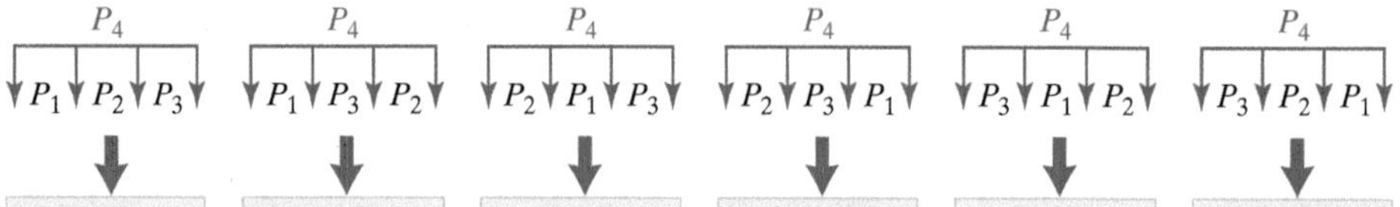

$P_1\ P_2\ P_3\ P_4$	$P_1\ P_3\ P_2\ P_4$	$P_2\ P_1\ P_3\ P_4$	$P_2\ P_3\ P_1\ P_4$	$P_3\ P_1\ P_2\ P_4$	$P_3\ P_2\ P_1\ P_4$
$P_1\ P_2\ P_4\ P_3$	$P_1\ P_3\ P_4\ P_2$	$P_2\ P_1\ P_4\ P_3$	$P_2\ P_3\ P_4\ P_1$	$P_3\ P_1\ P_4\ P_2$	$P_3\ P_2\ P_4\ P_1$
$P_1\ P_4\ P_2\ P_3$	$P_1\ P_4\ P_3\ P_2$	$P_2\ P_4\ P_1\ P_3$	$P_2\ P_4\ P_3\ P_1$	$P_3\ P_4\ P_1\ P_2$	$P_3\ P_4\ P_2\ P_1$
$P_4\ P_1\ P_2\ P_3$	$P_4\ P_1\ P_3\ P_2$	$P_4\ P_2\ P_1\ P_3$	$P_4\ P_2\ P_3\ P_1$	$P_4\ P_3\ P_1\ P_2$	$P_4\ P_3\ P_2\ P_1$

FIGURE 2-2 The 24 permutations of P_1, P_2, P_3, and P_4.

Note that $6 = 3 \times 2 \times 1 = 3!$ and $24 = 4 \times 3 \times 2 \times 1 = 4!$. Generalizing the idea in Example 2.21 gives the following important fact:

- **Number of permutations.** There are $N! = N \times (N-1) \times \ldots \times 3 \times 2 \times 1$ different permutations of N objects.

The connection between sequential coalitions and permutations is pretty straightforward: A sequential coalition of N players is just a permutation of the players. This leads to the following:

- **Number of sequential coalitions.** A weighted voting system with N players has $N!$ sequential coalitions.

EXAMPLE 2.22 PERMUTATIONS WITH A PLAYER IN A SPECIFIED POSITION

In Example 2.21 we generated the 24 permutations of P_1, P_2, P_3, P_4 by putting P_4 in each of 4 possible slots in a permutation of P_1, P_2, P_3. This means that there are 6 coalitions with P_4 in last place, 6 more with P_4 in third place, 6 with P_4 in second place, and 6 with P_4 at the head of the line (read Fig. 2-2 horizontally). What is true for P_4 is true for each of the other players: There are 6 permutations with P_3 in last place, 6 more with P_3 in third place, 6 with P_3 in second place, and 6 with P_3 at the head of the line. Same for P_2 and P_1.

The observations made in Example 2.22 can be generalized to any player in any position in any weighted voting system.

- **Number of sequential coalitions with _P_ in the _k_th position.** Let _P_ be a player in a weighted voting system with _N_ players and _k_ an arbitrary position between first and last. There are $(N-1)!$ sequential coalitions with _P_ in the _k_th position.

Conclusion

In this chapter we discussed weighted voting—voting situations in which the voters (called players) control different numbers of votes. The idea behind weighted voting is that sometimes we want to give some players more power than others over the outcome of the voting. Weighted voting is used in partnerships where some partners own a larger share than others; in international bodies where some countries are more influential than others; in county boards where some districts are bigger than others; in the Electoral College where the big states have more votes than the small states; and even at home, where Mom has more votes than anyone else when deciding where the family goes on vacation.

The big fallacy in weighted voting is the idea that the power of the players is proportional to the number of votes they control. In this chapter we saw examples of players with a few votes but plenty of power as well as players with many votes and no power. If power were proportional to votes, computing the power of the players in a weighted voting system would be not only easy but also very uninteresting. Because power is not proportional to votes, computing power is harder but much more interesting.

In this chapter we looked at the two most commonly used ways to compute the distribution of power among the players in a weighted voting system: the _Banzhaf power distribution_ and _the Shapley-Shubik power distribution_. These two approaches provide two different ways to measure power, and, while they occasionally agree (Example 2.19 The Electoral College), they can also differ significantly (Examples 2.14 and 2.18 The U.N. Security Council). Of the two, which one is better?

Unfortunately, there is no simple answer. Both are useful, and in some sense the choice is subjective. Perhaps the best way to evaluate them is to think of them as being based on a slightly different set of assumptions. The idea behind Banzhaf power is that players are free to come and go, negotiating their allegiance for power (somewhat like professional athletes since the advent of free agency). Underlying Shapley-Shubik power is the assumption that when a player joins a coalition the player is making a commitment to stay. In the latter case a player's power is generated by its ability to be in the right place at the right time.

In practice the choice of which method to use for measuring power is based on which of the assumptions better fits the specifics of the situation. Contrary to what we've often come to expect, mathematics does not give us the answer, just the tools that might help us make an informed decision.

KEY CONCEPTS

2.1 An Introduction to Weighted Voting

- **weighted voting system:** a formal voting arrangement where the voters are not necessarily equal in terms of the number of votes they control, **38**
- **motion:** a vote between two options (Yes and No), **38**
- **player:** a voter in a weighted voting system, **38**
- **weight:** of a player, the number of votes controlled by the player, **38**
- **quota:** the minimum number of votes required to pass a motion, **38**
- **dictator:** a player whose weight is bigger or equal to the quota, **40**
- **veto power:** the power to keep the remaining players from passing a motion, **40**

2.2 Banzhaf Power

- **coalition:** a set of players that join forces and agree to vote together, **41**
- **grand coalition:** the coalition consisting of all the players, **41**
- **winning coalition:** a coalition with enough votes to carry a motion, **42**
- **losing coalition:** a coalition that doesn't have enough votes to carry a motion, **42**
- **critical player:** in a winning coalition, a player without whom the coalition would be a losing coalition, **42**
- **critical count:** for each player, the number of winning coalitions in which the player is a critical player, **42**
- **Banzhaf power index:** for each player, the ratio B/T, in which B is the player's critical count and T is the total critical count for all the players, **42**
- **Banzhaf power distribution:** a list consisting of the Banzhaf power indexes of all the players, **42**

2.3 Shapley-Shubik Power

- **sequential coalition:** an ordered listing of all the players, **50**
- **factorial:** for a positive integer N, the product of all the integers from 1 to N, ($N! = 1 \times 2 \times 3 \times \cdots \times N$), **50**
- **pivotal player:** in a sequential coalition, as the votes are tallied from left to right, the first player whose votes make the total equal to or higher than the quota, **50**
- **pivotal count:** for each player, the number of sequential coalitions in which the player is a pivotal player, **50**
- **Shapley-Shubik power index:** for each player, the ratio $SS/N!$, where SS is the player's pivotal count and N is the number of players, **50**
- **Shapley-Shubik power distribution:** a list consisting of the Shapley-Shubik power indexes of all the players, **50**

2.4 Subsets and Permutations

- **permutation:** an ordered arrangement of a set of objects, **56**

EXERCISES

WALKING

2.1 Weighted Voting

1. **Nassau County Board of Supervisors (1990).** Table 2-13 shows the six districts in Nassau County and their votes in the County Board of Supervisors in 1990. Suppose the quota was set at 60% or more of the votes. Describe this weighted voting system using the standard notation $[q: w_1, w_2, \ldots, w_N]$.

District	Weight
Hempstead #1	30
Hempstead #2	28
Oyster Bay	22
North Hempstead	21
Long Beach	2
Glen Cove	2

■ TABLE 2-13

2. **The European Union Council (2010).** Table 2-14 shows the weights of the member nations in the European Union Council of Ministers in 2010. Suppose the quota is set at 74% or more of the votes.

   (a) Find the value of N (the number of players in this weighted voting system).

   (b) Find the value of V (the total number of votes in the system).

   (c) Describe this weighted voting system using the standard notation $[q: w_1, w_2, \ldots, w_N]$.

Member nation	Weight
France, Germany, Italy, United Kingdom	29
Spain, Poland	27
Romania	14
Netherlands	13
Belgium, Greece, Czech Republic, Hungary, Portugal	12
Austria, Bulgaria, Sweden	10
Denmark, Ireland, Lithuania, Slovakia, Finland	7
Cyprus, Estonia, Latvia, Luxembourg, Slovenia	4
Malta	3

■ TABLE 2-14

3. Consider the weighted voting system $[q: 6, 4, 3, 3, 2, 2]$.

   (a) What is the smallest value that the quota q can take?

   (b) What is the largest value that the quota q can take?

   (c) What is the value of the quota if *at least* three-fourths of the votes are required to pass a motion?

   (d) What is the value of the quota if *more* than three-fourths of the votes are required to pass a motion?

4. Consider the weighted voting system $[q: 10, 6, 5, 4, 2]$.

   (a) What is the smallest value that the quota q can take?

   (b) What is the largest value that the quota q can take?

   (c) What is the value of the quota if *at least* two-thirds of the votes are required to pass a motion?

   (d) What is the value of the quota if *more* than two-thirds of the votes are required to pass a motion?

5. In each of the following weighted voting systems, determine which players, if any, have veto power.

   (a) $[7: 4, 3, 3, 2]$

   (b) $[9: 4, 3, 3, 2]$

   (c) $[10: 4, 3, 3, 2]$

   (d) $[11: 4, 3, 3, 2]$

6. In each of the following weighted voting systems, determine which players, if any, have veto power.

   (a) $[9: 8, 4, 2, 1]$

   (b) $[12: 8, 4, 2, 1]$

   (c) $[14: 8, 4, 2, 1]$

   (d) $[15: 8, 4, 2, 1]$

7. Consider the weighted voting system $[q: 7, 5, 3]$. Find the *smallest* value of q for which

   (a) all three players have veto power.

   (b) P_2 has veto power but P_3 does not.

8. Consider the weighted voting system $[q: 10, 8, 6, 4, 2]$. Find the *smallest* value of q for which

   (a) all five players have veto power.

   (b) P_3 has veto power but P_4 does not.

9. A committee has four members (P_1, P_2, P_3, and P_4). In this committee P_1 has twice as many votes as P_2; P_2 has twice as many votes as P_3; P_3 and P_4 have the same number of votes. The quota is $q = 49$. For each of the given definitions of the *quota*, describe the committee using the notation $[q: w_1, w_2, w_3, w_4]$. (*Hint*: Write the weighted voting system as $[49: 4x, 2x, x, x]$, and then solve for x.)

   (a) The quota is defined as a *simple majority* of the votes.

   (b) The quota is defined as *more than two-thirds* of the votes.

   (c) The quota is defined as *more than three-fourths* of the votes.

10. A committee has six members (P_1, P_2, P_3, P_4, P_5, and P_6). In this committee P_1 has twice as many votes as P_2; P_2 and P_3 each has twice as many votes as P_4; P_4 has twice as many votes as P_5; P_5 and P_6 have the same number of votes. The quota is $q = 121$. For each of the given definitions of the *quota*, describe the committee using the notation $[q: w_1, w_2, w_3, w_4, w_5, w_6]$. (*Hint*: Write the weighted voting system as $[121: 8x, 4x, 4x, 2x, x, x]$, and then solve for x.)

   (a) The quota is defined as a *simple majority* of the votes.

   (b) The quota is defined as *more than two-thirds* of the votes.

   (c) The quota is defined as *more than three-fourths* of the votes.

2.2 Banzhaf Power

11. Consider the weighted voting system $[q: 7, 5, 3]$.

   (a) What is the weight of the coalition formed by P_1 and P_3?

   (b) For what values of the quota q is the coalition formed by P_1 and P_3 a winning coalition?

   (c) For what values of the quota q is the coalition formed by P_1 and P_3 a losing coalition?

12. Consider the weighted voting system $[q: 10, 8, 6, 4, 2]$.

   (a) What is the weight of the coalition formed by P_2, P_3, and P_4?

   (b) For what values of the quota q is the coalition formed by P_2, P_3, and P_4 a winning coalition?

   (c) For what values of the quota q is the coalition formed by P_2, P_3, and P_4 a losing coalition?

13. A weighted voting system with four players has the following winning coalitions (with critical players underlined):

   $\{\underline{P_1}, \underline{P_2}, \underline{P_3}\}, \{\underline{P_1}, \underline{P_2}, \underline{P_4}\}, \{\underline{P_1}, \underline{P_2}, P_3, P_4\}$.

   Find the Banzhaf power distribution of this weighted voting system.

14. A weighted voting system with five players has the following winning coalitions (with critical players underlined):

   $\{\underline{P_1}, \underline{P_2}, \underline{P_3}\}, \{\underline{P_1}, \underline{P_2}, \underline{P_4}\}, \{\underline{P_1}, \underline{P_2}, P_3, P_4\},$
   $\{\underline{P_1}, \underline{P_2}, \underline{P_3}, P_5\}, \{\underline{P_1}, \underline{P_2}, \underline{P_4}, P_5\}, \{\underline{P_1}, \underline{P_3}, \underline{P_4}, P_5\},$
   $\{\underline{P_1}, P_2, P_3, P_4, P_5\}$.

Find the Banzhaf power distribution of this weighted voting system.

15. Consider the weighted voting system $[10: 6, 5, 4, 2]$. $m=9$

   (a) Which players are critical in the winning coalition $\{P_1, P_2, P_4\}$?

   (b) Write down all winning coalitions.

   (c) Find the Banzhaf power distribution of this weighted voting system.

16. Consider the weighted voting system $[5: 3, 2, 1, 1]$.

   (a) Which players are critical in the winning coalition $\{P_1, P_3, P_4\}$?

   (b) Write down all winning coalitions.

   (c) Find the Banzhaf power distribution of this weighted voting system.

17. (a) Find the Banzhaf power distribution of the weighted voting system $[6: 5, 2, 1]$.

   (b) Find the Banzhaf power distribution of the weighted voting system $[3: 2, 1, 1]$. Compare your answers in (a) and (b).

18. (a) Find the Banzhaf power distribution of the weighted voting system $[7: 5, 2, 1]$.

   (b) Find the Banzhaf power distribution of the weighted voting system $[5: 3, 2, 1]$. Compare your answers in (a) and (b).

19. Consider the weighted voting system $[q: 5, 4, 3, 2, 1]$. Find the Banzhaf power distribution of this weighted voting system when

   (a) $q = 10$

   (b) $q = 11$

   (c) $q = 12$

   (d) $q = 15$

20. Consider the weighted voting system $[q: 8, 4, 2, 1]$. Find the Banzhaf power distribution of this weighted voting system when

   (a) $q = 8$

   (b) $q = 9$

   (c) $q = 10$

   (d) $q = 14$

21. In a weighted voting system with three players the winning coalitions are: $\{P_1, P_2\}$, $\{P_1, P_3\}$, and $\{P_1, P_2, P_3\}$.

   (a) Find the critical players in each winning coalition.

   (b) Find the Banzhaf power distribution of the weighted voting system.

22. In a weighted voting system with four players the winning coalitions are: $\{P_1, P_2\}$, $\{P_1, P_2, P_3\}$, $\{P_1, P_2, P_4\}$, and $\{P_1, P_2, P_3, P_4\}$.

(a) Find the critical players in each winning coalition.

(b) Find the Banzhaf power distribution of the weighted voting system.

23. The Nassau County (N.Y.) Board of Supervisors (1960s version). In the 1960s, the Nassau County Board of Supervisors operated as the weighted voting system $[58: 31, 31, 28, 21, 2, 2]$. Assume that the players are P_1 through P_6.

(a) List all the *two-* and *three-player* winning coalitions and find the critical players in each coalition.

(b) List all the winning coalitions that have P_4 as a member and find the critical players in each coalition.

(c) Use the results in (b) to find the Banzhaf power index of P_4.

(d) Use the results in (a) and (c) to find the Banzhaf power distribution of the weighted voting system.

24. The Nassau County Board of Supervisors (1990s version). In the 1990s, after a series of legal challenges, the Nassau County Board of Supervisors was redesigned to operate as the weighted voting system $[65: 30, 28, 22, 15, 7, 6]$.

(a) List all the *three-player* winning coalitions and find the critical players in each coalition.

(b) List all the *four-player* winning coalitions and find the critical players in each coalition. (*Hint*: There are 11 four-player winning coalitions.)

(c) List all the *five-player* winning coalitions and find the critical players in each coalition.

(d) Use the results in (a), (b), and (c) to find the Banzhaf power distribution of the weighted voting system.

25. A law firm is run by four partners $(A, B, C,$ and $D)$. Each partner has one vote and decisions are made by majority rule, but in the case of a 2-2 tie, the coalition with D (the junior partner) loses. (For example, $\{A, B\}$ wins, but $\{A, D\}$ loses.)

(a) List all the winning coalitions in this voting system and find the critical players in each.

(b) Find the Banzhaf power distribution in this law firm.

26. A law firm is run by four partners $(A, B, C,$ and $D)$. Each partner has one vote and decisions are made by majority rule, but in the case of a 2-2 tie, the coalition with A (the senior partner) wins.

(a) List all the winning coalitions in this voting system and the critical players in each.

(b) Find the Banzhaf power index of this law firm.

2.3 Shapley-Shubik Power

27. Table 2-15 shows the 24 sequential coalitions (with pivotal players underlined) in a weighted voting system with four players. Find the Shapley-Shubik power distribution of this weighted voting system.

$$\langle P_1, P_2, \underline{P_3}, P_4 \rangle \ \langle P_1, P_2, \underline{P_4}, P_3 \rangle \ \langle P_1, P_3, \underline{P_2}, P_4 \rangle \ \langle P_1, P_3, P_4, \underline{P_2} \rangle$$
$$\langle P_1, P_4, \underline{P_2}, P_3 \rangle \ \langle P_1, P_4, P_3, \underline{P_2} \rangle \ \langle P_2, P_1, \underline{P_3}, P_4 \rangle \ \langle P_2, P_1, \underline{P_4}, P_3 \rangle$$
$$\langle P_2, P_3, \underline{P_1}, P_4 \rangle \ \langle P_2, P_3, P_4, \underline{P_1} \rangle \ \langle P_2, P_4, \underline{P_1}, P_3 \rangle \ \langle P_2, P_4, P_3, \underline{P_1} \rangle$$
$$\langle P_3, P_1, \underline{P_2}, P_4 \rangle \ \langle P_3, P_1, P_4, \underline{P_2} \rangle \ \langle P_3, P_2, \underline{P_1}, P_4 \rangle \ \langle P_3, P_2, P_4, \underline{P_1} \rangle$$
$$\langle P_3, P_4, P_1, \underline{P_2} \rangle \ \langle P_3, P_4, P_2, \underline{P_1} \rangle \ \langle P_4, P_1, \underline{P_2}, P_3 \rangle \ \langle P_4, P_1, P_3, \underline{P_2} \rangle$$
$$\langle P_4, P_2, \underline{P_1}, P_3 \rangle \ \langle P_4, P_2, P_3, \underline{P_1} \rangle \ \langle P_4, P_3, P_1, \underline{P_2} \rangle \ \langle P_4, P_3, P_2, \underline{P_1} \rangle$$

■ **TABLE 2-15**

28. Table 2-16 shows the 24 sequential coalitions (with pivotal players underlined) in a weighted voting system with four players. Find the Shapley-Shubik power distribution of this weighted voting system.

$$\langle P_1, \underline{P_2}, P_3, P_4 \rangle \ \langle P_1, \underline{P_2}, P_4, P_3 \rangle \ \langle P_1, \underline{P_3}, P_2, P_4 \rangle \ \langle P_1, \underline{P_3}, P_4, P_2 \rangle$$
$$\langle P_1, P_4, \underline{P_2}, P_3 \rangle \ \langle P_1, P_4, \underline{P_3}, P_2 \rangle \ \langle P_2, \underline{P_1}, P_3, P_4 \rangle \ \langle P_2, \underline{P_1}, P_4, P_3 \rangle$$
$$\langle P_2, P_3, \underline{P_1}, P_4 \rangle \ \langle P_2, P_3, \underline{P_4}, P_1 \rangle \ \langle P_2, P_4, \underline{P_1}, P_3 \rangle \ \langle P_2, P_4, \underline{P_3}, P_1 \rangle$$
$$\langle P_3, \underline{P_1}, P_2, P_4 \rangle \ \langle P_3, \underline{P_1}, P_4, P_2 \rangle \ \langle P_3, P_2, \underline{P_1}, P_4 \rangle \ \langle P_3, P_2, \underline{P_4}, P_1 \rangle$$
$$\langle P_3, P_4, \underline{P_1}, P_2 \rangle \ \langle P_3, P_4, \underline{P_2}, P_1 \rangle \ \langle P_4, P_1, \underline{P_2}, P_3 \rangle \ \langle P_4, P_1, \underline{P_3}, P_2 \rangle$$
$$\langle P_4, P_2, \underline{P_1}, P_3 \rangle \ \langle P_4, P_2, \underline{P_3}, P_1 \rangle \ \langle P_4, P_3, \underline{P_1}, P_2 \rangle \ \langle P_4, P_3, \underline{P_2}, P_1 \rangle$$

■ **TABLE 2-16**

29. Consider the weighted voting system $[16: 9, 8, 7]$.

(a) Write down all the sequential coalitions, and in each sequential coalition identify the pivotal player.

(b) Find the Shapley-Shubik power distribution of this weighted voting system.

30. Consider the weighted voting system $[8: 7, 6, 2]$.

(a) Write down all the sequential coalitions, and in each sequential coalition identify the pivotal player.

(b) Find the Shapley-Shubik power distribution of this weighted voting system.

31. Find the Shapley-Shubik power distribution of each of the following weighted voting systems.

(a) $[15: 16, 8, 4, 1]$

(b) $[18: 16, 8, 4, 1]$

(c) $[24: 16, 8, 4, 1]$

(d) $[28: 16, 8, 4, 1]$

32. Find the Shapley-Shubik power distribution of each of the following weighted voting systems.

(a) $[8: 8, 4, 2, 1]$

(b) $[9: 8, 4, 2, 1]$

(c) $[12: 8, 4, 2, 1]$

(d) $[14: 8, 4, 2, 1]$

33. Find the Shapley-Shubik power distribution of each of the following weighted voting systems.

(a) $[51: 40, 30, 20, 10]$

(b) $[59: 40, 30, 20, 10]$ (*Hint:* Compare this situation with the one in (a).)

(c) $[60: 40, 30, 20, 10]$

34. Find the Shapley-Shubik power distribution of each of the following weighted voting systems.

(a) $[41: 40, 10, 10, 10]$

(b) $[49: 40, 10, 10, 10]$ (*Hint:* Compare this situation with the one in (a).)

(c) $[50: 40, 10, 10, 10]$

35. In a weighted voting system with three players the winning coalitions are: $\{P_1, P_2\}$, $\{P_1, P_3\}$, and $\{P_1, P_2, P_3\}$.

(a) List the sequential coalitions and identify the pivotal player in each one.

(b) Find the Shapley-Shubik power distribution of the weighted voting system.

36. In a weighted voting system with three players the winning coalitions are: $\{P_1, P_2\}$ and $\{P_1, P_2, P_3\}$.

(a) List the sequential coalitions and identify the pivotal player in each sequential coalition.

(b) Find the Shapley-Shubik power distribution of the weighted voting system.

37. Table 2-17 shows the 24 sequential coalitions in a weighted voting system with four players. In some cases the pivotal player is underlined, and in some cases it isn't. Find the Shapley-Shubik power distribution of this weighted voting system. (*Hint:* First find the pivotal player in the remaining sequential coalitions.)

$\langle P_1, \underline{P_2}, P_3, P_4 \rangle$	$\langle P_2, P_1, P_3, P_4 \rangle$	$\langle P_3, P_1, P_2, P_4 \rangle$	$\langle P_4, P_1, P_2, P_3 \rangle$
$\langle P_1, P_2, P_4, P_3 \rangle$	$\langle P_2, P_1, P_4, P_3 \rangle$	$\langle P_3, P_1, P_4, P_2 \rangle$	$\langle P_4, P_1, P_3, P_2 \rangle$
$\langle P_1, \underline{P_3}, P_2, P_4 \rangle$	$\langle P_2, P_3, \underline{P_1}, P_4 \rangle$	$\langle P_3, P_2, P_1, P_4 \rangle$	$\langle P_4, P_2, P_1, P_3 \rangle$
$\langle P_1, P_3, P_4, P_2 \rangle$	$\langle P_2, P_3, \underline{P_4}, P_1 \rangle$	$\langle P_3, P_2, P_4, P_1 \rangle$	$\langle P_4, P_2, P_3, P_1 \rangle$
$\langle P_1, P_4, \underline{P_2}, P_3 \rangle$	$\langle P_2, P_4, \underline{P_1}, P_3 \rangle$	$\langle P_3, P_4, \underline{P_1}, P_2 \rangle$	$\langle P_4, P_3, P_1, P_2 \rangle$
$\langle P_1, P_4, \underline{P_3}, P_2 \rangle$	$\langle P_2, P_4, \underline{P_3}, P_1 \rangle$	$\langle P_3, P_4, \underline{P_2}, P_1 \rangle$	$\langle P_4, P_3, P_2, P_1 \rangle$

■ TABLE 2-17

38. Table 2-18 shows the 24 sequential coalitions in a weighted voting system with four players. In some cases the pivotal player is underlined, and in some cases it isn't. Find the Shapley-Shubik power distribution of this weighted voting system. (*Hint:* First find the pivotal player in the remaining sequential coalitions.)

$\langle P_1, \underline{P_2}, P_3, P_4 \rangle$	$\langle P_2, P_1, P_3, P_4 \rangle$	$\langle P_3, P_1, P_2, P_4 \rangle$	$\langle P_4, P_1, P_2, P_3 \rangle$
$\langle P_1, P_2, P_4, P_3 \rangle$	$\langle P_2, P_1, P_4, P_3 \rangle$	$\langle P_3, P_1, P_4, P_2 \rangle$	$\langle P_4, P_1, P_3, P_2 \rangle$
$\langle P_1, P_3, \underline{P_2}, P_4 \rangle$	$\langle P_2, P_3, \underline{P_1}, P_4 \rangle$	$\langle P_3, P_2, P_1, P_4 \rangle$	$\langle P_4, P_2, P_1, P_3 \rangle$
$\langle P_1, P_3, \underline{P_4}, P_2 \rangle$	$\langle P_2, P_3, P_4, \underline{P_1}, \rangle$	$\langle P_3, P_2, P_4, P_1 \rangle$	$\langle P_4, P_2, P_3, P_1 \rangle$
$\langle P_1, P_4, \underline{P_2}, P_3 \rangle$	$\langle P_2, P_4, \underline{P_1}, P_3 \rangle$	$\langle P_3, P_4, \underline{P_1}, P_2 \rangle$	$\langle P_4, P_3, P_1, P_2 \rangle$
$\langle P_1, P_4, \underline{P_3}, P_2 \rangle$	$\langle P_2, P_4, P_3, P_1 \rangle$	$\langle P_3, P_4, P_2, P_1 \rangle$	$\langle P_4, P_3, P_2, P_1 \rangle$

■ TABLE 2-18

2.4 Subsets and Permutations

39. Let A be a set with 10 elements.

(a) Find the number of subsets of A.

(b) Find the number of subsets of A having one or more elements.

(c) Find the number of subsets of A having exactly one element.

(d) Find the number of subsets of A having two or more elements. [*Hint:* Use the answers to parts (b) and (c).]

40. Let A be a set with 12 elements.

(a) Find the number of subsets of A.

(b) Find the number of subsets of A having one or more elements.

(c) Find the number of subsets of A having exactly one element.

(d) Find the number of subsets of A having two or more elements. [*Hint:* Use the answers to parts (b) and (c).]

41. For a weighted voting system with 10 players,

(a) find the total number of coalitions.

(b) find the number of coalitions with two or more players.

42. Consider a weighted voting system with 12 players.

(a) Find the total number of coalitions in this weighted voting system.

(b) Find the number of coalitions with two or more players.

43. Consider a weighted voting system with six players (P_1 through P_6).

(a) Find the total number of coalitions in this weighted voting system.

(b) How many coalitions in this weighted voting system do not include P_1? (*Hint:* Think of all the possible coalitions of the remaining players.)

(c) How many coalitions in this weighted voting system do not include P_3? [*Hint:* Is this really different from (b)?]

(d) How many coalitions in this weighted voting system do not include both P_1 and P_3?

(e) How many coalitions in this weighted voting system include both P_1 and P_3? [*Hint*: Use your answers for (a) and (d).]

44. Consider a weighted voting system with five players (P_1 through P_5).

(a) Find the total number of coalitions in this weighted voting system.

(b) How many coalitions in this weighted voting system do not include P_1? (*Hint*: Think of all the possible coalitions of the remaining players.)

(c) How many coalitions in this weighted voting system do not include P_5? [*Hint*: Is this really different from (b)?]

(d) How many coalitions in this weighted voting system do not include P_1 or P_5?

(e) How many coalitions in this weighted voting system include both P_1 and P_5? [*Hint*: Use your answers for (a) and (d).]

For Exercises 45 through 48 you should use a calculator with a factorial key (typically, it's a key labeled either x! or n!). All scientific calculators and most business calculators have such a key.

45. Use a calculator to compute each of the following.

(a) 13!

(b) 18!

(c) 25!

(d) Suppose that you have a supercomputer that can list *one trillion* (10^{12}) sequential coalitions per second. Estimate (in years) how long it would take the computer to list all the sequential coalitions of 25 players.

46. Use a calculator to compute each of the following.

(a) 12!

(b) 15!

(c) 20!

(d) Suppose that you have a supercomputer that can list one billion (10^9) sequential coalitions per second. Estimate (in years) how long it would take the computer to list all the sequential coalitions of 20 players.

47. Use a calculator to compute each of the following.

(a) $\frac{13!}{3!}$ **(c)** $\frac{13!}{4!9!}$

(b) $\frac{13!}{3!10!}$ **(d)** $\frac{13!}{5!8!}$

48. Use a calculator to compute each of the following.

(a) $\frac{12!}{2!}$ **(c)** $\frac{12!}{3!9!}$

(b) $\frac{12!}{2!10!}$ **(d)** $\frac{12!}{4!8!}$

The purpose of Exercises 49 and 50 is for you to learn how to numerically manipulate factorials. If you use a calculator to answer these questions, you are defeating the purpose of the exercise. Please try Exercises 49 and 50 without using a calculator.

49. (a) Given that 10! = 3,628,800, find 9!

(b) Find $\frac{11!}{10!}$

(c) Find $\frac{11!}{9!}$

(d) Find $\frac{9!}{6!}$

(e) Find $\frac{101!}{99!}$

50. (a) Given that 20! = 2,432,902,008,176,640,000, find 19!

(b) Find $\frac{20!}{19!}$

(c) Find $\frac{201!}{199!}$

(d) Find $\frac{11!}{8!}$

51. Consider a weighted voting system with seven players (P_1 through P_7).

(a) Find the number of sequential coalitions in this weighted voting system.

(b) How many sequential coalitions in this weighted voting system have P_7 as the first player?

(c) How many sequential coalitions in this weighted voting system have P_7 as the last player?

(d) How many sequential coalitions in this weighted voting system do not have P_1 as the *first* player?

52. Consider a weighted voting system with six players (P_1 through P_6).

(a) Find the number of sequential coalitions in this weighted voting system.

(b) How many sequential coalitions in this weighted voting system have P_4 as the last player?

(c) How many sequential coalitions in this weighted voting system have P_4 as the *third* player?

(d) How many sequential coalitions in this weighted voting system do not have P_1 as the first player?

53. A law firm has seven partners: a senior partner (P_1) with 6 votes and six junior partners (P_2 through P_7) with 1 vote each. The quota is a *simple majority* of the votes. (This law firm operates as the weighted voting system $[7: 6, 1, 1, 1, 1, 1, 1]$.)

(a) In how many sequential coalitions is the senior partner P_1 the pivotal player? (*Hint*: First note that P_1 is the pivotal player in all sequential coalitions except those in which he is the first player.)

(b) Using your answer in (a), find the Shapley-Shubik power index of the senior partner P_1.

(c) Using your answer in (b), find the Shapley-Shubik power distribution in this law firm.

54. A law firm has six partners: a senior partner (P_1) with 5 votes and five junior partners (P_2 through P_6) with 1 vote each. The quota is a *simple majority* of the votes. (This law firm operates as the weighted voting system $[6: 5, 1, 1, 1, 1, 1]$.)

(a) In how many sequential coalitions is the senior partner P_1 the pivotal player? (*Hint*: First note that P_1 is the pivotal player in all sequential coalitions except those in which he is the first player.)

(b) Using your answer in (a), find the Shapley-Shubik power index of the senior partner P_1.

(c) Using your answer in (b), find the Shapley-Shubik power distribution in this law firm.

JOGGING

55. A partnership has four partners (P_1, P_2, P_3, and P_4). In this partnership P_1 has twice as many votes as P_2; P_2 has twice as many votes as P_3; P_3 has twice as many votes as P_4. The quota is a *simple majority* of the votes. Show that P_1 is always a *dictator*. (*Hint*: Write the weighted voting system in the form $[q: 8x, 4x, 2x, x]$, and express q in terms of x. Consider separately the case when x is even and the case when x is odd.)

56. In a weighted voting system with four players the winning coalitions are: $\{P_1, P_2, P_3\}$, $\{P_1, P_2, P_4\}$, $\{P_1, P_3, P_4\}$, and $\{P_1, P_2, P_3, P_4\}$.

(a) Find the Banzhaf power distribution of the weighted voting system.

(b) Find the Shapley-Shubik power distribution of the weighted voting system.

57. In a weighted voting system with three players, the six sequential coalitions (each with the pivotal player underlined) are: $\langle P_1, \underline{P_2}, P_3 \rangle$, $\langle P_1, \underline{P_3}, P_2 \rangle$, $\langle P_2, \underline{P_1}, P_3 \rangle$, $\langle P_2, P_3, \underline{P_1} \rangle$, $\langle P_3, \underline{P_1}, P_2 \rangle$, and $\langle P_3, P_2, \underline{P_1} \rangle$. Find the Banzhaf power distribution of the weighted voting system.

58. The Smith family has two parents (P_1 and P_2) and three children (c_1, c_2, and c_3). Family vacations are decided by a majority of the votes, but at least one parent must vote Yes (i.e., the three children don't have enough weight to carry the motion).

(a) If we use $[q: p, p, c, c, c]$ to describe this weighted voting system, find q, p, and c.

(b) Find the Banzhaf Power distribution of this weighted voting system.

59. A professional basketball team has four coaches, a head coach (H) and three assistant coaches (A_1, A_2, A_3). Player personnel decisions require at least three Yes votes, one of which must be H's.

(a) If we use $[q: h, a, a, a]$ to describe this weighted voting system, find q, h, and a.

(b) Find the Shapley-Shubik power distribution of the weighted voting system.

60. Veto power. A player P with weight w is said to have *veto power* if and only if $w < q$, and $V - w < q$ (where V denotes the total number of votes in the weighted voting system). Explain why each of the following is true:

(a) A player has veto power if and only if the player is a member of every winning coalition.

(b) A player has veto power if and only if the player is a critical player in the *grand* coalition.

61. Dummies. We defined a *dummy* as a player that is never critical. Explain why each of the following is true:

(a) If P is a dummy, then any winning coalition that contains P would also be a winning coalition without P.

(b) P is a dummy if and only if the Banzhaf power index of P is 0.

(c) P is a dummy if and only if the Shapley-Shubik power index of P is 0.

62. (a) Consider the weighted voting system $[22: 10, 10, 10, 10, 1]$. Are there any dummies? Explain your answer.

(b) Without doing any work [but using your answer for (a)], find the Banzhaf and Shapley-Shubik power distributions of this weighted voting system.

(c) Consider the weighted voting system $[q: 10, 10, 10, 10, 1]$. Find all the possible values of q for which P_5 is not a dummy.

(d) Consider the weighted voting system $[34: 10, 10, 10, 10, w]$. Find all positive integers w which make P_5 a dummy.

63. Consider the weighted voting system $[q: 8, 4, 1]$.

(a) What are the possible values of q?

(b) Which values of q result in a dictator? (Who? Why?)

(c) Which values of q result in exactly one player with veto power? (Who? Why?)

(d) Which values of q result in more than one player with veto power? (Who? Why?)

(e) Which values of q result in one or more dummies? (Who? Why?)

64. Consider the weighted voting system $[9: w, 5, 2, 1]$.

(a) What are the possible values of w?

(b) Which values of w result in a dictator? (Who? Why?)

(c) Which values of w result in a player with veto power? (Who? Why?)

(d) Which values of w result in one or more dummies? (Who? Why?)

65. (a) Verify that the weighted voting systems $[12: 7, 4, 3, 2]$ and $[24: 14, 8, 6, 4]$ result in exactly the same Banzhaf power distribution. (If you need to make calculations, do them for both systems side by side and look for patterns.)

(b) Based on your work in (a), explain why the two proportional weighted voting systems $[q: w_1, w_2, \ldots, w_N]$ and $[cq: cw_1, cw_2, \ldots, cw_N]$ always have the same Banzhaf power distribution.

66. (a) Verify that the weighted voting systems $[12: 7, 4, 3, 2]$ and $[24: 14, 8, 6, 4]$ result in exactly the same Shapley-Shubik power distribution. (If you need to make calculations, do them for both systems side by side and look for patterns.)

(b) Based on your work in (a), explain why the two proportional weighted voting systems $[q: w_1, w_2, \ldots, w_N]$ and $[cq: cw_1, cw_2, \ldots, cw_N]$ always have the same Shapley-Shubik power distribution.

67. A law firm has $N + 1$ partners: the senior partner with N votes, and N junior partners with one vote each. The quota is a simple majority of the votes. Find the Shapley-Shubik power distribution in this weighted voting system. (*Hint*: Try Exercise 53 or 54 first.)

68. Consider the generic weighted voting system $[q: w_1, w_2, \ldots, w_N]$. (Assume $w_1 \geq w_2 \geq \cdots \geq w_N$.)

(a) Find all the possible values of q for which no player has veto power.

(b) Find all the possible values of q for which every player has veto power.

(c) Find all the possible values of q for which P_i has veto power but P_{i+1} does not. (*Hint*: See Exercise 60.)

69. The weighted voting system $[8: 6, 4, 2, 1]$ represents a partnership among four partners (P_1, P_2, P_3, and you!). You are the partner with just one vote, and in this situation you have no power (you dummy!). Not wanting to remain a dummy, you offer to buy one vote. Each of the other four partners is willing to sell you one of their votes, and they are all asking the same price. From which partner should you buy in order to get as much power for your buck as possible? Use the Banzhaf power index for your calculations. Explain your answer.

70. The weighted voting system $[27: 10, 8, 6, 4, 2]$ represents a partnership among five people (P_1, P_2, P_3, P_4, and P_5). You are P_5, the one with two votes. You want to increase your power in the partnership and are prepared to buy one share (one share equals one vote) from any of the other partners. Partners P_1, P_2, and P_3 are each willing to sell cheap ($1000 for one share), but P_4 is not being quite as cooperative—she wants $5000 for one of her shares. Given that you still want to buy one share, from whom should you buy it? Use the Banzhaf power index for your calculations. Explain your answer.

71. The weighted voting system $[18: 10, 8, 6, 4, 2]$ represents a partnership among five people (P_1, P_2, P_3, P_4, and P_5). You are P_5, the one with two votes. You want to increase your power in the partnership and are prepared to buy shares (one share equals one vote) from any of the other partners.

(a) Suppose that each partner is willing to sell one share and that they are all asking the same price. Assuming that you decide to buy only one share, from which partner should you buy? Use the Banzhaf power index for your calculations.

(b) Suppose that each partner is willing to sell two shares and that they are all asking the same price. Assuming that you decide to buy two shares from a single partner, from which partner should you buy? Use the Banzhaf power index for your calculations.

(c) If you have the money and the cost per share is fixed, should you buy one share or two shares (from a single person)? Explain.

72. Mergers. Sometimes in a weighted voting system two or more players decide to merge—that is to say, to combine their votes and always vote the same way. (Note that a merger is different from a coalition—coalitions are temporary, whereas mergers are permanent.) For example, if in the weighted voting system $[7: 5, 3, 1]$ P_2 and P_3 were to merge, the weighted voting system would then become $[7: 5, 4]$. In this exercise we explore the effects of mergers on a player's power.

(a) Consider the weighted voting system $[4: 3, 2, 1]$. In Example 2.9 we saw that P_2 and P_3 each have a Banzhaf power index of $1/5$. Suppose that P_2 and P_3 merge and become a single player P^*. What is the Banzhaf power index of P^*?

(b) Consider the weighted voting system $[5: 3, 2, 1]$. Find first the Banzhaf power indexes of players P_2 and P_3 and then the Banzhaf power index of P^* (the merger of P_2 and P_3). Compare.

(c) Rework the problem in (b) for the weighted voting system $[6: 3, 2, 1]$.

(d) What are your conclusions from (a), (b), and (c)?

73. Decisive voting systems. A weighted voting system is called *decisive* if for every losing coalition, the coalition consisting of the remaining players (called the *complement*) must be a winning coalition.

(a) Show that the weighted voting system $[5: 4, 3, 2]$ is decisive.

(b) Show that the weighted voting system $[3: 2, 1, 1, 1]$ is decisive.

(c) Explain why any weighted voting system with a dictator is decisive.

(d) Find the number of winning coalitions in a decisive voting system with N players.

74. Equivalent voting systems. Two weighted voting systems are *equivalent* if they have the same number of players and exactly the same winning coalitions.

(a) Show that the weighted voting systems $[8: 5, 3, 2]$ and $[2: 1, 1, 0]$ are equivalent.

(b) Show that the weighted voting systems $[7: 4, 3, 2, 1]$ and $[5: 3, 2, 1, 1]$ are equivalent.

(c) Show that the weighted voting system discussed in Example 2.12 is equivalent to $[3: 1, 1, 1, 1, 1]$.

(d) Explain why equivalent weighted voting systems must have the same Banzhaf power distribution.

(e) Explain why equivalent weighted voting systems must have the same Shapley-Shubik power distribution.

75. Relative voting power. The *relative voting weight* w_i of a player P_i is the fraction of votes controlled by that player.

A player's Banzhaf power index β_i can differ considerably from his relative voting weight w_i. One indicator of the relation between Banzhaf power and relative voting weight is the ratio between the two (called the *relative Banzhaf voting power*): $\pi_i = \frac{\beta_i}{w_i}$.

(a) Compute the relative Banzhaf voting power of California in the Electoral College (see Table 2-11).

(b) Compute the relative Banzhaf voting power of each player in Example 2.13.

RUNNING

76. The Cleansburg City Council. Find the Banzhaf power distribution in the Cleansburg City Council discussed in Example 2.17.

77. The Fresno City Council. In Fresno, California, the city council consists of seven members (the mayor and six other council members). A motion can be passed by the mayor and at least three other council members, or by at least five of the six ordinary council members.

(a) Describe the Fresno City Council as a weighted voting system.

(b) Find the Shapley-Shubik power distribution for the Fresno City Council. (*Hint*: See Example 2.17 for some useful ideas.)

78. Suppose that in a weighted voting system there is a player A who hates another player P so much that he will always vote the opposite way of P, regardless of the issue. We will call A the *antagonist* of P.

(a) Suppose that in the weighted voting system $[8:5,4,3,2]$, P is the player with two votes and his antagonist A is the player with five votes. The other two players we'll call P_2 and P_3. What are the possible coalitions under these circumstances? What is the Banzhaf power distribution under these circumstances?

(b) Suppose that in a generic weighted voting system with N players there is a player P who has an antagonist A. How many coalitions are there under these circumstances?

(c) Give examples of weighted voting systems where a player A can

(i) increase his Banzhaf power index by becoming an antagonist of another player.

(ii) decrease his Banzhaf power index by becoming an antagonist of another player.

(d) Suppose that the antagonist A has more votes than his enemy P. What is a strategy that P can use to gain power at the expense of A?

79. (a) Give an example of a weighted voting system with four players and such that the Shapley-Shubik power index of P_1 is $\frac{3}{4}$.

(b) Show that in any weighted voting system with four players a player cannot have a Shapley-Shubik power index of more than $\frac{3}{4}$ unless he or she is a dictator.

(c) Show that in any weighted voting system with N players a player cannot have a Shapley-Shubik power index of more than $\frac{(N-1)}{N}$ unless he or she is a dictator.

(d) Give an example of a weighted voting system with N players and such that P_1 has a Shapley-Shubik power index of $\frac{(N-1)}{N}$.

80. (a) Explain why in any weighted voting system with N players a player with veto power must have a Banzhaf power index bigger than or equal to $\frac{1}{N}$.

(b) Explain why in any weighted voting system with N players a player with veto power must have a Shapley-Shubik power index bigger than or equal to $\frac{1}{N}$.

PROJECTS AND PAPERS

1 The Johnston Power Index

The Banzhaf and Shapley-Shubik power indexes are not the only two mathematical methods for measuring power. The Johnston power index is a subtle but rarely used variation of the Banzhaf power index in which the power of a player is based not only on how often he or she is critical in a coalition, but also on the number of other players in the coalition. Specifically, being a critical player in a coalition of 2 players contributes $\frac{1}{2}$ toward your power score; being critical in a coalition of 3 players contributes $\frac{1}{3}$ toward your power score; and being critical in a coalition of 10 contributes only $\frac{1}{10}$ toward your power score.

A player's *Johnston power score* is obtained by adding all such fractions over all coalitions in which the player is critical. The player's *Johnston power index* is his or her Johnston power score divided by the sum of all players' power scores.

Prepare a presentation on the Johnston power index. Include a mathematical description of the procedure for computing Johnston power, give examples, and compare the results with the ones obtained using the Banzhaf method. Include your own personal analysis of the merits of the Johnston method compared with the Banzhaf method.

2 The Past, Present, and Future of the Electoral College

Starting with the Constitutional Convention of 1776 and ending with the Bush-Gore presidential election of 2000, give a historical and political analysis of the Electoral College. You should address some or all of the following issues: How did the Electoral College get started? Why did some of the Founding Fathers want it? How did it evolve? What has been its impact over the years in affecting presidential elections? (Pay particular attention to the 2000 presidential election.) What does the future hold for the Electoral College? What are the prospects that it will be reformed or eliminated?

3 Mathematical Arguments in Favor of the Electoral College

As a method for electing the president, the Electoral College is widely criticized as being undemocratic. At the same time, different arguments have been made over the years to support the case that the Electoral College is not nearly as bad as it seems. Physicist Alan Natapoff has used mathematical ideas (many of which are connected to the material in this chapter) to argue that the Electoral College is a better system than a direct presidential election. A summary of Natapoff's arguments are given in the article "Math Against Tyranny," by Will Hively (*Discover*, Nov. 1996, 74–85). Write a paper explaining Natapoff's mathematical arguments in support of the Electoral College.

4 Banzhaf Power and the Law

John Banzhaf was a lawyer, and he made his original arguments on behalf of his mathematical method to measure power in court cases, most of which involved the Nassau County Board of Supervisors in New York State. (See the discussion in Example 2.13.) Among the more significant court cases were *Graham v. Board of Supervisors* (1966); *Bechtle v. Board of Supervisors* (1981); *League of Women Voters v. Board of Supervisors* (1983); and *Jackson v. Board of Supervisors* (1991). Other important legal cases based on the Banzhaf method for measuring power but not involving Nassau County were *Ianucci v. Board of Supervisors of Washington County* and *Morris v. Board of Estimate* (U.S. Supreme Court, 1989). Choose one or two of these cases, read their background, arguments, and the court's decision, and write a brief for each. This is a good project for pre-law and political science majors, but it might require access to a good law library.

PART 2

Management Science

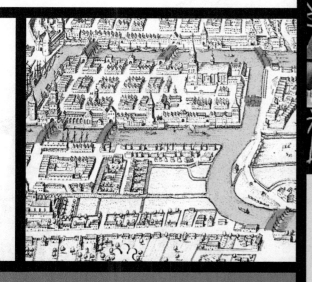

5 The Mathematics of Getting Around

Euler Paths and Circuits

United Parcel Service (UPS) is the largest package delivery company in the world. On a typical day UPS delivers roughly 15 million packages to over 6 million customers worldwide; on a busy day much more than that (the week before Christmas 2011, UPS delivered more than 120 million packages). Such remarkable feats of logistics require tremendous resources, superb organization, and (surprise!) a good dose of mathematics. In this chapter we will discuss some of the mathematical ideas that make this possible.

n a normal day a UPS driver delivers somewhere between 200 and 500 packages. In rural areas where there may be considerable distances between delivery points, the number is closer to 200; in highly populated urban areas where the delivery points are close to each other the number is closer to 500. But in both cases one of the keys to success in delivering all the packages is the efficiency of the delivery route. Efficient routing means, among other things, keeping *deadheading* (the term used to describe driving over the same section of road more than once) at a minimum, and this is where the mathematics comes in: How do you design a route that minimizes the total amount of "wasted" travel?

Problems like those faced by a UPS driver (or a FedEx driver, or a mail carrier for that matter) trying to minimize the total length of his or her route are known as *street-routing problems*, and they have applications to other types of situations such as routing garbage trucks, security patrols, tourist buses, and even late-night pizza deliveries.

Section 5.1 introduces the concept of a *street-routing problem* and shows examples in several different settings and applications. Keep in mind that many of the examples in this section are scaled down in size and scope to keep things simple—in real life the same application will occur on a much larger scale. Regardless of the scale, the mathematical theory behind street-routing problems is one and the same, and we owe much of this theory to the genius of one man—the Swiss mathematician Leonhard Euler. Euler's role was so significant that in this chapter we will see his last name (pronounced "oiler," by the way) used both as a noun (*Euler circuit, Euler path*) and as a verb (*eulerizing, semi-eulerizing*). Section 5.2 introduces *graphs*—the key mathematical tool that allows us to tackle street-routing problems— and some of the concepts and terminology associated with graphs. Section 5.3 gives the mathematical infrastructure needed to solve street-routing problems, consisting of three key facts (*Euler's Circuit Theorem, Euler's Path Theorem*, and the *Sum of Degrees Theorem*) and an algorithm known as *Fleury's Algorithm*. In Section 5.4 we will learn how to combine all the preceding ideas to develop the strategies needed to solve street-routing problems in general.

Leonhard Euler (1707–1783)

5.1  Street-Routing Problems

We will start this section with a brief discussion of routing problems. What is a **routing problem**? To put it in the most general way, routing problems are concerned with finding ways to route the delivery of *goods* and/or *services* to an assortment of *destinations*. The goods or services in question could be packages, mail, newspapers, pizzas, garbage collection, bus service, and so on. The delivery destinations could be homes, warehouses, distribution centers, terminals, and the like.

There are two basic questions that we are typically interested in when dealing with a routing problem. The first is called the *existence* question. The existence question is simple: Is an actual route possible? For most routing problems, the existence question is easy to answer, and the answer takes the form of a simple yes or no. When the answer to the existence question is yes, then a second question—the *optimization question*—comes into play. Of all the possible routes, which one is the *optimal route*? (*Optimal* here means "the best" when measured against some predetermined variable such as *cost*, *distance*, or *time*.) In most management science problems, the optimization question is where the action is.

In this chapter we will learn how to answer both the existence and optimization questions for a special class of routing problems known as **street-routing problems**. The common thread in all street-routing problems is what we might call, for lack of a better term, the *pass-through requirement*—the requirement that the route must pass at least once through some specified set of connections. In other words, in a street-routing problem the pass-through requirement means that each street (or bridge, or lane, or highway) within a defined area (be it a town, an area of town, or a subdivision) must be covered by the route. We will refer to these types of routes as *exhaustive routes*. The most common services that typically require exhaustive routing are mail delivery, police patrols, garbage collection, street sweeping, and snow removal. More exotic examples can be census taking, precinct walking, electric meter reading, routing parades, tour buses, and so on.

To clarify some of the ideas we will introduce several examples of street-routing problems (just the problems for now—their solutions will come later in the chapter).

EXAMPLE 5.1 THE SECURITY GUARD PROBLEM

After a rash of burglaries, a private security guard is hired to patrol the streets of the Sunnyside neighborhood shown in Fig. 5-1. The security guard's assignment is to make an exhaustive patrol, on foot, through the entire neighborhood. Obviously, he doesn't want to walk any more than what is necessary. His starting point is the corner of Elm and J streets across from the school (*S* in Fig. 5-1)—that's where he usually parks his car. (This is relevant because at the end of his patrol he needs to come back to *S* to pick up his car.) Being a practical person, the security guard would like the answers to the following questions:

1. Is it possible to start and end at *S*, cover every block of the neighborhood, and pass through each block *just once*?

2. If some of the blocks will have to be covered more than once, what is an *optimal* route that covers the entire neighborhood? ("Optimal" here means "with the minimal amount of walking.")

3. Can a better route (i.e., less walking) be found by choosing a different starting and ending point? We will answer all of these questions in Section 5.4.

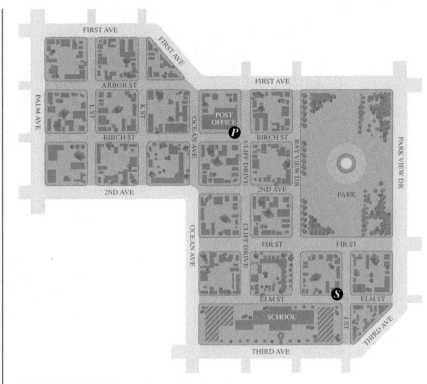

■ **FIGURE 5-1**   The Sunnyside neighborhood.

EXAMPLE 5.2   THE MAIL CARRIER PROBLEM

A mail carrier has to deliver mail in the same Sunnyside neighborhood (Fig. 5-1). The difference between the mail carrier's route and the security guard's route is that the mail carrier must make *two* passes through blocks with buildings on both sides of the street and only one pass through blocks with buildings on only one side of the street (and where there are no buildings on either side of the street, the mail carrier does not have to walk at all). In addition, the mail carrier has no choice as to her starting and ending points—she has to start and end her route at the local post office (*P* in Fig. 5-1). Much like the security guard, the mail carrier wants to find the optimal route that would allow her to cover the neighborhood with the least amount of walking. (Put yourself in her shoes and you would do the same—good weather or bad, she walks this route 300 days a year!)

EXAMPLE 5.3   THE UPS DRIVER PROBLEM

Now we consider the case of a UPS driver who must deliver packages around the Sunnyside neighborhood. The red crosses in Fig. 5-2 indicate the locations (homes or businesses) where packages are to be delivered (it's the week before Christmas so there is an unusually large number of packages to be delivered).

Unlike the mail carrier (required to pass through every block of the neighborhood where there are homes or businesses), the UPS driver has to pass only through those blocks where there are red crosses, and only once through such blocks (if the delivery is on the opposite side of the street he just crosses the street on foot). In addition, because of other deliveries, the UPS driver must enter the neighborhood through the street indicated by the "in" arrow and exit the neighborhood through the street indicated by the "out" arrow. Once again, we want to determine (and we will in Section 5.4) the most *efficient* route that will allow the UPS driver to deliver all those packages. The requirements for the route are (a) enter and exit the neighborhood where indicated in Fig. 5.2 and (b) pass through every block where there

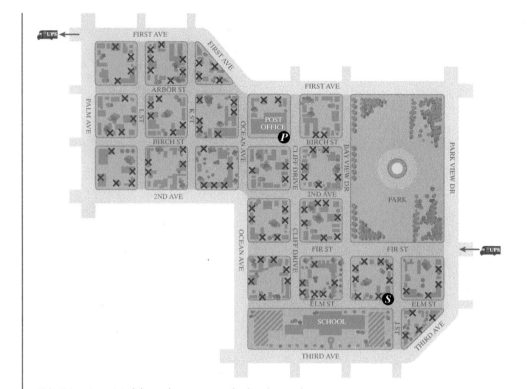

FIGURE 5-2 UPS delivery locations marked with a red cross.

are delivery locations marked with red crosses. [Note: In general, UPS drivers are mostly concerned with the total time it takes to complete their package deliveries rather than the total distance traveled, and often go out of their way to avoid left-turn signals or streets with a lot of traffic. This makes the routing problem more complicated; therefore, to keep things simple we will assume that in this example driving time is proportional to distance traveled (this happens, for example, when there is little or no traffic or when traffic moves evenly throughout the neighborhood). Under this assumption the most efficient route is still the shortest route.]

Our next example is primarily of historical interest. Euler was introduced to the Königsberg bridges puzzle in the early 1700s as a recreational puzzle that might potentially be solved using mathematical ideas, but nobody was clear as to what kind of mathematics was needed. Euler's great contribution was in developing a new mathematical theory (now known as *graph theory*) that could be used to solve the bridges puzzle as well as much more practical and complex problems. We will be introduced to Euler's ideas in the next three sections.

EXAMPLE 5.4   THE KÖNIGSBERG BRIDGES PUZZLE

This story starts in the 1700s in the medieval town of Königsberg, in Eastern Europe. A map of the city at that time is shown in Fig. 5-3, with the river Pregel running through town, the two islands on the river, and the north and south banks all connected by the seven bridges shown in red. (*Note*: Present-day Königsberg has a different layout, as two of the bridges no longer exist.) A little game played by the locals at the time was to try to take a walk around town fully crossing every bridge once and only once (i.e., no bridge could be skipped and no bridge could be crossed twice). Nobody was able to do this successfully and a widely held belief in the town was that such a walk was indeed impossible. What was asked of Euler was to rigorously prove this. He did this, and much more. We will soon learn how he did it.

KONINGSBERGA

A. *Das Schlos*.
B. *Alt Steuer Kirch.*
C. *S. Niclaus.*
D. *S. Barbara.*
E. *Stayheinsche Kirch.*
F. *Die Domkirch.*
G. *Das Collegium.*
H. *Rathaus im Kneiphof.*
I. *Das Closter.*
K. *Haberbergische Kirch.*
L. *Haber kirch.*
M. *Hospital.*

FIGURE 5-3 Map of the medieval town of Königsberg (Prussia) in the 1700s.

If we think of the bridges as playing a role analogous to that of the streets in the Sunnyside neighborhood, the Königsberg bridges puzzle becomes another street-routing problem. The negative answer to the puzzle means that no route that satisfies the restrictions of the problem (pass through each bridge once and only once) exists.

Our next example is an expanded and modernized version of the Königsberg bridges problem.

EXAMPLE 5.5 THE BRIDGES OF MADISON COUNTY

Madison County is a quaint old place, famous for its beautiful bridges. The Madison River runs through the county, and there are four islands ($A, B, C,$ and D) and 11 bridges joining the islands to both banks of the river (R and L) and one another (Fig. 5-4). A famous photographer is hired to take pictures of each of the 11 bridges for a national magazine. The photographer needs to drive across each bridge once for the photo shoot. The problem is that there is a $25 toll (the locals call it a "maintenance tax") every time an out-of-town visitor drives across a bridge, and the photographer wants to minimize the total cost of the trip. The street-routing problem here is to find a route that passes through each bridge at least once and recrosses as few bridges as possible. Moreover, the photographer can start the route on either bank of the river and, likewise, end it on either bank of the river.

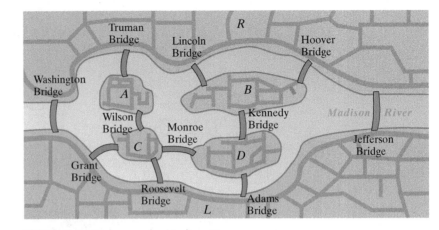

FIGURE 5-4 Bridges on the Madison River.

5.2 An Introduction to Graphs

 A note of warning: The graphs we will be discussing here have no relation to the graphs of functions you may have studied in algebra or calculus.

The key tool we will use to tackle the street-routing problems introduced in Section 5.1 is the notion of a **graph**. The most common way to describe a *graph* is by means of a picture. The basic elements of such a picture are a set of "dots" called the **vertices** of the graph and a collection of "lines" called the **edges** of the graph. (Unfortunately, this terminology is not universal. In some applications the word "nodes" is used for the vertices and the word "links" is used for the edges. We will stick to vertices and edges as much as possible.) On the surface, that's all there is to it—edges connecting vertices. Below the surface there is a surprisingly rich theory. Let's look at a few examples first.

EXAMPLE 5.6   BASIC GRAPH CONCEPTS

Figure 5-5 shows several examples of graphs. We will discuss each separately.

- Figure 5-5(a) shows a graph with six vertices labeled A, B, C, D, E, and F (it is customary to use capital letters to label the vertices of a graph). For convenience we refer to the set of vertices of a graph as the **vertex set**. In this graph, the vertex set is $\{A, B, C, D, E, F\}$. The graph has 11 edges (described by listing, in any order, the two vertices that are connected by the edge): AB, AD, BC, etc.

  □ When two vertices are connected by an edge we say that they are **adjacent vertices**. Thus, A and B are adjacent vertices, but A and E are not adjacent. The edge connecting B with itself is written as BB and is called a **loop**. Vertices C and D are connected twice (i.e., by two separate edges), so when we list the edges we include CD twice. Similarly, vertices E and F are connected by three edges, so we list EF three times. We refer to edges that appear more than once as **multiple edges**.

  □ The complete list of edges of the graph, the **edge list**, is AB, AD, BB, BC, BE, CD, CD, DE, EF, EF, EF.

  □ The number of edges that meet at each vertex is called the **degree** of the vertex and is denoted by $\deg(X)$. In this graph we have $\deg(A) = 2$, $\deg(B) = 5$ (please note that the loop contributes 2 to the degree of the vertex), $\deg(C) = 3$, $\deg(D) = 4$, $\deg(E) = 5$, and $\deg(F) = 3$. It will be important in the next section to distinguish between vertices depending on whether their degree is an odd or an even number. We will refer to vertices like B, C, E, and F with an odd degree as **odd vertices** and to vertices with an even degree like A and D as **even vertices**.

- Figure 5-5(b) is very similar to Fig. 5-5(a)—the only difference is the way the edge BE is drawn. In Fig. 5-5(a) edges AD and BE cross each other, but the

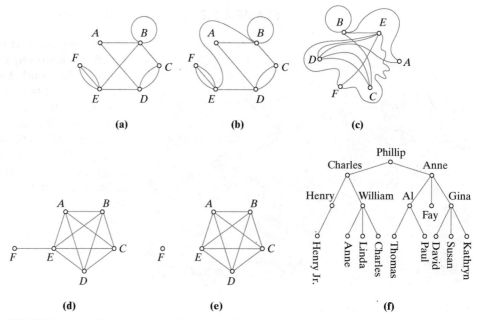

FIGURE 5-5 (a), (b), and (c) are all pictures of the same graph; (d) is a simple, connected graph; (e) is a simple, disconnected graph; and (f) is a graph labeled with names instead of letters.

crossing point is not a vertex of the graph—it's just an irrelevant crossing point. Fig. 5-5(b) gets around the crossing by drawing the edge in a more convoluted way, but the way we draw an edge is itself irrelevant. The key point here is that as graphs, Figs. 5-5(a) and 5-5(b) are the same. Both have exactly the same vertices and exactly the same edge list.

- Figure 5-5(c) take the idea one step further—it is in fact, another rendering of the graph shown in Figs. 5-5(a) and (b). The vertices have been moved around and put in different positions, and the edges are funky—no other way to describe it. Despite all the funkiness, this graph conveys exactly the same information that the graph in Fig. 5-5(a) does. You can check it out— same set of vertices and same edge list. The moral here is that while graphs are indeed pictures connecting "dots" with "lines," it is not the specific picture that matters but the story that the picture tells: which dots are connected to each other and which aren't. We can move the vertices around, and we can draw the edges any funky way we want (straight line, curved line, wavy line, etc.)—none of that matters. The only thing that matters is the set of vertices and the list of edges.

- Figure 5-5(d) shows a graph with six vertices. Vertices A, B, C, D, and E form what is known as a **clique**—each vertex is connected to each of the other four. Vertex F, on the other hand, is connected to only one other vertex. This graph has no loops or multiple edges. Graphs without loops or multiple edges are called **simple graphs**. There are many applications of graphs where loops and multiple edges cannot occur, and we have to deal only with simple graphs. (In Examples 5.7 and 5.8 we will see two applications where only simple graphs occur.)

- Figure 5-5(e) shows a graph very similar to the one in Fig. 5-5(d). The only difference between the two is the absence of the edge EF. In this graph there are no edges connecting F to any other vertex. For obvious reasons, F is called an **isolated** vertex. This graph is made up of two separate and disconnected "pieces"—the clique formed by the vertices A, B, C, D, and E and the isolated vertex F. Because the graph is not made of a single "piece," we say that the graph is **disconnected**, and the separate pieces that make up the graph are called the *components* of the graph.

- Figure 5-5(f) shows a connected simple graph. The vertices of this graph are names (there is no rule about what the labels of a vertex can be). Can you guess what this graph might possibly represent?

EXAMPLE 5.7   AIRLINE ROUTE MAPS

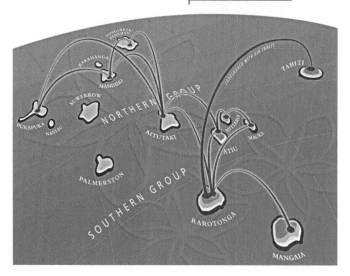

Figure 5-6 shows the route map for a very small airline called Air Rarotonga. Air Rarotonga serves just 10 islands in the South Pacific, and the route map shows the direct flights that are available between the various islands. In essence, the route map is a graph whose vertices are the islands. An edge connects two islands if there is a direct flight between them. No direct flight, no edge. The picture makes a slight attempt to respect geographical facts (the bigger islands are drawn larger but certainly not to scale, and they sit in the ocean more or less as shown), but the point of an airline route map is to show if there is a direct flight from point X to point Y, and, in that regard, accurate geography is not all that important.

FIGURE 5-6   Air Rarotonga route map.

EXAMPLE 5.8   THE FACEBOOK SOCIAL GRAPH

Do you know who your friends' friends are? In the off-line world—where friendships are tight and relationships are personal—you probably have some idea. In the Facebook world—where "friendships" are cheap—you probably have a fairly limited picture of the complex web of friendships that connect your own set of Facebook friends.

But worry no more. Thanks to the Facebook Social Graph (FSG), you can have a complete picture of how your Facebook friends are connected. The FSG is a Facebook app available for free to anyone on Facebook. [To create your own FSG (and you are strongly encouraged to do it now, not just for the curiosity factor but because it will help you navigate this example) go to your Facebook account, click on "Apps and Games," find "Social Graph" (you may have to do a search for it) and click "Allow."]

The vertices of the FSG are all your Facebook friends. You are not included because it is understood that you are a friend of everyone on the graph. An edge connecting two of your friends means that they are friends. Fig. 5-7 shows the FSG of a real person (who will remain nameless), but the FSG is at its most useful when used in a dynamic way. When you run the mouse over a particular friend X, the app will highlight all the connections between X and your other

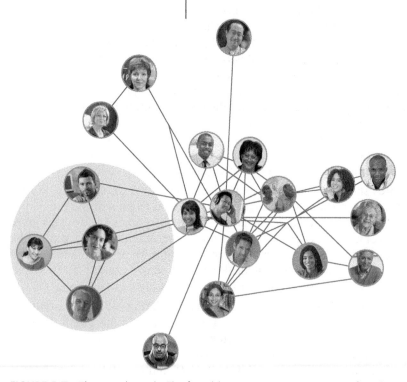

FIGURE 5-7   The social graph: The friendship connections among your friends.

friends. Some X's are "hubs" connected to many people (if you are married it is very likely that your spouse is a hub, since you typically share most of your friends); other X's might be isolated vertices (the guy sitting next to you on the airplane with whom you exchanged pleasantries and ended up being a Facebook friend). The FSG also highlights "clusters" of friendships. These clusters represent groups of individuals who are all friends with each other (your high school buddies perhaps, or coworkers, or family).

The main point of Examples 5.7 and 5.8 is to highlight how powerful (and useful) the concept of a graph can be. Granted, the Air Rarotonga route map is small (just right to illustrate the point), but if you think big you can imagine a United Airlines route map instead, with hundreds of destinations and thousands of flights connecting them. The fundamental idea is still the same—graphs convey visually a tremendous amount of information that would be hard to convey in any other form. Can you imagine describing the complex web of relationships in your Facebook Social Graph or in a United Airlines route map any other way? Airline route maps and friendship graphs are always simple graphs, without loops (airlines don't routinely schedule flights that go around in circles, and by definition, friendship is a connection between two different persons) or multiple edges (either there are direct flights connecting X and Y or there aren't, and X and Y are either friends or they aren't).

EXAMPLE 5.9   PATHS AND CIRCUITS

We say that two edges are **adjacent edges** when they share a common vertex. In Fig. 5-8 for example, AB is adjacent to AC and AD (they share vertex A), as well as to BC, BF, and BE (they share vertex B). A sequence of *distinct* edges each adjacent to the next is called a **path**, and the number of edges in the path is called the **length** of the path. For example in Fig. 5-8, the edges AB, BF, and FG form a path of length 3. A good way to think of a path is as a real-world path—a way to "hike" along the edges of the graph, traveling along the first edge, then the next, and so on. To shorten the notation, we describe the path by just listing the vertices in sequence separated by commas. For example A, B, F, G describes the path formed by the edges AB, BF, and FG.

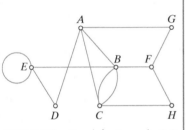

FIGURE 5-8   *Graph for Example 5.9.*

Here are a few more examples of paths in Fig. 5-8:

- A, B is a path of length 1. Any edge can be thought of as a path of length 1—not very interesting, but it allows us to apply the concept of a path even to single edges.

- A, B, C, A, D, E is a path of length 5 starting at A and ending at E. The path goes through vertex A a second time, but that's OK. It is permissible for a path to revisit some of the vertices. On the other hand, A, C, B, A, C does not meet the definition of a path because the edges of the path cannot be revisited and here AC is traveled twice. So, in a path it's OK to revisit some of the vertices but not OK to revisit any edges.

- A, B, C, A, D, E, E, B is a path of length 7. Notice that this "trip" is possible because of the loop at E.

- A, B, C, A, D, E, B, C is also a legal path of length 7. Here we can use the edge BC twice because there are in fact two distinct edges connecting B and C.

When a trip along the edges of the graph closes back on itself (i.e., starts and ends with the same vertex) we specifically call it a **circuit** rather than a path. Thus, we will restrict the term *path* to open-ended trips and the word *circuit* to closed trips. Here are a few examples of circuits in Fig. 5-8:

- A, D, E, B, A is a circuit of length 4. Even though it appears like the circuit designates A as the starting (and ending) vertex, a circuit is independent of where we designate the start. In other words, the same circuit can be written as D, E, B, A, D or E, B, A, D, E, etc. They are all the same circuit, but we have to choose one (arbitrary) vertex to start the list.

- B, C, B is a circuit of length 2. This is possible because of the double edge BC. On the other hand, B, A, B is not a circuit because the edge AB is being traveled twice. (Just as in a path, the edges of a circuit have to be distinct.)

- E, E is a circuit of length 1. A loop is the only way to have a circuit of length 1.

In Example 5.9 we saw several examples of paths (and circuits) that are part of the graph in Fig. 5-8, but the important idea we will discuss next in this: Can the path (or circuit) be the entire graph, not just a part of it? In other words, we want to consider the possibility of a path (or a circuit) that *exhausts* all the edges of the graph.

An **Euler path** (named after Leonhard Euler) is a path that covers *all* the edges of the graph. Likewise, an **Euler circuit** is a circuit that covers all the edges of the graph. In other words, we have an Euler path (or circuit) when the entire graph can be written as a path (or circuit).

EXAMPLE 5.10   EULER PATHS AND EULER CIRCUITS

Figures 5-9, 5-10, and 5-11 illustrate the three possibilities that can occur:

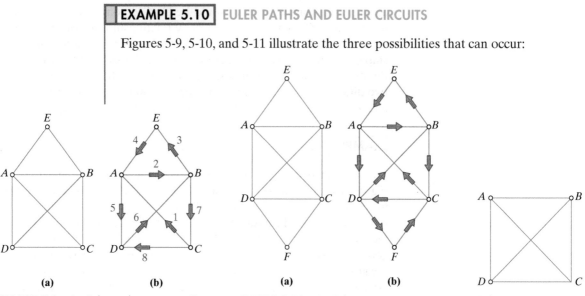

FIGURE 5-9   An Euler path starting at C and ending at D.

FIGURE 5-10   An Euler circuit.

FIGURE 5-11   No Euler path or circuit.

- The graph in Fig. 5-9(a) has an Euler path—in fact, it has several. One of the possible Euler paths is shown in Fig. 5-9(b). The path starts at C and ends at D—just follow the arrows and you will be able to "trace" the edges of the graph without retracing any (just like in elementary school).

- The graph in Fig. 5-10(a) has many possible Euler circuits. One of them is shown in Fig. 5-10(b). Just follow the arrows. Unlike the Euler path in Fig. 5-9(b), the arrows are not numbered. You can start this circuit at any vertex of the graph, follow the arrows, and you will return to the starting vertex having covered all the edges once.

- The graph in Fig. 5-11 has neither an Euler path nor an Euler circuit. That's the way it goes sometimes—some graphs just don't have it!

We introduced the idea of a *connected* or *disconnected* graph in Example 5.6. Formally, we say that a graph is **connected** if you can get from any vertex to any other vertex along some path of the graph. Informally, this says that you can get from any point to any other point by "hiking" along the edges of the graph. Even more informally, it means that the graph is made of one "piece." A graph that is not connected is called **disconnected** and consists of at least two (maybe more) separate "pieces" we call the **components** of the graph.

EXAMPLE 5.11   BRIDGES

Figure 5-12 shows three different graphs. The graph in Fig. 5-12(a) is connected; the graph in Fig. 5-12(b) is disconnected and has two components; the graph in Fig. 5-12(c) is disconnected and has three components (the isolated vertex *G* is a component—that's as small a component as you can get!).

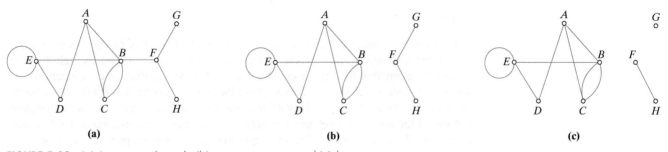

FIGURE 5-12 (a) A connected graph, (b) two components, and (c) three components.

Notice that the only difference between the *disconnected* graph in Fig. 5-12(b) and the *connected* graph in Fig. 5-12(a) is the edge BF. Think of *BF* as a "bridge" that connects the two components of the graph in Fig. 5-12(b). Not surprisingly, we call such an edge a *bridge*. A **bridge** in a connected graph is an edge that keeps the graph connected—if the bridge were not there, the graph would be disconnected. The graph in Fig. 5-12(a) has three bridges: *BF*, *FG*, and *FH*.

For the reader's convenience, Table 5-1 shows a summary of the basic graph concepts we have seen so far.

Vertices
- **adjacent:** any two vertices connected by an edge
- **vertex set:** the set of vertices in a graph
- **degree:** number of edges meeting at the vertex
- **odd (even):** degree is an odd (even) number
- **isolated:** no edges connecting the vertex (i.e., degree is 0)

Edges
- **adjacent:** two edges that share a vertex
- **loop:** an edge that connects a vertex with itself
- **multiple edges:** more than one edge connecting the same two vertices
- **edge list:** a list of all the edges in a graph
- **bridge:** an edge in a connected graph without which the graph would be disconnected

---

Paths and circuits
- **path:** a sequence of edges each adjacent to the next, with no edge included more than once, and starting and ending at different vertices
- **circuit:** same as a path, but starting and ending at the same vertex
- **Euler path:** a path that covers all the edges of the graph
- **Euler circuit:** a circuit that covers all the edges of the graph
- **length:** number of edges in a path or a circuit

Graphs
- **simple:** a graph with no loops or multiple edges
- **connected:** there is a path going from any vertex to any other vertex
- **disconnected:** not connected; consisting of two or more components
- **clique:** a set of completely interconnected vertices in the graph (every vertex is connected to every other vertex by an edge)

■ **TABLE 5-1**   Glossary of basic graph concepts

Graphs as Models

One of Euler's most important insights was that certain types of problems can be conveniently rephrased as graph problems and that, in fact, graphs are just the right tool for describing many real-life situations. The notion of using a mathematical concept to describe and solve a real-life problem is one of the oldest and grandest traditions in mathematics. It is called *modeling*. Unwittingly, we have all done simple forms of modeling before, all the way back to elementary school. Every time we turn a word problem into an arithmetic calculation, an algebraic equation, or a geometric picture, we are modeling. We can now add to our repertoire one more tool for modeling: graph models.

In the next set of examples we are going to illustrate how we can use graphs to *model* some of the street-routing problems introduced in Section 5.1.

EXAMPLE 5.12   MODELING THE BRIDGES OF KÖNIGSBERG PUZZLE

The Königsberg bridges puzzle introduced in Example 5.4 asked whether it was possible to take a stroll through the old city of Königsberg and cross each of the seven bridges once and only once. Figure 5-13 shows the evolution of a graph model that we can use to answer this question. Figure 5-13(a) shows the original map of the city in the 1700s. Figure 5-13(b) is a "leaner" version of the map, with lots of obviously irrelevant details removed. A little further reflection should convince us that many details in Fig. 5-13(b) are still irrelevant to the question. The shape and size of the islands, the width of the river, the lengths of the bridges—none of these things really matter. So, then, what does matter? Surprisingly little. *The only thing that truly matters to the solution of this problem is the relationship between land masses (islands and banks) and bridges.* Which land masses are connected to each other and by how many bridges? This information is captured by the red edges in Fig. 5-13(c). Thus, when we strip the map of all its superfluous information, we end up with the graph model shown in Fig. 5-13(d). The four vertices of the graph represent each of the four land masses; the edges represent the seven bridges. In this graph an *Euler circuit* would represent a stroll around the town that crosses each bridge once and ends back at the starting point; an *Euler path* would represent a stroll that crosses each bridge once but does not return to the starting point.

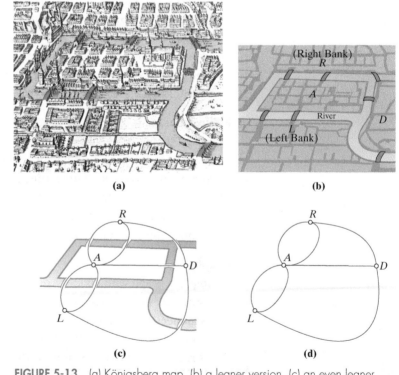

FIGURE 5-13 (a) Königsberg map, (b) a leaner version, (c) an even leaner version, and (d) the graph model.

As big moments go this one may not seem like much, but Euler's idea to turn a puzzle about walking across bridges in a quaint medieval city into an abstract question about graphs was a "eureka" moment in the history of mathematics.

EXAMPLE 5.13   MODELING THE SECURITY GUARD PROBLEM

In Example 5.1 we were introduced to the problem of the security guard who needs to walk the streets of the Sunnyside neighborhood [Fig. 5-14(a)]. The graph in Fig. 5-14(b)—where each edge represents a block of the neighborhood and each vertex an intersection—is a graph model of this problem. The questions raised in Example 5.1 can now be formulated in the language of graphs.

1. Does the graph in Fig. 5-14(b) have an Euler circuit that starts and ends at *S*?
2. What is the fewest number of edges that have to be added to the graph so that there is an Euler circuit?

We will learn how to answer such questions in the next couple of sections.

EXAMPLE 5.14   MODELING THE MAIL CARRIER PROBLEM

Unlike the security guard, the mail carrier in Example 5.2 must make two passes through every block that has homes on both sides of the street (she has to physically place the mail in the mailboxes), must make one pass through blocks that have homes on only one side of the street, and does not have to walk along blocks where there are no houses. In this situation an appropriate graph model requires two edges on the blocks that have homes on both sides of the street, one edge for the blocks that have homes on only one side of the street, and no edges for blocks having no homes on either side of the street. The graph that models this situation is shown in Fig. 5-14(c).

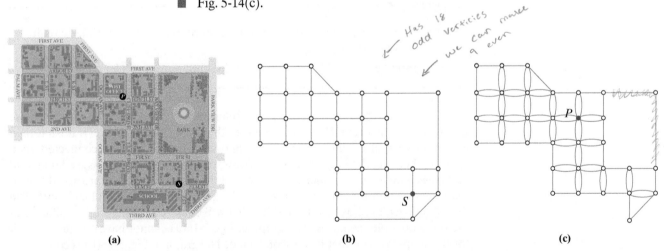

FIGURE 5-14   (a) The Sunnyside neighborhood. (b) A graph model for the security guard. (c) A graph model for the mail carrier.

EXAMPLE 5.15   MODELING THE UPS DRIVER PROBLEM

In Example 5.3 we discussed the UPS driver street-routing problem. The circumstances for the UPS driver are slightly different than those of the mail carrier. First, the UPS driver has to cover only those blocks where he has packages to deliver, shown by the red crosses in Fig. 5-15(a). Second, because of other deliveries outside the neighborhood, his route requires that he enter and exit the neighborhood at opposite ends, as shown in Fig. 5-15(a). Third, the driver can deliver packages on both sides of the street in a single pass. Taking all of these factors into account, we use the graph in Fig. 5-15(b) as a model for the UPS driver problem, with the required starting and ending points of the route shown in red.

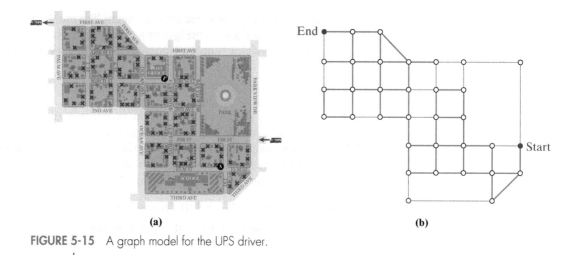

FIGURE 5-15 A graph model for the UPS driver.

5.3 Euler's Theorems and Fleury's Algorithm

In this section we are going to develop the basic theory that will allow us to determine if a graph has an Euler circuit, an Euler path, or neither. This is important because, as we saw in the previous section, what are Euler circuit or Euler path questions in theory are real-life street-routing questions in practice. The three theorems we are going to see next (all due to Euler) are surprisingly simple and yet tremendously useful.

■ EULER'S CIRCUIT THEOREM

- If a graph is *connected* and *every vertex is even*, then it has an Euler circuit (at least one, usually more).

- If a graph has *any odd vertices*, then it does not have an Euler circuit.

If we want to know if a graph has an Euler circuit or not, here is how we can use Euler's circuit theorem. First we make sure the graph is connected. (If it isn't, then no matter what else, an Euler circuit is impossible.) If the graph is connected, then we start checking the degrees of the vertices, one by one. As soon as we hit an odd vertex, we know that an Euler circuit is out of the question. If there are no odd vertices, then we know that the answer is yes—the graph does have an Euler circuit! (The theorem doesn't tell us how to find it—that will come soon.) Figure 5-16 illustrates the three possible scenarios. The graph in Fig. 5-16(a) cannot have an Euler circuit for the simple reason that it is disconnected. The graph in Fig. 5-16(b) is connected, but we can quickly spot odd vertices (*C* is one of them; there are others). This graph has no Euler circuits either. But the graph in Fig. 5-16(c) is connected and all the vertices are even. This graph does have Euler circuits.

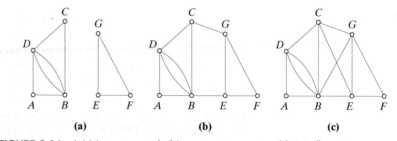

FIGURE 5-16 (a) Not connected; (b) some vertices are odd; (c) all vertices are even.

The basic idea behind Euler's circuit theorem is that as we travel along an Euler circuit, every time we go through a vertex we use up two different edges at that vertex—one to come in and one to go out. We can keep doing this as long as the vertices are even. A single odd vertex means that at some point we are going to come into it and not be able to get out. An analogous theorem will work with Euler paths, but now we do need odd vertices for the starting and ending points of the path. All the other vertices have to be even. Thus, we have the following theorem.

EULER'S PATH THEOREM

- If a graph is *connected* and has *exactly two odd vertices*, then it has an Euler path (at least one, usually more). Any such path must start at one of the odd vertices and end at the other one.

- If a graph has *more than two* odd vertices, then it cannot have an Euler path.

EXAMPLE 5.16   THE BRIDGES OF KÖNIGSBERG PUZZLE SOLVED

Back to the Königsberg bridges problem. In Example 5.12 we saw that the layout of the bridges in the old city can be modeled by the graph in Fig. 5-17(a). This graph has four odd vertices; thus, neither an Euler circuit nor an Euler path can exist. We now have an unequivocal answer to the puzzle: *There is no possible way anyone can walk across all the bridges without having to recross some of them!* How many bridges will need to be recrossed? It depends. If we want to start and end in the same place, we must recross at least two of the bridges. One of the many possible routes is shown in Fig. 5-17(b). In this route the bridge connecting *L* and *D* is crossed twice, and so is one of the two bridges connecting *A* and *R*. If we are allowed to start and end in different places, we can do it by recrossing just one of the bridges. One possible route starting at *A*, crossing bridge *LD* twice, and ending at *R* is shown in Fig. 5-17(c).

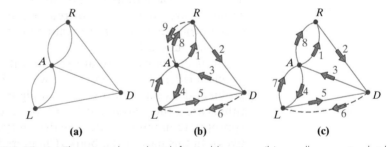

FIGURE 5-17   (a) The original graph with four odd vertices; (b) a walk recrossing bridges *DL* and *RA*; (c) a walk recrossing bridge *DL* only.

Euler's circuit theorem deals with graphs with zero odd vertices, whereas Euler's path theorem deals with graphs with two or more odd vertices. The only scenario not covered by the two theorems is that of graphs with just *one* odd vertex. Euler's third theorem rules out this possibility—a graph cannot have just one odd vertex. In fact, Euler's third theorem says much more.

EULER'S SUM OF DEGREES THEOREM

- The sum of the degrees of all the vertices of a graph equals twice the number of edges (and, therefore, is an even number).

- A graph always has an even number of *odd* vertices.

Euler's sum of degrees theorem is based on the following basic observation: Take any edge—let's call it *XY*. The edge contributes once to the degree of vertex *X* and once to the degree of vertex *Y*, so, in all, that edge makes a total contribution of 2 to the sum of the degrees. Thus, when the degrees of all the vertices of a graph are added, the total is twice the number of edges. Since the total sum is an even number, it is impossible to have just one odd vertex, or three odd vertices, or five odd vertices, and so on. To put it in a slightly different way, *the odd vertices of a graph always come in twos.*

Table 5-2 is a summary of Euler's three theorems. It shows the relationship between the number of odd vertices in a connected graph G and the existence of Euler paths or Euler circuits. (The assumption that G is connected is essential—a disconnected graph cannot have Euler paths or circuits regardless of what else is going on.)

Number of odd vertices	Conclusion
0	G has Euler circuit
2	G has Euler path
4, 6, 8, . . .	G has neither
1, 3, 5, . . .	This is impossible!

■ **TABLE 5-2** Euler's theorems (summary)

Euler's theorems help us answer the following existence question: Does the graph have an Euler circuit, an Euler path, or neither? But when the graph has an Euler circuit or path, how do we find it? For small graphs, simple trial-and-error usually works fine, but real-life applications sometimes involve graphs with hundreds, or even thousands, of vertices. In these cases a trial-and-error approach is out of the question, and what is needed is a systematic strategy that tells us how to create an Euler circuit or path. In other words, we need an *algorithm*.

Fleury's Algorithm

There are many types of problems that can be solved by simply following a set of procedural rules—very specific rules like *when you get to this point, do this, . . . after you finish this, do that*, and so on. Given a specific problem X, an **algorithm** for solving X is a set of *procedural rules* that, when followed, always lead to some sort of "solution" to X. X need not be a mathematics problem—algorithms are used, sometimes unwittingly, in all walks of life: directions to find someone's house, the instructions for assembling a new bike, and a recipe for baking an apple pie are all examples of real-life algorithms. A useful analogy is to think of the problem as a *dish* we want to prepare and the algorithm as a *recipe* for preparing that dish.

In many cases, there are several different algorithms for solving the same problem (there is more than one way to bake an apple pie); in other cases, the problem does not lend itself to an algorithmic solution. In mathematics, algorithms are either *formula* driven (you just apply the formula or formulas to the appropriate inputs) or *directive* driven (you must follow a specific set of directives). In this part of the book (Chapters 5 through 8) we will discuss many important algorithms of the latter type.

Algorithms may be complicated but are rarely difficult. (There is a world of difference between complicated and difficult—accounting is complicated, calculus is difficult!) You don't have to be a brilliant and creative thinker to implement most algorithms—you just have to learn how to follow instructions carefully and methodically. For most of the algorithms we will discuss in this and the next three chapters, the key to success is simple: practice, practice, and more practice!

We will now turn our attention to an algorithm that finds an *Euler circuit* or an *Euler path* in a connected graph. Technically speaking, these are two separate algorithms, but in essence they are identical, so they can be described as one. (The algorithm we will give here is attributed to a Frenchman by the name of M. Fleury, who is alleged to have published a description of the algorithm in 1885. Other than his connection to this algorithm, little else is known about Monsieur Fleury.)

The idea behind Fleury's algorithm can be paraphrased by that old piece of folk wisdom: *Don't burn your bridges behind you*. In graph theory the word *bridge* has a very specific meaning—it is the only edge connecting two separate sections (call

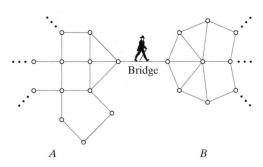

FIGURE 5-18 The bridge separates the two sections. Once you cross from *A* to *B*, the only way to get back to *A* is by recrossing the bridge.

them *A* and *B*) of a graph, as illustrated in Fig. 5-18. This means that if you are in *A*, you can only get to *B* by crossing the bridge. If you do that and then want to get back to *A*, you will need to recross that same bridge. It follows that if you don't want to recross bridges, you better finish your business at *A* before you move on to *B*.

Thus, Fleury's algorithm is based on a simple principle: To find an Euler circuit or an Euler path, *bridges are the last edges you want to cross*. Only do it if you have no choice! Simple enough, but there is a rub: The graph whose bridges we are supposed to avoid is not necessarily the original graph of the problem. Instead, it is that part of the original graph that has yet to be traveled. The point is this: Once we travel along an edge, we are done with it! We will never cross it again, so from that point on, as far as we are concerned, it is as if that edge never existed. Our only concern is how we are going to get around in the *yet-to-be-traveled* part of the graph. Thus, when we talk about bridges that we want to leave as a last resort, we are really referring to *bridges of the to-be-traveled part of the graph*.

┌─■ FLEURY'S ALGORITHM FOR FINDING AN EULER CIRCUIT (PATH) ─┐

- **Preliminaries.** Make sure that the graph is connected and either (1) has no odd vertices (circuit) or (2) has just two odd vertices (path).
- **Start.** Choose a starting vertex. [In case (1) this can be any vertex; in case (2) it must be one of the two *odd* vertices.]
- **Intermediate steps.** At each step, if you have a choice, *don't choose a bridge of the yet-to-be-traveled part* of the graph. However, if you have only one choice, take it.
- **End.** When you can't travel any more, the circuit (path) is complete. [In case (1) you will be back at the starting vertex; in case (2) you will end at the other odd vertex.]

■ For a completely different algorithm, known as **Hierholzer's algorithm**, see Exercise 75.

■ **MyMathLab®**
The applet *Euler Paths and Euler Circuits* in the Applets section of MyMathLab allows you to practice Fleury's algorithm using this approach.*

The only complicated aspect of Fleury's algorithm is the bookkeeping. With each new step, the untraveled part of the graph changes and there may be new bridges formed. Thus, in implementing Fleury's algorithm it is critical to separate the *past* (the part of the graph that has already been traveled) from the *future* (the part of the graph that still needs to be traveled). While there are many different ways to accomplish this (you are certainly encouraged to come up with one of your own), a fairly reliable way goes like this: Start with *two* copies of the graph. Copy 1 is to keep track of the "future"; copy 2 is to keep track of the "past." Every time you travel along an edge, *erase* the edge from copy 1, but mark it (say in red) and label it with the appropriate number on copy 2. As you move forward, copy 1 gets smaller and copy 2 gets redder. At the end, copy 1 has disappeared; copy 2 shows the actual Euler circuit or path.

It's time to look at a couple of examples.

┃ EXAMPLE 5.17 ┃ IMPLEMENTING FLEURY'S ALGORITHM

The graph in Fig. 5-19(a) is a very simple graph—it would be easier to find an Euler circuit just by trial-and-error than by using Fleury's algorithm. Nonetheless, we will do it using Fleury's algorithm. The real purpose of the example is to see the algorithm at work. Each step of the algorithm is explained in Figs. 5-19(b) through (h).

*MyMathLab code required.

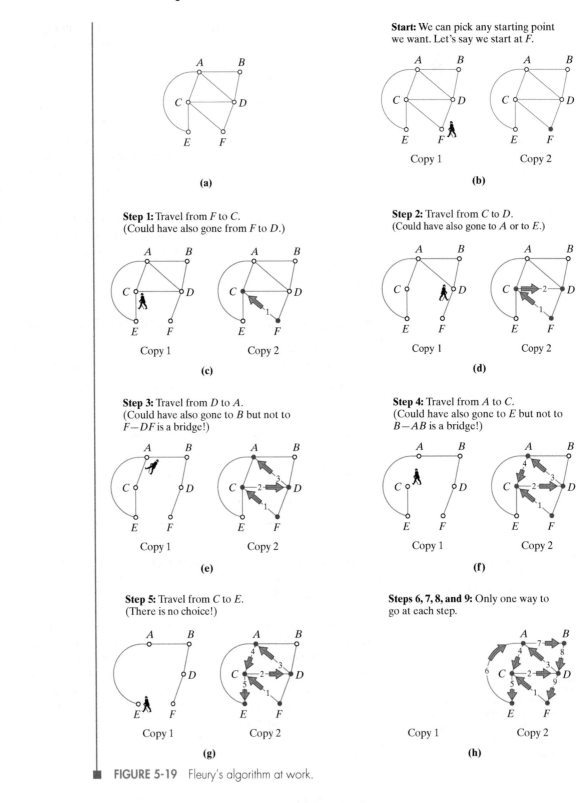

Start: We can pick any starting point we want. Let's say we start at *F*.

Step 1: Travel from *F* to *C*. (Could have also gone from *F* to *D*.)

Step 2: Travel from *C* to *D*. (Could have also gone to *A* or to *E*.)

Step 3: Travel from *D* to *A*. (Could have also gone to *B* but not to *F*—*DF* is a bridge!)

Step 4: Travel from *A* to *C*. (Could have also gone to *E* but not to *B*—*AB* is a bridge!)

Step 5: Travel from *C* to *E*. (There is no choice!)

Steps 6, 7, 8, and 9: Only one way to go at each step.

FIGURE 5-19   Fleury's algorithm at work.

EXAMPLE 5.18   FLEURY'S ALGORITHM FOR EULER PATHS

We will apply Fleury's algorithm to the graph in Figure 5-20. Since it would be a little impractical to show each step of the algorithm with a separate picture as we did in Example 5.17, you are going to have to do some of the work. Start by making two copies of the graph. (If you haven't already done so, get some paper, a pencil, and an eraser.)

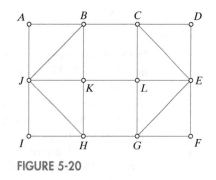

FIGURE 5-20

- **Start.** This graph has two odd vertices, E and J. We can pick either one as the starting vertex. Let's start at J.

- **Step 1.** From J we have five choices, all of which are OK. We'll randomly pick K. (Erase JK on copy 1, and mark and label JK with a 1 on copy 2.)

- **Step 2.** From K we have three choices (B, L, or H). Any of these choices is OK. Say we choose B. (Now erase KB from copy 1 and mark and label KB with a 2 on copy 2.)

- **Step 3.** From B we have three choices (A, C, or J). Any of these choices is OK. Say we choose C. (Now erase BC from copy 1 and mark and label BC with a 3 on copy 2.)

- **Step 4.** From C we have three choices (D, E, or L). Any of these choices is OK. Say we choose L. (EML—that's shorthand for erase, mark, and label.)

- **Step 5.** From L we have three choices (E, G, or K). Any of these choices is OK. Say we choose K. (EML.)

- **Step 6.** From K we have only one choice—to H. Without further ado, we choose H. (EML.)

- **Step 7.** From H we have three choices (G, I, or J). But for the first time, one of the choices is a bad choice. We should not choose G, as HG is a bridge of the yet-to-be-traveled part of the graph (Fig. 5-21). Either of the other two choices is OK. Say we choose J. (EML.)

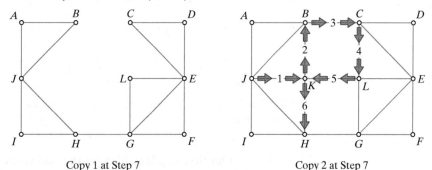

Copy 1 at Step 7   Copy 2 at Step 7

FIGURE 5-21

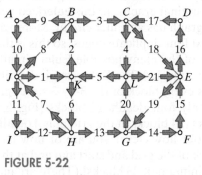

FIGURE 5-22

- **Step 8.** From J we have three choices (A, B, or I), but we should not choose I, as JI has just become a bridge. Either of the other two choices is OK. Say we choose B. (EML)

- **Steps 9 through 13.** Each time we have only one choice. From B we have to go to A, then to J, I, H, and G.

- **Steps 14 through 21.** Not to belabor the point, let's just cut to the chase. The rest of the path is given by G, F, E, D, C, E, G, L, E. There are many possible endings, and you should find a different one by yourself.

The completed Euler path (one of hundreds of possible ones) is shown in Fig. 5-22.

5.4 Eulerizing and Semi-Eulerizing Graphs

In this section we will finally answer some of the street-routing problems introduced in Section 5.1. The common thread in all these problems is to find routes that (1) cover all the edges of the graph that models the original problem and (2) recross the fewest number of edges. The first requirement typically comes with the problem; the second requirement comes from the desire to be as efficient as possible. In many applications, each edge represents a unit of cost. The more edges along the route, the higher the cost of the route. In a street-routing problem the first pass along an edge is a requirement of the job. Any additional pass along that edge represents a wasted expense (these extra passes are often described as *deadhead* travel). Thus, an optimal route is one with the fewest number of deadhead edges. (This is only true under the assumption that each edge equals one unit of cost.)

We are now going to see how the theory developed in the preceding sections will help us design optimal street routes for graphs with many (more than two) odd vertices. The key idea is that we can turn odd vertices into even vertices by adding "duplicate" edges in strategic places.

Eulerizations

| **EXAMPLE 5.19** | COVERING A 3-BY-3 STREET GRID |

The graph in Fig. 5-23(a) models a 3-block-by-3-block street grid. The graph has 24 edges, each representing a block of the street grid. How can we find an optimal route that covers all the blocks of the street grid and ends back at the starting point?

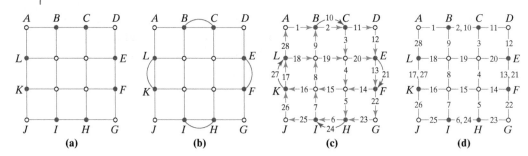

FIGURE 5-23   (a) The original graph model (odd vertices shown in red); (b) an optimal eularization; (c) an Euler circuit; (d) an optimal route on the street grid.

Our first step is to identify the odd vertices in the graph model. This graph has eight odd vertices (*B*, *C*, *E*, *F*, *H*, *I*, *K*, and *L*), shown in red. When we add a duplicate copy of edges *BC*, *EF*, *HI*, and *KL*, we get the graph in Fig. 5-23(b). This is called an **eulerization** of the original graph—in this **eulerized** version the vertices are all even, so we know this graph has an Euler circuit. Moreover, with eight odd vertices we need to add *at least* four duplicate edges, so this is the best we can do.

Figure 5-23(c) shows one of the many possible Euler circuits, with the edges numbered in the order they are traveled. The Euler circuit described in Fig. 5-23(c) represents a route that covers every block of the 3-by-3 street grid and ends back at the starting point, using only four deadhead blocks [Fig. 5-23(d)]. The total length of this route is 28 blocks (24 blocks in the grid plus 4 deadhead blocks), and this route is optimal—no matter how clever you are or how hard you try, if you want to travel along each block of the grid and start and end at the same point, you will have to pass through a minimum of 28 blocks! (There are many other ways to do it using just 28 blocks, but none with fewer than 28.)

EXAMPLE 5.20   COVERING A 4-BY-4 STREET GRID

The graph in Fig. 5-24(a) models a 4-block-by-4-block street grid consisting of 40 blocks. The 12 odd vertices in the graph are shown in red. We want to find a route that covers each of the 40 blocks of the street grid, ends back at the starting point, and has the fewest number of deadhead blocks. To do this, we first eulerize the graph by adding the fewest possible number of edges. Figure 5-24(b) shows how *not to do it!* This graph violates the cardinal rule of eulerization—you can only duplicate edges that are part of the original graph. Edges *DF* and *NL* are new edges, not duplicates, so Fig. 5-24(b) is out! Figure 5-24(c) shows a legal eulerization, but it is not optimal, as it is obvious that we could have accomplished the same thing by adding fewer duplicate edges. Figure 5-24(d) shows an *optimal eulerization* of the original graph—one of several possible. Once we have an optimal eulerization, we have the blueprint for the optimal route on the street grid. Regardless of the specific details, we now know that the route will travel along 48 blocks—the 40 original blocks in the grid plus 8 deadhead blocks. A route can be found by using Fleury's algorithm on the graph shown in Fig. 5-24(a). We leave the details to the reader. (By the way, in a grid such as this one, a route can be easily found using common sense and trial and error.)

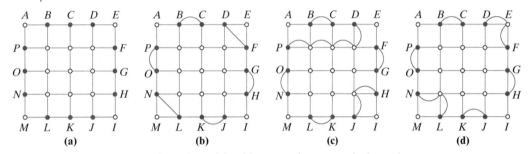

FIGURE 5-24 (a) The original graph model (odd vertices shown in red). (b) Bad move — *DF* and *NL* were not edges of the original graph! (c) An eulerization, but not an optimal one! (d) One of the many possible optimal eulerizations.

EXAMPLE 5.21   THE SECURITY GUARD PROBLEM SOLVED

We are now ready to solve the security guard street-routing problem introduced in Example 5.1 and subsequently modeled in Example 5.13. Let's recap the story: The security guard is required to walk each block of the Sunnyside neighborhood at least once and he wants to deadhead as few blocks as possible. He usually parks his car at *S* (there is a donut shop on that corner) and needs to end his route back at the car. Figure 5-25 shows the evolution of a solution: Fig. 5-25(a) shows the original neighborhood that the security guard must cover; Fig. 5-25(b) shows the graph model of the problem (with the 18 odd vertices of the graph highlighted in red); Fig. 5-25(c) shows an eulerization of the graph in (b), with the 9 duplicate edges shown in red. This is the fewest number of edges required to eulerize the graph in Fig. 5-25(b), so the eulerization is optimal. The eulerized graph in Fig. 5-25(c) has all even vertices, and an Euler circuit can be found. Since a circuit can be started at any vertex we will start the circuit at *S*. Figure 5-25(d) shows one of the many possible optimal routes for the security guard (just follow the numbers). Note that using a different starting vertex will not make the route shorter, so the security guard can continue parking in front of the donut shop—it will not hurt!

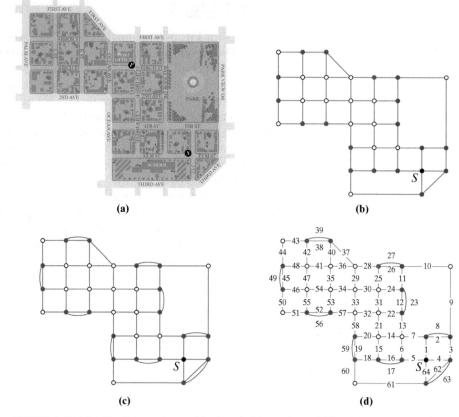

FIGURE 5-25 (a) The Sunnyside neighborhood; (b) graph model for the security guard problem; (c) an optimal eulerization of (b); (d) an optimal route for the security guard.

| **EXAMPLE 5.22** | THE MAIL CARRIER PROBLEM SOLVED |

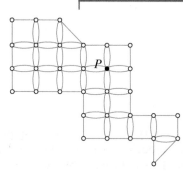

FIGURE 5-26 Graph model for the mail carrier.

The solution to the mail carrier problem follows essentially the same story line as the one for the security guard. Let's recap this story: The mail carrier needs to start and end her route at the post office (P), cover both sides of the street when there are buildings on both sides, and cover just one side on blocks where there are buildings on only one side, with no need to cover any streets where there are no buildings (like the back side of the park and the school). Fig. 5-26 shows the graph model for the mail carrier (see Example 5.14). The interesting thing about this graph is that every vertex is already even (there are some vertices of degree 2 in the corners, there are a couple of vertices of degree 6, and there are lots of vertices of degrees 4 and 8). This means that the graph does not have to be eulerized, as it has Euler circuits in its present form. An optimal route for the mail carrier can be found by finding an Euler circuit of the graph that starts and ends at P. We know how to do that and leave it as an exercise for the reader to find such a route. There are hundreds of possible routes that will work. (*Note*: Although Fleury's algorithm is a sure bet, in a case like this trial and error is almost guaranteed to work best.)

Semi-Eulerizations

In cases where a street route is not required to end back where it started (either because we can choose to start and end in different places or because the starting and ending points are required to be different) we are looking for Euler paths, rather than Euler circuits. In these cases we are looking for a graph that has two odd verti-ces and the rest even. We need the two odd vertices to give us a starting and ending point for our route. The process of adding additional edges to a graph so that all the vertices except two are even is called a **semi-eulerization**, and we say that the graph has been *semi-eulerized*.

EXAMPLE 5.23 THE BRIDGES OF MADISON COUNTY SOLVED

In Example 5.5 we introduced the problem of routing a photographer across all the bridges in Madison County, shown in Fig. 5-27(a). To recap the story: The pho-tographer needs to cross each of the 11 bridges at least once (for her photo shoot). Each crossing of a bridge costs $25, and the photographer is on a tight budget, so she wants to cover all the bridges once but recross as few bridges as possible. The other relevant fact is that the photographer can start her trip at either bank of the river and end the trip at either bank of the river. Figure 5-27(b) is a graph model of the Madison bridges layout. A la Euler, we let the vertices represent the land masses and the edges represent the bridges. The graph has four odd vertices (R, L, B, and D). The photographer can start the shoot at either bank and end at either bank—say she chooses to start the route at R and end it at L. Figure 5-27(c) shows a semi-eulerization of the graph in (b), with R and L left as odd vertices, and the edge BD (i.e., the Kennedy bridge) recrossed so that now B and D are even vertices. The numbers in Fig. 5-27(c) show one possible optimal route for the photographer, with a total of 12 bridge crossings and a total cost of $300.

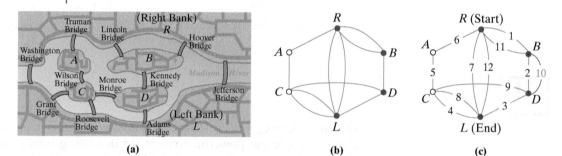

FIGURE 5-27   (a) The original layout; (b) graph model; (c) semi-eulerization of (b) and an optimal route.

EXAMPLE 5.24 THE UPS DRIVER PROBLEM DECONSTRUCTED

In Example 5.3 we introduced the street-routing problem facing a UPS driver who has to make package deliveries around the Sunnyside neighborhood during the Christmas season. Figure 5-28(a) shows all the locations (marked with red crosses) where the driver must deliver packages. Figure 5-28(b) shows the graph model of the problem (see Example 5.15), with the odd vertices highlighted in red. Two of those odd vertices happen to be the designated starting and ending points of his route. We solve this problem by finding an optimal semi-eulerization of the graph with the starting and ending points left alone. One optimal semi-eulerization is shown in Fig. 5-28(c). It has 10 additional edges shown in red. These represent the deadhead blocks the driver will have to cover a second time. The last step is to find an Euler path in Fig. 5-28(c) with the designated starting and ending points—that would give us an optimal route. This can be done using Fleury's algorithm (or trial and error), and we leave this final detail as an exercise for the UPS driver.

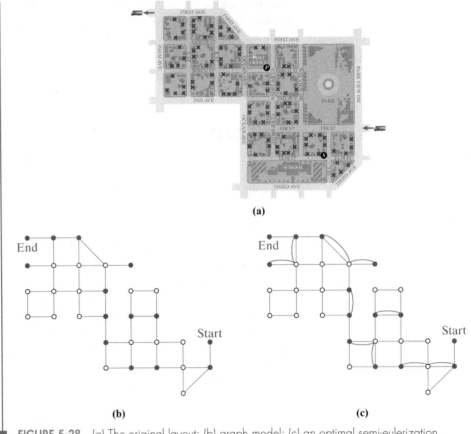

FIGURE 5-28   (a) The original layout; (b) graph model; (c) an optimal semi-eulerization.

Conclusion

In this chapter we got our first introduction to two fundamental ideas. First, we learned about a simple but powerful concept for describing relationships within a set of objects—the concept of a *graph*. This idea can be traced back to Euler, some 270 years ago. Since then, the study of graphs has grown into one of the most important and useful branches of modern mathematics.

The second important idea of this chapter is the concept of a *graph model*. Every time we take a real-life problem and turn it into a mathematical problem, we are, in effect, modeling. Unwittingly, we have all done some form of mathematical modeling at one time or another—first using arithmetic and later using equations and functions to describe real-life situations. In this chapter we learned about a new type of modeling called graph modeling, in which we use graphs and the mathematical theory of graphs to solve certain types of routing problems.

By necessity, the routing problems that we solved in this chapter were fairly simplistic—crossing a few bridges, patrolling a small neighborhood, routing a UPS driver. We should not be deceived by the simplicity of these examples—larger-scale variations on these themes have significant practical importance. In many big cities, where the efficient routing of municipal services (police patrols, garbage collection, etc.) is a major issue, the very theory that we developed in this chapter is being used on a large scale, the only difference being that many of the more tedious details are mechanized and carried out by a computer. (In New York City, for example, garbage collection, curb sweeping, snow removal, and other municipal services have been scheduled and organized using graph models since the 1970s, and the improved efficiency has yielded savings estimated in the tens of millions of dollars a year.)

KEY CONCEPTS

5.1 Street-Routing Problems

- **routing problems:** problems concerned with routing the delivery of goods or services to a set of destinations, **140**
- **street-routing problems:** problems where a specified set of connections (roads, bridges, edges) must be traveled at least once, **140**

5.2 An Introduction to Graphs

- **vertex set:** the set of vertices of a graph, **144**
- **edge list:** a list of all the edges of a graph, **144**
- **adjacent vertices:** two vertices connected by an edge, **144**
- **loop:** an edge that connects a vertex with itself, **144**
- **multiple edges:** two or more edges connecting the same two vertices, **144**
- **degree:** number of edges meeting at the vertex, **144**
- **odd (even) vertex:** a vertex of odd (even) degree, **145**
- **clique:** a set of vertices with the property that any two are adjacent, **145**
- **simple graph:** a graph with no loops or multiple edges, **145**
- **isolated vertex:** a vertex of degree 0, **145**
- **adjacent edges:** two edges with a shared vertex, **147**
- **path:** a sequence of edges each adjacent to the next, with no edge included more than once, and starting and ending at different vertices, **147**
- **circuit:** same as a path but starting and ending at the same vertex, **147**
- **length:** number of edges in a path or a circuit, **147**
- **Euler path:** a path that travels along each edge of a graph once and only once, **148**
- **Euler circuit:** a circuit that travels along each edge of a graph once and only once, **148**
- **connected graph:** a graph such that there is a path going from any vertex to any other vertex, **148**
- **disconnected graph:** a graph that is not connected; it has two or more connected components, **148**
- **components:** the connected "pieces" that make up a graph, **148**
- **bridge:** an edge in a connected graph without which the graph would be disconnected, **149**

5.3 Euler's Theorems and Fleury's Algorithm

- **Euler's Circuit Theorem:** a connected graph has an Euler circuit if and only if all vertices are even, **152**
- **Euler's Path Theorem:** a connected graph has an Euler path if and only it has two odd vertices, **153**
- **Euler's Sum of Degrees Theorem:** the sum of the degrees of all the vertices equals twice the number of edges, **153**
- **algorithm:** a set of procedural rules that when followed produces the answer to some problem, **154**

■ **Fleury's algorithm:** an algorithm for finding Euler circuits or Euler paths in a graph; it builds the Euler circuit (path) edge by edge—choosing a bridge of the yet-to-be traveled part of the graph only when there is no other choice, **154**

5.4 Eulerizing and Semi-Eulerizing Graphs

■ **eulerization:** the process of duplicating edges in a graph to make it have all even vertices, **158**

■ **semi-eulerization:** the process of duplicating edges in a graph to make it have all but two even vertices, **161**

EXERCISES

WALKING

5.1 Street-Routing Problems

No exercises for this section.

5.2 An Introduction to Graphs

1. For the graph shown in Fig. 5-29,

   (a) give the vertex set.

   (b) give the edge list.

   (c) give the degree of each vertex.

   (d) draw a version of the graph without crossing points.

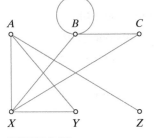

FIGURE 5-29

2. For the graph shown in Fig. 5-30,

   (a) give the vertex set.

   (b) give the edge list.

   (c) give the degree of each vertex.

   (d) sraw a version of the graph without crossing points.

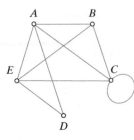

FIGURE 5-30

3. For the graph shown in Fig. 5-31,

   (a) give the vertex set.

   (b) give the edge list.

   (c) give the degree of each vertex.

   (d) give the number of components of the graph.

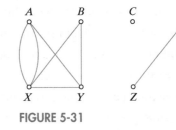

FIGURE 5-31

4. For the graph shown in Fig. 5-32,

   (a) give the vertex set.

   (b) give the edge list.

   (c) give the degree of each vertex.

   (d) give the number of components of the graph.

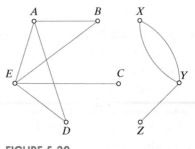

FIGURE 5-32

5. Consider the graph with vertex set $\{K, R, S, T, W\}$ and edge list $RS, RT, TT, TS, SW, WW, WS$. Draw two different pictures of the graph.

6. Consider the graph with vertex set $\{A, B, C, D, E\}$ and edge list $AC, AE, BD, BE, CA, CD, CE, DE$. Draw two different pictures of the graph.

7. Consider the graph with vertex set $\{A, B, C, D, E\}$ and edge list AD, AE, BC, BD, DD, DE. Without drawing a picture of the graph,

   (a) list all the vertices adjacent to D.

   (b) list all the edges adjacent to BD.

   (c) find the degree of D.

   (d) find the sum of the degrees of the vertices.

8. Consider the graph with vertex set $\{A, B, C, X, Y, Z\}$ and edge list $AX, AY, AZ, BB, CX, CY, CZ, YY$. Without drawing a picture of the graph,

   (a) list all the vertices adjacent to Y.

   (b) list all the edges adjacent to AY.

   (c) find the degree of Y.

   (d) find the sum of the degrees of the vertices.

9. (a) Give an example of a connected graph with six vertices such that each vertex has degree 2.

   (b) Give an example of a disconnected graph with six vertices such that each vertex has degree 2.

   (c) Give an example of a graph with six vertices such that each vertex has degree 1.

10. (a) Give an example of a connected graph with eight vertices such that each vertex has degree 3.

    (b) Give an example of a disconnected graph with eight vertices such that each vertex has degree 3.

    (c) Give an example of a graph with eight vertices such that each vertex has degree 1.

11. Consider the graph in Fig. 5-33.

    (a) Find a path from C to F passing through vertex B but not through vertex D.

    (b) Find a path from C to F passing through both vertex B and vertex D.

    (c) Find a path of length 4 from C to F.

    (d) Find a path of length 7 from C to F.

    (e) How many paths are there from C to A?

    (f) How many paths are there from H to F?

    (g) How many paths are there from C to F?

12. Consider the graph in Fig. 5-33.

    (a) Find a path from D to E passing through vertex G only once.

    (b) Find a path from D to E passing through vertex G twice.

    (c) Find a path of length 4 from D to E.

    (d) Find a path of length 8 from D to E.

    (e) How many paths are there from D to A?

    (f) How many paths are there from H to E?

    (g) How many paths are there from D to E?

13. Consider the graph in Fig. 5-33.

    (a) Find all circuits of length 1.

    (b) Find all circuits of length 2.

    (c) Find all circuits of length 3.

    (d) Find all circuits of length 4.

    (e) What is the total number of circuits in the graph?

14. Consider the graph in Fig. 5-34.

    (a) Find all circuits of length 1.

    (b) Find all circuits of length 2.

    (c) Find all circuits of length 3.

    (d) Find all circuits of length 4.

    (e) Find all circuits of length 5.

    (f) What is the total number of circuits in the graph?

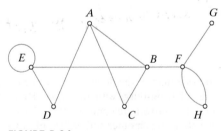

FIGURE 5-34

15. List all the bridges in each of the following graphs:

    (a) the graph in Fig. 5-33.

    (b) the graph with vertex set $\{A, B, C, D, E\}$ and edge list AB, AE, BC, CD, DE.

    (c) the graph with vertex set $\{A, B, C, D, E\}$ and edge list AB, BC, BE, CD.

16. List all the bridges in each of the following graphs:

    (a) the graph in Fig. 5-34.

    (b) the graph with vertex set $\{A, B, C, D, E\}$ and edge list AB, AD, AE, BC, CE, DE.

    (c) the graph with vertex set $\{A, B, C, D, E\}$ and edge list AB, BC, CD, DE.

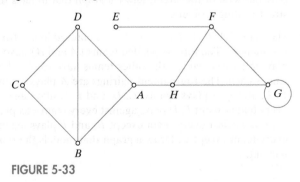

FIGURE 5-33

17. Consider the graph in Fig. 5-35.

(a) Find the largest clique in this graph.

(b) List all the bridges in this graph.

(c) If you remove *all* the bridges from the graph, how many components will the resulting graph have?

(d) Find the *shortest* path (i.e., the path with least length) from C to J. What is the length of the shortest path?

(e) Find a *longest* path from C to J. What is the length of a longest path?

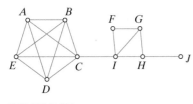

FIGURE 5-35

18. Consider the graph in Fig. 5-36.

(a) Find the largest clique in this graph.

(b) List all the bridges in this graph.

(c) If you remove *all* the bridges from the graph, how many components will the resulting graph have?

(d) Find the *shortest* path (i.e., the path with least length) from E to J. What is the length of the shortest path?

(e) What is the length of a *longest* path from E to J?

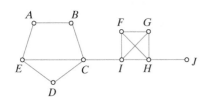

FIGURE 5-36

19. Figure 5-37 shows a map of the downtown area of the picturesque hamlet of Kingsburg, with the Kings River running through the downtown area and the three islands (A, B, and C) connected to each other and both banks by seven bridges. You have been hired by the Kingsburg Chamber of Commerce to organize the annual downtown parade. Part of your job is to plan the route for the parade. Draw a graph that models the layout of Kingsburg.

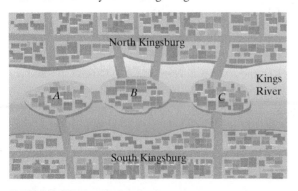

FIGURE 5-37

20. Figure 5-38 is a map of downtown Royalton, showing the Royalton River running through the downtown area and the three islands (A, B, and C) connected to each other and both banks by eight bridges. The Downtown Athletic Club wants to design the route for a marathon through the downtown area. Draw a graph that models the layout of Royalton.

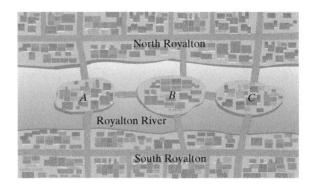

FIGURE 5-38

21. A night watchman must walk the streets of the Green Hills subdivision shown in Fig. 5-39. The night watchman needs to walk only once along each block. Draw a graph that models this street-routing problem.

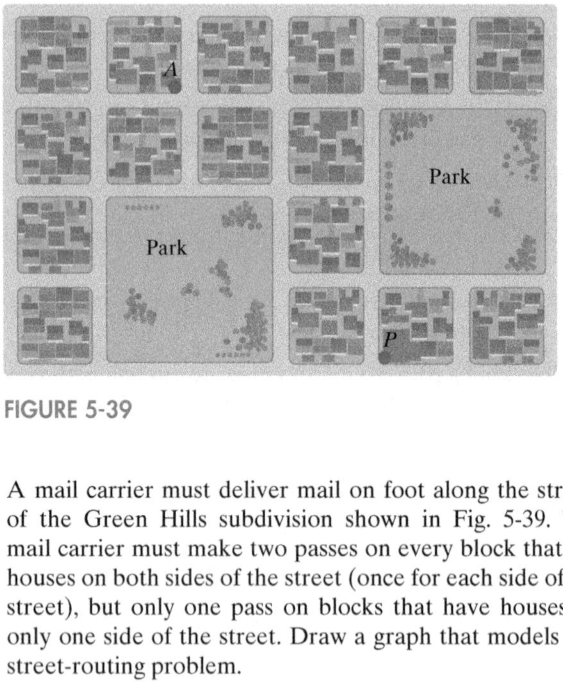

FIGURE 5-39

22. A mail carrier must deliver mail on foot along the streets of the Green Hills subdivision shown in Fig. 5-39. The mail carrier must make two passes on every block that has houses on both sides of the street (once for each side of the street), but only one pass on blocks that have houses on only one side of the street. Draw a graph that models this street-routing problem.

23. Six teams (A, B, C, D, E, and F) are entered in a softball tournament. The top two seeded teams (A and B) have to play only three games; the other teams have to play four games each. The tournament pairings are A plays against C, E, and F; B plays against C, D, and F; C plays against every team except F; D plays against every team except A; E plays against every team except B; and F plays against every team except C. Draw a graph that models the tournament.

24. The Kangaroo Lodge of Madison County has 10 members ($A, B, C, D, E, F, G, H, I,$ and J). The club has five working committees: the Rules Committee ($A, C, D, E, I,$ and J), the Public Relations Committee ($B, C, D, H, I,$ and J), the Guest Speaker Committee ($A, D, E, F,$ and H), the New Year's Eve Party Committee ($D, F, G, H,$ and I), and the Fund Raising Committee ($B, D, F, H,$ and J).

   (a) Suppose we are interested in knowing which pairs of members are on the same committee. Draw a graph that models this problem. (*Hint*: Let the vertices of the graph represent the members.)

   (b) Suppose we are interested in knowing which committees have members in common. Draw a graph that models this problem. (*Hint*: Let the vertices of the graph represent the committees.)

25. Table 5-3 summarizes the Facebook friendships between a group of eight individuals [an F indicates that the individuals (row and column) are Facebook friends]. Draw a graph that models the set of friendships in the group. (Use the first letter of the name to label the vertices.)

	Fred	Pat	Mac	Ben	Tom	Hale	Zac	Cher
Fred		F			F	F		
Pat	F				F	F		F
Mac				F			F	
Ben		F	F				F	
Tom	F	F				F		
Hale	F	F			F			F
Zac			F	F				
Cher		F				F		

■ **TABLE 5-3**

26. The Dean of Students' office wants to know how the seven general education courses selected by incoming freshmen are clustered. For each pair of general education courses, if 30 or more incoming freshmen register for both courses, the courses are defined as being "significantly linked." Table 5-4 shows all the significant links between general education courses (indicated by a 1). Draw a graph that models the significant links between the general education courses. (Use the first letter of each course to label the vertices of the graph.)

	Math	Chemistry	Biology	English	Physics	History	Art
Math		1	1	1	1		
Chemistry	1		1				
Biology	1	1		1		1	
English	1		1		1	1	1
Physics	1			1		1	1
History			1	1	1		1
Art				1	1	1	

■ **TABLE 5-4**

27. Figure 5-40 shows the downtown area of the small village of Kenton. The village wants to have a Fourth of July parade that passes through all the blocks of the downtown area, except for the 14 blocks highlighted in yellow, which the police department considers unsafe for the parade route. Draw a graph that models this street-routing problem.

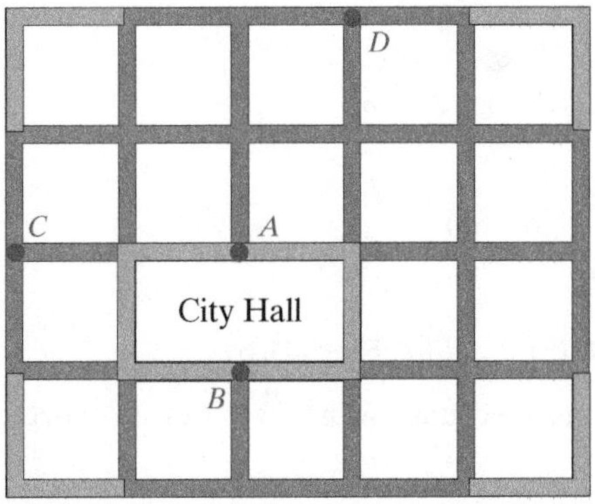

FIGURE 5-40

28. Figure 5-40 shows the downtown area of the small village of Kenton. At regular intervals at night, a police officer must patrol every downtown block at least once, and each of the six blocks along City Hall at least twice. Draw a graph that models this street-routing problem.

5.3 Euler's Theorems and Fleury's Algorithm

In Exercises 29 through 34 choose from one of the following answers and provide a short explanation for your answer.

(A) the graph has an Euler circuit.

(B) the graph has an Euler path.

(C) the graph has neither an Euler circuit nor an Euler path.

(D) the graph may or may not have an Euler circuit.

(E) the graph may or may not have an Euler path. You do not have to show an actual path or circuit.

29. (a) Fig. 5-41(a)   **(b)** Fig. 5-41(b)

(c) A graph with six vertices, all of degree 2

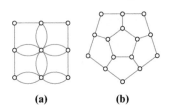

(a)   (b)

FIGURE 5-41

30. (a) Fig. 5-42(a)   **(b)** Fig. 5-42(b)

(c) A graph with eight vertices: six vertices of degree 2 and two vertices of degree 3

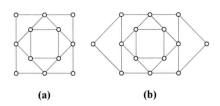

(a)   (b)

FIGURE 5-42

31. (a) Fig. 5-43(a)   **(b)** Fig. 5-43(b)

(c) A disconnected graph with six vertices, all of degree 2

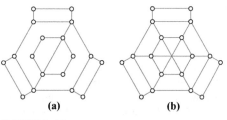

(a)   (b)

FIGURE 5-43

32. (a) Fig. 5-44(a)   **(b)** Fig. 5-44(b)

(c) A disconnected graph with eight vertices: six vertices of degree 2 and two vertices of degree 3

① Connected 2
② 2 ODD
So it has 4
Euler path

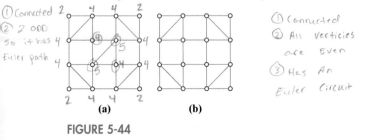

① Connected
② All verticies are Even
③ Has An Euler Circuit

(a)   (b)

FIGURE 5-44

33. (a) Fig. 5-45(a)   **(b)** Fig. 5-45(b)

(c) A graph with six vertices, all of degree 1. [*Hint*: Try Exercise 9(c) first.]

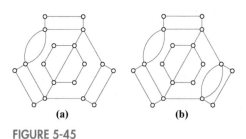

(a)   (b)

FIGURE 5-45

34. (a) Fig. 5-46(a)   **(b)** Fig. 5-46(b)

(c) A graph with eight vertices, all of degree 1.

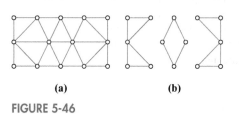

(a)   (b)

FIGURE 5-46

35. Find an Euler circuit for the graph in Fig. 5-47. Show your answer by labeling the edges 1, 2, 3, and so on in the order in which they are traveled.

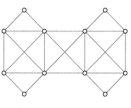

FIGURE 5-47

36. Find an Euler circuit for the graph in Fig. 5-48. Show your answer by labeling the edges 1, 2, 3, and so on in the order in which they can be traveled.

FIGURE 5-48

37. Find an Euler path for the graph in Fig. 5-49. Show your answer by labeling the edges 1, 2, 3, and so on in the order in which they are traveled.

FIGURE 5-49

38. Find an Euler path for the graph in Fig. 5-50. Show your answer by labeling the edges 1, 2, 3, and so on in the order in which they are traveled.

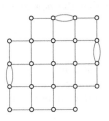

FIGURE 5-50

39. Find an Euler circuit for the graph in Fig. 5-51. Use *B* as the starting and ending point of the circuit. Show your answer by labeling the edges 1, 2, 3, and so on in the order in which they are traveled.

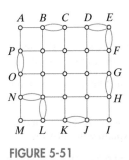

FIGURE 5-51

40. Find an Euler circuit for the graph in Fig. 5-52. Use *S* as the starting and ending point of the circuit. Show your answer by labeling the edges 1, 2, 3, and so on in the order in which they are traveled.

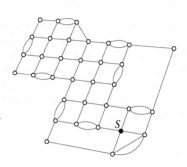

FIGURE 5-52

41. Suppose you are using Fleury's algorithm to find an Euler circuit for a graph and you are in the middle of the process. The graph in Fig. 5-53 shows both the already traveled part of the graph (the red edges) and the yet-to-be traveled part of the graph (the blue edges).

(a) Suppose you are standing at *P*. What edge(s) could you choose next?

(b) Suppose you are standing at *B*. What edge should you *not* choose next?

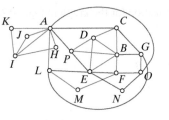

FIGURE 5-53

42. Suppose you are using Fleury's algorithm to find an Euler circuit for a graph and you are in the middle of the process. The graph in Fig. 5-53 shows both the already traveled part of the graph (the red edges) and the yet-to-be traveled part of the graph (the blue edges).

(a) Suppose you are standing at *C*. What edge(s) could you choose next?

(b) Suppose you are standing at *A*. What edge should you *not* choose next?

5.4 Eulerizing and Semi-Eulerizating Graphs

43. Find an optimal eulerization for the graph in Fig. 5-54.

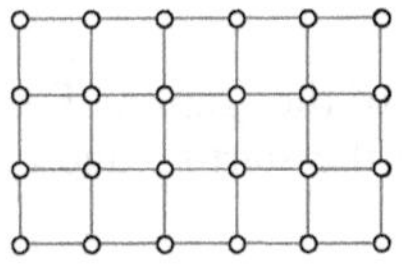

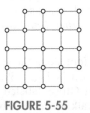

FIGURE 5-54

44. Find an optimal eulerization for the graph in Fig. 5-55.

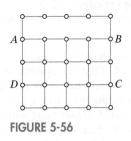

FIGURE 5-55

45. Find an optimal eulerization for the graph in Fig. 5-56.

A ○—○—○—○—○ B
D ○—○—○—○—○ C

FIGURE 5-56

46. Find an optimal eulerization for the graph in Fig. 5-57.

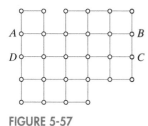

FIGURE 5-57

47. Find an optimal semi-eulerization for the graph in Fig. 5-56. You are free to choose the starting and ending vertices.

48. Find an optimal semi-eulerization for the graph in Fig. 5-57. You are free to choose the starting and ending vertices.

49. Find an optimal semi-eulerization of the graph in Figure 5-56 when *A* and *D* are required to be the starting and ending points of the route.

50. Find an optimal semi-eulerization of the graph in Figure 5-57 when *A* and *B* are required to be the starting and ending points of the route.

51. Find an optimal semi-eulerization of the graph in Figure 5-56 when *B* and *C* are required to be the starting and ending points of the route.

52. Find an optimal semi-eulerization of the graph in Fig. 5-57 when *A* and *D* are required to be the starting and ending points of the route.

53. A security guard must patrol on foot the streets of the Green Hills subdivision shown in Fig. 5-39. The security guard wants to start and end his walk at the corner labeled *A*, and he needs to cover each block of the subdivision at least once. Find an optimal route for the security guard. Describe the route by labeling the edges 1, 2, 3, and so on in the order in which they are traveled. (*Hint*: You should do Exercise 21 first.)

54. A mail carrier must deliver mail on foot along the streets of the Green Hills subdivision shown in Fig. 5-39. His route must start and end at the Post Office, labeled *P* in the figure. The mail carrier must walk along each block twice if there are houses on both sides of the street and once along blocks where there are houses on only one side of the street. Find an optimal route for the mail carrier. Describe the route by labeling the edges 1, 2, 3, and so on in the order in which they are traveled. (*Hint*: You should do Exercise 22 first.)

55. This exercise refers to the Fourth of July parade problem introduced in Exercise 27. Find an optimal route for the parade that starts at *A* and ends at *B* (see Fig. 5-40). Describe the route by labeling the edges 1, 2, 3, . . . etc. in the order they are traveled. [*Hint*: Start with the graph model for the parade route (see Exercise 27); then find an optimal semi-eulerization of the graph that leaves *A* and *B* odd; then find an Euler path in this new graph.]

56. This exercise refers to the Fourth of July parade problem introduced in Exercise 27. Find an optimal route for the parade that starts at *C* and ends at *D* (see Fig.

5-40). Describe the route by labeling the edges 1, 2, 3, . . . etc. in the order they are traveled. [*Hint*: Start with the graph model for the parade route (see Exercise 27); then find an optimal semi-eulerization of the graph that leaves *C* and *D* odd; then find an Euler path in this new graph.]

JOGGING

57. Assume you want to trace the diagram of a basketball court shown in Fig. 5-58 without retracing any lines. How many times would you have to lift your pencil to do it? Explain.

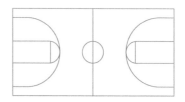

FIGURE 5-58

58. (a) Explain why in every graph the sum of the degrees of all the vertices equals twice the number of edges.

(b) Explain why every graph must have an even number of odd vertices.

59. If *G* is a connected graph with no bridges, how many vertices of degree 1 can *G* have? Explain your answer.

60. Regular graphs. A graph is called *regular* if every vertex has the same degree. Let *G* be a connected regular graph with *N* vertices.

(a) Explain why if *N* is odd, then *G* must have an Euler circuit.

(b) When *N* is even, then *G* may or may not have an Euler circuit. Give examples of both situations.

61. Complete bipartite graphs. A complete bipartite graph is a graph having the property that the vertices of the graph can be divided into two groups *A* and *B* and each vertex in *A* is adjacent to each vertex in *B*, as shown in Fig. 5-59. Two vertices in *A* are never adjacent, and neither are two vertices in *B*. Let *m* and *n* denote the number of vertices in *A* and *B*, respectively, and assume $m \leq n$.

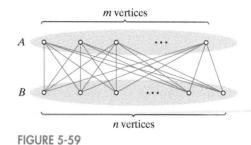

FIGURE 5-59

(a) Describe all the possible values of *m* and *n* for which the complete bipartite graph has an Euler circuit. (*Hint*: There are infinitely many values of *m* and *n*.)

(b) Describe all the possible values of m and n for which the complete bipartite graph has an Euler path.

62. Consider the following game. You are given N vertices and are required to build a graph by adding edges connecting these vertices. Each time you add an edge you must pay \$1. You can stop when the graph is connected.

(a) Describe the strategy that will cost you the least amount of money.

(b) What is the minimum amount of money needed to build the graph? (Give your answer in terms of N.)

63. Consider the following game. You are given N vertices and allowed to build a graph by adding edges connecting these vertices. For each edge you can add, you make \$1. You are not allowed to add loops or multiple edges, and you must stop before the graph is connected (i.e., the graph you end up with must be disconnected).

(a) Describe the strategy that will give you the greatest amount of money.

(b) What is the maximum amount of money you can make building the graph? (Give your answer in terms of N.)

64. Figure 5-60 shows a map of the downtown area of the picturesque hamlet of Kingsburg. You have been hired by the Kingsburg Chamber of Commerce to organize the annual downtown parade. Part of your job is to plan the route for the parade. An *optimal* parade route is one that keeps the bridge crossings to a minimum and yet crosses each of the seven bridges in the downtown area at least once.

(a) Find an optimal parade route if the parade is supposed to start in North Kingsburg but can end anywhere.

(b) Find an optimal parade route if the parade is supposed to start in North Kingsburg and end in South Kingsburg.

(c) Find an optimal parade route if the parade is supposed to start in North Kingsburg and end on island B.

(d) Find an optimal parade route if the parade is supposed to start in North Kingsburg and end on island A.

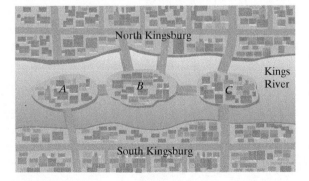

FIGURE 5-60

65. A policeman has to patrol on foot the streets of the subdivision shown in Fig. 5-61. The policeman needs to start his route at the police station, located at X, and end the route at the local coffee shop, located at Y. He needs to cover each block of the subdivision at least once, but he wants to make his route as efficient as possible and duplicate the fewest possible number of blocks.

(a) How many blocks will he have to duplicate in an optimal trip through the subdivision?

(b) Describe an optimal trip through the subdivision. Label the edges 1, 2, 3, and so on in the order the policeman would travel them.

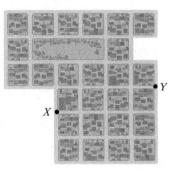

FIGURE 5-61

Exercises 66 through 68 refer to Example 5.23. In this example, the problem is to find an optimal route (i.e., a route with the fewest bridge crossings) for a photographer who needs to cross each of the 11 bridges of Madison County for a photo shoot. The layout of the 11 bridges is shown in Fig. 5-62. You may find it helpful to review Example 5.23 before trying these two exercises.

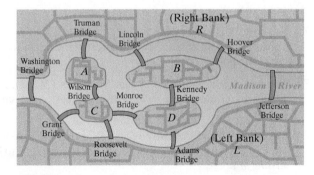

FIGURE 5-62

66. Describe an optimal route for the photographer if the route must start at B and end at L.

67. Describe an optimal route for the photographer if the route must start and end in D and the first bridge crossed must be the Adams Bridge.

68. Describe an optimal route for the photographer if the route must start and end in the same place, the first bridge crossed must be the Adams bridge, and the last bridge crossed must be the Grant Bridge.

69. This exercise comes to you courtesy of Euler himself. Here is the question in Euler's own words, accompanied by the diagram shown in Fig. 5-63.

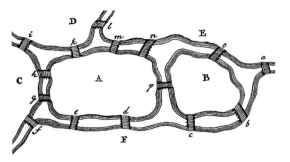

FIGURE 5-63

> *Let us take an example of two islands with four rivers forming the surrounding water. There are fifteen bridges marked a, b, c, d, etc., across the water around the islands and the adjoining rivers. The question is whether a journey can be arranged that will pass over all the bridges but not over any of them more than once.*

What is the answer to Euler's question? If the "journey" is possible, describe it. If it isn't, explain why not.

RUNNING

70. Suppose G is a connected graph with N vertices, all of even degree. Let k denote the number of bridges in G. Find the value(s) of k. Explain your answer.

71. Suppose G is a connected graph with $N - 2$ even vertices and two odd vertices. Let k denote the number of bridges in G. Find all the possible values of k. Explain your answer.

72. Suppose G is a disconnected graph with exactly two odd vertices. Explain why the two odd vertices must be in the same component of the graph.

73. Suppose G is a simple graph with N vertices ($N \geq 2$). Explain why G must have at least two vertices of the same degree.

74. Kissing circuits. When two circuits in a graph have no edges in common but share a common vertex v, they are said to be *kissing at v*.

(a) For the graph shown in Fig. 5-64, find a circuit kissing the circuit A, D, C, A (there is only one), and find two different circuits kissing the circuit A, B, D, A.

(b) Suppose G is a connected graph and every vertex in G is even. Explain why the following statement is true: *If a circuit in G has no kissing circuits, then that circuit must be an Euler circuit.*

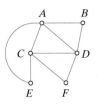

FIGURE 5-64

75. Hierholzer's algorithm. *Hierholzer's algorithm* is another algorithm for finding an Euler circuit in a graph. The basic idea behind Hierholzer's algorithm is to start with an arbitrary circuit and then enlarge it by patching to it a *kissing circuit*, continuing this way and making larger and larger circuits until the circuit cannot be enlarged any farther. (For the definition of kissing circuits, see Exercise 74.) More formally, Hierholzer's algorithm is as follows:

Step 1. Start with an arbitrary circuit C_0.

Step 2. Find a kissing circuit to C_0. If there are no kissing circuits to C_0, then you are finished—C_0 is itself an Euler circuit of the graph [see Exercise 74(b)]. If there is a kissing circuit to C_0, let's call it K_0, and let V denote the vertex at which the two circuits kiss. Go to Step 3.

Step 3. Let C_1 denote the circuit obtained by "patching" K_0 to C_0 at vertex V (i.e., start at V, travel along C_0 back to V, and then travel along K_0 back again to V). Now find a kissing circuit to C_1. (If there are no kissing circuits to C_1, then you are finished—C_1 is your Euler circuit.) If there is a kissing circuit to C_1, let's call it K_1, and let W denote the vertex at which the two circuits kiss. Go to Step 4.

Steps 4, 5, and so on. Continue this way until there are no more kissing circuits available.

(a) Use Hierholzer's algorithm to find an Euler circuit for the graph shown in Fig. 5-65 (this is the graph model for the mail carrier in Example 5.14).

(b) Describe a modification of Hierholzer's algorithm that allows you to find an Euler path in a connected graph having exactly two vertices of odd degree. (*Hint*: A path can also have a kissing circuit.)

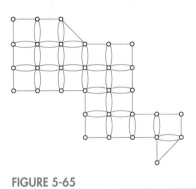

FIGURE 5-65

PROJECTS AND PAPERS

1 Original Sources

Whenever possible, it is instructive to read about a great discovery from the original source. Euler's landmark paper in graph theory with his solution to the Königsberg bridge problem was published in 1736. Luckily, the paper was written in a very readable style and the full English translation can be found in the following article: "The Bridges of Konigsberg," by Leonhard Euler (translated by James Newman), *Scientific American*, vol. 89 (1953), pp. 66–70.

Write a summary/analysis of Euler's original paper. Include (1) a description of how Euler originally tackled the Königsberg bridge problem, (2) a discussion of Euler's general conclusions, and (3) a discussion of Euler's approach toward finding an Euler circuit/path.

2 Computer Representation of Graphs

In many real-life routing problems, we have to deal with very large graphs—a graph could have thousands of vertices and tens of thousands of edges. In these cases algorithms such as Fleury's algorithm (as well as others we will study in later chapters) are done by computer. Unlike humans, computers are not very good at interpreting pictures, so the first step in using computers to perform computations with graphs is to describe the graph in a way the computer can understand it. The two most common ways to do so are by means of matrices.

In this project you are asked to write a short research paper describing the use of matrices to represent graphs. Explain (1) what is a **matrix**, (2) what is the **adjacency matrix** of a graph, and (3) what is the **incidence matrix** of a graph. Illustrate some of the graph concepts from this chapter (degrees of vertices, multiple edges, loops, etc.) in matrix terms. Include plenty of examples. You can find definitions and information on adjacency and incidence matrices of graphs in many graph theory books.

3 The Chinese Postman Problem

A *weighted graph* is a graph in which the edges are assigned positive numbers called weights. The weights represent distances, times, or costs. Finding optimal routes that cover *all* the edges of a *weighted graph* is a problem known as the *Chinese postman problem*. (Chinese postman problems are a generalization of *Euler circuit* problems and, as a general rule, are much harder to solve, but most of the concepts developed in this chapter still apply.)

In this project you are asked to prepare a presentation on the Chinese postman problem for your class.

Some suggestions: (1) Give several examples to illustrate Chinese postman problems and how they differ from corresponding Euler circuit problems. (2) Describe some possible real-life applications of Chinese postman problems. (3) Discuss how to solve a Chinese postman problem in the simplest cases when the weighted graph has no odd vertices or has only two odd vertices (these cases can be solved using techniques learned in this chapter). (4) Give a rough outline of how one might attempt to solve a Chinese postman problem for a graph with four odd vertices.

6 The Mathematics of Touring

Traveling Salesman Problems

The Mars Science Laboratory *Curiosity* is a six-wheeled rover that looks like a dune buggy on steroids and cost NASA $2.5 billion to build and launch. *Curiosity*, loaded with fancy cameras and all kinds of scientific instruments, left Cape Canaveral, Florida, on November 26, 2011 and landed on the Gale crater region of Mars on August 6, 2012. *Curiosity*'s mission is to explore an area around the Gale crater where planetary scientists believe there is a good chance of finding chemical and biological markers that might be evidence of past or present life. To put it simply, *Curiosity* is on the hunt for tiny Martians, dead or alive.

*C*uriosity is built not for speed (it can cover only 600 to 700 feet per day) but rather for endurance and the ability to move over and around obstacles that might appear in its path. In other words, *Curiosity* is a rugged *traveler*, moving slowly but steadily through various locations on the rough and uncharted territory that is the surface of Mars. The less time *Curiosity* has to spend moving around, the more time it has to conduct its experiments, so one of the key aspects of *Curiosity*'s mission is to optimize its travels. This is where the mathematics comes in.

The general problem of optimizing the route of a *traveler* that must visit a specified set of *locations* is known as the *traveling salesman problem* (TSP). This name is misleading, and the typical *traveling salesman problem* has nothing to do with a traveling salesperson—the name applies to many important real-life problems, including the routing of a $2.5- billion roving laboratory on the surface of Mars.

This chapter starts with a general description of what constitutes a TSP, followed by several real-life examples of TSPs (Section 6.1). In Section 6.2 we introduce and discuss the key mathematical concepts that are used to model a TSP (*Hamilton circuits*, *Hamilton paths*, and *complete graphs*). In Sections 6.3, 6.4, and 6.5, we introduce four different algorithms for solving TSPs: the *brute-force*, *nearest-neighbor*, *repetitive nearest-neighbor*, and *cheapest-link* algorithms, and use these algorithms to "solve" the TSPs introduced in Section 6.1. In these sections we also discuss the pros and cons of the various algorithms and introduce the concepts of *inefficient* and *approximate* algorithms.

Flyby view of the Gale Crater, Mars. The interior of the black oval region is the intended playground for *Curiosity*'s exploits.

175

6.1 What Is a Traveling Salesman Problem?

The term *traveling salesman problem* (TSP) is catchy but a bit misleading, since most of the time the problems that fall under this heading have nothing to do with salespeople living out of a suitcase. The expression "traveling salesman" has traditionally been used as a convenient metaphor for many different real-life problems that share a common mathematical structure.

The three elements common to all TSPs (from now on we simply refer to any traveling salesman problem as a TSP) are the following:

- **A traveler.** The traveler could be a person (or a group), an object (a bus, a truck, an unmanned rover, etc.); it could even be a bee.

- **A set of sites.** These are the places or locations the traveler must visit. We will use N to denote the number of sites.

- **A set of costs.** These are positive numbers associated with the expense of traveling from a site to another site. Here the "cost" variable is not restricted to just *monetary* cost—it can also represent *distance* traveled or *time* spent on travel.

A *solution* to a TSP is a "trip" that starts and ends at a site and visits all the other sites once (but only once). We call such a trip a **tour**. An *optimal solution* (**optimal tour**) is a tour of minimal *total cost*. (Notice that we used *a tour* rather than *the tour*—in general a TSP has more than one optimal solution.)

Let's now look at some examples that should help clarify the types of problems we call TSPs. We will not solve any of these TSPs in this section, but we will discuss solutions in later sections.

EXAMPLE 6.1 A REAL TRAVELING SALESMAN'S TSP

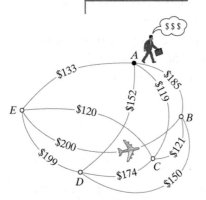

FIGURE 6-1 Cost of travel between cities.

Willy "the Traveler" is a traveling salesman who spends a lot of time on the road calling on customers. He is planning his next business trip, where he will visit customers in five cities we will call A, B, C, D, and E for short ($N = 5$). Since A is Willy's hometown, he needs to start and end his trip at A.

The graph in Fig. 6-1 shows the *cost* (in dollars) of a one-way ticket between any pair of cities (for simplicity we are assuming the cost of a one-way ticket is the same regardless of the direction of travel—something that is not always true in the crazy world of modern airline ticket prices). Like most people, Willy hates to waste money, so among the many possible ways he can organize the sales tour Willy wants to find the *cheapest* (i.e., an *optimal tour*). We will see the solution to Willy's TSP in Section 6.3, but if you want to give it a try on your own now, please feel free to do so.

EXAMPLE 6.2 THE INTERPLANETARY MISSION TSP

It is the year 2050. An unmanned mission to explore the outer planetary moons in our solar system is about to be launched from Earth. The mission is scheduled to visit Callisto, Ganymede, Io, Mimas, and Titan (the first three are moons of Jupiter; the last two of Saturn), collect rock samples at each, and then return to Earth with the loot. The graph in Fig. 6-2 shows the time (in years) required for exploration and travel between any two moons, as well as between Earth and any moon.

This is a long mission, and one of the obvious goals of the mission is to complete it in the least time. In this TSP, the *traveler* is the expedition spaceship, the *sites* are the moons plus the starting and ending site Earth ($N = 6$), and the *cost variable* is time. As in Example 6.1, the goal is to find an optimal tour. We will solve the interplanetary moons TSP in Sections 6.3, 6.4, and 6.5.

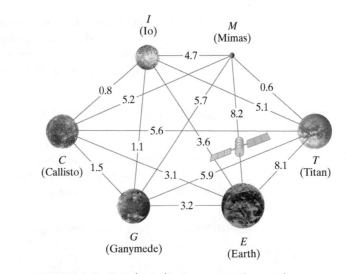

FIGURE 6-2 Travel time between moons (in years).

EXAMPLE 6.3 THE *CURIOSITY* TSP

The story of the Mars Science Laboratory nicknamed *Curiosity* was introduced in the chapter opener. *Curiosity* is a six-wheeled $2.5-billion rover loaded with cameras and instruments that roams around a region of Mars known as the Gale crater, collecting rocks and doing chemical and biological assays of the soil. The primary mission objective is to look for evidence of the existence of life (past or present) on Martian soil. The mission is expected to last approximately one Martian year (23 months), and *Curiosity* is a slow traveler (about 660 feet a day), so efficient planning of its travels is a critical part of the mission. The specific details of where *Curiosity* is to roam were not available at the time of the writing of this example, so the details that follow are a fictional but realistic version of how the mission might evolve.

Figure 6-3(a) is a graph showing seven locations around the Gale crater (called G_1 through G_7) that *Curiosity* is going to visit, with G_1 being the landing site. The numbers on each edge represent travel distances in meters. [To make some of these distances meaningful, consider the fact that *Curiosity* can cover only about 200 m a day, so the trek from say G_2 to G_5 (8000 m) would take roughly 40 days.] Note that in the graph the edges are not drawn to scale—as in any graph, the positioning of the vertices is irrelevant and the only data that are relevant in this case are the numbers (distances) associated with each edge. In spite of a conscious effort to render the graph as clear and readable as possible, it's hard to get around the fact that there are a lot of numbers in the picture and things get pretty crowded. The distance chart in Fig. 6-3(b) provides exactly the same information as the graph in Fig. 6-3(a) but is a little easier to work with. [For TSPs with more than six sites ($N > 6$), a chart is generally preferable to a graph.]

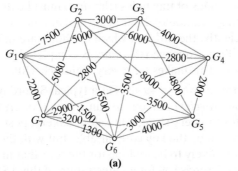

	G_1	G_2	G_3	G_4	G_5	G_6	G_7
G_1	*	7500	5000	2800	3500	1500	2200
G_2	7500	*	3000	6000	8000	6500	5000
G_3	5000	3000	*	4000	4800	3500	2800
G_4	2800	6000	4000	*	2000	3000	2900
G_5	3500	8000	4800	2000	*	4000	3200
G_6	1500	6500	3500	3000	4000	*	1300
G_7	2200	5000	2800	2900	3200	1300	*

(a)   (b)

FIGURE 6-3 Distance between locations (in meters) for the *Curiosity* TSP.

Given the harsh conditions on Mars, *Curiosity*'s tour will be long and full of risks. As one might imagine, the goal is to find a tour that minimizes distance and thus takes the least amount of travel time. In this TSP, *Curiosity* is the traveler, $N = 7$, and the cost variable is distance. We will solve the *Curiosity* TSP in Section 6.5.

EXAMPLE 6.4   THE CONCERT TOUR TSP

The indie rock band Luna Park is planning a concert tour. The 10 cities booked for the tour (including the band's home base *A*) and the distances between them are given in the mileage chart shown in Fig. 6-4. (Note that in this example we made no attempt to display the distances in a graph—to say the least, it would be messy.)

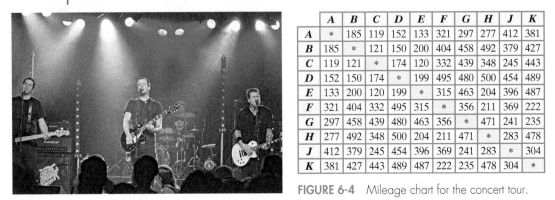

	A	*B*	*C*	*D*	*E*	*F*	*G*	*H*	*J*	*K*
A	*	185	119	152	133	321	297	277	412	381
B	185	*	121	150	200	404	458	492	379	427
C	119	121	*	174	120	332	439	348	245	443
D	152	150	174	*	199	495	480	500	454	489
E	133	200	120	199	*	315	463	204	396	487
F	321	404	332	495	315	*	356	211	369	222
G	297	458	439	480	463	356	*	471	241	235
H	277	492	348	500	204	211	471	*	283	478
J	412	379	245	454	396	369	241	283	*	304
K	381	427	443	489	487	222	235	478	304	*

FIGURE 6-4   Mileage chart for the concert tour.

The goal is to find the *shortest* (i.e., optimal) concert tour. In this TSP the *traveler* is the rock band (and their entourage), the *sites* are the cities in the concert tour ($N = 10$), and the *cost variable* is distance traveled. We will discuss and partially solve the concert tour TSP in Section 6.4.

Beyond the TSPs introduced in Examples 6.1 through 6.4 (we will follow through on these later in the chapter), the following is a short list of other real-world applications where TSPs arise:

- **School buses.** A school bus (the *traveler*) picks up children in the morning and drops them off at the end of the day at designated stops (the *sites*). On a typical rural school bus route there may be 20 to 30 such stops. With school buses, total time on the bus is always the most important variable (students have to get to school on time), and there is a known time of travel (the *cost*) between any two bus stops. Since children must be picked up at every bus stop, a *tour* of all the sites (starting and ending at the school) is required. Since the bus repeats its route every day during the school year, finding an *optimal tour* is crucial.

- **Circuit boards.** In the process of fabricating integrated-circuit boards, tens of thousands of tiny holes (the *sites*) must be drilled in each board. This is done by using a stationary laser beam and moving the board (the *traveler*). To do this efficiently, the order in which the holes are drilled should be such that the entire drilling sequence (the *tour*) is completed in the least amount of time (*optimal cost*). This makes for a very high-tech TSP.

- **Errands around town.** On a typical Saturday morning, an average Joe or Jane (the *traveler*) sets out to run a bunch of errands around town, visiting various sites (grocery store, hair salon, bakery, post office). When gas was cheap, *time* used to be the key *cost* variable, but with the cost of gas these days, people are more likely to be looking for the tour that minimizes the total *distance* traveled (see Exercise 59 for an illustration of this TSP).

- **Bees do it.** In 2010, scientists at the University of London studying the travel patterns of foraging bumblebees as they search for their food source (flower nectar) made a surprising discovery: The bees fly from flower to flower not in the order in which they originally discover the flowers but in the order that gives the shortest overall route. In other words, the bees are routing their foraging trips by solving a TSP. Scientists still don't understand what methods bumblebees use to solve such complex mathematical problems, but the answer is clearly not by doing numerical calculations—the brain of a bee is the size of a grain of sand. Understanding the shortcuts that allow a humble bumblebee to solve a TSP is important, as it may be possible to program the same shortcuts in modern computer algorithms used to solve large-scale TSPs.

6.2 Hamilton Paths and Circuits

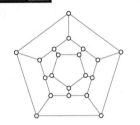

FIGURE 6-5   Hamilton's Icosian game.

In 1857, the Irish mathematician Sir William Rowan Hamilton invented a board game the purpose of which was to find a trip along the edges of the graph shown in Fig. 6-5 that visited each of the vertices once and only once, returning at the end to the starting vertex. (You may want to try your hand at it—the solution is shown on page 205.) Hamilton tried to market the game to make a little money, but he ended up just selling the rights to a London dealer for 25 pounds.

The only reason the story of Hamilton's Icosian game is of any interest to us is that it illustrates an important concept in this chapter—that of traveling along the edges of a connected graph with the purpose of visiting each and every one of the *vertices* once (but only once). This leads to the following two definitions:

- **Hamilton path.** A *Hamilton path* in a connected graph is a path that visits all the vertices of the graph once and only once.

- **Hamilton circuit.** A *Hamilton circuit* in a connected graph is a circuit that visits all the vertices of the graph once and only once.

In spite of the similarities in the definitions, Hamilton paths and circuits are very different from Euler paths and circuits and the two should not be confused. With Hamilton the name of the game is to visit all the *vertices* of the graph once; with Euler the name of the game is to pass through all the *edges* of the graph once.

EXAMPLE 6.5   GRAPHS WITHOUT HAMILTON CIRCUITS

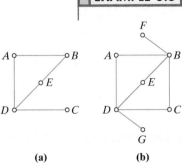

(a)   **(b)**

FIGURE 6-6

Figure 6.6 shows two graphs. The graph in Fig. 6.6(a) has no Hamilton circuits because once you visit *C* you are stuck there. On the other hand, the graph has several Hamilton paths. One of them is *C*, *D*, *E*, *B*, *A*; another one is *C*, *D*, *A*, *B*, *E*. We can *reverse* those two paths and get two more: *A*, *B*, *E*, *D*, *C* and *E*, *B*, *A*, *D*, *C*. Clearly, the Hamilton path has to start or end at *C*, so the four Hamilton paths listed above are the only ones possible. Note that the graph has two odd vertices, so from Euler's theorem for paths (page 153) we know that it has Euler paths as well.

The graph in Fig. 6.6(b) has no Hamilton circuits because once you visit *F* (or *G*) you are stuck there. Nor does the graph have Hamilton paths: The path has to start at either *F* or *G* and end at the other one, and there is no way to visit the other five vertices without going through some vertices more than once. Note that this graph also has two odd vertices, so we know that it has an Euler path.

EXAMPLE 6.6 LISTING HAMILTON CIRCUITS AND PATHS

The graph in Fig. 6.7(a) has no Euler circuits or paths (it has four odd vertices) but has lots of Hamilton circuits. We are going to try to list them all. To organize ourselves we will list the Hamilton circuits using A as the starting and ending point of the circuit. We'll start by going clockwise around the outside square and taking the "detour" to visit E at different times in the trip. This gives the following four Hamilton circuits: (1) A, B, C, D, E, A; (2) A, B, C, E, D, A; (3) A, B, E, C, D, A; and (4) A, E, B, C, D, A. [Figure 6-7(b) illustrates circuit (1) A, B, C, D, E, A]. We can also go around the outside square counterclockwise and get four more Hamilton circuits: (5) A, D, C, B, E, A; (6) A, D, C, E, B, A; (7) A, D, E, C, B, A; and (8) A, E, D, C, B, A. Notice that these last four are reversals of the first four.

What about Hamilton circuits that start at a different vertex—say for example B? Fortunately, we won't have to worry about finding more Hamilton circuits by changing the starting vertex. Any Hamilton circuit that starts and ends at B can be reinterpreted as a Hamilton circuit that starts and ends at A (or any other vertex, for that matter). For example, the circuit B, C, D, E, A, B is just the circuit A, B, C, D, E, A written in a different way [Fig. 6-7(b)]. In other words, a Hamilton circuit is defined by the ordering of the vertices and is independent of which vertex is used as the starting and ending point. This helps a great deal—*once we are sure that we listed all the Hamilton circuits that start and end at A, we know that we have listed all of them!* We will use this observation repeatedly in the next section.

In general, a graph has many more Hamilton paths than circuits. For one thing, each Hamilton circuit can be "broken" into a Hamilton path by deleting one of the edges of the circuit. For example, we can take the Hamilton circuit A, B, C, D, E, A shown in Fig. 6-7(b) and delete EA. This gives the Hamilton path A, B, C, D, E shown in Fig. 6-7(c). We can delete any other edge as well. If we delete CD from the Hamilton circuit A, B, C, D, E, A, we get the Hamilton path D, E, A, B, C [you can see this best if you look again at Fig. 6-7(b) and pretend the edge CD is gone]. You can do this with any of the eight Hamilton circuits of the graph—delete one of its edges and create a Hamilton path. This generates lots of Hamilton paths, so we will not list them all. On top of that, a graph can have Hamilton paths that are not "broken" Hamilton circuits. Figure 6-7(d) shows the Hamilton path A, B, E, D, C. This is not a path we would get from a Hamilton circuit—if it were we would be able to close it into a circuit, but to get from C back to A we would have to go through E once again. There are eight different Hamilton paths that do not come from Hamilton circuits, and we leave it to the reader to find the other seven (Exercise 9).

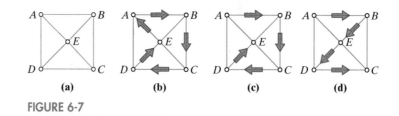

(a)   **(b)**   **(c)**   **(d)**

FIGURE 6-7

The following is a recap of the key points we should take away from Examples 6.5 and 6.6:

- Some graphs have neither Hamilton paths nor Hamilton circuits [see Fig. 6-6 (b)].
- Some graphs have Hamilton paths but no Hamilton circuits [see Fig. 6-6(a)].
- Any graph that has Hamilton circuits will automatically have Hamilton paths because you can always "break" a Hamilton circuit into a Hamilton path by deleting one of the edges of the circuit [see Figs. 6-7(b) and (c)].
- A graph can have Hamilton paths that do not come from a "broken" Hamilton circuit [see Fig. 6-7(d)].

- A Hamilton circuit or path can be reversed (i.e., traveled in the opposite direction). This gives a different Hamilton circuit or path. (Reversing the Hamilton circuit A, B, C, D, E, A gives the Hamilton circuit A, E, D, C, B, A.)
- The same Hamilton circuit can be written in many different ways by changing the chosen starting vertex. [A, B, C, D, E, A and B, C, D, E, A, B are two different descriptions of the Hamilton circuit in Fig. 6-7(b).]

Complete Graphs

A simple graph (i.e., no loops or multiple edges) in which the vertices are completely interconnected (every vertex is connected to every other vertex) is called a **complete graph**. Complete graphs are denoted by the symbol K_N, where N is the number of vertices. Figure 6-8 shows the complete graphs for $N = 3, 4, 5,$ and 6.

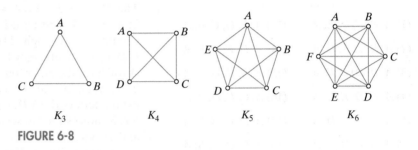

K_3 K_4 K_5 K_6

FIGURE 6-8

Listed below are four key properties of K_N:

1. The *degree* of every vertex in K_N is $N - 1$.
2. The number of *edges* in K_N is $\frac{N(N-1)}{2}$.
3. The number of *Hamilton paths* in K_N is $N! = 1 \times 2 \times 3 \times \cdots \times N$.
4. The number of *Hamilton circuits* in K_N is $(N-1)! = 1 \times 2 \times 3 \times \cdots \times (N-1)$.

Property (1) follows from the definition of K_N: since every vertex is adjacent to each of the other $N - 1$ vertices, the degree of each vertex is $N - 1$. Property (2) follows from property (1) and Euler's sum of degrees theorem (page 153): Since each vertex has degree $N - 1$, the sum of all the degrees is $N(N - 1)$ and the number of edges is $\frac{N(N-1)}{2}$. Properties (3) and (4) require a little more detailed explanation, so we will start by exploring in some detail the Hamilton circuits and paths in K_4 and K_5.

EXAMPLE 6.7 | HAMILTON CIRCUITS AND PATHS IN K_4

The six Hamilton circuits in K_4 are shown in Fig. 6-9. Listed using A as the starting and ending vertex they are: (a) A, B, C, D, A; (b) A, D, B, C, A; (c) A, B, D, C, A; and their respective reversals (d) A, D, C, B, A; (e) A, C, B, D, A; (f) A, C, D, B, A.

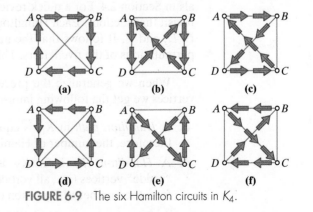

(a)   (b)   (c)

(d)   (e)   (f)

FIGURE 6-9 The six Hamilton circuits in K_4.

How do we know that Fig. 6-9 shows all possible Hamilton circuits? In a complete graph you can go from any vertex to any other vertex. Starting at A one can go to either B, C, or D; from there to either of the other two, from there to the only one left, and finally come back to A. This gives us $3 \times 2 \times 1 = 6$ different possibilities.

Each of the six Hamilton circuits can be broken into four different Hamilton paths (by deleting one of the edges). For example, the circuit in Fig. 6-9(a) gives us the following four Hamilton paths: (1) A, B, C, D; (2) B, C, D, A; (3) C, D, A, B; and (4) D, A, B, C. All in all, we get $6 \times 4 = 24$ Hamilton paths. Since the graph is complete, any Hamilton path can be closed into a Hamilton circuit (just join the starting and ending vertices of the path). It follows that there are no other possible Hamilton paths—just the 24 obtained from Hamilton circuits.

EXAMPLE 6.8   HAMILTON CIRCUITS AND PATHS IN K_5

(1) A, B, C, D, E, A	(13) A, E, D, C, B, A
(2) A, B, C, E, D, A	(14) A, D, E, C, B, A
(3) A, B, D, C, E, A	(15) A, E, C, D, B, A
(4) A, B, D, E, C, A	(16) A, C, E, D, B, A
(5) A, B, E, C, D, A	(17) A, D, C, E, B, A
(6) A, B, E, D, C, A	(18) A, C, D, E, B, A
(7) A, C, B, D, E, A	(19) A, E, D, B, C, A
(8) A, C, B, E, D, A	(20) A, D, E, B, C, A
(9) A, C, D, B, E, A	(21) A, E, B, D, C, A
(10) A, C, E, B, D, A	(22) A, D, B, E, C, A
(11) A, D, B, C, E, A	(23) A, E, C, B, D, A
(12) A, D, C, B, E, A	(24) A, E, B, C, D, A

■ **TABLE 6-1**   The 24 Hamilton circuits in K_5

The $4! = 1 \times 2 \times 3 \times 4 = 24$ Hamilton circuits in K_5 are shown in Table 6-1, written using A as the starting and ending vertex. Circuits (13) through (24) are the reversals of circuits (1) through (12), respectively. Any Hamilton circuit that starts and ends with A will have the other four "inside" vertices (B, C, D, and E) listed in between in some order. There are $4 \times 3 \times 2 \times 1 = 24$ ways to list the letters B, C, D, and E in order: 4 choices for the first letter, 3 choices for the second letter, 2 choices for the third letter, and a single choice for the last letter. This explains why Table 6-1 is a complete list of all the possible Hamilton circuits in K_5.

There are $24 \times 5 = 120$ Hamilton paths in K_5. For obvious reasons, we are not going to list them, but by now we should know how to generate them: Take any of the 24 Hamilton circuits and break it up by deleting one of its five edges. Figure 6-10 shows three of the 120 possible Hamilton paths: Fig. 6-10(a) is obtained by deleting edge DA from circuit (2) on Table 6-1, and Fig. 6-10(b) is obtained by deleting edge BC from circuit (11). We leave it as an exercise for the reader to figure out how the Hamilton path in Fig. 6-10(c) comes about.

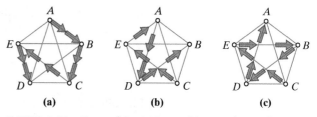

(a)   **(b)**   **(c)**

FIGURE 6-10   Three of the 120 possible Hamilton paths in K_5.

Another way to count the number of Hamilton paths in K_5 is to think in terms of *permutations*. (We first introduced permutations and their connection to factorials in Section 2.4. For a quick review of these concepts the reader is encouraged to revisit that section.) Each Hamilton path in K_5 is a permutation of the letters A, B, C, D, and E. It follows that the number of Hamilton paths equals the number of permutations of the five letters. This number is $5! = 120$.

When we generalize the preceding observations to a complete graph with N vertices we get the following improved version of properties (3) and (4):

3. A *Hamilton path* in K_N is equivalent to a *permutation of the N vertices*, and, therefore, the number of Hamilton paths is $N!$

4. A *Hamilton circuit* in K_N is equivalent to a permutation of the $N - 1$ "inside" vertices (i.e., all vertices except the starting/ending vertex), and, therefore, the number of Hamilton circuits is $(N - 1)!$

Table 6-2 shows the number of Hamilton circuits in K_N for $N = 3$ through 12. The numbers get big fast: K_{10} has 362,800 Hamilton circuits; K_{11} has over 3.6 million; K_{12} has close to 40 million. To understand the implications of how fast these numbers grow, imagine that you want to make a list of all the Hamilton circuits in K_N (like we did in Table 6-1 for K_5). Suppose you work really fast and can write down a Hamilton circuit each second and that you are superhuman and can do this 24 hours a day, 7 days a week. It would then take you over four days to write down all the Hamilton circuits in K_{10}, over a month to write down all the Hamilton circuits in K_{11}, and well over a year to write down all the Hamilton circuits in K_{12}.

A computer, of course, can do the job a lot faster than even the fastest human. Let's say, for the sake of argument, that you have unlimited access to SUPERHERO, the fastest computer on the planet and that SUPERHERO can generate one *quadrillion* (i.e., a million billion) Hamilton circuits per second. SUPERHERO could crank out the Hamilton circuits of K_{12} in a matter of nanoseconds. Problem solved! Not so fast. Let's up the ante a little and try to use SUPERHERO to generate the Hamilton circuits for K_{25}. Surprise! It would take SUPERHERO 20 years to do it! Table 6-3 shows how long it would take for even the world's fastest supercomputer to generate the Hamilton circuits in K_N for values of N ranging from 21 to 30. The numbers are beyond comprehension, and the implications will become clear in the next section.

N	Hamilton circuits
3	2
4	6
5	24
6	120
7	720
8	5040
9	40,320
10	362,880
11	3,628,800
12	39,916,800

■ TABLE 6-2

N	SUPERHERO computation time
21	40 minutes
22	14 hours
23	13 days
24	10 months
25	20 years
26	500 years
27	13,000 years
28	350,000 years
29	9.7 million years
30	280 million years

■ TABLE 6-3

6.3 The Brute-Force Algorithm

We start this section with the TSP introduced in Example 6.1.

EXAMPLE 6.9 THE REAL TRAVELING SALESMAN'S TSP SOLVED

In Example 6.1 we left Willy the traveling salesman hanging. What Willy would like from us, most of all, is to help him find the optimal (in this case *cheapest*) tour of the five cities in his sales territory. The cost of travel between any two cities is shown in Fig. 6.11 (this is exactly the same figure as Fig. 6-1). Notice that the underlying graph in Fig. 6-11 is just a fancy version of K_5 (five vertices each adjacent to the other four) with numbers associated with each of the 10 edges. In this TSP the numbers represent the cost of travel (in either direction) along that edge.

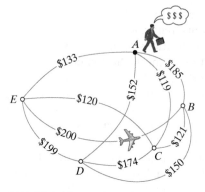

FIGURE 6-11

Table 6-4 lists the 24 possible tours that Willy could potentially take. The first and third columns of Table 6-4 gives the 24 different Hamilton circuits in K_5. This part is an exact copy of Table 6-1. Notice once again that the list is organized so that each tour in the third column is the reversed version of the corresponding tour in the first column. Listing the tours this way saves a lot of work because the cost of a tour is the same regardless of the direction of travel: Once we know the cost of a tour we know the cost of its reversal. (Please note that this is true only because we made the assumption that the cost of travel between two cities is the same regardless of the direction of travel. When the costs vary with the direction of travel then the shortcut won't work.) The middle column shows the total cost of each tour and the calculation that leads to it (for each tour just add the costs of the edges that make the tour).

Tour	Total cost	Tour
(1) A, B, C, D, E, A	$185 + 121 + 174 + 199 + 133 = 812$	(13) A, E, D, C, B, A
(2) A, B, C, E, D, A	$185 + 121 + 120 + 199 + 152 = 777$	(14) A, D, E, C, B, A
(3) A, B, D, C, E, A	$185 + 150 + 174 + 120 + 133 = 762$	(15) A, E, C, D, B, A
(4) A, B, D, E, C, A	$185 + 150 + 199 + 120 + 119 = 773$	(16) A, C, E, D, B, A
(5) A, B, E, C, D, A	$185 + 200 + 120 + 174 + 152 = 831$	(17) A, D, C, E, B, A
(6) A, B, E, D, C, A	$185 + 200 + 199 + 174 + 119 = 877$	(18) A, C, D, E, B, A
(7) A, C, B, D, E, A	$119 + 121 + 150 + 199 + 133 = 722$	(19) A, E, D, B, C, A
(8) A, C, B, E, D, A	$119 + 121 + 200 + 199 + 152 = 791$	(20) A, D, E, B, C, A
(9) A, C, D, B, E, A	$119 + 174 + 150 + 200 + 133 = 776$	(21) A, E, B, D, C, A
(10) A, C, E, B, D, A	$119 + 120 + 200 + 150 + 152 = 741$	(22) A, D, B, E, C, A
(11) A, D, B, C, E, A	$152 + 150 + 121 + 120 + 133 = 676$	(23) A, E, C, B, D, A
(12) A, D, C, B, E, A	$152 + 174 + 121 + 200 + 133 = 780$	(24) A, E, B, C, D, A

■ **TABLE 6-4**   The 24 possible tours in Example 6-9 and their costs, with the optimal tour(s), highlighted

Once we have the complete list of tours and their respective costs, we just choose the optimal tour(s). In this case, the optimal tours are (11) and its reversal (23). The cost is $676. Figure 6-12 shows both optimal tours.

A final note on Willy's sales trip: Was doing all this work worth it? In this case, yes. If Willy just chose the order of the cities at random, the worst-case scenario would be tour (6) or (18), costing $877. With just a little effort we found an optimal tour costing $676—a potential savings of $201.

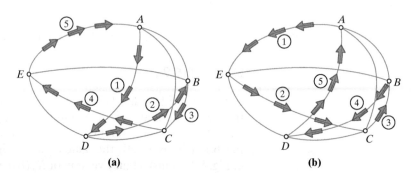

FIGURE 6-12   The two optimal tours for Willy's trip. (Total travel cost = $676.)

Before moving on to other TSP examples, let's connect a few dots. Our general assumption for a TSP is that there is a way to get from any location to any other location. If we think of the locations as the vertices of a graph, this means that every TSP has an underlying graph that is a complete graph K_N. In addition to the underlying graph, there are costs associated with each edge. A graph that has numbers associated with its edges is called a **weighted graph**, and the numbers are called **weights**. A tour in a TSP translates to a Hamilton circuit in the underlying graph, and an optimal tour translates into a Hamilton circuit of least total weight.

In short, the TSP is the concrete, real-life problem and its reformulation in terms of Hamilton circuits in a complete weighted graph is the mathematical model that represents the problem. In this model, *locations are vertices, costs are weights, tours are Hamilton circuits,* and *optimal tours are Hamilton circuits of least total weight.*

We can describe now the approach we used in Example 6.9 to solve Willy's TSP in a somewhat more formal language: We made a list of all possible Hamilton circuits (first and third columns of Table 6-4), calculated the total weight of each (middle column of Table 6-4), and picked the circuits with least total weight. This strategy is formally known as the **brute-force algorithm**.

┌─■THE BRUTE-FORCE ALGORITHM ─────────────────────────

- **Step 1.** Make a list of all the Hamilton circuits of the underlying graph K_N.
- **Step 2.** Calculate the total weight of each Hamilton circuit.
- **Step 3.** Choose a Hamilton circuit with least total weight.

> **❝** In theory, there is no difference between theory and practice. In practice, there is. **❞**
>
> *– Yogi Berra*

The brute-force algorithm is based on a simple idea—when you have a finite number of options, try them all and you will always be able to determine which one is the best. In theory, we should be able to use the brute-force algorithm to solve any TSP. In practice, we can solve only small TSPs this way. It's easy to say "make a list of all the Hamilton circuits . . ."— doing it is something else. Just take a look again at Table 6-3. It would take the world's fastest supercomputer 20 years to do it with K_{25}; 280 millions years to do it with K_{30}. And keep in mind that in real-world applications a TSP with $N = 30$ locations is considered small. In some cases, a TSP might involve 50 or even 100 locations.

The brute-force algorithm is a classic example of what is formally known as an **inefficient algorithm**—an algorithm for which the computational effort needed to carry out the steps of the algorithm grows disproportionately with the size of the problem. The trouble with inefficient algorithms is that they can only be used to solve small problems and, therefore, have limited practical use. Even the world's fastest computer would be of little use when trying to solve a TSP with $N = 25$ locations using the brute-force algorithm.

Before we conclude this section we tackle one more example of how we might use the brute-force algorithm to solve a TSP.

EXAMPLE 6.10   THE INTERPLANETARY MISSION TSP SOLVED

We are revisiting the TSP introduced in Example 6-2. In this TSP the goal is to find the *fastest* tour for an interplanetary mission to five of the outer moons in our solar system. Moreover, the tour has to start and end at our home planet, Earth. This makes it a TSP with $N = 6$ vertices. Figure 6-13(a) shows the mission time (in years) for travel between any two moons and between Earth and any moon.

To use the brute-force algorithm we would start with a list of all the possible Hamilton circuits using Earth as the starting and ending vertex. The problem is that this list has $5! = 120$ different Hamilton circuits. That's more work than we care to do, so a full list is out of the question. Imagine now that we get a hint: The first stop in an optimal tour is Callisto. How much help is that? A lot. It means that the optimal tour must be a Hamilton circuit of the form $E, C, *, *, *, *, E$. The $*$'s

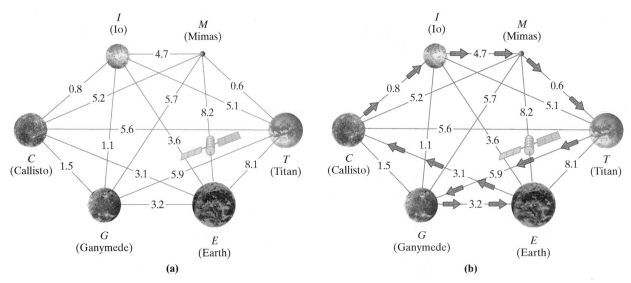

FIGURE 6-13 (a) Graph model for the interplanetary mission TSP. (b) An optimal tour.

are the letters *G*, *I*, *M*, and *T* in some order. Since there are only 4! = 24 possible permutations of these four letters, the brute-force algorithm becomes much more manageable: We make a list of the 24 Hamilton circuits of the form *E*, *C*, *, *, *, *, *E*, find their weights, and pick one (there are several) of least total weight. One of the optimal tours is shown in Fig. 6-13(b). The total length of this tour is 18.3 years. We leave it to the reader to verify the details.

6.4 The Nearest-Neighbor and Repetitive Nearest-Neighbor Algorithms

In this section we introduce a new method for solving TSPs called the *nearest-neighbor algorithm* (NNA). We will illustrate the basic idea of the nearest-neighbor algorithm using the interplanetary mission TSP once again. We found an optimal tour for this TSP in Example 6.10, so the point now is to see how the NNA does it.

EXAMPLE 6.11 THE INTERPLANETARY MISSION TSP
AND THE NEAREST-NEIGHBOR ALGORITHM

Look at the graph in Fig. 6-13(a) once again and imagine planning the mission. Starting from Earth we could choose any of the moons for our first stop. Of all the choices, Callisto makes the most sense because in terms of travel time it is Earth's "nearest neighbor": Among the edges connecting *E* to the other vertices, *EC* is the one with the smallest weight. (Technically speaking we should call *C* the "smallest weight" neighbor, but that sounds a bit strange, so we use *nearest neighbor* as a generic term for the vertex connected by the edge of least weight.)

So we made it to Callisto. Where to next? Following the same logic, we choose to go to Callisto's nearest neighbor Io. From Io we go to Ganymede (the nearest neighbor we have not yet been to), from Ganymede to Mimas, from Mimas to Titan (the last moon left), and finally from Titan the mission comes back to Earth. This tour, called the *nearest-neighbor tour*, is shown in Fig. 6-14. The total length of this tour is 19.4 years, and that's a bit of bad news. In Example 6.10 we found an optimal tour with total length 18.3 years—this tour is more than a year longer.

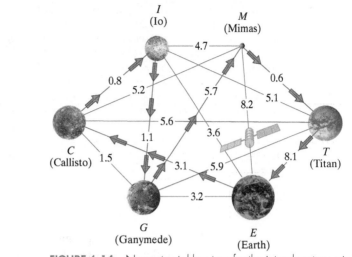

FIGURE 6-14   Nearest-neighbor tour for the interplanetary mission TSP.

Example 6.11 illustrates a common situation when trying to find solutions to TSPs. We can come up with very simple and fast methods for finding "good" tours, but these methods cut corners and don't necessarily produce the "best" (optimal) tour.

Formally, we will use the term **approximate algorithm** to describe any algorithm for solving TSPs that produces a tour, but not necessarily an optimal tour. The *nearest-neighbor* algorithm is an example of an *approximate* algorithm. We will discuss a different approximate algorithm called the *cheapest-link* algorithm in Section 6.5, and in Chapter 8 we will see approximate algorithms for solving a different type of problem (not a TSP).

Obviously, approximate algorithms are important and useful. The question is why? Why do we bother with methods that give *approximate* solutions when our objective is to find an *optimal* solution? The answer is that we are making a tradeoff between the solution and the amount of effort it takes to find it. Like in many walks of life, the choice is between perfection and expediency. If it takes 20 years to find the optimal tour in a TSP with $N = 25$ locations but we can find a *suboptimal* tour (i.e., a tour that is close to optimal) in a matter of minutes, shouldn't we consider the second a better option? Approximate algorithms are the mathematical version of the commonly used strategy of cutting corners for the sake of expediency.

To illustrate the usefulness of the nearest-neighbor algorithm we will now tackle a TSP with $N = 10$ cities.

EXAMPLE 6.12   THE CONCERT TOUR TSP AND THE NNA

In Example 6.4 we were introduced to the indie rock band Luna Park, just about to embark on a 10-city concert tour. Figure 6-15(a) shows the distances (in miles) between any two cities. Because the band members all live at A, the tour needs to start and end at A. The goal is to find the optimal (shortest distance) tour.

This is a TSP with $N = 10$ locations. Notice that we don't see a complete weighted graph, but the mileage chart provides exactly the same information as the graph would (and it does it in a much cleaner way). The only way we know for finding an optimal tour is the brute-force algorithm, and to use brute force would mean making a list of $9! = 362,880$ possible Hamilton circuits. Obviously, we are not about to do that, at least not without help. But, we now know of a quick-and-dirty shortcut—the nearest-neighbor algorithm. Let's try it and see what we get.

To implement the nearest-neighbor algorithm from a chart we use the following strategy: Start with the row labeled A, and look for the smallest number in that row. That number (119) identifies A's nearest neighbor, in this case C. We now go to row C and look for C's nearest neighbor. [Before we do that, it helps to cross out

	A	B	C	D	E	F	G	H	J	K
A	*	185	119	152	133	321	297	277	412	381
B	185	*	121	150	200	404	458	492	379	427
C	119	121	*	174	120	332	439	348	245	443
D	152	150	174	*	199	495	480	500	454	489
E	133	200	120	199	*	315	463	204	396	487
F	321	404	332	495	315	*	356	211	369	222
G	297	458	439	480	463	356	*	471	241	235
H	277	492	348	500	204	211	471	*	283	478
J	412	379	245	454	396	369	241	283	*	304
K	381	427	443	489	487	222	235	478	304	*

(a)

	Ⓐ	B	Ⓒ	Ⓓ	Ⓔ	F	G	H	J	K
A	*	185	119	152	133	321	297	277	412	381
B	185	*	121	150	200	404	458	492	379	427
C	119	121	*	174	120	332	439	348	245	443
D	152	150	174	*	199	495	480	500	454	489
E	133	200	120	199	*	315	463	204	396	487
F	321	404	332	495	315	*	356	211	369	222
G	297	458	439	480	463	356	*	471	241	235
H	277	492	348	500	204	211	471	*	283	478
J	412	379	245	454	396	369	241	283	*	304
K	381	427	443	489	487	222	235	478	304	*

(b)

FIGURE 6-15 (a) Mileage chart for the concert tour TSP. (b) The chart after the first four steps of the NNA (A, C, E, D, . . .).

the column for C (this helps make sure we don't go back to C in the middle of the tour). For similar reasons we also crossed out the A-column.] The smallest number available in row C is 120, and it identifies C's nearest-neighbor E. We now cross out the E-column and go to row E, looking for a nearest-neighbor. The smallest number available in row E is 199, and it identifies E's nearest-neighbor D. We cross out the D-column and continue [Fig. 6-15(b) shows the mileage chart at this point]: From D to its nearest-available neighbor B (150), from B to J (379), from J to G (241), from G to K (235), from K to F (222), from F to the only city left H (211), and finally end the tour by returning to A (277). This is the nearest-neighbor tour: A, C, E, D, B, J, G, K, F, H, A, and it has a total length of 2153 miles.

Example 6.12 clearly illustrates the tradeoff between perfection and expediency. We found a concert tour for the band, and it took only a few minutes, and we did it without the aid of a computer. That's the good news. But how good is the solution we found? More specifically, how much longer is the nearest-neighbor tour found in Example 6.12 than the optimal tour? To answer this question, we would need to know how long the optimal tour is. With the aid of a computer, special software, and a fair amount of effort, I was able to find the answer: The optimal concert tour has a total length of 1914 miles. This information allows us to look back and judge the "goodness" of the solution we found in Example 6.12. We do this by introducing the concept of *relative error*.

- **Relative error of a tour.** Let C denote the total cost of a given tour and *Opt* denote the total cost of the optimal tour. The *relative error* ε of the tour is given by $\varepsilon = \dfrac{C - Opt}{Opt}$.

The best way to think of the relative error is as a *percent* (i.e., the amount of error expressed as a percent of the optimal solution).

We are now ready to pass judgment on the nearest-neighbor tour we found in Example 6.12: The relative error of the tour is $\varepsilon = \dfrac{2153 - 1914}{1914} \approx 0.1249 = 12.49\%$. Is a relative error of 12.49% good or bad? The answer very much depends on the circumstances: When cost is a critical variable—say, for example, the timing of an interplanetary mission—an error of 12.49% is high. When cost is less critical—say, for example, the distance covered by a rock band traveling around in a fancy motor coach—an error of 12.49% might be OK.

The Repetitive Nearest-Neighbor Algorithm

One of the interesting features of the nearest-neighbor algorithm is that the tour it produces depends on the choice of starting vertex. For the same TSP, a change in the choice of starting vertex can produce a different nearest-neighbor tour. (Note that this does not imply that the tours are always different—we might change the starting vertex and still get the same tour.) This observation can help us squeeze better tours from the nearest-neighbor algorithm: Each time we try a different starting vertex there is the chance we might get an improved tour; the more vertices we try, the better our chances. This is the key idea behind a refinement of the nearest-neighbor algorithm known as the *repetitive nearest-neighbor* algorithm. Our next example illustrates how this strategy works.

EXAMPLE 6.13 THE CONCERT TOUR TSP REVISITED

Nearest-Neighbor tour	Total length
(1) $A, C, E, D, B, J, G, K, F, H, A$	2153
(2) $B, C, A, E, D, J, G, K, F, H, B$	2427
(3) $C, A, E, D, B, J, G, K, F, H, C$	2237
(4) $D, B, C, A, E, H, F, K, G, J, D$	2090
(5) $E, C, A, D, B, J, G, K, F, H, E$	2033
(6) $F, H, E, C, A, D, B, J, G, K, F$	2033
(7) $G, K, F, H, E, C, A, D, B, J, G$	2033
(8) $H, E, C, A, D, B, J, G, K, F, H$	2033
(9) $J, G, K, F, H, E, C, A, D, B, J$	2033
(10) $K, F, H, E, C, A, D, B, J, G, K$	2033

■ **TABLE 6-5** Nearest-neighbor tours for every possible starting vertex

In Example 6.12 we used the nearest-neighbor algorithm to find a concert tour for the Luna Park rock band (this is the TSP introduced in Example 6.4). We used A as the starting and ending vertex because the band lives at A, so in some sense we had no choice. The tour we found had a total length of 2153 miles.

We are going to try the same thing again but now will use B as the starting and ending vertex. (Let's disregard for now the fact that the tour really needs to start and end at A. We'll deal with that issue later.) From B we go to its nearest-neighbor C, from C to its nearest-neighbor A, from A to E, and so on. The work is a little tedious, but we can finish the tour in a matter of minutes. We leave the details to the enterprising reader, but the bottom line is that we end up with the tour $B, C, A, E, D, J, G, K, F, H, B$ with a total length of 2427 miles.

We will now repeat this process, using each of the other vertices as the starting/ending vertex and finding the corresponding nearest-neighbor tour. Figuring a couple of minutes per vertex, the process might take about 20 minutes. Table 6-5 summarizes the results. The first column shows the 10 nearest-neighbor tours obtained by running over all possible starting/ending vertices; the second column shows the total length of each tour. We are looking for the best among these. Tours (5) through (10) are all tied for best, each with a total length of 2033 miles. We can take any one of these tours, and get a nice improvement over the original tour we found in Example 6.12.

What about the fact that none of these tours starts and ends at A? That's easy to fix. We can take any of these tours and rewrite them so that they start and end at A. When we do that, regardless of which one we use, we get the tour $A, D, B, J, G, K, F, H, E, C, A$. We call this tour *the repetitive nearest-neighbor tour*. It is not an optimal tour, but an improvement over the nearest-neighbor tour nonetheless. (This tour has a relative error $\varepsilon = \frac{2033 - 1914}{1914} \approx 0.0622 = 6.22\%$.)

We conclude this section with a formal description of the *nearest-neighbor* and *repetitive nearest-neighbor* algorithms.

┌─ ■ **THE NEAREST-NEIGHBOR ALGORITHM** ─────

- **Start:** Start at the designated starting vertex. If there is no designated starting vertex pick any vertex.

- **First step:** From the starting vertex go to its *nearest neighbor* (i.e., the vertex for which the corresponding edge has the smallest weight).

- **Middle steps:** From each vertex go to its *nearest neighbor*, choosing only among *the vertices that haven't been yet visited*. (If there is more than one nearest neighbor choose among them at random.) Keep doing this until all the vertices have been visited.

- **Last step:** From the last vertex return to the starting vertex. The tour that we get is called the **nearest-neighbor** tour.

┌───┐
■THE REPETITIVE NEAREST-NEIGHBOR ALGORITHM

- ■ Let X be any vertex. Find the nearest-neighbor tour with X as the starting vertex, and calculate the cost of this tour.
- ■ Repeat the process with each of the other vertices of the graph as the starting vertex.
- ■ Of the nearest-neighbor tours thus obtained, choose one with least cost. If necessary, rewrite the tour so that it starts at the designated starting vertex. The tour that we get is called the **repetitive nearest-neighbor** tour.
└───┘

6.5 The Cheapest-Link Algorithm

Last, but not least, we will introduce a completely different *approximate* algorithm for solving TSPs called the *cheapest-link algorithm* (CLA). (The term "cheapest link" is used here to mean the same thing as "edge of least cost," and the algorithm could just as well be called the "edge of least cost algorithm," but "cheapest link" sounds a little better.) The idea is to piece together a tour by looking at all the possible *links* (i.e., edges) and always choosing the *cheapest* link available (with a couple of restrictions that we will discuss later). Unlike the nearest-neighbor algorithm, the order in which we piece the tour together has nothing to do with the order in which the vertices will be visited. It sounds complicated, but it's not. We will illustrate the cheapest-link algorithm by revisiting some by now familiar examples, starting with the interplanetary mission TSP (Examples 6.2, 6.10, and 6.11). This is an important example in terms of understanding the inner workings of the cheapest-link algorithm—you are encouraged to read it carefully. It is also long, and doodling along will help you keep up with the details. Paper, a pencil, and a red pen are strongly recommended.

| **EXAMPLE 6.14** | THE INTERPLANETARY MISSION TSP AND THE CLA

The graph in Fig. 6-16(a) is a repeat of Fig. 6-2. The weights of the edges represent the cost (in this case time) of travel between any two locations. We will now show how the cheapest-link algorithm handles this TSP.

- ■ Step 1. We start by scanning the graph in Fig. 6-16(a) looking for the *cheapest link (edge)*. Here the cheapest link is the one connecting Mimas and Titan (0.6 years). [For convenience we'll denote it by *MT* (0.6).] We select that link and indicate that we are doing so by highlighting it in red.
- ■ Step 2. We go back to scanning the graph looking for the *next cheapest link*. We find *CI* (0.8) and proceed to highlight it in red. (Notice that the two red links are not connected, but it doesn't matter at this point.)

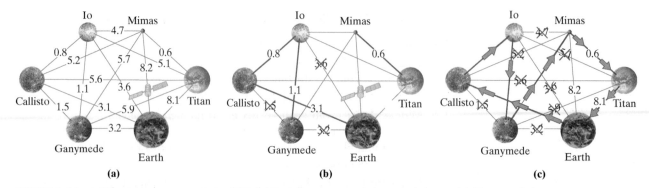

FIGURE 6-16 (a) The interplanetary mission TSP. (b) Partially constructed cheapest-link tour. (c) Cheapest-link tour after completion.

- **Step 3.** Once again, we scan the graph looking for the next cheapest link and find *IG* (1.1). We highlight it in red.

- **Step 4.** The next cheapest link in the graph is *CG* (1.5). We pick up our red pen and are about to highlight the link when we suddenly realize that this is not a good move. A red *CG* means that we would be forming a red circuit *C, I, G, C*. But tours (Hamilton circuits) can't contain partial circuits, so any edge that forms a partial circuit must be ruled out. (For convenience, we call this the *partial-circuit rule*.) So, even though *CG* is the next available cheapest link, we can't choose it because of the partial-circuit rule. We indicate this fact by ✕-ing out *CG* (the ✕ is like a little marker saying "do not travel along this link"). So, we try again. After *CG*, the next cheapest link is *CE* (3.1). No problem here, so we select it and highlight it in red.

- **Step 5.** The next cheapest link in the graph is *EG* (3.2). If we were to highlight *GE* in red we would be forming the partial red circuit *E, G, I, C, E*. Because of the partial-circuit rule, we must ✕-out *EG*. We scan the graph again and find that the next cheapest link is *IE*. If we were to highlight *IE* in red we would have the following problem: *three* red edges (*IE, IG,* and *IC*) meeting at one vertex. This is not possible in a tour, since it would require visiting that vertex more than once. (For convenience, we call this the *three-edge rule*.) So we ✕-out *IE* as well. [If you are doodling along with this narration, your picture at this point should look something like Fig. 6-16(b).] The next four cheapest links in order are *IM* (4.7), *IT* (5.1), *CM* (5.2), and *CT* (5.6). They all have to be ruled out because of the three-edge rule. This leads us to *GM* (5.7). This edge works, so we select it and highlight it in red.

- **Step 6.** Since *N* = 6 this should be the last step. The last step is a little easier than the others—there should be only one way to close the circuit. Looking at the graph we see that *E* and *T* are the two loose ends that need to be connected. We do that by adding the link *ET*. Now we are done.

This is the end of the busywork. We found a Hamilton circuit in the graph and from it we get two different tours, depending on the direction we choose to travel. Going clockwise gives the *cheapest-link tour E, C, I, G, M, T, E* with a total length of 19.4 years. Going counterclockwise gives us the reverse tour.

Notice that for the interplanetary mission TSP, the cheapest-link tour we just found is exactly the same as the nearest-neighbor tour we found in Example 6.11. This is a coincidence, and we should not read too much into it. In general, the cheapest-link tour is different from the nearest-neighbor tour, and there is no superiority of one over the other—sometimes the cheapest-link tour is better, sometimes it's the other way around.

A formal description of the cheapest-link algorithm is given below.

THE CHEAPEST-LINK ALGORITHM

- **Step 1.** Pick the *cheapest link* available. (If there is more than one, randomly pick one among the cheapest links.) Highlight the link in red (or any other color).

- **Step 2.** Pick the next cheapest link available and highlight it.

- **Steps 3, 4, . . ., N − 1.** Continue picking and highlighting the cheapest available link that (a) does not violate the *partial-circuit* rule (i.e., does not close a partial circuit) or (b) does not violate the *three-edge* rule (i.e., does not create three edges meeting at the same vertex).

- **Step N.** Connect the two vertices that close the red circuit. Once we have the Hamilton circuit, we can add a direction of travel (clockwise or counterclockwise). Either one gives us a **cheapest-link tour**.

Our next example illustrates how to implement the cheapest-link algorithm when we have to work from a chart rather than a graph. The main difficulty in this situation is that it is not easy to spot violations of the *partial-circuit* and *three-edge* rules when looking at a chart. A simple way around this difficulty is to create an auxiliary picture of the tour as it is being built, one edge at a time.

EXAMPLE 6.15   THE *CURIOSITY* TSP AND THE CLA

We are finally going to take a look at the *Curiosity* TSP introduced in the chapter opener and described in Example 6.3. The seven locations (G_1 through G_7) that the Mars rover *Curiosity* must visit and the distances (in meters) between pairs of locations are given in Fig. 6-17(a). We will use the cheapest-link algorithm working directly out of the distance chart. All we will need is an additional auxiliary graph that will help us visualize the links as we move through the steps of the algorithm. Figure 6-17(b) shows the auxiliary graph when we start—a blank slate of seven vertices G_1 through G_7 and no edges.

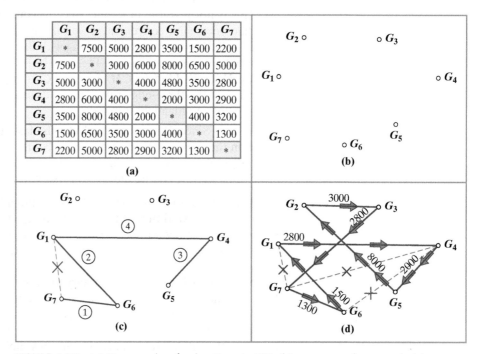

	G_1	G_2	G_3	G_4	G_5	G_6	G_7
G_1	*	7500	5000	2800	3500	1500	2200
G_2	7500	*	3000	6000	8000	6500	5000
G_3	5000	3000	*	4000	4800	3500	2800
G_4	2800	6000	4000	*	2000	3000	2900
G_5	3500	8000	4800	2000	*	4000	3200
G_6	1500	6500	3500	3000	4000	*	1300
G_7	2200	5000	2800	2900	3200	1300	*

(a)

FIGURE 6-17   (a) Distance chart for the *Curiosity* TSP, (b) starting auxiliary graph, (c) auxiliary graph at Step 4, and (d) cheapest-link tour (21,400 m).

- **Step 1.** We scan the distance chart looking for the smallest possible number. (*Note*: In a distance chart the half below the diagonal is the mirror image of the half above the diagonal, so we have to scan only one of the two halves.) The smallest number is 1300, and it belongs to the edge G_6G_7. This is the cheapest link, and we select it. We indicate this by connecting G_6 and G_7 in the auxiliary graph.

- **Step 2.** We scan the distance chart again looking for the next smallest number. The number is 1500, and it belongs to the edge G_1G_6. We select this edge and indicate that we are doing so by connecting G_1 and G_6 in the auxiliary graph.

- **Step 3.** The next smallest number in the chart is 2000, and it belongs to the edge G_4G_5. We select this edge and connect G_4 to G_5 in the auxiliary graph.

- **Step 4.** The next smallest number in the chart is 2200, and it belongs to the edge G_1G_7. When we go to the auxiliary graph we see that we can't select this edge because it would create the circuit G_1, G_7, G_6, G_1—a violation of the partial-circuit rule. We X-out G_1G_7 and scan the chart again, looking for the next smallest number after 2200. Here there is a tie with two entries equal to 2800: G_1G_4 and G_3G_7. We choose randomly one of these, say G_1G_4. This one is OK, and we select it by adding that edge to the auxiliary graph. At this point the auxiliary graph looks like Fig. 6-17(c).

- **Step 5.** We now try G_3G_7, the other edge with a cost of 2800. It works, so we add the edge G_3G_7 to the auxiliary graph.

- **Step 6.** The next smallest number in the chart is 2900, and it belongs to the edge G_4G_7. When we look at the auxiliary graph, we can see that this edge won't work because it would create a violation of the three-edge rule, both at G_4 and at G_7. So, we X-out the edge and look for the next smallest number. There are two entries tied at 3000: G_4G_6 and G_2G_3. Say we try G_4G_6 first. This choice violates both the three-edge and partial-circuit rules, so we X-it out. The second edge with weight 3000 is G_2G_3, and this one works. We select it, and add the edge to the auxiliary graph.

- **Step 7.** This is the last step, so we can go directly to the auxiliary graph. We see that the only way to close the Hamilton circuit is to add the edge G_2G_5.

We now have a Hamilton circuit. A *cheapest-link tour* is shown in Fig. 6-17(d): $G_1, G_4, G_5, G_2, G_3, G_7, G_6, G_1$. The total length is 21,400 m. (Traveling in the opposite direction gives the other cheapest-link tour).

How good is the cheapest-link tour we found in Example 6.15? At this point we have nothing to compare it with, so we just don't know. We will be able to answer the question in our next (and last) example.

EXAMPLE 6.16 THE *CURIOSITY* TSP AND THE NNA

We know only one way to find the optimal tour for the *Curiosity* TSP—use the brute-force algorithm, but this would require us to create a list with $6! = 720$ Hamilton circuits. That's a lot of circuits to check out by hand.

A less ambitious approach is to try the nearest-neighbor algorithm and hope we get a good approximate tour. We leave the details as an exercise for the reader, but here it is: the *nearest-neighbor tour* (starting at G_1) is $G_1, G_6, G_7, G_3, G_2, G_4, G_5, G_1$ [Fig. 6-18(b)]. The total length of this tour is 20,100 m. This is a respectable improvement over the cheapest-link tour found in Example 6.15.

	G_1	G_2	G_3	G_4	G_5	G_6	G_7
G_1	*	7500	5000	2800	3500	1500	2200
G_2	7500	*	3000	6000	8000	6500	5000
G_3	5000	3000	*	4000	4800	3500	2800
G_4	2800	6000	4000	*	2000	3000	2900
G_5	3500	8000	4800	2000	*	4000	3200
G_6	1500	6500	3500	3000	4000	*	1300
G_7	2200	5000	2800	2900	3200	1300	*

(a)

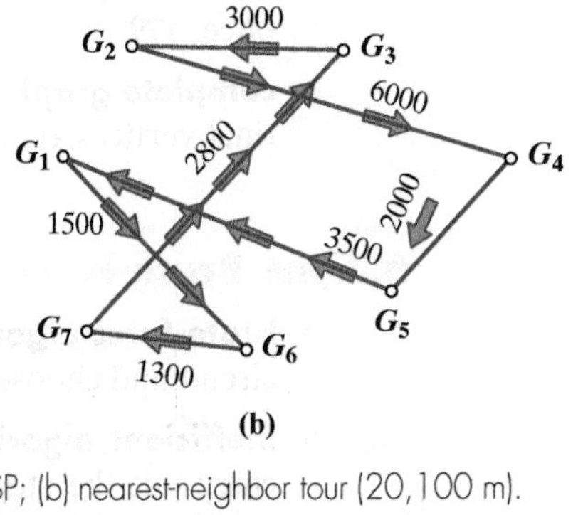

(b)

FIGURE 6-18 (a) Distance chart for the *Curiosity* TSP; (b) nearest-neighbor tour (20,100 m).

Out of curiosity, we decided to find, once and for all, an *optimal tour* for *Curiosity*. Using a computer and the brute-force algorithm we checked all 720 Hamilton circuits and came up with a surprise: There are several optimal tours, and one of them happens to be the nearest-neighbor tour shown in Fig. 6-18(b). In other words, in the case of the *Curiosity* TSP the nearest-neighbor algorithm (in a sense the most basic of all TSP algorithms) produced optimal solution—a nice (and lucky) turn of events. Too bad we can't count on this happening on a consistent basis. Well, maybe next chapter.

Conclusion

TSP is the acronym for *traveling salesman problem*. TSPs are some of the most important and perplexing problems in modern mathematics. Important because there is a wide range of real-life applications that can be modeled by TSPs, and perplexing because nobody knows a general algorithm for finding optimal solutions to TSPs that works no matter how large the number of vertices is. It's likely that an *optimal and efficient general algorithm for solving TSPs is a mathematical impossibility* along the lines of Arrow's Impossibility Theorem in Chapter 1, but unlike Arrow, nobody has been able to prove this as a mathematical fact. Great fame and fortune await the first person that can do this.

Alternatively, there are many good *approximate algorithms* that can produce *suboptimal* (i.e., approximate) solutions to TSPs even when the number of vertices is very large. These algorithms represent a departure from the traditional notion that a math problem can have only one answer or that an answer is either right or wrong. In this chapter we discussed several *approximate algorithms* for solving TSPs and learned an important lesson: some math problems can have a perfect solution or an approximate solution. When the perfect solution is beyond the human ability to compute it, a good approximate solution that is easy to compute is not such a bad thing. Regardless of how we choose to tackle *traveling salesman problems*, the acronym TSP should not stand for *Totally Stumped and Perplexed*.

KEY CONCEPTS

6.1 What Is a Traveling Salesman Problem?

- **tour:** a trip that starts and ends at a site and visits all the other sites exactly once, **176**
- **optimal tour:** a tour of minimal total cost, **176**
- **TSP:** an acronym for *traveling salesman problem*, **176**

6.2 Hamilton Paths and Circuits

- **Hamilton circuit:** a circuit that visits all the vertices of a connected graph once and only once, **179**
- **Hamilton path:** a path that visits all the vertices of a connected graph once and only once, **179**
- **complete graph (K_N):** a graph with no loops or multiple edges such that any two distinct vertices are connected by an edge, **181**

6.3 The Brute-Force Algorithm

- **brute-force algorithm:** an algorithm that checks the cost of every possible Hamilton circuit and chooses the optimal one, **185**
- **inefficient algorithm:** an algorithm for which the computational effort needed to carry out the steps of the algorithm grows disproportionately with the size of the problem, **185**

6.4 The Nearest-Neighbor and Repetitive Nearest-Neighbor Algorithms

- **approximate algorithm:** an algorithm that produces a solution, but not necessarily an optimal solution, **187**
- **nearest-neighbor algorithm:** starts at a designated vertex and at each step it visits the nearest neighbor (among the vertices not yet visited) until the tour is completed, **186, 189**

■ **relative error:** for a tour with cost C, the ratio, $\frac{C - Opt}{Opt}$ (usually expressed in the form of a percentage), where Opt is the cost of an optimal tour, **188**

■ **repetitive nearest-neighbor algorithm:** finds the nearest-neighbor tour for each possible starting vertex and chooses the one of least cost among them, **188, 190**

■ **nearest-neighbor tour:** the tour obtained using the nearest-neighbor algorithm, **189**

■ **repetitive nearest-neighbor tour:** a tour obtained using the nearest-neighbor algorithm, **190**

6.5 The Cheapest-Link Algorithm

■ **partial-circuit rule:** a Hamilton circuit (tour) cannot contain any partial circuits, **191**

■ **three-edge rule:** a Hamilton circuit (tour) cannot have three edges coming out of a vertex, **191**

■ **cheapest-link algorithm:** at each step chooses the cheapest link available that does not violate the partial-circuit rule or the three-edge rule, **191**

■ **cheapest-link tour:** a tour obtained using the cheapest-link algorithm, **191**

◰ EXERCISES

WALKING

6.1 What Is a Traveling Salesman Problem?

No exercises for this section.

6.2 Hamilton Paths and Circuits

1. For the graph shown in Fig. 6-19,

   (a) find three different Hamilton circuits.

   (b) find a Hamilton path that starts at A and ends at B.

   (c) find a Hamilton path that starts at D and ends at F.

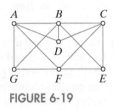

FIGURE 6-19

2. For the graph shown in Fig. 6-20,

   (a) find three different Hamilton circuits.

   (b) find a Hamilton path that starts at A and ends at B.

   (c) find a Hamilton path that starts at F and ends at I.

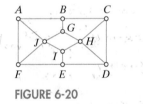

FIGURE 6-20

3. Find all possible Hamilton circuits in the graph in Fig. 6-21. Write your answers using A as the starting/ending vertex.

FIGURE 6-21

4. Find all possible Hamilton circuits in the graph in Fig. 6-22. Write your answers using A as the starting/ending vertex.

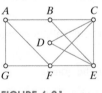

FIGURE 6-22

5. For the graph shown in Fig. 6-23,

   (a) find a Hamilton path that starts at *A* and ends at *E*.

   (b) find a Hamilton circuit that starts at *A* and ends with the edge *EA*.

   (c) find a Hamilton path that starts at *A* and ends at *C*.

   (d) find a Hamilton path that starts at *F* and ends at *G*.

FIGURE 6-23

6. For the graph shown in Fig. 6-24,

   (a) find a Hamilton path that starts at *A* and ends at *E*.

   (b) find a Hamilton circuit that starts at *A* and ends with the edge *EA*.

   (c) find a Hamilton path that starts at *A* and ends at *G*.

   (d) find a Hamilton path that starts at *F* and ends at *G*.

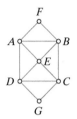

FIGURE 6-24

7. Suppose *D*, *G*, *E*, *A*, *H*, *C*, *B*, *F*, *D* is a Hamilton circuit in a graph.

   (a) Find the number of vertices in the graph.

   (b) Write the Hamilton circuit using *A* as the starting/ending vertex.

   (c) Find two different Hamilton paths in the graph that start at *A*.

8. Suppose *G*, *B*, *D*, *C*, *A*, *F*, *E*, *G* is a Hamilton circuit in a graph.

   (a) Find the number of vertices in the graph.

   (b) Write the Hamilton circuit using *F* as the starting/ending vertex.

   (c) Find two different Hamilton paths in the graph that start at *F*.

9. Consider the graph in Fig. 6-25.

   (a) Find the five Hamilton paths that can be obtained by "breaking" the Hamilton circuit *B,A,D,E,C,B* (i.e., by deleting just one edge from the circuit).

   (b) Find the eight Hamilton paths that do not come from "broken" Hamilton circuits (i.e., cannot be closed into a Hamilton circuit). (*Hint*: See Example 6.6).

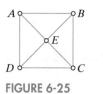

FIGURE 6-25

10. Consider the graph in Fig. 6-26.

   (a) Find all the Hamilton circuits in the graph, using *B* as the starting/ending vertex. (*Hint*: There are five Hamilton circuits and another five that are reversals of the first five.)

   (b) Find the four Hamilton paths that start at *B* and do not come from "broken" Hamilton circuits (i.e., cannot be closed into a Hamilton circuit).

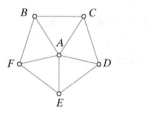

FIGURE 6-26

11. Consider the graph in Fig. 6-27.

   (a) Find all the Hamilton circuits in the graph, using *A* as the starting/ending vertex. You don't have to list both a circuit and its reversal—you can just list one from each pair.

   (b) Find all the Hamilton paths that do not come from "broken" Hamilton circuits (i.e., cannot be closed into a Hamilton circuit). You don't have to list both a path and its reversal—you can just list one from each pair.

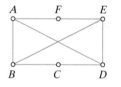

FIGURE 6-27

12. Consider the graph in Fig. 6-28.

   (a) Find all the Hamilton circuits in the graph, using *A* as the starting/ending vertex. You don't have to list both a circuit and its reversal—you can just list one from each pair.

   (b) Find all the Hamilton paths that do not come from "broken" Hamilton circuits (i.e., cannot be closed into a Hamilton circuit). You don't have to list both a path and its reversal—you can just list one from each pair. (*Hint*: Such paths must either start or end at *C*. You can just list all the paths that start at *C*— the ones that end at *C* are their reversals.)

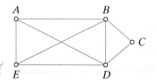

FIGURE 6-28

13. For the graph shown in Fig. 6-29,

 (a) find a Hamilton path that starts at A and ends at F.

 (b) find a Hamilton path that starts at K and ends at E.

 (c) explain why the graph has no Hamilton path that starts at C.

 (d) explain why the graph has no Hamilton circuits.

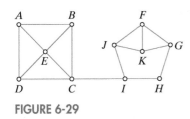

FIGURE 6-29

14. For the graph shown in Fig. 6-30,

 (a) find a Hamilton path that starts at B.

 (b) find a Hamilton path that starts at E.

 (c) explain why the graph has no Hamilton path that starts at A or at C.

 (d) explain why the graph has no Hamilton circuit.

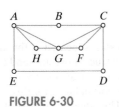

FIGURE 6-30

15. Explain why the graph shown in Fig. 6-31 has neither Hamilton circuits nor Hamilton paths.

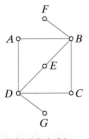

FIGURE 6-31

16. Explain why the graph shown in Fig. 6-32 has no Hamilton circuit but does have a Hamilton path.

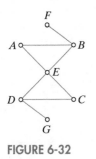

FIGURE 6-32

17. For the weighted graph shown in Fig. 6-33,

 (a) find the weight of edge BD.

 (b) find a Hamilton circuit that starts with edge BD, and give its weight.

 (c) find a Hamilton circuit that ends with edge DB, and give its weight.

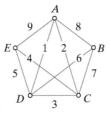

FIGURE 6-33

18. For the weighted graph shown in Fig. 6-34,

 (a) find the weight of edge AD.

 (b) find a Hamilton circuit that starts with edge AD, and give its weight.

 (c) find a Hamilton circuit that ends with edge DA, and give its weight.

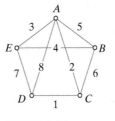

FIGURE 6-34

19. For the weighted graph shown in Fig. 6-35,

 (a) find a Hamilton path that starts at A and ends at C, and give its weight.

 (b) find a second Hamilton path that starts at A and ends at C, and give its weight.

 (c) find the optimal (least weight) Hamilton path that starts at A and ends at C, and give its weight.

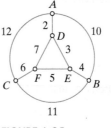

FIGURE 6-35

20. For the weighted graph shown in Fig. 6-36,

(a) find a Hamilton path that starts at B and ends at D, and give its weight.

(b) find a second Hamilton path that starts at B and ends at D, and give its weight.

(c) find the optimal (least weight) Hamilton path that starts at B and ends at D, and give its weight.

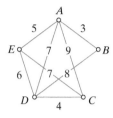

FIGURE 6-36

21. Suppose you have a supercomputer that can generate one *billion* Hamilton circuits per second.

(a) Estimate (in years) how long it would take the supercomputer to generate all the Hamilton circuits in K_{21}.

(b) Estimate (in years) how long it would take the supercomputer to generate all the Hamilton circuits in K_{22}.

22. Suppose you have a supercomputer that can generate one *trillion* Hamilton circuits per second.

(a) Estimate (in years) how long it would take the supercomputer to generate all the Hamilton circuits in K_{26}.

(b) Estimate (in years) how long it would take the supercomputer to generate all the Hamilton circuits in K_{27}.

23. (a) How many edges are there in K_{20}?

(b) How many edges are there in K_{21}?

(c) If the number of edges in K_{50} is x and the number of edges in K_{51} is y, what is the value of $y - x$?

24. (a) How many edges are there in K_{200}?

(b) How many edges are there in K_{201}?

(c) If the number of edges in K_{500} is x and the number of edges in K_{501} is y, what is the value of $y - x$?

25. In each case, find the value of N.

(a) K_N has 120 distinct Hamilton circuits.

(b) K_N has 45 edges.

(c) K_N has 20,100 edges.

26. In each case, find the value of N.

(a) K_N has 720 distinct Hamilton circuits.

(b) K_N has 66 edges.

(c) K_N has 80,200 edges.

6.3 The Brute-Force Algorithm

27. Find an optimal tour for the TSP given in Fig. 6-37, and give its cost.

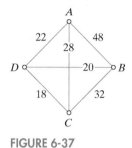

FIGURE 6-37

28. Find an optimal tour for the TSP given in Fig. 6-38, and give its cost.

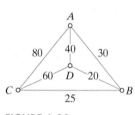

FIGURE 6-38

29. A truck must deliver furniture to stores located in five different cities $A, B, C, D,$ and E. The truck must start and end its route at A. The time (in hours) for travel between the cities is given in Fig. 6-39. Find an optimal tour for this TSP and give its cost in hours. (*Hint*: The edge AD is part of an optimal tour.)

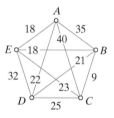

FIGURE 6-39

30. A social worker starts from her home A, must visit clients at $B, C, D,$ and E (in any order), and return home to A at the end of the day. The graph in Fig. 6-40 shows the distance (in miles) between the five locations. Find an optimal tour for this TSP, and give its cost in miles. (*Hint*: The edge AC is part of an optimal tour.)

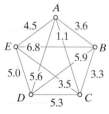

FIGURE 6-40

31. You are planning to visit four cities A, B, C, and D. Table 6-6 shows the time (in hours) that it takes to travel by car between any two cities. Find an optimal tour for this TSP that starts and ends at B.

	A	B	C	D
A	*	12	6	14
B	12	*	17	15
C	6	17	*	11
D	14	15	11	*

■ **TABLE 6-6**

32. An unmanned rover must be routed to visit four sites labeled A, B, C, and D on the surface of the moon. Table 6-7 shows the distance (in kilometers) between any two sites. Assuming the rover landed at C, find an optimal tour.

	A	B	C	D
A	0	4	18	16
B	4	0	17	13
C	18	17	0	7
D	16	13	7	0

■ **TABLE 6-7**

33. Consider a TSP with nine vertices labeled A through I.

(a) How many tours are of the form $A, G, \ldots, A$? (*Hint:* The remaining seven letters can be rearranged in any sequence.)

(b) How many tours are of the form $B, \ldots, E, B$?

(c) How many tours are of the form $A, D, \ldots, F, A$?

34. Consider a TSP with 11 vertices labeled A through K.

(a) How many tours are of the form $A, B, \ldots, A$? (*Hint:* The remaining nine letters can be rearranged in any sequence.)

(b) How many tours are of the form $C, \ldots, K, C$?

(c) How many tours are of the form $D, B, \ldots, K, D$?

6.4 The Nearest-Neighbor and Repetitive Nearest-Neighbor Algorithms

35. For the weighted graph shown in Fig. 6-41, (i) find the indicated tour, and (ii) give its cost. (*Note:* This is the TSP introduced in Example 6.1.)

(a) The nearest-neighbor tour with starting vertex B

(b) The nearest-neighbor tour with starting vertex C

(c) The nearest-neighbor tour with starting vertex D

(d) The nearest-neighbor tour with starting vertex E

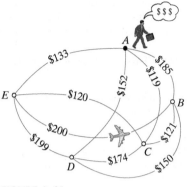

FIGURE 6-41

36. A delivery service must deliver packages at Buckman (B), Chatfield (C), Dayton (D), and Evansville (E) and then return to Arlington (A), the home base. Figure 6-42 shows a graph of the estimated travel times (in minutes) between the cities.

(a) Find the nearest-neighbor tour with starting vertex A. Give the total travel time of this tour.

(b) Find the nearest-neighbor tour with starting vertex D. Write the tour as it would be traveled if starting and ending at A. Give the total travel time of this tour.

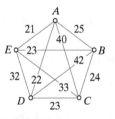

FIGURE 6-42 .

37. The Brute-Force Bandits is a rock band planning a five-city concert tour. The cities and the distances (in miles) between them are given in the weighted graph shown in Fig. 6-43. The tour must start and end at A. The cost of the chartered bus in which the band is traveling is $8 per mile.

(a) Find the nearest-neighbor tour with starting vertex A. Give the cost (in $) of this tour.

(b) Find the nearest-neighbor tour with starting vertex B. Write the tour as it would be traveled by the band, starting and ending at A. Give the cost (in $) of this tour.

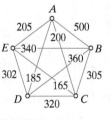

FIGURE 6-43

38. A space mission is scheduled to visit the moons Callisto (*C*), Ganymede (*G*), Io (*I*), Mimas (*M*), and Titan (*T*) to collect rock samples at each and then return to Earth (*E*). The travel times (in years) are given in the weighted graph shown in Fig. 6-44. (*Note*: This is the interplanetary TSP discussed in Example 6.11.)

(a) Find the nearest-neighbor tour with starting vertex *E*. Give the total travel time of this tour.

(b) Find the nearest-neighbor tour with starting vertex *T*. Write the tour as it would be traveled by an expedition starting and ending at *E*. Give the total travel time of this tour.

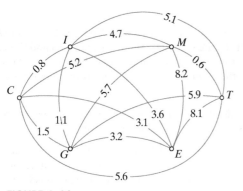

FIGURE 6-44

39. This exercise refers to the furniture truck TSP introduced in Exercise 29 (see Fig. 6-39).

(a) Find the nearest-neighbor tour starting at *A*.

(b) Find the nearest-neighbor tour starting at *B*, and give the answer using *A* as the starting/ending city.

40. This exercise refers to the social worker TSP introduced in Exercise 30 (see Fig. 6-40).

(a) Find the nearest-neighbor tour starting at *A*.

(b) Find the nearest-neighbor tour starting at *C*, and give the answer using *A* as the starting/ending city.

41. Darren is a sales rep whose territory consists of the six cities in the mileage chart shown in Fig. 6-45. Darren wants to visit customers at each of the cities, starting and ending his

Mileage Chart

	Atlanta	Columbus	Kansas City	Minneapolis	Pierre	Tulsa
Atlanta	*	533	798	1068	1361	772
Columbus	533	*	656	713	1071	802
Kansas City	798	656	*	447	592	248
Minneapolis	1068	713	447	*	394	695
Pierre	1361	1071	592	394	*	760
Tulsa	772	802	248	695	760	*

FIGURE 6-45

trip in his home city of Atlanta. His travel costs (gas, insurance, etc.) average $0.75 per mile.

(a) Find the nearest-neighbor tour with Atlanta as the starting city. What is the total cost of this tour?

(b) Find the nearest-neighbor tour using Kansas City as the starting city. Write the tour as it would be traveled by Darren, who must start and end the trip in Atlanta. What is the total cost of this tour?

42. The Platonic Cowboys are a country and western band based in Nashville. The Cowboys are planning a concert tour to the seven cities in the mileage chart shown in Fig. 6-46.

(a) Find the nearest-neighbor tour with Nashville as the starting city. What is the total length of this tour?

(b) Find the nearest-neighbor tour using St. Louis as the starting city. Write the tour as it would be traveled by the band, which must start and end the tour in Nashville. What is the total length of this tour?

Mileage Chart

	Boston	Dallas	Houston	Louisville	Nashville	Pittsburgh	St. Louis
Boston	*	1748	1804	941	1088	561	1141
Dallas	1748	*	243	819	660	1204	630
Houston	1804	243	*	928	769	1313	779
Louisville	941	819	928	*	168	388	263
Nashville	1088	660	769	168	*	553	299
Pittsburgh	561	1204	1313	388	553	*	588
St. Louis	1141	630	779	263	299	588	*

FIGURE 6-46

43. Find the repetitive nearest-neighbor tour (and give its cost) for the furniture truck TSP discussed in Exercises 29 and 39 (see Fig. 6-39).

44. Find the repetitive nearest-neighbor tour for the social worker TSP discussed in Exercises 30 and 40 (see Fig. 6-40).

45. This exercise is a continuation of Darren's sales trip problem (Exercise 41). Find the repetitive nearest-neighbor tour, and give the total cost for this tour. Write the answer using Atlanta as the starting city.

46. This exercise is a continuation of the Platonic Cowboys concert tour (Exercise 42). Find the repetitive nearest-neighbor tour, and give the total mileage for this tour. Write the answer using Nashville as the starting city.

47. Suppose that in solving a TSP you use the nearest-neighbor algorithm and find a nearest-neighbor tour with a total cost of $13,500. Suppose that you later find out that the cost of an optimal tour is $12,000. What was the relative error of your nearest-neighbor tour? Express your answer as a percentage, rounded to the nearest tenth of a percent.

48. Suppose that in solving a TSP you use the nearest-neighbor algorithm and find a nearest-neighbor tour with a total length of 21,400 miles. Suppose that you later find out that the length of an optimal tour is 20,100 miles. What was the relative error of your nearest-neighbor tour? Express your answer as a percentage, rounded to the nearest tenth of a percent.

6.5 Cheapest-Link Algorithm

49. Find the cheapest-link tour (and give its cost) for the furniture truck TSP discussed in Exercise 29 (see Fig. 6-39).

50. Find the cheapest-link tour for the social worker TSP discussed in Exercise 30 (see Fig. 6-40).

51. For the Brute-Force Bandits concert tour discussed in Exercise 37, find the cheapest-link tour, and give the bus cost for this tour (see Fig. 6-43).

52. For the weighted graph shown in Fig. 6-47, find the cheapest-link tour. Write the tour using B as the starting vertex.

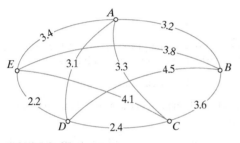

FIGURE 6-47

53. For Darren's sales trip problem discussed in Exercise 41, find the cheapest-link tour, and give the total cost for this tour (see Fig. 6-45).

54. For the Platonic Cowboys concert tour discussed in Exercise 42, find the cheapest-link tour, and give the total mileage for this tour (see Fig. 6-46).

55. A rover on the planet Mercuria has to visit six sites labeled A through F. Figure 6-48 shows the time (in days) for the rover to travel between any two sites.

(a) Find the cheapest-link tour for these sites and give its length.

(b) Given that the tour A, B, D, F, C, E, A is an optimal tour, find the relative error of the cheapest-link tour found in (a).

	A	B	C	D	E	F
A	*	11	19	16	9	10
B	11	*	20	13	17	15
C	19	20	*	21	13	11
D	16	13	21	*	12	16
E	9	17	13	12	*	14
F	10	15	11	16	14	*

FIGURE 6-48

56. A robotic laser must drill holes on five sites ($A, B, C, D,$ and E) in a microprocessor chip. At the end, the laser must return to its starting position A and start all over. Figure 6-49 shows the time (in seconds) it takes the laser arm to move from one site to another. In this TSP, a tour is a sequence of drilling locations starting and ending at A.

(a) Find the cheapest-link tour and its length.

(b) Given that the tour A, D, B, E, C, A is an optimal tour, find the relative error of the cheapest-link tour found in (a).

	A	B	C	D	E
A	*	1.2	0.7	1.0	1.3
B	1.2	*	0.9	0.8	1.1
C	0.7	0.9	*	1.2	0.8
D	1.0	0.8	1.2	*	0.9
E	1.3	1.1	0.8	0.9	*

FIGURE 6-49

JOGGING

57. Suppose that in solving a TSP you find an approximate solution with a cost of $1614, and suppose that you later find out that the relative error of your solution was 7.6%. What was the cost of the optimal solution?

58. Suppose that in solving a TSP you find an approximate solution with a cost of $2508, and suppose that you later find out that the relative error of your solution was 4.5%. What was the cost of the optimal solution?

59. You have a busy day ahead of you. You must run the following errands (in no particular order): Go to the post office, deposit a check at the bank, pick up some French bread at the deli, visit a friend at the hospital, and get a haircut at Karl's Beauty Salon. You must start and end at home. Each block on the map shown in Fig. 6-50 is exactly 1 mile.

(a) Draw a weighted graph modeling to this problem.

(b) Find an optimal tour for running all the errands. (Use any algorithm you think is appropriate.)

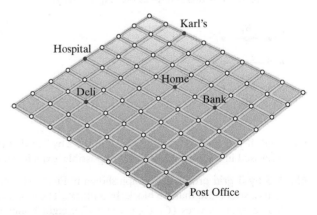

FIGURE 6-50

In Exercises 60 and 61, you are scheduling a dinner party for six people (A, B, C, D, E, and F). The guests are to be seated around a circular table, and you want to arrange the seating so that each guest is seated between two friends (i.e., the guests to the left and to the right are friends of the guest in between). You can assume that all friendships are mutual (when X is a friend of Y, Y is also a friend of X).

60. Suppose that you are told that all possible friendships can be deduced from the following information:

A is friends with *B* and *F*; *B* is friends with *A*, *C*, and *E*; *C* is friends with *B*, *D*, *E*, and *F*; *E* is friends with *B*, *C*, *D*, and *F*.

(a) Draw a "friendship graph" for the dinner guests.

(b) Find a possible seating arrangement for the party.

(c) Is there a possible seating arrangement in which *B* and *E* are seated next to each other? If there is, find it. If there isn't, explain why not.

61. Suppose that you are told that all possible friendships can be deduced from the following information:

A is friends with *C*, *D*, *E*, and *F*; *B* is friends with *C*, *D*, and *E*; *C* is friends with *A*, *B*, and *E*; *D* is friends with *A*, *B*, and *E*.

Explain why it is impossible to have a seating arrangement in which each guest is seated between friends.

62. If the number of edges in K_{500} is x and the number of edges in K_{502} is y, what is the value of $y - x$?

63. A 2 by 2 grid graph. The graph shown in Fig. 6-51 represents a street grid that is 2 blocks by 2 blocks. (Such a graph is called a *2 by 2 grid graph*.) For convenience, the vertices are labeled by type: corner vertices C_1, C_2, C_3, and C_4, boundary vertices B_1, B_2, B_3, and B_4, and the interior vertex *I*.

(a) Find a Hamilton path in the graph that starts at *I*.

(b) Find a Hamilton path in the graph that starts at one of the corner vertices and ends at a different corner vertex.

(c) Find a Hamilton path that starts at one of the corner vertices and ends at *I*.

(d) Find (if you can) a Hamilton path that starts at one of the corner vertices and ends at one of the boundary vertices. If this is impossible, explain why.

FIGURE 6-51

64. Find (if you can) a Hamilton circuit in the 2 by 2 grid graph discussed in Exercise 63. If this is impossible, explain why.

65. A 3 by 3 grid graph. The graph shown in Fig. 6-52 represents a street grid that is 3 blocks by 3 blocks. The graph has four corner vertices (C_1, C_2, C_3, and C_4), eight boundary vertices (B_1 through B_8), and four interior vertices (I_1, I_2, I_3, and I_4).

(a) Find a Hamilton circuit in the graph.

(b) Find a Hamilton path in the graph that starts at one of the corner vertices and ends at a different corner vertex.

(c) Find (if you can) a Hamilton path that starts at one of the corner vertices and ends at one of the interior vertices. If this is impossible, explain why.

(d) Given any two adjacent vertices of the graph, explain why there always is a Hamilton path that starts at one and ends at the other one.

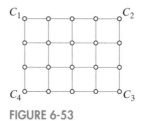

FIGURE 6-52

66. A 3 by 4 grid graph. The graph shown in Fig. 6-53 represents a street grid that is 3 blocks by 4 blocks.

(a) Draw a Hamilton circuit in the graph.

(b) Draw a Hamilton path in the graph that starts at C_1 and ends at C_3.

(c) Draw (if you can) a Hamilton path in the graph that starts at C_1 and ends at C_2. If this is impossible, explain why.

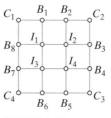

FIGURE 6-53

67. Explain why the cheapest edge in any graph is always part of the Hamilton circuit obtained using the nearest-neighbor algorithm.

68. (a) Explain why a graph that has a bridge cannot have a Hamilton circuit.

(b) Give an example of a graph with bridges that has a Hamilton path.

69. Nick is a traveling salesman. His territory consists of the 11 cities shown on the mileage chart in Fig. 6-54. Nick must find a tour that starts and ends in Dallas (that's his home) and visits each of the other 10 cities.

(a) Find a nearest-neighbor tour that starts at Dallas.

(b) Find the cheapest-link tour.

Mileage Chart

	Atlanta	Boston	Buffalo	Chicago	Columbus	Dallas	Denver	Houston	Kansas City	Louisville	Memphis
Atlanta	*	1037	859	674	533	795	1398	789	798	382	371
Boston	1037	*	446	963	735	1748	1949	1804	1391	941	1293
Buffalo	859	446	*	522	326	1346	1508	1460	966	532	899
Chicago	674	963	522	*	308	917	996	1067	499	292	530
Columbus	533	735	326	308	*	1028	1229	1137	656	209	576
Dallas	795	1748	1346	917	1028	*	781	243	489	819	452
Denver	1398	1949	1508	996	1229	781	*	1019	600	1120	1040
Houston	789	1804	1460	1067	1137	243	1019	*	710	928	561
Kansas City	798	1391	966	499	656	489	600	710	*	520	451
Louisville	382	941	532	292	209	819	1120	928	520	*	367
Memphis	371	1293	899	530	576	452	1040	561	451	367	*

FIGURE 6-54

70. Julie is the marketing manager for a small software company based in Boston. She is planning a sales trip to Michigan to visit customers in each of the nine cities shown on the mileage chart in Fig. 6-55. She can fly from Boston to any one of the cities and fly out of any one of the cities back to Boston for the same price (call the arrival city A and the departure city D). Her plan is to pick up a rental car at A, drive to each of the other cities, and drop off the rental car at the last city D. Slightly complicating the situation is that Michigan has two separate peninsulas—an upper peninsula and a lower peninsula—and the only way to get from one to the other is through the Mackinaw Bridge connecting Cheboygan to Sault Ste. Marie. (There is a $3 toll to cross the bridge in either direction.)

(a) Suppose that the rental car company charges 39 cents per mile plus a drop off fee of $250 if A and D are different cities (there is no charge if $A = D$). Find the optimal (cheapest) route and give the total cost.

(b) Suppose that the rental car company charges 49 cents per mile but the car can be returned to any city without a drop off fee. Find the optimal route and give the total cost.

RUNNING

71. Complete bipartite graphs. A complete bipartite graph is a graph with the property that the vertices can be divided into two sets A and B and each vertex in set A is adjacent to each of the vertices in set B. There are no other edges! If there are m vertices in set A and n vertices in set B, the complete bipartite graph is written as $K_{n,n}$. Figure 6-56 shows a generic bipartite graph.

(a) For $n > 1$, the complete bipartite graphs of the form $K_{m,n}$ all have Hamilton circuits. Explain why.

Mileage Chart

	Detroit	Lansing	Grand Rapids	Flint	Cheboygan	Sault Ste. Marie	Marquette	Escanaba	Menominee
Detroit	*	90	158	68	280				
Lansing	90	*	68	56	221				
Grand Rapids	158	68	*	114	233				
Flint	68	56	114	*	215				
Cheboygan	280	221	233	215	*	78			
Sault Ste. Marie					78	*	164	174	227
Marquette						164	*	67	120
Escanaba						174	67	*	55
Menominee						227	120	55	*

FIGURE 6-55 .

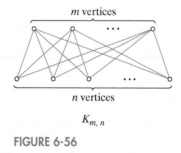

m vertices

n vertices

$K_{m,n}$

FIGURE 6-56

(b) If the difference between m and n is exactly 1 (i.e., $|m - n| = 1$), the complete bipartite graph $K_{m,n}$ has a Hamilton path. Explain why.

(c) When the difference between m and n is more than 1, then the complete bipartite graph $K_{m,n}$ has neither a Hamilton circuit nor a Hamilton path. Explain why.

72. *m* by *n* grid graphs. An m by n grid graph represents a rectangular street grid that is m blocks by n blocks, as indicated in Fig. 6-57. (You should try Exercises 63 through 66 before you try this one.)

(a) If m and n are both odd, then the m by n grid graph has a Hamilton circuit. Describe the circuit by drawing it on a generic graph.

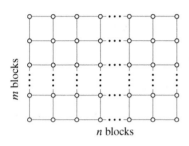

FIGURE 6-57

(b) If either m or n is even and the other one is odd, then the m by n grid graph has a Hamilton circuit. Describe the circuit by drawing it on a generic graph.

(c) If m and n are both even, then the m by n grid graph does not have a Hamilton circuit. Explain why a Hamilton circuit is impossible.

73. Ore's theorem. A connected graph with N vertices is said to satisfy *Ore's condition* if $\deg(X) + \deg(Y) \geq N$ for every pair of vertices X and Y of the graph. Ore's theorem states that *if a graph satisfies Ore's condition, then it has a Hamilton circuit.*

(a) Explain why the complete bipartite graph $K_{n,n}$ (see Exercise 71) satisfies Ore's condition.

(b) Explain why for $m \neq n$, the complete bipartite graph $K_{m,n}$ (see Exercise 71) does *not* satisfy Ore's condition.

(c) Ore's condition is sufficient to guarantee that a connected graph has a Hamilton circuit but is not a necessary condition. Give an example of a graph that has a Hamilton circuit but does not satisfy Ore's condition.

74. Dirac's theorem. If G is a connected graph with N vertices and $\deg(X) \geq \frac{N}{2}$ for every vertex X, then G has a Hamilton circuit. Explain why Dirac's theorem is a direct consequence of Ore's theorem.

PROJECTS AND PAPERS

1 The Nearest-Insertion Algorithm

The *nearest-insertion algorithm* is another approximate algorithm used for tackling TSPs. The basic idea of the algorithm is to start with a subcircuit (a circuit that includes some, but not all, of the vertices) and enlarge it, one step at a time, by adding an extra vertex—the one that is closest to some vertex in the circuit. By the time we have added all of the vertices, we have a full-fledged Hamilton circuit.

In this project, you should prepare a class presentation on the nearest-insertion algorithm. Your presentation should include a detailed description of the algorithm, at least two carefully worked-out examples, and a comparison of the nearest-insertion and the nearest-neighbor algorithms.

2 Computing with DNA

DNA is the basic molecule of life—it encodes the genetic information that characterizes all living organisms. Due to the recent great advances in biochemistry, scientists can now snip, splice, and recombine segments of DNA almost at will. In 1994, Leonard Adleman, a professor of computer science at the University of Southern California, was able to encode a graph representing seven cities into a set of DNA segments and to use the chemical reactions of the DNA fragments to uncover the existence of a Hamilton path in the graph. Basically, he was able to use the biochemistry of DNA to solve a graph theory problem. While the actual problem solved was insignificant, the idea was revolutionary, as it opened the door for the possibility of someday using DNA computers to solve problems beyond the reach of even the most powerful of today's electronic computers.

Write a research paper telling the story of Adleman's landmark discovery. How did he encode the graph into DNA? How did he extract the mathematical solution (Hamilton path) from the chemical solution? What other kinds of problems might be solved using DNA computing? What are the implications of Adleman's discovery for the future of computing?

3 Ant Colony Optimization

An individual ant is, by most standards, a dumb little creature, but collectively an entire ant colony can perform surprising feats of teamwork (such as lifting and carrying large leaves or branches) and self-organize to solve remarkably complex problems (finding the shortest route to a food source, optimizing foraging strategies, managing a smooth and steady traffic flow in congested ant highways). The ability of ants and other social insects to perform sophisticated group tasks goes by the name of *swarm intelligence*. Since ants don't talk to each other and don't have bosses telling them what to do, swarm intelligence is a decentralized, spontaneous type of intelligence that has many potential applications at the human scale. In recent years, computer scientists have been able to approach many difficult optimization problems (including TSPs) using *ant colony optimization* software (i.e., computer programs that use *virtual ants* to imitate the problem-solving strategies of real ants).

Write a research paper describing the concept of swarm intelligence and some of the recent developments in ant colony optimization methods and, in particular, the use of virtual ant algorithms for solving TSPs.

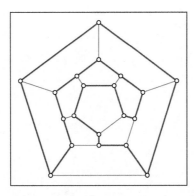

Solution to Hamilton's Icosian game
(Fig. 6-5, page 179).

PART 3

Growth

News Now

Outbreak H1N1 Flu (Swine Flu)

The influenza virus is relatively unique in its ability to change shift. For example, the swine flu of 1918 was named H1N1, found to have changed its hemagglutinin molecules (doub Scientists believe that these ch... a swine was mixed... sources, such as if an influe... RNA, or missence n... a new strain that ...ne influenza virus, or a... ...ions c... after a number of... ...outbreak...

dexes	Last	Change
trials*	13265.47	-208.10
Composite*	2562.24	-37.10
*1458.95	-23.71	-1.6
ire 5000*	14710.78	-227.
2000*	777.83	-13.

Last	%		High	Low
36.95		3	1	83.0
19.		1	1	18.6
0.20	0	1	2	9.5
15.05	1.69		15.49	14.41

CURRENT POPULATION
of the UNITED STATES

200 000 000

AN ADDITIONAL AMERICAN EVERY 14 SECONDS

A birth every 8½ seconds   A death every 17 seconds   An immigrant every 60 seconds   An emigrant every 29 minutes

9 Population Growth Models

There Is Strength in Numbers

There is a big clock—located inside the U.S. Department of Commerce Building in Washington, D.C.—that instead of keeping time keeps the official count of the U.S. population. The *United States Population Clock* is really a digital display operated by the Census Bureau that shows a big number: the official resident population of the United States at the moment you are looking at it—citizens and noncitizens included. (A *virtual* version of the real clock can be found at *www.census.gov/population/www/popclockus.html*.)

f you stare at the U.S. population clock for more than just a few seconds you will see the count go up by 1. What happened? Did some hospital call the Census Bureau with news that another baby had just been born? No. The ticking of the U.S. population clock is based on a mathematical model for the growth of the U.S. population. Like any other model, this is not intended to be a perfect representation of reality but just an approximation—that number on the clock is, in fact, almost certain to be wrong.

So, if the population figure in the clock is wrong, what is the clock good for? You'd be surprised. This is the remarkable thing about population models—they are incredibly useful (for the "big picture") notwithstanding the fact that they are typically wrong (in the small details). In spite of their lack of accuracy, population models are successfully used by economists to make economic forecasts, by epidemiologists to project (and prepare for) epidemics, by urban planners to plan the future of cities, by demographers to develop population pyramids, by biologists to study animal populations, and so on.

In this chapter we will look at three different mathematical models of population growth. We start by introducing the concept of a number *sequence* followed by a brief general discussion of *population sequences* and the role they play in modeling population growth (Section 9.1). In Section 9.2 we introduce the *linear growth model* and the concept of an *arithmetic sequence*, we learn about an important formula called the *arithmetic sum formula*, and we discuss several real-life applications—including the Census Bureau model for the U.S. population—of linear growth. In Section 9.3 we introduce the *exponential growth model* and the concept of a *geometric sequence*, we learn about another important formula called the *geometric sum formula*, and we discuss examples of exponential growth in biological populations (much more on exponential growth will come in Chapter 10). Finally, in Section 9.4 we introduce the *logistic growth model* and the *logistic equation*, and we discuss examples of logistic growth in animal populations.

CURRENT POPULATION of the UNITED STATES

200 000 000

AN ADDITIONAL AMERICAN EVERY 14 SECONDS

9.1 Sequences and Population Sequences

Sequences

In mathematics the word *sequence* has a very specific meaning: A **sequence** is an infinite, ordered list of numbers. In principle, the numbers can be any type of number—positive, negative, zero, rational, or irrational. The individual numbers in a sequence are called the **terms** of the sequence.

The simplest way to describe a sequence is using a list format—start writing the terms of the sequence, in order, separated by commas. The list, however, is infinite, so at some point one has to stop writing. At that point, a "..." is added as a symbolic way of saying "and so on." For lack of a better term, we will call this the **infinite list** description of the sequence.

How many terms should we write at the front end before we appeal to the "..."? This is a subjective decision, but the idea is to write enough terms so that a reasonable third party looking at the sequence can figure out how the sequence continues. No matter what we do, the "..." is always a leap of faith, and we should strive to make that leap as small as possible. Some sequences become clear with four or five terms, others take more.

EXAMPLE 9.1   HOW MANY TERMS ARE ENOUGH?

- Consider the sequence that starts with 1, 2, 4, 8, 16, 32, ... We could have continued writing down terms, but it seems reasonable to assume that at this point most people would agree that the sequence continues with 64, 128, ... The leap of faith here is small.

- Consider the sequence that starts with 3, 5, 7, ... Are there enough terms here so that we can figure out what comes next? A good guess is that the sequence continues with 9, 11, 13, ... but this is not the only reasonable guess. Perhaps the sequence is intending to describe the odd prime numbers, and in that case the next three terms of the sequence would be 11, 13, 17, ... We can conclude that 3, 5, 7, ... does not provide enough terms to draw a clear conclusion about the sequence and that a decent description should have included a few additional terms.

- Consider the sequence that starts with 1, 11, 21, 1211, 111221, 312211, 13112221, 1113213211, 31131211131221, ... These are the first nine terms of the sequence—can you guess what the tenth term is? Even after nine terms, what comes next is far from obvious. (This sequence represents an interesting and challenging puzzle, and we leave it to the reader to try to find the next term and decipher the puzzle. Give it a try! The answer is given on page 291.)

The main lesson to be drawn from Example 9.1 is that describing a sequence using an infinite list is simple and convenient, but it doesn't work all that well with the more exotic sequences. Are there other ways? Yes. Before we get to them, we introduce some useful notation for sequences.

- **Sequence notation.** A generic sequence can be written in infinite list form as

$$A_1, A_2, A_3, A_4, A_5, \ldots$$

The A is a variable representing a symbolic name for the sequence. Each term of the sequence is described by the sequence name and a numerical subscript that represents the position of the term in the sequence. You may think of the subscript as the "address" of the term. This notation makes it possible to conveniently describe any term by its position in the sequence: A_{10} represents the 10th term, A_{100} represents the 100th term, and A_N represents a term in a generic position N in the sequence.

The aforementioned notation makes it possible to describe some sequences by just giving an **explicit formula** for the generic Nth term of the sequence. That formula then is used with $N = 1$ for the first term, $N = 2$ for the second term, and so on.

EXAMPLE 9.2   SEQUENCES DESCRIBED BY A NICE FORMULA

Consider the sequence defined by the formula $A_N = 2^N + 1$. The first four terms of this sequence are

$$A_1 = 2^1 + 1 = 3, A_2 = 2^2 + 1 = 5, A_3 = 2^3 + 1 = 9, \text{ and } A_4 = 2^4 + 1 = 17.$$

If we are interested in the 10th term, we just plug $N = 10$ into the formula and get $A_{10} = 2^{10} + 1 = 1025$. If we are interested in the 100th term of the sequence we apply the formula once again and get $A_{100} = 2^{100} + 1$. Oops! What now? This is a huge number, and it may or may not be worth spelling it out in full. It is often the case that leaving the answer as $A_{100} = 2^{100} + 1$ makes more sense than writing down a 31-digit number, but if you really must have it, then here it is:

$$A_{100} = 1,267,650,600,228,229,401,496,703,205,377.$$

Example 9.2 worked out well because the formula defining the sequence was fairly simple. (Yes, the terms get very large, but that is a separate issue.) Unfortunately, as our next example shows, sometimes we will have to deal with sequences defined by some pretty complicated explicit formulas.

EXAMPLE 9.3   SEQUENCES DESCRIBED BY A NOT SO NICE FORMULA

A very important and much-studied sequence is called the *Fibonacci sequence*, named after the Italian mathematician Leonardo Pisano, better known as Fibonacci (circa 1175–1250). The next two examples give a brief introduction to the Fibonacci sequence.

There are several alternative formulas that can be used to define the Fibonacci sequence, and here is one of them (using F to represent the terms of the sequence):

- Fibonacci sequence (version 1): $F_N = \left[\!\left[\left(\dfrac{1 + \sqrt{5}}{2} \right)^N \!\!/ \sqrt{5} \right]\!\right]$.

   ($[\![\ ]\!]$ means round the number inside the brackets to the nearest integer).

To calculate the terms of this sequence using such a nasty formula is going to require at the very least a good calculator. You might want to confirm this with your own calculator or computer, but the first seven terms generated by the formula are as follows: $F_1 = [\![0.72\ldots]\!] = 1$, $F_2 = [\![1.17\ldots]\!] = 1$, $F_3 = [\![1.89\ldots]\!] = 2$, $F_4 = [\![3.06\ldots]\!] = 3$, $F_5 = [\![4.95\ldots]\!] = 5$, $F_6 = [\![8.02\ldots]\!] = 8$, and $F_7 = [\![12.98\ldots]\!] = 13$.

With this formula we don't have to compute the terms in sequential order—if we want to (and with the right equipment), we can dive directly into deeper waters: $F_{12} = [\![144.0013\ldots]\!] = 144$; $F_{25} = [\![75024.999\ldots]\!] = 75025$, and so on.

An alternative way to describe a sequence is to use a *recursive* formula. In contrast to an explicit formula, a **recursive formula** defines a term of a sequence using previous terms of the sequence. A recursive formula is not always possible, but when it is, it can provide a much nicer definition for a sequence than an explicit formula. A case in point is the Fibonacci sequence.

EXAMPLE 9.4 RECURSIVE FORMULA FOR THE FIBONACCI SEQUENCE

The recursive formula for the Fibonacci sequence is surprisingly simple, especially when compared to the explicit formula given in Example 9.3. It is amazing that the two definitions describe the same sequence.

- Fibonacci sequence (version 2): $F_N = F_{N-1} + F_{N-2}$, and $F_1 = 1$, $F_2 = 1$.

The key part of the above formula is the recursive rule $F_N = F_{N-1} + F_{N-2}$. Stated in plain English, the rule says that each term of the sequence is obtained by adding its two preceding terms. Since this rule cannot be applied to the first two terms (neither has two preceding terms to work with), the first two terms must be given separately.

Applying the recursive formula requires us to find the terms of the sequence in order. The first two terms, $F_1 = 1$, $F_2 = 1$, are given in the definition. The next term comes from the recursive formula: $F_3 = F_2 + F_1 = 1 + 1 = 2$. Another turn of the crank gives $F_4 = F_3 + F_2 = 2 + 1 = 3$. Do it again, and we get $F_5 = F_4 + F_3 = 3 + 2 = 5$. We can continue this way generating, in order, the terms of the sequence for as long as we want, and the beauty of it is that all we have to do to find each term is add the previous two numbers.

Here is the Fibonacci sequence written in infinite list form: 1, 1, 2, 3, 5, 8, 13, 21, 34, 55, 89, 144, 233, ...

Examples 9.3 and 9.4 illustrate the fact that the same sequence can be defined in two completely different ways. In the case of the Fibonacci sequence, we saw first a definition based on a nasty looking *explicit* formula (version 1) and then a different definition based on a beautifully simple *recursive* formula (version 2). It is tempting to declare the latter version clearly superior to the first, but before we do so, there is one important detail to consider—with the recursive formula we cannot find a term of the sequence unless we know the terms that come before it. Think of computing a value of F_N as analogous to getting to the peak of a mountain. The recursive formula is the mathematical version of climbing up to the peak one step at a time; the explicit formula is the mathematical version of being dropped at the peak by a helicopter.

As an example, consider the problem of finding the value of F_{100}. To find this number using the recursive formula we will first have to find F_{99} and F_{98}, and before we can find those values we will have to find and F_{97} and F_{96}, and so on down the line. Each step of this journey is simple (add two numbers), but there are a lot of steps. In contrast, if we use the explicit formula we have to carry out one calculation—it is not an easy one, but it can be done with the right tools (a good scientific calculator or a computer program). Which is better? You decide.

Population Sequences

For the rest of this chapter we will focus on special types of sequences called *population sequences*. For starters, let's clarify the meaning of the word **population**. In its original meaning, the word refers to human populations (the Latin root of the word is *populus*, which means "people") but over time the scope of the word has been expanded to apply to many other "things"—animals, bacteria, viruses, Web sites, plastic bags, money, etc. The main characteristic shared by all these "things" is that their quantities change over time, and to track the ebb and flow of these changes we use a *population sequence*.

A **population sequence** describes the size of a population as it changes over time, measured in discrete time intervals. A population sequence starts with an *initial* population (you have to start somewhere), and it is customary to think of the start as time zero. The size of the population at time zero is the first term of the population sequence. After some time goes by (it may be years, hours, seconds, or even nanoseconds), there is a "change" in the population—up, down, or it may even stay unchanged. We call this change a *transition*, and the population after the first transition is the *first generation*. The size of the *first* generation is the *second* term of the population sequence. After another transition the population is in its second generation, and the size of the *second* generation is given by the *third* term of the population sequence. The population sequence continues this way, each term describing the size of the population at a particular generation.

Notice that in the above description there is a slight mismatch between the generations and the terms of the population sequence: The first generation is represented by the second term of the sequence, the second generation by the third term, and so on. This is a little annoyance that can be fixed by starting the subscripts of the population sequence at $N = 0$. This means that for population sequences we will adopt a slightly different notation than the one we use with ordinary sequences.

■ **Population sequence notation.** A generic population sequence is described by

$$P_0, P_1, P_2, P_3, P_4, \ldots$$

where P_0 is the size of the initial population, P_1 is the size of the population in the first generation, P_2 is the size of the population in the second generation, and so on (Fig. 9-1).

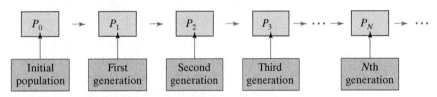

FIGURE 9-1 A generic population sequence. P_N is the size of the population in the Nth generation.

A convenient way to visualize a population sequence is with a **time-series graph**. In a typical two-dimensional, time-series graph, the horizontal axis is used to represent time and the vertical axis is used to represent the size of the population. The terms of the sequence are represented by either isolated points, as in Fig. 9-2(a), or by points connected with lines, as in Fig. 9-2(b). The former is called a **scatter plot**, the latter a **line graph**.

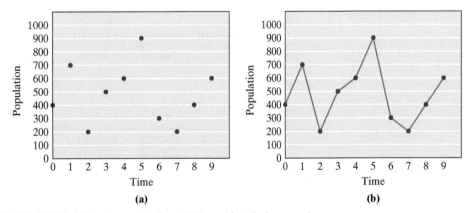

FIGURE 9-2 Time-series graphs: (a) scatter plot; (b) line graph.

EXAMPLE 9.5 FIBONACCI'S RABBITS

More than eight centuries ago, in his seminal book *Liber Abaci* published in 1202, Fibonacci proposed the following population growth problem:

> *A man puts one pair of rabbits in a certain place entirely surrounded by a wall. How many pairs of rabbits can be produced from that pair in a year if the nature of these rabbits is such that every month each pair bears a new pair which from the second month on becomes productive?*

Fibonacci's description of the problem can be restated into the following three facts: (1) each month, each pair (male/female) of *mature* (he called them productive) rabbits produces a pair of baby rabbits, (2) it takes one month for a pair of baby rabbits to become mature, and (3) the initial population consists of one pair (male/female) of baby rabbits.

We can use a population sequence to track the evolution of the rabbit population over time. (Since everything is stated in terms of male/female pairs, we will let the terms of the sequence represent pairs of rabbits.)

- Start: $P_0 = 1$. [The initial population has one pair (male/female) of baby rabbits.]
- Month 1: $P_1 = 1$. [The starting pair becomes mature.]
- Month 2: $P_2 = 2$. [The mature pair produces a baby pair. There are now two pairs—the original pair and their baby pair.]
- Month 3: $P_3 = 3$. [The mature pair in month 2 produces another baby pair; the baby pair in month 2 becomes mature. There are now two mature pairs and one baby pair.]
- Month 4: $P_4 = 5$. [Each of the two mature pairs in month 3 produces a baby pair; the baby pair in month 3 becomes mature. There are now three mature pairs and two baby pairs.]

We can keep going this way, but a better idea is to try to find a general rule that describes what is going on. In month N we have P_N pairs—some are mature pairs and some are baby pairs. Because rabbits become mature the month after they are born, the number of mature pairs in month N equals the *total number* of pairs in month $N - 1$. This number is P_{N-1}. Because every mature pair produces a baby pair the following month, the number of baby pairs in month N equals the *number of mature* pairs in month $N - 1$, which in turn equals the total number of pairs in month $N - 2$. This number is P_{N-2}.

Figure 9-3 illustrates the generational changes for the first six generations. The blue arrows in the figure represent the fact that the number of baby pairs each month equals the number of mature pairs the previous month; the red arrows represent the fact that every pair of rabbits (baby or mature) is a mature pair one month later.

	Initial population	First generation	Second generation	Third generation	Fourth generation	Fifth generation	Sixth generation
Time	0	1 month	2 months	3 months	4 months	5 months	6 months
Baby pairs	1	0	1	1	2	3	5
Mature pairs	0	1	1	2	3	5	8
Total pairs	$P_0 = 1$	$P_1 = 1$	$P_2 = 2$	$P_3 = 3$	$P_4 = 5$	$P_5 = 8$	$P_6 = 13$

FIGURE 9-3 Fibonacci's rabbits: P_N is the number of male/female pairs in the Nth generation.

We now have a nice recursive formula for the rabbit population in month N: $P_N = P_{N-1} + P_{N-2}$, and starting terms $P_0 = 1, P_1 = 1$. We can use this formula to track the growth of the rabbit population over a 12-month period and answer Fibonacci's original question ("how many pairs of rabbits . . . in a year?"):

$$P_0 = 1, P_1 = 1, P_2 = 2, P_3 = 3, P_4 = 5, P_5 = 8, P_6 = 13,$$
$$P_7 = 21, P_8 = 34, P_9 = 55, P_{10} = 89, P_{11} = 144, P_{12} = 233.$$

There is an obvious connection between the population sequence describing the growth of the rabbit population in Example 9.5 and the Fibonacci sequence discussed in Example 9.4. Other than a change in notation (the F's changed to P's and

the subscripts started at 0 instead of 1), they are the same sequence.

Fibonacci's description of how his rabbit population would grow was an oversimplified *mathematical model* of how real-life rabbit populations live and breed. In real life, things are quite a bit more complicated: real rabbits are not monogamous, produce litters of varying sizes, die, and so on. We can't capture all the variables that affect a rabbit population in a simple equation, and Fibonacci never intended to do that.

In practical terms, then, is there any value to simplified mathematical models that attempt to describe the complex behavior of populations? The answer is Yes. We can make very good predictions about the ebb and flow of a population over time even when we don't have a completely realistic set of rules describing the population's behavior. Mathematical models that describe population growth are based on a "big-picture" principle: Capture the variables that are really influential in determining how the population changes over time, put them into an equation (or several equations in the case of more complicated models) describing how these variables interact, and forget about the small details. In the next three sections we will put this idea into practice and explore three classic models of population "growth." [A cautionary note on the terminology: When discussing populations, the word *growth* takes on a very general meaning—growth can be *positive* (the numbers go up), *negative* (the numbers go down), or *zero* (the numbers stay the same).]

9.2 The Linear Growth Model

A population grows according to a **linear growth** model if in each generation the population changes by a constant amount. When a population grows according to a linear growth model, that population grows *linearly*, and the population sequence is called an *arithmetic sequence*. Linear growth and arithmetic sequences go hand in hand, but they are not synonymous. *Linear growth* is a term we use to describe a special type of population growth, while an *arithmetic sequence* is an abstract concept that describes a special type of number sequence.

Linear growth models occur mostly when studying *inanimate* populations—that is, populations of things that are not alive and, therefore, do not reproduce. Our first two examples are made-up, but describe typical real-life situations involving linear growth.

EXAMPLE 9.6 HOW MUCH GARBAGE CAN WE TAKE?

The city of Cleansburg is considering a new law that would restrict the monthly amount of garbage allowed to be dumped in the local landfill to a maximum of 120 tons a month. There is a concern among local officials that unless this restriction on dumping is imposed, the landfill will reach its maximum capacity of 20,000 tons in a few years. Currently, there are 8000 tons of garbage in the landfill. Suppose the law is passed right now, and the landfill collects the maximum allowed (120 tons) of garbage each month from here on. (a) How much garbage will there be in the landfill five years from now? (b) How long would it take the landfill to reach its maximum capacity of 20,000 tons?

We can answer these questions by modeling the amount of garbage in the landfill as a population that grows according to a linear growth model. A very simple way to think of the growth of the garbage population is the following: Start with an initial population of $P_0 = 8000$ tons and *each month add 120 tons to whatever the garbage population was in the previous month*. This formulation gives the *recursive* formula $P_N = P_{N-1} + 120$, with $P_0 = 8000$ to get things started. Figure 9-4 illustrates the first few terms of the population sequence based on the recursive formula. For the purposes of answering the questions posed at the start of this example, the recursive formula is not particularly convenient. Five years, for example, equals 60 months, and we would prefer to find the value of P_{60} without having to compute the first 59 terms in the sequence.

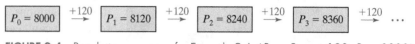

FIGURE 9-4 Population sequence for Example 9.6 ($P_N = P_{N-1} + 120$, $P_0 = 8000$).

We can get a nice explicit formula for the growth of the garbage population using a slightly different interpretation: *In any given month N, the amount of garbage in the landfill equals the original 8000 tons plus 120 tons for each month that has passed.* This formulation gives the *explicit* formula $P_N = 8000 + 120 \times N$. Figure 9-5 illustrates the growth of the population viewed in terms of the explicit formula.

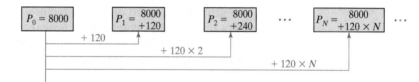

FIGURE 9-5 Population sequence for Example 9.6 ($P_N = 8000 + 120 \times N$).

The explicit formula $P_N = 8000 + 120 \times N$ will allow us to quickly answer the two questions raised at the start of the example. (a) After five years (60 months), the garbage population in the landfill is given by $P_{60} = 8000 + 120 \times 60 = 8000 + 7200 = 15{,}200$. (b) If X represents the month the landfill reaches its maximum capacity of 20,000, then $20{,}000 = 8000 + 120X$. Solving for X gives $X = 100$ months. The landfill will be maxed out 8 years and 4 months from now.

The line graph in Fig. 9-6 shows the projections for the garbage population in the landfill until the landfill reaches its maximum capacity. Not surprisingly, the line graph forms a straight line. This is always true in a linear growth model (and the reason for the name *linear*)—the growth of the population follows a straight line.

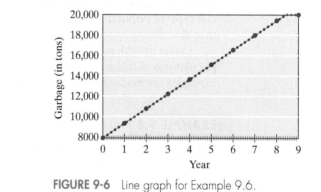

FIGURE 9-6 Line graph for Example 9.6.

EXAMPLE 9.7 NEGATIVE GROWTH AND DONUTS

Crunchy Donuts is a chain of donut stores. At the height of their popularity, Crunchy Donuts were the rage—people stood in line for hours (OK, maybe minutes) for a chance to bite into a warm Crunchy. But times have changed. Bad management and changes in people's eating habits have forced Crunchy Donuts Corporation to start closing stores. On January 1, 2012 Crunchy Donuts had 1290 stores open for business, but since then it has been closing stores at the rate of 60 stores a month. If they continue closing stores at this rate, how long will they stay in business? When will that very last Crunchy be consumed?

We will model the number of Crunchy Donut stores still open as a population with the generations changing once a month—not exactly how things happen but a good approximation of reality. What makes this example different from Example 9.6 is that here we have *negative* linear growth: The population is declining at a constant rate of 60 stores a month.

The simplest way to deal with negative linear growth is to let d be negative. Here $d = -60$, and the population "sequence" written in list form is

$$1290, 1230, 1170, 1110, \ldots, ???$$

Here is the reason for the strange "???" at the end and for the word *sequence* being inside quotation marks: In this situation the list is not infinite—at some point the numbers will become negative, but a negative number of donut stores doesn't make sense. In fact, what we really have here is a finite list that starts as an arithmetic sequence but stops right before the terms become negative numbers.

We can find the number of generations it takes before the terms become negative by setting the explicit formula for the Nth term of the sequence equal to 0 and then solving the equation for N. When N is not an integer (as is often the case) we round it *down* to the nearest integer. Here are the steps applied to our model:

1. Explicit formula for the Nth term set equal to 0: $P_N = 1290 - 60N = 0$.

2. Solve above equation for N: $1290 = 60N \Rightarrow N = \frac{1290}{60} = 21.5$.

3. The last positive term of the population sequence is $P_{21} = 1290 - 60 \times 21 = 30$.

$P_{21} = 30$ means that on October 1, 2013 (21 months after January 1, 2012) the model predicts that Crunchy Donuts will be down to 30 stores and sometime around the middle of October someone will be eating the last Crunchy ever. This is only a model, but it's still sad to see them go.

We will now generalize the ideas introduced in Examples 9.6 and 9.7 and introduce some useful terminology.

- A population grows *linearly* (i.e., according to a linear growth model) if in each generation the population changes by a constant amount d. The constant d is called the **common difference** and the population sequence is an **arithmetic sequence**.

- When d is positive we have *positive growth* (i.e., the population is increasing); when d is negative we have *negative growth* (i.e., the population is decreasing); when $d = 0$ we have *zero growth* (i.e., the population stays constant).

- A population that grows linearly, with initial population P_0 and common difference d, is described by the population sequence

$$P_0, P_0 + d, P_0 + 2d, P_0 + 3d, P_0 + 4d, \ldots$$

Since a population sequence cannot have negative terms, in the case of negative growth the "sequence" ends at the last positive term.

- An *explicit* formula for the Nth term of the population sequence is $P_N = P_0 + Nd$; a *recursive* formula for the Nth term of the population sequence ($N \neq 0$) is $P_N = P_{N-1} + d$.

- The line graph describing a population that grows linearly is always a straight line. When $d > 0$ the line graph has positive slope [Fig. 9-7(a)]; when $d < 0$ the line graph has negative slope [Fig. 9-7(b)]; when $d = 0$ the line graph is horizontal [Fig. 9-7(c)].

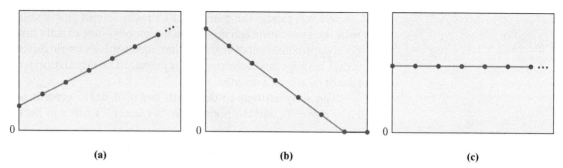

(a)　　　　　　**(b)**　　　　　　**(c)**

FIGURE 9-7 Linear growth. (a) $d > 0$, (b) $d < 0$, and (c) $d = 0$.

Our next example illustrates an important model of population growth. In this model the population grows on a straight line for a while, then the model is recalibrated and the population grows on a different straight line, and so on. This type of growth is called *piecewise linear*.

EXAMPLE 9.8 A SHORT-TERM MODEL OF THE U.S. POPULATION

The U.S. Census Bureau runs a virtual population clock that shows the official United States population at any moment in time. If you go right now to *www.census.gov/population/www /popclockus.html* you can find out what the official United States population is at this moment. If you go back a minute later the numbers will have changed. Why and how did they change?

The ticking of the population clock is based on a mathematical model for the growth of the U.S. population developed by the Census Bureau. The Census Bureau model is based on a combination of just three variables (the Census Bureau refers to these as the *component settings* for the model): (1) the average frequency of births in the United States, (2) the average frequency of deaths in the United States, and (3) the average frequency of international *net migration* into the United States. These component settings are recalibrated each month to account for seasonal changes, but throughout each monthly period they remain constant. This means that the short-term (monthly) model of the U.S. population growth is a linear growth model, and a line graph showing the population growth throughout one month is a line segment. Figure 9-8(a) shows the line graph for the U.S. population from January 1 to February 1, 2012. It is a straight line. If we look at two consecutive months, the line graph consists of two separate line segments, but it need not be a straight line. Figure 9-8(b) shows the line graph for the U.S. population from September 1 to November 15, 2011. It looks almost like a straight line, but it isn't—there is a change of slope at the start of each month.

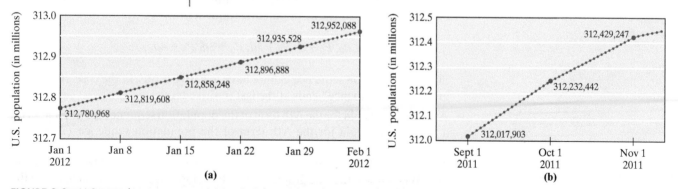

FIGURE 9-8 U.S. population estimates: (a) Jan. 1–Feb. 1, 2012 (linear growth); (b) Sept. 1–Nov. 15, 2011 (piecewise linear growth). (*Source:* U.S. Census Bureau, Population Division.)

At the time of the writing of this example (January, 2012), the three component settings for the month were (1) one birth every 8 seconds, (2) one death every 12 seconds, and (3) one international migrant (net) every 45 seconds. These three numbers are combined into an average net gain of one person every 15.65 seconds. [Here is how you get the 15.65 seconds (if you have the stomach to deal with parts of a person): (1) one birth every 8 seconds is equivalent to $(1/8)$th of a person born every second, (2) one death every 12 seconds is equivalent to $(1/12)$th of a person dying every second, and (3) one net migrant every 45 seconds is equivalent to $(1/45)$th of a person migrating into the United States every second. The net result is that the U.S. population grows by $(1/8) - (1/12) + (1/45) \approx 0.0639$ parts of a person per second. This is equivalent to one person every $\frac{1}{0.0639} \approx 15.65$ seconds.] This number stays constant throughout the month: One person gained every 15.65 seconds means 230 persons added every hour, 5520 persons added each day, and a grand total gain of 171,120 persons for the month of January, 2012 [Fig. 9-8(a)].

EXAMPLE 9.9 REDUCING SINGLE-USE PLASTIC BAG CONSUMPTION

According to the Environmental Protection Agency, about 380 billion plastic bags are consumed each year in the United States. Of these, only about 1% are recycled—the remaining 99% end up in landfills or polluting waterways, rivers, and oceans. (*Source:* U.S. Environmental Protection Agency, *www.epa.gov.*)

Of the 380 billion plastic bags consumed, an estimated 100 billion are *single-use* plastic bags of the type used at the grocery store for bagging groceries. The typical fate of a single-use plastic bag is to be neither reused nor recycled. As shopping consumers we can do something about this—take reusable cloth bags with us when we go grocery shopping. But how much of a dent can this minor change in grocery shopping habits make on the overall problem?

In the United States, on average, 450 single-use plastic grocery bags are consumed each year by each shopping adult in the population. Giving it a positive spin, for each shopping adult that stops using single-use plastic bags at the grocery store, 450 single-use plastic bags can be subtracted from the 100 billion consumed each year. That's not much. But suppose that instead of thinking in terms of individuals we thought in terms of population percentages. There are roughly 210 million shopping-age adults in the U.S. population. For each 1% of this population that stops using single-use plastic bags, 0.945 billion bags (i.e., 945 million) can be subtracted from the 100 billion consumed each year.

This gives us a realistic linear growth model for annual consumption of single-use plastic bags: $P_N = 100 - (0.945)N$, in which P_N represents the annual number of single-use plastic bags consumed (in billions) and N represents the percent of the adult U.S. population that switches to the use of reusable cloth bags.

Figure 9.9 shows a line graph for this model. It shows that it is indeed possible to make a dent in the single-use plastic bag problem.

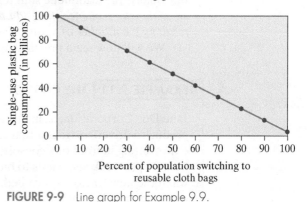

FIGURE 9-9 Line graph for Example 9.9.

The Arithmetic Sum Formula

Suppose you are given an arithmetic sequence—say, 5, 8, 11, 14, 17, . . .—and you are asked to add a few of its terms. How would you do it? When it's just a very few, you would probably just add them term by term: $5 + 8 + 11 + 14 + \cdots$, but what if you were asked to add lots of terms—say the first 500 terms—of the sequence? Adding 500 numbers, even with a calculator, does not seem like a very enticing idea. Fortunately, there is a nice trick that allows us to easily add any number of consecutive terms in any arithmetic sequence. Before giving the general formula, let's see the trick in action.

EXAMPLE 9.10 ADDING THE FIRST 500 TERMS OF 5, 8, 11, 14, . . .

Since a population sequence starts with P_0, the first 500 terms are $P_0, P_1, P_2, \ldots, P_{499}$. In the particular case of the sequence 5, 8, 11, 14, 17, . . . we have $P_0 = 5$, $d = 3$, and $P_{499} = 5 + 3 \times 499 = 1502$. The sum we want to find is

$$S = 5 + 8 + 11 + \cdots + 1496 + 1499 + 1502.$$

Now here comes the trick: (1) write the sum in the normal way, (2) below the first sum, write the sum again but do it backwards (and make sure the +signs are lined up), (3) add the columns, term by term. In our case, we get

(1) $S = \quad 5 + \quad 8 + \quad 11 + \cdots + 1496 + 1499 + 1502.$
(2) $S = 1502 + 1499 + 1496 + \cdots + \quad 11 + \quad 8 + \quad 5.$
(3) $2S = 1507 + 1507 + 1507 + \cdots + 1507 + 1507 + 1507.$

The key is that what happened in (3) is no coincidence. In each column we get the same number: $1507 = 5 + 1502 =$ (starting term) + (ending term). Rewriting (3) as $2S = 500 \times 1507$ and solving for S gives the sum we want: $S = \frac{1507 \times 500}{2} = 376{,}750.$

We will now generalize the trick we used in the preceding example. In the solution $S = \frac{1507 \times 500}{2}$ the 1507 represents the sum of the starting and ending terms, the 500 represents the number of terms being added, and the 2 is just a 2. The generalization of this observation gives the **arithmetic sum formula**.

■ ARITHMETIC SUM FORMULA

If $P_0, P_1, P_2, \ldots$ are the terms of an arithmetic sequence, then

$$P_0 + P_1 + P_2 + \cdots + P_{N-1} = \frac{(P_0 + P_{N-1})N}{2}.$$

Informally, the arithmetic sum formula says *to find the sum of consecutive terms of an arithmetic sequence, first add the first and the last terms of the sum, multiply the result by the number of terms being added, and divide by two.*

We will now see a practical application of the arithmetic sum formula.

EXAMPLE 9.11 THE COST OF BUILDING UP INVENTORY

Jane Doe Corporation, a small tractor manufacturer, has developed a radically new product: a driverless tractor that can be controlled remotely with a joystick by an operator sitting in front of a console. The company can manufacture a maximum of 30 tractors per week and wants to build up its inventory to meet the projected demand when the new tractor is unveiled. The plan is to go into an accelerated production schedule ahead of the product launch date. The company will produce 30 tractors each week for a period of 72 weeks and place the tractors in storage at a cost of $10 per tractor per week. How much should the company budget for storage costs over the 72-week production period?

Table 9-1 shows the weekly storage cost starting at the end of week 1 (the start of storage) and ending at the end of week 72. The storage costs represent the first 72 terms of an arithmetic sequence that starts with $300 and ends with $21,600. The arithmetic sum formula gives the total storage costs over the 72-week production period: $\frac{(\$300 + \$21,600) \times 72}{2} = \$788,400$.

Week	0	1	2	3	...	70	71	72
Production	0	30	30	30	...	30	30	30
Storage cost	0	$300	$600	$900	...	$21,000	$21,300	$21,600

TABLE 9-1 Weekly storage costs for new tractors

Sometimes the use of the arithmetic sum formula requires us to do a little detective work, as in the case where we are given just the first term and last term of the sum and the common difference d of the arithmetic sequence.

EXAMPLE 9.12 $(4 + 13 + 22 + \cdots + 922) = ?$

Suppose you are asked to add the terms of an arithmetic sequence with common difference $d = 9$. The first term in the sum is 4; the last term is 922. To use the arithmetic sum formula we need to know how many terms we are adding. Call that number N. Then $922 = P_{N-1}$ (remember, we start at P_0). On the other hand, the explicit formula for linear growth gives $P_{N-1} = 4 + 9(N-1)$. Combining the two gives $922 = 4 + 9(N-1) = 9N - 5 \Rightarrow 9N = 927 \Rightarrow N = 103$. We now have what we need to use the arithmetic sum formula:

$$4 + 13 + 22 + \cdots + 922 = \frac{(4 + 922) \times 103}{2} = 47,689.$$

9.3 The Exponential Growth Model

Imagine you are presented with the following choice: (1) You can have $100,000, to be paid to you one month from today, or (2) you can have 1 penny today, 2 pennies tomorrow, 4 pennies the day after tomorrow, and so on—each day doubling your payoff from the day before—for a full month (say 31 days). Which of the two options would you choose? We'll come back to this question later in the section, but you should make your choice now, and no cheating—once you make your choice you have to stay with it.

Before we start a full discussion of exponential growth, we need to spend a little time explaining the mathematical meaning of the term *growth rate*. In this chapter we will focus on growth rates as they apply to population models, but the concept applies to many other situations besides populations. In Chapter 10, for example, we will discuss growth rates again, but in the context of money and finance.

When the size of a population "grows" from some value X to some new value Y, we want to describe the growth in relative terms, so that the growth in going from $X = 2$ to $Y = 4$ is the same as the growth in going from $X = 50$ to $Y = 100$.

- **Growth rate.** The *growth rate r* of a population as it changes from an initial value X (the *baseline*) to a new value Y (the *end-value*) is given by the ratio $r = \frac{Y - X}{X}$. (*Note*: It is customary to express growth rates in terms of percentages, so, as a final step, r is converted to a percent.)

One important thing to keep in mind about the definition of growth rate is that it is not symmetric—the growth rate when the baseline is X and the end-value is Y is very different from the growth rate when the baseline is Y and the end-value is X.

| **EXAMPLE 9.13** | GROWTH RATES, END-VALUES, AND BASELINES |

Table 9-2 shows the growth rates for several different baseline/end-value combinations. The first column of Table 9-2 shows the baseline population X, the second column shows the value for the new population Y, and the third column shows the computation of the growth rate r. All the computations except for (6) can and should be done without the use of a calculator.

Sometimes we are given the baseline X and the growth rate r and need to compute the end-value Y. If we solve the equation $r = \frac{Y - X}{X}$ for Y, we get $Y = rX + X = (r + 1)X$. In this formula r must be in fractional or decimal form. Table 9-3 shows several examples of the computation of the end-value Y given the baseline X and the growth rate r.

The last variation of this theme is to compute the baseline X given the end-value Y and the growth rate r. The formula for X in terms of Y and r is $X = \frac{Y}{r + 1}$. It is just a twisted version of the formula $Y = (r + 1)X$.

	Baseline X	End-value Y	Growth rate $r = \frac{(Y - X)}{X}$
(1)	2	4	$\frac{(4 - 2)}{2} = 1 = 100\%$
(2)	50	100	$\frac{(100 - 50)}{50} = 1 = 100\%$
(3)	100	50	$\frac{(50 - 100)}{100} = -\frac{1}{2} = -50\%$
(4)	10	12	$\frac{(12 - 10)}{10} = \frac{2}{10} = 20\%$
(5)	10	7.5	$\frac{(7.5 - 10)}{10} = -\frac{2.5}{10} = -25\%$
(6)	1321	1472	$\frac{(1472 - 1321)}{1321} \approx 11.43\%$

■ **TABLE 9-2**   Computation of growth rates

	Baseline X	Growth rate r	End-value $Y = (r + 1)X$
(1)	50	$100\% = 1$	$2 \times 50 = 100$
(2)	50	$-100\% = -1$	$0 \times 50 = 0$
(3)	50	$50\% = 0.5$	$1.5 \times 50 = 75$
(4)	100	$-20\% = -0.2$	$0.8 \times 100 = 80$
(5)	37,314	$5.4\% = 0.054$	$1.054 \times 37,314$
(6)	37,314	$-5.4\% = -0.054$	$0.946 \times 37,314$

■ **TABLE 9-3**   Computation of end-values

We are finally ready to define *exponential growth*.

- A population grows **exponentially** if in each generation the population "grows" by the same constant *factor R* called the **common ratio**. In this case the population sequence takes the form

$$P_0, P_1 = RP_0, P_2 = R^2P_0, P_3 = R^3P_0, P_4 = R^4P_0, \ldots \quad (1)$$

(Note the difference between linear and exponential growth: In linear growth we *add* a fixed constant, in exponential growth we *multiply* by a fixed constant.)

- An *explicit* formula for the Nth term of the population sequence given in equation (1) is $P_N = R^N P_0$; a *recursive* formula for the Nth term of the population sequence $(N \neq 0)$ is $P_N = RP_{N-1}$.

- Any numerical sequence in which a term is obtained by multiplying the preceding term by the same constant R is called a **geometric sequence**. While geometric sequences in general can have negative terms $(1, -2, 4, -8, \ldots$ is a geometric sequence with $R = -2)$, population sequences cannot have any negative terms. This implies that for population sequences we must include the assumption that $R \geq 0$.

- If a population sequence grows exponentially, the *growth rate* from one generation to the next is constant. If we call this constant growth rate r, we can describe the population sequence in a slightly different form:

$$P_0, P_1 = (1 + r)P_0, P_2 = (1 + r)^2 P_0, P_3 = (1 + r)^3 P_0, P_4 = (1 + r)^4 P_0, \ldots \quad (2)$$

Equations (1) and (2) are two different versions of the same sequence connected by the relation $R = (1 + r)$. In other words, the *common ratio* equals *one plus the growth rate*.

- The relation $R = (1 + r)$ combined with the restriction $R \geq 0$ imposes a restriction on the values of the growth rate: $r \geq -1$ (i.e., a population growth rate cannot go below $-1 = -100\%$). When $R > 1$ the growth rate r is positive and the line-graph of the population sequence is increasing [Fig. 9-10(a)]; when $0 < R < 1$ the growth rate r is negative and the line-graph of the population sequence is decreasing [Fig. 9-10(b)]; when $R = 1$ the growth rate r is zero and the line-graph of the population sequence is horizontal [Fig. 9-10(c)]; and finally, $R = 0$ means $r = -1$ and a total collapse of the population—it becomes extinct after one generation [Fig. 9-10(d)]. (This last scenario is so unusual as to be practically impossible, but in the next section we will see a model that makes the possibility of extinction much more realistic.)

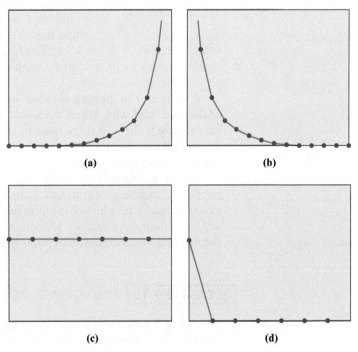

(a)   (b)

(c)   (d)

FIGURE 9-10 Exponential growth. (a) $R > 1$ $(r > 0)$, (b) $0 < R < 1$ $(-1 < r < 0)$, (c) $R = 1$ $(r = 0)$, (d) $R = 0$ $(r = -1)$.

Exponential growth models are useful to describe the growth of living organisms such as bacteria and viruses, the growth of human or animal populations under unrestricted breeding conditions, and even the growth of intellectual products such as e-mails, Web pages, and data sets. In all real-life applications, exponential growth is assumed to occur only for a limited amount of time—there is always a point at which exponential growth stops because the conditions that support the model can no longer be sustained. Our next example illustrates this point.

EXAMPLE 9.14 THE SPREAD OF AN EPIDEMIC

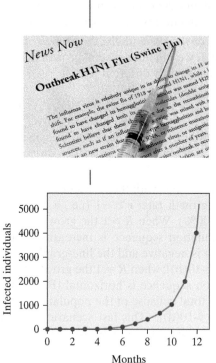

FIGURE 9-11   The first year of an epidemic.

In their early stages, infectious diseases such as HIV or the swine flu spread following an exponential growth model—each infected individual infects roughly the same number of healthy individuals over a given period of time. Formally, this translates into the recursive formula $P_N = (1 + r)P_{N-1}$ where P_N denotes the number of infected individuals in the population at time N and r denotes the growth rate of the infection.

Every epidemic starts with an original group of infected individuals called "population zero." Let's consider an epidemic in which "population zero" consists of just one infected individual ($P_0 = 1$) and such that, on average, each infected individual transmits the disease to one healthy individual each month. This means that every month the number of infected individuals doubles and the growth rate is $r = 1 = 100\%$. Under this model the number of infected individuals N months after the start of the epidemic is given by $P_N = 2^N$.

Figure 9-11 shows the growth of the epidemic during its first year. By the end of the first year the number of infected individuals is $P_{12} = 2^{12} = 4096$. That's not too bad. But suppose that no vaccines are found to slow down the epidemic and the growth rate for infected individuals continues at 100% per month. At the end of the second year the number of infected individuals would equal $P_{24} = 2^{24} = 16,777,216$. Eight months after that the number of infected individuals would equal $P_{32} = 2^{32} \approx 4.3$ billion (more than half of the world's population); one month later every person on the planet would be infected.

Example 9.14 illustrates what happens when exponential growth continues unchecked, and why, when modeling epidemics, exponential growth is a realistic model for a while, but there must be a point in time where the rate of infection has to level off and the model must change. Otherwise, the human race would have been wiped out many times over.

Our next example shows the flip side of an epidemic—how vaccines and good public health policy help to eradicate a disease. Smallpox and polio are two examples of diseases that have been practically eradicated, but to keep things simple we will use a fictitious example. (A detailed discussion of the development of the polio vaccine and the eradication of polio is given in Chapter 14.)

EXAMPLE 9.15 ERADICATING THE GAMMA VIRUS INFECTION

Thanks to a new vaccine and good public health policy, the number of reported cases of the Gamma virus infection has been *dropping* by 70% a year since 2010, when there were 1 million reported cases of the infection. If the present rate continues, how many reported cases of Gamma virus infection can we predict by the year 2016? How long will it take to eradicate the virus?

In this example we are dealing with negative exponential growth. The growth rate is $r = -70\% = -0.7$, and the common ratio is $R = 1 - 0.7 = 0.3$. The initial population is $P_0 = 1,000,000$.

According to the model, the number of cases of the Gamma virus in 2016 should be $P_6 = 1{,}000{,}000 \times (0.3)^6 = 729$. By 2017 this number will drop to about 220 cases $(729 \times 0.3 = 218.7)$, by 2018 to about 66 cases, by 2019 to about 20 cases, and by 2020 to 6 cases.

The story of the eradication of the Gamma virus is illustrated in Figure 9-12.

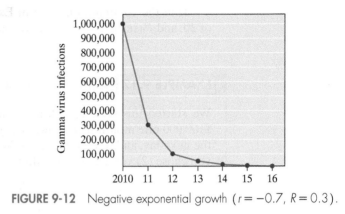

FIGURE 9-12 Negative exponential growth $(r = -0.7, R = 0.3)$.

The Geometric Sum Formula

Suppose you want to find the sum of the first 100 (or 1000) terms of a geometric sequence. Just as with arithmetic sequences, there is a handy formula that will allow us to do it without having to actually add the terms. We will call this formula the **geometric sum formula**. Here we will give the formula first and then explain how it can be derived.

■ GEOMETRIC SUM FORMULA

$$P_0 + RP_0 + R^2 P_0 + \cdots + R^{N-1}P_0 = \frac{(R^N - 1)P_0}{R - 1}$$

(*Note:* The geometric sum formula works for all values of R with one important exception: When $R = 1$ the denominator on the right-hand side equals 0, and the formula does not work. When $R = 1$, however, no fancy formula is needed: Each term of the sum equals P_0 and the sum equals NP_0.)

The next example illustrates how the geometric sum formula can be derived using a trick analogous to the one we used to derive the arithmetic sum formula.

EXAMPLE 9.16   ADDING THE FIRST 20 TERMS OF 5, 15, 45, 135, . . .

The sequence 5, 15, 45, 135, . . . is a geometric sequence with $R = 3$. Let's call S the sum of the first 20 terms of the sequence. Then,

$$S = 5 + 3 \times 5 + 3^2 \times 5 + 3^3 \times 5 + \cdots + 3^{19} \times 5 \qquad (1)$$

(The sum ends with the term $3^{19} \times 5$ because it starts with $5 = 3^0 \times 5$.)

If we multiply both sides of equation (1) by $R = 3$ we get

$$3S = 3 \times 5 + 3^2 \times 5 + 3^3 \times 5 + \cdots + 3^{19} \times 5 + 3^{20} \times 5 \qquad (2)$$

If you compare the terms in equation (2) to those in equation (1) you can see most of them are the same. Subtracting equation (1) from equation (2) gets rid of a lot of stuff (try it and you'll see) and gives us equation (3):

$$3S - S = 3^{20} \times 5 - 5 \qquad (3)$$

With a little housekeeping on both sides of equation (3) we get

$$S = \frac{(3^{20} - 1) \times 5}{2} = 8,716,961,000.$$

If in the computation done in Example 9.16 we use R instead of 3, N instead of 20, and P_0 instead of 5 we get the general version of the geometric sum formula.

| **EXAMPLE 9.17** | A MONTH'S WORTH OF DOUBLING PENNIES |

We started this section with a unique proposition: (1) Take a lump payment of $100,000 one month from now, or (2) take 1 cent today, 2 cents tomorrow, 4 cents the next day, and so on for 31 days. Which one did you think was the better offer? If you chose (2) you were wise. After 31 days, you would have a grand total of

$$1 + 2 + 2^2 + 2^3 + \cdots + 2^{30} \text{ cents.}$$

This is a geometric sum with $R = 2$ and $P_0 = 1$. Applying the geometric sum formula gives $1 + 2 + 2^2 + 2^3 + \cdots + 2^{30} = \frac{2^{31} - 1}{2 - 1} = 2^{31} - 1 = 2,147,483,647$ cents. That's $21,474,836 plus some spare change! (Yes, that's right—$21 million plus!)

The geometric sum formula has many important and interesting applications to finance (amortizing loans, calculating the value of an annuity, etc.), and we will discuss some of these applications in Chapter 10.

9.4 The Logistic Growth Model

One of the key tenets of population biology is the idea that there is an inverse relation between the growth rate of a population and its density. Small populations have plenty of room to spread out and grow, and thus their growth rates tend to be high. As the population density increases, however, there is less room to grow and there is more competition for resources—the growth rate tends to taper off. Sometimes the population density is so high that resources become scarce or depleted, leading to negative population growth or even to extinction.

The effects of population density on growth rates were studied in the 1950s by behavioral psychologist John B. Calhoun. Calhoun's now classic studies showed that when rats were placed in a closed environment, their behavior and growth rates were normal as long as the rats were not too crowded. When their environment became too crowded, the rats started to exhibit abnormal behaviors, such as infertility and cannibalism, which effectively put a brake on the rats' growth rate. In extreme cases, the entire rat population became extinct.

Calhoun's experiments with rats are but one classic illustration of the general principle that a *population's growth rate is negatively impacted by the population's density.*

This principle is particularly important in cases in which the population is confined to a limited environment. Population biologists call such an environment the **habitat**. The habitat might be a cage (as in Calhoun's rat experiments), a lake (for a population of fish), a garden (for a population of snails), and, of course, Earth itself (everyone's habitat).

In 1838, the Belgian mathematician Pierre François Verhulst proposed a mathematical model of population growth for species living within a fixed habitat. Verhulst called his model the **logistic growth model**.

The logistic growth model is based on two principles:

1. Every biological population living in a confined habitat has a natural inter-generational growth rate that we call the **growth parameter** of that population. The growth parameter of a population depends on the kind of species that makes up the population and the nature of its habitat—a population of beetles in a garden has a different growth parameter than a population of gorillas in the rainforest, and a population of gorillas in the rainforest has a different growth parameter than a population of gorillas in a zoo. Given a specific species and a specific habitat for that species, we will assume the growth parameter is a constant we will denote by r.

2. The actual growth rate of a specific population living in a specific habitat depends not just on the growth parameter r (otherwise we would have an exponential growth model) but also on the amount of "elbow room" available for the population to grow (a variable that changes from generation to generation). When the population is small (relative to the size of the habitat) and there is plenty of elbow room for the population to grow, the growth rate is roughly equal to the growth parameter r and the population grows more or less exponentially [Fig. 9-13(a)]. As the population gets bigger and there is less space for the population to grow, the growth rate gets proportionally smaller [Fig. 9-13(b)]. Sometimes there is a switch to negative growth, and the population starts decreasing for a few generations to get back to a more sustainable level [Fig. 9-13(c)].

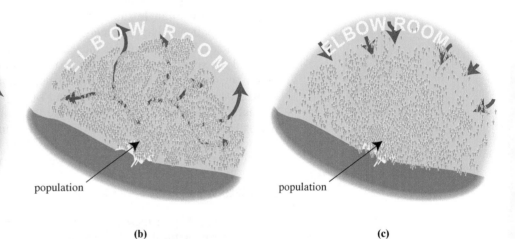

(a)   **(b)**   **(c)**

FIGURE 9-13 (a) Growth rate approximately r, (b) growth rate gets smaller, and (c) negative growth rate.

We will now discuss how the two loosely stated principles above can be formalized into a mathematical model. The first step is to quantify the concept of "elbow room" in a habitat. This can be done by introducing a related concept: the *carrying capacity*. For a given species and a given habitat, the **carrying capacity** C of a habitat is the *maximum* number of individuals that the habitat can carry. Once we accept the idea that each habitat has a carrying capacity C for a particular population, we can quantify the amount of "elbow room" for that population as the difference $(C - P_N)$ where P_N is the size of the population in the Nth generation.

The simplest way to put populations, habitats, carrying capacity, and elbow room into a mathematical model is to combine the population size P_N and the carrying capacity C into a single fraction $p_N = \frac{P_N}{C}$, the **p-value** of the population. The p-value of a population represents the fraction (or percentage) of the carrying capacity that is occupied by that population and is analogous to the occupancy rate at a hotel. Using p-values makes things a lot easier. We don't really worry about what the carrying capacity C of the habitat is—the p-value has already taken that into account: A p-value of 0.6 means that the population is occupying 60% of the carrying capacity of the habitat; a p-value of 1 means 100% occupancy of the habitat. Using p-values we can also express the relative elbow room for a population in its habitat:

The relative elbow room for the Nth generation is $(1 - p_N)$. [Think of $(1 - p_N)$ as the difference between 100% occupancy and the current occupancy rate at the Habitat Hotel.]

We are finally ready to put all of the aforementioned together. Everything will be expressed in terms of population p-values.

- In the Nth generation, the p-value of the population is p_N and the amount of elbow room for that population is $(1 - p_N)$.

- The growth rate of the population in going from the Nth generation to the next generation is proportional to the growth parameter r and the amount of elbow room $(1 - p_N)$, i.e.,

$$\text{growth rate for the } N\text{th generation} = r(1 - p_N).$$

- In any given generation, the growth rate times the size of the population equals the size of the population in the next generation, i.e.,

$$p_{N+1} = r(1 - p_N)p_N.$$

- **Logistic equation.** The equation $p_{N+1} = r(1 - p_N)p_N$ is called the *logistic equation*. It gives a recursive formula for the growth of a population under the logistic growth model.

Using the logistic equation, we can analyze the behavior of any population living in a fixed habitat. In the next few examples, we will explore the remarkable population patterns that can emerge from the logistic equation. All we will need for our "ecological experiments" is the value p_0 of the starting population (this number is called the **seed**), the value of the growth parameter r, and a good calculator, or better yet, a spreadsheet. [A note of warning: all p-values are expressed as decimals between 0 (the population is extinct) and 1 (the population has completely filled up the habitat). The calculations were done in a computer and carried to 16 decimal places before being rounded off to 3 or 4 decimal places. You are encouraged to follow along with your own calculator, but don't be surprised if the numbers don't match exactly. Round-off errors are a way of life with the logistic equation.]

EXAMPLE 9.18 A STABLE EQUILIBRIUM

Fish farming is big business these days, so you decide to give it a try. You have access to a large, natural pond in which you plan to set up a rainbow trout hatchery. The carrying capacity of the pond is $C = 10,000$ fish, and the growth parameter of this type of rainbow trout is $r = 2.5$. We will use the logistic equation to model the growth of the fish population in your pond.

You start by seeding the pond with an initial population of 2000 rainbow trout (i.e., 20% of the pond's carrying capacity, or $p_0 = 0.2$). After the first year (trout have an annual hatching season) the population is given by

$$p_1 = r(1 - p_0)p_0 = 2.5 \times (1 - 0.2) \times (0.2) = 0.4$$

The population of the pond has doubled, and things are looking good! Unfortunately, most of the fish are small fry and not ready to be sent to market. After the second year the population of the pond is given by

$$p_2 = 2.5 \times (1 - 0.4) \times (0.4) = 0.6$$

The population is no longer doubling, but the hatchery is still doing well. You are looking forward to even better yields after the third year. But on the third year you get a big surprise:

$$p_3 = 2.5 \times (1 - 0.6) \times (0.6) = 0.6$$

Stubbornly, you wait for better luck the next year, but

$$p_4 = 2.5 \times (1 - 0.6) \times (0.6) = 0.6$$

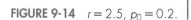

FIGURE 9-14 $r = 2.5$, $p_0 = 0.2$.

From the second year on, the hatchery is stuck at 60% of the pond capacity—nothing is going to change unless external forces come into play. We describe this situation as one in which the population is at a *stable equilibrium*. Figure 9-14 shows a line graph of the pond's fish population for the first four years.

EXAMPLE 9.19 AN ATTRACTING POINT

Consider the same setting as in Example 9.18 (same pond and the same variety of rainbow trout with $r = 2.5$), but suppose you initially seed the pond with 3000 rainbow trout (30% of the pond's carrying capacity). How will the fish population grow if we start with $p_0 = 0.3$?

The first six years of population growth are as follows:

$$p_1 = 2.5 \times (1 - 0.3) \times (0.3) = 0.525$$
$$p_2 = 2.5 \times (1 - 0.525) \times (0.525) \approx 0.6234$$
$$p_3 = 2.5 \times (1 - 0.6234) \times (0.6234) \approx 0.5869$$
$$p_4 = 2.5 \times (1 - 0.5869) \times (0.5869) \approx 0.6061$$
$$p_5 = 2.5 \times (1 - 0.6061) \times (0.6061) \approx 0.5968$$
$$p_6 = 2.5 \times (1 - 0.5968) \times (0.5968) \approx 0.6016$$

Clearly, something different is happening here. The trout population appears to be fluctuating—up, down, up again, back down—but always hovering near the value of 0.6. We leave it to the reader to verify that as one continues with the population sequence, the p-values inch closer and closer to 0.6 in an oscillating (up, down, up, down, ...) manner. The value 0.6 is called an *attracting point* of the population sequence. Figure 9-15 shows a line graph of the pond's fish population for the first six years.

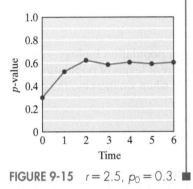

FIGURE 9-15 $r = 2.5$, $p_0 = 0.3$.

EXAMPLE 9.20 COMPLEMENTARY SEEDS

In Example 9.19 we seeded the pond at 30% of its carrying capacity ($p_0 = 0.3$). If we seed the pond with the complementary seed $p_0 = 1 - 0.3 = 0.7$, we end up with the same populations:

$$p_1 = 2.5 \times 0.3 \times 0.7 = 2.5 \times 0.7 \times 0.3 = 0.525$$
$$p_2 = 2.5 \times (1 - 0.525) \times (0.525) \approx 0.6234$$

and so on.

Example 9.20 points to a simple but useful general rule about logistic growth—the seeds p_0 and $(1 - p_0)$ always produce the same population sequence. This follows because in the expression $p_1 = r(1 - p_0)p_0$, p_0 and $(1 - p_0)$ play interchangeable roles—if you change p_0 to $(1 - p_0)$, then you are also changing $(1 - p_0)$ to p_0. Nothing gained, nothing lost! Once the values match in the first generation, the rest of the p-values follow suit. The moral of this observation is that you should never seed your pond at higher than 50% of its carrying capacity.

EXAMPLE 9.21 A TWO-CYCLE PATTERN

You decided that farming rainbow trout is too difficult. You are moving on to raising something easier—goldfish. The particular variety of goldfish you will grow has growth parameter $r = 3.1$.

Suppose you start by seeding a tank at 20% of its carrying capacity ($p_0 = 0.2$). The first 16 p-values of the goldfish population (for brevity, the details are left to the reader) are

$$p_0 = 0.2, \qquad p_1 = 0.496, \qquad p_2 \approx 0.775, \qquad p_3 \approx 0.541,$$
$$p_4 \approx 0.770, \qquad p_5 \approx 0.549, \qquad p_6 \approx 0.767, \qquad p_7 \approx 0.553,$$
$$p_8 \approx 0.766, \qquad p_9 \approx 0.555, \qquad p_{10} \approx 0.766, \qquad p_{11} \approx 0.556,$$
$$p_{12} \approx 0.765, \qquad p_{13} \approx 0.557, \qquad p_{14} \approx 0.765, \qquad p_{15} \approx 0.557, \qquad \ldots$$

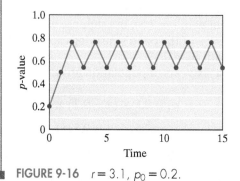

An interesting pattern emerges here. After a few breeding seasons, the population settles into a two-cycle pattern, alternating between a high-population period at 0.765 and a low-population period at 0.557. Figure 9-16 convincingly illustrates the oscillating nature of the population sequence.

FIGURE 9-16 $r = 3.1$, $p_0 = 0.2$.

Example 9.21 describes a situation not unusual in population biology—animal populations that alternate cyclically between two different levels of population density. Even more complex cyclical patterns are possible when we increase the growth parameter just a little.

EXAMPLE 9.22   A FOUR-CYCLE PATTERN

You are now out of the fish-farming business and have acquired an interest in entomology—the study of insects. Let's apply the logistic growth model to study the population growth of a type of flour beetle with growth parameter $r = 3.5$. The seed will be $p_0 = 0.44$. (There is no particular significance to the choice of the seed—you can change the seed and you will still get an interesting population sequence.)

Following are a few specially selected p-values. We leave it to the reader to verify these numbers and fill in the missing details.

$$p_0 = 0.440, \qquad p_1 \approx 0.862, \qquad p_2 \approx 0.415, \qquad p_3 \approx 0.850,$$
$$p_4 \approx 0.446, \qquad p_5 \approx 0.865, \qquad \ldots \qquad\qquad p_{20} \approx 0.497,$$
$$p_{21} \approx 0.875, \qquad p_{22} \approx 0.383, \qquad p_{23} \approx 0.827, \qquad p_{24} \approx 0.501,$$
$$p_{25} \approx 0.875, \qquad \ldots$$

It took a while, but we can now see a pattern: Since $p_{25} = p_{21}$, the population will repeat itself in a four-period cycle ($p_{26} = p_{22}$, $p_{27} = p_{23}$, $p_{28} = p_{24}$, $p_{29} = p_{25} = p_{21}$, etc.), an interesting and surprising turn of events. Figure 9-17 shows the line graph of the first 26 p-values.

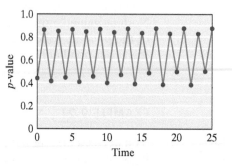

FIGURE 9-17 $r = 3.5$, $p_0 = 0.44$.

The cyclical behavior exhibited in Example 9-22 is not unusual, and many insect populations follow cyclical patterns of various lengths—7-year locusts, 17-year cicadas, and so on.

In the logistic growth model, the highest allowed value of the growth parameter r is $r = 4$. (For $r > 4$ the p-values can fall outside the permissible range.) Our last example illustrates what happens when $r = 4$.

EXAMPLE 9.23 A RANDOM PATTERN

Suppose the seed is $p_0 = 0.2$ and $r = 4$. Below are the p-values p_0 through p_{20}.

$p_0 = 0.2$, $p_1 = 0.64$, $p_2 \approx 0.9216$, $p_3 \approx 0.289$,

$p_4 \approx 0.8219$, $p_5 \approx 0.5854$, $p_6 \approx 0.9708$, $p_7 \approx 0.1133$,

$p_8 \approx 0.402$, $p_9 \approx 0.9616$, $p_{10} \approx 0.1478$, $p_{11} \approx 0.5039$,

$p_{12} \approx 0.9999$, $p_{13} \approx 0.0004$, $p_{14} \approx 0.001$, $p_{15} \approx 0.0039$,

$p_{16} \approx 0.0157$, $p_{17} \approx 0.0617$, $p_{18} \approx 0.2317$, $p_{19} \approx 0.7121$, $p_{20} = 0.82$.

Figure 9-18 is a line graph plotting these p-values.

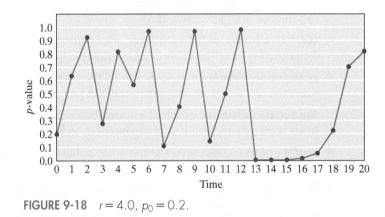

FIGURE 9-18 $r = 4.0$, $p_0 = 0.2$.

The surprise here is the absence of any predictable pattern. In fact, no matter how much further we continue computing p-values, we will find no pattern—to an outside observer the p-values for this population sequence appear to be quite erratic and seemingly random. Of course, we know better—they are all coming from the logistic equation.

The logistic growth model exhibits many interesting surprises. In addition to Exercises 57 through 62 you are encouraged to experiment on your own much like we did in the preceding examples: Choose a seed p_0 between 0 and 0.5, choose an r between 3 and 4, and let her (the logistic equation) rip!

 Conclusion

In this chapter we discussed three classic models of population growth. In the *linear growth model*, the population is described by an *arithmetic sequence* of the form $P_0, P_0 + d, P_0 + 2d, P_0 + 3d, \ldots$. In each transition period the population grows by the addition of a fixed amount d called the *common difference*. Linear growth is most common in situations in which there is no "breeding" such as populations of inanimate objects—commodities, resources, garbage, and so on.

In the *exponential growth model*, the population is described by a *geometric sequence* of the form $P_0, RP_0, R^2P_0, R^3P_0, \ldots$. In each transition period the population grows by multiplication by a positive constant R called the *common ratio*. Exponential growth is typical of situations in which there is some form of "breeding" in the population and the amount of breeding is directly proportional to the size of the population.

In the *logistic growth model* populations are described in relative terms by the logistic equation $p_{N+1} = r(1 - p_N)p_N$. This model is used to describe the growth of biological populations living in a fixed habitat and whose growth rates are in direct proportion to the amount of "elbow room" in the habitat. When confined to a single-species habitat, many animal populations grow according to the logistic growth model.

KEY CONCEPTS

9.1 Sequences and Population Sequences

- **sequence:** an ordered, infinite list of numbers, **262**
- **term:** the individual numbers in a sequence, **262**
- **explicit formula:** for a sequence, a formula that gives the Nth term explicitly, without the use of other terms, **263**
- **recursive formula:** for a sequence, a formula that gives the Nth term of the sequence as a function of other terms of the sequence, **263**
- **population sequence:** a sequence of the form $P_0, P_1, P_2, P_3, \ldots$, where P_N represents the size of the population in the Nth generation, **264**
- **time-series graph:** a graph of a population sequence where time is measured on the horizontal axis and the size of the population is measured on the vertical axis, **265**
- **scatter-plot:** a times-series graph with isolated points representing the values of a population sequence, **265**
- **line graph:** a times-series graph where the values (points) are connected with lines, **265**

9.2 The Linear Growth Model

- **linear growth:** a model of population growth based on the recursive rule $P_N = P_{N-1} + d$, where d is a constant, **267**
- **arithmetic sequence:** a sequence of the form $P_0, P_0 + d, P_0 + 2d, P_0 + 3d, \ldots$, **267**
- **common difference:** the constant difference d between successive terms of an arithmetic sequence $(d = P_N - P_{N-1})$, **269**
- **arithmetic sum formula:** gives the sum of N consecutive terms of an arithmetic sequence $\left[(\text{first term} + \text{last term}) \times \frac{N}{2} \right]$, **272**

9.3 The Exponential Growth Model

- **growth rate:** the ratio $\frac{(Y - X)}{X}$ as a variable changes from a baseline value X to an end-value Y, **274**
- **exponential growth:** a model of population growth based on the recursive rule $P_N = RP_{N-1}$, where R is a non-negative constant, **274**
- **common ratio:** the constant ratio R between successive terms of a geometric sequence, $\left(R = \frac{P_N}{P_{N-1}} \right)$, **274**
- **geometric sequence:** a sequence of the form $P_0, RP_0, R^2P_0, R^3P_0, \ldots$, **275**
- **geometric sum formula:** gives the sum of N consecutive terms of a geometric sequence with common ratio R, $\left[(\text{first term})\frac{(R^N - 1)}{(R - 1)} \right]$, **277**

9.4 The Logistic Growth Model

- **habitat:** a confined geographical area inhabited by a population, **278**
- **logistic growth model:** a model of population growth based on the logistic equation, **278**
- **growth parameter:** the natural, unrestricted growth rate of a species in a specific habitat, **279**
- **carrying capacity:** the maximum number of individuals of a given species that a habitat can carry, **279**
- **p-value:** the ratio $\frac{P}{C}$ where P is the size of the population and C is the carrying capacity of the habitat; it represents the fraction or percent of the habitat occupied by the population, **279**
- **logistic equation:** the recursive equation $p_{N+1} = r(1 - p_N)p_N$, where p_N is the p-value of the population in the Nth generation and r is the growth parameter of the species, **280**

EXERCISES

WALKING

9.1 Sequences and Population Sequences

1. Consider the sequence defined by the explicit formula $A_N = N^2 + 1$.

(a) Find A_1.

(b) Find A_{100}.

(c) Suppose $A_N = 10$. Find N.

2. Consider the sequence defined by the explicit formula $A_N = 3^N - 2$.

(a) Find A_3.

(b) Use a calculator to find A_{15}.

(c) Suppose $A_N = 79$. Find N.

3. Consider the sequence defined by the explicit formula $A_N = \frac{4N}{N+3}$.

(a) Find A_1.

(b) Find A_9.

(c) Suppose $A_N = \frac{5}{2}$. Find N.

4. Consider the sequence defined by the explicit formula $A_N = \frac{2N+3}{3N-1}$.

(a) Find A_1.

(b) Find A_{100}.

(c) Suppose $A_N = 1$. Find N.

5. Consider the sequence defined by the explicit formula $A_N = (-1)^{N+1}$.

(a) Find A_1.

(b) Find A_{100}.

(c) Find all values of N for which $A_N = 1$.

6. Consider the sequence defined by the explicit formula $A_N = \left(-\frac{1}{N}\right)^{N-1}$.

(a) Find A_1.

(b) Find A_4.

(c) Find all values of N for which A_N is positive.

7. Consider the sequence defined by the recursive formula $A_N = 2A_{N-1} + A_{N-2}$ and starting with $A_1 = 1$, $A_2 = 1$.

(a) List the next four terms of the sequence.

(b) Find A_8.

8. Consider the sequence defined by the recursive formula $A_N = A_{N-1} + 2A_{N-2}$ and starting with $A_1 = 1$, $A_2 = 1$.

(a) List the next four terms of the sequence.

(b) Find A_8.

9. Consider the sequence defined by the recursive formula $A_N = A_{N-1} - 2A_{N-2}$ and starting with $A_1 = 1$, $A_2 = -1$.

(a) List the next four terms of the sequence.

(b) Find A_8.

10. Consider the sequence defined by the recursive formula $A_N = 2A_{N-1} - 3A_{N-2}$ and starting with $A_1 = -1$, $A_2 = 1$.

(a) List the next four terms of the sequence.

(b) Find A_8.

11. Consider the sequence 1, 4, 9, 16, 25, ...

- **(a)** List the next two terms of the sequence.

- **(b)** Assuming the sequence is denoted by $A_1, A_2, A_3, \ldots$, give an explicit formula for A_N.

- **(c)** Assuming the sequence is denoted by $P_0, P_1, P_2, \ldots$, give an explicit formula for P_N.

12. Consider the sequence 1, 2, 6, 24, 120, ...

- **(a)** List the next two terms of the sequence.

- **(b)** Assuming the sequence is denoted by $A_1, A_2, A_3, \ldots$, give an explicit formula for A_N.

- **(c)** Assuming the sequence is denoted by $P_0, P_1, P_2, \ldots$, give an explicit formula for P_N.

13. Consider the sequence 0, 1, 3, 6, 10, 15, 21, ...

- **(a)** List the next two terms of the sequence.

- **(b)** Assuming the sequence is denoted by $A_1, A_2, A_3, \ldots$, give an explicit formula for A_N.

- **(c)** Assuming the sequence is denoted by $P_0, P_1, P_2, \ldots$, give an explicit formula for P_N.

14. Consider the sequence 2, 3, 5, 9, 17, 33, ...

- **(a)** List the next two terms of the sequence.

- **(b)** Assuming the sequence is denoted by $A_1, A_2, A_3, \ldots$, give an explicit formula for A_N.

- **(c)** Assuming the sequence is denoted by $P_0, P_1, P_2, \ldots$, give an explicit formula for P_N.

15. Consider the sequence $1, \frac{8}{5}, 2, \frac{16}{7}, \frac{20}{8}, \ldots$.

- **(a)** List the next two terms of the sequence.

- **(b)** If the notation for the sequence is $A_1, A_2, A_3, \ldots$, give an explicit formula for A_N.

16. Consider the sequence $3, 2, \frac{5}{4}, \frac{6}{8}, \frac{7}{16}, \ldots$.

- **(a)** List the next two terms of the sequence.

- **(b)** If the notation for the sequence is $A_1, A_2, A_3, \ldots$, give an explicit formula for A_N.

17. Airlines would like to board passengers in the order of decreasing seat numbers (largest seat number first, second largest next, and so on), but passengers don't like this policy and refuse to go along. If two passengers randomly board a plane the probability that they board in order of decreasing seat numbers is $\frac{1}{2}$; if three passengers randomly board a plane the probability that they board in order of decreasing seat numbers is $\frac{1}{6}$; if four passengers randomly board a plane the probability that they board in order of decreasing seat numbers is $\frac{1}{24}$; and if five passengers randomly board a plane, the probability that they board in order of decreasing seat numbers is $\frac{1}{120}$. Using the sequence $\frac{1}{2}, \frac{1}{6}, \frac{1}{24}, \frac{1}{120}, \ldots$ as your guide,

- **(a)** determine the probability that if six passengers randomly board a plane they board in order of decreasing seat numbers.

- **(b)** determine the probability that if 12 passengers randomly board a plane they board in order of decreasing seat numbers.

18. When two fair coins are tossed the probability of tossing two heads is $\frac{1}{4}$; when three fair coins are tossed the probability of tossing two heads and one tail is $\frac{3}{8}$; when four fair coins are tossed the probability of tossing two heads and two tails is $\frac{6}{16}$; when five fair coins are tossed the probability of tossing two heads and three tails is $\frac{10}{32}$. Using the sequence $\frac{1}{4}, \frac{3}{8}, \frac{6}{16}, \frac{10}{32}, \ldots$ as your guide,

- **(a)** determine the probability of tossing two heads and four tails when six fair coins are tossed.

- **(b)** determine the probability of tossing two heads and 10 tails when 12 fair coins are tossed. (*Hint:* Find an explicit formula first.)

9.2 The Linear Growth Model

19. Consider a population that grows linearly following the recursive formula $P_N = P_{N-1} + 125$, with initial population $P_0 = 80$.

- **(a)** Find P_1, P_2, and P_3.

- **(b)** Give an explicit formula for P_N.

- **(c)** Find P_{100}.

20. Consider a population that grows linearly following the recursive formula $P_N = P_{N-1} + 23$, with initial population $P_0 = 57$.

- **(a)** Find P_1, P_2, and P_3.

- **(b)** Give an explicit formula for P_N.

- **(c)** Find P_{200}.

21. Consider a population that grows linearly following the recursive formula $P_N = P_{N-1} - 25$, with initial population $P_0 = 578$.

- **(a)** Find P_1, P_2, and P_3.

- **(b)** Give an explicit formula for P_N.

- **(c)** Find P_{23}.

22. Consider a population that grows linearly following the recursive formula $P_N = P_{N-1} - 111$, with initial population $P_0 = 11,111$.

- **(a)** Find P_1, P_2, and P_3.

- **(b)** Give an explicit formula for P_N.

- **(c)** Find P_{100}.

23. Consider a population that grows linearly, with $P_0 = 8$ and $P_{10} = 38$.

- **(a)** Give an explicit formula for P_N.

- **(b)** Find P_{50}.

24. Consider a population that grows linearly, with $P_5 = 37$ and $P_7 = 47$.

   (a) Find P_0.

   (b) Give an explicit formula for P_N.

   (c) Find P_{100}.

25. Official unemployment rates for the U.S. population are reported on a monthly basis by the Bureau of Labor Statistics. For the period October, 2011, through January, 2012, the official unemployment rates were 8.9% (Oct.), 8.7% (Nov.), 8.5% (Dec.), and 8.3% (Jan.). (*Source:* U.S. Bureau of Labor Statistics, *www.bls.gov*.) If the unemployment rates were to continue to decrease following a linear model,

   (a) predict the unemployment rate on January, 2013.

   (b) predict when the United States would reach a zero unemployment rate.

26. The world population reached 6 billion people in 1999 and 7 billion in 2012. (*Source:* Negative Population Growth, *www.npg.org*.) Assuming a linear growth model for the world population,

   (a) predict the year when the world population would reach 8 billion.

   (b) predict the world population in 2020.

27. The Social Security Administration uses a linear growth model to estimate life expectancy in the United States. The model uses the explicit formula $L_N = 66.17 + 0.96N$ where L_N is the life expectancy of a person born in the year $1995 + N$ (i.e., $N = 0$ corresponds to 1995 as the year of birth, $N = 1$ corresponds to 1996 as the year of birth, and so on). (*Source:* Social Security Administration, *www.socialsecurity.gov*.)

   (a) Assuming the model continues to work indefinitely, estimate the life expectancy of a person born in 2012.

   (b) Assuming the model continues to work indefinitely, what year will you have to be born so that your life expectancy is 90?

28. While the number of smokers for the general adult population is decreasing, it is not decreasing equally across all subpopulations (and for some groups it is actually increasing). For the 18-to-24 age group, the number of smokers was 8 million in 1965 and 6.3 million in 2009. (*Source:* "Trends in Tobacco Use," American Lung Association, 2011.) Assuming the number of smokers in the 18-to-24 age group continues decreasing according to a negative linear growth model,

   (a) predict the number of smokers in the 18-to-24 age group in 2015 (round your answer to the nearest thousand).

   (b) predict in what year the number of smokers in the 18-to-24 age group will reach 5 million.

29. Use the arithmetic sum formula to find the sum
$$\underbrace{2 + 7 + 12 + \cdots + 497}_{100 \text{ terms}}.$$

30. Use the arithmetic sum formula to find the sum
$$\underbrace{21 + 28 + 35 + \cdots + 413}_{57 \text{ terms}}.$$

31. The first two terms of an arithmetic sequence are 12 and 15.

   (a) The number 309 is which term of the arithmetic sequence?

   (b) Find $12 + 15 + 18 + \cdots + 309$.

32. An arithmetic sequence has first term 1 and common difference 9.

   (a) The number 2701 is which term of the arithmetic sequence?

   (b) Find $1 + 10 + 19 + \cdots + 2701$.

33. Consider a population that grows according to a linear growth model. The initial population is $P_0 = 23$, and the common difference is $d = 7$.

   (a) Find $P_0 + P_1 + P_2 + \cdots + P_{999}$.

   (b) Find $P_{100} + P_{101} + \cdots + P_{999}$.

34. Consider a population that grows according to a linear growth model. The initial population is $P_0 = 7$, and the population in the first generation is $P_1 = 11$.

   (a) Find $P_0 + P_1 + P_2 + \cdots + P_{500}$.

   (b) Find $P_{100} + P_{101} + \cdots + P_{500}$.

35. The city of Lightsville currently has 137 streetlights. As part of an urban renewal program, the city council has decided to install and have operational 2 additional streetlights at the end of each week for the next 52 weeks. Each streetlight costs $1 to operate for 1 week.

   (a) How many streetlights will the city have at the end of 38 weeks?

   (b) How many streetlights will the city have at the end of N weeks? (Assume $N \le 52$.)

   (c) What is the cost of operating the original 137 lights for 52 weeks?

   (d) What is the additional cost for operating the newly installed lights for the 52-week period during which they are being installed?

36. A manufacturer currently has on hand 387 widgets. During the next 2 years, the manufacturer will be increasing his inventory by 37 widgets per week. (Assume that there are exactly 52 weeks in one year.) Each widget costs 10 cents a week to store.

   (a) How many widgets will the manufacturer have on hand after 20 weeks?

   (b) How many widgets will the manufacturer have on hand after N weeks? (Assume $N \le 104$.)

   (c) What is the cost of storing the original 387 widgets for 2 years (104 weeks)?

   (d) What is the additional cost of storing the increased inventory of widgets for the next 2 years?

9.3 The Exponential Growth Model

37. A population grows according to an exponential growth model. The initial population is $P_0 = 11$ and the common ratio is $R = 1.25$.

(a) Find P_1.

(b) Find P_9.

(c) Give an explicit formula for P_N.

38. A population grows according to an exponential growth model, with $P_0 = 8$ and $P_1 = 12$.

(a) Find the common ratio R.

(b) Find P_9.

(c) Give an explicit formula for P_N.

39. A population grows according to the recursive rule $P_N = 4P_{N-1}$, with initial population $P_0 = 5$.

(a) Find P_1, P_2, and P_3.

(b) Give an explicit formula for P_N.

(c) How many generations will it take for the population to reach 1 million?

40. A population *decays* according to an exponential growth model, with $P_0 = 3072$ and common ratio $R = 0.75$.

(a) Find P_5.

(b) Give an explicit formula for P_N.

(c) How many generations will it take for the population to fall below 200?

41. Crime in Happyville is on the rise. Each year the number of crimes committed increases by 50%. Assume that there were 200 crimes committed in 2010, and let P_N denote the number of crimes committed in the year $2010 + N$.

(a) Give a recursive description of P_N.

(b) Give an explicit description of P_N.

(c) If the trend continues, approximately how many crimes will be committed in Happyville in the year 2020?

42. Since 2010, when 100,000 cases were reported, each year the number of new cases of equine flu has decreased by 20%. Let P_N denote the number of new cases of equine flu in the year $2010 + N$.

(a) Give a recursive description of P_N.

(b) Give an explicit description of P_N.

(c) If the trend continues, approximately how many new cases of equine flu will be reported in the year 2025?

43. In 2010 the number of mathematics majors at Bright State University was 425; in 2011 the number of mathematics majors was 463. Find the growth rate (expressed as a percent) of mathematics majors from 2010 to 2011.

44. Avian influenza A(H5N1) is a particularly virulent strain of the bird flu. In 2008 there were 44 cases of avian influenza A(H5N1) confirmed worldwide; in 2009 the number of confirmed cases worldwide was 73. (*Source:* World Health Organization, *www.who.int.*) Find the growth rate in the number of confirmed cases worldwide of avian influenza A(H5N1) from 2008 to 2009. Express your answer as a percent.

45. In 2010 the undergraduate enrollment at Bright State University was 19,753; in 2011 the undergraduate enrollment was 17,389. Find the "growth" rate in the undergraduate enrollment from 2010 to 2011. Give your answer as a percent.

46. In 2009 there were 73 cases of avian influenza A(H5N1) confirmed worldwide; in 2010 the number of confirmed cases worldwide was 48. (*Source:* World Health Organization, *www.who.int.*) Find the "growth" rate in the number of confirmed cases worldwide of avian influenza A(H5N1). Give your answer as a percent.

47. Consider the geometric sequence $P_0 = 2, P_1 = 6, P_2 = 18, \ldots$.

(a) Find the common ratio R.

(b) Use the geometric sum formula to find the sum $P_0 + P_1 + \cdots + P_{20}$.

48. Consider the geometric sequence $P_0 = 4, P_1 = 6, P_2 = 9, \ldots$

(a) Find the common ratio R.

(b) Use the geometric sum formula to find the sum $P_0 + P_1 + \cdots + P_{24}$.

49. Consider the geometric sequence $P_0 = 4, P_1 = 2, P_2 = 1, \ldots$

(a) Find the common ratio R.

(b) Use the geometric sum formula to find the sum $P_0 + P_1 + \cdots + P_{11}$.

50. Consider the geometric sequence $P_0 = 10, P_1 = 2, P_2 = 0.4, \ldots$.

(a) Find the common ratio R.

(b) Use the geometric sum formula to find the sum $P_0 + P_1 + \cdots + P_{24}$.

51. In April, 2010, the month Apple introduced the iPad, there were 300,000 iPads sold. One month later, in May, 2010, one million iPads were sold. (*Source:* Fortune, *www.fortune.com.*) If iPad sales had continued to grow at the same rate for the rest of 2010 (they didn't), find the total number of iPads that would have been sold from April through December of 2010.

52. The NCAA college basketball tournament brackets start with 64 teams. The tournament is a "single-elimination" tournament, which means that once a team loses a game they are eliminated from the tournament. In the first round 64 teams play 32 games. In the second round there are 32 teams left and 16 games played. This continues until the final round, in which there are two teams left and they play for the championship. The total number of games played is given by the geometric sum $32 + 16 + \cdots + 2 + 1$.

(a) Use the geometric sum formula to find a numerical expression that gives the total number of games played, and verify that this total is 63.

(b) Imagine an expanded version of the NCAA tournament that starts with 1024 teams in the first round. Find the total number of games played in this "super-tournament."

9.4 The Logistic Growth Model

53. A population grows according to the logistic growth model, with growth parameter $r = 0.8$. Starting with an initial population given by $p_0 = 0.3$,

(a) find p_1.

(b) find p_2.

(c) determine what percent of the habitat's carrying capacity is taken up by the third generation.

54. A population grows according to the logistic growth model, with growth parameter $r = 0.6$. Starting with an initial population given by $p_0 = 0.7$,

(a) find p_1.

(b) find p_2.

(c) determine what percent of the habitat's carrying capacity is taken up by the third generation.

55. For the population discussed in Exercise 53 $(r = 0.8, p_0 = 0.3)$,

(a) find the values of p_1 through p_{10}.

(b) what does the logistic growth model predict in the long term for this population?

56. For the population discussed in Exercise 54 $(r = 0.6, p_0 = 0.7)$,

(a) find the values of p_1 through p_{10}.

(b) what does the logistic growth model predict in the long term for this population?

57. A population grows according to the logistic growth model, with growth parameter $r = 1.8$. Starting with an initial population given by $p_0 = 0.4$,

(a) find the values of p_1 through p_{10}.

(b) what does the logistic growth model predict in the long term for this population?

58. A population grows according to the logistic growth model, with growth parameter $r = 1.5$. Starting with an initial population given by $p_0 = 0.8$,

(a) find the values of p_1 through p_{10}.

(b) what does the logistic growth model predict in the long term for this population?

59. A population grows according to the logistic growth model, with growth parameter $r = 2.8$. Starting with an initial population given by $p_0 = 0.15$,

(a) find the values of p_1 through p_{10}.

(b) what does the logistic growth model predict in the long term for this population?

60. A population grows according to the logistic growth model, with growth parameter $r = 2.5$. Starting with an initial population given by $p_0 = 0.2$,

(a) find the values of p_1 through p_{10}.

(b) what does the logistic growth model predict in the long term for this population?

61. A population grows according to the logistic growth model, with growth parameter $r = 3.25$. Starting with an initial population given by $p_0 = 0.2$,

(a) find the values of p_1 through p_{10}.

(b) what does the logistic growth model predict in the long term for this population?

62. A population grows according to the logistic growth model, with growth parameter $r = 3.51$. Starting with an initial population given by $p_0 = 0.4$,

(a) find the values of p_1 through p_{10}.

(b) what does the logistic growth model predict in the long term for this population?

JOGGING

63. Each of the following sequences follows a linear, an exponential, or a logistic growth model. For each sequence, determine which model applies (if more than one applies, then indicate all the ones that apply).

(a) $2, 4, 8, 16, 32, \ldots$

(b) $2, 4, 6, 8, 10, \ldots$

(c) $0.8, 0.4, 0.6, 0.6, 0.6, \ldots$

(d) $0.81, 0.27, 0.09, 0.03, 0.01, \ldots$

(e) $0.49512, 0.81242, 0.49528, 0.81243, 0.49528, \ldots$

(f) $0.9, 0.75, 0.6, 0.45, 0.3, \ldots$

(g) $0.7, 0.7, 0.7, 0.7, 0.7, \ldots$

64. Each of the line graphs shown in Figs. 9-19 through 9-24 describes a population that grows according to a linear, an exponential, or a logistic model. For each line graph, determine which model applies.

(a)

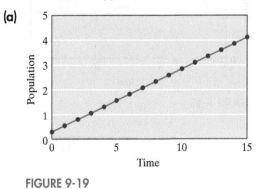

FIGURE 9-19

(b)

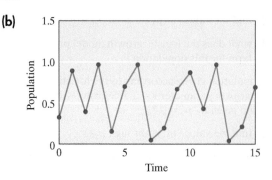

FIGURE 9-20

(c)

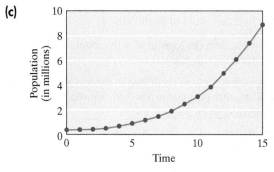

FIGURE 9-21

(d)

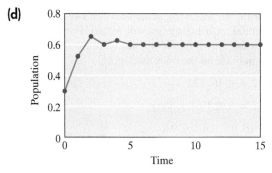

FIGURE 9-22

(e)

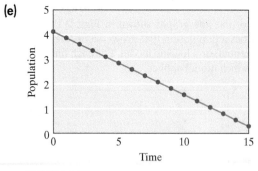

FIGURE 9-23

(f)

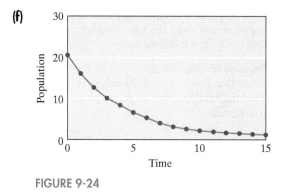

FIGURE 9-24

65. Show that the sum of the first N terms of an arithmetic sequence with first term c and common difference d is
$$\frac{N}{2}\left[2c + (N-1)d\right].$$

66. Compute the sum
$$1 + 1 + 2 + \frac{1}{2} + 4 + \frac{1}{4} + 8 + \frac{1}{8} + \cdots + 4096 + \frac{1}{4096}$$

67. Suppose that $P_0, P_1, P_2, \ldots, P_N$ are the terms of a geometric sequence. Suppose, moreover, that the sequence satisfies the recursive rule $P_N = P_{N-1} + P_{N-2}$, for $N \geq 2$. Find the common ratio R.

68. (a) Find a right triangle whose sides are consecutive terms of an arithmetic sequence with common difference $d = 2$.

(b) Find a right triangle whose sides are consecutive terms of a geometric sequence with common ratio R.

69. Give an example of a geometric sequence in which P_0, P_1, P_2, and P_3 are integers, and all the terms from P_4 on are fractions.

70. Consider a population that grows according to the logistic growth model with initial population given by $p_0 = 0.7$. What growth parameter r would keep the population constant?

71. Suppose that you are in charge of stocking a lake with a certain type of alligator with a growth parameter $r = 0.8$. Assuming that the population of alligators grows according to the logistic growth model, is it possible for you to stock the lake so that the alligator population is constant? Explain.

72. Consider a population that grows according to the logistic growth model with growth parameter $r \, (r > 1)$. Find p_0 in terms of r so that the population is constant.

RUNNING

73. The purpose of this exercise is to understand why we assume that, under the logistic growth model, the growth parameter r is between 0 and 4.

(a) What does the logistic equation give for p_{N+1} if $p_N = 0.5$ and $r > 4$? Is this a problem?

(b) What does the logistic equation predict for future generations if $p_N = 0.5$ and $r = 4$?

(c) If $0 \leq p \leq 1$, what is the largest possible value of $(1 - p)p$?

(d) Explain why, if $0 < p_0 < 1$ and $0 < r < 4$, then $0 < p_N < 1$, for every positive integer N.

74. Suppose $r > 3$. Using the logistic growth model, find a population p_0 such that $p_0 = p_2 = p_4 \ldots$, but $p_0 \neq p_1$.

75. Show that if $P_0, P_1, P_2, \ldots$ is an arithmetic sequence, then $2^{P_0}, 2^{P_1}, 2^{P_2}, \ldots$ must be a geometric sequence.

◱ PROJECTS AND PAPERS

1 The Malthusian Doctrine

In 1798, Thomas Malthus wrote his famous *Essay on the Principle of Population*. In this essay, Malthus put forth the principle that population grows according to an exponential growth model, whereas food and resources grow according to a linear growth model. Based on this doctrine, Malthus predicted that humankind was doomed to a future where the supply of food and other resources would be unable to keep pace with the needs of the world's population.

Write an analysis paper detailing some of the consequences of Malthus's doctrine. Does the doctrine apply in a modern technological world? Can the doctrine be the explanation for the famines in sub-Saharan Africa? Discuss the many possible criticisms that can be leveled against Malthus's doctrine. To what extent do you agree with Malthus's doctrine?

2 A Logistic Growth Model for the United States Population

The logistic growth model, first discovered by Verhulst, was rediscovered in 1920 by the American population ecologists Raymond Pearl and Lowell Reed. Pearl and Reed compared the population data for the United States between 1790 and 1920 with what would be predicted using a logistic equation and found that the numbers produced by the equation and the real data matched quite well.

In this project, you are to read and analyze Pearl and Reed's 1920s paper. "On the Rate of Growth of the Population of the United States since 1790 and Its Mathematical Representation," *Proceedings of the National Academy of Sciences USA*, 6 (June 1920), 275–288. Here are some suggested questions you may want to discuss: Is the logistic model a good model to use with human populations? What might be a reasonable estimate for the carrying capacity of the United States?

3 World Population Growth

How do demographers model world population? Is this different from how they model, say, the population of the United States? How does this process compare with that used by biologists in determining the size of a future salmon spawn?

In this project, you will compare and contrast the process demographers use to model human population growth with that which biologists use to model animal populations.

Solution to Example 9.1(c):

The sequence 1, 11, 21, 1211, 111221, 312211, 13112221, 1113213211, 31131211131221, . . . is obtained by calling out each number (as if you were reading it out to someone else). Calling out the last number "one three, two ones, one three, one one, one two, three ones, one three, one one, two twos, one one" gives the next number: 13211311123113112211.

PART 5

Statistics

14 Censuses, Surveys, Polls, and Studies

The Joys of Collecting Data

How many mountain gorillas are left in the wild? How many people live in the United States? What percentage of voters plans to vote for the Republican Party candidate in the next election? Is hormone replacement therapy a risk factor for breast cancer in older women? Does an aspirin a day help prevent heart disease? Does coffee make you live longer?

Each one of these questions has an answer, and if you dig around you might even find it. And if you dig a little harder you might find more than one answer, and most likely, the answers will contradict each other. Which means that some of the answers out there might be wrong.

Right or wrong, there are some questions in life that cannot be answered without data. Data are the clay with which we build the statistical bricks that inform much of our modern world. The purpose of collecting data is to make hypotheses, draw conclusions, and find explanations for what is happening around us. Our conclusions and explanations are only as good as the data we collect, and collecting good reliable data is a lot harder than it seems.

An interesting data collection story lurks behind every piece of statistical information. How was the data collected? By whom? Why? When? For how long? Who funded the effort? In this chapter we will explore a few basic ideas and issues in data collection. Most of the relevant issues and ideas are introduced through real-life examples and case studies. The chapter has lots of stories and no mathematical formulas (well, maybe two little ones).

> ❝Data! Data! Data!❞ he cried impatiently. "I can't make bricks without clay. ❞
>
> – *Sherlock Holmes*

One of the most basic purposes of data collection is *enumeration*: "How many X's are there?" or "How many X's have characteristic C?" Answers to these types of questions can be answered by a census, or estimated by using samples. We discuss this topic in Section 14.1. In Section 14.2 we discuss *measurement* questions. These are questions for which some characteristic or behavior must be measured, including opinions and intentions. Typically, these questions are answered through surveys and public opinion polls. The most difficult data collection questions are cause and effect questions: Does X cause Y? These are the types of questions that affect us most—diet, medications, exercise, behavior are all stepchildren of cause and effect. We discuss data collection methods for cause and effect questions in Section 14.3.

14.1 Enumeration

enu·mer·ate: to ascertain the number of 99

– *Merriam-Webster Dictionary**

The most basic enumeration questions are questions of the form *How many X's are there?* To have a definitive, unequivocal answer to a question of this type, it is essential that the set of *X*'s being counted—called the *population*—be clearly defined.

■ **Population.** This is the term we use to describe the set of "individuals" being *enumerated* (i.e., counted). The individuals may be people, animals, plants, or inanimate objects. A population is well-defined when given an individual we can clearly determine if the individual belongs to the population (and, therefore, should be counted) or not.

Typically, the members of the population are indivisible things, so the answer to an enumeration question of the type *How many X's are there?* is a positive integer or zero (for enumeration purposes we don't count parts of a person or an animal, and even inanimate objects are counted in terms of whole units). The standard convention is to use the letter *N* to denote the size of a population and to refer to a population count as the *N-value* of the population.

■ **N-value.** A positive integer (or zero) that is alleged to be a count of the number of individuals in a given population.

cen·sus: a usually complete enumeration of a population 99

– *Merriam-Webster Dictionary**

There are essentially two ways to find the *N*-value of a given population: do a *complete head count* (this is just a commonly used metaphor—we can do "head counts" even for objects that don't have heads), or do only a *partial head count* and use this partial information to estimate the *N*-value of the population. The first approach is called a *census*; the second approach is called (in very broad terms) a *survey*. We will illustrate both of these strategies next.

Censuses for Enumeration

> **EXAMPLE 14.1** HUNTING FOR BUFFALO (NICKELS)
>
> A buffalo nickel is a historic, collectible coin whose value is definitely more than the five-cent face value of the coin—depending on its condition and the year it was minted, a buffalo nickel can be worth anywhere from a few dollars to several thousand dollars. If you have some in your possession, it makes sense to set them aside and not comingle them with ordinary nickels.
>
> Imagine that you have a very large coin jar where you have thrown your spare change over the years, and you know for a fact that there are some buffalo nickels in that jar (you remember throwing some in the jar when you were a kid). Imagine that you have some spare time and you need some extra cash, so you decide to hunt down the buffalo nickels, enumerate them, and eventually sell them to a coin dealer.
>
> What is the population for this example? As is often the case, here the population is defined by the purpose of the enumeration: Since you are only interested in the buffalo nickels, they constitute the population of interest, and the number of buffalo nickels in the jar is the *N*-value you are after. (Had you been interested in how much money is in the jar, the population of interest would be the entire set of coins in the jar, with a separate tally for nickels, dimes, quarters, etc.)
>
> To find your *N*-value, your only reasonable option in this situation is to conduct a *census* of the buffalo nickels in your coin jar. This may be a

*By permission. From *Merriam-Webster's Collegiate® Dictionary, 11th Edition* ©2012 by Merriam-Webster, Incorporated (*www.Merriam-Webster.com*).

little time-consuming, but not hard—you are counting inanimate objects, and unlike humans and animals (more on that soon) inanimate objects are quite cooperative when it comes to a head count. To conduct your census you dump all the coins out of the jar and go through them one by one. Each time you find a buffalo nickel you set it aside and add one to your tally. When you have gone through all the coins in the jar you have completed the census. Ka-ching!

Censuses become considerably more complicated when you are enumerating animal populations. Unlike buffalo nickels or other inanimate species, most animal species live in large and tough habitats, move around, hide from humans, and some species, say tigers, like to snack on the people trying to enumerate them. Moreover, a full census for an entire animal species requires a lot of planning and tends to be quite expensive. Currently, efforts to accurately enumerate the members of a species by means of a census are very rare and reserved for species that are critically endangered. One such species is the mountain gorilla.

EXAMPLE 14.2   HOW MANY MOUNTAIN GORILLAS ARE LEFT IN THE WILD?

Mountain gorillas (*Gorilla beringei beringei*) in the wild can only be found in central Africa, in a relatively small natural habitat consisting of four contiguous national parks (one in Rwanda, two in Uganda and one in the Democratic Republic of Congo).

Due to loss of habitat and poaching, the mountain gorilla population had been in decline for decades and became (and still is) critically endangered—there were less than 300 mountain gorillas in the wild left in 1985. Since then, thanks to a worldwide conservation effort (nudged by the success of the movie *Gorillas in the Mist*), poaching has been greatly reduced and the mountain gorilla population is slowly coming back. A census conducted in March and April of 2010 had a total count of 786 mountain gorillas living in the wild. A new census is being organized for 2012–2013.

To understand how much effort goes into an animal population census, consider the planning for the next mountain gorilla census.

- The census will be conducted by seven different teams of researchers who will sweep different regions of the gorilla's natural habitat in a coordinated fashion.
- As the gorillas move around in small groups, a research team will follow behind a particular group for three days and enumerate the number of individuals in the group.
- To enumerate the number of individuals in a group, the research team will use their nests as a *proxy*. This means that, rather than counting the gorillas directly (that would require following the group too closely), the team will count the number of nests left behind (each gorilla builds his or her own new nest to sleep in each night).
- To make sure that the counts are completely accurate, samples of fecal matter (i.e., gorilla poop) will be collected from each nest for later analysis. The poop sample serves as a *second proxy*—it provides the DNA markers that uniquely identify each individual. To insure accuracy, samples will be collected from nests on three consecutive nights.
- It will take about nine months after the field work is finished to analyze the data and release a new *N*-value for the mountain gorilla population. (The data should be available sometime in 2013.)

One would think that accurately enumerating human populations should be a lot easier than enumerating animals in the wild, but this is not always the case. What is the population of the United States? We have a rough idea but not an exact count, in spite of the fact that we spend billions of dollars trying.

EXAMPLE 14.3   HOW MANY PEOPLE LIVE IN THE UNITED STATES?

This is an example of an enumeration question whose answer changes by the minute, and yet there is a current, up-to-date answer that you can easily find: Go to *www.census.gov/population/www/popclockus.html*. This Web site is the virtual version of the United States population clock maintained by the U.S. Census Bureau. (Check it out now and see what the current number is!) To be clear about what that number represents: It is the official *N*-value for the *resident population* of the United States, and it enumerates everyone—citizens, permanent residents, illegal aliens, visitors, and tourists—physically present in the United States at that moment in time.

How is the Census Bureau able to keep track of the *N*-value of a population that essentially changes by the minute? There are two parts to the answer: (1) establishing a baseline, and (2) using that baseline as the initial population together with a mathematical model that projects how that population changes over time. We discussed part (2) in detail in Chapter 9, Example 9.8 (*A Short-Term Model of the U.S. Population*), so in this example we will focus on describing how the baseline is set. This is where *the Census* comes in.

Every 10 years, the United States conducts a census of its population, officially called the United States Population Census but most commonly referred to (at least in the United States) as *the Census*. While most countries conduct periodic censuses of their populations, the United States is the only country where the population census is required by the country's constitution.

> 66 . . . this was an outstanding census. When this fact is added to prior positive evaluations, the American public can be proud of the *2010 Census* their participation made possible. 99
>
> *– Robert Graves, Director of the Census Bureau*

Accurately enumerating a population as large and diverse as that of the United States is practically impossible, but we try it anyway (it is required by law). The amount of effort and money spent on this enumeration is staggering. The 2010 U.S. Census involved hiring 635,000 enumerators and cost around $13 billion—roughly $42 per head counted. (We will describe in more detail the inner workings of the U.S. Census in Case Study 1 at the end of this section.)

The final official tally for the 2010 Census: On April 1, 2010 (Census Day), the resident population of the United States was $N = 308,745,538$. While nobody expected this number to be right on, post-enumeration surveys (using a more sophisticated methodology than just counting heads) showed that the official count was off by roughly 36,000 heads too many. This may seem like a lot of heads to overcount after spending that much money, but it represents a relative error of just 0.012%. By traditional U.S. Census standards the 2010 Census was a big success.

Surveys for Enumeration

In this chapter we use the word *survey* in its broadest meaning: Any strategy that uses a *sample* from a *population* to draw conclusions about the entire population is a survey (even when there are no questionnaires to fill or phone calls to answer). When the nurse draws a sample of blood from your arm and the sample is used to measure your white cell count, in the broadest sense of the word she is in fact conducting a survey. The working assumption is that the blood drawn from your arm is a good representative of the rest of your blood.

One way to think of a survey is as the flip side of a census. (A census involves *every* individual in the population; a survey only involves *some* individuals.) Before we look at some examples of how surveys are used to estimate population counts, we introduce a few useful terms.

- **Survey.** A data collection strategy that uses a sample to draw inferences about a population.
- **Sample.** A subset of the population chosen to be the providers of information in a survey.
- **Sampling.** The act of selecting a sample.
- **Statistic.** A numerical estimate of some measurable characteristic of a population obtained from a sample.
- **Parameter.** A true measurement of some characteristic of a population. In general, a *parameter* is an unknown quantity, and a *statistic* is an educated guess as to what that unknown quantity might be.

Surveys are used to measure characteristics of a population or to predict the future actions of a group of individuals (we will cover these uses in the next section), but surveys can also be used to estimate the N-value of a population. We will discuss this particular use of surveys in the next couple of examples.

EXAMPLE 14.4 DEFECTIVE LIGHTBULBS: ONE-SAMPLE ESTIMATION

Have you ever bought an electronic product, taken it home, and found out it is defective? When the product is a big-ticket item like a computer or a plasma TV, buying a lemon is especially frustrating; but, even for minor items like a lightbulb, it can be aggravating (you climb on a step ladder, remove the old lightbulb, screw in the new lightbulb, flip the switch, no light, @%#!).

To minimize the problem of factory defectives, manufacturers do quality control tests on their products before shipping. For big-ticket items, every single item is factory tested for quality control, but for cheaper items like lightbulbs this is not cost-effective, so the quality control testing is done using a sample.

Imagine you are quality control manager for a lightbulb manufacturer. The lightbulbs come out of the assembly line in batches of 100,000. The manufacturer's specs are that if the batch has more than 2500 defective bulbs (2.5%) the batch cannot be shipped. In this situation the population of interest consists of the defective lightbulbs in the batch, but testing the entire batch of 100,000 to enumerate the defectives is too time-consuming and expensive. Instead, you have a sample of 800 selected and tested. Out of the 800 lightbulbs tested, 17 turn out to be defective.

We can now estimate the total number of defective lightbulbs in the batch by assuming that *the proportion of defectives in the entire batch is approximately the same as the proportion of defectives in the sample.* In other words, $\frac{17}{800} \approx \frac{N}{100,000}$. Solving for N gives an estimate (i.e., a statistic) of $N \approx 2125$ defectives in the batch, well under the allowed quota of 2500. We will never know the exact number of defective lightbulbs in the batch (the parameter) unless we test the entire batch, but we feel confident that this shipment is good to go. (We will revisit the issue of confidence in our statistic in Chapter 17, but that's another story.)

The underlying assumption of the sampling method used in Example 14.4 [sometimes called *one-sample* (or *single-sample*) *estimation*] is that the percentage of defectives in the sample is roughly the same as the percentage of defectives in the entire batch. To insure that this assumption is valid, the sample has to be carefully chosen and be sufficiently large. We will discuss what "carefully chosen" and "sufficiently large" mean in greater detail in Section 14.2.

The general description of **one-sample estimation** is as follows: Suppose we have a general population of known size P (in our last example, $P = 100,000$ lightbulbs) and we want to find the N-value of a subpopulation having some specified characteristic (for example, being a defective lightbulb). We can estimate this N-value by carefully choosing a sample of size n (in our last example $n = 800$) and counting the number of individuals in that sample having that particular characteristic. Call that number k (in our last example, $k = 17$). Then, if we assume that the percentage of individuals with the desired characteristic is roughly the same in both the sample and the general population, we get $\frac{k}{n} \approx \frac{N}{P}$. Solving for N gives $N \approx \left(\frac{k}{n}\right)P$.

We can only estimate the N-value of a subpopulation using a sample if we know P, the size of the general population. In many real-life applications we don't. There is, however, an extremely useful sampling method that allows us to estimate the N-value of any population called *two-sample estimation*, and more commonly as the *capture-recapture* method. The most common application of this method is in the study of fish and wildlife populations (thus the name *capture-recapture*), and it involves taking two consecutive samples of the population (thus the name *two-sample estimation*). We will illustrate the method with an example first and then give a general description.

| **EXAMPLE 14.5**   COUNTING FISH POPULATIONS: CAPTURE-RECAPTURE |

Imagine you are a wildlife biologist studying the ecosystem in a small lake. A major player in this lake is the northern pike—a voracious carnivore that eats the hatchlings of other fish such as trout and salmon. To maintain a healthy ecosystem, the population of pike has to be controlled, and this requires taking regular measurements of the N-value of the pike population in the lake. Here's how you do this.

- **Step 1 (the capture).** You capture the first sample of pike, tag them (gently—you want to avoid harming them in any way), and release them back into the lake. Let's say in this case the first sample consists of $n_1 = 200$ pike. Once you release the tagged pike back into the lake, you can assume that the percentage of tagged pike in the lake is given by the ratio $\frac{200}{N}$ (remember, N is your unknown).

- **Step 2 (the recapture).** After waiting awhile (you want the released fish to disperse naturally throughout the lake) you capture a second sample of pike and count the number of pike in the second sample that have tags. Let's say that the second sample consisted of $n_2 = 150$ pike, of which $k = 21$ had tags. This means that the percentage of tagged pike in the sample is given by the ratio $\frac{21}{150}$ (we won't worry about the computations yet).

The working assumption now is that *the percentage of tagged pike in the sample is roughly the same as the percentage of tagged pike in the lake*. In other words, $\frac{21}{150} \approx \frac{200}{N}$. Solving for N gives $N \approx \frac{200 \times 150}{21} = 1428.57$. Since the number of pike in the lake has to be a whole number we round the estimate to $N = 1429$.

The underlying assumption of the capture-recapture method is that both samples (the capture sample and the recapture sample) are good representatives of the entire population, and for this to happen, several requirements have to be met:

(1) The chances of being captured are the same for all members of the population.

(2) The chances of being recaptured are the same for both tagged and untagged individuals.

(3) The general population remains unchanged between the capture and the recapture (i.e., no births, deaths, or escapes).

(4) The tags do not come off.

When these requirements are met (or mostly met), the capture-recapture method gives very good estimates of a population size.

The capture-recapture method has many other applications beyond wildlife ecology. It is used in epidemiology to estimate the number of individuals infected with a particular disease, and it is used in public health to estimate birth rates and death rates in a particular population.

The general description of the **two-sample estimation** (or **capture–recapture**) method (borrowing the terminology of wildlife ecology) is as follows:

- **Step 1 (the capture).** Choose a sample of the population consisting of n_1 individuals. "Tag" the individuals in the sample. Release the tagged individuals back into the general population.

  ["Tag" is a metaphor for giving the individuals an identifying mark—it could be anything from an ink dot on a dorsal fin to an asterisk on a spreadsheet. The two most important things about the tag are that (1) it should not harm the individual and (2) it should not come off in the time between the capture and the recapture.]

- **Step 2 (the recapture).** Choose a second sample of the population consisting of n_2 individuals and count the number of tagged individuals in the second sample. Let k denote the number of tagged individuals in the second sample.

- **Step 3.** Set up the proportion $\frac{k}{n_2} \approx \frac{n_1}{N}$, and solve for N. When the value of N is not a whole number, round it to the nearest whole number.

We conclude this section with Case Study 1, a general discussion of the United States Census, the role it plays in our lives, and the statistical issues that are involved.

| CASE STUDY 1 | THE UNITED STATES CENSUS

Article 1, Section 2, of the U.S. Constitution mandates that a national census be conducted every 10 years. The original purpose of the national census was to "count heads" for a twofold purpose: *taxes* and *political representation* (i.e., the apportionment of seats in the House of Representatives to the states based on their populations—a topic we discussed at length in Chapter 4). Like many other parts of the Constitution, Article 1, Section 2, was a compromise of many conflicting interests: The census count was to exclude "Indians not taxed" and to count slaves as "three-fifths of a free Person."

> 66 [An] Enumeration shall be made within three Years after the first Meeting of the Congress of the United States, and within every subsequent Term of ten Years, in such Manner as they [Congress] shall by Law direct. 99
>
> – Article 1, Section 2, U.S. Constitution

Today, the scope of the U.S. Census has been greatly expanded by the Fourteenth Amendment and by the courts to count the full "resident population" of the United States on Census Day (April 1 of every year that ends with 0). The modern census does a lot more than give the national population count: It provides a complete breakdown of the population by state, county, city, etc.; it collects demographic information about the population (gender, age, ethnicity, marital status, etc.); and it collects economic information (income, employment, housing, etc.).

The data collected by the U.S. Census is considered a vital part of the nation's economic and political infrastructure—it's impossible to imagine the United States functioning without the census data. Among other things, the census data is used to

- apportion the seats in the House of Representatives,
- redraw legislative districts within each state,
- allocate federal tax dollars to states, counties, cities, and municipalities,
- develop plans for the future by federal, state, and local governments,

■ collect vital government data such as the Consumer Price Index and the Current Population Survey, and

■ develop strategic plans for production and services by business and industry.

All the data collected by the Census is obtained through some form of sampling (they are all statistics, rather than parameters) except for one—the national and individual state populations are required by law to be collected by means of a full census. (So ruled the *Supreme Court in 1999 in Department of Commerce et al. v. United States House of Representatives et al.*)

Table 14-1 shows the population count from the last three national censuses, the approximate cost of each, the cost per head counted, and the estimated error (undercount/overcount) in each case (+ indicates an overcount, – an undercount). All it takes is a look at Table 14-1 to see that the U.S. Census is an incredibly expensive data collection effort that (except for the 2010 Census) does not produce very good data and misses a lot of people. (Ironically, to obtain a more accurate count and estimate the error in the official count, the Census Bureau uses a *post-enumeration* survey based on the capture-recapture method—cheaper, more efficient, and more accurate). So, why do we continue spending billions on a flawed data collection system? Good question.

Year	N	Cost	Cost per person	Error
1990	248,709,873	~$2.5 billion	~$10	−4 million
2000	281,421,906	~$4.5 billion	~$16	−1.4 million
2010	308,745,538	~$13 billion	~$42	+36,000

■ **TABLE 14-1**   Cost and performance of U.S. Census (last three censuses)

14.2 Measurement

Finding the *N*-value of a population is, in a sense, the simplest data collection problem there is (not to say that it is easy, as we have learned by now). In most situations we don't need to perform any measurements or ask any questions—we just count (either the sample or the entire population). Things become quite a bit trickier when the information we want requires more than just counting heads: What is the median home price in California? What is your cholesterol level? What is the level of customer satisfaction with our company's customer service? What percentage of voters will vote Republican in the next election?, etc. The data needed to answer these types of questions require either some sort of *measurement* (tracking home sales in a real estate database, counting cholesterol molecules) or some form of question/answer interaction (*How would you rate our customer service? If the election were held today, would you vote for the Republican Party's candidate?* etc.). We will use the term **measurement problem** to describe both situations (the point being that asking questions to assess people's opinions or intentions is also a form of measurement).

The typical way to answer a measurement problem is to conduct a survey (called a **poll** when the measurements require asking questions and recording answers). The three basic steps in any survey or poll are: (1) sampling (i.e., choosing the sample—or samples if more than one sample is required), (2) "measuring" the individuals in the sample, and (3) drawing inferences about the population from the measurements in the sample. Each of these three steps sounds simple enough, but there is a lot of devil in the details. For the rest of this chapter we will focus on step 1. We will discuss steps 2 and 3 in Chapters 15 and 17.

Sampling

The basic philosophy behind sampling is simple and well understood—if you choose a "good" sample you can get reasonably reliable data about the population by measuring just the individuals in the sample (you can never draw perfectly accurate data from a sample). Conversely, if your sample is not good (statisticians call it *biased*), then any conclusions you draw from the sample are unreliable.

A good sample is one that is "representative" of the population and is large enough to cover the variability in the population. The preceding sentence is a bit vague to say the least, and we will try to clarify its meaning in the remainder of this section, but let's start with the issue of sample size.

When the population is highly homogeneous, then a small sample is good enough to represent the entire population. Take, for example, blood samples for lab testing: All it takes is a small blood sample drawn from an arm to get reliable data about all kinds of measures—white and red cell counts, cholesterol levels, sugar levels, etc. A small blood sample is a good enough sample because a person's blood is essentially the same throughout the body. At the other end of the spectrum, when a population is very heterogeneous, a large sample is necessary (but not sufficient) if the sample is going to represent all the variability in the population. What's important to keep in mind is that it's not the size of the population that dictates the size of a good sample but rather the variability in the population. That's why a sample of 1500 people can be good enough to represent the population of a small city, a large city, or the whole country.

It is a customary to use n to denote the size of a sample (to distinguish it from N, the size of the population). The ratio n/N is called the **sampling proportion**, and is typically expressed as a percentage.

> ❝ Whether you poll the United States or New York State or Baton Rouge . . . you need . . . the same number of interviews or sample [size]. It's no mystery really—if a cook has two pots of soup on the stove, one far larger than the other, and thoroughly stirs them both, he doesn't have to take more spoonfuls from one than the other to sample the taste accurately. ❞
>
> *– George Gallup*

EXAMPLE 14.6   DEFECTIVE LIGHTBULBS: SAMPLING PROPORTION

In Example 14.4 we used a sample of $n = 800$ lightbulbs taken from a batch of $N = 100,000$ to determine the number of defective lightbulbs in the batch. In this example we are lucky—we know both n and N and we can compute the sampling proportion easily: $n/N = 0.008 = 0.8\%$.

While a sampling proportion of 0.8% may seem very small (and in many applications it would be), it is more than adequate in this situation. Lightbulbs are fairly homogeneous objects (no moving parts and just a very few elements that could go bad), so a sample of $n = 800$ is large enough for this population. A more relevant question is, How was the sample chosen?

Choosing a "good" sample is the most important and complex part of the data collection process. But how do we know if a sample is a "good" sample or not? The key lies in the idea of "equal opportunity"—we want every member of the population to have an equal chance of being included in the sample. When some members of the population are less likely to be selected for the sample than others (even if it is unintentional) we have a **biased sample** (or **sampling bias**), and a biased sample is an unreliable sample. To restate the point, in a survey, reliable measurements of a population are only possible when using an *unbiased* sample.

Depending on the nature of the population, choosing an unbiased sample can be difficult, sometimes impossible. There are many reasons why a sample can be biased, and we will illustrate some of them next.

Target population

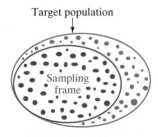

FIGURE 14-1 The sample is selected from the red part of the population. Gray individuals have zero chance of being in the sample.

Selection Bias

When the selection of the sample has a built-in tendency (whether intentional or not) to exclude a particular group or characteristic within the population, we say that the survey suffers from **selection bias**.

One significant example of selection bias occurs when the *sampling frame* for a survey is different from the *target population*. As the name indicates, the **target population** is the population to which the conclusions of the survey apply—in other words the population the survey is talking about. The **sampling frame** is the population from which the sample is drawn. Ideally, the two should be the same but sometimes they are not, and in that case there will be individuals in the population that have zero chance of being selected for the sample (Fig. 14-1).

The distinction between the target population and the sampling frame presents a very significant problem for polls that try to predict the results of an election. The target population for such a poll consists of the people that are going to vote in the election, but how do you identify that group? The conventional approach is to use registered voters as the sampling frame, but using registered voters does not always work out very well, as shown in the next example.

EXAMPLE 14.7   PRE-ELECTION POLLS: REGISTERED v. LIKELY VOTERS

A CNN/USA Today/Gallup poll conducted right before the November 2, 2004, national election asked the following question: "If the election for Congress were being held today, which party's candidate would you vote for in your congressional district, the Democratic Party's candidate or the Republican Party's candidate?"

When the question was asked of 1866 *registered* voters nationwide, the results of the poll were 49% for the Democratic Party candidate, 47% for the Republican Party candidate, 4% undecided.

When exactly the same question was asked of 1573 *likely* voters nationwide, the results of the poll were 50% for the Republican Party candidate, 47% for the Democratic Party candidate, 3% undecided.

Clearly, one of the two polls had to be wrong, because in the first poll the Democrats beat out the Republicans, whereas in the second poll it was the other way around. The only significant difference between the two polls was the choice of the sampling frame—in the first poll the sampling frame consisted of *all registered voters*, and in the second poll the sampling frame consisted of *all likely voters*. Although neither one faithfully represents the target population of *actual voters*, using likely voters instead of registered voters for the sampling frame gives much more reliable data. (The second poll predicted very closely the average results of the 2004 congressional races across the nation.)

So, why don't all pre-election polls use likely voters as a sampling frame instead of registered voters? The answer is economics. Registered voters are relatively easy to identify—every county registrar can produce an accurate list of registered voters. Not every registered voter votes, though, and it is much harder to identify those who are "likely" to vote. (What is the definition of *likely* anyway?) Typically, one has to look at demographic factors (age, ethnicity, etc.) as well as past voting behavior to figure out who is likely to vote and who isn't. Doing that takes a lot more effort, time, and money.

Convenience Sampling

There is always a cost (effort, time, money) associated with collecting data, and it is a truism that this cost is proportional to the quality of the data collected—the better the data, the more effort required to collect it. It follows that the temptation to take shortcuts when collecting data is always there and that data collected "on the cheap" should always be scrutinized carefully. One commonly used shortcut in sampling is known as **convenience sampling**. In convenience sampling the selection of which individuals are in the sample is dictated by what is easiest or cheapest for the people collecting the data.

A classic example of convenience sampling is when interviewers set up at a fixed location such as a mall or outside a supermarket and ask passersby to be part of a public opinion poll. A different type of convenience sampling occurs when the sample is based on self-selection—the sample consists of those individuals who volunteer to be in it. *Self-selection bias* is the reason why many Area Code 800 polls ("Call 1-800-YOU-NUTS to express your opinion on the new tax proposal . . .") are not to be trusted. Even worse are the Area Code 900 polls, for which an individual has to actually pay (sometimes as much as $2) to be in the sample. A sample consisting entirely of individuals who paid to be in the sample is not likely to be a representative sample of general public opinion.

Convenience sampling is not always bad—at times there is no other choice or the alternatives are so expensive that they have to be ruled out. We should keep in mind, however, that data collected through convenience sampling are naturally tainted and should always be scrutinized (that's why we always want to get to the details of *how* the data were collected).

Our next case study is a famous case in the history of pre-election polls, and it illustrates the many things that can go wrong when a biased sample is selected—even when it is a very large sample.

| CASE STUDY 2 | THE 1936 *LITERARY DIGEST* POLL

The U.S. presidential election of 1936 pitted Alfred Landon, the Republican governor of Kansas, against the incumbent Democratic President, Franklin D. Roosevelt. At the time of the election, the nation had not yet emerged from the Great Depression, and economic issues such as unemployment and government spending were the dominant themes of the campaign.

The *Literary Digest*, one of the most respected magazines of the time, conducted a poll a couple of weeks before the election. The magazine had used polls to accurately predict the results of every presidential election since 1916, and their 1936 poll was the largest and most ambitious poll ever. The *sampling frame* for the *Literary Digest* poll consisted of an enormous list of names that included (1) every person listed in a telephone directory anywhere in the United States, (2) every person on a magazine subscription list, and (3) every person listed on the roster of a club or professional association. From this sampling frame a list of about 10 million names was created, and every name on this list was mailed a mock ballot and asked to mark it and return it to the magazine.

One cannot help but be impressed by the sheer scope and ambition of the 1936 *Literary Digest* poll, as well as the magazine's unbounded confidence in its accuracy. In its issue of August 22, 1936, the *Literary Digest* crowed:

> *Once again, [we are] asking more than ten million voters—one out of four, representing every county in the United States—to settle November's election in October.*
>
> *Next week, the first answers from these ten million will begin the incoming tide of marked ballots, to be triple-checked, verified, five-times cross-classified and totaled. When the last figure has been totted and checked, if past experience is a criterion, the country will know to within a fraction of 1 percent the actual popular vote of forty million [voters].*

Based on the poll results, the *Literary Digest* predicted a landslide victory for Landon with 57% of the vote, against Roosevelt's 43%. Amazingly, the election turned out to be a landslide victory for Roosevelt with 62% of the vote, against 38% for Landon. The difference between the poll's prediction and the actual election results was a whopping 19%, the largest error ever in a major public opinion poll.

The results damaged the credibility of the magazine so much so that soon after the election its sales dried up and it went out of business—the victim of a major statistical blunder.

For the same election, a young pollster named George Gallup was able to predict accurately a victory for Roosevelt using a sample of "only" 50,000 people. In fact, Gallup *also* publicly predicted, to within 1%, the incorrect results that the *Literary Digest* would get using a sample of just 3000 people taken from the same sampling frame the magazine was using. What went wrong with the *Literary Digest* poll and why was Gallup able to do so much better?

The first thing seriously wrong with the *Literary Digest* poll was the sampling frame, consisting of names taken from telephone directories, lists of magazine subscribers, rosters of club members, and so on. Telephones in 1936 were something of a luxury, and magazine subscriptions and club memberships even more so, at a time when 9 million people were unemployed. When it came to economic status the *Literary Digest* sample was far from being a representative cross section of the voters. This was a critical problem, because voters often vote on economic issues, and given the economic conditions of the time, this was especially true in 1936.

The second serious problem with the *Literary Digest* poll was the issue of *nonresponse bias*. In a typical poll it is understood that not every individual is willing to respond to the request to participate (and in a democracy we cannot force them to do so). Those individuals who do not respond to the poll are called *nonrespondents*, and those who do are called *respondents*. The percentage of respondents out of the total sample is called the **response rate**. For the *Literary Digest* poll, out of a sample of 10 million people who were mailed a mock ballot only about 2.4 million mailed a ballot back, resulting in a 24% response rate. When the response rate to a poll is low, the poll is said to suffer from **nonresponse bias**. (Exactly at what point the response rate is to be considered low depends on the circumstances and nature of the poll, but a response rate of 24% is generally considered very low.)

Nonresponse bias can be viewed as a special type of selection bias—it excludes from the sample reluctant and uninterested people. Since reluctant and uninterested people can represent a significant slice of the population, we don't want them excluded from the sample. But getting reluctant, uninterested, and apathetic slugs to participate in a survey is a conundrum—in a free country we cannot force people to participate, and bribing them with money or chocolate chip cookies is not always a practical solution.

One of the significant problems with the *Literary Digest* poll was that the poll was conducted by mail. This approach is the most likely to magnify nonresponse bias, because people often consider a mailed questionnaire just another form of junk mail. Of course, given the size of their sample, the *Literary Digest* hardly had a choice. This illustrates another important point: Bigger is not better, and a big sample can be more of a liability than an asset.

Quota Sampling

Quota sampling is a systematic effort to force the sample to be representative of a given population through the use of quotas—the sample should have so many women, so many men, so many blacks, so many whites, so many people living in urban areas, so many people living in rural areas, and so on. The proportions in each category in the sample should be the same as those in the population. If we can assume that every important characteristic of the population is taken into account when the quotas are set up, it is reasonable to expect that the sample will be representative of the population and produce reliable data.

Our next historical example illustrates some of the difficulties with the assumptions behind quota sampling.

EXAMPLE 14.8 THE 1948 PRESIDENTIAL ELECTION: QUOTA SAMPLING

"Ain't the way I heard it," Truman gloats while holding an early edition of the *Chicago Daily Tribune* in which the headline erroneously claimed a Dewey victory based on the predictions of all the polls.

George Gallup had introduced quota sampling as early as 1935 and had used it successfully to predict the winner of the 1936, 1940, and 1944 presidential elections. Quota sampling thus acquired the reputation of being a "scientifically reliable" sampling method, and by the 1948 presidential election all three major national polls—the Gallup poll, the Roper poll, and the Crossley poll—used quota sampling to make their pre-election predictions.

For the 1948 election between Thomas Dewey and Harry Truman, Gallup conducted a poll with a sample of approximately 3250 people. Each individual in the sample was interviewed in person by a professional interviewer to minimize nonresponse bias, and each interviewer was given a very detailed set of quotas to meet—for example, 7 white males under 40 living in a rural area, 5 black males over 40 living in a rural area, 6 white females under 40 living in an urban area, and so on. By the time all the interviewers met their quotas, the entire sample was expected to accurately represent the entire population in every respect: gender, race, age, and so on.

Based on his sample, Gallup predicted that Dewey, the Republican candidate, would win the election with 49.5% of the vote to Truman's 44.5% (with third-party candidates Strom Thurmond and Henry Wallace accounting for the remaining 6%). The Roper and Crossley polls also predicted an easy victory for Dewey. (In fact, after an early September poll showed Truman trailing Dewey by 13 percentage points, Roper announced that he would discontinue polling since the outcome was already so obvious.) The actual results of the election turned out to be almost the exact reverse of Gallup's prediction: Truman got 49.9% and Dewey 44.5% of the national vote.

Truman's victory was a great surprise to the nation as a whole. So convinced was the *Chicago Daily Tribune* of Dewey's victory that it went to press on its early edition for November 4, 1948, with the headline "Dewey defeats Truman." The picture of Truman holding aloft a copy of the *Tribune* and his famous retort "Ain't the way I heard it" have become part of our national folklore.

To pollsters and statisticians, the erroneous predictions of the 1948 election had two lessons: (1) *Poll until election day*, and (2) *quota sampling is intrinsically flawed*.

What's wrong with quota sampling? After all, the basic idea behind it appears to be a good one: Force the sample to be a representative cross section of the population by having each important characteristic of the population proportionally represented in the sample. Since income is an important factor in determining how people vote, the sample should have all income groups represented in the same proportion as the population at large. The same should be true for gender, race, age, and so on. Right away, we can see a potential problem: Where do we stop? No matter how careful we might be, we might miss some criterion that would affect the way people vote, and the sample could be deficient in this regard.

An even more serious flaw in quota sampling is that, other than meeting the quotas, the interviewers are free to choose whom they interview. This opens the door to selection bias. Looking back over the history of quota sampling, we can see a clear tendency to overestimate the Republican vote. In 1936, using quota sampling, Gallup predicted that the Republican candidate would get 44% of the vote, but the actual number was 38%. In 1940, the prediction was 48%, and the actual vote was 45%; in 1944, the prediction was 48%, and the actual vote was 46%. Gallup was able to predict the winner correctly in each of these elections, mostly because the spread between the candidates was large enough to cover the error. In 1948, Gallup (and all the other pollsters) simply ran out of luck.

The failure of quota sampling as a method for getting representative samples has a simple moral: *Even with the most carefully laid plans, human intervention in choosing the sample can result in selection bias.*

Random Sampling

The best alternative to human selection is to let the *laws of chance* determine the selection of a sample. Sampling methods that use randomness as part of their design are known as **random sampling** methods, and any sample obtained through random sampling is called a **random sample** (or a *probability sample*).

The idea behind random sampling is that the decision as to which individuals should or should not be in the sample is best left to chance because the laws of chance are better than human design in coming up with a representative sample. At first, this idea seems somewhat counterintuitive. How can a process based on random selection guarantee an unbiased sample? Isn't it possible to get by sheer bad luck a sample that is very biased (say, for example, a sample consisting of males only)? In theory, such an outcome is possible, but in practice, when the sample is large enough, the odds of it happening are so low that we can pretty much rule it out.

Most present-day methods of quality control in industry, corporate audits in business, and public opinion polling are based on random sampling. The reliability of data collected by random sampling methods is supported by both practical experience and mathematical theory. (We will discuss some of the details of this theory in Chapter 17.)

The most basic form of random sampling is called **simple random sampling**. It is based on the same principle as a lottery: Any set of numbers of a given size has an equal chance of being chosen as any other set of numbers of the same size. Thus, if a lottery ticket consists of six winning numbers, a fair lottery is one in which any combination of six numbers has the same chance of winning as any other combination of six numbers. In sampling, this means that any group of members of the population should have the same chance of being the sample as any other group of the same size.

| **EXAMPLE 14.9** | DEFECTIVE LIGHTBULBS: SIMPLE RANDOM SAMPLING

We introduced the idea of sampling as a tool for quality control in Example 14.4, and in Example 14.6 we followed up with a discussion of the sample size. The last part of the story is the method for choosing the sample, and for most quality-control testing situations, simple random sampling is the method of choice.

Suppose we want to choose a sample of $n = 800$ lightbulbs out of a batch of $N = 100,000$ lightbulbs coming out of an assembly line. The first step is to use a computer program to randomly draw 800 different numbers between 1 and 100,000. This can be done in a matter of seconds. Say that the 800 numbers chosen by the computer are 74, 159, 311, etc. Then, as the lightbulbs move out of the production line the 74th, 159th, 311th, etc. bulbs are selected and tested. With robotic arms, the whole process can be implemented seamlessly and without any human intervention.

In theory, simple random sampling is easy to implement. We put the name of each individual in the population in "a hat," mix the names well, and then draw as many names as we need for our sample. Of course "a hat" is just a metaphor. If our population is 100 million voters and we want to choose a simple random sample of 1500, we will not be putting all 100 million names in a real hat and then drawing 1500 names one by one. These days, the "hat" is a computer database containing a list of members of the population. A computer program then randomly selects the names. This is a fine idea for easily accessible populations such as lightbulbs coming off of an assembly line, but a hopeless one when it comes to national surveys and public opinion polls.

Implementing simple random sampling in national public opinion polls raises problems of expediency and cost. Interviewing hundreds of individuals chosen by simple random sampling means chasing people all over the country, a task that requires an inordinate amount of time and money. For most public opinion polls—especially those done on a regular basis—the time and money needed to do this are simply not available.

The alternative to simple random sampling used nowadays for national surveys and public opinion polls is a sampling method known as **stratified sampling**. The basic idea of stratified sampling is to break the sampling frame into categories, called **strata**, and then (unlike quota sampling) *randomly* choose a sample from these strata. The chosen strata are then further divided into categories, called substrata, and a random sample is taken from these substrata. The selected substrata are further subdivided, a random sample is taken from them, and so on. The process goes on for a predetermined number of steps (usually four or five).

Our next example illustrates how stratified sampling is used to conduct *national public opinion polls*. Basic variations of the same idea can be used at the state, city, or local level. The specific details, of course, will be different.

EXAMPLE 14.10 PUBLIC OPINION POLLS: STRATIFIED SAMPLING

In national public opinion polls the *strata* and *substrata* are defined by a combination of geographic and demographic criteria. For example, the nation is first divided into "size of community" *strata* (big cities, medium cities, small cities, villages, rural areas, etc.). The strata are then subdivided by geographical region (New England, Middle Atlantic, East Central, etc.). This is the first layer of substrata. Within each geographical region and within each size of community stratum some communities (called *sampling locations*) are selected by simple random sampling. The selected sampling locations are the only places where interviews will be conducted. Next, each of the selected sampling locations is further subdivided into geographical units called *wards*. This is the second layer of substrata. Within each sampling location some of the wards are selected using simple random sampling. The selected wards are then divided into smaller units, called *precincts* (third layer), and within each ward some of its precincts are selected by simple random sampling. At the last stage, *households* (fourth layer) are selected from within each precinct by simple random sampling. The interviewers are then given specific instructions as to which households in their assigned area they must conduct interviews in and the order that they must follow.

The efficiency of stratified sampling compared with simple random sampling in terms of cost and time is clear. The members of the sample are clustered in well-defined and easily manageable areas, significantly reducing the cost of conducting interviews as well as the response time needed to collect the data. For a large, heterogeneous nation like the United States, stratified sampling has generally proved to be a reliable way to collect national data.

We conclude this section with a list of basic concepts concerning surveys and sampling.

- **Survey.** A data collection strategy based on using information from a sample to draw conclusions about a general population.
- **Sample.** A subset of the population chosen to be the providers of information in a survey.
- **Sampling.** The act of choosing a sample.
- **Sampling proportion.** The proportion of the population represented by the sample.
- **Statistic.** A numerical measurement of some characteristic of a population obtained using a sample. A statistic is always an estimate of the real measurement.
- **Parameter.** An exact (accurate) measurement of some characteristic of a population. A parameter is the real measurement we would like to have.
- **Sampling error.** The difference between a parameter and the estimate for that parameter (i.e., the statistic) obtained from a sample.
- **Sampling variability.** The natural variability in the statistics obtained by different samples of the same population, even when the samples are chosen using the same methodology.
- **Sampling bias.** This occurs when some members of the population are less likely to be selected for the sample than others (even if it is unintentional).
- **Sampling frame.** The population from which a sample is drawn (not necessarily the same as the target population).
- **Response rate.** The percentage of respondents in a poll out of the total sample size.
- **Nonresponse bias.** A type of bias that is the result of too many nonrespondents (i.e., low response rates).
- **Convenience sampling.** A sampling strategy based on the convenience factor: Individuals that can be reached conveniently have a high chance of being included in the sample; individuals whose access is more inconvenient have little or no chance of being included in the sample.
- **Self-selection bias.** A type of bias that occurs when the sample consists of individuals that volunteer to be in the sample (i.e., self-select).
- **Quota sampling.** A sampling method that uses quotas as a way to force the sample to be representative of the population.
- **Simple random sampling.** A sampling method in which any group of individuals in a population has the same chance of being in the sample as any other group of equal size.
- **Stratified sampling.** A sampling method that uses several layers of strata and substrata and chooses the sample by a process of random selection within each layer.

14.3 Cause and Effect

Good news, bad news. When it comes to the connections between our lifestyle habits (diet, exercise, smoking, pill popping, etc.) and our health and well-being (longevity, weight control, chances of disease, etc.), the news is full of both good and bad: "coffee is good for you—you will live longer if you drink a few cups a day"; "HRT is bad for you—it increases your chances of getting breast cancer."

How much should we trust these types of pronouncements? And what should we do when the information is conflicting ("X is good for you; Oops! On second thought, X is really bad for you; No, actually X is kind of good for you after all!"). Our next example illustrates how serious this issue can be.

| **EXAMPLE 14.11** | HORMONE REPLACEMENT THERAPY |

Hormone replacement therapy (HRT) is basically a form of estrogen replacement and is an accepted and widely used therapy to treat the symptoms of menopause in women. No controversy there. The question is whether women after menopause should continue HRT, and if so, what are the benefits of doing so? Here is a chronology of the answers:

- *Nurses' Health Study*, 1985: Good news! Women taking estrogen had one-third the number of heart attacks than women who didn't. Hormone replacement therapy (estrogen plus progestin) becomes a highly recommended treatment for preventing heart disease (as well as osteoporosis) in postmenopausal women. By 2001, 15 million prescriptions for HRT are filled annually and about 5 million are for postmenopausal women.

- *Women's Health Initiative Study*, 2002: Bad news! Hormone replacement therapy significantly increases the risk of heart disease and breast cancer, and is a risk factor for stroke. Its only health benefit is for preventing osteoporosis and possibly colorectal cancer. Hormone replacement therapy is no longer recommended as a general therapy for older women (it is still recommended as an effective therapy for women during menopause).

- *Women's Health Initiative Follow-up*, 2007: Mixed news! Hormone replacement therapy offers protection against heart disease for women that start taking it during menopause but increases the risk of heart disease for women who start taking it after menopause.

- *Women's Health Initiative Follow-up II*, 2009: Bad news! Hormone replacement therapy significantly increases the risk of breast cancer in menopausal and postmenopausal women.

" There is very strong evidence that estrogen plus progestin causes breast cancer. You start women on hormones and within five years their risk of breast cancer is clearly elevated. You stop the hormones and within one year their risk is essentially back to normal. It's reasonably convincing cause and effect data. "

– Marcia Stefanik,
Women's Health Initiative Follow-up II

The relation between HRT and heart disease or breast cancer in older women is one of thousands of important cause-and-effect questions that still remain unanswered, and women are left to struggle weighing the good and the bad. Why?

A typical cause-and-effect statement (at least the kind that makes the news) takes the form *treatment X causes result Y*. The treatment *X* might be a food, a drug, a therapy, or a lifestyle habit such as exercise, and the result *Y* a disease, a health benefit, or a behavioral change. These types of questions are incredibly difficult to answer definitively because there is a huge difference between *correlation* and *causation*, and yet it is very difficult to separate one from the other. A **correlation** (or **association**) between two events *X* and *Y* occurs when there is an observed mutual relationship between the two events. A **causation** (or **casual relationship**) between *X* and *Y* occurs when one event is the cause of the other one.

An observed correlation between two events *X* and *Y* [Fig. 14-2(a)] can occur for many reasons: Maybe *X* is the cause and *Y* is the effect [Fig. 14-2(b)], or Y is the cause and *X* is the effect [Fig. 14-2(c)], or both *X* and *Y* are effects of a common cause C [Fig. 14-2(d)], or *X* and *Y* are the effects of two different correlated causes [Fig. 14-2(e)]. It follows that trying to establish a cause-and-effect relationship between two events just because a correlation is observed is tricky to say the least.

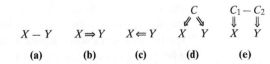

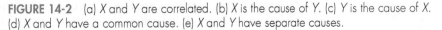

FIGURE 14-2   (a) *X* and *Y* are correlated. (b) *X* is the cause of *Y*. (c) *Y* is the cause of *X*. (d) *X* and *Y* have a common cause. (e) *X* and *Y* have separate causes.

In general, finding a correlation between a treatment and an observed result is easy. The difficult part is establishing that the correlation is indeed due to some cause-effect relation. In the rest of this section we will illustrate the complexities of establishing cause and effect from observed correlations.

EXAMPLE 14.12   DOES DRINKING COFFEE HELP YOU LIVE LONGER?

In mid May 2012 a big story made the headlines: a major study showing that drinking coffee helps you live longer. For those of us who often wonder—as we sip another double espresso—what our coffee addiction does to us, this was a great bit of news. Can it really be true?

The coffee finding came from the *NIH-AARP Diet and Health Study*—a very large *observational study* sponsored by the National Institutes of Health (NIH). In an observational study individuals are tracked for an extensive period of time and records are kept of their lifestyle factors (diet, physical activity, smoking, alcohol consumption, etc.) as well as disease rates and general health. Whenever a correlation between a lifestyle factor X and an observed change Y is found, a hypothesis is formulated: *Could X be a cause of Y?* Let's check out the 'coffee causes longevity hypothesis' in a little more detail.

The NIH-AARP study involved 400,000 subjects living in the United States aged 50 to 71. Initially, the subjects were given an extensive survey concerning their health, nutrition, and lifestyle habits and then were tracked for 12 years for health status, life span, and causes of death if they had indeed died.

One of the lifestyle factors considered was coffee consumption, and the initial correlation found by the researchers was that the non-coffee drinkers lived longer than coffee drinkers. (During the 12-year period of the study, 19% of the men and 15% of the women coffee-drinkers died, but among non-coffee drinkers the death rates dropped to 13% men and 10% women.) These correlations would point towards the hypothesis that coffee is bad for you, but it turned out that coffee drinking is also positively correlated with smoking: Coffee drinkers are more likely to be smokers than non-coffee drinkers. This raises the possibility that it is really the smoking that is bad for you and not the coffee. Similar correlations were found between coffee drinking and a host of other lifestyle factors: Coffee drinkers consume more alcohol, consume more red meat, have lower levels of physical activity, and consume fewer fruits and vegetables. Any one of these (or a combination of several) could be the cause of the observed effect.

However, once the researchers *controlled* for smoking (comparing longevity among non-smoking coffee drinkers with longevity among non-smoking noncoffee drinkers) the tables were turned: Coffee consumption was correlated with living longer and with a reduced incidence of cancer and heart disease. The same positive correlation showed up when the researchers controlled for other *confounding variables*—alcohol consumption, body mass index (BMI), age, ethnicity, marital status, physical activity, consumption of red meat, and (for postmenopausal women) use or nonuse of HRT. The general conclusion of the study was that men who drank two or more cups of a day had a 10% better chance of living through the study than those who didn't, and for women the advantage was 13%.

While the NIH-AARP study raises the tantalizing possibility that coffee might help us live longer and healthier lives, the evidence is far from conclusive. Observational studies cannot prove a cause and effect relationship—they can only suggest the possibility that one might exist. The NIH-AARP study had many flaws—the lifestyle factors were self-reported and people are known to fudge the truth (if you smoked three packs a day, would your really put that down in a questionnaire?), the lifestyle data was collected only at the beginning of the study (what about those who changed their lifestyle in the middle of the study?), and there were many other possible confounding variables (high cholesterol, high blood pressure, type of health insurance, etc.) that were not *considered*. No doubt there will be follow-up studies to clarify things a bit. In the meantime, if you are a coffee drinker enjoy your cup of java. If you are not, don't start now.

One of the problems with cause and effect findings is that they often get a lot of coverage in the press—the more surprising and unexpected the finding the more coverage it gets. Some findings can result in a major shift in public health policy, and this is a serious issue when the finding turns out to be false. This is illustrated in our next example.

EXAMPLE 14.13 THE ALAR SCARE

Alar is a chemical used by apple growers to regulate the rate at which apples ripen. Until 1989, practically all apples sold in grocery stores were sprayed with Alar. But in 1989 Alar became bad news, denounced in newspapers and on TV as a potent cancer-causing agent and a primary cause of cancer in children. As a result of these reports, people stopped buying apples, schools all over the country removed apple juice from their lunch menus, and the Washington State apple industry lost an estimated $375 million.

The case against Alar was based on a single 1973 study in which laboratory mice were exposed to the active chemicals in Alar. The dosage used in the study was eight times greater than the maximum tolerated dosage—a concentration at which even harmless substances can produce tissue damage. In fact, a child would have to eat about 200,000 apples a day to be exposed to an equivalent dosage of the chemical. Subsequent studies conducted by the National Cancer Institute and the Environmental Protection Agency failed to show any correlation between Alar and cancer in children.

While it is generally accepted now that Alar does not cause cancer, because of potential legal liability, it is no longer used. The Alar scare turned out to be a false alarm based on a poor understanding of the statistical evidence. Unfortunately, it left in its wake a long list of casualties, among them the apple industry, the product's manufacturer, the media, and the public's confidence in the system.

Clinical Studies

A second approach to establishing a cause and effect relationship between a treatment and a result is a **clinical study** (or **clinical trial**). Clinical studies are used to demonstrate that a treatment X (usually a drug, a vaccine, or a therapy) is *effective*. (For simplicity we will call X an *effective treatment* if X helps cure a disease or improves the condition of a patient.) The only way to be sure that X is an effective treatment is to isolate X from other possible causes (**confounding variables**) that could explain the same effect.

The classic way to isolate a treatment X from all other possible confounding variables is to use a **controlled study**. In a controlled study the subjects are divided into groups—some groups (called the *treatment groups*) are the ones that get the treatment; the other groups (called the *control groups*) don't get the treatment. The control groups are there for comparison purposes only—they give the experimenters a baseline to see if the treatment groups do better or not. If the treatment groups show better results than the control groups, then there is good reason to suspect that the treatment might be an effective treatment.

To eliminate the many potential confounding variables that can bias its results, a well-designed controlled study should have control and treatment groups that are similar in every characteristic other than the fact that one group is being treated and the other one is not. (It would be a very bad idea, for example, to have a treatment group that is all female and a control group that is all male.) The most reliable way to get equally representative treatment and control groups is to use a *randomized controlled study*. In a **randomized controlled study**, the subjects are assigned to the treatment group or the control group randomly.

When the randomization part of a randomized controlled study is properly done, treatment and control groups can be assumed to be statistically similar. But there is still one major difference between the two groups that can significantly affect the validity of the study—a critical confounding variable known as the *placebo effect*. The **placebo effect** follows from the generally accepted principle that *just the idea that one is getting a treatment can produce positive results*. Thus, when subjects in a study are getting a pill or a vaccine or some other kind of treatment, how can the researchers separate positive results that are consequences of the treatment itself from those that might be caused by the placebo effect? When possible, the standard way to handle this problem is to give the control group a *placebo*. A **placebo** is a *make-believe* form of treatment—a harmless pill, an injection of saline solution, or any other fake type of treatment intended to look like the real treatment. A controlled study in which the subjects in the control group are given a placebo is called a **controlled placebo study**.

By giving all subjects a seemingly equal treatment (the treatment group gets the real treatment and the control group gets a placebo that looks like the real treatment), we do not eliminate the placebo effect but rather control it—whatever its effect might be, it affects all subjects equally. It goes without saying that the use of placebos is pointless if the subject knows he or she is getting a placebo. Thus, a second key element of a good controlled placebo study is that all subjects be kept in the dark as to whether they are being treated with a real treatment or a placebo. A study in which neither the members of the treatment group nor the members of the control group know to which of the two groups they belong is called a **blind study**.

Blindness is a key requirement of a controlled placebo study but not the only one. To keep the interpretation of the results (which can often be ambiguous) totally objective, it is important that the scientists conducting the study and collecting the data also be in the dark when it comes to who got the treatment and who got the placebo. A controlled placebo study in which neither the subjects nor the scientists conducting the experiment know which subjects are in the treatment group and which are in the control group is called a **double-blind study**.

Our next case study illustrates one of the most famous and important double-blind studies in the annals of clinical research.

| CASE STUDY 3 | THE 1954 SALK POLIO VACCINE FIELD TRIALS

Polio (infantile paralysis) has been practically eradicated in the Western world. In the first half of the twentieth century, however, it was a major public health problem. Over one-half million cases of polio were reported between 1930 and 1950, and the actual number may have been considerably higher.

Because polio attacks mostly children and because its effects can be so serious (paralysis or death), eradication of the disease became a top public health priority in the United States. By the late 1940s, it was known that polio is a virus and, as such, can best be treated by a vaccine that is itself made up of a virus. The vaccine virus can be a closely related virus that does not have the same harmful effects, or it can be the actual virus that produces the disease but that has been killed by a special treatment. The former is known as a *live-virus vaccine*, the latter as a *killed-virus vaccine*. In response to either vaccine, the body is known to produce *antibodies* that remain in the system and give the individual immunity against an attack by the real virus.

Both the live-virus and the killed-virus approaches have their advantages and disadvantages. The live-virus approach produces a stronger reaction and better immunity, but at the same time, it is also more likely to cause a harmful reaction and, in some cases, even to produce the very disease it is supposed to prevent. The killed-virus approach is safer in terms of the likelihood of producing a harmful reaction, but it is also less effective in providing the desired level of immunity.

These facts are important because they help us understand the extraordinary amount of caution that went into the design of the study that tested the effectiveness of the polio vaccine. By 1953, several potential vaccines had been developed, one of the more promising of which was a killed-virus vaccine developed by Jonas Salk at the University of Pittsburgh. The killed-virus approach was chosen because there was a great potential risk in testing a live-virus vaccine in a large-scale study. (A large-scale study was needed to collect enough information on polio, which, in the 1950s, had a rate of incidence among children of about 1 in 2000.)

The testing of any new vaccine or drug creates many ethical dilemmas that have to be taken into account in the design of the study. With a killed-virus vaccine the risk of harmful consequences produced by the vaccine itself is small, so one possible approach would have been to distribute the vaccine widely among the population and then follow up on whether there was a decline in the national incidence of polio in subsequent years. This approach, which was not possible at the time because supplies were limited, is called the *vital statistics* approach and is the simplest way to test a vaccine. This is essentially the way the smallpox vaccine was determined to be effective. The problem with such an approach for polio is that polio is an epidemic type of disease, which means that there is a great variation in the incidence of the disease from one year to the next. In 1952, there were close to 60,000 reported cases of polio in the United States, but in 1953, the number of reported cases had dropped to almost half that (about 35,000). Since no vaccine or treatment was used, the cause of the drop was the natural variability typical of epidemic diseases. But if an ineffective polio vaccine had been tested in 1952 without a control group, the observed effect of a large drop in the incidence of polio in 1953 could have been incorrectly interpreted as statistical evidence that the vaccine worked.

The final decision on how best to test the effectiveness of the Salk vaccine was left to an advisory committee of doctors, public officials, and statisticians convened by the National Foundation for Infantile Paralysis and the Public Health Service. It was a highly controversial decision, but at the end, a large-scale, randomized, double-blind, controlled placebo study was chosen. Approximately 750,000 children were randomly selected to participate in the study. Of these, about 340,000 declined to participate, and another 8500 dropped out in the middle of the experiment. The remaining children were randomly divided into two groups—a treatment group and a control group—with approximately 200,000 children in each group. Neither the families of the children nor the researchers collecting the data knew if a particular child was getting the actual vaccine or a shot of harmless solution. The latter was critical because polio is not an easy disease to diagnose—it comes in many different forms and degrees. Sometimes it can be a borderline call, and if the doctor collecting the data had prior knowledge of whether the subject had received the real vaccine or the placebo, the diagnosis could have been subjectively tipped one way or the other.

A summary of the results of the Salk vaccine field trials is shown in Table 14-2. These data were taken as conclusive evidence that the Salk vaccine was an effective treatment for polio, and on the basis of this study, a massive inoculation campaign was put into effect. Today, all children are routinely inoculated against polio, and the disease has essentially been eradicated in the United States.

	Number of children	Number of reported cases of polio	Number of paralytic cases of polio	Number of fatal cases of polio
Treatment group	200,745	82	33	0
Control group	201,229	162	115	4
Declined to participate in the study	338,778	182*	121*	0*
Dropped out in the middle	8,484	2*	1*	0*
Total	749,236	428	270	4

*These figures are not a reliable indicator of the actual number of cases—they are only self-reported cases.
[*Source:* Adapted from Thomas Francis, Jr., et al., "An Evaluation of the 1954 Poliomyelitis Vaccine Trials—Summary Report," *American Journal of Public Health*, 45 (1955), 25.]

■ **TABLE 14-2**   Results of the Salk vaccine field trials

Conclusion

In this chapter we have discussed different methods for collecting data. In principle, the most accurate method is a *census*, a method that relies on collecting data from each member of the population. In most cases, because of considerations of cost and time, a census is an unrealistic strategy. When data are collected from only a subset of the population (called a *sample*), the data collection method is called a *survey*. The most important rule in designing good surveys is to eliminate or minimize *sample bias*. Today, almost all strategies for collecting data are based on surveys in which the laws of chance are used to determine how the sample is selected, and these methods for collecting data are called *random sampling* methods. Random sampling is the best way known to minimize or eliminate sample bias. Two of the most common random sampling methods are *simple random sampling* and *stratified sampling*. In some special situations, other more complicated types of random sampling can be used.

Sometimes identifying the sample is not enough. In cases in which cause-and-effect questions are involved, the data may come to the surface only after an extensive study has been carried out. The critical issue in establishing that there is a true cause and effect relation between two events is to distinguish between *correlations* and *causations*. The two most commonly used strategies for doing this are *observational studies* and *controlled double-blind placebo studies*. Both of these strategies are nowadays used (and sometimes abused) to settle issues affecting every aspect of our lives. We can thank this area of statistics for many breakthroughs in social science, medicine, and public health, as well as for the constant and dire warnings about our health, our diet, and against practically anything that is fun.

KEY CONCEPTS

14.1 Enumeration

- **population:** The set of individuals (humans, animals or inanimate objects) being enumerated, **416**
- **N-value:** The count giving the number of individuals in a given population, **416**
- **census:** a complete enumeration of a population, **416**
- **survey:** a data collection strategy that uses a sample to draw inferences about a population, **419**
- **sample:** a subset of the population chosen to be the providers of information in a survey, **419**
- **sampling:** the act of selecting a sample, **419**
- **statistic:** a numerical estimate of some measurable characteristic of a population obtained from a sample, **419**
- **parameter:** a true measurement of some characteristic of a population, **419**
- **one-sample estimation:** a method for estimating the size of a subpopulation using a sample, **419**
- **two-sample estimation (capture-recapture):** a method for estimating the size of a population using two samples, **421**

14.2 Measurement

- **poll:** a survey in which the data collection involves asking questions and recording answers, **422**

- **sampling proportion:** the percentage or proportion of the population represented by the sample, **423**

- **biased sample (sampling bias):** a sample in which not every member of the population had an equal chance of being included, **423**

- **selection bias:** a bias that occurs when some members of the population have no chance of being included in the sample, **424**

- **target population:** the population to which the conclusions of the survey apply, **424**

- **sampling frame:** the population from which the sample is drawn, **424**

- **convenience sampling:** a sampling strategy based on selecting the most convenient individuals to be in the sample, **425**

- **self-selection bias:** a type of bias that results when the sample consists of individuals who volunteer to be in the sample, **425**

- **quota sampling:** a sampling method that uses quotas as a way to force the sample to be representative of the population, **426**

- **response rate:** the percentage of respondents in a poll out of the total sample size, **426**

- **nonresponse bias:** a type of bias that results from having low response rates, **426**

- **simple random sampling:** a sampling method where any group of individuals in a population has the same chance of being in the sample as any other group of equal size, **428**

- **stratified sampling:** a sampling method that uses several layers of strata and sub-strata and chooses the sample by a process of random selection within each layer, **429**

- **sampling error:** the difference between a parameter and a statistic obtained from a sample, **430**

- **sampling variability:** the natural variability in the statistics obtained by different samples of the same population, even when the samples are chosen using the same methodology, **430**

14.3 Cause and Effect

- **correlation (association):** between two events X and Y; occurs when there is an observed mutual relationship between the two events, **431**

- **causation (causal relationship):** between two events X and Y; occurs when one event is the cause of the other one, **431**

- **observational study:** a study where individuals are tracked for an extensive period of time to look for correlations between lifestyle factors and disease or wellness factors, **432**

- **confounding variable:** an alternative possible cause for an observed effect; not the hypothetical cause, **433**

- **clinical study (clinical trial):** a study intended to demonstrate that a specific treatment is effective in treating some disease or symptom, **433**

- **controlled study:** a study in which the subjects are divided into treatment groups and control groups, **433**

- **randomized controlled study:** the assignment of subjects to treatment and control groups is done at random, **433**

- **placebo:** a fake treatment; intended to make the subject believe he or she is being treated, **434**

- **controlled placebo study:** a study in which the subjects in the control groups are given a placebo, **434**

■ **blind study:** a study in which the subjects don't know if they are getting the treatment or the placebo, **434**

■ **double-blind study:** a study in which neither the subjects nor the experimenters know who is getting the real treatment and who is getting the placebo, **434**

 **EXERCISES**

WALKING

14.1 Enumeration

1. As part of a sixth-grade class project the teacher brings to class a large jar containing 200 gumballs of two different colors: red and green. Andy is asked to draw a sample of his own choosing and estimate the number of red gumballs in the jar. Andy draws a sample of 25 gumballs, of which 8 are red and 17 are green. Use Andy's sample to estimate the number of red gumballs in the jar.

2. As part of a sixth-grade class project the teacher brings to class a large jar containing 200 gumballs of two different colors: red and green. Brianna is asked to draw a sample of her own choosing and estimate the number of red gumballs in the jar. Brianna draws a sample of 40 gumballs, of which 14 are red and 26 are green. Use Brianna's sample to estimate the number of red gumballs in the jar.

3. Madison County has a population of 34,522 people. The county hospital is interested in estimating the number of people in the county with blood-type A–. To do this they test blood samples from 253 patients. Out of this group, 17 have blood-type A–. Use this sample to estimate the number of people in Madison County with blood-type A–.

4. Madison County has a population of 34,522 people. The county hospital is interested in estimating the number of people in the county with blood-type AB+. To do this they test blood samples from 527 patients. Out of this group, 22 have blood-type AB+. Use this sample to estimate the number of people in Madison County with blood-type AB+.

5. A big concert was held at the Bowl. Men and women had to go through separate lines to get into the concert (the men had to be frisked for weapons). Once everyone was inside, total attendance at the concert had to be recorded. The turnstile counters on the female entrance showed a total count of 1542 females, but the turnstile counters on the male entrance were broken and there was no exact record of how many males attended. A sample taken from the 200 seats in Section A showed 79 males in that section. Using the male count in Section A estimate the number of people attending the concert.

6. A large jar contains an unknown number of red gumballs and 150 green gumballs. As part of a seventh-grade class project the teacher asks Carlos to estimate the total number of gumballs in the jar using a sample. Carlos draws a sample of 50 gumballs, of which 19 are red and 31 are green. Use Carlos' sample to estimate the number of gumballs in the jar.

7. You want to estimate how many fish there are in a small pond. Let's suppose that you first capture $n_1 = 500$ fish, tag them, and throw them back into the pond. After a couple of days you go back to the pond and capture $n_2 = 120$ fish, of which $k = 30$ are tagged. Estimate the number of fish in the pond.

8. To estimate the population in a rookery, 4965 fur seal pups were captured and tagged in early August. In late August, 900 fur seal pups were captured. Of these, 218 had been tagged. Based on these figures, estimate the population of fur seal pups in the rookery. [*Source:* Chapman and Johnson, "Estimation of Fur Seal Pup Populations by Randomized Sampling," *Transactions of the American Fisheries Society*, 97 (July 1968), 264–270.]

9. To count whale populations, the "capture" is done by means of a photograph, and the "tagging" is done by identifying each captured whale through their unique individual pigmentation and markings. To estimate the population of gray whales in a region of the Pacific between Northern California and Southeast Alaska, 121 gray whales were "captured" and "tagged" in 2007. In 2008, 172 whales were "recaptured." Of these, 76 had been "tagged" in the 2007 survey. Based on these figures, estimate the population of gray whales in the region. [*Source:* Calambokidis, J., J.L. Laake and A. Klimek, "Abundance and population structure of seasonal gray whales in the Pacific Northwest, 1998–2008." Paper IWC/62/BRG32 submitted to the *International Whaling Commission Scientific Committee*, 2010.]

10. The critically endangered Maui's dolphin is currently restricted to a relatively small stretch of coastline along the west coast of New Zealand's North Island. The dolphins are "captured" by just collecting samples of DNA and "tagged" by identifying their DNA fingerprint. A 2010–2011 capture-recapture study "captured" and "tagged" 26 Maui's dolphins in 2010. In 2011, 27 Maui's dolphins were "recaptured" and through their DNA, 12 were identified as having been "tagged" in 2010. Based on these figures, estimate the population of Maui's dolphins in 2011. [*Source:* Oremus, M., et al, "Distribution, group characteristics and movements of the critically endangered Maui's Dolphin (*Cephalorhynchus hectori maui*)." *Endangered Species Research*, preprint.]

Exercises 11 and 12 refer to Chapman's correction. Chapman's correction is a small tweak on the final formula used in two-sample estimation. Using the same three input variables n_1 (size of the first sample), n_2 (size of the second sample), and k (number of tagged individuals in the second sample), Chapman's correction is given by the formula $\frac{k+1}{n_2+1} \approx \frac{n_1+1}{N+1}$. Solving for N gives Chapman's correction estimate for the size of the population.

11. Use Chapman's correction to estimate the population of gray whales described in Exercise 9. Compare the two answers.

12. Use Chapman's correction to estimate the population of Maui's dolphins described in Exercise 10. Compare the two answers.

13. Starting in 2004, a study to determine the number of lake sturgeon on Rainy River and Lake of the Woods on the United States–Canada border was conducted by the Canadian Ministry of Natural Resources, the Minnesota Department of Natural Resources, and the Rainy River First Nations. Using the capture-recapture method, the size of the population of lake sturgeon on Rainy River and Lake of the Woods was estimated at $N = 160{,}286$. In the capture phase of the study, 1700 lake sturgeon were caught, tagged, and released. Of these tagged sturgeon, seven were recaptured during the recapture phase of the study. Based on these figures, estimate the number of sturgeon caught in the recapture phase of the study. [*Source:* Dan Gauthier, "Lake of the Woods Sturgeon Population Recovering," *Daily Miner and News* (Kenora, Ont.), June 11, 2005, p. 31.]

14. A 2004 study conducted at Utah Lake using the capture-recapture method estimated the carp population in the lake to be about 1.1 million. Over a period of 15 days, workers captured, tagged, and released 24,000 carp. In the recapture phase of the study 10,300 carp were recaptured. Estimate how many of the carp that were recaptured had tags. [*Source:* Brett Prettyman, "With Carp Cooking Utah Lake, It's Time to Eat," *Salt Lake Tribune*, July 15, 2004, p. D3.]

14.2 Measurement

15. Name the sampling method that best describes each situation. Choose your answer from the following (A) simple random sampling, (B) convenience sampling, (C) quota sampling, (D) stratified sampling, (E) census.

(a) George wants to know how the rest of the class did on the last quiz. He peeks at the scores of a few students sitting right next to him. Based on what he sees, he concludes that nobody did very well.

(b) Eureka High School has 400 freshmen, 300 sophomores, 300 juniors, and 200 seniors. The student newspaper conducts a poll asking students if the football coach should be fired. The student newspaper randomly selects 20 freshmen, 15 sophomores, 15 juniors, and 10 seniors for the poll.

(c) For the last football game of the season, the coach chooses the three captains by putting the names of all the players in a hat and drawing three names. (Maybe that's why they are trying to fire him!)

(d) For the last football game of the season, the coach chooses the three captains by putting the names of all the *seniors* in a hat and drawing three names.

16. An audit is performed on last year's 15,000 student-aid packages given out by the financial aid office at Tasmania State University. Roughly half of the student-aid packages were less than $1000 (Category 1), about one-fourth were between $1000 and $5000 (Category 2), and another quarter were over $5000 (Category 3). For each audit described below, name the sampling method that best describes it. Choose your answer from the following: (A) simple random sampling, (B) convenience sampling, (C) quota sampling, (D) stratified sampling, (E) census.

(a) The auditor reviews all 15,000 student-aid packages.

(b) The auditor randomly selects 200 student-aid packages in Category 1, 100 student-aid packages in Category 2, and 100 transactions in Category 3.

(c) The auditor reviews the first 500 student-aid packages that he comes across.

(d) The auditor first separates the student-aid packages by school (Agriculture, Arts and Humanities, Engineering, Nursing, Social Science, Science, and Mathematics). Three of these schools are selected at random and further subdivided by major. Ten majors are randomly selected within each selected school, and then 20 students are randomly selected from each of the selected majors.

Exercises 17 through 20 refer to the following story: The city of Cleansburg has 8325 registered voters. There is an election for mayor of Cleansburg, and there are three candidates for the position: Smith, Jones, and Brown. The day before the election a telephone poll of 680 randomly chosen registered voters produced the following results: 306 people surveyed indicated that they would vote for Smith, 272 indicated that they would vote for Jones and 102 indicated that they would vote for Brown.

17. (a) Describe the population for this survey.

(b) Describe the sample for this survey.

(c) Name the sampling method used for this survey.

18. (a) Give the sampling proportion for this survey.

(b) Give the sample statistic estimating the percentage of the vote going to Smith.

19. Given that in the actual election Smith received 42% of the vote, Jones 43% of the vote, and Brown 15% of the vote, find the sampling errors in the survey expressed as percentages.

20. Do you think that the sampling error in this example was due primarily to sampling bias or to chance? Explain your answer.

Exercises 21 through 24 refer to the following story: The 1250 students at Eureka High School are having an election for Homecoming King. The candidates are Tomlinson (captain of the football team), Garcia (class president), and Marsalis (member of the marching band). At the football game a week before the election, a pre-election poll was taken of students as they entered the stadium gates. Of the students who attended the game, 203 planned to vote for Tomlinson, 42 planned to vote for Garcia, and 105 planned to vote for Marsalis.

21. (a) Describe the sample for this survey.

(b) Give the sampling proportion for this survey.

22. Name the sampling method used for this survey.

23. (a) Compare and contrast the population and the sampling frame for this survey.

(b) Is the sampling error a result of sampling variability or of sample bias? Explain

24. (a) Give the sample statistics estimating the percentage of the vote going to each candidate.

(b) A week after this survey, Garcia was elected Homecoming King with 51% of the vote, Marsalis got 30% of the vote, and Tomlinson came in last with 19% of the vote. Find the sampling errors in the survey expressed as percentages.

Exercises 25 through 28 refer to the following story: The Cleansburg Planning Department is trying to determine what percent of the people in the city want to spend public funds to revitalize the downtown mall. To do so, the department decides to conduct a survey. Five professional interviewers are hired. Each interviewer is asked to pick a street corner of his or her choice within the city limits, and every day between 4:00 P.M. and 6:00 P.M. the interviewers are supposed to ask each passerby if he or she wishes to respond to a survey sponsored by Cleansburg City Hall. If the response is yes, the follow-up question is asked: Are you in favor of spending public funds to revitalize the downtown mall? The interviewers are asked to return to the same street corner as many days as are necessary until each has conducted a total of 100 interviews. The results of the survey are shown in Table 14-3.

Interviewer	Yes[a]	No[b]	Nonrespondents[c]
A	35	65	321
B	21	79	208
C	58	42	103
D	78	22	87
E[d]	12	63	594

[a]In favor of spending public funds to revitalize the downtown mall.
[b]Opposed to spending public funds to revitalize the downtown mall.
[c]Declined to be interviewed or had no opinion.
[d] Got frustrated and quit.

■ **TABLE 14-3**

25. (a) Describe as specifically as you can the target population for this survey.

(b) Compare and contrast the target population and the sampling frame for this survey.

26. (a) What is the size of the sample?

(b) Calculate the response rate in this survey. Was this survey subject to nonresponse bias?

27. (a) Can you explain the big difference in the data from interviewer to interviewer?

(b) One of the interviewers conducted the interviews at a street corner downtown. Which interviewer? Explain.

(c) Do you think the survey was subject to selection bias? Explain.

(d) Was the sampling method used in this survey the same as quota sampling? Explain.

28. Do you think this was a good survey? If you were a consultant to the Cleansburg Planning Department, could you suggest some improvements? Be specific.

*Exercises 29 through 32 refer to the following story: The dean of students at Tasmania State University wants to determine how many undergraduates at TSU are familiar with a new financial aid program offered by the university. There are 15,000 undergraduates at TSU, so it is too expensive to conduct a census. The following sampling method is used to choose a representative sample of undergraduates to poll. Start with the registrar's alphabetical listing containing the names of all undergraduates. Randomly pick a number between 1 and 100, and count that far down the list. Take that name and every 100th name after it. For example, if the random number chosen is 73, then pick the 73rd, 173rd, 273rd, and so forth, names on the list. (The sampling method illustrated in this survey is known as **systematic sampling**.)*

29. (a) Compare and contrast the sampling frame and the target population for this survey.

(b) Give the exact N-value of the population.

30. (a) Find the sampling proportion.

(b) Suppose that the survey had a response rate of 90%. Find the size n of the sample.

31. (a) Explain why the method used for choosing the sample is not simple random sampling.

(b) If 100% of those responding claimed that they were not familiar with the new financial aid program offered by the university, is this result more likely due to sampling variability or to sample bias? Explain.

32. (a) Suppose that the survey had a response rate of 90% and that 108 students responded that they were not familiar with the new financial aid program. Give a statistic for the total number of students at the university who were not familiar with the new financial aid program.

(b) Do you think the results of this survey will be reliable? Explain.

Exercises 33 and 34 refer to the following story: An orange grower wishes to compute the average yield from his orchard. The orchard contains three varieties of trees: 50% of his trees are of variety A, 25% of variety B, and 25% of variety C.

33. (a) Suppose that the grower samples randomly from 300 trees of variety A, 150 trees of variety B, and 150 trees of variety C. What type of sampling is being used?

(b) Suppose that the grower selects for his sample a 10 by 30 rectangular block of 300 trees of variety A, a 10 by 15 rectangular block of 150 trees of variety B, and a 10 by 15 rectangular block of 150 trees of variety C. What type of sampling is being used?

34. (a) Suppose that in his survey, the grower found that each tree of variety A averages 100 oranges, each tree of variety B averages 50 oranges, and each tree of variety

C averages 70 oranges. Estimate the average yield per tree of his orchard.

(b) Is the yield you found in (a) a parameter or a statistic? Explain.

35. You are a fruit wholesaler. You have just received 250 crates of pineapples: 75 crates came from supplier A, 75 crates from supplier B, and 100 crates from supplier C. You wish to determine if the pineapples are good enough to ship to your best customers by inspecting a sample of $n = 20$ crates. Describe how you might implement each of the following sampling methods.

(a) Simple random sampling

(b) Convenience sampling

(c) Stratified sampling

(d) Quota sampling

36. For each of the following situations, determine if the sample is representative of the population. Explain your answer.

(a) To determine if the chicken is well done, you sample one of the wings.

(b) To determine if the statistics test you are taking is easy or difficult, you look at the first three questions on the test and then make up your mind.

(c) To determine if you have a viral infection, the doctor draws 10 ml of blood from your arm and tests the blood.

(d) To determine how well liked a person is, you look up the number of friends the person has on Facebook.

14.3 Cause and Effect

Exercises 37 through 40 refer to the following story: The manufacturer of a new vitamin (vitamin X) decides to sponsor a study to determine the vitamin's effectiveness in curing the common cold. Five hundred college students having a cold were recruited from colleges in the San Diego area and were paid to participate as subjects in this study. The subjects were each given two tablets of vitamin X a day. Based on information provided by the subjects themselves, 457 of the 500 subjects were cured of their colds within 3 days. (The average number of days a cold lasts is 4.87 days.) As a result of this study, the manufacturer launched an advertising campaign based on the claim that "vitamin X is more than 90% effective in curing the common cold."

37. (a) Describe as specifically as you can the target population for the study.

(b) Describe the sampling frame for the study.

(c) Describe the sample used for the study.

38. (a) Was the study a controlled study? Explain.

(b) List four possible causes other than the effectiveness of vitamin X itself that could have confounded the results of the study.

39. List four different problems with the study that indicate poor design.

40. Make some suggestions for improving the study.

Exercises 41 through 44 refer to a clinical study conducted at the Houston Veterans Administration Medical Center on the effectiveness of knee surgery to cure degenerative arthritis (osteoarthritis) of the knee. Of the 324 individuals who met the inclusion criteria for the study, 144 declined to participate. The researchers randomly divided the remaining 180 subjects into three groups: One group received a type of arthroscopic knee surgery called debridement; a second group received a type of arthroscopic knee surgery called lavage; and a third group received skin incisions to make it look like they had had arthroscopic knee surgery, but no actual surgery was performed. The patients in the study did not know which group they were in and in particular did not know if they were receiving the real surgery or simulated surgery. All the patients who participated in the study were evaluated for two years after the procedure. In the two-year follow-up, all three groups said that they had slightly less pain and better knee movement, but the "fake" surgery group often reported the best results. [Source: New England Journal of Medicine, 347, no. 2 (July 11, 2002): 81–88.]

41. (a) Describe as specifically as you can the target population for this study.

(b) Describe the sample.

42. (a) Was the sample chosen by random sampling? Explain.

(b) Was this study a controlled placebo experiment? Explain.

(c) Describe the treatment group(s) in this study.

43. (a) Could this study be considered a randomized controlled study? Explain.

(b) Was this Study blind, double blind, or neither?

44. As a result of this study, the Department of Veterans Affairs issued an advisory to its doctors recommending that they stop using arthroscopic knee surgery for patients suffering from osteoarthritis. Do you agree or disagree with the advisory? Explain your answer.

Exercises 45 through 48 refer to a clinical trial named APPROVe designed to determine whether Vioxx, a medication used for arthritis and acute pain, was effective in preventing the recurrence of colorectal polyps in patients with a history of colorectal adenomas. APPROVe was conducted between 2002 and 2003 and involved 2586 participants, all of whom had a history of colorectal adenomas. The participants were randomly divided into two groups: 1287 were given 25 milligrams of Vioxx daily for the duration of the clinical trial (originally intended to last three years), and 1299 patients were given a placebo. Neither the participants nor the doctors involved in the clinical trial knew who was in which group. During the trial, 72 of the participants had cardiovascular events (mostly heart attacks or strokes). Later it was found that 46 of these people were from the group taking the Vioxx and only 26 were from the group taking the placebo. Based on these results, the clinical trial was stopped in 2003 and Vioxx was taken off the market in 2004.

45. Describe as specifically as you can the target population for APPROVe.

46. Describe the sample for APPROVe.

47. (a) Describe the control and treatment groups in APPROVe.

(b) APPROVe can be described as a *double-blind, randomized controlled placebo study.* Explain why each of these terms applies.

48. What conclusions would you draw from APPROVe?

Exercises 49 through 52 refer to a study on the effectiveness of an HPV (human papilloma virus) vaccine conducted between October 1998 and November 1999. HPV is the most common sexually transmitted infection—more than 20 million Americans are infected with HPV—but most HPV infections are benign, and in most cases infected individuals are not even aware they are infected. (On the other hand, some HPV infections can lead to cervical cancer in women.) The researchers recruited 2392 women from 16 different centers across the United States to participate in the study through advertisements on college campuses and in the surrounding communities. To be eligible to participate in the study, the subjects had to meet the following criteria: (1) be a female between 16 and 23 years of age, (2) not be pregnant, (3) have no prior abnormal Pap smears, and (4) report to have had sexual relations with no more than five men. At each center, half of the participants were randomly selected to receive the HPV vaccine, and the other half received a placebo injection. After 17.4 months, the incidence of HPV infection was 3.8 per 100 woman-years at risk in the placebo group and 0 per 100 woman-years at risk in the vaccine group. In addition, all nine cases of HPV-related cervical precancerous growths occurred among the placebo recipients. [Source: New England Journal of Medicine, 347, no. 21 (November 21, 2002): 1645–1651.]

49. (a) Describe as specifically as you can the target population for the study.

(b) Describe the sampling frame for the study.

50. (a) Describe the sample for the study.

(b) Was the sample chosen using random sampling? Explain.

51. (a) Describe the treatment group in the study.

(b) Could this study be considered a double-blind, randomized controlled placebo study? Explain.

52. Carefully state what a legitimate conclusion from this study might be.

Exercises 53 through 56 refer to a landmark study conducted in 1896 in Denmark by Dr. Johannes Fibiger, who went on to receive the Nobel Prize in Medicine in 1926. The purpose of the study was to determine the effectiveness of a new serum for treating diphtheria, a common and often deadly respiratory disease in those days. Fibiger conducted his study over a one-year period (May 1896–April 1897) in one particular Copenhagen hospital. New diphtheria patients admitted to the hospital received different treatments based on the day of admission. In one set of days (call them "even" days for convenience), the patients were treated with the new serum daily and received the standard treatment. Patients admitted on alternate days (the "odd" days) received just the standard treatment. Over the one-year period of the study, eight of the 239 patients admitted on the "even" days and treated with the serum died, whereas 30 of the 245 patients admitted on the "odd" days died.

53. (a) Describe as specifically as you can the target population for Fibiger's study.

(b) Describe the sampling frame for the study.

54. (a) Describe the sample for Fibiger's study.

(b) Is selection bias a possible problem in this study? Explain.

55. (a) Describe the control and treatment groups in Fibiger's study.

(b) What conclusions would you draw from Fibiger's study? Explain.

56. In a different study on the effectiveness of the diphtheria serum conducted prior to Fibiger's study, patients in one Copenhagen hospital were chosen to be in the treatment group and were given the new serum, whereas patients in a different Copenhagen hospital were chosen to be in the control group and were given the standard treatment. Fibiger did not believe that the results of this earlier study could be trusted. What are some possible confounding variables that may have affected the results of this earlier study?

Exercises 57 through 60 refer to a study conducted between 2008 and 2010 on the effectiveness of saw palmetto fruit extracts at treating lower urinary tract symptoms in men with prostate enlargement. (Saw palmetto is a widely used over-the-counter supplement for treating urinary tract symptoms.) In the study, 369 men aged 45 years or older were randomly divided into a group taking a daily placebo and a group taking saw palmetto. Participants were nonpaid volunteers recruited at 11 North American sites. All had moderately impaired urinary flow. Because the saw palmetto extract has a mild odor, the doses were administered using gelcaps to eliminate the odor. In an analysis of the 306 men who completed the 72-week trial, both groups had similar small improvements in mean symptom scores, but saw palmetto conferred no benefit over placebo on symptom scores or on any secondary outcomes. [Source: Journal of the American Medical Association, 306(12), 2011, 1344–1351.]

57. (a) Describe as specifically as you can the target population for the study.

(b) Compare and contrast the sampling frame and target population for the study.

58. (a) Describe the sample for the study.

(b) Was the sample chosen using random sampling? Explain.

59. (a) Describe the treatment group in the study.

(b) Explain why the experimenters took the trouble to cover the mild odor of saw palmetto to the point of packaging the doses in the form of gelcaps.

(c) Was this study a blind, randomized, controlled placebo study? Explain.

60. If you were a 55-year-old male with an enlarged prostate taking saw palmetto daily, how might you react to this study?

JOGGING

61. Imagine you have a very large coin jar full of nickels, dimes, and quarters. You would like to know how much money you have in the jar, but you don't want to go through the trouble of counting all the coins. You decide to estimate how many nickels, dimes, and quarters are in the jar using the two-sample estimation method. After shaking the jar well, you draw a first sample of 150 coins and get

36 quarters, 45 nickels, and 69 dimes. Using a permanent ink marker you tag each of the 150 coins with a black dot and put the coins back in the jar, shake the jar really well to let the tagged coins mix well with the rest, and draw a second sample of 100 coins. The second sample has 28 quarters, 29 nickels, and 43 dimes. Of these, 4 quarters, 5 nickels, and 8 dimes have black dots. Estimate how much money is in the jar. (*Hint*: You will need a separate calculation for estimating the quarters, nickels, and dimes in the jar.)

62. One implicit assumption when using the capture-recapture method to estimate the size of a population is that the capture process is truly random, with all individuals having the same likelihood of being captured. Sometimes that is not true, and some populations have a large number of individuals that are "trap-happy" individuals (more prone to capture than others, more likely to take the bait, less cagey, slower, dumber, etc.). If that were the case, would the capture-recapture method be likely to *underestimate* or *overestimate* the size of the population? Explain your answer.

63. One implicit assumption when using the capture-recapture method to estimate the size of a population is that when individuals are tagged in the capture stage, these individuals are not affected in any harmful way by the tags. Sometimes, though, tagged individuals become affected, with the tags often making them more likely prey to predators (imagine, for example, tagging fish with bright yellow tags that make them stand out or tagging a bird on a wing in such a way that it affects its ability to fly). If that were the case, would the capture-recapture method be likely to *underestimate* or *overestimate* the size of the population? Explain your answer.

64. **Informal surveys.** In everyday life we are constantly involved in activities that can be described as *informal surveys*, often without even realizing it. Here are some examples.

    (i) Al gets up in the morning and wants to know what kind of day it is going to be, so he peeks out the window. He doesn't see any dark clouds, so he figures it's not going to rain.

    (ii) Betty takes a sip from a cup of coffee and burns her lips. She concludes that the coffee is too hot and decides to add a tad of cold water to it.

    (iii) Carla got her first Math 101 exam back with a C grade on it. The students sitting on each side of her also received C grades. She concludes that the entire Math 101 class received a C on the first exam.

    For each of the preceding examples,

    (a) describe the population.

    (b) discuss whether the sample is random or not.

    (c) discuss the validity of the conclusions drawn. (There is no right or wrong answer to this question, but you should be able to make a reasonable case for your position.)

65. Read the examples of informal surveys given in Exercise 64. Give three new examples of your own. Make them as different as possible from the ones given in Exercise 64 [changing coffee to soup in (ii) is not a new example].

66. **Leading-question bias.** The way the questions in many surveys are phrased can itself be a source of bias. When a question is worded in such a way as to predispose the respondent to provide a particular response, the results of the survey are tainted by a special type of bias called *leading-question bias*. The following is an extreme hypothetical situation intended to drive the point home.

In an effort to find out how the American taxpayer feels about a tax increase, the Institute for Tax Reform conducts a "scientific" one-question poll.

Are you in favor of paying higher taxes to bail the federal government out of its disastrous economic policies and its mismanagement of the federal budget? Yes____. No____.

Ninety-five percent of the respondents answered no.

    (a) Explain why the results of this survey might be invalid.

    (b) Rephrase the question in a neutral way. Pay particular attention to highly charged words.

    (c) Make up your own (more subtle) example of leading-question bias. Analyze the critical words that are the cause of bias.

67. **Question order bias.** In July 1999, a Gallup poll of 1061 people asked the following two questions:

    ■ *As you may know, former Major League Baseball player Pete Rose is ineligible for baseball's Hall of Fame because of charges that he gambled on baseball games. Do you think he should or should not be eligible for admission to the Hall of Fame?*

    ■ *As you may know, former Major League Baseball player Shoeless Joe Jackson is ineligible for baseball's Hall of Fame because of charges that he took money from gamblers in exchange for fixing the 1919 World Series. Do you think he should or should not be eligible for admission to the Hall of Fame?*

The order in which the questions were asked was random: Approximately half of the people polled were asked about Rose first and Jackson second; the other half were asked about Jackson first and Rose second. When the order of the questions was Rose first and Jackson second, 64% of the respondents said that Rose should be eligible for admission to the Hall of Fame and 33% said that Jackson should be eligible for admission to the Hall of Fame. When the order of the questions was Jackson first and Rose second, 52% said that Rose should be eligible for admission to the Hall of Fame and 45% said that Jackson should be eligible for admission to the Hall of Fame. Explain why you think each player's support for eligibility was less (by 12% in each case) when the player was second in the order of the questions.

68. Today, most consumer marketing surveys are conducted by telephone. In selecting a sample of households that are representative of all the households in a given geographical area, the two basic techniques used are (1) randomly selecting telephone numbers to call from the local telephone directory or directories and (2) using a computer to randomly generate seven-digit numbers to try that are compatible with the local phone numbers.

(a) Briefly discuss the advantages and disadvantages of each technique. In your opinion, which of the two will produce the more reliable data? Explain.

(b) Suppose that you are trying to market burglar alarms in New York City. Which of the two techniques for selecting the sample would you use? Explain your reasons.

69. The following two surveys were conducted in January 1991 to assess how the American public viewed media coverage of the Persian Gulf war. Survey 1 was an Area Code 900 telephone poll survey conducted by *ABC News*. Viewers were asked to call a certain 900 number if they believed that the media were doing a good job of covering the war and a different 900 number if they believed that the media were not doing a good job in covering the war. Each call cost 50 cents. Of the 60,000 respondents, 83% believed that the media were not doing a good job. Survey 2 was a telephone poll of 1500 randomly selected households across the United States conducted by the *Times-Mirror* survey organization. In this poll, 80% of the respondents indicated that they approved of the press coverage of the war.

(a) Briefly discuss survey 1, indicating any possible types of bias.

(b) Briefly discuss survey 2, indicating any possible types of bias.

(c) Can you explain the discrepancy between the results of the two surveys?

(d) In your opinion, which of the two surveys gives the more reliable data?

70. An article in the *Providence Journal* about automobile accident fatalities includes the following observation: "Forty-two percent of all fatalities occurred on Friday, Saturday, and Sunday, apparently because of increased drinking on the weekends."

(a) Give a possible argument as to why the conclusion drawn may not be justified by the data.

(b) Give a different possible argument as to why the conclusion drawn may be justified by the data after all.

71. (a) For the capture-recapture method to give a reasonable estimate of N, what assumptions about the two samples must be true?

(b) Give reasons why the assumptions in (a) may not hold true in many situations.

72. Consider the following hypothetical survey designed to find out what percentage of people cheat on their income taxes.

Fifteen hundred taxpayers are randomly selected from the Internal Revenue Service (IRS) rolls. These individuals are then interviewed in person by representatives of the IRS and read the following statement.

"This survey is for information purposes only. Your answer will be held in strict confidence. Have you ever cheated on your income taxes? Yes____. No____."

Twelve percent of the respondents answered yes.

(a) Explain why the above figure might be unreliable.

(b) Can you think of ways in which a survey of this type might be designed so that more reliable information could be obtained? In particular, discuss who should be sponsoring the survey and how the interviews should be carried out.

RUNNING

73. One of the problems with the capture-recapture method is that in some animal populations there are individuals that are trap-happy (easy to trap) and others that are more cagey and hard to trap. Too many trap-happy individuals can skew the data (see Exercise 62). A **removal method** is a method for estimating the N-value of a population that takes into account the existence of trap-happy individuals by trapping them and removing them. In the first "capture," individuals from the general population are trapped, counted, and removed from the habitat so that they can't be trapped again. In the "recapture," individuals from the remaining population (those that had not been trapped before) are trapped and counted. The number of individuals trapped in the capture can be denoted by pN, where p denotes the fraction of the population trapped and N is the size of the population. The number of individuals left after the removal is $(1-p)N$. If we assume that the number of individuals trapped in each capture represents the same fraction of the population, then the number of individuals trapped in the recapture should be $p(1-p)N$. From the two equations ($pN =$ number of individuals trapped in the capture; $p(1-p)N =$ number of individuals trapped in the recapture) we can solve for N and get an estimate of the population.

Suppose 250 individuals are trapped in the capture stage and removed from the population, and 150 individuals are trapped in the recapture stage. Estimate the size of the population.

74. **Darroch's method.** is a method for estimating the size of a population using multiple (more than two) captures. For example, suppose that there are four captures of sizes $n_1, n_2, n_3,$ and n_4, respectively, and let M be the total number of *distinct* individuals caught in the four captures (i.e., an individual that is captured in more than one capture is counted only once). Darroch's method gives the estimate for N as the unique solution of the equation $\left(1 - \frac{M}{N}\right) = \left(1 - \frac{n_1}{N}\right)\left(1 - \frac{n_2}{N}\right)\left(1 - \frac{n_3}{N}\right)\left(1 - \frac{n_4}{N}\right)$.

(a) Suppose that we are estimating the size of a population of fish in a pond using four separate captures. The sizes of the captures are $n_1 = 30$, $n_2 = 15$, $n_3 = 22$, and $n_4 = 45$. The number of distinct fish caught is $M = 75$. Estimate the size of the population using Darroch's formula.

(b) Show that with just two captures Darroch's method gives the same answer as the capture-recapture method.

PROJECTS AND PAPERS

1 What's the Latest?

In this project you are to do an in-depth report on a recent study. Find a recent article from a newspaper or news magazine reporting the results of a major study and write an analysis of the study. Discuss the extent to which the article gives the reader enough information to assess the validity of the study's conclusions. If in your opinion there is information missing in the article, generate a list of questions that would help you further assess the validity of the study's conclusions. Pay particular attention to the ideas and concepts discussed in this chapter, including the target population, sample size, sampling bias, randomness, controls, and so on.

2 The Placebo Effect: Myth or Reality?

There is no consensus among researchers conducting clinical studies as to the true impact of the placebo effect. According to some researchers, as many as 30% of patients in a clinical trial can be affected by it; according to others, the placebo effect is a myth.

Write a paper on the *placebo effect*. Discuss the history of this idea, the most recent controversies regarding whether it truly exists or not and why is it important to determine its true impact.

3 Ethical Issues in Clinical Studies

Until the world was exposed to the atrocities committed by Nazi physicians during World War II, there was little consensus regarding the ethics of medical experiments involving human subjects. Following the trial of the Nazi physicians in 1946, the Nuremberg Code of Ethics was developed to deal with the ethics of clinical studies on human subjects. Sadly, unethical experimentation continued. In the Tuskegee syphilis study starting in 1932, 600 low-income African American males (400 infected with syphilis) were monitored. Even though a proven cure (penicillin) became available in the 1950s, the study continued until 1972 with participants denied treatment. As many as 100 subjects died from the disease.

In this project you are to write a paper summarizing current ethical standards for the treatment of humans in experimental studies.

15 Graphs, Charts, and Numbers

The Data Show and Tell

In 2011 a total of 1,647,123 college-bound students took the SAT. Put them all in one place and you would have the fifth largest city in the United States—a third larger than Dallas and twice as large as San Francisco. Each of the 1,647,123 tests taken generated several numbers: individual sub scores in three separate subject areas (Mathematics, Critical Thinking, and Writing), and percentiles for each subject area plus a composite percentile for the entire test. Put it all together and you have more than 10 million numbers to play with—a vast sea of mysterious but potentially useful data.

When it comes to rapid mental processing, we humans do well with images and words, but not so well with numbers. Psychologists have found that a typical human mind can juggle the relationships between six, at most seven, numbers at one time. Anything beyond that requires a more deliberate and purposeful effort. Certainly, by the time you get to a dozen or more numbers, some organization and management of the *data* will be required. And what about managing and organizing a *data set* of more than 10 million numbers? No worries.

There are essentially two major strategies for describing a large data set. One of them is to take advantage of the human mind's great talent for visualization and describe the data using pictures (graphs and charts). In Section 15.1 we cover some of the standard graphical tools for describing data—*bar charts, pictograms, pie charts, and histograms*—and discuss a few basic rules for when and how to use each. The second strategy for describing a large data set is to use *numerical summaries*. While a few numbers can't tell the full story behind 10 million numbers, it's amazing how much mileage one can get from a few well-chosen numerical summaries. In Section 15.2 we cover the classic numerical summaries for a data set—*averages* (*means*), *medians*, *quartiles*, *percentiles*, and *five-number summaries*. All of these numerical summaries help us identify where the data set sits in relation to the possible values that the data could take and are called *measures of location*. A second group of useful numbers consists of those that provide information about the *spread* of the data set. In Section 15.3 we briefly discuss the three most commonly used *measures of spread*—the range, the interquartile range, and the standard deviation.

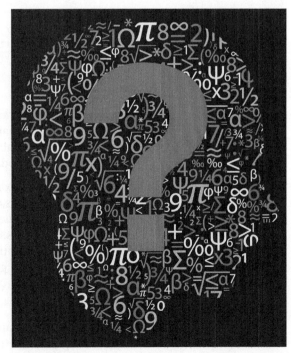

15.1 Graphs and Charts

The old adage "a picture is worth 1000 words" is even more valid when applied to numbers instead of words. A single, well-chosen graphical display can say a lot about the patterns that lie hidden within a bunch of numbers, especially when there are a lot of them numbers. OK, we are going to need a slightly more formal terminology than "them numbers," so we start with a couple of basic definitions.

- **Data set.** A *data set* is a collection of numbers that represent all the values obtained when measuring some characteristic of a population (such as a test score, a stock price, a sales figure, etc.). [*Note*: Technically speaking a data set is not a set because repeated numbers are included—in a real set, repeats are not included.]

- **Data point.** Each of the individual numbers in a data set is called a *data point*. In all the data sets we will consider in this chapter, the data points will be rational numbers (either whole numbers, decimals, or percentages). We will let N denote the total number of data points in the data set, and we will refer to N as the *size* of the data set.

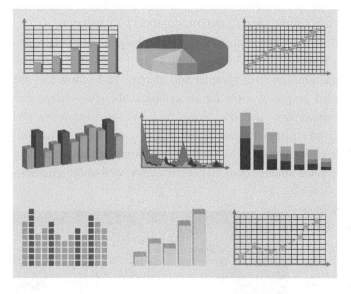

Creating a graphical representation of a data set is somewhat like taking a photograph, except that instead of taking snapshots of people or nature we are creating a picture of the data. And, just like photography is a skill that can be elevated into an art form, creating the most appropriate and efficient graph or chart for a data set is both a skill and an art. In this section we are only going to cover the most basic types of graphs and charts, and discuss when to use one or the other.

The choice of what is the most appropriate type of graph or chart to use in graphically displaying a data set depends on many criteria, and many of these criteria are not quantifiable: Who is your audience? Do you have a message? Are you trying sell a product or idea? Are you looking for particular patterns? To keep things simple, we will focus on two basic but critical questions: (1) How large is the data set? and (2) Does the data represent a *discrete* or a *continuous* variable?

- **Discrete variable.** A discrete variable is one in which the values of the variable can only change by minimum increments. In other words, two different values of the variable cannot be arbitrarily close to each other—there is a minimum gap required.

A classic example of a discrete variable is a test score. If the test is multiple-choice then it is obvious—the minimum gap between two scores is one point (assuming each question is worth a point). Even when the scoring is more refined, such as in an essay, there is a minimum gap between scores—half a point, a quarter of a point, a tenth of a point. There is always a limit as to how far the person doing the scoring can go in finessing the differences between essays.

- **Continuous variables.** Continuous variables are variables that can take infinitely many values, and those values can differ by arbitrarily small amounts.

A good example of a continuous variable is the measured distance between two points. In theory, two different distance measurements could differ by an inch, a tenth of an inch, or one-millionth of an inch—there is no minimum gap that must separate the two. (In practice, of course, there is the problem of how refined can our measurement be—if the difference between the two distances is one-millionth of an inch we probably won't be able to measure the difference.)

The case of money (especially when we are dealing with large sums) is particularly interesting because money is really a discrete variable (the minimum gap between two sums of money is one cent), but it is usually described as if it were a continuous variable. In other words, when two large sums of money differ by a penny we will think of that difference as being "infinitely small."

Bar Graphs, Pictograms, and Line Graphs

We will start our exploration of data sets and their graphical representations with a fictitious example. Except for the details, this example represents a situation familiar to every college student.

EXAMPLE 15.1 STAT 101 MIDTERM SCORES

As usual, the day after the midterm exam in his Stat 101 class, Dr. Blackbeard has posted the scores online (Table 15-1). The data set consists of $N = 75$ data points (the number of students who took the test). Each data point (listed under the "Score" columns) is an integer between 0 and 25 (Dr. Blackbeard gives no partial credit). Note that the numbers listed under the "ID" columns are not data points—they are the last four digits of the student IDs used as substitutes for their names to protect the students' rights of privacy.

ID	Score	ID	Score	ID	Score	ID	Score	ID	Score
1257	12	2651	10	4355	8	6336	11	8007	13
1297	16	2658	11	4396	7	6510	13	8041	9
1348	11	2794	9	4445	11	6622	11	8129	11
1379	24	2795	13	4787	11	6754	8	8366	13
1450	9	2833	10	4855	14	6798	9	8493	8
1506	10	2905	10	4944	6	6873	9	8522	8
1731	14	3269	13	5298	11	6931	12	8664	10
1753	8	3284	15	5434	13	7041	13	8767	7
1818	12	3310	11	5604	10	7196	13	9128	10
2030	12	3596	9	5644	9	7292	12	9380	9
2058	11	3906	14	5689	11	7362	10	9424	10
2462	10	4042	10	5736	10	7503	10	9541	8
2489	11	4124	12	5852	9	7616	14	9928	15
2542	10	4204	12	5877	9	7629	14	9953	11
2619	1	4224	10	5906	12	7961	12	9973	10

■ **TABLE 15-1**   Stat 101 midterm scores ($N = 75$)

Like students everywhere, the students in the Stat 101 class have one question foremost on their mind when they look at Table 15-1: How did I do? Each student can answer this question directly from the table. It's the next question that is statistically much more interesting. How did the class as a whole do?

The first step in organizing the data set in Table 15-1 is to create a **frequency table** such as Table 15-2. In this table, the number below each score gives the *frequency* of the score—that is, the number of students getting that particular score. We can readily see from Table 15-2 that there was one student with a score of 1, one with a score of 6, two with a score of 7, six with a score of 8, and so on. Notice that the scores with a frequency of zero are not listed in the table.

Score	1	6	7	8	9	10	11	12	13	14	15	16	24
Frequency	1	1	2	6	10	16	13	9	8	5	2	1	1

■ **TABLE 15-2**   Frequency table for the Stat 101 midterm scores

Table 15-2 shows that the $N = 75$ scores fall into $M = 13$ different **actual values** $(1, 6, 7, \ldots, 15, 16, 24)$. If we think of the actual values as "bins" where we can place the data, we get a graph such as the one shown in Fig. 15-1(a). A slightly simpler version of the same idea is shown in Fig. 15-1(b).

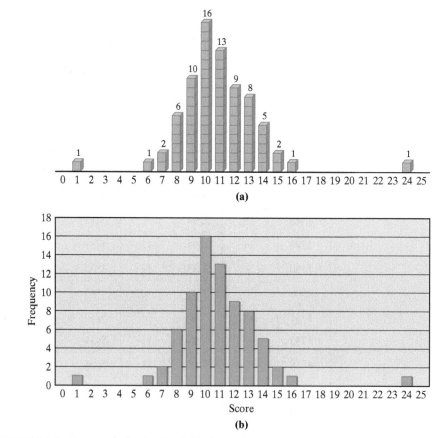

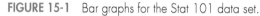

■ FIGURE 15-1   Bar graphs for the Stat 101 data set.

Figures 15-1(a) and (b) are both examples of a type of graph called a **bar graph**. Figure 15-1(a) is the fancier, 3D version; Fig. 15-1(b) is a more plain 2D version, but they both illustrate the data set equally well. When looking at either one, one of the first things we would notice are the two *outliers* (i.e., data points that do not fit-in with the rest of the data). In the Stat 101 data set there are two obvious outliers—the score of 24 (head and shoulders above the rest of the class) and the score of 1 (lagging way behind the pack).

Sometimes it is useful to draw a bar graph using *relative frequencies*—that is, making the heights of the bars represent percentages of the population. Figure 15-2 shows a *relative frequency bar graph* for the Stat 101 data set. Notice that we indicated on the graph that we are dealing with percentages rather than absolute frequencies and that the size of the data set is $N = 75$. This allows anyone who wishes to do so to compute the actual frequencies. For example, Fig. 15-2 indicates that 12% of the 75 students scored a 12 on the exam, so the actual frequency is given by $75 \times 0.12 = 9$ students. The change from actual frequencies to percentages (or vice versa) does not change the shape of the graph—it is basically a change of scale.

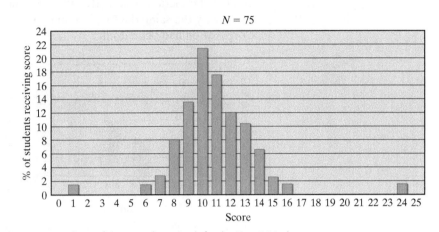

FIGURE 15-2 Relative frequency bar graph for the Stat 101 data set.

Relative frequency bar graphs are especially convenient when we have a very large data set (N is in the thousands or more) but a relatively small number of actual values. In these cases the frequencies for each bar tend to be very large and it is much easier to handle things using percentages.

While the term *bar graph* is most commonly used for graphs like the ones in Figs. 15-1 and 15-2, there is no rule that mandates that the columns have to take the form of bars. Sometimes the "bins" can be filled with symbolic images that can add a little extra flair or subtly influence the content of the information given by the graph. Dr. Blackbeard, for example, might have chosen to display the midterm data using a graph like the one shown in Fig. 15-3, which conveys the same information as the original bar graph and includes a subtle individual message to each student.

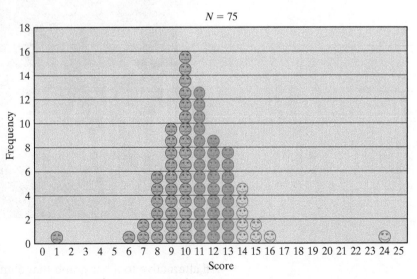

FIGURE 15-3 Pictogram for the Stat 101 data set.

Frequency charts that use icons or symbolic images instead of bars to display the frequencies are commonly referred to as **pictograms**. The point of a pictogram is that a graph is often used not only to inform but also to impress and persuade, and, in such cases, a well-chosen icon or image can be a more effective tool than just a bar.

EXAMPLE 15.2   SELLING THE XYZ CORPORATION

Figure 15-4(a) is a pictogram showing the growth in yearly sales of the XYZ Corporation between 2008 and 2013. It's a good picture to show at a shareholders meeting, but the picture is actually quite misleading. Figure 15-4(b) shows a pictogram for exactly the same data with a much more accurate picture of how well the XYZ Corporation had been doing.

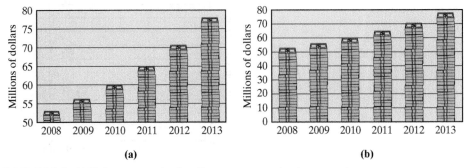

FIGURE 15-4   XYZ Corp. annual sales. Two pictograms for the same data set.

The difference between the two pictograms can be attributed to a couple of standard tricks of the trade: (1) stretching the scale of the vertical axis and (2) "cheating" on the choice of starting value on the vertical axis. As an educated consumer, you should always be on the lookout for these tricks. In graphical descriptions of data, a fine line separates objectivity from propaganda. (For more on this topic, see Project 1.)

For convenience let's call the number of bars in a bar graph M. In a typical bar graph M is a number in single or double digits, and rarely will you see a bar graph with $M > 100$. Even if you push the columns together and make them really skinny you can only fit so many in a reasonably sized window. Figure 15-5 shows a bar graph with $M = 80$, and that is already pushing the upper limit of what a reasonably sized bar graph can accommodate.

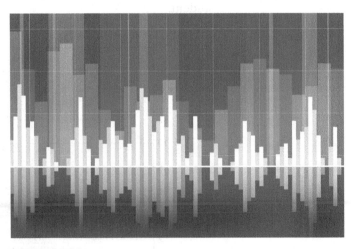

FIGURE 15-5

An alternative to a bar graph that eliminates the need for bars is a line graph. In a **line graph**, instead of bars we use points (small circles or small squares) with adjacent points connected by lines [Fig. 15-6(a)]. Line graphs are particularly useful when the number of values plotted is large [Fig. 15-6(b)], or when the graph represents a *time-series* (i.e., the horizontal axis represents a time variable) such as when tracking the price of a company's stock in a stock market [Fig. 15-6(c)].

(a)   (b)   (c)

FIGURE 15-6

EXAMPLE 15.3 GM, FORD, AND TOYOTA MONTHLY SALES (2008–2012)

Figure 15-7 shows three separate line graphs superimposed on a single time line. Each line graph represents a different automaker (GM, Ford, and Toyota), and the data shows monthly light-vehicle sales (i.e., trucks are not included) for the period January 2008 through May 2012. (*Source:* The *Wall Street Journal, http://graphics .wsj/documents/WSJ-US-Autosales/index.php*.)

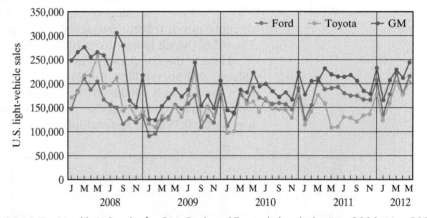

FIGURE 15-7   Monthly U.S. sales for GM, Ford, and Toyota light vehicles (Jan. 2008–May 2012).

This graph illustrates how a good graphical display can pack a lot of useful information. First, there are a lot of data being displayed—53 different data points for each manufacturer, 159 data points in all, and yet, the graph does not appear crowded. This would be much harder to accomplish using bar graphs. Secondly, there is a lot of useful information lurking behind the visible patterns in the data—we can see the big drop in sales for all three automakers at the end of 2008 (the aftermath of the Big Recession of 2008), we can see the sales spiking every December (Christmas bonuses, dealers trying to meet their annual quotas), we can see the 2012 sales climbing back to 2008 levels, and so on. When properly done, a statistical graph can be a great exploratory tool—all you have to do is look at it carefully and ask the right questions.

Categorical Variables and Pie Charts

A variable need not always represent a measurable quantity—variables can also describe non-numerical characteristics of a population such as gender, ethnicity, nationality, emotions, feelings, actions, etc. Variables of this type are called **categorical** (or **qualitative**) variables.

In some ways, categorical variables must be treated differently from numerical variables—you can't add, rescale, or average categories—but when it comes to graphical displays of data, categorical variables can be treated much like discrete numerical variables.

EXAMPLE 15.4 HOW DO COLLEGE STUDENTS SPEND THEIR DAY?

Activity	Hours
Sleep	8.4
Leisure/Sports	3.6
Work	3.0
Education	3.4
Eat/Drink	1.1
Grooming	0.8
Travel	1.5
Other	2.2
Total	**24**

■ **TABLE 15-3** Time use of a typical college student

Table 15-3 shows a breakdown of how a typical full-time university or college student spends a typical nonholiday weekday. Time use is broken into eight major categories, including the catch-all category "Other." (*Source:* Bureau of Labor Statistics, *American Time Use Survey*. Data include individuals, ages 15 to 49, who were enrolled full time at a university or college. Data include nonholiday weekdays and are averages for 2006–2010.)

Figure 15-8(a) is a bar graph for the data in Table 15-3. The only difference between this bar graph and the others we saw earlier is the absence of a horizontal axis. Since the data is categorical, there is no number line or time line for the placement of the columns. In fact, other than making sure that the bottoms of the columns are aligned, you can position the columns any way you want.

Figure 15-8(b) is a *pie chart* representing the data in Table 15-3. In a **pie chart**, the categories take the form of wedges of pie (or slices of pizza, if you prefer), with the size of each wedge (measured by the central angle of the wedge) proportional to the frequency of that category. To calculate the central angle for a category (in degrees) we first convert the frequency of that category into a relative frequency (i.e., a percentage) and then use the fact that $1\% = 3.6°$ (which follows from $100\% = 360°$).

Here is the computation of the central angle corresponding to the category "Sleep" (8.4 hours): First, $8.4/24 = 0.35 = 35\%$; then, $35 \times 3.6° = 126°$. [These two steps can be nicely combined into a single calculation: $(8.4/24) \times 360° = 126°$. This works because converting the 0.35 to 35% and multiplying by 3.6 is the same as leaving the 0.35 alone and multiplying by 360.]

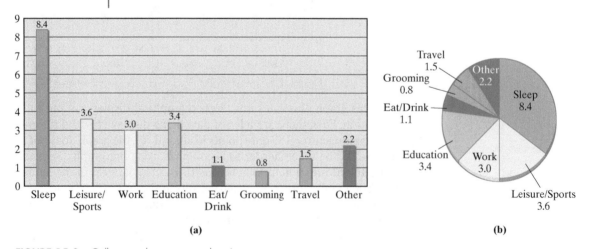

(a)   (b)

FIGURE 15-8 College and university students' time use.

In general, the computation of the central angle for a category doesn't always work out as nicely as it did for the Sleep category, and typically you end up with fractions of a degree. You can decide how accurate you want to be in your central angle measurements, but rounding the number to the nearest degree is typically more than good enough. Table 15-4 shows the calculations for the central angles of all eight categories in Table 15-3.

Activity	Hours	Central angle
Sleep	8.4	$(8.4/24) \times 360° = 126°$
Leisure/Sports	3.6	$(3.6/24) \times 360° = 54°$
Work	3.0	$(3.0/24) \times 360° = 45°$
Education	3.4	$(3.4/24) \times 360° = 51°$
Eat/Drink	1.1	$(1.1/24) \times 360° \approx 16°$
Grooming	0.8	$(0.8/24) \times 360° = 12°$
Travel	1.5	$(1.5/24) \times 360° \approx 23°$
Other	2.2	$(2.2/24) \times 360° = 33°$
Total	**24**	**360°**

■ TABLE 15-4   Central angle on pie chart for Table 15-3

Sometimes a variable starts out as a numerical variable, but then, as a matter of convenience, it is converted into a categorical variable. You are certainly familiar with one of the classic examples of this—your numerical scores (in an exam, or in a course) converted into categories (grades A, B, C, D, or F) according to some artificial scale [e.g., A = 90–100, B = 80–89, C = 70–79, D = 60–69, F = 0–59 or some variation thereof. (Have you ever wondered why it's not A = 80–100, B = 60–79, C = 40–59, D = 20–39, F = 0–19?)].

EXAMPLE 15.5 STAT 101 MIDTERM GRADES

We are going to take a second look at the midterm scores in Prof. Blackbeard's Stat 101 section (Example 15.1). The midterm score is a numerical variable that can take integer values between 0 and 25. Prof. Blackbeard's grading scale is A = 18–25, B = 14–17, C = 11–13, D = 9–10, and F = 0–8. (This is a somewhat unusual way to scale for grades, but Prof. Blackbeard is a pretty unusual guy and has his own ideas about how to do things.)

Table 15-5 is the categorical (grade) version of the original numerical (score) frequency table (Table 15-2, page 450). One A and 36 D's and F's. What's up with that?

Figure 15-9(a) is a bar graph for the data in Table 15-5. Figure 15-9(b) is the corresponding pie chart. In the pie chart, each student represents an angle of $\frac{360°}{75} = 4.8°$. Rounding the central angles to the nearest degree gives angles of 5° for A, 38° for B, 144° for C, 125° for D, and 48° for F. In both cases, the small size of the A category creates a bit of a scaling problem; but, other than that, both images do a good job of conveying the results.

Grade	A	B	C	D	F
Frequency	1	8	30	26	10

■ TABLE 15-5   Grade distribution for Stat 101 midterm

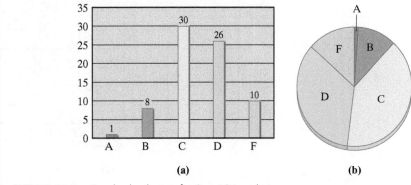

(a)   (b)

■ FIGURE 15-9   Grade distribution for Stat 101 midterm.

Converting numerical data into categorical data is particularly useful in situations involving large populations and large numbers of possible values for the measurements of the population. Our next example illustrates an important application of this idea.

EXAMPLE 15.6 SAT MATH SCORES (2011)

The college dreams and aspirations of millions of high school seniors often ride on their SAT scores. The SAT is divided into three subject areas (Math, Critical Reading, and Writing), with separate scores in each subject area that range from a minimum of 200 to a maximum of 800 points and going up in increments of 10 points. There is a total of 61 possible such scores (200, 210, 220, . . . , 790, 800) for each subject area—that's a lot of possibilities. In this example, we will look at the 2011 Math scores only (see Exercises 15 and 16 for the Critical Reading and Writing scores).

A total of $N = 1,647,123$ college-bound seniors took the SAT in 2011. A full breakdown of the number of students by individual score would require a frequency table with 61 entries, or a bar graph with 61 columns, or a pie chart with 61 wedges. For most purposes, that's a case of too much information! As an alternative, the results are broken into six score ranges called **class intervals**: 200–290, 300–390, . . . , 600–690, and 700–800. (Think of these class intervals as analogous to letter grades except that there are no letters.) The first five class intervals contain 10 possible scores; the last class interval contains 11 possible scores.

The second column of Table 15-6 shows the aggregate results of the 2011 SAT Mathematics section. (*Source*: 2011 College Bound Seniors: Total Group Report. Copyright © 2011. The College Board. *www.collegeboard.org*. Reproduced with permission.) With numbers as large as these, it is somewhat easier to work with percentages of the population in each class interval (column 3). Figure 15-10(a) is a relative frequency bar graph for the data in column 3 of Table 15-6; Fig. 15-10(b) shows the corresponding pie chart.

Score range	Number of test-takers	Percentage of test-takers
700–800	111,893	6.8%
600–690	304,037	18.5%
500–590	481,170	29.2%
400–490	498,944	30.3%
300–390	210,645	12.8%
200–290	40,434	2.4%
Total	$N = \mathbf{1,647,123}$	**100%**

■ **TABLE 15-6**   2011 SAT Mathematics test scores.

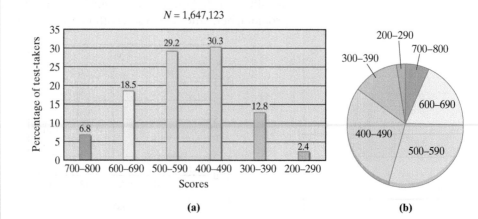

(a)   **(b)**

Continuous Variables and Histograms

When a numerical variable is continuous, its possible values can vary by infinitesimally small increments. As a consequence, there are no gaps between the class intervals, and our old way of doing things (using separate columns for each actual value or category) will no longer work. In this case we use a variation of a bar graph called a **histogram**. We illustrate the concept of a histogram in the next example.

EXAMPLE 15.7   STARTING SALARIES OF TSU GRADUATES

Suppose we want to use a graph to display the distribution of starting salaries of the 2012 graduating class at Tasmania State University ($N = 3258$).

The starting salaries range from a low of $40,350 to a high of $74,800. Based on this range and the amount of detail we want to show, we must decide on the length of the class intervals. A reasonable choice would be to use class intervals defined in increments of $5000. Table 15-7 is a frequency table for the salaries based on these class intervals. We chose a starting value of $40,000 for convenience. The third column in the table shows the data as a percentage of the population (rounded to the nearest percentage point).

The histogram showing the relative frequency of each class interval is shown in Fig. 15-11.

Salary	Frequency	Percentage
40,000⁺–45,000	228	7%
45,000⁺–50,000	456	14%
50,000⁺–55,000	1043	32%
55,000⁺–60,000	912	28%
60,000⁺–65,000	391	12%
65,000⁺–70,000	163	5%
70,000⁺–75,000	65	2%
Total	**3258**	**100%**

■ **TABLE 15-7**   Starting salaries of 2012 TSU graduates

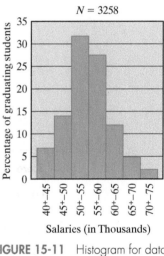

FIGURE 15-11   Histogram for data in Table 15-7.

As we can see, a histogram is very similar to a bar graph. Several important distinctions must be made, however. To begin with, because a histogram is used for continuous variables, there can be no gaps between the class intervals, and it follows, therefore, that the columns of a histogram must touch each other. In addition, we must decide how to handle a value that falls exactly on the boundary between two class intervals. Should it always belong to the class interval to the left or to the one to the right? This is called the *endpoint convention*. The "plus" superscripts in Table 15-7 and Fig. 15-11 indicate how we chose to deal with the endpoint convention in Example 15.7. A starting salary of exactly $50,000, for example, would be listed under the 45,000⁺–50,000 class interval rather than the 50,000⁺–55,000 class interval.

When creating histograms, we should try, as much as possible, to define class intervals of equal size. When the class intervals are significantly different in size, the rules for creating a histogram are considerably more complicated, since it is no longer appropriate to use the heights of the columns to indicate the frequencies of the class intervals. (For more details on histograms with class intervals of unequal lengths, see Exercises 73 and 74.)

15.2 Means, Medians, and Percentiles

As useful as bar graphs, pie charts, and histograms can be in describing data, in some circumstances (for example, in everyday conversation) a graph is not readily available and we have to resort to other means of description. One of the most convenient and commonly used devices is to use numerical summaries of the data. In this section we will discuss a few of the more frequently used numerical summaries for a data set.

The Average

The most commonly used number for summarizing a data set is the *average*, also called the *mean*. (There is no universal agreement as to which of these names is a better choice—in some settings *mean* is a better choice than *average*, in other settings it's the other way around. In this chapter we will use whichever seems the better choice at the moment.)

- **Average (mean).** The average A of a set of N numbers is found by adding the numbers and dividing the total by N. In other words, the average of the data set $d_1, d_2, d_3, \ldots, d_N$, is $A = (d_1 + d_2 + \cdots + d_N)/N$.

EXAMPLE 15.8   AVERAGE SCORE IN THE STAT 101 MIDTERM

In this example we will find the average test score in the Stat 101 exam first introduced in Example 15.1. To find this average we need to add all the test scores and divide by 75. The addition of the 75 test scores can be simplified considerably if we use a frequency table. (Table 15-8 is the same as Table 15-2, shown again for the reader's convenience.)

Score	1	6	7	8	9	10	11	12	13	14	15	16	24
Frequency	1	1	2	6	10	16	13	9	8	5	2	1	1

■ **TABLE 15-8**   Frequency table for the Stat 101 data set

From the frequency table we can find the sum S of all the test scores as follows: Multiply each test score by its corresponding frequency, and then add these products. Thus, the sum of all the test scores is

$$S = (1 \times 1) + (6 \times 1) + (7 \times 2) + (8 \times 6) + \cdots + (16 \times 1) + (24 \times 1) = 814$$

If we divide this sum by $N = 75$, we get the average test score A (rounded to two decimal places): $A = 814/75 \approx 10.85$ points.

In general, to find the average A of a data set given by a frequency table such as Table 15-9 we do the following:

- Step 1. $S = d_1 f_1 + d_2 f_2 + \cdots + d_k f_k$.
- Step 2. $N = f_1 + f_2 + \cdots + f_k$.
- Step 3. $A = S/N$.

Value	Frequency
d_1	f_1
d_2	f_2
$\vdots$	$\vdots$
d_k	f_k

■ **TABLE 15-9**

When dealing with data sets that have outliers, averages can be quite misleading. As our next example illustrates, even a single outlier can have a big effect on the average.

EXAMPLE 15.9 STARTING SALARIES OF PHILOSOPHY MAJORS

Imagine that you just read in the paper the following remarkable tidbit: *The average starting salary of 2011 Tasmania State University graduates with a philosophy major was $76,400 a year!* This is quite an impressive number, but before we all rush out to change majors, let's point out that one of those philosophy majors happened to be basketball star "Hoops" Tallman, who is now doing his thing in the NBA for a starting salary of $3.5 million a year.

If we were to take this one outlier out of the population of 75 philosophy majors, we would have a more realistic picture of what philosophy majors are making. Here is how we can do it:

- The total of all 75 salaries is 75 times the average salary:
  $75 \times \$76,400 = \$5,730,000$
- The total of the other 74 salaries (excluding Hoops's cool 3.5 mill):
  $\$5,730,000 - \$3,500,000 = \$2,230,000$
- The average of the remaining 74 salaries: $\$2,230,000/74 \approx \$30,135$

Percentiles

While a single numerical summary—such as the average—can be useful, it is rarely sufficient to give a meaningful description of a data set. A better picture of the data set can be presented by using a well-organized cadre of numerical summaries. The most common way to do this is by means of *percentiles*.

- **Percentiles.** The *pth percentile* of a data set is a number X_p such that $p\%$ of the data is smaller or equal to X_p and $(100 - p)\%$ of the data is bigger or equal to X_p.

Many college students are familiar with percentiles, if for no other reason than the way they pop up in SAT reports. In all SAT reports, a given score—say a score of 620 in the Mathematics section—is identified with a percentile—say the 81st percentile. This can be interpreted to mean that 81% of those taking the test scored 620 *or less*, or, looking up instead of down, that 19% of those taking the test scored 620 *or more*.

There are several different ways to compute percentiles that will satisfy the definition, and different statistics books describe different methods. We will illustrate one such method below.

The first step in finding the *p*th *percentile* of a data set of N numbers is to *sort the numbers from smallest to largest*. Let's denote the sorted data values by $d_1, d_2, d_3, \ldots, d_N$, where d_1 represents the smallest number in the data set, d_2 the second smallest number, and so on. Sometimes we will also need to talk about the average of two consecutive numbers in the sorted list, so we will use more unusual subscripts such as $d_{3.5}$ to represent the average of the data values d_3 and d_4, $d_{7.5}$ to represent the average of the data values d_7 and d_8, and so on.

The next, and most important, step is to identify which d represents the *p*th percentile of the data set. To do this, we compute the *p*th *percent of* N, which we will call the **locator** and denote it by the letter L. [In other words, $L = \left(\frac{p}{100}\right)N$.] If L happens to be a whole number, then the *p*th *percentile* will be $d_{L.5}$ (the average of d_L and d_{L+1}). If L is not a whole number, then the *p*th *percentile* will be d_{L^+}, where L^+ represents the value of L *rounded up*.

The procedure for finding the *p*th *percentile* of a data set is summarized as follows:

FINDING THE *p*TH PERCENTILE OF A DATA SET

- **Step 0.** Sort the data set from smallest to largest. Let $d_1, d_2, d_3, \ldots, d_N$ represent the sorted data.
- **Step 1.** Find the locator $L = \left(\frac{p}{100}\right)N$.
- **Step 2.** Depending on whether L is a whole number or not, the *p*th *percentile* is given by
  - $d_{L.5}$ if L is a whole number.
  - d_{L^+} if L is not a whole number (L^+ is L rounded up).

The following example illustrates the procedure for finding percentiles of a data set.

EXAMPLE 15.10   SCHOLARSHIPS BY PERCENTILE

To reward good academic performance from its athletes, Tasmania State University has a program in which athletes with GPAs in the 80th or higher percentile of their team's GPAs get a $5000 scholarship and athletes with GPAs in the 55th or higher percentile of their team's GPAs who did not get the $5000 scholarship get a $2000 scholarship.

The women's volleyball team has $N = 15$ players on the roster. A list of their GPAs is as follows:

3.42, 3.91, 3.33, 3.65, 3.57, 3.45, 4.0, 3.71, 3.35, 3.82, 3.67, 3.88, 3.76, 3.41, 3.62

The sorted list of GPAs (from smallest to largest) is:

3.33, 3.35, 3.41, 3.42, 3.45, 3.57, 3.62, 3.65, 3.67, 3.71, 3.76, 3.82, 3.88, 3.91, 4.0

- **$5000 scholarships:** The locator for the 80th percentile is $(0.8) \times 15 = 12$. Here the locator is a whole number, so the 80th percentile is given by $d_{12.5} = 3.85$ (the average between $d_{12} = 3.82$ and $d_{13} = 3.88$). Thus, three students (the ones with GPAs of 3.88, 3.91, and 4.0) get $5000 scholarships.
- **$2000 scholarships:** The locator for the 55th percentile is $(0.55) \times 15 = 8.25$. This locator is not a whole number, so we round it up to 9, and the 55th percentile is given by $d_9 = 3.67$. Thus, the students with GPAs of 3.67, 3.71, 3.76, and 3.82 (all students with GPAs of 3.67 or higher except the ones that already received $5000 scholarships) get $2000 scholarships.

The Median and the Quartiles

The 50th percentile of a data set is known as the **median** and denoted by M. The median splits a data set into two halves—half of the data is smaller or equal to the median and half of the data is bigger or equal to the median.

We can find the median by simply applying the definition of percentile with $p = 50$, but the bottom line comes down to this: (1) when N is *odd*, the median is the data point in position $(N + 1)/2$ of the sorted data set; (2) when N is *even*, the median is the average of the data points in positions $N/2$ and $N/2 + 1$ of the sorted data set. [All of the preceding follows from the fact that the locator for the median is $L = \frac{N}{2}$. When N is even, L is an integer; when N is odd, L is not an integer.]

┌───┐
■ FINDING THE MEDIAN OF A DATA SET

- Sort the data set from smallest to largest. Let $d_1, d_2, d_3, \ldots, d_N$ represent the sorted data.
- If N is odd, the median is $d_{(N+1)/2}$.
- If N is even, the median is the average of $d_{N/2}$ and $d_{(N/2)+1}$.
└───┘

After the median, the next most commonly used set of percentiles are the **quartiles**. The *first quartile* (denoted by Q_1) is the 25th percentile, and the *third quartile* (denoted by Q_3) is the 75th percentile of the data set.

EXAMPLE 15.11 HOME PRICES IN GREEN HILLS

During the last year, 11 homes sold in the Green Hills subdivision. The selling prices, in chronological order, were \$267,000, \$252,000, \$228,000, \$234,000, \$292,000, \$263,000, \$221,000, \$245,000, \$270,000, \$238,000, and \$255,000. We are going to find the *median* and the *quartiles* of the $N = 11$ home prices.

Sorting the home prices from smallest to largest (and dropping the 000's) gives the sorted list

$$221, 228, 234, 238, 245, 252, 255, 263, 267, 270, 292$$

The locator for the median is $(0.5) \times 11 = 5.5$, the locator for the first quartile is $(0.25) \times 11 = 2.75$, and the locator for the third quartile is $(0.75) \times 11 = 8.25$. Since these locators are not whole numbers, they must be rounded up: 5.5 to 6, 2.75 to 3, and 8.25 to 9. Thus, the median home price is given by $d_6 = 252$ (i.e., $M = \$252,000$), the first quartile is given by $d_3 = 234$ (i.e., $Q_1 = \$234,000$), and the third quartile is given by $d_9 = 267$ (i.e., $Q_3 = \$267,000$).

Oops! Just this morning a home sold in Green Hills for \$264,000. We need to recalculate the median and quartiles for what are now $N = 12$ home prices.

We can use the sorted data set that we already had—all we have to do is insert the new home price (264) in the right spot (remember, we drop the 000's!). This gives

$$221, 228, 234, 238, 245, 252, 255, 263, \mathbf{264}, 267, 270, 292$$

Now $N = 12$ and in this case the median is the average of $d_6 = 252$ and $d_7 = 255$. It follows that the median home price is $M = \$253,500$. The locator for the first quartile is $0.25 \times 12 = 3$. Since the locator is a whole number, the first quartile is the average of $d_3 = 234$ and $d_4 = 238$ (i.e., $Q_1 = \$236,000$). Similarly, the third quartile is $Q_3 = 265,500$ (the average of $d_9 = 264$ and $d_{10} = 267$).

EXAMPLE 15.12 MEDIAN AND QUARTILES FOR THE STAT 101 MIDTERM

We will now find the median and quartile scores for the Stat 101 data set (shown again in Table 15-10).

Score	1	6	7	8	9	10	11	12	13	14	15	16	24
Frequency	1	1	2	6	10	16	13	9	8	5	2	1	1

■ TABLE 15-10 Frequency table for the Stat 101 data set

Having the frequency table available eliminates the need for sorting the scores—the frequency table has, in fact, done this for us. Here $N = 75$ (odd), so the median is the thirty-eighth score (counting from the left) in the frequency table. To find the thirty-eighth number in Table 15-10, we tally frequencies as we move from left to right: $1 + 1 = 2$; $1 + 1 + 2 = 4$; $1 + 1 + 2 + 6 = 10$; $1 + 1 + 2 + 6 + 10 = 20$; $1 + 1 + 2 + 6 + 10 + 16 = 36$. At this point, we know that the 36th test score on the list is a 10 (the last of the 10's) and the next 13 scores are all 11's. We can conclude that the 38th test score is 11. Thus, $M = 11$.

The locator for the first quartile is $L = (0.25) \times 75 = 18.75$. Thus, $Q_1 = d_{19}$. To find the nineteenth score in the frequency table, we tally frequencies from left to right: $1 + 1 = 2$; $1 + 1 + 2 = 4$; $1 + 1 + 2 + 6 = 10$; $1 + 1 + 2 + 6 + 10 = 20$. At this point we realize that $d_{10} = 8$ (the last of the 8's) and that d_{11} through d_{20} all equal 9. Hence, the first quartile of the Stat 101 midterm scores is $Q_1 = d_{19} = 9$.

Since the first and third quartiles are at an equal "distance" from the two ends of the sorted data set, a quick way to locate the third quartile now is to look for the nineteenth score in the frequency table when we count frequencies *from right to left*. We leave it to the reader to verify that the third quartile of the Stat 101 data set is $Q_3 = 12$.

> **EXAMPLE 15.13**   MEDIAN AND QUARTILES FOR 2011 SAT MATH SCORES

In this example we continue the discussion of the 2011 SAT Math scores introduced in Example 15.6. Recall that the number of college-bound students taking the test was $N = 1{,}647{,}123$. As reported by the College Board, the median score in the test was $M = 510$, the first quartile score was $Q_1 = 430$, and the third quartile was $Q_3 = 600$. What can we make of this information?

Let's start with the median. From $N = 1{,}647{,}123$ (an odd number), we can conclude that the median (510 points) is the 823,562nd score in the sorted list of test scores. This means that there were *at least* 823,562 students who scored 510 or less in the math section of the 2011 SAT. Why did we use "at least" in the preceding sentence? Could there have been more than that number who scored 510 or less? Yes, almost surely. Since the number of students who scored 510 is in the thousands, it is very unlikely that the 823,562nd score will be the last of the group of 510s.

In a similar vein, we can conclude that there were at least 411,781 scores of $Q_1 = 430$ or less [the locator for the first quartile is $(0.25) \times 1{,}647{,}123 = 411{,}780.75$] and at least 1,235,343 scores of $Q_3 = 600$ or less.

A note of warning: Medians, quartiles, and general percentiles are often computed using statistical calculators or statistical software packages, which is all well and fine since the whole process can be a bit tedious. The problem is that there is no universally agreed upon procedure for computing percentiles, so different types of calculators and different statistical packages may give different answers from each other and from those given in this book for quartiles and other percentiles (everyone agrees on the median). *Keep this in mind when doing the exercises*—the answer given by your calculator may be slightly different from the one you would get from the procedure we use in the book.

The Five-Number Summary

A common way to summarize a large data set is by means of its *five-number summary*. The **five-number summary** is given by (1) the smallest value in the data set (called the *Min*), (2) the *first quartile* Q_1, (3) the *median M*, (4) the *third quartile* Q_3, and (5) the largest value in the data set (called the *Max*). These five numbers together often tell us a great deal about the data.

> **EXAMPLE 15.14**   FIVE-NUMBER SUMMARY FOR THE STAT 101 MIDTERM

For the Stat 101 data set, the five-number summary is $Min = 1$, $Q_1 = 9$, $M = 11$, $Q_3 = 12$, $Max = 24$ (see Example 15.12). What useful information can we get out of this?

Right away we can see that the $N = 75$ test scores were not evenly spread out over the range of possible scores. For example, from $M = 11$ and $Q_3 = 12$ we can conclude that 25% or more of the class (that means at least 19 students) scored either 11 or 12 on the test. At the same time, from $Q_3 = 12$ and $Max = 24$ we can conclude that at most 18 students had scores in the 13–24 point range. Using similar arguments, we can conclude that at least 19 students had scores between $Q_1 = 9$ and $M = 11$ points and at most 18 students scored in the 1–8 point range.

The "big picture" we get from the five-number summary of the Stat 101 test scores is that there was a lot of bunching up in a narrow band of scores (at least half of the students in the class scored in the range 9–12 points), and the rest of the class was all over the place. In general, this type of "lumpy" distribution of test scores is indicative of a test with an uneven level of difficulty—a bunch of easy questions and a bunch of really hard questions with little in between. (Having seen the data, we know that the *Min* and *Max* scores were both outliers and that if we disregard these two outliers, the test results don't look quite so bad. Of course, there is no way to pick this up from just the five-number summary.)

Box Plots

Invented in 1977 by statistician John Tukey, a *box plot* (also known as a *box-and-whisker* plot) is a picture of the five-number summary of a data set. The **box plot** consists of a rectangular box that sits above a number line representing the data values and extends from the first quartile Q_1 to the third quartile Q_3 on that number line. A vertical line crosses the box, indicating the position of the median M. On both sides of the box are "whiskers" extending to the smallest value, *Min*, and largest value, *Max*, of the data. Figure 15-12 shows a generic box plot for a data set.

Figure 15-13(a) shows a box plot for the Stat 101 data set (see Example 15.12). The long whiskers in this box plot are largely due to the outliers 1 and 24. Figure 15-13(b) shows a variation of the same box plot, but with the two outliers, marked with two crosses, segregated from the rest of the data. (When there are outliers, it is useful to segregate them from the rest of the data set—we think of outliers as "anomalies" within the data set.)

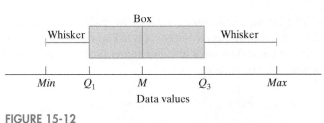

FIGURE 15-12

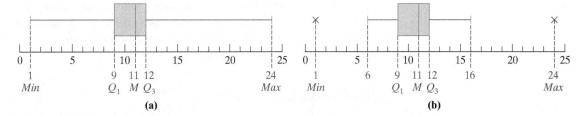

FIGURE 15-13 (a) Box plot for the Stat 101 data set. (b) Same box plot with the outliers separated from the rest of the data.

Box plots are particularly useful when comparing similar data for two or more populations. This is illustrated in the next example.

| **EXAMPLE 15.15** | COMPARING AGRICULTURE AND ENGINEERING SALARIES |

Figure 15-14 shows box plots for the starting salaries of two different populations: first-year agriculture and engineering graduates of Tasmania State University.

Superimposing the two box plots on the same scale allows us to make some useful comparisons. It is clear, for instance, that engineering graduates are doing better overall than agriculture graduates, even though at the very top levels agriculture graduates are better paid. Another interesting point is that the median salary of agriculture graduates ($43,000) is less than the first quartile of the salaries of engineering graduates ($45,000). The very short whisker on the left side of the agriculture box plot tells us that

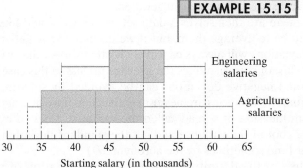

FIGURE 15-14 Comparison of starting salaries of first-year graduates in agriculture and engineering.

the bottom 25% of agriculture salaries are concentrated in a very narrow salary range ($33,000–$35,000). We can also see that agriculture salaries are much more spread out than engineering salaries, even though most of the spread occurs at the higher end of the salary scale.

15.3 Ranges and Standard Deviations

There are several different ways to describe the spread of a data set; in this section we will describe the three most commonly used ones.

- **The range.** The range R of a data set is given by the difference between the highest and lowest values of the data ($R = Max - Min$).

The range is most useful when there are no outliers in the data. In the presence of outliers the range tells a distorted story. For example, the range of the test scores in the Stat 101 exam (Example 15.1) is $24 - 1 = 23$ points, an indication of a big spread within the scores (i.e., a very heterogeneous group of students). True enough, but if we discount the two outliers, the remaining 73 test scores would have a much smaller range of $16 - 6 = 10$ points.

To eliminate the possible distortion caused by outliers, a common practice when measuring the spread of a data set is to use the *interquartile range*, denoted by the acronym *IQR*.

- **The interquartile range.** The interquartile range *IQR* is the difference between the third quartile and the first quartile ($IQR = Q_3 - Q_1$). The *IQR* tells us how spread out the middle 50% of the data values are. For many types of real-world data, the *IQR* is a useful measure of spread.

EXAMPLE 15.16   RANGE AND IQR FOR 2011 SAT MATH SCORES

The five-number summary for the 2011 SAT Math scores (see Example 15.13) was $Min = 200$ (yes, there were a few jokers who missed every question!), $Q_1 = 430$, $M = 510$, $Q_3 = 600$, $Max = 800$ (there are still a few geniuses around!). It follows that the 2011 SAT Math scores had a range of 600 points ($800 - 200 = 600$) and an *IQR* of 170 points ($IQR = 600 - 430 = 170$).

The Standard Deviation

The most important and most commonly used measure of spread for a data set is the *standard deviation*. The key concept for understanding the standard deviation is the concept of *deviation from the mean*. If A is the average of the data set and x is an arbitrary data value, the difference $x - A$ is x's *deviation from the mean*. The deviations from the mean tell us how "far" the data values are from the average value of the data. The idea is to use this information to figure out how spread out the data is. There are, unfortunately, several steps before we can get there.

The deviations from the mean are themselves a data set, which we would like to summarize. One way would be to average them, but if we do that, the negative deviations and the positive deviations will always cancel each other out so that we end up with an average of 0. This, of course, makes the average useless in this case. The cancellation of positive and negative deviations can be avoided by squaring each of the deviations. The squared deviations are never negative, and if we average them out, we get an important measure of spread called the **variance**, denoted by V. Finally, we take the square root of the variance and get the **standard deviation**, denoted by the Greek letter σ (and sometimes by the acronym SD).

The following is an outline of the definition of the standard deviation of a data set.

┌──┐
THE STANDARD DEVIATION OF A DATA SET

- Let A denote the mean of the data set. For each number x in the data set, compute its *deviation from the mean* $(x - A)$ and *square* each of these numbers. These numbers are called the *squared deviations*.
- Find the average of the squared deviations. This number is called the *variance V*.
- The *standard deviation* is the square root of the variance $\left(\sigma = \sqrt{V}\right)$.
└──┘

Standard deviations of large data sets are not fun to calculate by hand, and they are rarely found that way. The standard procedure for calculating standard deviations is to use a computer or a good scientific or business calculator, often preprogrammed to do all the steps automatically. Be that as it may, it is still important to understand what's behind the computation of a standard deviation, even when the actual grunt work is going to be performed by a machine.

EXAMPLE 15.17 CALCULATION OF A SD

Over the course of the semester, Angela turned in all of her homework assignments. Her grades in the 10 assignments (sorted from lowest to highest) were 85, 86, 87, 88, 89, 91, 92, 93, 94, and 95. Our goal in this example is to calculate the standard deviation of this data set the old-fashioned way (i.e., doing our own grunt work).

The first step is to find the mean A of the data set. It's not hard to see that $A = 90$. We are lucky—this is a nice round number! The second step is to calculate the *deviations from the mean* and then the *squared deviations*. The details are shown in the second and third columns of Table 15-11. When we average the squared deviations, we get $(25 + 16 + 9 + 4 + 1 + 1 + 4 + 9 + 16 + 25)/10 = 11$. This means that the variance is $V = 11$ and, thus, the standard deviation (rounded to one decimal place) is $\sigma = \sqrt{11} \approx 3.3$ points.

x	$(x - 90)$	$(x - 90)^2$
85	−5	25
86	−4	16
87	−3	9
88	−2	4
89	−1	1
91	1	1
92	2	4
93	3	9
94	4	16
95	5	25

■ TABLE 15-11

Standard deviations are measured in the same units as the original data, so in Example 15.17 the standard deviation of Angela's homework scores was roughly 3.3 points. What should we make of this fact? It is clear from just a casual look at Angela's homework scores that she was pretty consistent in her homework, never straying too much above or below her average score of 90 points. The standard deviation is, in effect, a way to measure this degree of consistency (or lack thereof). A small standard deviation tells us that the data are consistent and the spread of the data is small, as is the case with Angela's homework scores.

The ultimate in consistency within a data set is when all the data values are the same (like Angela's friend Chloe, who got a 20 in every homework assignment). When this happens the standard deviation is 0. On the other hand, when there is a lot of inconsistency within the data set, we are going to get a large standard deviation. This is illustrated by Angela's other friend, Tiki, whose homework scores were 5, 15, 25, 35, 45, 55, 65, 75, 85, and 95. We would expect the standard deviation of this data set to be quite large—in fact, it is almost 29 points.

The standard deviation is arguably the most important and frequently used measure of data spread. Yet it is not a particularly intuitive concept. Here are a few basic guidelines that recap our preceding discussion:

- The standard deviation of a data set is measured in the same units as the original data. For example, if the data are points on a test, then the standard deviation is also given in points. Conversely, if the standard deviation is given in dollars, then we can conclude that the original data must have been money—home prices, salaries, or something like that. For sure, the data couldn't have been test scores on an exam.

- It is pointless to compare standard deviations of data sets that are given in different units. Even for data sets that are given in the same units—say, for example, test scores—the underlying scale should be the same. We should not try to compare standard deviations for SAT scores measured on a scale of 200–800 points with standard deviations of a set of homework assignments measured on a scale of 0–100 points.

- For data sets that are based on the same underlying scale, a comparison of standard deviations can tell us something about the spread of the data. If the standard deviation is small, we can conclude that the data points are all bunched together—there is very little spread. As the standard deviation increases, we can conclude that the data points are beginning to spread out. The more spread out they are, the larger the standard deviation becomes. A standard deviation of 0 means that all data values are the same.

As a measure of spread, the standard deviation is particularly useful for analyzing real-life data. We will come to appreciate its importance in this context in Chapter 17.

Conclusion

Graphical summaries of data can be produced by bar graphs, pictograms, pie charts, histograms, and so on. (There are many other types of graphical descriptions that we did not discuss in the chapter.) The kind of graph that is the most appropriate for a situation depends on many factors, and creating a good "picture" of a data set is as much an art as a science.

> " Statistical reasoning will one day be as necessary for efficient citizenship as the ability to read and write. "
>
> – H. G. Wells

Numerical summaries of data, when properly used, help us understand the overall pattern of a data set without getting bogged down in the details. They fall into two categories: (1) measures of location, such as the *average*, the *median*, and the *quartiles*, and (2) measures of spread, such as the *range*, the *interquartile range*, and the *standard deviation*. Sometimes we even combine numerical summaries and graphical displays, as in the case of the *box plot*. We touched upon all of these in this chapter, but the subject is a big one, and by necessity we only scratched the surface.

In this day and age, we are all consumers of data, and at one time or another, we are likely to be providers of data as well. Thus, understanding the basics of how data are organized and summarized has become an essential requirement for personal success and good citizenship.

KEY CONCEPTS

15.1 Graphs and Charts

- **data set:** a collection of numbers that represent all the values obtained when measuring some characteristic of a population, **448**

- **data point:** an individual number in a data set, **448**

- **discrete variable:** a variable that can only take on a discrete set of values—there is a minimum gap between two possible values of the variable, **448**

- **continuous variable:** a variable that can take on infinitely many values and those values can differ by arbitrarily small amounts, **448**

- **actual value:** each of the distinct values taken on by the variable in a data set, **450**

- **bar graph:** a graph with bars (columns) representing each of the actual values in the data set. The height of each column represents the frequency of that value in the data set, **450**

- **frequency table:** a table showing the frequency of each actual value in a data set, **450**

- **pictogram:** a variation of a bar graph that uses icons or symbolic images to represent the frequencies of the actual values in a data set, **452**

- **line graph:** a graph where the values of the data are given by points with adjacent points connected by a line, **452**

- **categorical (qualitative) variable:** a variable that takes on non-numerical values, **453**

- **pie chart:** a chart consisting of a circle broken up into wedges. Each wedge represents a category, with the size of the wedge proportional to the relative frequency of the corresponding category, **454**

- **class interval:** a category consisting of a range of numerical values, **456**

- **histogram:** a variation of a bar graph used to describe frequencies of class intervals in the case of a continuous variable, **457**

15.2 Means, Medians, and Percentiles

- **average (mean):** given a data set consisting of the numbers $d_1, d_2, \ldots, d_N$, their average is the number $A = (d_1 + d_2 + \cdots + d_N)/N$, **458**

- **percentile:** given a data set, the pth percentile of the data set is a number X_p such that $p\%$ of the numbers in the data set are smaller or equal to X_p and $(100 - p)\%$ of the numbers in the data set are bigger or equal to X_p, **459**

- **locator:** the locator for the pth percentile of a data set consisting of N numbers is the number $L = \left(\frac{p}{100}\right)N$, **459**

- **median:** the median M of a data set is the 50th percentile of the data set—half the numbers in the data set are smaller or equal to M, half are bigger or equal to M, **460**

- **quartiles:** the first quartile Q_1 is the 25th percentile of a data set; the third quartile Q_3 is the 75th percentile, **461**

- **five-number summary:** a summary of the data set consisting of the *Min* (smallest value in the data set), the first quartile Q_1, the median *M*, the third quartile Q_3, and the *Max* (largest value in the data set), **462**

- **box plot (box and whisker plot):** **463**

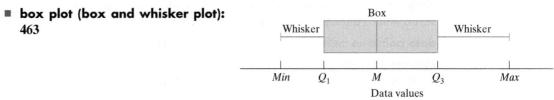

15.3 Ranges and Standard Deviations

- **range:** the range *R* of a data set is the difference between the largest and the smallest values in the data set $(R = Max - Min)$, **464**

- **interquartile range:** the interquartile range *IQR* of a data set is the difference between the third and first quartiles of the data set $(IQR = Q_3 - Q_1)$, **464**

- **variance:** the variance *V* of a data set is the average of the squared differences between the data points and the average of the data set [i.e., for each data point *d*, compute $(d - A)^2$; *V* is the average of these numbers], **465**

- **standard deviation:** the standard deviation σ of a data set is the square root of the variance of the data set, $(\sigma = \sqrt{V})$, **465**

EXERCISES

WALKING

 Graphs and Charts

Exercises 1 through 4 refer to the data set shown in Table 15-12. The table shows the scores on a Chem 103 test consisting of 10 questions worth 10 points each.

Student ID	Score	Student ID	Score
1362	50	4315	70
1486	70	4719	70
1721	80	4951	60
1932	60	5321	60
2489	70	5872	100
2766	10	6433	50
2877	80	6921	50
2964	60	8317	70
3217	70	8854	100
3588	80	8964	80
3780	80	9158	60
3921	60	9347	60
4107	40		

■ **TABLE 15-12**   Chem 103 test scores

1. **(a)** Make a frequency table for the Chem 103 test scores.

   (b) Draw a bar graph for the data in Table 15-12.

2. Draw a line graph for the data in Table 15-12.

3. Suppose that the grading scale for the test is A: 80–100; B: 70–79; C: 60–69; D: 50–59; and F: 0–49.

   (a) Make a frequency table for the distribution of the test grades.

   (b) Draw a relative frequency bar graph for the test grades.

4. Suppose that the grading scale for the test is A: 80–100; B: 70–79; C: 60–69; D: 50–59; and F: 0–49.

   (a) What percentage of the students who took the test got a grade of D?

   (b) In a pie chart showing the distribution of the test grades, what is the size of the central angle (in degrees) of the "wedge" representing the grade of D?

   (c) Draw a pie chart showing the distribution of the test grades. Give the central angles for each wedge in the pie chart (round your answer to the nearest degree).

Exercises 5 through 10 refer to Table 15-13, which gives the home-to-school distance d (measured to the closest one-half mile) for each kindergarten student at Cleansburg Elementary School.

Student ID	d	Student ID	d
1362	1.5	3921	5.0
1486	2.0	4355	1.0
1587	1.0	4454	1.5
1877	0.0	4561	1.5
1932	1.5	5482	2.5
1946	0.0	5533	1.5
2103	2.5	5717	8.5
2877	1.0	6307	1.5
2964	0.5	6573	0.5
3491	0.0	8436	3.0
3588	0.5	8592	0.0
3711	1.5	8964	2.0
3780	2.0	9205	0.5
		9658	6.0

■ **TABLE 15-13**   Home-to-school distance

5. **(a)** Make a frequency table for the distances in Table 15-13.

   (b) Draw a line graph for the data in Table 15-13.

6. Draw a bar graph for the data in Table 15-13.

7. Draw a bar graph for the home-to-school distances for the kindergarteners at Cleansburg Elementary School using the following class intervals:

Very close: Less than 1 mile

Close: 1 mile up to and including 1.5 miles

Nearby: 2 miles up to and including 2.5 miles

Not too far: 3 miles up to and including 4.5 miles

Far: 5 miles or more

8. Draw a bar graph for the home-to-school distances for the kindergarteners at Cleansburg Elementary School using the following class intervals:

Zone A: 1.5 miles or less

Zone B: more than 1.5 miles up to and including 2.5 miles

Zone C: more than 2.5 miles up to and including 3.5 miles

Zone D: more than 3.5 miles

9. Using the class intervals given in Exercise 7, draw a pie chart for the home-to-school distances for the kindergarteners at Cleansburg Elementary School. Give the central angles for each wedge of the pie chart. Round your answer to the nearest degree.

10. Using the class intervals given in Exercise 8, draw a pie chart for the home-to-school distances for the kindergarteners at Cleansburg Elementary School. Give the central angles for each wedge of the pie chart. Round your answer to the nearest degree.

Exercises 11 and 12 refer to the bar graph shown in Fig. 15-15 describing the scores of a group of students on a 10-point math quiz.

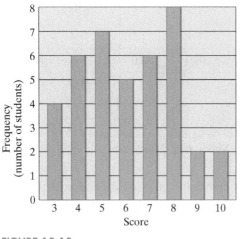

FIGURE 15-15

11. (a) How many students took the math quiz?

(b) What percentage of the students scored 2 points?

(c) If a grade of 6 or more was needed to pass the quiz, what percentage of the students passed? (Round your answer to the nearest percent.)

12. Draw a relative frequency bar graph showing the results of the quiz.

Exercises 13 and 14 refer to the pie chart in Fig. 15-16.

Cause of Death in U.S. Among 18- to 22-Year-Olds (2005)
N = 19,548

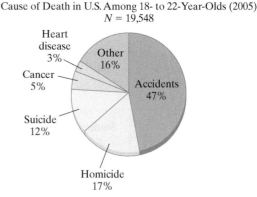

Source: Centers for Disease Control and Prevention, *www.cdc.gov.*

FIGURE 15-16

13. (a) Is cause of death a quantitative or a qualitative variable?

(b) Use the data provided in the pie chart to estimate the number of 18- to 22-year-olds who died in the United States in 2005 due to an accident.

14. Use the data provided in the pie chart to estimate the number of 18- to 22-year-olds who died in the United States in 2005 for each category shown in the pie chart.

15. Table 15-14 shows the class interval frequencies for the 2011 Critical Reading scores on the SAT. Draw a relative frequency bar graph for the data in Table 15-14.

Score range	Number of test-takers
700–800	76,565
600–690	256,676
500–590	480,588
400–490	531,429
300–390	247,836
200–290	54,029
Total	N = 1,647,123

Source: 2011 College Bound Seniors: Total Group Report. Copyright © 2011. The College Board. *www.collegeboard .org.* Reproduced with permission.

■ **TABLE 15-14** 2011 SAT Critical Reading Scores

16. Table 15-15 shows the class interval frequencies for the 2011 Writing scores on the SAT. Draw a pie chart for the data in Table 15-15. Indicate the degree of the central angle for each wedge of the pie chart (rounded to the nearest degree).

Score range	Number of test-takers
700–800	72,386
600–690	225,070
500–590	454,773
400–490	556,340
300–390	285,730
200–290	52,824
Total	$N = 1,647,123$

Source: 2011 College Bound Seniors: Total Group Report. Copyright © 2011. The College Board. *www.collegeboard.org.* Reproduced with permission.

■ **TABLE 15-15**   2011 SAT Writing scores

17. Table 15-16 shows the percentage of U.S. working married couples in which the wife's income is higher than the husband's (1999–2009).

(a) Draw a pictogram for the data in Table 15-16. Assume you are trying to convince your audience that things are looking great for women in the workplace and that women's salaries are catching up to men's very quickly.

(b) Draw a different pictogram for the data in Table 15-16, where you are trying to convince your audience that women's salaries are catching up with men's very slowly.

Year	1999	2000	2001	2002	2003	2004
Percent	28.9	29.9	30.7	31.9	32.4	32.6
Year	2005	2006	2007	2008	2009	
Percent	33.0	33.4	33.5	34.5	37.7	

Source: Bureau of Labor Statistics, *www.bls.gov.*

■ **TABLE 15-16**

18. Table 15-17 shows the percentage of U.S. workers who are members of unions (2000–2011).

(a) Draw a pictogram for the data in Table 15-17. Assume you are trying to convince your audience that unions are holding their own and that the percentage of union members in the workforce is steady.

(b) Draw a different pictogram for the data in Table 15-17, where you are trying to convince your audience that there is a steep decline in union membership in the U.S. workforce.

Year	2000	2001	2002	2003	2004	2005
Percent	13.4	13.3	13.3	12.9	12.5	12.5
Year	2006	2007	2008	2009	2010	2011
Percent	12.0	12.1	12.4	12.3	11.9	11.8

Source: Bureau of Labor Statistics, *www.bls.gov.*

■ **TABLE 15-17**   Percentage of unionized U.S. workers

Exercises 19 and 20 refer to Table 15-18, which shows the birth weights (in ounces) of the 625 babies born in Cleansburg hospitals in 2012.

More than	Less than or equal to	Frequencies	More than	Less than or equal to	Frequencies
48	60	15	108	120	184
60	72	24	120	132	142
72	84	41	132	144	26
84	96	67	144	156	5
96	108	119	156	168	2

■ **TABLE 15-18**   Cleansburg birth weights (in ounces)

19. (a) Give the length of each class interval (in ounces).

(b) Suppose that a baby weighs exactly 5 pounds 4 ounces. To what class interval does she belong? Describe the endpoint convention.

(c) Draw the histogram describing the 2012 birth weights in Cleansburg using the class intervals given in Table 15-18.

20. (a) Write a new frequency table for the birth weights in Cleansburg using class intervals of length equal to 24 ounces. Use the same endpoint convention as the one used in Table 15-18.

(b) Draw the histogram corresponding to the frequency table found in (a).

Exercises 21 and 22 refer to the two histograms shown in Fig. 15-17 summarizing the team payrolls in Major League Baseball (2008). The two histograms are based on the same data set but use slightly different class intervals. (You can assume that no team had a payroll that was exactly equal to a whole number of millions of dollars.)

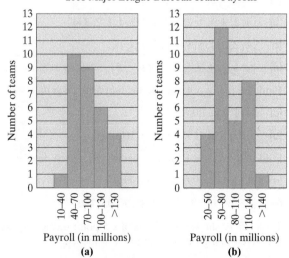

2008 Major League Baseball Team Payrolls

Source: ESPN, *sports.espn.go.com/mlb/teams/salaries?team=min*

FIGURE 15-17

21. (a) How many teams in Major League Baseball had a payroll of more than $110 million in 2008?

(b) How many teams had a payroll of between $130 million and $140 million in 2008?

22. (a) How many teams in Major League Baseball had a payroll of less than $100 million in 2008?

(b) Given that the team with the lowest payroll (the Florida Marlins) had a payroll of $22,650,000, determine the number of teams with a payroll of between $40 million and $50 million in 2008.

15.2 Means, Medians, and Percentiles

23. Consider the data set $\{3, -5, 7, 4, 8, 2, 8, -3, -6\}$.

(a) Find the average A of the data set.

(b) Find the median M of the data set.

(c) Consider the data set $\{3, -5, 7, 4, 8, 2, 8, -3, -6, 2\}$ obtained by adding one more data point to the original data set. Find the average and median of this data set.

24. Consider the data set $\{-4, 6, 8, -5.2, 10.4, 10, 12.6, -13\}$

(a) Find the average A of the data set.

(b) Find the median M of the data set.

(c) Consider the data set $\{-4, 6, 8, -5.2, 10.4, 10, 12.6\}$ having one less data point than the original set. Find the average and the median of this data set.

25. Find the average A and the median M of each data set.

(a) $\{0, 1, 2, 3, 4, 5, 6, 7, 8, 9\}$

(b) $\{1, 2, 3, 4, 5, 6, 7, 8, 9\}$

(c) $\{1, 2, 3, 4, 5, 6, 7, 8, 9, 10\}$

(d) $\{a, 2a, 3a, 4a, 5a, 6a, 7a, 8a, 9a, 10a\}$

26. Find the average A and the median M of each data set.

(a) $\{1, 2, 1, 2, 1, 2, 1, 2, 1, 2\}$

(b) $\{1, 2, 3, 4, 1, 2, 3, 4, 1, 2, 3, 4, 1, 2, 3, 4\}$

(c) $\{1, 2, 3, 4, 5, 5, 4, 3, 2, 1\}$

(d) $\{a, b, c, d, d, c, b, a, a, b, c, d\}$, where $a < b < c < d$.

27. Find the average A and the median M of each data set.

(a) $\{5, 10, 15, 20, 25, 60\}$

(b) $\{105, 110, 115, 120, 125, 160\}$

28. Find the average A and the median M of each data set.

(a) $\{5, 10, 15, 20, 25, 30, 35, 40, 45, 50\}$

(b) $\{55, 60, 65, 70, 75, 80, 85, 90, 95, 100\}$

29. Table 15-19 shows the results of a 5-point musical aptitude test given to a group of first-grade students.

(a) Find the average aptitude score.

(b) Find the median aptitude score.

Aptitude score	0	1	2	3	4	5
Frequency	24	16	20	12	5	3

■ TABLE 15-19

30. Table 15-20 shows the ages of the firefighters in the Cleansburg Fire Department.

Age	25	27	28	29	30
Frequency	2	7	6	9	15
Age	31	32	33	37	39
Frequency	12	9	9	6	4

■ TABLE 15-20

(a) Find the average age of the Cleansburg firefighters rounded to two decimal places.

(b) Find the median age of the Cleansburg firefighters.

31. Table 15-21 shows the relative frequencies of the scores of a group of students on a philosophy quiz.

Score	4	5	6	7	8
Relative frequency	7%	11%	19%	24%	39%

■ TABLE 15-21

(a) Find the average quiz score.

(b) Find the median quiz score.

32. Table 15-22 shows the relative frequencies of the scores of a group of students on a 10-point math quiz.

Score	3	4	5	6	7	8	9
Relative frequency	8%	12%	16%	20%	18%	14%	12%

■ TABLE 15-22

(a) Find the average quiz score rounded to two decimal places.

(b) Find the median quiz score.

33. Consider the data set $\{-5, 7, 4, 8, 2, 8, -3, -6\}$.

(a) Find the first quartile Q_1 of the data set.

(b) Find the third quartile Q_3 of the data set.

(c) Consider the data set $\{-5, 7, 4, 8, 2, 8, -3, -6, 2\}$ obtained by adding one more data point to the original data set. Find the first and third quartiles of this data set.

34. Consider the data set $\{-4, 6, 8, -5.2, 10.4, 10, 12.6, -13\}$.

(a) Find the first quartile Q_1 of the data set.

(b) Find the third quartile Q_3 of the data set.

(c) Consider the data set $\{-4, 6, 8, -5.2, 10.4, 10, 12.6\}$ obtained by deleting one data point from the original data set. Find the first and third quartiles of this data set.

35. For each data set, find the 75th and the 90th percentiles.

(a) $\{1, 2, 3, 4, \ldots, 98, 99, 100\}$

(b) $\{0, 1, 2, 3, 4, \ldots, 98, 99, 100\}$

(c) $\{1, 2, 3, 4, \ldots, 98, 99\}$

(d) $\{1, 2, 3, 4, \ldots, 98\}$

36. For each data set, find the 10th and the 25th percentiles.

(a) $\{1, 2, 3, \ldots, 49, 50, 50, 49, \ldots, 3, 2, 1\}$

(b) $\{1, 2, 3, \ldots, 49, 50, 49, \ldots, 3, 2, 1\}$

(c) $\{1, 2, 3, \ldots, 49, 49, \ldots, 3, 2, 1\}$

37. This exercise refers to the age distribution in the Cleansburg Fire Department shown in Table 15-20 (Exercise 30).

(a) Find the first quartile of the data set.

(b) Find the third quartile of the data set.

(c) Find the 90th percentile of the data set.

38. This exercise refers to the math quiz scores shown in Table 15-22 (Exercise 32).

(a) Find the first quartile of the data set.

(b) Find the third quartile of the data set.

(c) Find the 70th percentile of the data set.

Exercise 39 and 40 refer to the 2011 SAT scores. In 2011, a total of $N = 1,647,123$ college-bound students took the SAT test. Assume that the test scores are sorted from lowest to highest and that the sorted data set is $\{d_1, d_2, \ldots, d_{1,647,123}\}$.

39. (a) Determine the position of the median M.

(b) Determine the position of the first quartile Q_1.

(c) Determine the position of the 80th percentile score X_{80}.

40. (a) Determine the position of the third quartile Q_3.

(b) Determine the position of the 90th percentile score X_{90}.

41. Consider the data set $\{-5, 7, 4, 8, 2, 8, -3, -6\}$.

(a) Find the five-number summary of the data set. [Use the results of Exercises 23(b) and 33.]

(b) Draw a box plot for the data set.

42. Consider the data set $\{-4, 6, 8, -5.2, 10.4, 10, 12.6, -13\}$.

(a) Find the five-number summary of the data set. [See Exercises 24(b) and 34.]

(b) Draw a box plot for the data set.

43. This exercise refers to the distribution of ages in the Cleansburg Fire Department shown in Table 15-20 (see Exercises 30 and 37).

(a) Find the five-number summary of the data set.

(b) Draw a box plot for the data set.

44. This exercise refers to the distribution of math quiz scores shown in Table 15-22 (see Exercises 32 and 38).

(a) Find the five-number summary of the data set.

(b) Draw a box plot for the data set.

Exercises 45 and 46 refer to the two box plots in Fig. 15-18 showing the starting salaries of Tasmania State University first-year graduates in agriculture and engineering. (These are the two box plots discussed in Example 15.15.)

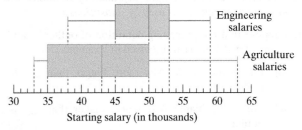

FIGURE 15-18

45. (a) What is the median salary for agriculture majors?

(b) What is the median salary for engineering majors?

(c) Explain how we can tell that the median salary for engineering majors is the same as the third quartile salary for agriculture majors.

46. (a) Fill in the blank: Of the 612 engineering graduates, at most ___ had a starting salary greater than $45,000.

(b) Fill in the blank: If there were 240 agriculture graduates with starting salaries of $35,000 or less, the total number of agriculture graduates is approximately ___.

15.3 Ranges and Standard Deviations

47. For the data set $\{-5, 7, 4, 8, 2, 8, -3, -6\}$, find

(a) the range.

(b) the interquartile range (see Exercise 33).

48. For the data set $\{-4, 6, 8, -5.2, 10, 4, 10, 12.6, -13\}$, find

(a) the range.

(b) the interquartile range (see Exercise 34).

49. A realty company has sold $N = 341$ homes in the last year. The five-number summary for the sale prices is $Min = \$97,000$, $Q_1 = \$115,000$, $M = \$143,000$, $Q_3 = \$156,000$, and $Max = \$249,000$.

(a) Find the interquartile range of the home sale prices.

(b) How many homes sold for a price between $115,000 and $156,000 (inclusive)? (*Note*: If you don't believe that you have enough information to give an exact answer, you should give the answer in the form of "at least ___" or "at most ___.")

50. This exercise refers to the starting salaries of Tasmania State University first-year graduates in agriculture and engineering discussed in Exercises 45 and 46.

(a) Estimate the range for the starting salaries of agriculture majors.

(b) Estimate the interquartile range for the starting salaries of engineering majors.

*For Exercises 51 through 54, you should use the following definition of an outlier: An **outlier** is any data value that is above the third quartile by more than 1.5 times the IQR [Outlier $> Q_3 + 1.5(IQR)$] or below the first quartile by more than 1.5 times the IQR [Outlier $< Q_1 - 1.5(IQR)$]. (Note: There is no one universally agreed upon definition of an outlier; this is but one of several definitions used by statisticians.)*

51. Suppose that the preceding definition of outlier is applied to the Stat 101 data set discussed in Example 15.14.

(a) Fill in the blank: Any score bigger than ___ is an outlier.

(b) Fill in the blank: Any score smaller than ___ is an outlier.

(c) Find the outliers (if there are any) in the Stat 101 data set.

52. Using the preceding definition, find the outliers (if there are any) in the City of Cleansburg Fire Department data set discussed in Exercises 30 and 37. (*Hint:* Do Exercise 37 first.)

53. The distribution of the heights (in inches) of 18-year-old U.S. males has first quartile $Q_1 = 67$ in. and third quartile $Q_3 = 71$ in. Using the preceding definition, determine which heights correspond to outliers.

54. The distribution of the heights (in inches) of 18-year-old U.S. females has first quartile $Q_1 = 62.5$ in. and third quartile $Q_3 = 66$ in. Using the preceding definition, determine which heights correspond to outliers.

The purpose of Exercises 55 through 58 is to practice computing standard deviations by using the definition. Granted, computing standard deviations this way is not the way it is generally done in practice; a good calculator (or a computer package) will do it much faster and more accurately. The point is that computing a few standard deviations the old-fashioned way should help you understand the concept a little better. If you use a calculator or a computer to answer these exercises, you are defeating their purpose.

55. Find the standard deviation of each of the following data sets.

(a) $\{5, 5, 5, 5\}$

(b) $\{0, 5, 5, 10\}$

(c) $\{0, 10, 10, 20\}$

56. Find the standard deviation of each of the following data sets.

(a) $\{3, 3, 3, 3\}$

(b) $\{0, 6, 6, 8\}$

(c) $\{-6, 0, 0, 18\}$

57. The Karstens family loves to read. The parents keep track of the number of books read each month by each of the 5 children in the family. For the month of June, the number of books read by the children was 11, 8, 10, 7, and 4. Find the mean and the standard deviation of the number of books read by the Karstens children during the month of June (round your answer to the nearest hundredth).

58. Tom and Joe love to hike the trails around Cleansburg during the summer. This summer they went on hikes of 7, 14, 18, 6, and 15 miles. Find the mean and the standard deviation of the length of the hikes Tom and Joe took this summer (round your answer to the nearest hundredth).

JOGGING

*Exercises 59 and 60 refer to the mode of a data set. The **mode** of a data set is the data point that occurs with the highest frequency. When there are several data points (or categories) tied for the most frequent, each of them is a mode, but if all data points have the same frequency, rather than say that every data point is a mode, it is customary to say that there is no mode.*

59. (a) Find the mode of the data set given by Table 15-20 (Exercise 30).

(b) Find the mode of the data set given by Fig. 15-15 (Exercises 11 and 12).

60. (a) Find the mode category for the data set described by the pie chart in Fig. 15-19(a).

(b) Find the mode category for the data set shown in Fig. 15-19(b). If there is no mode, your answer should indicate so.

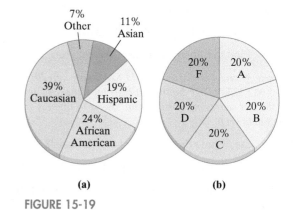

(a)   (b)

FIGURE 15-19

61. Mike's average on the first five exams in Econ 1A is 88. What must he earn on the next exam to raise his overall average to 90?

62. Sarah's overall average in Physics 101 was 93%. Her average was based on four exams each worth 100 points and a final worth 200 points. What is the lowest possible score she could have made on the first exam?

63. In 2011, $N = 1,647,123$ students took the SAT. Table 15-15 shows the class interval frequencies for the scores in the Writing section of the test. Use the data in Table 15-15 and the fact that the median score was $M = 480$ to give lower and upper estimates for the number of students that had scores between 200 and 480.

64. Explain each of the following statements regarding the median score in one of the SAT sections:

(a) If the number of test-takers N is odd, then the median score must end in 0.

(b) If the number of test-takers N is even, then the median score can end in 0 or 5, but the chances that it will end in 5 are very low.

65. In 2006, the median SAT score was the average of $d_{732,872}$ and $d_{732,873}$, where $\{d_1, d_2, \ldots, d_N\}$ denotes the data set of all SAT scores ordered from lowest to highest. Determine the number of students N who took the SAT in 2006.

66. In 2004, the third quartile of the SAT scores was $d_{1,064,256}$, where $\{d_1, d_2, \ldots, d_N\}$ denotes the data set of all SAT scores ordered from lowest to highest. Determine the number of students N who took the SAT in 2004.

67. (a) Give an example of 10 numbers with an average less than the median.

(b) Give an example of 10 numbers with a median less than the average.

(c) Give an example of 10 numbers with an average less than the first quartile.

(d) Give an example of 10 numbers with an average more than the third quartile.

68. Suppose that the average of 10 numbers is 7.5 and that the smallest of them is $Min = 3$.

(a) What is the smallest possible value of Max?

(b) What is the largest possible value of Max?

69. This exercise refers to the 2008 payrolls of major league baseball teams summarized by the histograms in Fig. 15-20 (This is Fig. 15-17 in Exercises 21 and 22.) Using the information shown in the figure, it can be determined that the median payroll of 2008 baseball teams falls somewhere between $70 million and $80 million. Explain how.

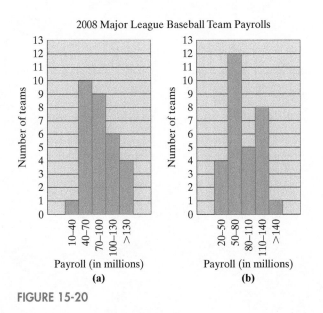

2008 Major League Baseball Team Payrolls

FIGURE 15-20

70. What happens to the five-number summary of the Stat 101 data set (see Example 15.14) if

(a) two points are added to each score?

(b) 10% is added to each score?

71. Let A denote the average and M the median of the data set $\{x_1, x_2, x_3, \ldots, x_N\}$.

Let c be any constant.

(a) Find the average of the data set $\{x_1 + c, x_2 + c, x_3 + c, \ldots, x_N + c\}$ expressed in terms of A and c.

(b) Find the median of the data set $\{x_1 + c, x_2 + c, x_3 + c, \ldots, x_N + c\}$ expressed in terms of M and c.

72. Explain why the data sets $\{x_1, x_2, x_3, \ldots, x_N\}$ and $\{x_1 + c, x_2 + c, x_3 + c, \ldots, x_N + c\}$ have

(a) the same range.

(b) the same standard deviation.

Exercises 73 and 74 refer to histograms with unequal class intervals. When sketching such histograms, the columns must be drawn so that the frequencies or percentages are proportional to the area of the column. Figure 15-21 illustrates this. If the column over class interval 1 represents 10% of the population, then the column over class interval 2, also representing 10% of the population, must be one-third as high, because the class interval is three times as large (Fig. 15-21).

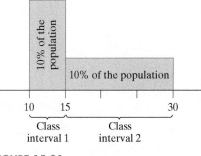

FIGURE 15-21

73. If the height of the column over the class interval 20–30 is one unit and the column represents 25% of the population, then

(a) how high should the column over the interval 30–35 be if 50% of the population falls into this class interval?

(b) how high should the column over the interval 35–45 be if 10% of the population falls into this class interval?

(c) how high should the column over the interval 45–60 be if 15% of the population falls into this class interval?

74. Two hundred senior citizens are tested for fitness and rated on their times on a one-mile walk. These ratings and associated frequencies are given in Table 15-23. Draw a histogram for these data based on the categories defined by the ratings in the table.

Time	Rating	Frequency
6^+ to 10 minutes	Fast	10
10^+ to 16 minutes	Fit	90
16^+ to 24 minutes	Average	80
24^+ to 40 minutes	Slow	20

■ **TABLE 15-23**

RUNNING

75. A data set is called **constant** if every value in the data set is the same. Explain why any data set with standard deviation 0 must be a constant data set.

76. Show that the standard deviation of any set of numbers is always less than or equal to the range of the set of numbers.

77. (a) Show that if $\{x_1, x_2, x_3, \ldots, x_N\}$ is a data set with mean A and standard deviation σ, then $\sigma\sqrt{N} \geq |x_i - A|$ for every data value x_i.

(b) Use (a) to show that every data value is bigger than or equal to $A - \sigma\sqrt{N}$ and smaller than or equal to $A + \sigma\sqrt{N}$ (i.e., for every data value x, $A - \sigma\sqrt{N} \leq x \leq A + \sigma\sqrt{N}$).

78. Show that if A is the mean and M is the median of the data set $\{1, 2, 3, \ldots, N\}$, then for all values of N, $A = M$.

79. Suppose that the standard deviation of the data set $\{x_1, x_2, x_3, \ldots, x_N\}$ is σ. Explain why the standard deviation of the data set $\{a \cdot x_1, a \cdot x_2, a \cdot x_3, \ldots, a \cdot x_N\}$ (where a is a positive number) is $a \cdot \sigma$.

80. Chebyshev's theorem. The Russian mathematician P. L. Chebyshev (1821–1894) showed that for any data set and any constant k greater than 1, at least $1 - (1/k^2)$ of the data must lie within k standard deviations on either side of the mean A. For example, when $k = 2$, this says that $1 - \frac{1}{4} = \frac{3}{4}$ (i.e., 75%) of the data must lie within two standard deviations of A (i.e., somewhere between $A - 2\sigma$ and $A + 2\sigma$).

(a) Using Chebyshev's theorem, what percentage of a data set must lie within three standard deviations of the mean?

(b) How many standard deviations on each side of the mean must we take to be assured of including 99% of the data?

(c) Suppose that the average of a data set is A. Explain why there is no number k of standard deviations for which we can be certain that 100% of the data lies within k standard deviations on either side of the mean A.

PROJECTS AND PAPERS

1 Lies, Damn Lies, and Statistics

Statistics are often used to exaggerate, distort, and misinform, and this is most commonly done by the misuse of graphs and charts. In this project you are to discuss the different graphical "tricks" that can be used to mislead or slant the information presented in a picture. Attempt to include items from recent newspapers, magazines, and other media.

2 Data in Your Daily Life

Which month is the best one to invest in the stock market? During which day of the week are you most likely to get into an automobile accident? Which airline is the safest to travel with? Who is the best place-kicker in the National Football League?

In this project, you are to formulate a question from everyday life (similar to one of the aforementioned questions) that is amenable to a statistical analysis. Then you will need to find relevant data that attempt to answer this question and summarize these data using the methods discussed in this chapter. Present your final conclusions and defend them using appropriate charts and graphs.

3 Book Review: *Curve Ball*

Baseball is the ultimate statistical sport, and statistics are as much a part of baseball as peanuts and Cracker Jack. The book *Curve Ball: Baseball, Statistics, and the Role of Chance in the Game* (Albert, Jim, and Jay Bennett, New York: Springer-Verlag, 2001) is a compilation of all sorts of fascinating statistical baseball issues, from how to better measure a player's offensive performance to what is the true value of home field advantage.

In this project you are to pick one of the many topics discussed in *Curve Ball* and write an analysis paper on the topic.

Taken from:

Finite Mathematics for Business, Economics, Life Sciences, and Social Sciences, Twelfth Edition, by Raymond A. Barnett, Michael R. Zieger, and Karl E. Byleen

Mathematics of Finance

3

Introduction

How do I choose the right loan for college? Would it be better to take the dealer's financing or the rebate for my new car? Should my parents refinance their home mortgage? To make wise decisions in such matters, you need a basic understanding of the mathematics of finance.

In Chapter 3 we study the mathematics of simple and compound interest, ordinary annuities, auto loans, and home mortgage loans (see Problems 27–30 in Section 3-4). You will need a calculator with logarithmic and exponential keys. A graphing calculator would be even better: It can help you visualize the rate at which an investment grows or the rate at which principal on a loan is amortized.

You may wish to review arithmetic and geometric sequences, discussed in Appendix B-2, before beginning this chapter.

Finally, to avoid repeating the following reminder many times, we emphasize it here: Throughout the chapter, **interest rates are to be converted to decimal form before they are used in a formula**.

3-1 Simple Interest

The Simple Interest Formula

Simple interest is used on short-term notes—often of duration less than 1 year. The concept of simple interest, however, forms the basis of much of the rest of the material developed in this chapter, for which time periods may be much longer than a year.

If you deposit a sum of money P in a savings account or if you borrow a sum of money P from a lender, then P is referred to as the **principal**. When money is borrowed—whether it is a savings institution borrowing from you when you deposit money in your account, or you borrowing from a lender—a fee is charged for the money borrowed. This fee is rent paid for the use of another's money, just as rent is paid for the use of another's house. The fee is called **interest**. It is usually computed as a percentage (called the **interest rate**)* of the principal over a given period of time. The interest rate, unless otherwise stated, is an annual rate. **Simple interest** is given by the following formula:

DEFINITION Simple Interest

$$I = Prt \tag{1}$$

where I = interest

P = principal

r = annual simple interest rate (written as a decimal)

t = time in years

For example, the interest on a loan of $100 at 12% for 9 months would be

$$I = Prt$$
$$= (100)(0.12)(0.75) \qquad \textit{Convert 12\% to a decimal (0.12)}$$
$$= \$9 \qquad \textit{and 9 months to years } \left(\tfrac{9}{12} = 0.75\right).$$

At the end of 9 months, the borrower would repay the principal ($100) plus the interest ($9), or a total of $109.

In general, if a principal P is borrowed at a rate r, then after t years, the borrower will owe the lender an amount A that will include the principal P plus the interest I. Since P is the amount that is borrowed now and A is the amount that must be paid back in the future, P is often referred to as the **present value** and A as the **future value**. The formula relating A and P follows:

THEOREM 1 Simple Interest

$$A = P + Prt$$
$$= P(1 + rt) \tag{2}$$

where A = amount, or future value

P = principal, or present value

r = annual simple interest rate (written as a decimal)

t = time in years

Given any three of the four variables A, P, r, and t in (2), we can solve for the fourth. The following examples illustrate several types of common problems that can be solved by using formula (2).

---

*If r is the interest rate written as a decimal, then $100r\%$ is the rate using %. For example, if $r = 0.12$, then $100r\% = 100(0.12)\% = 12\%$. The expressions 0.12 and 12% are equivalent.

EXAMPLE 1   **Total Amount Due on a Loan** Find the total amount due on a loan of $800 at 9% simple interest at the end of 4 months.

SOLUTION To find the amount A (future value) due in 4 months, we use formula (2) with $P = 800$, $r = 0.09$, and $t = \frac{4}{12} = \frac{1}{3}$ year. Thus,

$$A = P(1 + rt)$$
$$= 800\left[1 + 0.09\left(\tfrac{1}{3}\right)\right]$$
$$= 800(1.03)$$
$$= \$824$$

Matched Problem 1   Find the total amount due on a loan of $500 at 12% simple interest at the end of 30 months.

EXPLORE & DISCUSS 1

(A) Your sister has loaned you $1,000 with the understanding that you will repay the principal plus 4% simple interest when you can. How much would you owe her if you repaid the loan after 1 year? After 2 years? After 5 years? After 10 years?

(B) How is the interest after 10 years related to the interest after 1 year? After 2 years? After 5 years?

(C) Explain why your answers are consistent with the fact that for simple interest, the graph of future value as a function of time is a straight line (Fig. 1).

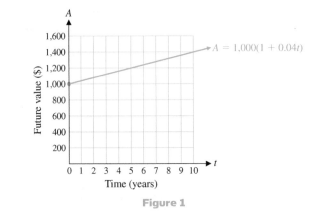

Figure 1

EXAMPLE 2   **Present Value of an Investment** If you want to earn an annual rate of 10% on your investments, how much (to the nearest cent) should you pay for a note that will be worth $5,000 in 9 months?

SOLUTION We again use formula (2), but now we are interested in finding the principal P (present value), given $A = \$5,000$, $r = 0.1$, and $t = \frac{9}{12} = 0.75$ year. Thus,

$$A = P(1 + rt)$$
$$5,000 = P[1 + 0.1(0.75)]$$ *Replace A, r, and t with the given*
$$5,000 = (1.075)P$$ *values, and solve for P.*
$$P = \$4,651.16$$

Matched Problem 2   Repeat Example 2 with a time period of 6 months.

CONCEPTUAL INSIGHT

If we consider future value A as a function of time t with the present value P and the annual rate r being fixed, then $A = P + Prt$ is a linear function of t with y intercept P and slope Pr. For example, if $P = 1,000$ and $r = 0.04$ (Fig. 1), then

$$A = 1,000(1 + 0.04t) = 1,000 + 40t$$

is a linear function with y intercept 1,000 and slope 40.

Simple Interest and Investments

EXAMPLE 3 **Interest Rate Earned on a Note** T-bills (Treasury bills) are one of the instruments that the U.S. Treasury Department uses to finance the public debt. If you buy a 180-day T-bill with a maturity value of $10,000 for $9,893.78, what annual simple interest rate will you earn? (Express answer as a percentage, correct to three decimal places.)

SOLUTION Again we use formula (2), but this time we are interested in finding r, given $P = \$9,893.78$, $A = \$10,000$, and $t = 180/360 = 0.5$ year.*

$$A = P(1 + rt) \qquad \text{\textit{Replace P, A, and t with the}}$$
$$10,000 = 9,893.78(1 + 0.5r) \qquad \text{\textit{given values, and solve for r.}}$$
$$10,000 = 9,893.78 + 4,946.89r$$
$$106.22 = 4,946.89r$$
$$r = \frac{106.22}{4,946.89} \approx 0.02147 \quad \text{or} \quad 2.147\%$$

Matched Problem 3 Repeat Example 3, assuming that you pay $9,828.74 for the T-bill.

EXAMPLE 4 **Interest Rate Earned on an Investment** Suppose that after buying a new car you decide to sell your old car to a friend. You accept a 270-day note for $3,500 at 10% simple interest as payment. (Both principal and interest are paid at the end of 270 days.) Sixty days later you find that you need the money and sell the note to a third party for $3,550. What annual interest rate will the third party receive for the investment? Express the answer as a percentage, correct to three decimal places.

SOLUTION **Step 1** Find the amount that will be paid at the end of 270 days to the holder of the note.

$$A = P(1 + rt)$$
$$= \$3,500\left[1 + (0.1)\left(\tfrac{270}{360}\right)\right]$$
$$= \$3,762.50$$

Step 2 For the third party, we are to find the annual rate of interest r required to make $3,550 grow to $3,762.50 in 210 days ($270 - 60$); that is, we are to find r (which is to be converted to 100 r%), given $A = \$3,762.50$, $P = \$3,550$, and $t = \frac{210}{360}$.

$$A = P + Prt \qquad \text{\textit{Solve for r.}}$$
$$r = \frac{A - P}{Pt}$$
$$r = \frac{3,762.50 - 3,550}{(3,550)\left(\tfrac{210}{360}\right)} \approx 0.102\,62 \quad \text{or} \quad 10.262\%$$

Matched Problem 4 Repeat Example 4 assuming that 90 days after it was initially signed, the note was sold to a third party for $3,500.

---

*In situations that involve days, some institutions use a 360-day year, called a banker's year, to simplify calculations. In this section, we will use a 360-day year. In other sections, we will use a 365-day year. The choice will always be clearly stated.

Some online discount brokerage firms offer flat rates for trading stock, but many still charge commissions based on the transaction amount (principal). Table 1 shows the commission schedule for one of these firms.

Table 1	Commission Schedule
Principal	**Commission**
$0–$2,499	$29 + 1.6% of principal
$2,500–$9,999	$49 + 0.8% of principal
$10,000+	$99 + 0.3% of principal

EXAMPLE 5   **Interest on an Investment**   An investor purchases 50 shares of a stock at $47.52 per share. After 200 days, the investor sells the stock for $52.19 per share. Using Table 1, find the annual rate of interest earned by this investment. Express the answer as a percentage, correct to three decimal places.

SOLUTION   The principal referred to in Table 1 is the value of the stock. The total cost for the investor is the cost of the stock plus the commission:

$$47.52(50) = \$2,376 \qquad \textit{Principal}$$
$$29 + 0.016(2,376) = \$67.02 \qquad \textit{Commission, using line 1 of Table 1}$$
$$2,376 + 67.02 = \$2,443.02 \qquad \textit{Total investment}$$

When the stock is sold, the commission is subtracted from the proceeds of the sale and the remainder is returned to the investor:

$$52.19(50) = \$2,609.50 \qquad \textit{Principal}$$
$$49 + 0.008(2,609.50) = \$69.88 \qquad \textit{Commission, using line 2 of Table 1}$$
$$2,609.50 - 69.88 = \$2,539.62 \qquad \textit{Total return}$$

Now using formula (2) with $A = 2,539.62$, $P = 2,443.02$, and $t = \dfrac{200}{360} = \dfrac{5}{9}$, we have

$$A = P(1 + rt)$$
$$2,539.62 = 2,443.02\left(1 + \frac{5}{9}r\right)$$
$$= 2,443.02 + 1,357.23r$$
$$96.60 = 1,357.23r$$
$$r = \frac{96.60}{1,357.23} \approx 0.07117 \quad \text{or} \quad 7.117\%$$

Matched Problem 5   Repeat Example 5 if 500 shares of stock were purchased for $17.64 per share and sold 270 days later for $22.36 per share.

CONCEPTUAL INSIGHT

The commission schedule in Table 1 specifies a piecewise defined function C with independent variable p, the principal (see Section 2-2).

$$C = \begin{cases} 29 + 0.016p & \text{if } 0 \le p < 2,500 \\ 49 + 0.008p & \text{if } 2,500 \le p < 10,000 \\ 99 + 0.003p & \text{if } 10,000 \le p \end{cases}$$

Exercises 3-1

A

In Problems 1–8, convert the given interest rate to decimal form if it is given as a percentage, and to a percentage if it is given in decimal form.

1. 3%

2. 5.25%

3. 0.105

4. 0.08

5. 4.75%

6. 16%

7. 0.21

8. 0.005

In Problems 9–16, convert the given time period to years, in fraction form, assuming a 360-day year [this assumption does not affect the number of quarters (4), months (12), or weeks (52) in a year].

9. 4 months

10. 39 weeks

11. 240 days

12. 6 quarters

13. 12 weeks

14. 10 months

15. 2 quarters

16. 30 days

In Problems 17–24, use formula (1) for simple interest to find each of the indicated quantities.

17. $P = \$300; r = 7\%; t = 2$ years; $I = ?$

18. $P = \$950; r = 9\%; t = 1$ year; $I = ?$

19. $I = \$36; r = 4\%; t = 6$ months; $P = ?$

20. $I = \$15; r = 8\%; t = 3$ quarters; $P = ?$

21. $I = \$48; P = \$600; t = 240$ days; $r = ?$

22. $I = \$28; P = \$700; t = 13$ weeks; $r = ?$

23. $I = \$60; P = \$2,400; r = 5\%; t = ?$

24. $I = \$96; P = \$3,200; r = 4\%; t = ?$

B

In Problems 25–32, use formula (2) for the amount to find each of the indicated quantities.

25. $P = \$4,500; r = 10\%; t = 1$ quarter; $A = ?$

26. $P = \$3,000; r = 4.5\%; t = 30$ days; $A = ?$

27. $A = \$910; r = 16\%; t = 13$ weeks; $P = ?$

28. $A = \$6,608; r = 24\%; t = 3$ quarters; $P = ?$

29. $A = \$14,560; P = \$13,000; t = 4$ months; $r = ?$

30. $A = \$22,135; P = \$19,000; t = 39$ weeks; $r = ?$

31. $A = \$736; P = \$640; r = 15\%; t = ?$

32. $A = \$410; P = \$400; r = 10\%; t = ?$

C

In Problems 33–38, solve each formula for the indicated variable.

33. $I = Prt$; for r

34. $I = Prt$; for P

35. $A = P + Prt$; for P

36. $A = P + Prt$; for r

37. $A = P(1 + rt)$; for t

38. $I = Prt$; for t

39. Discuss the similarities and differences in the graphs of future value A as a function of time t if $1,000 is invested at simple interest at rates of 4%, 8%, and 12%, respectively (see the figure).

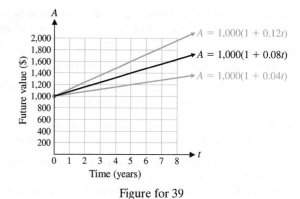

Figure for 39

40. Discuss the similarities and differences in the graphs of future value A as a function of time t for loans of $400, $800, and $1,200, respectively, each at 7.5% simple interest (see the figure).

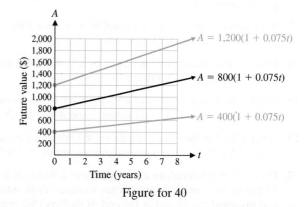

Figure for 40

Applications*

In all problems involving days, a 360-day year is assumed. When annual rates are requested as an answer, express the rate as a percentage, correct to three decimal places. Round dollar amounts to the nearest cent.

41. If $3,000 is loaned for 4 months at a 4.5% annual rate, how much interest is earned?

42. If $5,000 is loaned for 9 months at a 6.2% annual rate, how much interest is earned?

43. How much interest will you have to pay for a credit card balance of $554 that is 1 month overdue, if a 20% annual rate is charged?

*The authors wish to thank Professor Roy Luke of Pierce College and Professor Dennis Pence of Western Michigan University for their many useful suggestions of applications for this chapter.

44. A department store charges an 18% annual rate for overdue accounts. How much interest will be owed on an $835 account that is 2 months overdue?

45. A loan of $7,260 was repaid at the end of 8 months. What size repayment check (principal and interest) was written, if an 8% annual rate of interest was charged?

46. A loan of $10,000 was repaid at the end of 6 months. What amount (principal and interest) was repaid, if a 6.5% annual rate of interest was charged?

47. A loan of $4,000 was repaid at the end of 10 months with a check for $4,270. What annual rate of interest was charged?

48. A check for $3,097.50 was used to retire a 5-month $3,000 loan. What annual rate of interest was charged?

49. If you paid $30 to a loan company for the use of $1,000 for 60 days, what annual rate of interest did they charge?

50. If you paid $120 to a loan company for the use of $2,000 for 90 days, what annual rate of interest did they charge?

51. A radio commercial for a loan company states: "You only pay 29¢ a day for each $500 borrowed." If you borrow $1,500 for 120 days, what amount will you repay, and what annual interest rate is the company charging?

52. George finds a company that charges 59¢ per day for each $1,000 borrowed. If he borrows $3,000 for 60 days, what amount will he repay, and what annual interest rate will he pay the company?

53. What annual interest rate is earned by a 13-week T-bill with a maturity value of $1,000 that sells for $989.37?

54. What annual interest rate is earned by a 33-day T-bill with a maturity value of $1,000 that sells for $996.16?

55. What is the purchase price of a 50-day T-bill with a maturity value of $1,000 that earns an annual interest rate of 5.53%?

56. What is the purchase price of a 26-week T-bill with a maturity value of $1,000 that earns an annual interest rate of 4.903%?

57. For services rendered, an attorney accepts a 90-day note for $5,500 at 8% simple interest from a client. (Both interest and principal are repaid at the end of 90 days.) Wishing to use her money sooner, the attorney sells the note to a third party for $5,560 after 30 days. What annual interest rate will the third party receive for the investment?

58. To complete the sale of a house, the seller accepts a 180-day note for $10,000 at 7% simple interest. (Both interest and principal are repaid at the end of 180 days.) Wishing to use the money sooner for the purchase of another house, the seller sells the note to a third party for $10,124 after 60 days. What annual interest rate will the third party receive for the investment?

Use the commission schedule from Company A shown in Table 2 to find the annual rate of interest earned by each investment in Problems 59 and 60.

Table 2   Company A

Principal	Commission
Under $3,000	$25 + 1.8% of principal
$3,000–$10,000	$37 + 1.4% of principal
Over $10,000	$107 + 0.7% of principal

59. An investor purchases 200 shares at $14.20 a share, holds the stock for 39 weeks, and then sells the stock for $15.75 a share.

60. An investor purchases 450 shares at $21.40 a share, holds the stock for 26 weeks, and then sells the stock for $24.60 a share.

Use the commission schedule from Company B shown in Table 3 to find the annual rate of interest earned by each investment in Problems 61 and 62.

Table 3   Company B

Principal	Commission
Under $3,000	$32 + 1.8% of principal
$3,000–$10,000	$56 + 1% of principal
Over $10,000	$106 + 0.5% of principal

61. An investor purchases 215 shares at $45.75 a share, holds the stock for 300 days, and then sells the stock for $51.90 a share.

62. An investor purchases 75 shares at $37.90 a share, holds the stock for 150 days, and then sells the stock for $41.20 a share.

Many tax preparation firms offer their clients a refund anticipation loan (RAL). For a fee, the firm will give a client his refund when the return is filed. The loan is repaid when the IRS refund is sent to the firm. The RAL fee is equivalent to the interest charge for a loan. The schedule in Table 4 is from a major RAL lender. Use this schedule to find the annual rate of interest for the RALs in Problems 63–66.

Table 4

RAL Amount	RAL Fee
$0–$500	$29.00
$501–$1,000	$39.00
$1,001–$1,500	$49.00
$1,501–$2,000	$69.00
$2,001–$5,000	$89.00

63. A client receives a $475 RAL, which is paid back in 20 days.

64. A client receives a $1,100 RAL, which is paid back in 30 days.

65. A client receives a $1,900 RAL, which is paid back in 15 days.

66. A client receives a $3,000 RAL, which is paid back in 25 days.

Answers to Matched Problems

1. $650

2. $4,761.90

3. 3.485%

4. 15.0%

5. 31.439%

3-2 Compound and Continuous Compound Interest

- Compound Interest
- Continuous Compound Interest
- Growth and Time
- Annual Percentage Yield

Compound Interest

If at the end of a payment period the interest due is reinvested at the same rate, then the interest as well as the original principal will earn interest during the next payment period. Interest paid on interest reinvested is called **compound interest**.

For example, suppose you deposit $1,000 in a bank that pays 8% compounded quarterly. How much will the bank owe you at the end of a year? *Compounding quarterly* means that earned interest is paid to your account at the end of each 3-month period and that interest as well as the principal earns interest for the next quarter. Using the simple interest formula (2) from the preceding section, we compute the amount in the account at the end of the first quarter after interest has been paid:

$$A = P(1 + rt)$$
$$= 1,000\left[1 + 0.08\left(\tfrac{1}{4}\right)\right]$$
$$= 1,000(1.02) = \$1,020$$

Now, $1,020 is your new principal for the second quarter. At the end of the second quarter, after interest is paid, the account will have

$$A = \$1,020\left[1 + 0.08\left(\tfrac{1}{4}\right)\right]$$
$$= \$1,020(1.02) = \$1,040.40$$

Similarly, at the end of the third quarter, you will have

$$A = \$1,040.40\left[1 + 0.08\left(\tfrac{1}{4}\right)\right]$$
$$= \$1,040.40(1.02) = \$1,061.21$$

Finally, at the end of the fourth quarter, the account will have

$$A = \$1,061.21\left[1 + 0.08\left(\tfrac{1}{4}\right)\right]$$
$$= \$1,061.21(1.02) = \$1,082.43$$

How does this compounded amount compare with simple interest? The amount with simple interest would be

$$A = P(1 + rt)$$
$$= \$1,000[1 + 0.08(1)]$$
$$= \$1,000(1.08) = \$1,080$$

We see that compounding quarterly yields $2.43 more than simple interest would provide.

Let's look over the calculations for compound interest above to see if we can uncover a pattern that might lead to a general formula for computing compound interest:

$$A = 1,000(1.02) \qquad \text{End of first quarter}$$
$$A = [1,000(1.02)](1.02) = 1,000(1.02)^2 \qquad \text{End of second quarter}$$
$$A = [1,000(1.02)^2](1.02) = 1,000(1.02)^3 \qquad \text{End of third quarter}$$
$$A = [1,000(1.02)^3](1.02) = 1,000(1.02)^4 \qquad \text{End of fourth quarter}$$

It appears that at the end of n quarters, we would have

$$A = 1,000(1.02)^n \qquad \text{End of } n\text{th quarter}$$

or

$$A = 1,000\left[1 + 0.08\left(\tfrac{1}{4}\right)\right]^n$$
$$= 1,000\left[1 + \tfrac{0.08}{4}\right]^n$$

where $\frac{0.08}{4} = 0.02$ is the interest rate per quarter. Since interest rates are generally quoted as *annual nominal rates*, the **rate per compounding period** is found by dividing the annual nominal rate by the number of compounding periods per year.

In general, if P is the principal earning interest compounded m times a year at an annual rate of r, then (by repeated use of the simple interest formula, using $i = r/m$, the rate per period) the amount A at the end of each period is

$A = P(1 + i)$ 　　　　　　　　　　　　　　　End of the first period

$A = [P(1 + i)](1 + i) = P(1 + i)^2$ 　　　　End of second period

$A = [P(1 + i)^2](1 + i) = P(1 + i)^3$ 　　　End of third period

$\vdots$

$A = [P(1 + i)^{n-1}](1 + i) = P(1 + i)^n$ 　　End of nth period

We summarize this important result in Theorem 1:

THEOREM 1   Compound Interest

$$A = P(1 + i)^n \tag{1}$$

where $i = r/m$ and $A =$ amount (future value) at the end of n periods

$P =$ principal (present value)

$r =$ annual nominal rate*

$m =$ number of compounding periods per year

$i =$ rate per compounding period

$n =$ total number of compounding periods

---

*This is often shortened to "annual rate" or just "rate."

EXAMPLE 1   **Comparing Interest for Various Compounding Periods** If \$1,000 is invested at 8% compounded

(A) annually, 　　　　　　　　　(B) semiannually,

(C) quarterly, 　　　　　　　　　(D) monthly,

what is the amount after 5 years? Write answers to the nearest cent.

SOLUTION   (A) Compounding annually means that there is one interest payment period per year. So, $n = 5$ and $i = r = 0.08$.

$A = P(1 + i)^n$

$\quad = 1,000(1 + 0.08)^5$ 　　Use a calculator.

$\quad = 1,000(1.469\ 328)$

$\quad = \$1,469.33$ 　　　　　　Interest earned $= A - P = \$469.33$.

(B) Compounding semiannually means that there are two interest payment periods per year. The number of payment periods in 5 years is $n = 2(5) = 10$, and the interest rate per period is

$$i = \frac{r}{m} = \frac{0.08}{2} = 0.04$$

$A = P(1 + i)^n$

$\quad = 1,000(1 + 0.04)^{10}$ 　Use a calculator.

$\quad = 1,000(1.480\ 244)$

$\quad = \$1,480.24$ 　　　　　　Interest earned $= A - P = \$480.24$.

(C) Compounding quarterly means that there are four interest payments per year. So, $n = 4(5) = 20$ and $i = \frac{0.08}{4} = 0.02$.

$A = P(1 + i)^n$

$\quad = 1,000(1 + 0.02)^{20}$ 　　Use a calculator.

$\quad = 1,000(1.485\ 947)$

$\quad = \$1,485.95$ 　　　　　　Interest earned $= A - P = \$485.95$.

(D) Compounding monthly means that there are twelve interest payments per year. So, $n = 12(5) = 60$ and $i = \frac{0.08}{12} = 0.006\,66\overline{6}.*$

$$A = P(1 + i)^n$$

$$= 1,000\left(1 + \frac{0.08}{12}\right)^{60} \qquad \text{Use a calculator.}$$

$$= 1,000(1.489\,846)$$

$$= \$1,489.85 \qquad \text{Interest earned} = A - P = \$489.85.$$

Matched Problem 1 Repeat Example 1 with an annual interest rate of 6% over an 8-year period.

Continuous Compound Interest

In Example 1, we considered an investment of $1,000 at an annual rate of 8%. We calculated the amount after 5 years for interest compounded annually, semiannually, quarterly, and monthly. What would happen to the amount if interest were compounded daily, or every minute, or every second?

Although the difference in amounts in Example 1 between compounding semi-annually and annually is $1,480.24 − $1,469.33 = $10.91, the difference between compounding monthly and quarterly is only $1.489.85 − $1,485.95 = $3.90. This suggests that as the number m of compounding periods per year increases without bound, the amount will approach some limiting value. To see that this is indeed the case, we rewrite the amount A as follows:

$$A = P(1 + i)^n \qquad \text{Substitute } i = \frac{r}{m}, n = mt.$$

$$= P\left(1 + \frac{r}{m}\right)^{mt} \qquad \text{Multiply the exponent by } \frac{r}{r}(=1).$$

$$= P\left(1 + \frac{r}{m}\right)^{(m/r)rt} \qquad \text{Let } x = \frac{m}{r}; \text{ then } \frac{1}{x} = \frac{r}{m}.$$

$$= P\left(1 + \frac{1}{x}\right)^{xrt} \qquad \text{Use a law of exponents: } a^{xy} = (a^x)^y.$$

$$= P\left[\left(1 + \frac{1}{x}\right)^x\right]^{rt}$$

As the number m of compounding periods increases without bound, so does x. So the expression in square brackets gets close to the irrational number $e \approx 2.7183$, and the amount approaches the limiting value

$$A = Pe^{rt} = 1,000e^{0.08(5)} \approx \$1,491.8247$$

In other words, no matter how often interest is compounded, the amount in the account after 5 years will never equal or exceed $1,491.83. Therefore, the interest $I(= A - P)$ will never equal or exceed $491.83 (Fig. 1).

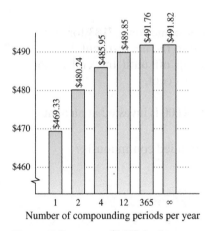

Figure 1 Interest on $1,000 for 5 years at 8% with various compounding periods

Number of compounding periods per year

CONCEPTUAL INSIGHT

One column in Figure 1 is labeled with the symbol ∞, read as "infinity." This symbol does not represent a real number. We use ∞ to denote the process of allowing m, the number of compounding periods per year, to get larger and larger with no upper limit on its size.

The formula we have obtained, $A = Pe^{rt}$, is known as the **continuous compound interest formula**. It is used when interest is **compounded continuously**; that is, when the number of compounding periods per year increases without bound.

---

*Recall that the bar over the 6 indicates a repeating decimal expansion. Rounding i to a small number of decimal places, such as 0.007 or 0.0067, can result in round-off errors. To avoid this, use as many decimal places for i as your calculator is capable of displaying.

THEOREM 2 Continuous Compound Interest Formula

If a principal P is invested at an annual rate r (expressed as a decimal) compounded continuously, then the amount A in the account at the end of t years is given by

$$A = Pe^{rt} \qquad\qquad (2)$$

EXAMPLE 2 **Compounding Daily and Continuously** What amount will an account have after 2 years if $5,000 is invested at an annual rate of 8%

(A) compounded daily? (B) compounded continuously?

Compute answers to the nearest cent.

SOLUTION (A) Use the compounded interest formula

$$A = P\left(1 + \frac{r}{m}\right)^{mt}$$

with $P = 5{,}000$, $r = 0.08$, $m = 365$, and $t = 2$:

$$A = 5{,}000\left(1 + \frac{0.08}{365}\right)^{(365)(2)} \qquad \text{Use a calculator.}$$

$$= \$5{,}867.45$$

(B) Use the continuous compound interest formula

$$A = Pe^{rt}$$

with $P = 5{,}000$, $r = 0.08$, and $t = 2$:

$$A = 5{,}000e^{(0.08)(2)} \qquad \text{Use a calculator.}$$

$$= \$5{,}867.55$$

⚠ **CAUTION** In Example 2B, do not use the approximation 2.7183 for e; it is not accurate enough to compute the correct amount to the nearest cent. Instead, use your calculator's built-in e. Avoid any rounding off until the end of the calculation, when you round the amount to the nearest cent.

Matched Problem 2 What amount will an account have after 1.5 years if $8,000 is invested at an annual rate of 9%

(A) compounded weekly? (B) compounded continuously?

Compute answers to the nearest cent.

CONCEPTUAL INSIGHT

The continuous compound interest formula $A = Pe^{rt}$ is identical, except for the names of the variables, to the equation $y = ce^{kt}$ that we used to model population growth in Section 2-5. Like the growth of an investment that earns continuous compound interest, we usually consider the population growth of a country to be continuous: Births and deaths occur all the time, not just at the end of a month or quarter.

Growth and Time

How much should you invest now to have a given amount at a future date? What annual rate of return have your investments earned? How long will it take your investment to double in value? The formulas for compound interest and continuous compound interest can be used to answer such questions. If the values of all but one of the variables in the formula are known, then we can solve for the remaining variable.

EXAMPLE 3   **Finding Present Value** How much should you invest now at 10% to have $8,000 toward the purchase of a car in 5 years if interest is

(A) compounded quarterly?   (B) compounded continuously?

SOLUTION   (A) We are given a future value $A = \$8,000$ for a compound interest investment, and we need to find the present value P given $i = \frac{0.10}{4} = 0.025$ and $n = 4(5) = 20$.

$$A = P(1 + i)^n$$
$$8{,}000 = P(1 + 0.025)^{20}$$
$$P = \frac{8{,}000}{(1 + 0.025)^{20}} \quad \text{Use a calculator.}$$
$$= \frac{8{,}000}{1.638\ 616}$$
$$= \$4{,}882.17$$

Your initial investment of $4,882.17 will grow to $8,000 in 5 years.

(B) We are given $A = \$8,000$ for an investment at continuous compound interest, and we need to find the present value P given $r = 0.10$ and $t = 5$.

$$A = Pe^{rt}$$
$$8{,}000 = Pe^{0.10(5)}$$
$$P = \frac{8{,}000}{e^{0.10(5)}} \quad \text{Use a calculator.}$$
$$P = \$4{,}852.25$$

Your initial investment of $4,852.25 will grow to $8,000 in 5 years.

Matched Problem 3   How much should new parents invest at 8% to have $80,000 toward their child's college education in 17 years if interest is

(A) compounded semiannually?   (B) compounded continuously?

A graphing calculator is a useful tool for studying compound interest. In Figure 2, we use a spreadsheet to illustrate the growth of the investment in Example 3A both numerically and graphically. Similar results can be obtained from most graphing calculators.

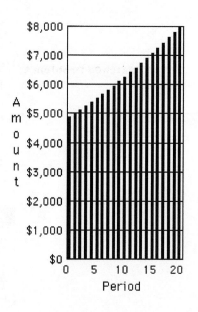

	A	B	C
1	Period	Interest	Amount
2	0		$4,882.17
3	1	$122.05	$5,004.22
4	2	$125.11	$5,129.33
5	3	$128.23	$5,257.56
6	4	$131.44	$5,389.00
7	5	$134.73	$5,523.73
8	6	$138.09	$5,661.82
9	7	$141.55	$5,803.37
10	8	$145.08	$5,948.45
11	9	$148.71	$6,097.16
12	10	$152.43	$6,249.59
13	11	$156.24	$6,405.83
14	12	$160.15	$6,565.98
15	13	$164.15	$6,730.13
16	14	$168.25	$6,898.38
17	15	$172.46	$7,070.84
18	16	$176.77	$7,247.61
19	17	$181.19	$7,428.80
20	18	$185.72	$7,614.52
21	19	$190.36	$7,804.88
22	20	$195.12	$8,000.00

Figure 2 Growth of $4,882.17 at 10% compounded quarterly for 5 years

Solving the compound interest formula or the continuous compound interest formula for r enables us to determine the rate of growth of an investment.

EXAMPLE 4   Computing Growth Rate   Figure 3 shows that a $10,000 investment in a growth-oriented mutual fund over a recent 10-year period would have grown to $126,000. What annual nominal rate would produce the same growth if interest was:

(A) compounded annually?   (B) compounded continuously?

Express answers as percentages, rounded to three decimal places.

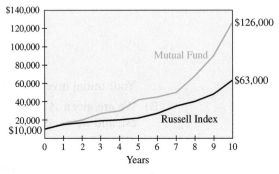

Figure 3 Growth of a $10,000 investment

SOLUTION   (A) $126{,}000 = 10{,}000(1 + r)^{10}$

$12.6 = (1 + r)^{10}$

$\sqrt[10]{12.6} = 1 + r$

$r = \sqrt[10]{12.6} - 1 = 0.28836$ or   28.836%

(B) $126{,}000 = 10{,}000e^{r(10)}$

$12.6 = e^{10r}$ *Take ln of both sides.*

$\ln 12.6 = 10r$

$r = \dfrac{\ln 12.6}{10} = 0.25337$ or   25.337%

Matched Problem 4   The Russell Index tracks the average performance of various groups of stocks. Figure 3 shows that, on average, a $10,000 investment in midcap growth funds over a recent 10-year period would have grown to $63,000. What annual nominal rate would produce the same growth if interest were

(A) compounded annually?   (B) compounded continuously?

Express answers as percentages, rounded to three decimal places.

CONCEPTUAL INSIGHT

We can solve $A = P(1 + i)^n$ for n using a property of logarithms:

$$\log_b M^p = p \log_b M$$

Theoretically, any base can be used for the logarithm, but most calculators only evaluate logarithms with base 10 (denoted log) or base e (denoted ln).

Finally, if we solve the compound interest formula for n (or the continuous compound interest formula for t), we can determine the **growth time** of an investment—the time it takes a given principal to grow to a particular value (the shorter the time, the greater the return on the investment).

Example 5 illustrates three methods for solving for growth time.

EXAMPLE 5   Computing Growth Time   How long will it take $10,000 to grow to $12,000 if it is invested at 9% compounded monthly?

SOLUTION   Method 1. Use logarithms and a calculator:

$$A = P(1 + i)^n$$

$$12{,}000 = 10{,}000\left(1 + \frac{0.09}{12}\right)^n$$

$$1.2 = 1.0075^n$$

Now, solve for n by taking logarithms of both sides:

$$\ln 1.2 = \ln 1.0075^n \qquad \textit{We choose the natural logarithm (base e)}$$

$$\ln 1.2 = n \ln 1.0075 \qquad \textit{and use the property } \ln M^p = p \ln M.$$

$$n = \frac{\ln 1.2}{\ln 1.0075}$$

$$\approx 24.40 \approx 25 \text{ months} \quad \text{or} \quad 2 \text{ years and 1 month}$$

Note: 24.40 is rounded up to 25 to guarantee reaching $12,000 since interest is paid at the end of each month.

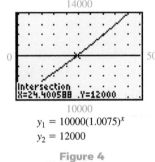

14000

0   50

Intersection
X=24.400588 Y=12000

10000

$y_1 = 10000(1.0075)^x$
$y_2 = 12000$

Figure 4

Method 2. Use a graphing calculator: To solve this problem using graphical approximation techniques, we graph both sides of the equation $12{,}000 = 10{,}000(1.0075)^n$ and find that the graphs intersect at $x = n = 24.40$ months (Fig. 4). So, the growth time is 25 months.

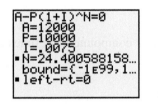

A-P(1+I)^N=0
 A=12000
 P=10000
 I=.0075
▪N=24.400588158…
 bound=(-1ᴇ99,1…
▪left-rt=0

(B)

Figure 5 TI-84 equation solver

Method 3. Most graphing calculators have an approximation process that is referred to as **equation solver**. Figure 5 shows the equation solver on a TI-84. Notice that this solver requires that one side of the equation is equal to zero (see the first line in Fig. 5). After entering values for three of the four variables, the solver will approximate the value of the remaining variable. Once again, we see that the growth time is 25 months (Fig. 5).

Matched Problem 5   How long will it take $10,000 to grow to $25,000 if it is invested at 8% compounded quarterly?

Annual Percentage Yield

Table 1 lists the rate and compounding period for certificates of deposit (CDs) recently offered by three banks. How can we tell which of these CDs has the best return?

Table 1 Certificates of Deposit (CDs)		
Bank	**Rate**	**Compounded**
Advanta	4.93%	monthly
DeepGreen	4.95%	daily
Charter One	4.97%	quarterly
Liberty	4.94%	continuously

EXPLORE & DISCUSS 1 Determine the value after 1 year of a $1,000 CD purchased from each of the banks in Table 1. Which CD offers the greatest return? Which offers the least return?

If a principal P is invested at an annual rate r compounded m times a year, then the amount after 1 year is

$$A = P\left(1 + \frac{r}{m}\right)^m$$

The simple interest rate that will produce the same amount A in 1 year is called the **annual percentage yield** (APY). To find the APY, we proceed as follows:

$$\begin{pmatrix} \text{amount at} \\ \text{simple interest} \\ \text{after 1 year} \end{pmatrix} = \begin{pmatrix} \text{amount at} \\ \text{compound interest} \\ \text{after 1 year} \end{pmatrix}$$

$$P(1 + \text{APY}) = P\left(1 + \frac{r}{m}\right)^m \qquad \text{Divide both sides by } P.$$

$$1 + \text{APY} = \left(1 + \frac{r}{m}\right)^m \qquad \text{Isolate APY on the left side.}$$

$$\text{APY} = \left(1 + \frac{r}{m}\right)^m - 1$$

If interest is compounded continuously, then the amount after 1 year is $A = Pe^r$. So to find the annual percentage yield, we solve the equation

$$P(1 + \text{APY}) = Pe^r$$

for APY, obtaining $\text{APY} = e^r - 1$. We summarize our results in Theorem 3.

THEOREM 3   Annual Percentage Yield

If a principal is invested at the annual (nominal) rate r compounded m times a year, then the annual percentage yield is

$$\text{APY} = \left(1 + \frac{r}{m}\right)^m - 1$$

If a principal is invested at the annual (nominal) rate r compounded continuously, then the annual percentage yield is

$$\text{APY} = e^r - 1$$

The annual percentage yield is also referred to as the **effective rate** or **true interest rate**.

Compound rates with different compounding periods cannot be compared directly (see Explore & Discuss 1). But since the annual percentage yield is a simple interest rate, the annual percentage yields for two different compound rates can be compared.

EXAMPLE 6   Using APY to Compare Investments   Find the APYs (expressed as a percentage, correct to three decimal places) for each of the banks in Table 1 and compare these CDs.

SOLUTION

$$\text{Advanta: APY} = \left(1 + \frac{0.0493}{12}\right)^{12} - 1 = 0.05043 \quad \text{or} \quad 5.043\%$$

$$\text{DeepGreen: APY} = \left(1 + \frac{0.0495}{365}\right)^{365} - 1 = 0.05074 \quad \text{or} \quad 5.074\%$$

$$\text{Charter One: APY} = \left(1 + \frac{0.0497}{4}\right)^{4} - 1 = 0.05063 \quad \text{or} \quad 5.063\%$$

$$\text{Liberty: APY} = e^{0.0494} - 1 = 0.05064 \quad \text{or} \quad 5.064\%$$

Comparing these APYs, we conclude that the DeepGreen CD will have the largest return and the Advanta CD will have the smallest.

Matched Problem 6   Southern Pacific Bank recently offered a 1-year CD that paid 4.8% compounded daily and Washington Savings Bank offered one that paid 4.85% compounded quarterly. Find the APY (expressed as a percentage, correct to three decimal places) for each CD. Which has the higher return?

EXAMPLE 7   **Computing the Annual Nominal Rate Given the APY** A savings and loan wants to offer a CD with a monthly compounding rate that has an APY of 7.5%. What annual nominal rate compounded monthly should they use? Check with a graphing calculator.

SOLUTION

$$\text{APY} = \left(1 + \frac{r}{m}\right)^m - 1$$

$$0.075 = \left(1 + \frac{r}{12}\right)^{12} - 1$$

$$1.075 = \left(1 + \frac{r}{12}\right)^{12}$$

$$\sqrt[12]{1.075} = 1 + \frac{r}{12}$$

$$\sqrt[12]{1.075} - 1 = \frac{r}{12}$$

$$r = 12(\sqrt[12]{1.075} - 1) \qquad \textit{Use a calculator.}$$

$$= 0.072\,539 \quad \text{or} \quad 7.254\%$$

```
A-(1+R/M)^M+1=0
 A=.075
•R=.0725390282
 M=12
 bound={-1E99,1…
•left-rt=0
```

Figure 6 TI-84 equation solver

So, an annual nominal rate of 7.254% compounded monthly is equivalent to an APY of 7.5%.

CHECK   We use an equation solver on a graphing calculator to check this result (Fig. 6).

Matched Problem 7   What is the annual nominal rate compounded quarterly for a bond that has an APY of 5.8%?

⚠ **CAUTION** Each compound interest problem involves two interest rates. Referring to Example 5, $r = 0.09$ or 9% is the annual nominal compounding rate, and $i = r/12 = 0.0075$ or 0.75% is the interest rate per month. Do not confuse these two rates by using r in place of i in the compound interest formula. If interest is compounded annually, then $i = r/1 = r$. In all other cases, r and i are not the same.

EXPLORE & DISCUSS 2

(A) Which would be the better way to invest $1,000: at 9% simple interest for 10 years, or at 7% compounded monthly for 10 years?

(B) Explain why the graph of future value as a function of time is a straight line for simple interest, but for compound interest the graph curves upward (see Fig. 7).

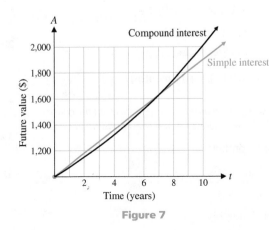

Figure 7

CONCEPTUAL INSIGHT

The two curves in Figure 7 intersect at $t = 0$ and again near $t = 7$. The t coordinate of each intersection point is a solution of the equation

$$1,000(1 + 0.09t) = 1,000(1 + 0.07/12)^{12t}$$

Don't try to use algebra to solve this equation. It can't be done. But the solutions are easily approximated on a graphing calculator (Fig. 8).

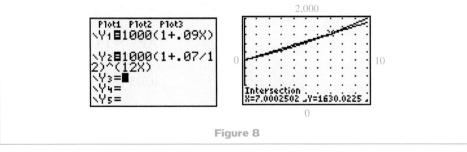

Figure 8

Exercises 3-2

Find all dollar amounts to the nearest cent. When an interest rate is requested as an answer, express the rate as a percentage correct to two decimal places, unless directed otherwise. In all problems involving days, use a 365-day year.

A

In Problems 1–4, use compound interest formula (1) to find each of the indicated values.

1. $P = \$5,000; i = 0.005; n = 36; A = ?$

2. $P = \$2,800; i = 0.003; n = 24; A = ?$

3. $A = \$8,000; i = 0.02; n = 32; P = ?$

4. $A = \$15,000; i = 0.01; n = 28; P = ?$

In Problems 5–12, use the continuous compound interest formula (2) to find each of the indicated values.

5. $P = \$2,450; r = 8.12\%; t = 3\text{ years}; A = ?$

6. $P = \$995; r = 22\%; t = 2\text{ years}; A = ?$

7. $A = \$6,300; r = 9.45\%; t = 8\text{ years}; P = ?$

8. $A = \$19,000; r = 7.69\%; t = 5\text{ years}; P = ?$

9. $A = \$88,000; P = \$71,153; r = 8.5\%; t = ?$

10. $A = \$32,982; P = \$27,200; r = 5.93\%; t = ?$

11. $A = \$15,875; P = \$12,100; t = 48\text{ months}; r = ?$

12. $A = \$23,600; P = \$19,150; t = 60\text{ months}; r = ?$

In Problems 13–18, use the given annual interest rate r and the compounding period to find i, the interest rate per compounding period.

13. 9% compounded monthly

14. 6% compounded quarterly

15. 14.6% compounded daily

16. 15% compounded monthly

17. 4.8% compounded quarterly

18. 3.2% compounded semiannually

In Problems 19–24, use the given interest rate i per compounding period to find r, the annual rate.

19. 0.395% per month   **20.** 0.012% per day

21. 0.9% per quarter   **22.** 0.175% per month

23. 2.1% per half year   **24.** 1.4% per quarter

B

25. If \$100 is invested at 6% compounded
(A) annually   (B) quarterly   (C) monthly
what is the amount after 4 years? How much interest is earned?

26. If \$2,000 is invested at 7% compounded
(A) annually   (B) quarterly   (C) monthly
what is the amount after 5 years? How much interest is earned?

27. If \$5,000 is invested at 5% compounded monthly, what is the amount after
(A) 2 years?   (B) 4 years?

28. If \$20,000 is invested at 4% compounded monthly, what is the amount after
(A) 5 years?   (B) 8 years?

29. If \$8,000 is invested at 7% compounded continuously, what is the amount after 6 years?

30. If \$23,000 is invested at 13.5% compounded continuously, what is the amount after 15 years?

31. Discuss the similarities and the differences in the graphs of future value A as a function of time t if \$1,000 is invested for 8 years and interest is compounded monthly at annual rates of 4%, 8%, and 12%, respectively (see the figure).

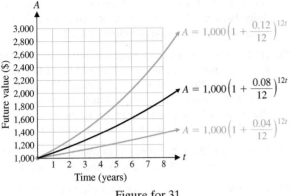

Figure for 31

✎ **32.** Discuss the similarities and differences in the graphs of future value A as a function of time t for loans of $4,000, $8,000, and $12,000, respectively, each at 7.5% compounded monthly for 8 years (see the figure).

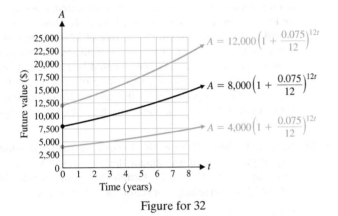

Figure for 32

33. If $1,000 is invested in an account that earns 9.75% compounded annually for 6 years, find the interest earned during each year and the amount in the account at the end of each year. Organize your results in a table.

34. If $2,000 is invested in an account that earns 8.25% compounded annually for 5 years, find the interest earned during each year and the amount in the account at the end of each year. Organize your results in a table.

35. If an investment company pays 6% compounded semiannually, how much should you deposit now to have $10,000

(A) 5 years from now?   (B) 10 years from now?

36. If an investment company pays 8% compounded quarterly, how much should you deposit now to have $6,000

(A) 3 years from now?   (B) 6 years from now?

37. If an investment earns 9% compounded continuously, how much should you deposit now to have $25,000

(A) 36 months from now?   (B) 9 years from now?

38. If an investment earns 12% compounded continuously, how much should you deposit now to have $4,800

(A) 48 months from now?   (B) 7 years from now?

39. What is the annual percentage yield (APY) for money invested at an annual rate of

(A) 3.9% compounded monthly?

(B) 2.3% compounded quarterly?

40. What is the annual percentage yield (APY) for money invested at an annual rate of

(A) 4.32% compounded monthly?

(B) 4.31% compounded daily?

41. What is the annual percentage yield (APY) for money invested at an annual rate of

(A) 5.15% compounded continuously?

(B) 5.20% compounded semiannually?

42. What is the annual percentage yield (APY) for money invested at an annual rate of

(A) 3.05% compounded quarterly?

(B) 2.95% compounded continuously?

43. How long will it take $4,000 to grow to $9,000 if it is invested at 7% compounded monthly?

44. How long will it take $5,000 to grow to $7,000 if it is invested at 6% compounded quarterly?

45. How long will it take $6,000 to grow to $8,600 if it is invested at 9.6% compounded continuously?

46. How long will it take $42,000 to grow to $60,276 if it is invested at 4.25% compounded continuously?

C

In Problems 47 and 48, use the compound interest formula (1) to find n to the nearest larger integer value.

47. $A = 2P; i = 0.06; n = ?$

48. $A = 2P; i = 0.05; n = ?$

49. How long will it take money to double if it is invested at

(A) 10% compounded quarterly?

(B) 12% compounded quarterly?

50. How long will it take money to double if it is invested at

(A) 8% compounded semiannually?

(B) 7% compounded semiannually?

51. How long will it take money to double if it is invested at

(A) 9% compounded continuously?

(B) 11% compounded continuously?

52. How long will it take money to double if it is invested at

(A) 21% compounded continuously?

(B) 33% compounded continuously?

Applications

53. A newborn child receives a $20,000 gift toward college from her grandparents. How much will the $20,000 be worth in 17 years if it is invested at 7% compounded quarterly?

54. A person with $14,000 is trying to decide whether to purchase a car now, or to invest the money at 6.5% compounded semiannually and then buy a more expensive car. How much will be available for the purchase of a car at the end of 3 years?

55. What will a $210,000 house cost 10 years from now if the inflation rate over that period averages 3% compounded annually?

56. If the inflation rate averages 4% per year compounded annually for the next 5 years, what will a car that costs $17,000 now cost 5 years from now?

57. Rental costs for office space have been going up at 4.8% per year compounded annually for the past 5 years. If office space rent is now $25 per square foot per month, what were the rental rates 5 years ago?

58. In a suburb, housing costs have been increasing at 5.2% per year compounded annually for the past 8 years. A house worth $260,000 now would have had what value 8 years ago?

59. If the population in a particular country is growing at 1.7% compounded continuously, how long will it take the population to double? (Round up to the next-higher year if not exact.)

60. If the world population is now about 6.5 billion people and is growing at 1.14% compounded continuously, how long will it take the population to grow to 10 billion people? (Round up to the next-higher year if not exact.)

61. Which is the better investment and why: 9% compounded monthly or 9.3% compounded annually?

62. Which is the better investment and why: 8% compounded quarterly or 8.3% compounded annually?

63. (A) If an investment of $100 were made in 1776, and if it earned 3% compounded quarterly, how much would it be worth in 2016?

(B) Discuss the effect of compounding interest monthly, daily, and continuously (rather than quarterly) on the $100 investment.

(C) Use a graphing calculator to graph the growth of the investment of part (A).

64. (A) Starting with formula (1), derive each of the following formulas:

$$P = \frac{A}{(1+i)^n}, \quad i = \left(\frac{A}{P}\right)^{1/n} - 1, \quad n = \frac{\ln A - \ln P}{\ln(1+i)}$$

(B) Explain why it is unnecessary to memorize the formulas above for $P, i,$ and n if you know formula (1).

65. A promissory note will pay $50,000 at maturity 6 years from now. If you pay $28,000 for the note now, what rate compounded continuously would you earn?

66. If you deposit $10,000 in a savings account now, what rate compounded continuously would be required for you to withdraw $12,500 at the end of 4 years?

67. You have saved $7,000 toward the purchase of a car costing $9,000. How long will the $7,000 have to be invested at 9% compounded monthly to grow to $9,000? (Round up to the next-higher month if not exact.)

68. A married couple has $15,000 toward the purchase of a house. For the house that the couple wants to buy, a down payment of $20,000 is required. How long will the money have to be invested at 7% compounded quarterly to grow to $20,000? (Round up to the next-higher quarter if not exact.)

69. An Individual Retirement Account (IRA) has $20,000 in it, and the owner decides not to add any more money to the

account other than interest earned at 6% compounded daily. How much will be in the account 35 years from now when the owner reaches retirement age?

70. If $1 had been placed in a bank account in the year 1066 and forgotten until now, how much would be in the account at the end of 2016 if the money earned 2% interest compounded annually? 2% simple interest? (Now you can see the power of compounding and why inactive accounts are closed after a relatively short period of time.)

71. How long will it take money to double if it is invested at 7% compounded daily? 8.2% compounded continuously?

72. How long will it take money to triple if it is invested at 5% compounded daily? 6% compounded continuously?

73. In a conversation with a friend, you note that you have two real estate investments, one that has doubled in value in the past 9 years and another that has doubled in value in the past 12 years. Your friend says that the first investment has been growing at approximately 8% compounded annually and the second at 6% compounded annually. How did your friend make these estimates? The **rule of 72** states that the annual compound rate of growth r of an investment that doubles in n years can be approximated by $r = 72/n$. Construct a table comparing the exact rate of growth and the approximate rate provided by the rule of 72 for doubling times of $n = 6, 7, \ldots, 12$ years. Round both rates to one decimal place.

74. Refer to Problem 73. Show that the exact annual compound rate of growth of an investment that doubles in n years is given by $r = 100(2^{1/n} - 1)$. Graph this equation and the rule of 72 on a graphing calculator for $5 \le n \le 20$.

Solve Problems 75–78 using graphical approximation techniques on a graphing calculator.

75. How long does it take for a $2,400 investment at 13% compounded quarterly to be worth more than a $3,000 investment at 6% compounded quarterly?

76. How long does it take for a $4,800 investment at 8% compounded monthly to be worth more than a $5,000 investment at 5% compounded monthly?

77. One investment pays 10% simple interest and another pays 7% compounded annually. Which investment would you choose? Why?

78. One investment pays 9% simple interest and another pays 6% compounded monthly. Which investment would you choose? Why?

79. What is the annual nominal rate compounded daily for a bond that has an annual percentage yield of 6.8%?

80. What is the annual nominal rate compounded monthly for a CD that has an annual percentage yield of 5.9%?

81. What annual nominal rate compounded monthly has the same annual percentage yield as 7% compounded continuously?

82. What annual nominal rate compounded continuously has the same annual percentage yield as 6% compounded monthly?

*Problems 83–86 refer to zero coupon bonds. A **zero coupon bond** is a bond that is sold now at a discount and will pay its **face value** at some time in the future when it matures—no interest payments are made.*

83. A zero coupon bond with a face value of $30,000 matures in 15 years. What should the bond be sold for now if its rate of return is to be 4.348% compounded annually?

84. A zero coupon bond with a face value of $20,000 matures in 10 years. What should the bond be sold for now if its rate of return is to be 4.194% compounded annually?

85. If you pay $4,126 for a 20-year zero coupon bond with a face value of $10,000, what is your annual compound rate of return?

86. If you pay $32,000 for a 5-year zero coupon bond with a face value of $40,000, what is your annual compound rate of return?

87. An online financial service listed the following money market accounts:

(A) Republic Bank: 4.31% compounded continuously

(B) Chase Bank: 4.35% compounded daily

(C) BankFirst: 4.36% compounded monthly

What is the annual percentage yield (to three decimal places) of each?

88. An online financial service listed the following 1-year CD accounts:

(A) Banking for CDs: 4.5% compounded quarterly

(B) Wingspan Bank: 4.6% compounded monthly

(C) Discover Bank: 4.6% compounded continuously

What is the annual percentage yield (to three decimal places) of each?

The buying and selling commission schedule shown at the top of the next column is from an online discount brokerage firm. Taking into consideration the buying and selling commissions in this schedule, find the annual compound rate of interest earned by each investment in Problems 89–92.

Transaction Size	Commission Rate
$0–$1,500	$29 + 2.5% of principal
$1,501–$6,000	$57 + 0.6% of principal
$6,001–$22,000	$75 + 0.30% of principal
$22,001–$50,000	$97 + 0.20% of principal
$50,001–$500,000	$147 + 0.10% of principal
$500,001+	$247 + 0.08% of principal

89. An investor purchases 100 shares of stock at $65 per share, holds the stock for 5 years, and then sells the stock for $125 a share.

90. An investor purchases 300 shares of stock at $95 per share, holds the stock for 3 years, and then sells the stock for $156 a share.

91. An investor purchases 200 shares of stock at $28 per share, holds the stock for 4 years, and then sells the stock for $55 a share.

92. An investor purchases 400 shares of stock at $48 per share, holds the stock for 6 years, and then sells the stock for $147 a share.

Answers to Matched Problems

1. (A) $1,593.85 (C) $1,610.32
(B) $1,604.71 (D) $1,614.14

2. (A) $9,155.23 **3.** (A) $21,084.17
(B) $9,156.29 (B) $20,532.86

4. (A) 20.208%
(B) 18.405%

5. 47 quarters, or 11 years and 3 quarters

6. Southern Pacific Bank: 4.917%
Washington Savings Bank: 4.939%
Washington Savings Bank has the higher return.

7. 5.678%

3-3   Future Value of an Annuity; Sinking Funds

- Future Value of an Annuity
- Sinking Funds
- Approximating Interest Rates

Future Value of an Annuity

An **annuity** is any sequence of equal periodic payments. If payments are made at the end of each time interval, then the annuity is called an **ordinary annuity**. We consider only ordinary annuities in this book. The amount, or **future value**, of an annuity is the sum of all payments plus all interest earned.

Suppose you decide to deposit $100 every 6 months into an account that pays 6% compounded semiannually. If you make six deposits, one at the end of each interest payment period, over 3 years, how much money will be in the account after the last deposit is made? To solve this problem, let's look at it in terms of a time line. Using the compound amount formula $A = P(1 + i)^n$, we can find the value of each deposit after it has earned compound interest up through the sixth deposit, as shown in Figure 1.

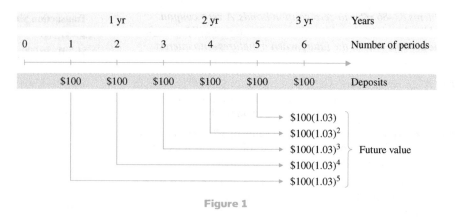

Figure 1

We could, of course, evaluate each of the future values in Figure 1 using a calculator and then add the results to find the amount in the account at the time of the sixth deposit—a tedious project at best. Instead, we take another approach, which leads directly to a formula that will produce the same result in a few steps (even when the number of deposits is very large). We start by writing the total amount in the account after the sixth deposit in the form

$$S = 100 + 100(1.03) + 100(1.03)^2 + 100(1.03)^3 + 100(1.03)^4 + 100(1.03)^5 \qquad (1)$$

We would like a simple way to sum these terms. Let us multiply each side of (1) by 1.03 to obtain

$$1.03S = 100(1.03) + 100(1.03)^2 + 100(1.03)^3 + 100(1.03)^4 + 100(1.03)^5 + 100(1.03)^6 \qquad (2)$$

Subtracting equation (1) from equation (2), left side from left side and right side from right side, we obtain

$$1.03S - S = 100(1.03)^6 - 100 \qquad \text{Notice how many terms drop out.}$$
$$0.03S = 100[(1.03)^6 - 1]$$
$$S = 100\frac{(1 + 0.03)^6 - 1}{0.03} \qquad \begin{array}{l}\text{We write } S \text{ in this form to} \\ \text{observe a general pattern.}\end{array} \qquad (3)$$

In general, if R is the periodic deposit, i the rate per period, and n the number of periods, then the future value is given by

$$S = R + R(1 + i) + R(1 + i)^2 + \cdots + R(1 + i)^{n-1} \qquad \begin{array}{l}\text{Note how this} \\ \text{compares to (1).}\end{array} \qquad (4)$$

and proceeding as in the above example, we obtain the general formula for the future value of an ordinary annuity:

$$S = R\frac{(1 + i)^n - 1}{i} \qquad \text{Note how this compares to (3).} \qquad (5)$$

Returning to the example above, we use a calculator to complete the problem:

$$S = 100\frac{(1.03)^6 - 1}{0.03} \qquad \begin{array}{l}\text{For improved accuracy, keep all values in the} \\ \text{calculator until the end; round to the} \\ \text{required number of decimal places.}\end{array}$$

$$= \$646.84$$

An alternative to the preceding computation of S is provided by the use of tables of values of certain functions of the mathematics of finance. One such function is the fractional factor of formula (5), denoted by the symbol $s_{\overline{n}i}$ (read "s angle n at i"):

$$s_{\overline{n}i} = \frac{(1 + i)^n - 1}{i}$$

CONCEPTUAL INSIGHT

In general, an expression of the form

$$a + ar + ar^2 + \cdots + ar^{n-1}$$

is called a finite geometric series (each term is obtained from the preceding term by multiplying by r). The sum of the terms of a finite geometric series is (see Section B-2)

$$a + ar + ar^2 + \cdots + ar^{n-1} = a\frac{r^n - 1}{r - 1}$$

If $a = R$ and $r = 1 + i$, then equation (4) is the sum of the terms of a finite geometric series and, using the preceding formula, we have

$$S = R + R(1 + i) + R(1 + i)^2 + \cdots + R(1 + i)^{n-1}$$

$$= R\frac{(1 + i)^n - 1}{1 + i - 1} \qquad a = R, r = 1 + i$$

$$= R\frac{(1 + i)^n - 1}{i} \qquad\qquad\qquad (5)$$

So formula (5) is really a direct consequence of the sum formula for a finite geometric series.

Tables found in books on finance and mathematical handbooks list values of $s_{\overline{n}|i}$ for various values of n and i. To complete the computation of S, R is multiplied by $s_{\overline{n}|i}$ as indicated by formula (5). (A main advantage of using a calculator rather than tables is that a calculator can handle many more situations than a table, no matter how large the table.)

It is common to use FV (future value) for S and PMT (payment) for R in formula (5). Making these changes, we have the formula in Theorem 1.

THEOREM 1   Future Value of an Ordinary Annuity

$$FV = PMT\frac{(1 + i)^n - 1}{i} = PMT s_{\overline{n}|i} \qquad (6)$$

where FV = future value (amount)

   PMT = periodic payment

   i = rate per period

   n = number of payments (periods)

Note: Payments are made at the end of each period.

EXAMPLE 1   **Future Value of an Ordinary Annuity** What is the value of an annuity at the end of 20 years if $2,000 is deposited each year into an account earning 8.5% compounded annually? How much of this value is interest?

SOLUTION   To find the value of the annuity, use formula (6) with $PMT = \$2,000$, $i = r = 0.085$, and $n = 20$.

$$FV = PMT\frac{(1 + i)^n - 1}{i}$$

$$= 2,000\frac{(1.085)^{20} - 1}{0.085} = \$96,754.03 \qquad \textit{Use a calculator.}$$

To find the amount of interest earned, subtract the total amount deposited in the annuity (20 payments of $2,000) from the total value of the annuity after the 20th payment.

Deposits = 20(2,000) = $40,000

Interest = value − deposits = 96,754.03 − 40,000 = $56,754.03

 Figure 2 on the next page, which was generated using a spreadsheet, illustrates the growth of this account over 20 years.

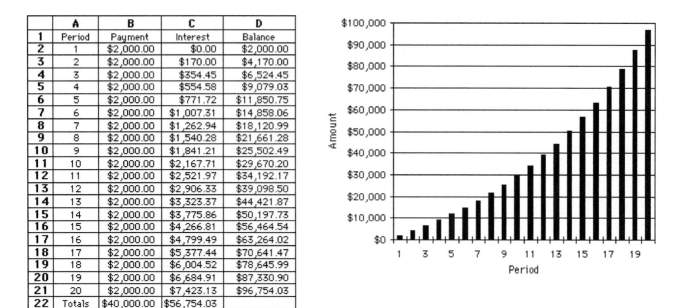

	A	B	C	D
1	Period	Payment	Interest	Balance
2	1	$2,000.00	$0.00	$2,000.00
3	2	$2,000.00	$170.00	$4,170.00
4	3	$2,000.00	$354.45	$6,524.45
5	4	$2,000.00	$554.58	$9,079.03
6	5	$2,000.00	$771.72	$11,850.75
7	6	$2,000.00	$1,007.31	$14,858.06
8	7	$2,000.00	$1,262.94	$18,120.99
9	8	$2,000.00	$1,540.28	$21,661.28
10	9	$2,000.00	$1,841.21	$25,502.49
11	10	$2,000.00	$2,167.71	$29,670.20
12	11	$2,000.00	$2,521.97	$34,192.17
13	12	$2,000.00	$2,906.33	$39,098.50
14	13	$2,000.00	$3,323.37	$44,421.87
15	14	$2,000.00	$3,775.86	$50,197.73
16	15	$2,000.00	$4,266.81	$56,464.54
17	16	$2,000.00	$4,799.49	$63,264.02
18	17	$2,000.00	$5,377.44	$70,641.47
19	18	$2,000.00	$6,004.52	$78,645.99
20	19	$2,000.00	$6,684.91	$87,330.90
21	20	$2,000.00	$7,423.13	$96,754.03
22	Totals	$40,000.00	$56,754.03	

Figure 2 Ordinary annuity at 8.5% compounded annually for 20 years

Matched Problem 1

What is the value of an annuity at the end of 10 years if $1,000 is deposited every 6 months into an account earning 8% compounded semiannually? How much of this value is interest?

The table in Figure 2 is called a **balance sheet**. Let's take a closer look at the construction of this table. The first line is a special case because the payment is made at the end of the period and no interest is earned. Each subsequent line of the table is computed as follows:

payment + interest + old balance = new balance

2,000 + 0.085(2,000) + 2,000 = 4,170   *Period 2*

2,000 + 0.085(4,170) + 4,170 = 6,524.45   *Period 3*

And so on. The amounts at the bottom of each column in the balance sheet agree with the results we obtained by using formula (6), as you would expect. Although balance sheets are appropriate for certain situations, we will concentrate on applications of formula (6). There are many important problems that can be solved only by using this formula.

EXPLORE & DISCUSS 1

(A) Discuss the similarities and differences in the graphs of future value *FV* as a function of time *t* for ordinary annuities in which $100 is deposited each month for 8 years and interest is compounded monthly at annual rates of 4%, 8%, and 12%, respectively (Fig. 3).

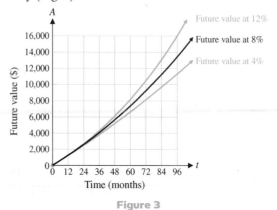

Figure 3

(B) Discuss the connections between the graph of the equation $y = 100t$, where *t* is time in months, and the graphs of part (A).

Sinking Funds

The formula for the future value of an ordinary annuity has another important application. Suppose the parents of a newborn child decide that on each of the child's birthdays up to the 17th year, they will deposit PMT in an account that pays 6% compounded annually. The money is to be used for college expenses. What should the annual deposit (PMT) be in order for the amount in the account to be $80,000 after the 17th deposit?

We are given FV, i, and n in formula (6), and we must find PMT:

$$FV = PMT\frac{(1 + i)^n - 1}{i}$$

$$80,000 = PMT\frac{(1.06)^{17} - 1}{0.06} \qquad \textit{Solve for PMT.}$$

$$PMT = 80,000\frac{0.06}{(1.06)^{17} - 1} \qquad \textit{Use a calculator.}$$

$$= \$2,835.58 \text{ per year}$$

An annuity of 17 annual deposits of $2,835.58 at 6% compounded annually will amount to $80,000 in 17 years.

This is an example of a *sinking fund problem*. In general, any account that is established for accumulating funds to meet future obligations or debts is called a **sinking fund**. If the payments are to be made in the form of an ordinary annuity, then we have only to solve formula (6) for the **sinking fund payment** PMT:

$$PMT = FV\frac{i}{(1 + i)^n - 1} \tag{7}$$

It is important to understand that formula (7), which is convenient to use, is simply a variation of formula (6). You can always find the sinking fund payment by first substituting the appropriate values into formula (6) and then solving for PMT, as we did in the college fund example discussed above. Or you can substitute directly into formula (7), as we do in the next example. Use whichever method is easier for you.

EXAMPLE 2   **Computing the Payment for a Sinking Fund**   A company estimates that it will have to replace a piece of equipment at a cost of $800,000 in 5 years. To have this money available in 5 years, a sinking fund is established by making equal monthly payments into an account paying 6.6% compounded monthly.

(A) How much should each payment be?

(B) How much interest is earned during the last year?

SOLUTION   (A) To find PMT, we can use either formula (6) or (7). We choose formula (7) with $FV = \$800,000$, $i = \frac{0.066}{12} = 0.0055$, and $n = 12 \cdot 5 = 60$:

$$PMT = FV\frac{i}{(1 + i)^n - 1}$$

$$= 800,000\frac{0.0055}{(1.0055)^{60} - 1}$$

$$= \$11,290.42 \text{ per month}$$

(B) To find the interest earned during the fifth year, we first use formula (6) with $PMT = \$11,290.42$, $i = 0.0055$, and $n = 12 \cdot 4 = 48$ to find the amount in the account after 4 years:

$$FV = PMT\frac{(1 + i)^n - 1}{i}$$

$$= 11,290.42\frac{(1.0055)^{48} - 1}{0.0055}$$

$$= \$618,277.04 \qquad \textit{Amount after 4 years}$$

During the 5th year, the amount in the account grew from \$618,277.04 to \$800,000. A portion of this growth was due to the 12 monthly payments of \$11,290.42. The remainder of the growth was interest. Thus,

$$800,000 - 618,277.04 = 181,722.96 \quad \text{Growth in the 5th year}$$
$$12 \cdot 11,290.42 = 135,485.04 \quad \text{Payments during the 5th year}$$
$$181,722.96 - 135,485.04 = \$46,237.92 \quad \text{Interest during the 5th year}$$

Matched Problem 2   A bond issue is approved for building a marina in a city. The city is required to make regular payments every 3 months into a sinking fund paying 5.4% compounded quarterly. At the end of 10 years, the bond obligation will be retired with a cost of \$5,000,000.

(A) What should each payment be?

(B) How much interest is earned during the 10th year?

EXAMPLE 3   Growth in an IRA Jane deposits \$2,000 annually into a Roth IRA that earns 6.85% compounded annually. (The interest earned by a Roth IRA is tax free.) Due to a change in employment, these deposits stop after 10 years, but the account continues to earn interest until Jane retires 25 years after the last deposit was made. How much is in the account when Jane retires?

SOLUTION   First, we use the future value formula with $PMT = \$2,000$, $i = 0.0685$, and $n = 10$ to find the amount in the account after 10 years:

$$FV = PMT \frac{(1 + i)^n - 1}{i}$$

$$= 2,000 \frac{(1.0685)^{10} - 1}{0.0685}$$

$$= \$27,437.89$$

Now we use the compound interest formula from Section 3-2 with $P = \$27,437.89$, $i = 0.0685$, and $n = 25$ to find the amount in the account when Jane retires:

$$A = P(1 + i)^n$$

$$= 27,437.89(1.0685)^{25}$$

$$= \$143,785.10$$

Matched Problem 3   Refer to Example 3. Mary starts a Roth IRA earning the same rate of interest at the time Jane stops making payments into her IRA. How much must Mary deposit each year for the next 25 years in order to have the same amount at retirement as Jane?

EXPLORE & DISCUSS 2   Refer to Example 3 and Matched Problem 3. What was the total amount Jane deposited in order to have \$143,785.10 at retirement? What was the total amount Mary deposited in order to have the same amount at retirement? Do you think it is advisable to start saving for retirement as early as possible?

Approximating Interest Rates

Algebra can be used to solve the future value formula (6) for *PMT* or *n* but not for *i*. However, graphical techniques or equation solvers can be used to approximate *i* to as many decimal places as desired.

EXAMPLE 4   **Approximating an Interest Rate**   A person makes monthly deposits of $100 into an ordinary annuity. After 30 years, the annuity is worth $160,000. What annual rate compounded monthly has this annuity earned during this 30-year period? Express the answer as a percentage, correct to two decimal places.

SOLUTION   Substituting $FV = \$160,000$, $PMT = \$100$, and $n = 30(12) = 360$ in (6) produces the following equation:

$$160,000 = 100\frac{(1 + i)^{360} - 1}{i}$$

We can approximate the solution to this equation by using graphical techniques (Figs. 4A, 4B) or an equation solver (Fig. 4C). From Figure 4B or 4C, we see that $i = 0.006\,956\,7$ and $12(i) = 0.083\,480\,4$. So the annual rate (to two decimal places) is $r = 8.35\%$.

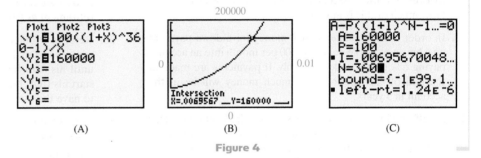

(A)   (B)   (C)

Figure 4

Matched Problem 4   A person makes annual deposits of $1,000 into an ordinary annuity. After 20 years, the annuity is worth $55,000. What annual compound rate has this annuity earned during this 20-year period? Express the answer as a percentage, correct to two decimal places.

Exercises 3-3

A

In Problems 1–8, find i (the rate per period) and n (the number of periods) for each annuity.

1. Quarterly deposits of $500 are made for 20 years into an annuity that pays 8% compounded quarterly.

2. Monthly deposits of $350 are made for 6 years into an annuity that pays 6% compounded monthly.

3. Semiannual deposits of $900 are made for 12 years into an annuity that pays 7.5% compounded semiannually.

4. Annual deposits of $2,500 are made for 15 years into an annuity that pays 6.25% compounded annually.

5. Monthly deposits of $235 are made for 4 years into an annuity that pays 9% compounded monthly.

6. Semiannual deposits of $1,900 are made for 7 years into an annuity that pays 8.5% compounded semiannually.

7. Annual deposits of $3,100 are made for 12 years into an annuity that pays 5.95% compounded annually.

8. Quarterly deposits of $1,200 are made for 18 years into an annuity that pays 7.6% compounded quarterly.

In Problems 9–16, use the future value formula (6) to find each of the indicated values.

9. $n = 20; i = 0.03; PMT = \$500; FV = ?$

10. $n = 25; i = 0.04; PMT = \$100; FV = ?$

11. $FV = \$5,000; n = 15; i = 0.01; PMT = ?$

12. $FV = \$2,500; n = 10; i = 0.08; PMT = ?$

B

13. $FV = \$4,000; i = 0.02; PMT = 200; n = ?$

14. $FV = \$8,000; i = 0.04; PMT = 500; n = ?$

15. $FV = \$7,600; PMT = \$500; n = 10; i = ?$
    (Round answer to two decimal places.)

16. $FV = \$4,100; PMT = \$100; n = 20; i = ?$
    (Round answer to two decimal places.)

C

17. Explain what is meant by an ordinary annuity.

18. Explain why no interest is credited to an ordinary annuity at the end of the first period.

19. Solve the future value formula (6) for n.

20. Solve the future value formula (6) for i if $n = 2$.

Applications

21. Guaranty Income Life offered an annuity that pays 6.65% compounded monthly. If $500 is deposited into this annuity every month, how much is in the account after 10 years? How much of this is interest?

22. USG Annuity and Life offered an annuity that pays 7.25% compounded monthly. If $1,000 is deposited into this annuity every month, how much is in the account after 15 years? How much of this is interest?

23. In order to accumulate enough money for a down payment on a house, a couple deposits $300 per month into an account paying 6% compounded monthly. If payments are made at the end of each period, how much money will be in the account in 5 years?

24. A self-employed person has a Keogh retirement plan. (This type of plan is free of taxes until money is withdrawn.) If deposits of $7,500 are made each year into an account paying 8% compounded annually, how much will be in the account after 20 years?

25. Sun America recently offered an annuity that pays 6.35% compounded monthly. What equal monthly deposit should be made into this annuity in order to have $200,000 in 15 years?

26. Recently, The Hartford offered an annuity that pays 5.5% compounded monthly. What equal monthly deposit should be made into this annuity in order to have $100,000 in 10 years?

27. A company estimates that it will need $100,000 in 8 years to replace a computer. If it establishes a sinking fund by making fixed monthly payments into an account paying 7.5% compounded monthly, how much should each payment be?

28. Parents have set up a sinking fund in order to have $120,000 in 15 years for their children's college education. How much should be paid semiannually into an account paying 6.8% compounded semiannually?

29. If $1,000 is deposited at the end of each year for 5 years into an ordinary annuity earning 8.32% compounded annually, construct a balance sheet showing the interest earned during each year and the balance at the end of each year.

30. If $2,000 is deposited at the end of each quarter for 2 years into an ordinary annuity earning 7.9% compounded quarterly, construct a balance sheet showing the interest earned during each quarter and the balance at the end of each quarter.

31. Beginning in January, a person plans to deposit $100 at the end of each month into an account earning 6% compounded monthly. Each year taxes must be paid on the interest earned during that year. Find the interest earned during each year for the first 3 years.

32. If $500 is deposited each quarter into an account paying 8% compounded quarterly for 3 years, find the interest earned during each of the 3 years.

33. Bob makes his first $1,000 deposit into an IRA earning 6.4% compounded annually on his 24th birthday and his last $1,000 deposit on his 35th birthday (12 equal deposits in all). With no additional deposits, the money in the IRA continues to earn 6.4% interest compounded annually until Bob retires on his 65th birthday. How much is in the IRA when Bob retires?

34. Refer to Problem 33. John procrastinates and does not make his first $1,000 deposit into an IRA until he is 36, but then he continues to deposit $1,000 each year until he is 65 (30 deposits in all). If John's IRA also earns 6.4% compounded annually, how much is in his IRA when he makes his last deposit on his 65th birthday?

35. Refer to Problems 33 and 34. How much would John have to deposit each year in order to have the same amount at retirement as Bob has?

36. Refer to Problems 33 and 34. Suppose that Bob decides to continue to make $1,000 deposits into his IRA every year until his 65th birthday. If John still waits until he is 36 to start his IRA, how much must he deposit each year in order to have the same amount at age 65 as Bob has?

37. Compubank, an online banking service, offered a money market account with an APY of 4.86%.

(A) If interest is compounded monthly, what is the equivalent annual nominal rate?

(B) If you wish to have $10,000 in this account after 4 years, what equal deposit should you make each month?

38. American Express's online banking division offered a money market account with an APY of 5.65%.

(A) If interest is compounded monthly, what is the equivalent annual nominal rate?

(B) If a company wishes to have $1,000,000 in this account after 8 years, what equal deposit should be made each month?

39. You can afford monthly deposits of $200 into an account that pays 5.7% compounded monthly. How long will it be until you have $7,000? (Round to the next-higher month if not exact.)

40. A company establishes a sinking fund for upgrading office equipment with monthly payments of $2,000 into an account paying 6.6% compounded monthly. How long will it be before the account has $100,000? (Round up to the next-higher month if not exact.)

In Problems 41–44, use graphical approximation techniques or an equation solver to approximate the desired interest rate. Express each answer as a percentage, correct to two decimal places.

41. A person makes annual payments of $1,000 into an ordinary annuity. At the end of 5 years, the amount in the annuity is $5,840. What annual nominal compounding rate has this annuity earned?

42. A person invests $2,000 annually in an IRA. At the end of 6 years, the amount in the fund is $14,000. What annual nominal compounding rate has this fund earned?

43. At the end of each month, an employee deposits $50 into a Christmas club fund. At the end of the year, the fund contains $620. What annual nominal rate compounded monthly has this fund earned?

44. At the end of each month, an employee deposits $80 into a credit union account. At the end of 2 years, the account contains $2,100. What annual nominal rate compounded monthly has this account earned?

In Problems 45 and 46, use graphical approximation techniques to answer the questions.

45. When would an ordinary annuity consisting of quarterly payments of $500 at 6% compounded quarterly be worth more than a principal of $5,000 invested at 4% simple interest?

46. When would an ordinary annuity consisting of monthly payments of $200 at 5% compounded monthly be worth more than a principal of $10,000 invested at 7.5% compounded monthly?

Answers to Matched Problems

1. Value: $29,778.08; interest: $9,778.08

2. (A) $95,094.67   (B) $248,628.89

3. $2,322.73   **4.** 9.64%

3-4 Present Value of an Annuity; Amortization

- Present Value of an Annuity
- Amortization
- Amortization Schedules
- General Problem-Solving Strategy

Present Value of an Annuity

How much should you deposit in an account paying 6% compounded semiannually in order to be able to withdraw $1,000 every 6 months for the next 3 years? (After the last payment is made, no money is to be left in the account.)

Actually, we are interested in finding the present value of each $1,000 that is paid out during the 3 years. We can do this by solving for P in the compound interest formula:

$$A = P(1 + i)^n$$

$$P = \frac{A}{(1 + i)^n} = A(1 + i)^{-n}$$

The rate per period is $i = \frac{0.06}{2} = 0.03$. The present value P of the first payment is $1,000(1.03)^{-1}$, the present value of the second payment is $1,000(1.03)^{-2}$, and so on. Figure 1 shows this in terms of a time line.

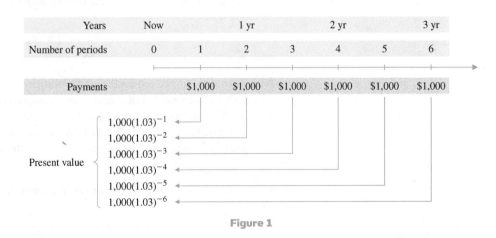

Figure 1

We could evaluate each of the present values in Figure 1 using a calculator and add the results to find the total present values of all the payments (which will be the amount needed now to buy the annuity). Since this is a tedious process, particularly when the number of payments is large, we will use the same device we used in the preceding section to produce a formula that will accomplish the same result in a couple of steps. We start by writing the sum of the present values in the form

$$P = 1,000(1.03)^{-1} + 1,000(1.03)^{-2} + \cdots + 1,000(1.03)^{-6} \qquad (1)$$

Multiplying both sides of equation (1) by 1.03, we obtain

$$1.03P = 1,000 + 1,000(1.03)^{-1} + \cdots + 1,000(1.03)^{-5} \qquad (2)$$

Now subtract equation (1) from equation (2):

$$1.03P - P = 1,000 - 1,000(1.03)^{-6} \qquad \text{Notice how many terms drop out.}$$

$$0.03P = 1,000[1 - (1 + 0.03)^{-6}]$$

$$P = 1,000\frac{1 - (1 + 0.03)^{-6}}{0.03} \qquad \begin{array}{l}\text{We write } P \text{ in this form to}\\ \text{observe a general pattern.}\end{array} \qquad (3)$$

In general, if R is the periodic payment, i the rate per period, and n the number of periods, then the present value of all payments is given by

$$P = R(1 + i)^{-1} + R(1 + i)^{-2} + \cdots + R(1 + i)^{-n} \qquad \begin{array}{l}\text{Note how this}\\ \text{compares to (1).}\end{array}$$

Proceeding as in the above example, we obtain the general formula for the present value of an ordinary annuity:

$$P = R\frac{1 - (1 + i)^{-n}}{i} \qquad \text{Note how this compares to (3).} \qquad (4)$$

Returning to the preceding example, we use a calculator to complete the problem:

$$P = 1,000\frac{1 - (1.03)^{-6}}{0.03}$$

$$= \$5,417.19$$

CONCEPTUAL INSIGHT

Formulas (3) and (4) can also be established by using the sum formula for a finite geometric series (see Section B-2):

$$a + ar + ar^2 + \cdots + ar^{n-1} = a\frac{r^n - 1}{r - 1}$$

The fractional factor of formula (4) may be denoted by the symbol $a_{\overline{n}i}$, read as "a angle n at i":

$$a_{\overline{n}i} = \frac{1 - (1 + i)^{-n}}{i}$$

An alternative approach to the computation of P is to use a table that gives values of $a_{\overline{n}i}$ for various values of n and i. The computation of P is then completed by multiplying R by $a_{\overline{n}i}$ as indicated by formula (4).

It is common to use PV (present value) for P and PMT (payment) for R in formula (4). Making these changes, we have the following:

THEOREM 1   Present Value of an Ordinary Annuity

$$PV = PMT\frac{1 - (1 + i)^{-n}}{i} = PMT a_{\overline{n}i} \qquad (5)$$

where PV = present value of all payments

PMT = periodic payment

i = rate per period

n = number of periods

Note: Payments are made at the end of each period.

EXAMPLE 1   **Present Value of an Annuity** What is the present value of an annuity that pays $200 per month for 5 years if money is worth 6% compounded monthly?

SOLUTION   To solve this problem, use formula (5) with $PMT = \$200, i = \frac{0.06}{12} = 0.005$, and $n = 12(5) = 60$:

$$PV = PMT\frac{1 - (1 + i)^{-n}}{i}$$

$$= 200\frac{1 - (1.005)^{-60}}{0.005} \quad \textit{Use a calculator.}$$

$$= \$10,345.11$$

Matched Problem 1   How much should you deposit in an account paying 8% compounded quarterly in order to receive quarterly payments of $1,000 for the next 4 years?

EXAMPLE 2   **Retirement Planning** Lincoln Benefit Life offered an ordinary annuity that earned 6.5% compounded annually. A person plans to make equal annual deposits into this account for 25 years and then make 20 equal annual withdrawals of $25,000, reducing the balance in the account to zero. How much must be deposited annually to accumulate sufficient funds to provide for these payments? How much total interest is earned during this entire 45-year process?

SOLUTION   This problem involves both future and present values. Figure 2 illustrates the flow of money into and out of the annuity.

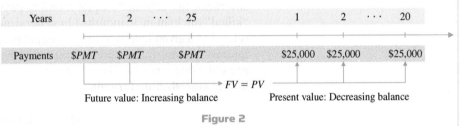

Figure 2

Since we are given the required withdrawals, we begin by finding the present value necessary to provide for these withdrawals. Using formula (5) with $PMT = \$25,000, i = 0.065$, and $n = 20$, we have

$$PV = PMT\frac{1 - (1 + i)^{-n}}{i}$$

$$= 25,000\frac{1 - (1.065)^{-20}}{0.065} \quad \textit{Use a calculator.}$$

$$= \$275,462.68$$

Now we find the deposits that will produce a future value of $275,462.68 in 25 years. Using formula (7) from Section 3-3 with $FV = \$275,462.68, i = 0.065$, and $n = 25$, we have

$$PMT = FV\frac{i}{(1 + i)^n - 1}$$

$$= 275,462.68\frac{0.065}{(1.065)^{25} - 1} \quad \textit{Use a calculator.}$$

$$= \$4,677.76$$

Thus, depositing $4,677.76 annually for 25 years will provide for 20 annual withdrawals of $25,000. The interest earned during the entire 45-year process is

$$\text{interest} = (\text{total withdrawals}) - (\text{total deposits})$$

$$= 20(25,000) - 25(\$4,677.76)$$

$$= \$383,056$$

Matched Problem 2   Refer to Example 2. If $2,000 is deposited annually for the first 25 years, how much can be withdrawn annually for the next 20 years?

Amortization

The present value formula for an ordinary annuity, formula (5), has another important use. Suppose that you borrow $5,000 from a bank to buy a car and agree to repay the loan in 36 equal monthly payments, including all interest due. If the bank charges 1% per month on the unpaid balance (12% per year compounded monthly), how much should each payment be to retire the total debt, including interest in 36 months?

Actually, the bank has bought an annuity from you. The question is: If the bank pays you $5,000 (present value) for an annuity paying them PMT per month for 36 months at 12% interest compounded monthly, what are the monthly payments (PMT)? (Note that the value of the annuity at the end of 36 months is zero.) To find PMT, we have only to use formula (5) with $PV = \$5,000, i = 0.01$, and $n = 36$:

$$PV = PMT \frac{1 - (1 + i)^{-n}}{i}$$

$$5,000 = PMT \frac{1 - (1.01)^{-36}}{0.01} \qquad \textit{Solve for PMT and use a calculator.}$$

$$PMT = \$166.07 \text{ per month}$$

At $166.07 per month, the car will be yours after 36 months. That is, you have *amortized* the debt in 36 equal monthly payments. (*Mort* means "death"; you have "killed" the loan in 36 months.) In general, **amortizing a debt** means that the debt is retired in a given length of time by equal periodic payments that include compound interest. We are interested in computing the equal periodic payments. Solving the present value formula (5) for PMT in terms of the other variables, we obtain the following **amortization formula**:

$$PMT = PV \frac{i}{1 - (1 + i)^{-n}} \qquad (6)$$

Formula (6) is simply a variation of formula (5), and either formula can be used to find the periodic payment PMT.

EXAMPLE 3   **Monthly Payment and Total Interest on an Amortized Debt**   Assume that you buy a television set for $800 and agree to pay for it in 18 equal monthly payments at $1\frac{1}{2}\%$ interest per month on the unpaid balance.

(A) How much are your payments?

(B) How much interest will you pay?

SOLUTION   (A) Use formula (6) with $PV = \$800, i = 0.015$, and $n = 18$:

$$PMT = PV \frac{i}{1 - (1 + i)^{-n}}$$

$$= 800 \frac{0.015}{1 - (1.015)^{-18}} \qquad \textit{Use a calculator.}$$

$$= \$51.04 \text{ per month}$$

(B) Total interest paid = (amount of all payments) − (initial loan)

$$= 18(\$51.04) - \$800$$

$$= \$118.72$$

Matched Problem 3   If you sell your car to someone for $2,400 and agree to finance it at 1% per month on the unpaid balance, how much should you receive each month to amortize the loan in 24 months? How much interest will you receive?

To purchase a home, a family plans to sign a mortgage of $70,000 at 8% on the unpaid balance. Discuss the advantages and disadvantages of a 20-year mortgage as opposed to a 30-year mortgage. Include a comparison of monthly payments and total interest paid.

Amortization Schedules

What happens if you are amortizing a debt with equal periodic payments and later decide to pay off the remainder of the debt in one lump-sum payment? This occurs each time a home with an outstanding mortgage is sold. In order to understand what happens in this situation, we must take a closer look at the amortization process. We begin with an example that allows us to examine the effect each payment has on the debt.

EXAMPLE 4   Constructing an Amortization Schedule   If you borrow $500 that you agree to repay in six equal monthly payments at 1% interest per month on the unpaid balance, how much of each monthly payment is used for interest and how much is used to reduce the unpaid balance?

SOLUTION   First, we compute the required monthly payment using formula (5) or (6). We choose formula (6) with $PV = \$500, i = 0.01$, and $n = 6$:

$$PMT = PV \frac{i}{1 - (1 + i)^{-n}}$$

$$= 500 \frac{0.01}{1 - (1.01)^{-6}} \qquad \text{Use a calculator.}$$

$$= \$86.27 \text{ per month}$$

At the end of the first month, the interest due is

$$\$500(0.01) = \$5.00$$

The amortization payment is divided into two parts, payment of the interest due and reduction of the unpaid balance (repayment of principal):

Monthly payment		Interest due		Unpaid balance: reduction
$86.27	=	$5.00	+	$81.27

The unpaid balance for the next month is

Previous unpaid balance		Unpaid balance reduction		New unpaid balance
$500.00	−	$81.27	=	$418.73

At the end of the second month, the interest due on the unpaid balance of $418.73 is

$$\$418.73(0.01) = \$4.19$$

Thus, at the end of the second month, the monthly payment of $86.27 covers interest and unpaid balance reduction as follows:

$$\$86.27 = \$4.19 + \$82.08$$

and the unpaid balance for the third month is

$$\$418.73 - \$82.08 = \$336.65$$

This process continues until all payments have been made and the unpaid balance is reduced to zero. The calculations for each month are listed in Table 1, often referred to as an **amortization schedule.**

In Table 1, notice that the last payment had to be increased by $0.03 in order to reduce the unpaid balance to zero. This small discrepancy is due to rounding the monthly payment and the entries in the interest column to two decimal places.

Table 1 Amortization Schedule

Payment Number	Payment	Interest	Unpaid Balance Reduction	Unpaid Balance
0				$500.00
1	$86.27	$5.00	$81.27	418.73
2	86.27	4.19	82.08	336.65
3	86.27	3.37	82.90	253.75
4	86.27	2.54	83.73	170.02
5	86.27	1.70	84.57	85.45
6	86.30	0.85	85.45	0.00
Totals	$517.65	$17.65	$500.00	

Matched Problem 4 Construct the amortization schedule for a $1,000 debt that is to be amortized in six equal monthly payments at 1.25% interest per month on the unpaid balance.

EXAMPLE 5 **Equity in a Home** A family purchased a home 10 years ago for $80,000. The home was financed by paying 20% down and signing a 30-year mortgage at 9% on the unpaid balance. The net market value of the house (amount received after subtracting all costs involved in selling the house) is now $120,000, and the family wishes to sell the house. How much equity (to the nearest dollar) does the family have in the house now after making 120 monthly payments?

[**Equity** = (current net market value) − (unpaid loan balance).]*

SOLUTION How can we find the unpaid loan balance after 10 years or 120 monthly payments? One way to proceed would be to construct an amortization schedule, but this would require a table with 120 lines. Fortunately, there is an easier way. The unpaid balance after 120 payments is the amount of the loan that can be paid off with the remaining 240 monthly payments (20 remaining years on the loan). Since the lending institution views a loan as an annuity that they bought from the family, **the unpaid balance of a loan with n remaining payments is the present value of that annuity and can be computed by using formula (5)**. Since formula (5) requires knowledge of the monthly payment, we compute PMT first using formula (6).

Step 1 Find the monthly payment:

$$PMT = PV \frac{i}{1 - (1 + i)^{-n}}$$

$PV = (0.80)(\$80,000) = \$64,000$

$i = \frac{0.09}{12} = 0.0075$

$$= 64,000 \frac{0.0075}{1 - (1.0075)^{-360}}$$

$n = 12(30) = 360$

$$= \$514.96 \text{ per month}$$

Use a calculator.

Step 2 Find the present value of a $514.96 per month, 20-year annuity:

$$PV = PMT \frac{1 - (1 + i)^{-n}}{i}$$

$PMT = \$514.96$

$n = 12(20) = 240$

$$= 514.96 \frac{1 - (1.0075)^{-240}}{0.0075}$$

$i = \frac{0.09}{12} = 0.0075$

Use a calculator.

$$= \$57,235$$

Unpaid loan balance

---

*If a family wants to sell a house and buy another, more expensive house, then the price of a new house that the family can afford to buy will often depend on the family's *equity* in the first house, where equity is defined by the equation given here. In refinancing a house or taking out an "equity loan," the new mortgage (or second mortgage) often will be based on the equity in the house.

Step 3 Find the equity:

equity = (current net market value) − (unpaid loan balance)

= $120,000 − $57,235

= $62,765

If the family sells the house for $120,000 net, the family will have $62,765 after paying off the unpaid loan balance of $57,235.

Matched Problem 5 A couple purchased a home 20 years ago for $65,000. The home was financed by paying 20% down and signing a 30-year mortgage at 8% on the unpaid balance. The net market value of the house is now $130,000, and the couple wishes to sell the house. How much equity (to the nearest dollar) does the couple have in the house now after making 240 monthly payments?

The unpaid loan balance in Example 5 may seem a surprisingly large amount to owe after having made payments for 10 years, but long-term amortizations start out with very small reductions in the unpaid balance. For example, the interest due at the end of the very first period of the loan in Example 5 was

$$\$64,000(0.0075) = \$480.00$$

The first monthly payment was divided as follows:

		Unpaid
Monthly	Interest	balance
payment	due	reduction
$514.96 −	$480.00 =	$34.96

Only $34.96 was applied to the unpaid balance.

EXPLORE & DISCUSS 2

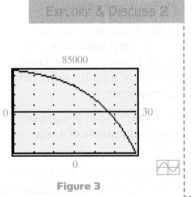

Figure 3

(A) A family has an $85,000, 30-year mortgage at 9.6% compounded monthly. Show that the monthly payments are $720.94.

(B) Explain why the equation

$$y = 720.94 \frac{1 - (1.008)^{-12(30-x)}}{0.008}$$

gives the unpaid balance of the loan after x years.

(C) Find the unpaid balance after 5 years, after 10 years, and after 15 years.

(D) When is the unpaid balance exactly half of the original $85,000?

(E) Solve part (D) using graphical approximation techniques on a graphing calculator (see Fig. 3).

EXAMPLE 6 **Automobile Financing** You have negotiated a price of $25,200 for a new Bison pickup truck. Now you must choose between 0% financing for 48 months or a $3,000 rebate. If you choose the rebate, you can obtain a credit union loan for the balance at 4.5% compounded monthly for 48 months. Which option should you choose?

SOLUTION   If you choose 0% financing, your monthly payment will be

$$PMT_1 = \frac{25{,}200}{48} = \$525$$

If you choose the \$3,000 rebate, and borrow \$22,200 at 4.5% compounded monthly for 48 months, the monthly payment is

$$PMT_2 = PV\frac{i}{1 - (1 + i)^{-n}} \qquad PV = \$22{,}200$$

$$= 22{,}200\frac{0.00375}{1 - 1.00375^{-48}} \qquad i = \frac{.045}{12} = 0.00375$$

$$= \$506.24 \qquad\qquad n = 48$$

You should choose the \$3,000 rebate. You will save $525 - 506.24 = \$18.76$ monthly or $48(18.76) = \$900.48$ over the life of the loan.

Matched Problem 6   Which option should you choose if your credit union raises its loan rate to 7.5% compounded monthly and all other data remain the same?

General Problem-Solving Strategy

After working the problems in Exercise 3-4, it is important to work the problems in the Review Exercise. This will give you valuable experience in distinguishing among the various types of problems we have considered in this chapter. It is impossible to completely categorize all the problems you will encounter, but you may find the following guidelines helpful in determining which of the four basic formulas is involved in a particular problem. Be aware that some problems may involve more than one of these formulas and others may not involve any of them.

SUMMARY   Strategy for Solving Mathematics of Finance Problems

Step 1   Determine whether the problem involves a single payment or a sequence of equal periodic payments. Simple and compound interest problems involve a single present value and a single future value. Ordinary annuities may be concerned with a present value or a future value but always involve a sequence of equal periodic payments.

Step 2   If a single payment is involved, determine whether simple or compound interest is used. Often simple interest is used for durations of a year or less and compound interest for longer periods.

Step 3   If a sequence of periodic payments is involved, determine whether the payments are being made into an account that is increasing in value—a future value problem—or the payments are being made out of an account that is decreasing in value—a present value problem. Remember that amortization problems always involve the present value of an ordinary annuity.

Steps 1–3 will help you choose the correct formula for a problem, as indicated in Figure 4. Then you must determine the values of the quantities in the formula that are given in the problem and those that must be computed, and solve the problem.

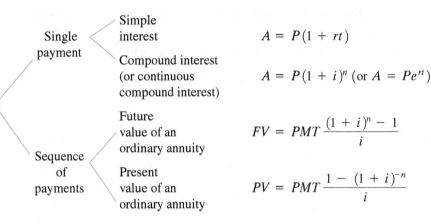

Figure 4 Selecting the correct formula for a problem

Exercises 3-4

A

In Problems 1–8, find i (the rate per period) and n (the number of periods) for each loan at the given annual rate.

1. Monthly payments of $245.65 are made for 4 years to repay a loan at 7.2% compounded monthly.

2. Semiannual payments of $3,200 are made for 12 years to repay a loan at 9.9% compounded semiannually.

3. Quarterly payments of $975 are made for 10 years to repay a loan at 9.9% compounded quarterly.

4. Annual payments of $1,045 are made for 5 years to repay a loan at 4.75% compounded annually.

5. Semiannual payments of $4,500 are made for 16 years to repay a loan at 5.05% compounded semiannually.

6. Quarterly payments of $610 are made for 6 years to repay loan at 8.24% compounded quarterly.

7. Annual payments of $5,195 are made for 9 years to repay a loan at 5.48% compounded annually.

8. Monthly payments of $433 are made for 3 years to repay a loan at 10.8% compounded monthly.

In Problems 9–20, use formula (5) or (6) to solve each problem.

9. $n = 30; i = 0.04; PMT = \$200; PV = ?$

10. $n = 40; i = 0.01; PMT = \$400; PV = ?$

B

11. $PV = \$40,000; n = 96; i = 0.0075; PMT = ?$

12. $PV = \$14,000; n = 72; i = 0.005; PMT = ?$

C

13. $PV = \$5,000; i = 0.01; PMT = \$200; n = ?$

14. $PV = \$20,000; i = 0.0175; PMT = \$500; n = ?$

15. $PV = \$9,000; PMT = \$600; n = 20; i = ?$
    (Round answer to three decimal places.)

16. $PV = \$12,000; PMT = \$400; n = 40; i = ?$
    (Round answer to three decimal places.)

17. Explain what is meant by the present value of an ordinary annuity.

18. Solve the present value formula (5) for n.

19. Explain how an ordinary annuity is involved when you take out an auto loan from a bank.

20. Explain why the last payment in an amortization schedule might differ from the other payments.

Applications

21. American General offers a 10-year ordinary annuity with a guaranteed rate of 6.65% compounded annually. How much should you pay for one of these annuities if you want to receive payments of $5,000 annually over the 10-year period?

22. American General offers a 7-year ordinary annuity with a guaranteed rate of 6.35% compounded annually. How much should you pay for one of these annuities if you want to receive payments of $10,000 annually over the 7-year period?

23. E-Loan, an online lending service, recently offered 36-month auto loans at 7.56% compounded monthly to applicants with good credit ratings. If you have a good credit rating and can afford monthly payments of $350, how much can you borrow from E-Loan? What is the total interest you will pay for this loan?

24. E-Loan recently offered 36-month auto loans at 9.84% compounded monthly to applicants with fair credit ratings. If you have a fair credit rating and can afford monthly payments of $350, how much can you borrow from E-Loan? What is the total interest you will pay for this loan?

25. If you buy a computer directly from the manufacturer for $2,500 and agree to repay it in 48 equal installments at 1.25% interest per month on the unpaid balance, how much

are your monthly payments? How much total interest will be paid?

26. If you buy a computer directly from the manufacturer for $3,500 and agree to repay it in 60 equal installments at 1.75% interest per month on the unpaid balance, how much are your monthly payments? How much total interest will be paid?

Problems 27 and 28 refer to the following ads.

27. Use the information given in the Bison sedan ad to determine if this is really 0% financing. If not, explain why and determine what rate a consumer would be charged for financing one of these sedans.

* Bison sedan, 0% down, 0% for 72 months   * Bison wagon, 0% down, 0% for 72 months

28. Use the information given in the Bison wagon ad to determine if this is really 0% financing. If not, explain why and determine what rate a consumer would be charged for financing one of these wagons.

29. You want to purchase an automobile for $27,300. The dealer offers you 0% financing for 60 months or a $5,000 rebate. You can obtain 6.3% financing for 60 months at the local bank. Which option should you choose? Explain.

30. You want to purchase an automobile for $28,500. The dealer offers you 0% financing for 60 months or a $6,000 rebate. You can obtain 6.2% financing for 60 months at the local bank. Which option should you choose? Explain.

31. A sailboat costs $35,000. You pay 20% down and amortize the rest with equal monthly payments over a 12-year period. If you must pay 8.75% compounded monthly, what is your monthly payment? How much interest will you pay?

32. A recreational vehicle costs $80,000. You pay 10% down and amortize the rest with equal monthly payments over a 7-year period. If you pay 9.25% compounded monthly, what is your monthly payment? How much interest will you pay?

33. Construct the amortization schedule for a $5,000 debt that is to be amortized in eight equal quarterly payments at 2.8% interest per quarter on the unpaid balance.

34. Construct the amortization schedule for a $10,000 debt that is to be amortized in six equal quarterly payments at 2.6% interest per quarter on the unpaid balance.

35. A woman borrows $6,000 at 9% compounded monthly, which is to be amortized over 3 years in equal monthly payments. For tax purposes, she needs to know the amount of interest paid during each year of the loan. Find the interest paid during the first year, the second year, and the third year of the loan. [*Hint:* Find the unpaid balance after 12 payments and after 24 payments.]

36. A man establishes an annuity for retirement by depositing $50,000 into an account that pays 7.2% compounded monthly. Equal monthly withdrawals will be made each month for 5 years, at which time the account will have a zero balance. Each year taxes must be paid on the interest earned by the account during that year. How much interest was earned during the first year? [*Hint:* The amount in the account at the end of the first year is the present value of a 4-year annuity.]

37. Some friends tell you that they paid $25,000 down on a new house and are to pay $525 per month for 30 years. If interest is 7.8% compounded monthly, what was the selling price of the house? How much interest will they pay in 30 years?

38. A family is thinking about buying a new house costing $120,000. The family must pay 20% down, and the rest is to be amortized over 30 years in equal monthly payments. If money costs 7.5% compounded monthly, what will the monthly payment be? How much total interest will be paid over 30 years?

39. A student receives a federally backed student loan of $6,000 at 3.5% interest compounded monthly. After finishing college in 2 years, the student must amortize the loan in the next 4 years by making equal monthly payments. What will the payments be and what total interest will the student pay? [*Hint:* This is a two-part problem. First, find the amount of the debt at the end of the first 2 years; then amortize this amount over the next 4 years.]

40. A person establishes a sinking fund for retirement by contributing $7,500 per year at the end of each year for 20 years. For the next 20 years, equal yearly payments are withdrawn, at the end of which time the account will have a zero balance. If money is worth 9% compounded annually, what yearly payments will the person receive for the last 20 years?

41. A family has a $150,000, 30-year mortgage at 6.1% compounded monthly. Find the monthly payment. Also find the unpaid balance after

   (A) 10 years
   (B) 20 years
   (C) 25 years

42. A family has a $210,000, 20-year mortgage at 6.75% compounded monthly. Find the monthly payment. Also find the unpaid balance after

   (A) 5 years
   (B) 10 years
   (C) 15 years

43. A family has a $129,000, 20-year mortgage at 7.2% compounded monthly.

   (A) Find the monthly payment and the total interest paid.
   (B) Suppose the family decides to add an extra $102.41 to its mortgage payment each month starting with the very first payment. How long will it take the family to pay off the mortgage? How much interest will be saved?

44. At the time they retire, a couple has $200,000 in an account that pays 8.4% compounded monthly.

   (A) If the couple decides to withdraw equal monthly payments for 10 years, at the end of which time the account will have a zero balance, how much should the couple withdraw each month?

(B) If the couple decides to withdraw $3,000 a month until the balance in the account is zero, how many withdrawals can the couple make?

45. An ordinary annuity that earns 7.5% compounded monthly has a current balance of $500,000. The owner of the account is about to retire and has to decide how much to withdraw from the account each month. Find the number of withdrawals under each of the following options:

(A) $5,000 monthly

(B) $4,000 monthly

(C) $3,000 monthly

46. Refer to Problem 45. If the account owner decides to withdraw $3,000 monthly, how much is in the account after 10 years? After 20 years? After 30 years?

47. An ordinary annuity pays 7.44% compounded monthly.

(A) A person deposits $100 monthly for 30 years and then makes equal monthly withdrawals for the next 15 years, reducing the balance to zero. What are the monthly withdrawals? How much interest is earned during the entire 45-year process?

(B) If the person wants to make withdrawals of $2,000 per month for the last 15 years, how much must be deposited monthly for the first 30 years?

48. An ordinary annuity pays 6.48% compounded monthly.

(A) A person wants to make equal monthly deposits into the account for 15 years in order to then make equal monthly withdrawals of $1,500 for the next 20 years, reducing the balance to zero. How much should be deposited each month for the first 15 years? What is the total interest earned during this 35-year process?

(B) If the person makes monthly deposits of $1,000 for the first 15 years, how much can be withdrawn monthly for the next 20 years?

49. A couple wishes to borrow money using the equity in its home for collateral. A loan company will loan the couple up to 70% of their equity. The couple purchased the home 12 years ago for $179,000. The home was financed by paying 20% down and signing a 30-year mortgage at 8.4% on the unpaid balance. Equal monthly payments were made to amortize the loan over the 30-year period. The net market value of the house is now $215,000. After making the 144th payment, the couple applied to the loan company for the maximum loan. How much (to the nearest dollar) will the couple receive?

50. A person purchased a house 10 years ago for $160,000. The house was financed by paying 20% down and signing a 30-year mortgage at 7.75% on the unpaid balance. Equal monthly payments were made to amortize the loan over a 30-year period. The owner now (after the 120th payment) wishes to refinance the house due to a need for additional cash. If the loan company agrees to a new 30-year mortgage of 80% of the new appraised value of the house, which is $225,000, how much cash (to the nearest dollar) will the owner receive after repaying the balance of the original mortgage?

51. A person purchased a $145,000 home 10 years ago by paying 20% down and signing a 30-year mortgage at 7.9% compounded monthly. Interest rates have dropped and the owner wants to refinance the unpaid balance by signing a new 20-year mortgage at 5.5% compounded monthly. How much interest will refinancing save?

52. A person purchased a $200,000 home 20 years ago by paying 20% down and signing a 30-year mortgage at 13.2% compounded monthly. Interest rates have dropped and the owner wants to refinance the unpaid balance by signing a new 10-year mortgage at 8.2% compounded monthly. How much interest will refinancing save?

53. Discuss the similarities and differences in the graphs of unpaid balance as a function of time for 30-year mortgages of $50,000, $75,000, and $100,000, respectively, each at 9% compounded monthly (see the figure). Include computations of the monthly payment and total interest paid in each case.

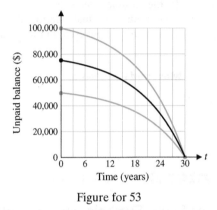

Figure for 53

54. Discuss the similarities and differences in the graphs of unpaid balance as a function of time for 30-year mortgages of $60,000 at rates of 7%, 10%, and 13%, respectively (see the figure). Include computations of the monthly payment and total interest paid in each case.

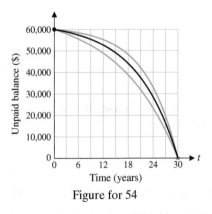

Figure for 54

In Problems 55–58, use graphical approximation techniques or an equation solver to approximate the desired interest rate. Express each answer as a percentage, correct to two decimal places.

55. A discount electronics store offers to let you pay for a $1,000 stereo in 12 equal $90 installments. The store claims that since you repay $1,080 in 1 year, the $80 finance charge represents an 8% annual rate. This would be true if you repaid the loan in a single payment at the end of the year. But since you start repayment after 1 month, this is an amortized loan, and 8% is not the correct rate. What is the annual nominal compounding rate for this loan?

56. A $2,000 computer can be financed by paying $100 per month for 2 years. What is the annual nominal compounding rate for this loan?

57. The owner of a small business has received two offers of purchase. The first prospective buyer offers to pay the owner $100,000 in cash now. The second offers to pay the owner $10,000 now and monthly payments of $1,200 for 10 years. In effect, the second buyer is asking the owner for a $90,000 loan. If the owner accepts the second offer, what annual nominal compounding rate will the owner receive for financing this purchase?

58. At the time they retire, a couple has $200,000 invested in an annuity. The couple can take the entire amount in a single payment, or receive monthly payments of $2,000 for 15 years. If the couple elects to receive the monthly payments, what annual nominal compounding rate will the couple earn on the money invested in the annuity?

Answers to Matched Problems

1. $13,577.71

2. $10,688.87

3. $PMT = $112.98/mo; total interest = $311.52

4.

Payment Number	Payment	Interest	Unpaid Balance Reduction	Unpaid Balance
0				$1,000.00
1	$ 174.03	$12.50	$ 161.53	838.47
2	174.03	10.48	163.55	674.92
3	174.03	8.44	165.59	509.33
4	174.03	6.37	167.66	341.67
5	174.03	4.27	169.76	171.91
6	174.06	2.15	171.91	0.00
Totals	$1,044.21	$44.21	$1,000.00	

5. $98,551

6. Choose the 0% financing.

Chapter 3 Review

Important Terms, Symbols, and Concepts

3-1 Simple Interest

EXAMPLES

- **Interest** is the fee paid for the use of a sum of money P, called the **principal**. **Simple interest** is given by

$$I = Prt$$

  where I = interest

  P = principal

  r = annual simple interest rate (written as a decimal)

  t = time in years

- If a principal P **(present value)** is borrowed, then the **amount** A **(future value)** is the total of the principal and the interest:

$$A = P + Prt$$
$$= P(1 + rt)$$

Ex. 1, p. 128
Ex. 2, p. 128
Ex. 3, p. 129
Ex. 4, p. 129
Ex. 5, p. 130

3-2 Compound and Continuous Compound Interest

- **Compound interest** is interest paid on the principal plus reinvested interest. The future and present values are related by

$$A = P(1 + i)^n$$

  where i = r/m and

  A = amount or future value

  P = principal or present value

  r = annual nominal rate (or just rate)

  m = number of compounding periods per year

  i = rate per compounding period

  n = total number of compounding periods

Ex. 1, p. 134

- If a principal P is invested at an annual rate r earning **continuous compound interest**, then the amount A after t years is given by

Ex. 2, p. 136
Ex. 3, p. 137
Ex. 4, p. 138

$$A = Pe^{rt}$$

- The **growth time** of an investment is the time it takes for a given principal to grow to a particular amount. Three methods for finding the growth time are as follows:

Ex. 5, p. 139

   1. Use logarithms and a calculator.

   2. Use graphical approximation on a graphing calculator.

   3. Use an **equation solver** on a graphing calculator or a computer.

- The **annual percentage yield** APY (also called the **effective rate** or **true interest rate**) is the simple interest rate that would earn the same amount as a given annual rate for which interest is compounded.

- If a principal is invested at the annual rate r compounded m times a year, then the annual percentage yield is given by

Ex. 6, p. 140
Ex. 7, p. 141

$$APY = \left(1 + \frac{r}{m}\right)^m - 1$$

- If a principal is invested at the annual rate r compounded continuously, then the annual percentage yield is given by

$$APY = e^r - 1$$

- A **zero coupon bond** is a bond that is sold now at a discount and will pay its **face value** at some time in the future when it matures.

3-3 Future Value of an Annuity; Sinking Funds

- An **annuity** is any sequence of equal periodic payments. If payments are made at the end of each time interval, then the annuity is called an **ordinary annuity**. The amount, or **future value**, of an annuity is the sum of all payments plus all interest earned and is given by

Ex. 1, p. 147
Ex. 3, p. 150
Ex. 4, p. 151

$$FV = PMT \frac{(1 + i)^n - 1}{i}$$

where FV = future value (amount)

   PMT = periodic payment

   i = rate per period

   n = number of payments (periods)

- A **balance sheet** is a table that shows the interest and balance for each payment of an annuity.

- An account that is established to accumulate funds to meet future obligations or debts is called a **sinking fund**. The **sinking fund payment** can be found by solving the future value formula for PMT:

Ex. 2, p. 149

$$PMT = FV \frac{i}{(1 + i)^n - 1}$$

3-4 Present Value of an Annuity; Amortization

- If equal payments are made from an account until the amount in the account is 0, the payment and the **present value** are related by the following formula:

Ex. 1, p. 155
Ex. 2, p. 155

$$PV = PMT \frac{1 - (1 + i)^{-n}}{i}$$

where PV = present value of all payments

   PMT = periodic payment

   i = rate per period

   n = number of periods

- **Amortizing** a debt means that the debt is retired in a given length of time by equal periodic payments that include compound interest. Solving the present value formula for the payment gives us the **amortization formula**:

Ex. 3, p. 156
Ex. 6, p. 159

$$PMT = PV \frac{i}{1 - (1 + i)^{-n}}$$

- An **amortization schedule** is a table that shows the interest due and the balance reduction for each payment of a loan.

Ex. 4, p. 157

- The **equity** in a property is the difference between the current net market value and the unpaid loan balance. The unpaid balance of a loan with n **remaining payments** is given by the present value formula.

Ex. 5, p. 158

- A strategy for solving problems in the mathematics of finance is presented on page 160.

Review Exercises

Work through all the problems in this chapter review and check your answers in the back of the book. Answers to all review problems are there along with section numbers in italics to indicate where each type of problem is discussed. Where weaknesses show up, review appropriate sections in the text.

A

In Problems 1–4, find the indicated quantity, given $A = P(1 + rt)$.

1. $A = ?; P = \$100; r = 9\%; t = 6$ months

2. $A = \$808; P = ?; r = 12\%; t = 1$ month

3. $A = \$212; P = \$200; r = 8\%; t = ?$

4. $A = \$4,120; P = \$4,000; r = ?; t = 6$ months

B

In Problems 5 and 6, find the indicated quantity, given $A = P(1 + i)^n$.

5. $A = ?; P = \$1,200; i = 0.005; n = 30$

6. $A = \$5,000; P = ?; i = 0.0075; n = 60$

In Problems 7 and 8, find the indicated quantity, given $A = Pe^{rt}$.

7. $A = ?; P = \$4,750; r = 6.8\%; t = 3$ years

8. $A = \$36,000; P = ?; r = 9.3\%; t = 60$ months

In Problems 9 and 10, find the indicated quantity, given

$$FV = PMT \frac{(1 + i)^n - 1}{i}$$

9. $FV = ?; PMT = \$1,000; i = 0.005; n = 60$

10. $FV = \$8,000; PMT = ?; i = 0.015; n = 48$

In Problems 11 and 12, find the indicated quantity, given

$$PV = PMT \frac{1 - (1 + i)^{-n}}{i}$$

11. $PV = ?; PMT = \$2,500; i = 0.02; n = 16$

12. $PV = \$8,000; PMT = ?; i = 0.0075; n = 60$

C

13. Solve the equation $2,500 = 1,000(1.06)^n$ for n to the nearest integer using:

    (A) Logarithms

    (B) Graphical approximation techniques or an equation solver on a graphing calculator

14. Solve the equation

$$5,000 = 100 \frac{(1.01)^n - 1}{0.01}$$

    for n to the nearest integer using:

    (A) Logarithms

    (B) Graphical approximation techniques or an equation solver on a graphing calculator.

Applications

Find all dollar amounts correct to the nearest cent. When an interest rate is requested as an answer, express the rate as a percentage, correct to two decimal places.

15. If you borrow \$3,000 at 14% simple interest for 10 months, how much will you owe in 10 months? How much interest will you pay?

16. Grandparents deposited \$6,000 into a grandchild's account toward a college education. How much money (to the nearest dollar) will be in the account 17 years from now if the account earns 7% compounded monthly?

17. How much should you pay for a corporate bond paying 6.6% compounded monthly in order to have \$25,000 in 10 years?

18. A savings account pays 5.4% compounded annually. Construct a balance sheet showing the interest earned during each year and the balance at the end of each year for 4 years if

    (A) A single deposit of \$400 is made at the beginning of the first year.

    (B) Four deposits of \$100 are made at the end of each year.

19. One investment pays 13% simple interest and another 9% compounded annually. Which investment would you choose? Why?

20. A $10,000 retirement account is left to earn interest at 7% compounded daily. How much money will be in the account 40 years from now when the owner reaches 65? (Use a 365-day year and round answer to the nearest dollar.)

21. A couple wishes to have $40,000 in 6 years for the down payment on a house. At what rate of interest compounded continuously must $25,000 be invested now to accomplish this goal?

22. Which is the better investment and why: 9% compounded quarterly or 9.25% compounded annually?

23. What is the value of an ordinary annuity at the end of 8 years if $200 per month is deposited into an account earning 7.2% compounded monthly? How much of this value is interest?

24. A credit card company charges a 22% annual rate for overdue accounts. How much interest will be owed on a $635 account 1 month overdue?

25. What will a $23,000 car cost (to the nearest dollar) 5 years from now if the inflation rate over that period averages 5% compounded annually?

26. What would the $23,000 car in Problem 25 have cost (to the nearest dollar) 5 years ago if the inflation rate over that period had averaged 5% compounded annually?

27. A loan of $2,500 was repaid at the end of 10 months with a check for $2,812.50. What annual rate of interest was charged?

28. You want to purchase an automobile for $21,600. The dealer offers you 0% financing for 48 months or a $3,000 rebate. You can obtain 4.8% financing for 48 months at the local bank. Which option should you choose? Explain.

29. Find the annual percentage yield on a CD earning 6.25% if interest is compounded

  (A) monthly.

  (B) continuously.

30. You have $5,000 toward the purchase of a boat that will cost $6,000. How long will it take the $5,000 to grow to $6,000 if it is invested at 9% compounded quarterly? (Round up to the next-higher quarter if not exact.)

31. How long will it take money to double if it is invested at 6% compounded monthly? 9% compounded monthly? (Round up to the next-higher month if not exact.)

32. Starting on his 21st birthday, and continuing on every birthday up to and including his 65th, John deposits $2,000 a year into an IRA. How much (to the nearest dollar) will be in the account on John's 65th birthday, if the account earns:

  (A) 7% compounded annually?

  (B) 11% compounded annually?

33. If you just sold a stock for $17,388.17 (net) that cost you $12,903.28 (net) 3 years ago, what annual compound rate of return did you make on your investment?

34. The table shows the fees for refund anticipation loans (RALs) offered by an online tax preparation firm. Find the annual rate of interest for each of the following loans.

  (A) A $400 RAL paid back in 15 days

  (B) A $1,800 RAL paid back in 21 days

RAL Amount	RAL Fee
$10–$500	$29.00
$501–$1,000	$39.00
$1,001–$1,500	$49.00
$1,501–$2,000	$69.00
$2,001–$5,000	$82.00

35. Lincoln Benefit Life offered an annuity that pays 5.5% compounded monthly. What equal monthly deposit should be made into this annuity in order to have $50,000 in 5 years?

36. A person wants to establish an annuity for retirement purposes. He wants to make quarterly deposits for 20 years so that he can then make quarterly withdrawals of $5,000 for 10 years. The annuity earns 7.32% interest compounded quarterly.

  (A) How much will have to be in the account at the time he retires?

  (B) How much should be deposited each quarter for 20 years in order to accumulate the required amount?

  (C) What is the total amount of interest earned during the 30-year period?

37. If you borrow $4,000 from an online lending firm for the purchase of a computer and agree to repay it in 48 equal installments at 0.9% interest per month on the unpaid balance, how much are your monthly payments? How much total interest will be paid?

38. A company decides to establish a sinking fund to replace a piece of equipment in 6 years at an estimated cost of $50,000. To accomplish this, they decide to make fixed monthly payments into an account that pays 6.12% compounded monthly. How much should each payment be?

39. How long will it take money to double if it is invested at 7.5% compounded daily? 7.5% compounded annually?

40. A student receives a student loan for $8,000 at 5.5% interest compounded monthly to help her finish the last 1.5 years of college. Starting 1 year after finishing college, the student must amortize the loan in the next 5 years by making equal monthly payments. What will the payments be and what total interest will the student pay?

41. If you invest $5,650 in an account paying 8.65% compounded continuously, how much money will be in the account at the end of 10 years?

42. A company makes a payment of $1,200 each month into a sinking fund that earns 6% compounded monthly. Use graphical approximation techniques on a graphing calculator to determine when the fund will be worth $100,000.

43. A couple has a $50,000, 20-year mortgage at 9% compounded monthly. Use graphical approximation techniques on a graphing calculator to determine when the unpaid balance will drop below $10,000.

44. A loan company advertises in the paper that you will pay only 8¢ a day for each $100 borrowed. What annual rate of interest are they charging? (Use a 360-day year.)

45. Construct the amortization schedule for a $1,000 debt that is to be amortized in four equal quarterly payments at 2.5% interest per quarter on the unpaid balance.

46. You can afford monthly deposits of only $300 into an account that pays 7.98% compounded monthly. How long will it be until you will have $9,000 to purchase a used car? (Round to the next-higher month if not exact.)

47. A company establishes a sinking fund for plant retooling in 6 years at an estimated cost of $850,000. How much should be invested semiannually into an account paying 8.76% compounded semiannually? How much interest will the account earn in the 6 years?

48. What is the annual nominal rate compounded monthly for a CD that has an annual percentage yield of 6.48%?

49. If you buy a 13-week T-bill with a maturity value of $5,000 for $4,922.15 from the U.S. Treasury Department, what annual interest rate will you earn?

50. In order to save enough money for the down payment on a condominium, a young couple deposits $200 each month into an account that pays 7.02% interest compounded monthly. If the couple needs $10,000 for a down payment, how many deposits will the couple have to make?

51. A business borrows $80,000 at 9.42% interest compounded monthly for 8 years.

(A) What is the monthly payment?

(B) What is the unpaid balance at the end of the first year?

(C) How much interest was paid during the first year?

52. You unexpectedly inherit $10,000 just after you have made the 72nd monthly payment on a 30-year mortgage of $60,000 at 8.2% compounded monthly. Discuss the relative merits of using the inheritance to reduce the principal of the loan or to buy a certificate of deposit paying 7% compounded monthly.

53. Your parents are considering a $75,000, 30-year mortgage to purchase a new home. The bank at which they have done business for many years offers a rate of 7.54% compounded monthly. A competitor is offering 6.87% compounded monthly. Would it be worthwhile for your parents to switch banks? Explain.

54. How much should a $5,000 face value zero coupon bond, maturing in 5 years, be sold for now, if its rate of return is to be 5.6% compounded annually?

55. If you pay $5,695 for a $10,000 face value zero coupon bond that matures in 10 years, what is your annual compound rate of return?

56. If an investor wants to earn an annual interest rate of 6.4% on a 26-week T-bill with a maturity value of $5,000, how much should the investor pay for the T-bill?

57. Two years ago you borrowed $10,000 at 12% interest compounded monthly, which was to be amortized over 5 years. Now you have acquired some additional funds and decide that you want to pay off this loan. What is the unpaid balance after making equal monthly payments for 2 years?

58. What annual nominal rate compounded monthly has the same annual percentage yield as 7.28% compounded quarterly?

59. (A) A man deposits $2,000 in an IRA on his 21st birthday and on each subsequent birthday up to, and including, his 29th (nine deposits in all). The account earns 8% compounded annually. If he leaves the money in the account without making any more deposits, how much will he have on his 65th birthday, assuming the account continues to earn the same rate of interest?

(B) How much would be in the account (to the nearest dollar) on his 65th birthday if he had started the deposits on his 30th birthday and continued making deposits on each birthday until (and including) his 65th birthday?

60. A promissory note will pay $27,000 at maturity 10 years from now. How much money should you be willing to pay now if money is worth 5.5% compounded continuously?

61. In a new housing development, the houses are selling for $100,000 and require a 20% down payment. The buyer is given a choice of 30-year or 15-year financing, both at 7.68% compounded monthly.

(A) What is the monthly payment for the 30-year choice? For the 15-year choice?

(B) What is the unpaid balance after 10 years for the 30-year choice? For the 15-year choice?

62. A loan company will loan up to 60% of the equity in a home. A family purchased their home 8 years ago for $83,000. The home was financed by paying 20% down and signing a 30-year mortgage at 8.4% for the balance. Equal monthly payments were made to amortize the loan over the 30-year period. The market value of the house is now $95,000. After making the 96th payment, the family applied to the loan company for the maximum loan. How much (to the nearest dollar) will the family receive?

63. A $600 stereo is financed for 6 months by making monthly payments of $110. What is the annual nominal compounding rate for this loan?

64. A person deposits $2,000 each year for 25 years into an IRA. When she retires immediately after making the 25th deposit, the IRA is worth $220,000.

(A) Find the interest rate earned by the IRA over the 25-year period leading up to retirement.

(B) Assume that the IRA continues to earn the interest rate found in part (A). How long can the retiree withdraw $30,000 per year? How long can she withdraw $24,000 per year?

ANSWERS TO SELECTED EXERCISES

Chapter 1

WALKING

1.1 Ballots and Preference Schedules

1. (a)

Number of voters	5	3	5	3	2	3
1st choice	A	A	C	D	D	B
2nd	B	D	E	C	C	E
3rd	C	B	D	B	B	A
4th	D	C	A	E	A	C
5th	E	E	B	A	E	D

3.

	37	36	24	13	5
1st	B	A	B	E	C
2nd	E	B	A	B	E
3rd	A	D	D	C	A
4th	C	C	E	A	D
5th	D	E	C	D	B

5.

	14	10	8	7	4
A	2	3	1	5	3
B	1	1	2	3	2
C	5	5	5	2	4
D	4	2	4	1	5
E	3	4	3	4	1

7. (a) 21 **(b)** 11 **(c)** C

9.

Number of voters	255	480	765
1st	L	C	M
2nd	M	M	L
3rd	C	L	C

1.2 Plurality Method

11. (a) C **(b)** C, B, A, D
13. (a) C **(b)** C, B, A, D
15. (a) D **(b)** D, C, B, A, E

17. (a) A **(b)** A, C, D, B, E
19. (a) A **(b)** A, C, D, B, E
21. (a) B **(b)** B, D, A, C

1.3 Borda Count Method

23. (a) C **(b)** C, D, B, A
25. A, C, D, B, E

27. Ingram (1304), Gerhart (1276), McCoy (1145), Suh (815)
29. A, D, B, C (D had 310 points).

1.4 Plurality With Elimination

31. (a) A **(b)** A, C, B, D
33. (a) C **(b)** C, B, A, D
35. (a) D **(b)** D, C, B, A, E

37. B, C, A, D, E
39. A

1.5 Pairwise Comparisons

41. (a) D **(b)** D, B, A, C
43. (a) C **(b)** C, D, A, B
45. D

47. A, B, C, E, D (B, C, and E have two points each, but in their head-to-head comparisons B beats C and E, and C beats E)
49. (a) 3 **(b)** C

1.6 Fairness Criteria

51. The winner under the Borda count method is B; the Condorcet candidate is A.
53. The winner under plurality is R; when F is eliminated H becomes the winner.
55. The winner under plurality-with-elimination is A; when C is eliminated E becomes the winner.

57. If X is the Condorcet candidate, then by definition X wins every pairwise comparison and is, therefore, the winner under the method of pairwise comparisons.
59. When a voter moves a candidate up in his or her ballot that candidate's Borda points increase. It follows that if X had the most Borda points and a voter changes his or her ballot to rank X higher, then X still has the most Borda points.

JOGGING

61. Suppose that A gets a first-place votes and B gets b first-place votes, where a > b. It is clear that candidate A wins the election under the plurality method, the plurality-with-elimination method, and the method of pairwise comparisons. Under the Borda count method, A gets $2a + b$ points while B gets $2b + a$ points. Since $a > b$, $2a + b > 2b + a$, and so again A wins the election.

63. The number of points under this variation is complementary to the number of points under the standard Borda count method: A first place is worth 1 point instead of N, a second place is worth 2 points instead of $N - 1, \ldots,$ a last place is worth N points instead of 1. It follows that having the fewest points here is equivalent to having the most points under the standard Borda count method, having the second fewest is equivalent to having the second most, and so on.

65. (a) 65

   (b) 34 second-place votes and 31 third-place votes

   (c) 31 second-place votes and 34 third-place votes

67. 5 points for each first-place vote, 3 points for each second-place vote, 1 point for each third-place vote

69. (a) C

   (b) A is a Condorcet candidate but is eliminated in the first round.

Number of voters	10	6	6	3	3
1st	B	A	A	D	C
2nd	C	B	C	A	A
3rd	D	D	B	C	B
4th	A	C	D	B	D

   (c) B wins under the Coombs method. However, if 8 voters move B from their third choice to their second choice, then C wins.

Number of voters	10	8	7	4
1st	B	C	C	A
2nd	A	A	B	B
3rd	C	B	A	C

Chapter 2

WALKING

2.1   Weighted Voting

1. $[63: 30, 28, 22, 21, 2, 2]$

3. (a) 11   **(b)** 20   **(c)** 15   **(d)** 16

5. (a) None   **(b)** P_1 **(c)** P_1, P_2, P_3 **(d)** P_1, P_2, P_3, P_4

7. (a) 13   **(b)** 11

9. (a) $[49: 48, 24, 12, 12]$ **(b)** $[49: 36, 18, 9, 9]$

   (c) $[49: 32, 16, 8, 8]$

2.2   Banzhaf Power

11. (a) 10   **(b)** $8, 9, 10$ **(c)** $11, 12, 13, 14, 15$

13. $\beta_1 = \frac{3}{8}; \beta_2 = \frac{3}{8}; \beta_3 = \frac{1}{8}; \beta_4 = \frac{1}{8}$

15. (a) P_1, P_2

   (b) $\{P_1, P_2\}, \{P_1, P_3\}, \{P_1, P_2, P_3\}, \{P_1, P_2, P_4\}, \{P_1, P_3, P_4\},$ $\{P_2, P_3, P_4\}, \{P_1, P_2, P_3, P_4\}$

   (c) $\beta_1 = \frac{5}{12}; \beta_2 = \frac{3}{12} = \frac{1}{4}; \beta_3 = \frac{3}{12} = \frac{1}{4}; \beta_4 = \frac{1}{12}$

17. (a) $\beta_1 = \frac{3}{5}; \beta_2 = \frac{1}{5}; \beta_3 = \frac{1}{5}$

   (b) $\beta_1 = \frac{3}{5}; \beta_2 = \frac{1}{5}; \beta_3 = \frac{1}{5}$. The Banzhaf power distributions in (a) and (b) are the same.

19. (a) $\beta_1 = \frac{8}{24}; \beta_2 = \frac{6}{24}; \beta_3 = \frac{4}{24}; \beta_4 = \frac{4}{24}; \beta_5 = \frac{2}{24}$

   (b) $\beta_1 = \frac{7}{19}; \beta_2 = \frac{5}{19}; \beta_3 = \frac{3}{19}; \beta_4 = \frac{3}{19}; \beta_5 = \frac{1}{19}$

   (c) $\beta_1 = \frac{5}{15}; \beta_2 = \frac{5}{15}; \beta_3 = \frac{3}{15}; \beta_4 = \frac{1}{15}; \beta_5 = \frac{1}{15}$

   (d) $\beta_1 = \frac{1}{5}; \beta_2 = \frac{1}{5}; \beta_3 = \frac{1}{5}; \beta_4 = \frac{1}{5}; \beta_5 = \frac{1}{5}$

21. (a) $\{P_1, P_2\}, \{P_1, P_3\}, \{P_1, P_2, P_3\}$

   (b) $\beta_1 = \frac{3}{5}; \beta_2 = \frac{1}{5}; \beta_3 = \frac{1}{5}$

23. (a) $\{P_1, P_2\}, \{P_1, P_3\}, \{P_2, P_3\}, \{P_1, P_2, P_3\}, \{P_1, P_2, P_4\},$ $\{P_1, P_2, P_5\}, \{P_1, P_2, P_6\}, \{P_1, P_3, P_4\}, \{P_1, P_3, P_5\},$ $\{P_1, P_3, P_6\}, \{P_2, P_3, P_4\}, \{P_2, P_3, P_5\}, \{P_2, P_3, P_6\}$

   (b) $\{P_1, P_2, P_4\}, \{P_1, P_3, P_4\}, \{P_2, P_3, P_4\}, \{P_1, P_2, P_3, P_4\},$ $\{P_1, P_2, P_4, P_5\}, \{P_1, P_2, P_4, P_6\}, \{P_1, P_3, P_4, P_5\},$ $\{P_1, P_3, P_4, P_6\}, \{P_2, P_3, P_4, P_5\}, \{P_2, P_3, P_4, P_6\},$ $\{P_1, P_2, P_3, P_4, P_5\}, \{P_1, P_2, P_3, P_4, P_6\}, \{P_1, P_2, P_4, P_5, P_6\},$ $\{P_1, P_3, P_4, P_5, P_6\}, \{P_2, P_3, P_4, P_5, P_6\},$ $\{P_1, P_2, P_3, P_4, P_5, P_6\}$

   (c) $\beta_4 = 0$

   (d) $\beta_1 = \frac{1}{3}; \beta_2 = \frac{1}{3}; \beta_3 = \frac{1}{3}; \beta_4 = 0; \beta_5 = 0; \beta_6 = 0$

25. (a) $\{A, B\}, \{A, C\}, \{B, C\}, \{A, B, C\}, \{A, B, D\}, \{A, C, D\}$ $\{B, C, D\}, \{A, B, C, D\}$

   (b) $A, B,$ and C have Banzhaf power index of $\frac{4}{12}$ each; D is a dummy.

2.3   Shapley-Shubik Power

27. $\sigma_1 = \frac{10}{24}; \sigma_2 = \frac{10}{24}; \sigma_3 = \frac{2}{24}; \sigma_4 = \frac{2}{24}$

29. (a) $\langle P_1, \underline{P_2}, P_3 \rangle, \langle P_1, \underline{P_3}, P_2 \rangle, \langle P_2, \underline{P_1}, P_3 \rangle, \langle P_2, P_3, \underline{P_1} \rangle,$ $\langle P_3, \underline{P_1}, P_2 \rangle, \langle P_3, P_2, \underline{P_1} \rangle$

   (b) $\sigma_1 = \frac{4}{6}; \sigma_2 = \frac{1}{6}; \sigma_3 = \frac{1}{6}$

31. (a) $\sigma_1 = 1; \sigma_2 = 0; \sigma_3 = 0; \sigma_4 = 0$

   (b) $\sigma_1 = \frac{4}{6}; \sigma_2 = \frac{1}{6}; \sigma_3 = \frac{1}{6}; \sigma_4 = 0$

   (c) $\sigma_1 = \frac{1}{2}; \sigma_2 = \frac{1}{2}; \sigma_3 = 0; \sigma_4 = 0$

   (d) $\sigma_1 = \frac{1}{3}; \sigma_2 = \frac{1}{3}; \sigma_3 = \frac{1}{3}; \sigma_4 = 0$

33. (a) $\sigma_1 = \frac{10}{24}; \sigma_2 = \frac{6}{24}; \sigma_3 = \frac{6}{24}; \sigma_4 = \frac{2}{24}$

   (b) $\sigma_1 = \frac{10}{24}; \sigma_2 = \frac{6}{24}; \sigma_3 = \frac{6}{24}; \sigma_4 = \frac{2}{24}$

   (c) $\sigma_1 = \frac{10}{24}; \sigma_2 = \frac{6}{24}; \sigma_3 = \frac{6}{24}; \sigma_4 = \frac{2}{24}$

35. (a) $\langle P_1, \underline{P_2}, P_3 \rangle, \langle P_1, \underline{P_3}, P_2 \rangle, \langle P_2, \underline{P_1}, P_3 \rangle, \langle P_2, P_3, \underline{P_1} \rangle,$ $\langle P_3, \underline{P_1}, P_2 \rangle, \langle P_3, P_2, \underline{P_1} \rangle$

   (b) $\sigma_1 = \frac{4}{6}; \sigma_2 = \frac{1}{6}; \sigma_3 = \frac{1}{6}$

37. $\sigma_1 = \frac{10}{24}; \sigma_2 = \frac{6}{24}; \sigma_3 = \frac{6}{24}; \sigma_4 = \frac{2}{24}$

2.4 Subsets and Permutations

39. (a) $2^{10} = 1024$ (b) 1023 (c) 10 (d) 1013
41. (a) 1023 (b) 1013
43. (a) 63 (b) 31 (c) 31 (d) 15 (e) 16
45. (a) 6,227,020,800

(b) 6,402,373,705,728,000

(c) 15,511,210,043,330,985,984,000,000

(d) 491,857 years

47. (a) 1,037,836,800 (b) 286 (c) 715 (d) 1287
49. (a) 362,880 (b) 11 (c) 110 (d) 504 (e) 10,100
51. (a) $7! = 5040$ (b) $6! = 720$ (c) $6! = 720$ (d) 4320
53. (a) 4320 (b) $\frac{4320}{5040} = \frac{6}{7}$

(c) $\sigma_1 = \frac{6}{7}; \sigma_2 = \sigma_3 = \sigma_4 = \sigma_5 = \sigma_6 = \sigma_7 = \frac{1}{42}$

JOGGING

55. If x is even, then $q = \frac{15x}{2} + 1 \le 8x$; if x is odd, then $q = \frac{15x+1}{2} \le 8x$.
57. $\beta_1 = \frac{3}{5}, \beta_2 = \frac{1}{5}, \beta_3 = \frac{1}{5}$
59. (a) $q = 4, h = 2, a = 1$. (Any answer with multiples of these numbers is also correct.)

(b) SS power index of the head coach is $\frac{1}{2}$; SS power index of each assistant coach is $\frac{1}{6}$

61. (a) Suppose that a winning coalition that contains P is not a winning coalition without P. Then P would be a critical player in that coalition, contradicting the fact that P is a dummy.

(b) P is a dummy $\Leftrightarrow P$ is never critical $\Leftrightarrow$ the numerator of its Banzhaf power index is 0 $\Leftrightarrow$ its Banzhaf power index is 0.

(c) Suppose that P is not a dummy. Then P is critical in some winning coalition. Let S denote the other players in that winning coalition. The sequential coalition with the players in S first (in any order) followed by P and then followed by the remaining players has P as its pivotal player. Thus, P's Shapley-Shubik power index is not zero. Conversely, if P's Shapley-Shubik power index is not zero, then P is pivotal in some sequential coalition. A coalition consisting of P together with the players preceding P in that sequential coalition is a winning coalition, and P is a critical player in it. Thus, P is not a dummy.

63. (a) $7 \le q \le 13$

(b) For $q = 7$ or $q = 8$, P_1 is a dictator because $\{P_1\}$ is a winning coalition.

(c) For $q = 9$, only P_1 has veto power because P_2 and P_3 together have only five votes.

(d) For $10 \le q \le 12$, both P_1 and P_2 have veto power because no motion can pass without both of their votes. For $q = 13$, all three players have veto power.

(e) For $q = 7$ or $q = 8$, both P_2 and P_3 are dummies because P_1 is a dictator. For $10 \le q \le 12$, P_3 is a dummy because all winning coalitions contain $\{P_1, P_2\}$, which is itself a winning coalition.

65. (a) Both have $\beta_1 = \frac{2}{5}, \beta_2 = \frac{1}{5}, \beta_3 = \frac{1}{5}$, and $\beta_4 = \frac{1}{5}$.

(b) In the weighted voting system $[q: w_1, w_2, \ldots, w_N]$, if P_k is critical in a coalition, then the sum of the weights of all the players in that coalition (including P_k) is at least q but the sum of the weights of all the players in the coalition except P_k is less than q. Consequently, if the weights of all the players in that coalition are multiplied by $c > 0$ ($c = 0$ would make no sense), then the sum of the weights of all the players in the coalition (including P_k) is at least cq but the sum of the weights of all the players in the coalition except P_k is less than cq. Therefore, P_k is critical in the same coalitions in the weighted voting system $[cq: cw_1, cw_2, \ldots, cw_N]$.

67. The senior partner has Shapley-Shubik power index $\frac{N}{N+1}$; each of the junior partners has Shapley-Shubik power index $\frac{1}{N(N+1)}$.

69. You should buy from P_3.

71. (a) You should buy from P_2.

(b) You should buy two votes from P_2.

(c) Buying a single vote from P_2 raises your power from $\frac{1}{25} = 4\%$ to $\frac{3}{25} = 12\%$. Buying a second vote from P_2 raises your power to $\frac{2}{13} \approx 15.4\%$.

73. (a) The losing coalitions are $\{P_1\}, \{P_2\}$, and $\{P_3\}$. The complements of these coalitions are $\{P_2, P_3\}, \{P_1, P_3\}$, and $\{P_1, P_2\}$, respectively, all of which are winning coalitions.

(b) The losing coalitions are $\{P_1\}, \{P_2\}, \{P_3\}, \{P_4\}, \{P_2, P_3\}, \{P_2, P_4\}$, and $\{P_3, P_4\}$. The complements of these coalitions are $\{P_2, P_3, P_4\}, \{P_1, P_3, P_4\}, \{P_1, P_2, P_4\}, \{P_1, P_2, P_3\}, \{P_1, P_4\}, \{P_1, P_3\}$, and $\{P_1, P_2\}$, respectively, all of which are winning coalitions.

(c) If P is a dictator, then the losing coalitions are all the coalitions without P; the winning coalitions are all the coalitions that include P.

(d) 2^{N-1}

75. (a) approximately 1.115 (relative voting weight $= \frac{55}{538}$; BPI $= 0.114$)

(b) $\frac{115}{93}, \frac{115}{93}, \frac{115}{84}, 0, 0, 0$

Chapter 5

WALKING

5.2 An Introduction to Graphs

1. (a) $\{A, B, C, X, Y, Z\}$

(b) $AX, AY, AZ, BB, BC, BX, CX, XY$

(c) $\deg(A) = 3, \deg(B) = 4, \deg(C) = 2, \deg(X) = 4,$
$\deg(Y) = 2, \deg(Z) = 1$

(d)

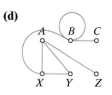

3. (a) $\{A, B, C, D, X, Y, Z\}$

   (b) $AX, AX, AY, BX, BY, DZ, XY$

   (c) $\deg(A) = 3, \deg(B) = 2, \deg(C) = 0, \deg(D) = 1,$
   $\deg(X) = 4, \deg(Y) = 3, \deg(Z) = 1$

   (d) 3

5.

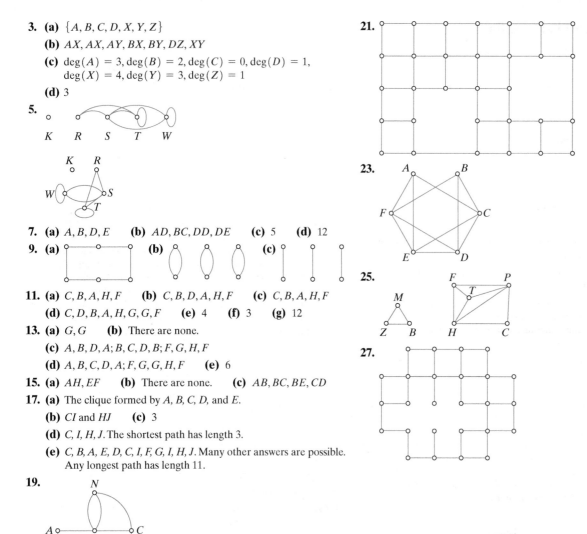

7. (a) A, B, D, E **(b)** AD, BC, DD, DE **(c)** 5   **(d)** 12

9. (a)   **(b)**   **(c)**

11. (a) C, B, A, H, F **(b)** C, B, D, A, H, F **(c)** C, B, A, H, F

   (d) C, D, B, A, H, G, G, F **(e)** 4   **(f)** 3   **(g)** 12

13. (a) G, G **(b)** There are none.

   (c) $A, B, D, A; B, C, D, B; F, G, H, F$

   (d) $A, B, C, D, A; F, G, G, H, F$ **(e)** 6

15. (a) AH, EF **(b)** There are none.   **(c)** AB, BC, BE, CD

17. (a) The clique formed by $A, B, C, D,$ and E.

   (b) CI and HJ **(c)** 3

   (d) C, I, H, J. The shortest path has length 3.

   (e) $C, B, A, E, D, C, I, F, G, I, H, J$. Many other answers are possible.
   Any longest path has length 11.

19.

21.

23.

25.

27.

5.3 Euler's Theorems and Fleury's Algorithm

29. (a) (A); all vertices are even.

   (b) (C); four vertices are odd.

   (c) (D); see Exercises 9(a) and 9(b).

31. (a) (C); four vertices are odd.

   (b) (A); all vertices are even.

   (c) (C); the graph is disconnected.

33. (a) (B); exactly two vertices are odd.

   (b) (A); all vertices are even.

   (c) (C); more than two vertices are odd.

35.

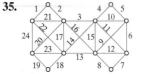

Other answers are possible.

37.

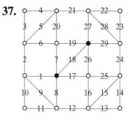

Other answers are possible.

39.

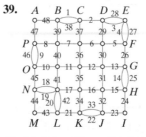

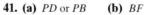

41. (a) PD or PB **(b)** BF

5.4 Eulerizing and Semi-Eulerizing Graphs

43.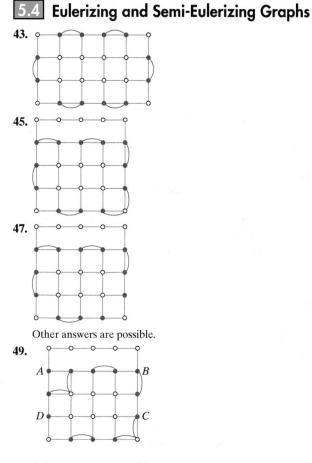

45.

47.

Other answers are possible.

49.

Other answers are possible.

51.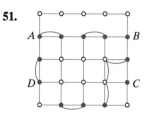

Other answers are possible.

53.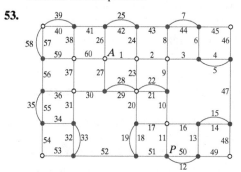

Many other answers are possible.

55.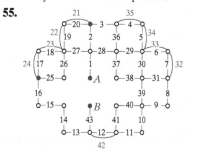

Many other answers are possible.

JOGGING

57. 6; there are 14 odd vertices. Two can be used as the starting and ending vertices. The remaining 12 can be paired so that each pair forces one lifting of the pencil.

59. None. If a vertex had degree 1, then the edge incident to that vertex would be a bridge.

61. (a) Both m and n must be even.

(b) $m = 1$ and $n = 1$, $m = 1$ and $n = 2$, or $m = 2$ and n is odd.

63. (a) Make a complete graph with $N - 1$ of the vertices, and leave the other vertex as an isolated vertex.

(b) $\frac{(N-1)(N-2)}{2}$ dollars

65. (a) 12

(b)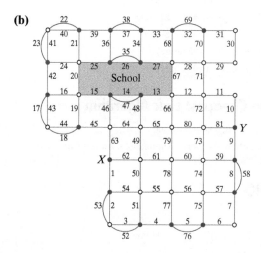

67. $D, L, R, L, C, A, R, B, R, B, D, C, L, D$. Others answers are possible.

69. Yes; one of the many possible journeys is given by crossing the bridges in the following order: $a, b, c, d, e, f, g, h, i, l, m, n, o, p, k$. (*Note*: Euler did not ask that the journey start and end at the same place.)

Chapter 6

WALKING

6.2 Hamilton Paths and Circuits

1. (a) 1. A, B, D, C, E, F, G, A;   **(b)** A, G, F, E, C, D, B
     2. A, D, C, E, B, G, F, A;   **(c)** D, A, G, B, C, E, F
     3. A, D, B, E, C, F, G, A

3. A, B, C, D, E, F, G, A; A, B, E, D, C, F, G, A and their mirror images

5. (a) A, F, B, C, G, D, E **(b)** A, F, B, C, G, D, E, A
   (c) A, F, B, E, D, G, C **(d)** F, A, B, E, D, C, G

7. (a) 8   **(b)** $A, H, C, B, F, D, G, E, A$
   (c) A, H, C, B, F, D, G, E and A, E, G, D, F, B, C, H

9. (a) B, A, D, E, C; A, D, E, C, B; D, E, C, B, A; E, C, B, A, D; C, B, A, D, E
   (b) A, B, E, D, C; A, D, E, B, C; B, A, E, C, D; B, C, E, A, D; C, B, E, D, A; C, D, E, B, A; D, C, E, A, B; D, A, E, C, B

11. (a) A, B, C, D, E, F, A and A, D, C, B E, F, A (or their reversals)
   (b) C, B, A, D, E, F; C, B, E, D, A, F; C, D, A, B, E, F and C, D, E, B, A, F (or their reversals)

13. (a) $A, B, E, D, C, I, H, G, K, J, F$
   (b) $K, J, F, G, H, I, C, D, A, B, E$

6.3 The Brute-Force Algorithm

27. A, C, B, D, A or its reversal; cost $= 102$

29. A, D, C, B, E, A or its reversal; cost $= 92$ hours

6.4 The Nearest-Neighbor and Repetitive Nearest-Neighbor Algorithm

35. (a) B, C, A, E, D, B; cost $= \$722$
   (b) C, A, E, D, B, C; cost $= \$722$
   (c) D, B, C, A, E, D; cost $= \$722$
   (d) E, C, A, D, B, E; cost $= \$741$

37. (a) A, D, E, C, B, A; cost $= \$11,656$
   (b) A, D, B, C, E, A; cost $= \$9,760$

39. (a) A, E, B, C, D, A (92 hours)
   (b) A, D, B, C, E, A (93 hours)

6.5 The Cheapest-Link Algorithm

51. B, E, C, A, D, B; cost $= \$10,000$

53. Atlanta, Columbus, Pierre, Minneapolis, Kansas City, Tulsa, Atlanta; cost $= \$2598.75$

JOGGING

57. $1500

59. (a)

(b) Home, Bank, Post Office, Deli, Hospital, Karl's, Home

(c) CI is a bridge of the graph connecting a "left half" and a "right half." If you start at C and go left, there is no way to get to the right half of the graph without going through C again. Conversely, if you start at C and cross over to the right half first, there is no way to get back to the left half without going through C again.

(d) No matter where you start, you would have to cross the bridge CI twice to visit every vertex and get back to where you started.

15. There is no Hamilton circuit since two vertices have degree 1. There is no Hamilton path since any such path must contain edges AB, BE, and BC, which would force vertex B to be visited more than once.

17. (a) 6   **(b)** B, D, A, E, C, B; weight $= 27$
   (c) The mirror image B, C, E, A, D, B; weight $= 27$

19. (a) A, D, F, E, B, C; weight $= 29$
   (b) A, B, E, D, F, C; weight $= 30$
   (c) A, D, F, E, B, C; weight $= 29$

21. (a) ≈ 77 years   **(b)** ≈ 1620 years

23. (a) 190   **(b)** 210   **(c)** 50

25. (a) $N = 6$ **(b)** $N = 10$ **(c)** $N = 201$

31. B, A, C, D, B or its reversal (44 hours)

33. (a) $7! = 5040$ **(b)** 5040   **(c)** $6! = 720$

41. (a) Atlanta, Columbus, Kansas City, Tulsa, Minneapolis, Pierre, Atlanta; cost $= \$2915.25$
   (b) Atlanta, Kansas City, Tulsa, Minneapolis, Pierre, Columbus, Atlanta; cost $= \$2804.25$

43. A, E, B, C, D, A or its reversal (92 hours)

45. Atlanta, Columbus, Minneapolis, Pierre, Kansas City, Tulsa, Atlanta; cost $= \$2439.00$

47. 12.5%

49. A, D, C, B, E, A or its reversal (92 hours)

55. (a) A, E, D, B, C, F, A or its reversal (75 days)
   (b) $\varepsilon = 2/73 \approx 2.74\%$

61. The graph describing the friendships among the guests does not have a Hamilton circuit. Thus, it is impossible to seat everyone around the table with friends on both sides.

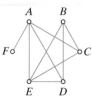

63. (a) $I, B_1, C_2, B_2, C_3, B_3, C_4, B_4, C_1$

(b) $C_1, B_1, C_2, B_2, I, B_4, C_4, B_3, C_3$

(c) $C_1, B_4, C_4, B_3, C_3, B_2, C_2, B_1, I$

(d) Suppose that we color the vertices of the grid graph with two colors [say black (*B*) and white (*W*)] with adjacent vertices having different colors (see figure). Since there are five black vertices and four white vertices and in any Hamilton path the vertices must alternate color, the only possible Hamilton paths are of the form *B, W, B, W, B, W, B, W, B*. Since every boundary vertex is white, it is impossible to end a Hamilton path on a boundary vertex.

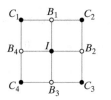

65. (a) $C_1, B_8, B_7, C_4, B_6, I_3, I_1, I_2, I_4, B_5, C_3, B_4, B_3, C_2, B_2, B_1, C_1$

(b) $C_1, B_8, B_7, C_4, B_6, I_3, I_1, B_1, B_2, I_2, I_4, B_5, C_3, B_4, B_3, C_2$

(c) $C_1, B_8, B_7, C_4, B_6, I_3, I_4, B_5, C_3, B_4, B_3, C_2, B_2, B_1, I_1, I_2$

(d) Suppose that *X* and *Y* are any two adjacent vertices. If we pick a Hamilton circuit that contains the edge *XY* and remove that edge, then we get a Hamilton path that has *X* and *Y* as its endpoints. (Finding a Hamilton circuit is relatively easy.)

67. Suppose that the cheapest edge in a graph is the edge joining vertices *X* and *Y*. Using the nearest-neighbor algorithm, we will eventually visit one of these vertices—suppose that the first one of these vertices we visit is *X*. Then, since edge *XY* is the cheapest edge in the graph and since we have not yet visited vertex *Y*, the nearest-neighbor algorithm will take us to *Y*.

69. (a) Dallas, Houston, Memphis, Louisville, Columbus, Chicago, Kansas City, Denver, Atlanta, Buffalo, Boston, Dallas.

(b) Dallas, Houston, Denver, Boston, Buffalo, Columbus, Louisville, Chicago, Atlanta, Memphis, Kansas City, Dallas.

Chapter 9

WALKING

9.1   Sequences and Population Sequences

1. (a) 2   (b) 10,001   (c) $N = 3$

3. (a) 1   (b) 3   (c) $N = 5$

5. (a) 1   (b) -1 (c) $N = 1, 3, 5, 7, \ldots$

7. (a) $A_3 = 3, A_4 = 7, A_5 = 17, A_6 = 41$ (b) $A_8 = 239$

9. (a) $A_3 = -3, A_4 = -1, A_5 = 5, A_6 = 7$ (b) $A_8 = -17$

11. (a) 36, 49   (b) $A_N = N^2$ (c) $P_N = (N+1)^2$

13. (a) 28, 36   (b) $A_N = N(N-1)/2$

(c) $P_N = N(N+1)/2$

15. (a) $\dfrac{24}{9}, \dfrac{28}{10}$ (b) $A_N = \dfrac{4N}{N+3}$

17. (a) $\dfrac{1}{720}$ (b) $\dfrac{1}{12!} = \dfrac{1}{479,001,600}$

9.2   The Linear Growth Model

19. (a) $P_1 = 205, P_2 = 330, P_3 = 455$ (b) $P_N = 80 + 125N$

(c) $P_{100} = 12,580$

21. (a) $P_1 = 553, P_2 = 528, P_3 = 503$ (b) $P_N = 578 - 25N$

(c) $P_{23} = 3$

23. (a) $P_N = 8 + 3N$ (b) $P_{50} = 158$

25. (a) 5.9%

(b) Sometime in July, 2015 (the unemployment rate for June, 2015, would be 0.1%).

27. (a) 82.49 years

(b) the life expectancy for someone born in 2020 would be 90.17 years

29. 24,950

31. (a) 100th term   (b) 16,050

33. (a) 3,519,500   (b) 3,482,550

35. (a) 213   (b) $137 + 2N$

(c) $7124   (d) $2652

9.3   The Exponential Growth Model

37. (a) 13.75   (b) $11 \times (1.25)^9 \approx 82$

(c) $P_N = 11 \times (1.25)^N$

39. (a) $P_1 = 20, P_2 = 80, P_3 = 320$ (b) $P_N = 5 \times 4^N$ (c) 9

41. (a) $P_N = (1.5) \times P_{N-1}$ with $P_0 = 200$

(b) $P_N = 200 \times (1.5)^N$ (c) approximately 11,500

43. $\sim 8.94\%$

45. $\sim -11.97\%$

47. (a) $R = 3$ (b) $\left[(3)^{21} - 1\right] \times \dfrac{2}{2} = 10,460,353,202$

49. (a) $R = 0.5$

(b) $\left[(0.5)^{12} - 1\right] \times \dfrac{4}{-0.5} \approx 7.998$

51. $\left[\left(\dfrac{10}{3}\right)^9 - 1\right] \times \dfrac{300,000}{\left(\dfrac{7}{3}\right)} \approx 6,531,976,726$

9.4   The Logistic Growth Model

53. (a) $p_1 = 0.1680$ (b) $p_2 \approx 0.1118$

(c) 7.945%

55. (a) $p_1 = 0.1680, p_2 \approx 0.1118, p_3 \approx 0.0795,$
$p_4 \approx 0.0585, p_5 \approx 0.0441, p_6 \approx 0.0337,$
$p_7 \approx 0.0261, p_8 \approx 0.0203, p_9 \approx 0.0159, p_{10} \approx 0.0125$

(b) extinction

57. (a) $p_1 = 0.4320, p_2 \approx 0.4417, p_3 \approx 0.4439,$
$p_4 \approx 0.4443, p_5 \approx 0.4444, p_6 \approx 0.4444,$
$p_7 \approx 0.4444, p_8 \approx 0.4444, p_9 \approx 0.4444, p_{10} \approx 0.4444$

(b) It stabilizes at 44.44% of the habitat's carrying capacity.

59. (a) $p_1 = 0.3570, p_2 \approx 0.6427, p_3 \approx 0.6429,$
$p_4 \approx 0.6428, p_5 \approx 0.6429, p_6 \approx 0.6428,$
$p_7 \approx 0.6429, p_8 \approx 0.6428, p_9 \approx 0.6429, p_{10} \approx 0.6428$

(b) It stabilizes at $\frac{9}{14} \approx 64.29\%$ of the habitat's carrying capacity.

61. (a) $p_1 = 0.5200, p_2 = 0.8112, p_3 \approx 0.4978, p_4 \approx 0.8125,$
$p_5 \approx 0.4952, p_6 \approx 0.8124, p_7 \approx 0.4953, p_8 \approx 0.8124,$
$p_9 \approx 0.4953, p_{10} \approx 0.8124$

(b) The population settles into a two-period cycle alternating between a high-population period at 81.24% and a low-population period at 49.53% of the habitat's carrying capacity.

JOGGING

63. (a) exponential **(b)** linear
(c) logistic **(d)** exponential
(e) logistic **(f)** linear
(g) linear, exponential, and logistic

65. The first N terms of the arithmetic sequence are $c, c + d, c + 2d, \ldots c + (N-1)d$. Their sum is

$$\frac{(c + [c + (N-1)d]) \times N}{2} = \frac{N}{2}[2c + (N-1)d].$$

67. $R = \dfrac{1 + \sqrt{5}}{2}$

69. $8, 4, 2, 1, \frac{1}{2}, \frac{1}{4}, \ldots$ (Many other answers are possible.)

71. No. A constant population would require $p_0 = p_1 = 0.8(1 - p_0)p_0$, so $1 = 0.8(1 - p_0)$ or $p_0 = -0.25$.

Chapter 14

WALKING

14.1 Enumeration

1. 64
3. 2320
5. 2549
7. 2000

9. 274
11. 273 (one less than under the standard capture-recapture formula).
13. 660

14.2 Measurement

15. (a) B **(b)** D **(c)** A **(d)** C

17. (a) the registered voters in Cleansburg

(b) the 680 registered voters polled by telephone

(c) simple random sampling

19. Smith: 3%; Jones: 3%; Brown: 0%

21. (a) The sample consisted of the 350 students attending the Eureka High School football game the week before the election.

(b) $\frac{350}{1250} = 28\%$

23. (a) The population consists of all 1250 students at Eureka High School, whereas the sampling frame consists only of those 350 students who attended the football game the week prior to the election.

(b) Mainly sampling bias. The sampling frame is not representative of the population.

25. (a) the citizens of Cleansburg

(b) The sampling frame is limited to that part of the target population that passes by a city street corner between 4:00 P.M. and 6:00 P.M.

27. (a) The choice of street corner could make a great deal of difference in the responses collected.

(b) Interviewer D. We are assuming that people who live or work downtown are much more likely to answer yes than people in other parts of town.

(c) Yes, for two main reasons: (1) People out on the street between 4 P.M. and 6 P.M. are not representative of the population at large.

For example, office and white-collar workers are much more likely to be in the sample than homemakers and schoolteachers. (2) The five street corners were chosen by the interviewers, and the passersby are unlikely to represent a cross section of the city.

(d) No. No attempt was made to use quotas to get a representative cross section of the population.

29. (a) The target population and the sampling frame both consist of all TSU undergraduates.

(b) 15,000

31. (a) In simple random sampling, any two members of the population have as much chance of both being in the sample as any other two, but in this sample, two people with the same last name — say Len Euler and Linda Euler — have no chance of being in the sample together.

(b) Sampling variability. The students sampled appear to be a representative cross section of all TSU undergraduates.

33. (a) Stratified sampling. **(b)** Quota sampling.

35. (a) Label the crates with numbers 1 through 250. Select 20 of these numbers at random (put the 250 numbers in a hat and draw out 20). Sample those 20 crates.

(b) Select the top 20 crates in the shipment (those easiest to access).

(c) Randomly sample 6 crates from supplier A, 6 crates from supplier B, and 8 crates from supplier C.

(d) Select any 6 crates from supplier A, any 6 crates from supplier B, and any 8 crates from supplier C.

14.3 Cause and Effect

37. (a) The target population consisted of anyone who could have a cold and would consider buying vitamin X (i.e., pretty much all adults).

(b) The sampling frame consisted of college students in the San Diego area having a cold at the time.

(c) The sample consisted of the 500 students that took vitamin X.

39. 1. Using college students—they are not a representative cross section of the population.

2. Using subjects only from the San Diego area.

3. Offering money as an incentive to participate.

4. Allowing self-reporting (the subjects themselves determine when their colds are over).

41. (a) All potential knee surgery patients.

(b) the 180 potential knee surgery patients at the Houston VA Medical Center who volunteered to be in the study

43. (a) Yes. The 180 patients in the study were assigned to a treatment group at random.

(b) Blind

45. The target population consisted of all people having a history of colorectal adenomas.

47. (a) The treatment group consisted of the 1287 patients who were given 25 milligrams of Vioxx daily. The control group consisted of the 1299 patients who were given a placebo.

(b) This clinical study was a controlled placebo study because there was a control group that did not receive the treatment, but instead received a placebo. It was a randomized controlled study because the 2586 participants were randomly divided into the treatment and control groups. The study was double blind because neither the participants nor the doctors involved in the study knew who was in each group.

49. (a) The target population consisted of women (particularly young women).

(b) The sampling frame consists of those women between 16 and 23 years of age who are not at high risk for HPV infection (i.e., those women having no prior abnormal Pap smears and at most five previous male sexual partners). Pregnant women are also excluded from the sampling frame due to the risks involved.

51. (a) The treatment group consisted of the women who received the HPV vaccine.

(b) This was a controlled placebo study because there was a control group that did not receive the treatment, but instead received a placebo injection. It was a randomized controlled study because the 2392 participants were randomly divided into the treatment and control groups. The study was likely double blind because neither the participants nor the medical personnel giving the injections knew who was in each group.

53. (a) The target population consisted of all people suffering from diphtheria.

(b) The sampling frame consisted of the individuals admitted to that particular Copenhagen hospital between May 1896 and April 1897 and having serious diptheria symptoms.

55. (a) The control group consisted of those patients admitted on the "odd" days who received just the standard treatment for diphtheria at the time. The treatment group consisted of those patients admitted on the "even" days who received both the new serum and the standard treatment.

(b) When the new serum was combined with the standard treatment, it proved effective in treating diphtheria.

57. (a) The target population consisted of men with prostate enlargement; particularly older men.

(b) The sampling frame consists of men aged 45 years or older having moderately impaired urinary flow. It appears to be a representative subset of the target population.

59. (a) The treatment group consisted of the group of volunteers that received saw palmetto daily.

(b) The saw palmetto odor would be a dead give away as to who was getting the treatment and who was getting a placebo. To make the study truly blind, the odor had to be covered up.

(c) Yes. There was a control group that received a placebo instead of the treatment, and the treatment group was randomized. We can infer the study was blind from the fact that an effort was made to hide the odor of the saw palmetto. From the description of the study there is no way to tell if the study was also double blind.

JOGGING

61. approx. $113.15 (252 quarters, 261 nickels, 371 dimes)

63. Capture-recapture would overestimate the true population. If the fraction of those tagged in the recapture appears lower than it is in reality, then the fraction of those tagged in the initial capture will also be computed as lower than the truth. This makes the total population appear larger than it really is.

65. Answers will vary.

67. Consideration of one exception made them less likely to consider a second exception.

69. (a) An Area Code 900 telephone poll represents an extreme case of selection bias. People who respond to these polls usually represent the extreme viewpoints (strongly for or strongly against), leaving out much of the middle of the road point of view. Economics also plays some role in the selection bias. (While 50 cents is not a lot of money anymore, poor people are much more likely to think twice before spending the money to express their opinion.)

(b) This survey was based on fairly standard modern-day polling techniques (random sample telephone interviews, etc.) but it had one subtle flaw. How reliable can a survey about the conduct of the newsmedia be when the survey itself is conducted by a newsmedia organization? ("The fox guarding the chicken-coop" syndrome.)

(c) Both surveys seem to have produced unreliable data—survey 1 overestimating the public's dissapproval of the role played by the newsmedia and survey 2 overestimating the public's support for the press coverage of the war.

(d) Any reasoned out answer should be acceptable. (Since Area Code 900 telephone polls are particularly unreliable, survey 2 gets our vote.)

71. (a) Both samples should be a representative cross section of the same population. In particular, it is essential that the first sample, after being released, be allowed to disperse evenly throughout the population, and that the population should not change between the time of the capture and the time of the recapture.

(b) It is possible (especially when dealing with elusive types of animals) that the very fact that the animals in the first sample allowed themselves to be captured makes such a sample biased (they could represent a slower, less cunning group). This type of bias is compounded with the animals that get captured the second time around. A second problem is the effect that the first capture can have on the captured animals. Sometimes the animal may be hurt (physically or emotionally), making it more (or less) likely to be captured the second time around. A third source of bias is the possibility that some of the tags will come off.

Chapter 15

WALKING

15.1 Graphs and Charts

1. (a)

Score	10	40	50	60	70	80	100
Frequency	1	1	3	7	6	5	2

(b)

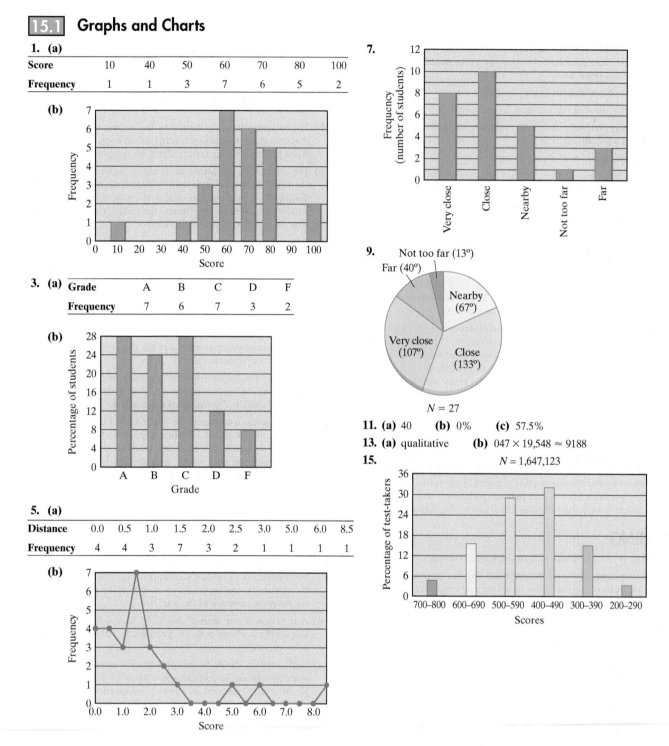

3. (a)

Grade	A	B	C	D	F
Frequency	7	6	7	3	2

(b)

5. (a)

Distance	0.0	0.5	1.0	1.5	2.0	2.5	3.0	5.0	6.0	8.5
Frequency	4	4	3	7	3	2	1	1	1	1

(b)

7.

9. $N = 27$

11. (a) 40   **(b)** 0%   **(c)** 57.5%

13. (a) qualitative   **(b)** $047 \times 19{,}548 \approx 9188$

15. $N = 1{,}647{,}123$

17. (a)

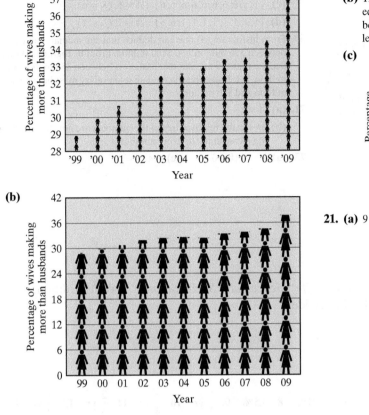

(b)

19. (a) 12 ounces

(b) The third class interval: "more than 72 ounces and less than or equal to 84 ounces." A value that falls exactly on the boundary between two class intervals belongs to the class interval to the left.

(c)

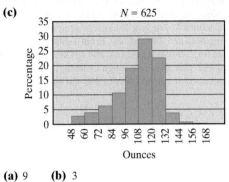

21. (a) 9 **(b)** 3

15.2 Means, Medians, and Percentiles

23. (a) $A = 2$ **(b)** $M = 3$ **(c)** $A = 2, M = 2.5$

25. (a) $A = 4.5, M = 4.5$ **(b)** $A = 5, \quad M = 5$
(c) $A = 5.5, M = 5.5$ **(d)** $A = 5.5a, \quad M = 5.5a$

27. (a) $A = 22.5, M = 17.5$ **(b)** $A = 122.5, M = 117.5$

29. (a) $A = 1.5875$ **(b)** $M = 1.5$

31. (a) $A = 6.77$ **(b)** $M = 7$

33. (a) $Q_1 = -4$ **(b)** $Q_3 = 7.5$ **(c)** $Q_1 = -3, Q_3 = 7$

35. (a) 75th percentile $= 75.5$, 90th percentile $= 90.5$
(b) 75th percentile $= 75$, 90th percentile $= 90$
(c) 75th percentile $= 75$, 90th percentile $= 90$
(d) 75th percentile $= 74$, 90th percentile $= 89$

37. (a) $Q_1 = 29$ **(b)** $Q_3 = 32$ **(c)** 37

39. (a) $M = d_{823,562}$ **(b)** $Q_1 = d_{411,781}$ **(c)** $X_{80} = d_{1,317,699}$

41. (a) $Min = -6, Q_1 = -4, M = 3, Q_3 = 7.5, Max = 8$

(b)

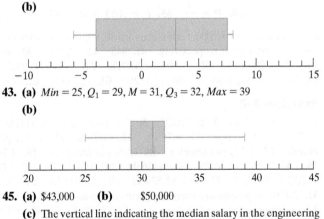

43. (a) $Min = 25, Q_1 = 29, M = 31, Q_3 = 32, Max = 39$
(b)

45. (a) $43,000 **(b)** $50,000

(c) The vertical line indicating the median salary in the engineering box plot is aligned with the right end of the box in the agriculture box plot.

15.3 Ranges and Standard Deviations

47. (a) 14 **(b)** 11.5

49. (a) $41,000 **(b)** at least 171 homes

51. (a) 16.5 **(b)** 4.5 **(c)** 1 and 24

53. heights less than 61 in. or greater than 77 in.

55. (a) 0 **(b)** $\dfrac{5\sqrt{2}}{2} \approx 3.5$ **(c)** $\sqrt{50} \approx 7.1$

57. Mean $= 8$ books, standard deviation $= 2.45$ books

JOGGING

59. (a) 30   **(b)** 8

61. 100

63. Somewhere between 823,562 and 894,894 students scored between 200 and 480. (Since the median was 480, we know that at least half of the test-takers scored 480 or less. That gives a minimum of 823,562 students scoring between 200 and 480. From Table 15-14 if we add the frequencies for 200–490 we get that 894,894 students scored between 200 and 490. This gives us a rough estimate for the maximum number of students that scored between 200 and 480.

65. 1,465,744

67. (a) $\{1, 1, 1, 1, 6, 6, 6, 6, 6, 6\}$ $(A = 4, M = 6)$

    (b) $\{1, 1, 1, 1, 1, 1, 1, 6, 6, 6\}$ $(A = 3, M = 1)$

    (c) $\{1, 1, 6, 6, 6, 6, 6, 6, 6, 6\}$ $(A = 5, Q_1 = 6)$

    (d) $\{1, 1, 1, 1, 1, 1, 1, 1, 6, 6\}$ $(A = 2, Q_3 = 1)$

69. From histogram (a) one can deduce that the median team salary is between \$70 million and \$100 million. From histogram (b) one can deduce that the median team salary is between \$50 million and \$80 million. It follows that the median team salary must be between \$70 million and \$80 million.

71. (a) $A + c$

    (b) $M + c$; the relative sizes of the numbers are not changed by adding a constant c to every number.

73. (a) 4   **(b)** 0.4   **(c)** 0.4

Taken from: *Finite Mathematics for Business, Economics, Life Sciences, and Social Sciences*, Twelfth Edition, by Raymond A. Barnett, Michael R. Zieger, and Karl E. Byleen

Chapter 3

Exercises 3–1

1. 0.03   **2.** 0.0525   **3.** 10.5%   **4.** 8%   **5.** 0.0475   **6.** 0.16   **7.** 21%   **8.** 0.5%   **9.** $\frac{1}{3}$ yr   **10.** $\frac{3}{4}$ yr   **11.** $\frac{2}{3}$ yr   **12.** $\frac{3}{2}$ yr   **13.** $\frac{3}{13}$ yr

14. $\frac{5}{6}$ yr   **15.** $\frac{1}{2}$ yr   **16.** $\frac{1}{12}$ yr   **17.** \$42   **18.** \$85.50   **19.** \$1,800   **20.** \$250   **21.** 0.12 or 12%   **22.** 0.16 or 16%   **23.** $\frac{1}{2}$ yr

24. $\frac{3}{4}$ yr   **25.** \$4,612.50   **26.** \$3,011.25   **27.** \$875   **28.** \$5,600   **29.** 0.36 or 36%   **30.** 0.22 or 22%   **31.** 1 yr   **32.** $\frac{1}{4}$ yr

33. $r = I/Pt$ **34.** $P = \dfrac{I}{rt}$ **35.** $P = A/(1 + rt)$ **36.** $r = \dfrac{A - P}{Pt}$ **37.** $t = \dfrac{A - P}{Pr}$ **38.** $t = \dfrac{I}{Pr}$ **39.** The graphs are linear, all with y intercept \$1,000; their slopes are 40, 80, and 120, respectively.   **40.** The graphs are linear, with y intercepts 400, 800, and 1,200, and slopes 30, 60, and 90, respectively.   **41.** \$45   **42.** \$232.50   **43.** \$9.23   **44.** \$25.05   **45.** \$7,647.20   **46.** \$10,325.00   **47.** 8.1%   **48.** 7.8%   **49.** 18%   **50.** 24%   **51.** \$1,604.40; 20.88%   **52.** \$3,106.20; 21.24%   **53.** 4.298%   **54.** 4.205%   **55.** \$992.38   **56.** \$976.07   **57.** 5.396%   **58.** 6.697%   **59.** 6.986%   **60.** 22.112%   **61.** 12.085%   **62.** 6.352%   **63.** 109.895%   **64.** 53.454%   **65.** 87.158%   **66.** 42.72%

Exercises 3–2

1. $A =$ \$5,983.40   **2.** \$3,008.71   **3.** $P =$ \$4,245.07   **4.** \$11,352.53   **5.** \$3,125.79   **6.** \$1,544.94   **7.** \$2,958.11   **8.** \$12,935.03   **9.** 2.5 yr   **10.** 3.25 yr   **11.** 6.789%   **12.** 4.179%   **13.** 0.75% per month   **14.** 1.5% per quarter   **15.** 0.04% per day   **16.** 1.25% per month   **17.** 1.2% per quarter   **18.** 1.6% per half-year   **19.** 4.74%   **20.** 4.38%   **21.** 3.6%   **22.** 2.1%   **23.** 4.2%   **24.** 5.6%   **25.** (A) \$126.25; \$26.25   (B) \$126.90; \$26.90   (C) \$127.05; \$27.05   **26.** (A) \$2,805.10; \$805.10   (B) \$2,829.56; \$829.56   (C) \$2,835.25; \$835.25   **27.** (A) \$5,524.71   (B) \$6,104.48   **28.** (A) \$24,419.93   (B) \$27,527.90   **29.** \$12,175.69   **30.** \$174,250.55   **31.** All three graphs are increasing, curve upward, and have the same y intercept; the greater the interest rate, the greater the increase. The amounts at the end of 8 years are \$1,376.40, \$1,892.46, and \$2,599.27, respectively.   **32.** All three graphs are increasing and curve upward; they have y intercepts 4,000, 8,000, and 12,000, respectively. The amounts at the end of 8 years are \$7,274.88, \$14,549.76, and \$21,824.64, respectively.

33.

Period	Interest	Amount
0		\$1,000.00
1	\$ 97.50	\$1,097.50
2	\$107.01	\$1,204.51
3	\$117.44	\$1,321.95
4	\$128.89	\$1,450.84
5	\$141.46	\$1,592.29
6	\$155.25	\$1,747.54

34.

Period	Interest	Amount
0		\$2,000.00
1	\$165.00	\$2,165.00
2	\$178.61	\$2,343.61
3	\$193.35	\$2,536.96
4	\$209.30	\$2,746.26
5	\$226.57	\$2,972.83

35. (A) \$7,440.94 (B) \$5,536.76 **36.** (A) \$4,730.96 (B) \$3,730.33 **37.** (A) \$19,084.49 (B) \$11,121.45 **38.** (A) \$2,970.16
(B) \$2,072.21 **39.** (A) 3.97% (B) 2.32% **40.** (A) 4.41% (B) 4.40% **41.** (A) 5.28% (B) 5.27% **42.** (A) 3.09%
(B) 2.99% **43.** $11\frac{2}{3}$ yr **44.** $5\frac{3}{4}$ yr **45.** 3.75 yr **46.** 8.5 yr **47.** $n \approx 12$ **48.** $n \approx 15$ **49.** (A) $7\frac{1}{4}$ yr (B) 6 yr **50.** (A) 9 yr
(B) $10\frac{1}{2}$ yr **51.** (A) 7.7 yr (B) 6.3 yr **52.** (A) 3.3 yr (B) 2.1 yr **53.** \$65,068.44 **54.** \$16,961.66 **55.** \$282,222.44
56. \$20,683.10 **57.** \$19.78 per ft^2 per mo **58.** \$173,319.50 **59.** 41 yr **60.** 38 yr
61. 9% compounded monthly, since its APY is 9.38%; the APY of 9.3% compounded annually is 9.3%
62. 8.3% compounded annually, since its APY is 8.3%; the APY of 8% compounded quarterly is 8.24%

63. (A) In 2016, 240 years after the signing, it
would be worth \$130,392.50.
(B) If interest were compounded monthly,
daily, or continuously, it would be
worth \$132,744.98, \$133,903.45, or
\$133,943.08, respectively.

(C)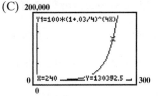

65. 9.66% **66.** 5.58% **67.** 2 yr, 10 mo **68.** 17 quarters of $4\frac{1}{4}$ yr **69.** \$163,295.21 **70.** \$147,966,422.56; \$19

71. 3,615 days; 8.453 yr **72.** 8,021 days; 18.310 yr **73.**

Years	Exact Rate	Rule of 72
6	12.2	12.0
7	10.4	10.3
8	9.1	9.0
9	8.0	8.0
10	7.2	7.2
11	6.5	6.5
12	5.9	6.0

74.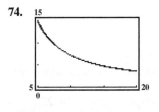

75. 14 quarters **76.** 17 months **77.** To maximize earnings, choose 10% simple interest for
investments lasting fewer than 11 years and 7% compound interest otherwise. **78.** To maximize
earnings, choose 9% simple interest for investments lasting fewer than 154 months, and 6%
compounded monthly otherwise. **79.** 6.58% **80.** 5.75% **81.** 7.02% **82.** 5.99%
83. \$15,843.80 **84.** \$13,261.81 **85.** 4.53% **86.** 4.56% **87.** (A) 4.404% (B) 4.446%
(C) 4.448% **88.** (A) 4.577% (B) 4.698% (C) 4.707% **89.** 13.44% **90.** 17.61%
91. 17.62% **92.** 20.30%

Exercises 3-3

1. $i = 0.02$; $n = 80$ **2.** $i = 0.005$; $n = 72$ **3.** $i = 0.0375$; $n = 24$ **4.** $i = 0.0625$; $n = 15$ **5.** $i = 0.0075$; $n = 48$ **6.** $i = 0.0425$;
$n = 14$ **7.** $i = 0.0595$; $n = 12$ **8.** $i = 0.019$; $n = 72$ **9.** $FV = \$13,435.19$ **10.** $FV = \$4,164.59$ **11.** $PMT = \$310.62$

12. $PMT = \$172.57$ **13.** $n = 17$ **14.** $n = 13$ **15.** $i = 0.09$ **16.** $i = 0.07$ **19.** $n = \dfrac{\ln\left(1 + i\dfrac{FV}{PMT}\right)}{\ln(1 + i)}$ **20.** $i = \dfrac{FV}{PMT} - 2$
21. Value: \$84,895.40; interest: \$24,895.40 **22.** Value = \$180,000; interest = \$143.943.07 **23.** \$20,931.01 **24.** \$343,214.73
25. \$667.43 **26.** \$626.93 **27.** \$763.39 **28.** \$2,363.07
29.

Period	Amount	Interest	Balance
1	\$1,000.00	\$ 0.00	\$1,000.00
2	\$1,000.00	\$ 83.20	\$2,083.20
3	\$1,000.00	\$173.32	\$3,256.52
4	\$1,000.00	\$270.94	\$4,527.46
5	\$1,000.00	\$376.69	\$5,904.15

30.

Period	Amount	Interest	Balance
1	\$2,000.00		\$2,000.00
2	\$2,000.00	\$39.50	\$4,039.50
3	\$2,000.00	\$79.78	\$6,119.28
4	\$2,000.00	\$120.86	\$8,240.14
5	\$2,000.00	\$162.74	\$10,402.88
6	\$2,000.00	\$205.46	\$12,608.34
7	\$2,000.00	\$249.01	\$14,857.35
8	\$2,000.00	\$293.43	\$17,150.78

31. First year: \$33.56; second year: \$109.64; third year: \$190.41 **32.** First year: \$60.80; second year: \$230.68; third year: \$414.56
33. \$111,050.77 **34.** \$84,852.51 **35.** \$1,308.75 **36.** \$2,308.75 **37.** (A) 4.755% (B) \$189.56 **38.** (A) 5.51% (B) \$8,312.47
39. 33 months **40.** 45 months **41.** 7.77% **42.** 6.14% **43.** 7.13% **44.** 9.24% **45.** After 11 quarterly payments **46.** After 66
monthly payments

Exercises 3–4

1. $i = 0.006$; $n = 48$ **2.** $i = 0.0495$; $n = 24$ **3.** $i = 0.02475$; $n = 40$ **4.** $i = 0.0475$; $n = 5$ **5.** $i = 0.02525$; $n = 32$ **6.** $i = 0.0206$; $n = 24$ **7.** $i = 0.0548$; $n = 9$ **8.** $i = 0.009$; $n = 36$ **9.** $PV = \$3,458.41$ **10.** $PV = \$13,133.87$ **11.** $PMT = \$586.01$

12. $PMT = \$232.02$ **13.** $n = 29$ **14.** $n = 70$ **15.** $i = 0.029$ **16.** $i = 0.015$ **18.** $n = -\dfrac{\ln\left(1 - i\,\dfrac{PV}{PMT}\right)}{\ln(1+i)}$ **21.** $\$35,693.18$

22. $\$55,135.98$ **23.** $\$11,241.81$; $\$1,358.19$ **24.** $\$10,872.23$; $\$1,727.77$ **25.** $\$69.58$; $\$839.84$ **26.** $\$94.69$; $\$2,181.40$ **27.** For 0% financing, the monthly payments should be $\$129.58$, not $\$179$. If a loan of $\$9,330$ is amortized in 72 payments of $\$179$, the rate is 11.29% compounded monthly.

28. For 0% financing, the monthly payments should be $\$176.25$, not $\$222$. If a loan of $\$12,690$ is amortized in 72 payments of $\$222$, the rate is 7.92% compounded monthly.

29. The monthly payments with 0% financing are $\$455$. If you take the rebate, the monthly payments are $\$434.24$. You should choose the rebate.

30. The monthly payments with 0% financing are $\$475$. If you take the rebate, the monthly payments will be $\$437.08$. You should choose the rebate.

31. $\$314.72$; $\$17,319.68$ **32.** $\$1,167.57$; $\$26,075.88$

33.

Payment Number	Payment	Interest	Unpaid Balance Reduction	Unpaid Balance
0				$5,000.00
1	$ 706.29	$140.00	$ 566.29	4,433.71
2	706.29	124.14	582.15	3,851.56
3	706.29	107.84	598.45	3,253.11
4	706.29	91.09	615.20	2,637.91
5	706.29	73.86	632.43	2,005.48
6	706.29	56.15	650.14	1,355.34
7	706.29	37.95	668.34	687.00
8	706.24	19.24	687.00	0.00
Totals	$5,650.27	$650.27	$5,000.00	

34.

Payment Number	Payment	Interest	Unpaid Balance Reduction	Unpaid Balance
0				$10,000.00
1	$1,821.58	$260.00	$1,561.58	8,438.42
2	1,821.58	219.40	1,602.18	6,836.24
3	1,821.58	177.74	1,643.84	5,192.40
4	1,821.58	135.00	1,686.58	3,505.82
5	1,821.58	91.15	1,730.43	1,775.39
6	1,821.55	46.16	1,775.39	0.00
Totals	$10,929.45	$929.45	$10,000.00	

35. First year: $\$466.05$; second year: $\$294.93$; third year: $\$107.82$
36. $\$3,319.03$ **37.** $\$97,929.78$; $\$116,070.22$
38. $\$671.25$; $\$145,650$ **39.** $\$143.85$/mo; $\$904.80$
40. $\$42,033.08$
41. Monthly payment: $\$908.99$
  (A) $\$125,862$ (B) $\$81,507$ (C) $\$46,905$
42. Monthly payment: $\$1,596.76$ (A) $\$180,443$
  (B) $\$139,061$ (C) $\$81,122$

43. (A) Monthly payment: $\$1,015.68$; interest: $\$114,763$ (B) 197 months; interest saved: $\$23,499$
44. 90 **45.** (A) 157 (B) 243 (C) The withdrawals continue forever. **46.** $\$522,241.29$; $\$569,216.34$; $\$668,430.68$
47. (A) Monthly withdrawals: $\$1,229.66$; total interest: $\$185,338.80$ (B) Monthly deposits: $\$162.65$ **48.** (A) $\$664.99$; $\$240,301.80$
(B) $\$2,255.69$ **49.** $\$65,584$ **50.** $\$68,299$ **51.** $\$34,692$ **52.** $\$40,227.60$ **53.** All three graphs are decreasing, curve downward, and have the same x intercept; the unpaid balances are always in the ratio 2:3:4. The monthly payments are $\$402.31$, $\$603.47$, and $\$804.62$, with total interest amounting to $\$94,831.60$, $\$142,249.20$, and $\$189,663.20$, respectively. **54.** All three graphs are decreasing, curve downward, and have the same x and y intercepts; the greater the interest rate, the greater the unpaid balance. The monthly payments are $\$399.18$, $\$526.54$, and $\$663.72$, with total interest amounting to $\$83,704.80$, $\$129,554.40$, and $\$178,939.20$, respectively.
55. 14.45% **56.** 18.16% **57.** 10.21% **58.** 8.76%

Review Exercises

1. $A = \$104.50$ *(3-1)* **2.** $P = \$800$ *(3-1)* **3.** $t = 0.75$ yr, or 9 mo *(3-1)* **4.** $r = 6\%$ *(3-1)* **5.** $A = \$1,393.68$ *(3-2)*
6. $P = \$3,193.50$ *(3-2)* **7.** $A = \$5,824.92$ *(3-2)* **8.** $P = \$22,612.86$ *(3-2)* **9.** $FV = \$69,770.03$ *(3-3)* **10.** $PMT = \$115.00$ *(3-3)*
11. $PV = \$33,944.27$ *(3-4)* **12.** $PMT = \$166.07$ *(3-4)* **13.** $n \approx 16$ *(3-2)* **14.** $n \approx 41$ *(3-3)* **15.** $\$3,350.00$; $\$350.00$ *(3-1)*
16. $\$19,654$ *(3-2)* **17.** $\$12,944.67$ *(3-2)*

18. (A)

Period	Interest	Amount
0		$400.00
1	$21.60	$421.60
2	$22.77	$444.37
3	$24.00	$468.36
4	$25.29	$493.65

(3-2)

(B)

Period	Interest	Payment	Balance
1		$100.00	$100.00
2	$ 5.40	$100.00	$205.40
3	$11.09	$100.00	$316.49
4	$17.09	$100.00	$433.58

(3-3)

19. To maximize earnings, choose 13% simple interest for investments lasting less than 9 years and 9% compound interest for investments lasting 9 years or more. *(3-2)*

20. $164,402 *(3-2)*   **21.** 7.83% *(3-2)*

22. 9% compounded quarterly, since its effective rate is 9.31%, while the effective rate of 9.25% compounded annually is 9.25% *(3-2)*

23. $25,861.65; $6,661.65 *(3-3)*   **24.** $11.64 *(3-1)*   **25.** $29,354 *(3-2)*   **26.** $18,021 *(3-2)*   **27.** 15% *(3-1)*

28. The monthly payments with 0% financing are $450. If you take the rebate, the monthly payments are $426.66. You should choose the rebate. *(3-4)*

29. (A) 6.43%   (B) 6.45% *(3-2)*   **30.** 2 yr, 3 mo *(3-2)*   **31.** 139 mo; 93 mo *(3-2)*   **32.** (A) $571,499   (B) $1,973,277 *(3-3)*

33. 10.45% *(3-2)*   **34.** (A) 174%   (B) 65.71% *(3-1)*   **35.** $725.89 *(3-3)*   **36.** (A) $140,945.57   (B) $789.65   (C) $136,828 *(3-3, 3-4)*

37. $102.99; $943.52 *(3-4)*   **38.** $576.48 *(3-3)*   **39.** 3,374 days; 10 yr *(3-2)*   **40.** $175.28; $2,516.80 *(3-4)*   **41.** $13,418.78 *(3-2)*

42. 5 yr, 10 mo *(3-3)*   **43.** 18 yr *(3-4)*   **44.** 28.8% *(3-1)*

45.

Payment Number	Payment	Interest	Unpaid Balance Reduction	Unpaid Balance
0				$1,000.00
1	$265.82	$25.00	$ 240.82	759.18
2	265.82	18.98	246.84	512.34
3	265.82	12.81	253.01	259.33
4	265.81	6.48	259.33	0.00
Totals	$1,063.27	$63.27	$1,000.00	

(3-4)

46. 28 months *(3-3)*

47. $55,347.48; $185,830.24 *(3-3)*

48. 6.30% *(3-2)*   **49.** 6.33% *(3-1)*

50. 44 deposits *(3-3)*

51. (A) $1,189.52   (B) $72,963.07   (C) $7,237.31 *(3-4)*

52. The certificate would be worth $53,394.30 when the 360th payment is made. By reducing the principal the loan would be paid off in 252 months. If the monthly payment were then invested at 7% compounded monthly, it would be worth $67,234.20 at the time of the 360th payment. *(3-2, 3-3, 3-4)*

53. The lower rate would save $12,247.20 in interest payments. *(3-4)*   **54.** $3,807.59 *(3-2)*   **55.** 5.79% *(3-2)*

56. $4,844.96 *(3-1)*   **57.** $6,697.11 *(3-4)*   **58.** 7.24% *(3-2)*   **59.** (A) $398,807   (B) $374,204 *(3-3)*

60. $15,577.64 *(3-2)*   **61.** (A) 30 yr: $569.26; 15 yr: $749.82   (B) 30 yr: $69,707.99; 15 yr: $37,260.74 *(3-4)*

62. $20,516 *(3-4)*   **63.** 33.52% *(3-4)*   **64.** (A) 10.74%   (B) 15 yr; 40 yr *(3-3)*

INDEX

PHOTO CREDITS

INDEX OF APPLICATIONS

INDEX OF APPLICATIONS (continued)